Modeling Using PRO|ENGINEER WILDFIRE 4.0

Sridhar S. Condoor
Saint Louis University

ISBN: 978-1-58503-377-5

SDC PUBLICATIONS

Schroff Development Corporation

www.schroff.com

Modeling Using PRO|ENGINEER W I L D F I R E 4.0 – A Click Away

This new book synergistically integrates the design process with the specific commands and procedures of Pro|ENGINEER through a unique presentation scheme. Users are first provided with the information about the design (part or assembly), and its design intent. Then, they see an overview of steps involved in modeling the part/assembly. This is accompanied by detailed instructions showing goals, steps and commands in a four-column presentation. The consistent approach is supplemented by many illustrations on each page. Each chapter adds new information while reinforcing key concepts.

Key Features of this book are:

- Models of real machine components and assemblies.
- A flexible four-column format page layout with several illustrations.
- Detailed instructions for creating good engineering drawings.
- Implementation of bottom-up and top-down approaches.
- Additional resources including exercise problems and "helpful hints" are provided at "http://parks.slu.edu/condoor."

TABLE OF CONTENTS

Preface

Over the past several years, I taught project-based design courses to engineering students. During the course of the projects, students found great difficulties in creating "real" parts and assembling them. Most books fall short in providing the reader with a consistent and systematic methodology for approaching even simple solid modeling tasks.

Graphics books do not deal with the solid modeling software in detail. On the other hand, solid modeling books do not handle both graphics and design topics well. This book is aimed at addressing this need and is based on the lecture notes developed to teach ProEngineer, graphics and along with aspects of design.

The focus of the text is on teaching actual design modeling using ProEngineer rather than teaching a set of commands. The book illustrates the part, drawing and assembly creation with several industrial examples. These parts fit together in the final chapters to form one large assembly.

Chapters are organized such that each chapter builds on previous chapters and introduces additional commands. It is a hands-on book where students are expected to work with ProEngineer. Several figures are used to illustrate each step. The book eliminates the frequent sight of students staring at the book and desperately trying to follow the instructions.

Modeling Using ProEngineer is a book for graphics and design courses from freshmen- to senior-level students in engineering. Practicing engineers will also find this book valuable. This book is aimed at the new generation of students who are:

- Highly computer literate (sometimes more literate than faculty).
- Not motivated in reading large volumes of information to do simple things.
- Hands-on when it comes to computers.

I hope this book will help you to use imagination and skill in the creation of functionally efficient and aesthetic objects.

I would like to thank faculty, staff, and friends at Saint Louis University for their continuous support and cooperation. I wish to thank the students who conceived and created the design examples possible. Also, I would like to acknowledge the support of the Parametric Technology Corporation.

About the Author

Sridhar S. Condoor received his Ph.D. from the Department of Mechanical Engineering at Texas A&M University. He received M.S. from the Indian Institute of Technology, Bombay and B.S. from Jawaharlal Nehru Technological University, Hyderabad, India. His research interests include many areas of Design Theory and Methodology, Computer Aided Design, Cognitive Science, and Mechatronics.

Condoor is the co-author of *Innovative Conceptual Design: Applications: Theory and Application of Parameter Analysis* (Cambridge University Press). He conducted several short-courses for both faculty and practicing engineers on design techniques. He coauthored several papers on various facets of design including design management, design theory, design principles, cognitive aspects of design and design education.

Condoor currently teaches at Saint Louis University – Parks College of Engineering & Aviation. He initiated the multidisciplinary design program with a strong emphasis on industry participation at Saint Louis University. He works with a diverse range of industries in creating new products, modeling existing products to understand the underlying physics, and developing automated manufacturing systems.

NOTES:

LESSON 1
INTRODUCTION

What is parametric, feature-based design?

Parametric Technologies Corporation (PTC) revolutionized the CAD industry in the late 1980s with the introduction of Pro|ENGINEER, the first parametric, feature-based solid modeling CAD system with a strong emphasis on design intent. Pro|ENGINEER provides a three-dimensional environment to create solid models, visualize objects, and analyze physical properties such as volume.

As opposed to two-dimensional drafting and three-dimensional Boolean modeling techniques, feature-based design is an intuitive system. A part is created systematically by incorporating one feature at a time. The feature names can, in fact, correspond to the physical features of the part. For instance, bolt head, socket, shank, threads, top chamfer, and bottom chamfer are the six key features defining a hexagonal socket head bolt (Refer to Fig. 1.1). In feature-based design, these features can be turned on/off, or resized with ease.

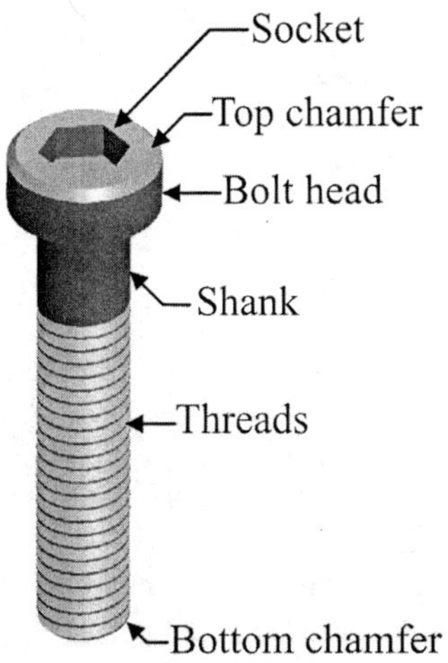

Fig. 1.1.

Features can be classified into *sketched* and *referenced* features. A sketched feature is created by sketching one or more two-dimensional section, and then sweeping the section along a predetermined path. For instance, the socket feature is formed by drawing a hexagon, extruding it along the bolt axis up to a predetermined depth, and removing the material contained within the extruded volume. Referenced features are pick-and-place features with predetermined shapes. Holes, rounds, and chamfers are three most used referenced features. They involve selecting the references such as edges to be chamfered.

The term *parametric design* refers to the modeling technique wherein the design features, parts and assemblies are based on parameters whose values determine the geometry. Modifying the value of a parameter not only changes the corresponding feature, but also all associated features. For instance, the top chamfer feature automatically readjusts to the changing height or diameter of the bolt head.

Pro|ENGINEER provides a practical way to develop flexible models that are easy to customize to suit the specific needs of customers. A designer can carry-out structural and thermal analysis, and motion simulation using ProMechanica in an integrated environment. The analysis leads to a deeper understanding of the design and helps in identifying product improvements. Photorealistic models and animation help in getting a feedback from the customers. Thus, a good of understanding of the software helps in the product life cycle management - wherein the product can be conceptualized, designed, and build through active collaboration of the product development team (design, analysis, and manufacturing engineers, and marketing personnel), suppliers, and consumers.

What is a parent-child relationship?

To create a new feature, the designer may reference prior features. The top chamfer in the bolt example (Refer to Fig. 1.1) uses the top edge of the bolt head as the reference. Now, the new feature (the top chamfer) naturally becomes a child of the referenced feature (the bolt head). Thus, feature-based design continuously creates child features, which depend on parent features for their existence. If the parent feature is deleted, then the user must delete, redefine, rollback, or reroute its child features. Note that it is not possible to reorder a child feature before the parent feature. In other words, one can't chamfer the edge of the bolt head before creating the bolt head feature.

The primary advantage of feature-based modeling lies in its ability to capture design intent. The term design intent refers to the governing relationship between the different features of the model. If the model captures the design intent, then changes can be made to the model effortlessly and they produce the intended behavior. On the other hand, a model with flawed design intent fails when modified or changes inappropriately. The parent-child relationship is useful to capture the design intent. Changes to the parent features automatically propagate to the child. For instance, if we increase the length of the shank, then the threads move along with it such that they start at the bottom of the shank. The parametric, feature-based design provides a useful way to capture the *design intent* – the threads starting at the bottom surface in this particular case.

To manage the design intent throughout the modeling process, the user should develop the proficiency in using different commands as well as strategies to capture the design intent. This book helps in both these aspects by requiring you to repeatedly practice different commands, while at the same time applying the commands to a diverse set of scenarios to develop your own set of strategies for capturing the design intent.

What is associative?

In Pro|ENGINEER, the user can work in several modes. Some of the key modes are:

Sketcher – for creating sections and sketches
Part – for modeling parts
Drawing – for creating engineering drawings
Assembly – for assembling parts

A designer can create a sketch, use the sketch to model a part, create engineering drawing of the part, and also use the part in an assembly. The designer can modify the dimension of the part in any one of these four modes. Pro|ENGINEER handles this situation well as all modes in Pro|ENGINEER are fully associative (Refer Fig. 1.2). In other words, changes made in one mode automatically propagate to the other modes. Thus, it maintains consistency of the model.

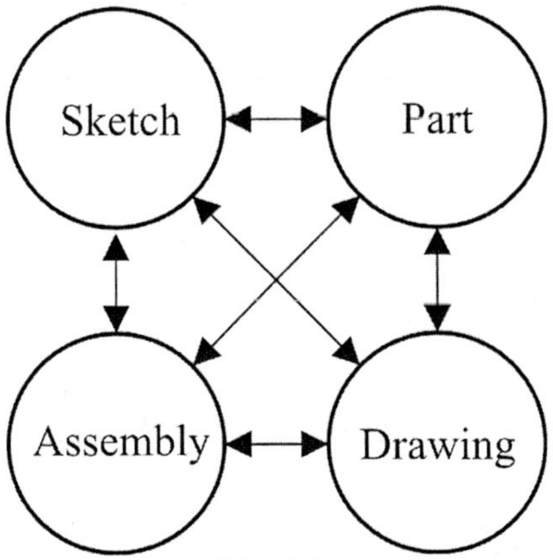

Fig. 1.2.

Organization of the book

This book is heavily dependent on examples to elucidate the fundamental concepts in solid modeling in general and Pro|ENGINEER in particular. The examples are carefully crafted and detailed in a way that clarifies the thought process undertaken and the actual commands used. The author has seen firsthand the value of the "coaching method" that takes the reader from modeling simple machine components such as bearings, to complex components such as helical gears, and then to the bottom-up and top-down assembly approaches. The examples are chosen to exemplify engineering design characteristics such as equations, data points and graphs.

The reader is encouraged to work with Pro|ENGINEER and follow the modeling process throughout the book. The combination of "theoretical" discussion of the solid modeling principles and the "hands-on" Pro|ENGINEER exercises has proved to be an effective method for this material to be learned.

Chapters 2 – 12 introduce the basic concepts in complex part modeling using simple features, professional drawing, and bottom-up assembly design. Chapters 13 – 20 expand on advanced features including top-down design approach. The chapters are organized so that each chapter adds new knowledge about solid modeling and reinforces the previous chapters. Thus, the readers can sharpen their skills while acquiring new ones. This continuous reinforcement of concepts is one of the key features of this book.

Each chapter is organized into four sections. The first section provides a background about the features and commands and then, details the part/assembly information including the functionality and the design intent. The second section shows the sequence of steps involved in modeling the part/assembly. Even though the book shows one modeling approach, the reader is encouraged to explore alternative approaches for creating the same part and identify their advantages and disadvantages. Then, the third section provides detailed procedure for creating the part/assembly in Pro|ENGINEER. The exercise set in each chapter reinforces the concepts and also, exposes the user to the full power of each feature.

The procedure for creating a part/assembly is organized in terms of goals (describe major objectives), steps (describe steps involved in satisfying the goal) and commands (actual Pro|ENGINEERcommands). Several illustrative figures are included on each page to assist the reader in modeling. The commands are coded to provide fast access to the commands. Fig. 1.3 describes the command codes.

Command Codes

UPPERCASE LETTERS – Main menu.

Lowercase Letters – Menu Manager.

Underlined Letters – To be typed by the user.

Italics – Select or click with mouse.

Default Option – Default option in the menu.

BUTTON – Menu button.

KEYBOARD – Keyboard entry (typically delete, enter or control keys).

★ – Tricky step or read the instructions carefully.

ICON – Click on the icon.

ICON>ICONS – Click on > to see the icons.

Fig. 1.3.

REMEMBER TO SAVE THE PARTS.

PARTS CREATED IN LESSONS 2, 6, 8, 9 AND 10 ARE REQUIRED FOR LESSONS 11 AND 12.

What are the main components of Pro|ENGINEER display? As shown in Fig. 1.4, the Pro|ENGINEER display consists of:

- **Graphics window:** Displays the model.
- **Navigator:** Displays files, model tree and favorites.
- **Main toolbar:** Allows access to all tools.
- **Feature creation toolbar:** Show shortcut icons to commonly used tools. These toolbars can be customized.
- **Dashboard:** Provides direct control of the part creation. It prompts the desired action.
- **Message window:** Provides a concise description of the tool when the cursor is placed on the tool. Also, aids the user in feature creation by providing instructions and feedback. The previous messages can be viewed by using the scroll bar. The window can be resized by dragging the lower edge of the window.

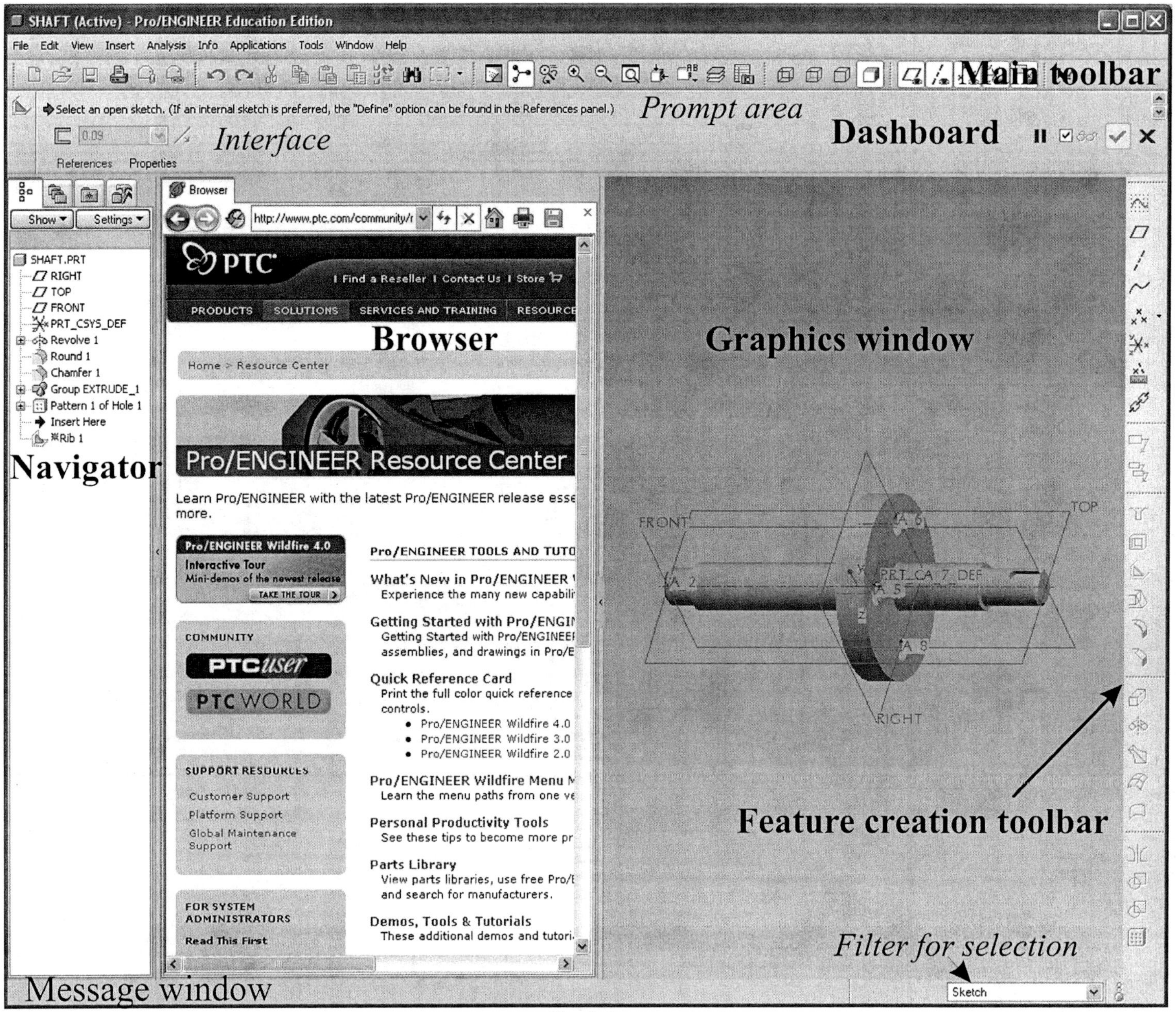

Fig. 1.4.

LESSON 2
BEARING

Learning Objectives

- Understand the concept of ***datum planes***.
- Explore the use of ***mouse*** for ***zoom***, ***spin***, and ***pan*** functions.
- Learn ***Extrude*** and ***Round*** features.
- Experiment with the use of ***model player*** and ***trail/training files***.

About Pro|ENGINEER files

When modeling, Pro|ENGINEER creates several files. Part files have an extension ".prt.X" where X represents the revision number. Each time a user saves a part, Pro|ENGINEER creates a new file. For instance, a part, say bearing, is saved for the first time, Pro|ENGINEER creates the file - bearing.prt.1. Subsequent saves, it creates "bearing.prt.2", "bearing.prt.3", "bearing.prt.4", and so on. A user can roll back to any previous version of the part by renaming that particular revision file and opening it. For most purposes, the last and latest version is sufficient. The previous versions can be deleted to optimize the disk space by selecting the following list of commands: **FILE → DELETE → OLDER VERSIONS**.

File Extensions

.sec	Section (or sketch)
.prt	Part
.mfg	Manufacturing process
.drw	Drawing
.frm	Format
.rep	Report
.dgm	Diagram
.lay	Layout
.mrk	Markup
.ptb	Pattern table
.stl	Stereolithography file
.txt	Trail or text file
.pro	Configuration file

Trail/Training Files

Pro|ENGINEER records all the commands, menu selections, and dialog choices in a file called "trail.txt." This file is useful in recreating a session or creating training files. The file can be edited using a text editor. Note that before playing the trail file, the file should be renamed. The following sequence of commands plays the trail file: **TOOLS → PLAY TRAIL/TRAINING FILES**.

Model Player

Model player is a useful tool to walk through a part model, and understand the design intent of the original designer. A user can initiate the model player using: **TOOLS → MODEL PLAYER**. Once started, it steps the user through each feature, and provides information about each feature.

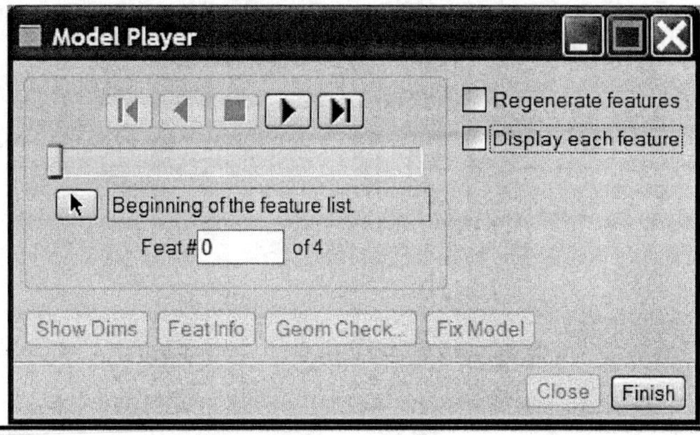

Extrude feature	
Useful for creating a solid protrusion, a cut, or a surface.	
Starting the feature	**INSERT → EXTRUDE**, or 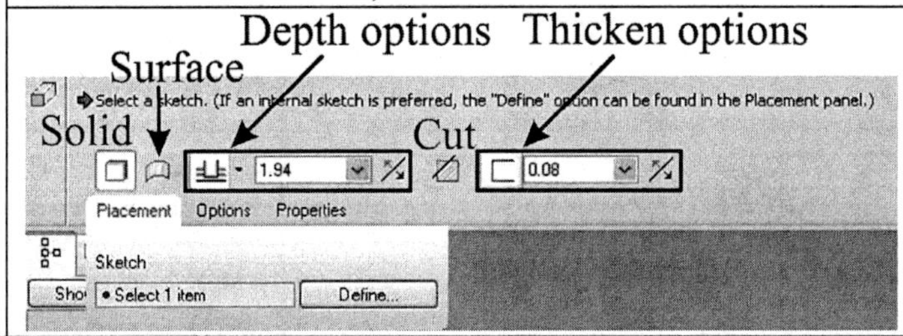
Solid	creates a solid
Surface	Creates a surface
Depth Options	specified depth both sides of the sketching plane by half the specified depth in each direction up to next surface where the extrusion stops when a surface is encountered intersect or extend with all surfaces intersect a specific surface where the user specifies the surface up to a selected point, curve, plane, or surface Flips the direction of extrusion
Cut	Removes the material when the option is highlighted
Thickness Options	Create a thin feature whose thickness is specified Adds thickness to the outside/inside/either sides of the sketch
Placement	**Define** to create a new section or redefine the existing one.

Examples	Extruding a circular section with different extrude option. 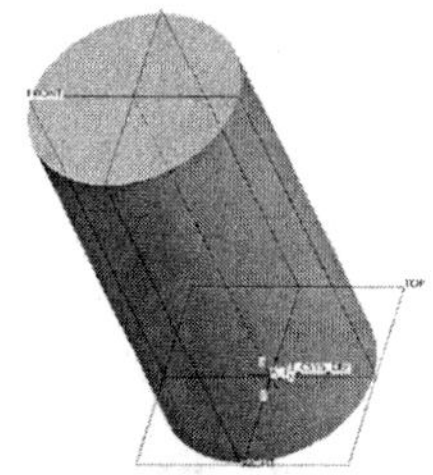 Extrude – Solid 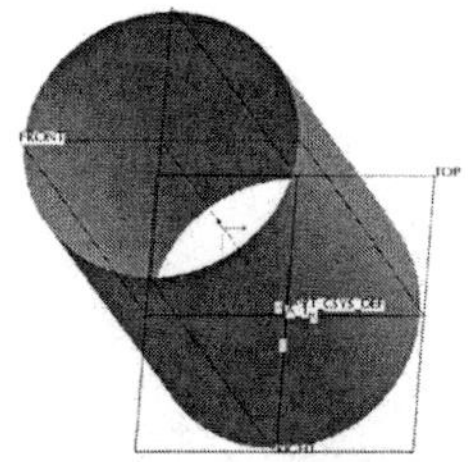 Extrude - Surface 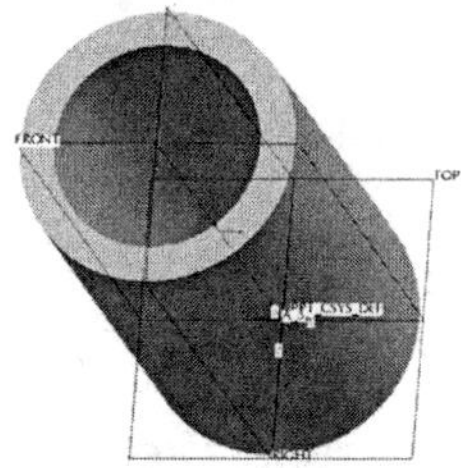 Extrude - Thin 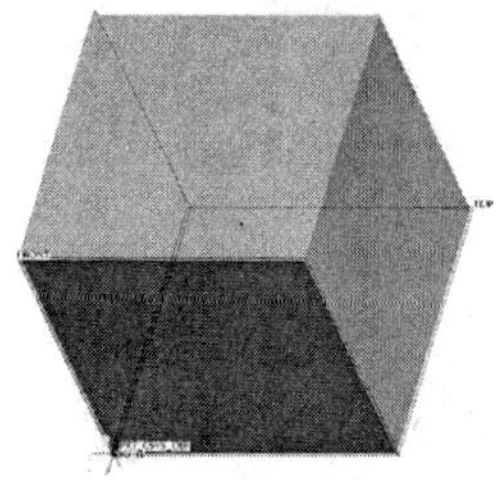 Block before extrude cut 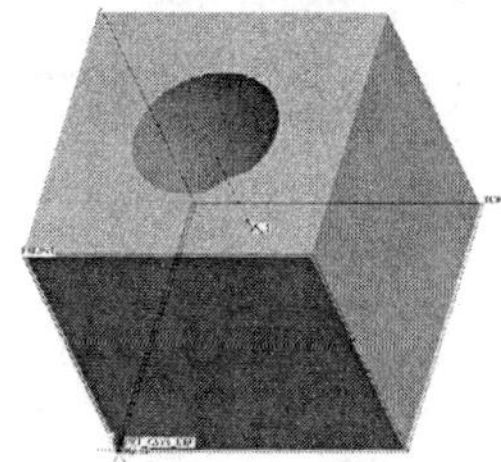 Extrude – Cut using a circular section

Round feature		
Useful for rounding edges.		
Starting the feature	INSERT → ROUND, or 	
	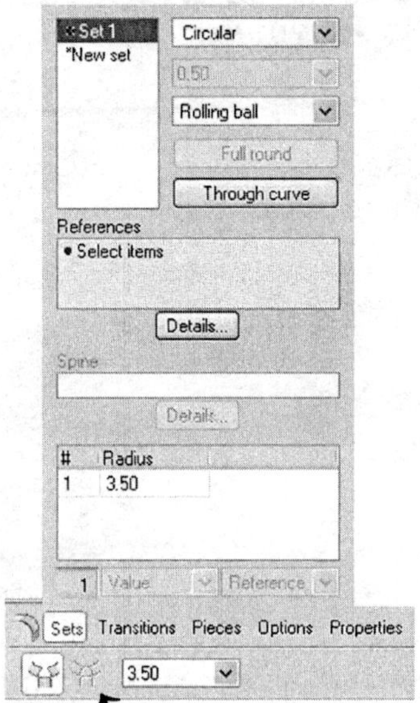 **Set mode** **Transition mode**	
Mode		By default, Pro|ENGINEER ngineer activates the set mode. In this mode, a user controls a set of round geometry using a single round dimension. When selecting a number of references (edges to be rounded), hold ***CTRL*** to place them in a single set.
		In the transition mode, a user specifies the filler geometry to transition between round geometries.
Shape of the section	Two basic geometries for round are circular and conic. The conic option provides a better control of the sharpness of the round.	
Rolling ball	The round is formed by rolling a spherical ball along the surfaces to which it is tangent. It is the default option.	
Normal to spine	The round is created by sweeping a conic section normal to a spine.	

Examples	 Constant round  Variable round  Full round 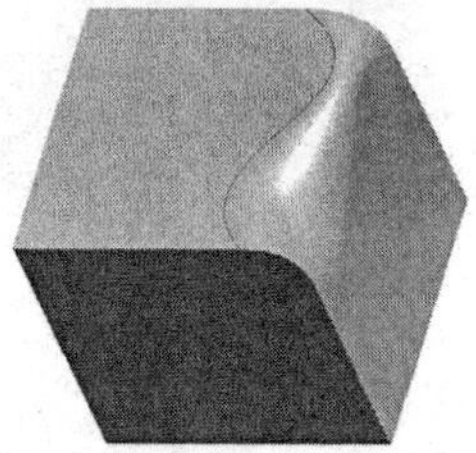 Round driven by a datum curve  D1 × D2 conic

Working Directory

The working directory is a designated area for Pro|ENGINEER to save its files. Pro|ENGINEER looks for files in the working directory. Note that if you retrieve a file from another directory and use **FILE → SAVE**, Pro|ENGINEER saves the file in the original directory, and not in the working directory. Use **SAVE AS** command to save it in the working directory.

Datum Planes

Pro|ENGINEER creates three default datum planes - FRONT, TOP and RIGHT - as the initial features to start the modeling process. Each datum plane has two sides marked by orange and black colors. In the standard orientation, only the orange sides are visible. The black color appears when the model is rotated. The orange side is considered to be the active side of the datum plane. The default part coordinate system "PRT-CSYS-DEF" is located at the intersection of the three datum planes. The spin center shown in Red, Green and Blue (RGB) color lines helps in rotating the model.

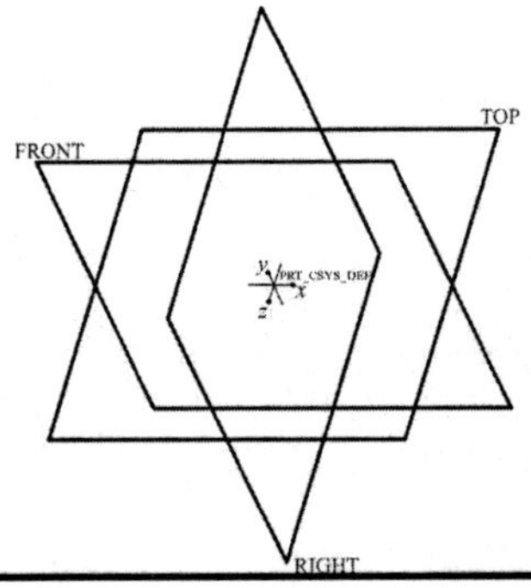

Background Information:

Bearings allow relative motion between two components while minimizing frictional losses. For instance, the main bearings in automobile allow the wheels to rotate relative to the axle. A rolling element bearing, one of the widely-used bearings, consist of an outer race and an inner race separated by rolling elements (either balls or cylinders). The rolling elements reduce friction by providing rolling contact. As bearings are purchased items, only the outer profile is modeled. As the rolling element bearings are typically mounted using an interference fit, the inner and outer diameters of the bearing are critical. For a proper assembly, the edges of the bearing are rounded, and therefore, the radius of the round is another critical dimension.

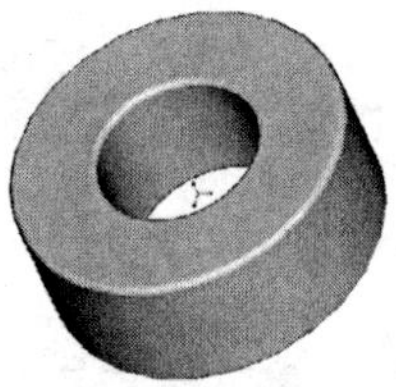

SEQUENCE OF STEPS

Step I - Extrude the base cylinder

1. Use "Extrude" feature.
2. Define the sketch plane
3. Sketch two circular sections
4. Define the depth of extrusion

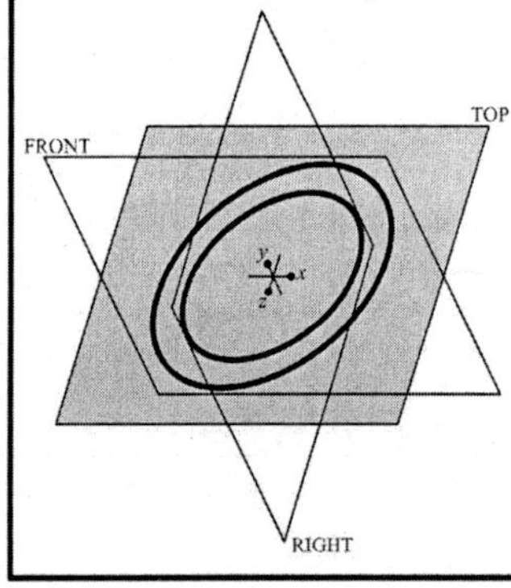

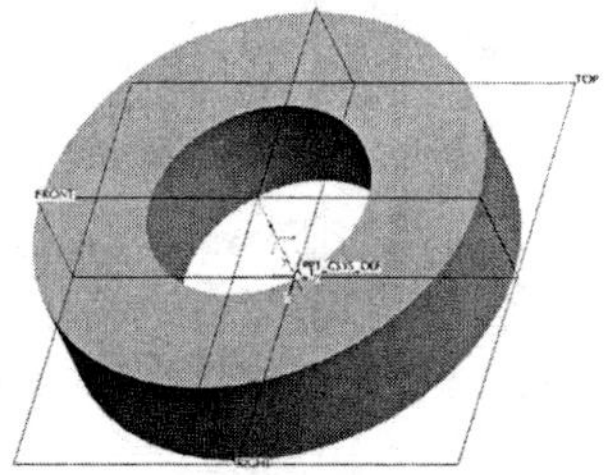

Step II - Round the edges of the base cylinder

1. Use "Round" feature
2. Specify the radius
3. Select the edges to be rounded

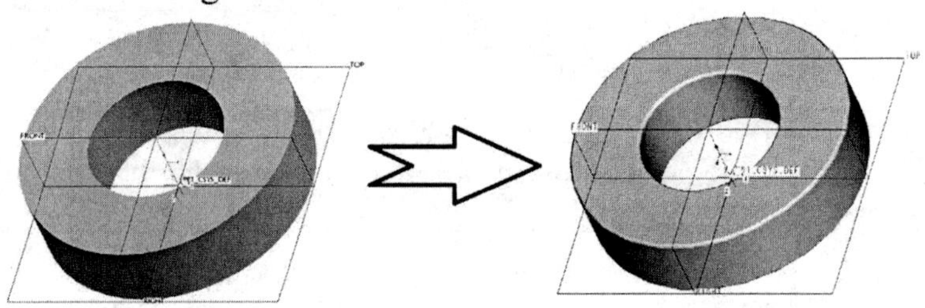

Goal	Step	Commands
Open a new file for the bearing part	1. Set up the working directory.	The working directory is a designated area for Pro|ENGINEER to save its files. Pro|ENGINEER looks for files in the working directory. Note that if you retrieve a file from another directory and use **FILE → SAVE**, Pro|ENGINEER saves the file in the original directory, and not in the working directory. Use **SAVE AS** command to save it in the working directory. **FILE → SET WORKING DIRECTORY →** ***Select the working directory*** **→ OK**
	2. Open a new file.	We will create the bearing as a solid part. **FILE → NEW →** ***Part*** **→** ***Solid*** **→ bearing → OK** Refer to Fig. 2.1. In the graphics window, Pro|ENGINEER displays the three default datum planes (FRONT, TOP, and RIGHT), and the default part coordinate system (PRT_CSYS_DEF) at the intersection of the three datum planes. Refer to Fig. 2.2.

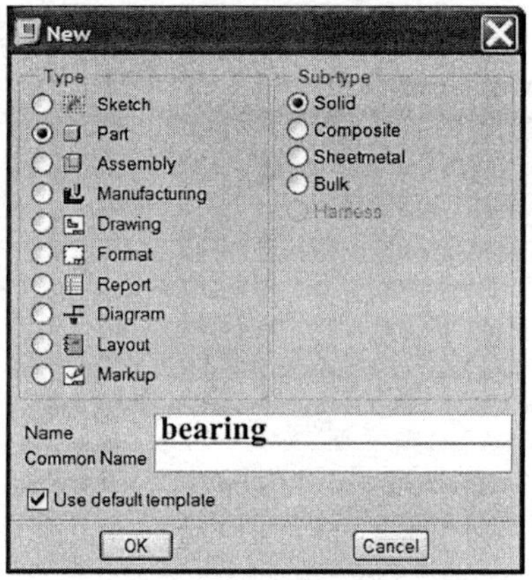

Fig. 2.1.

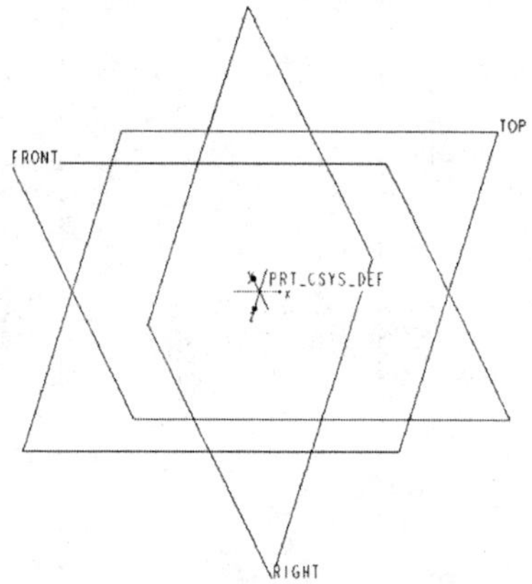

Fig. 2.2.

Goal	Step	Commands
Experiment with the mouse	3. Use the mouse to zoom, spin, and pan the model.	The user can spin, zoom, and pan the model by moving the mouse while holding middle mouse button, middle mouse and ***CTRL*** key, and middle mouse and ***SHIFT*** key respectively. Fig. 2.3 illustrates the mouse functions. The center of the zoom is always at the cursor location. The view can be scaled by a factor of 2 by holding ***SHIFT*** or ***CTRL*** key, and rotating the middle mouse button. Explore each of these functions. To get back to the default view, use the following command: **VIEW → ORIENTATION → STANDARD ORIENTATION** (or → **STANDARD ORIENTATION**) Refer to Fig. 2.4. The default view is typically set as trimetric. However, it can be changed to isometric or user-defined by using the following command: **VIEW → ORIENTATION → REORIENT → (Type)** ***Preferences*** **→ (Default orientation) Trimetric→ OK** Refer to Fig. 2.5.

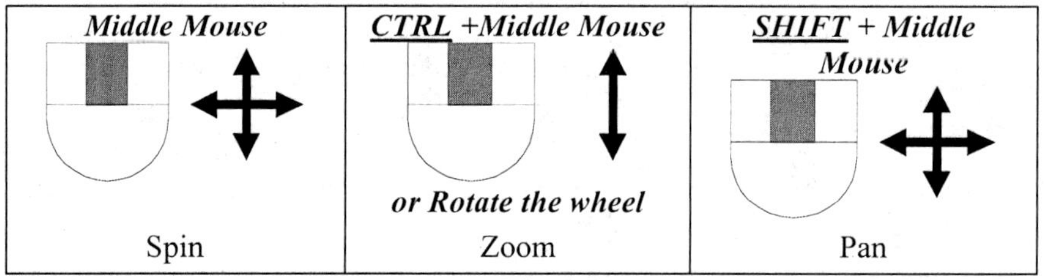

Fig. 2.3.

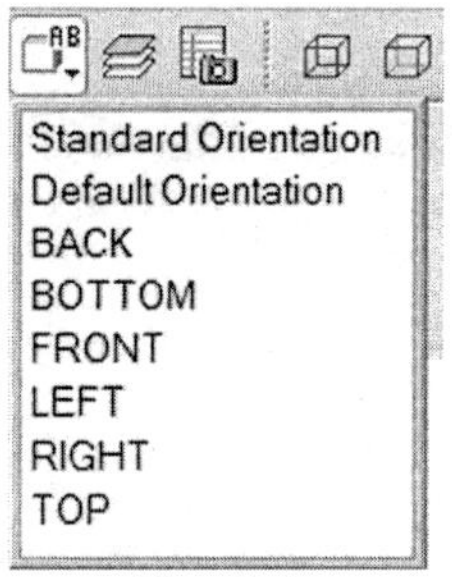

Fig. 2.4.

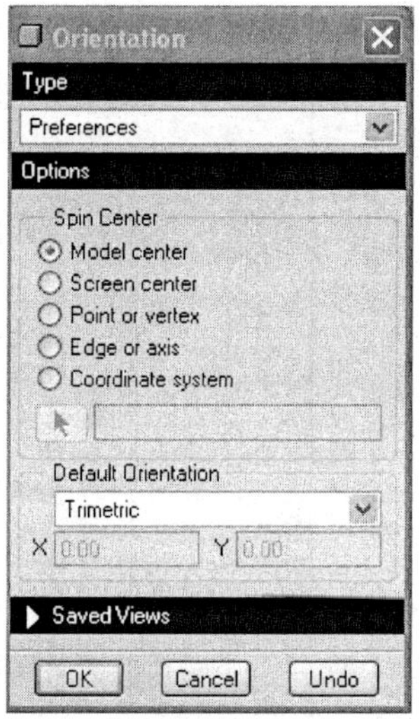

Fig. 2.5.

Goal	Step	Commands
Understand the datum planes	4. Understand the datum planes.	★Pro|ENGINEER creates three default datum planes - FRONT, TOP and RIGHT. Each datum plane has two sides marked by orange and black colors. These planes can be visualized by looking at Fig. 2.5 where the planes are shaded. In the standard orientation (shown in Figs. 2.2 and 2.5), only the orange sides are visible. The black color appears when the model is rotated. The orange side is considered to be the active side of the datum plane. In Figs. 2.2 and 2.5, the default part coordinate system "PRT-CSYS-DEF" is located at the intersection of three datum planes. The spin center shown in Red, Green and Blue (RGB) color lines helps in rotating the model.
Create the base cylinder	5. Start "Extrude" feature.	**INSERT → EXTRUDE** [Or *click*  in the feature toolbar – left side]

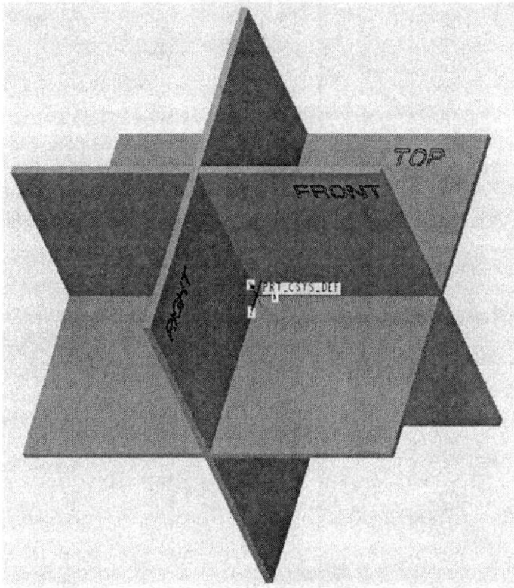

Fig. 2.5.

Goal	Step	Commands
Create the base cylinder (continued)	6. Define the sketching plane.	To select the sketch plane, ***click Placement*** **(in the dashboard) → Define** Refer to Fig. 2.6. Pro|ENGINEER brings up "Sketch" window where we define the sketch plane. Refer to Fig. 2.7. We are going to sketch the section on the TOP datum plane. Pro|ENGINEER highlights different planes as we move the mouse over them. ***Select the TOP datum plane in the graphics window or in the model tree by clicking on "TOP" →*** Refer to Fig. 2.8. The yellow arrow in the graphics window points to the view direction. Clicking "Flip" in the sketch window reverses the view direction. Pro|ENGINEER automatically orients the sketch plane by aligning the outward normal from the reference (the right datum plane) in the right direction. Refer to Fig. 2.8. **Sketch**

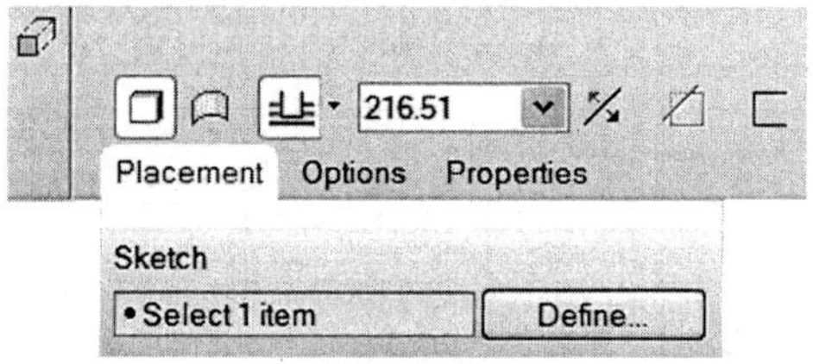

Fig. 2.6.

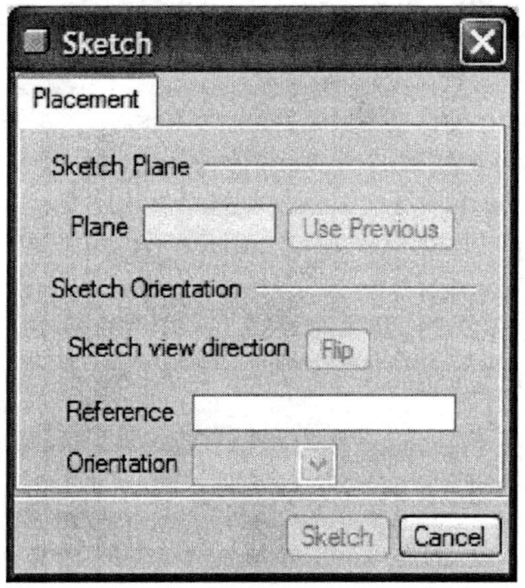

Fig. 2.7.

Fig. 2.8.

Goal	Step	Commands
Create the base cylinder (continued)	7. Identify and select references.	The screen changes to the sketcher mode. Activate "References" window by selecting: **SKETCH → REFERENCES →** The "References" window shows two references: F1(RIGHT) and F3(FRONT). Refer to Fig. 2.9. All dimensions are placed with respect to these two references. If necessary, additional references can be added to this list. It is advisable to select the references before sketching. Close
	8. Understand the orientation of the sketcher.	Holding the middle mouse button and moving the mouse rotates the model. ***Move the mouse holding Middle Mouse →*** To get back to the sketch view, use the following command: **VIEW → ORIENTATION → SKETCH ORIENTATION** (Or 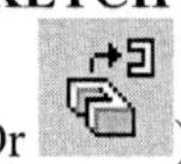)

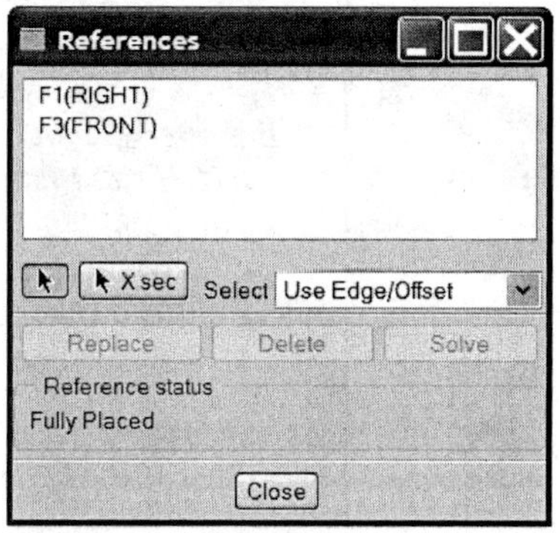

Fig. 2.9.

Goal	Step	Commands
Create the base cylinder (continued)	9. Draw an outer circle.	→ ***Select the center of the circle as the intersection of the FRONT and RIGHT datum planes →*** Refer to Fig. 2.10. The cursor snaps onto the intersection. ***Select a point to define the outer edge of the circle*** Refer to Fig. 2.10.
	10. Create an inner circle.	→ ***Select the center of the circle as the intersection of the FRONT and RIGHT datum planes → Select a point to define the inner circle*** Refer to Fig. 2.10.
	11. Modify the dimensions.	Pro|ENGINEER automatically places dimensions for the circles. A good practice is to modify smaller dimensions first. → ***Double click the inner diameter dimension → <u>1</u>→ <u>ENTER</u> → Double click the outer diameter dimension → <u>2</u> → <u>ENTER</u>*** Pro|ENGINEER automatically regenerates the section. Refer to Fig. 2.11.
	12. Exit sketcher.	✓

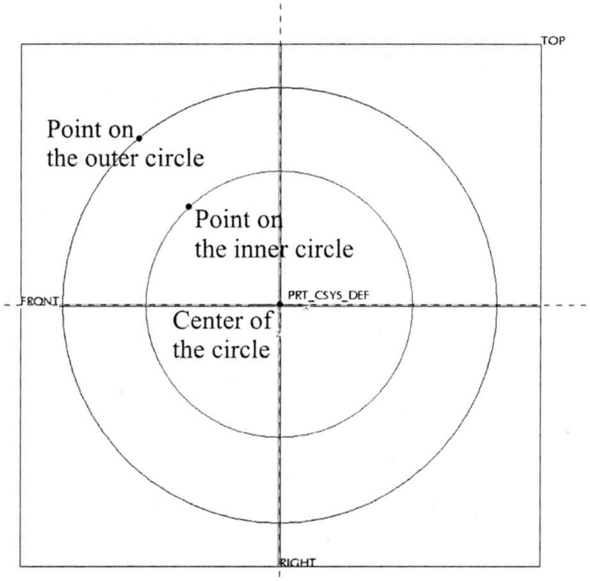

Fig. 2.10.

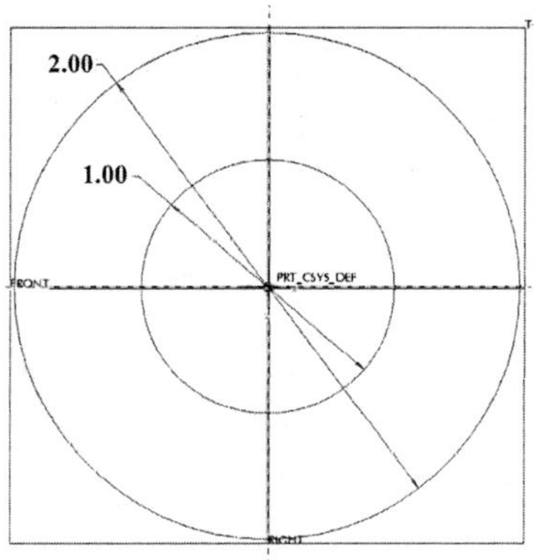

Fig. 2.11.

Goal	Step	Commands
Create the base cylinder (continued)	13. Define the depth.	The depth dimension appears in the dash and on the part. Modify the depth at one of these two places. Refer to Figs. 2.12 and 2.13. ***Select the depth dimension*** **→ <u>0.5</u> →** ***<u>ENTER</u>***
	14. Accept the feature creation.	Refer to Fig. 2.14.
Round the four edges	15. Round the four edges of the bearing.	**INSERT → ROUND (or)** **→** Specify the radius of the rounds to be 0.025. **<u>0.025</u> →** ***<u>ENTER</u>*** **→** Refer to Fig. 2.15. ***Select the four edges to be rounded while holding <u>CTRL</u>*** **→** The four edges are rounded regardless of the ***<u>CTRL</u>*** key. Holding ***CTRL*** puts the four edge rounds in one round set. Therefore, one parameter, the radius of the round, controls the geometry of all the rounds. Refer to Fig. 2.16. Refer to Fig. 2.17.

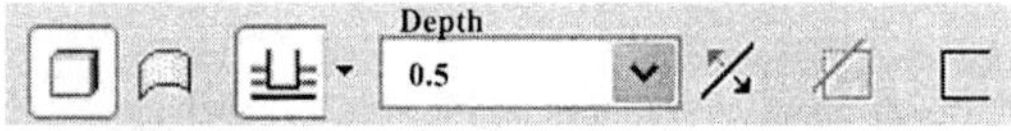

Fig. 2.12.

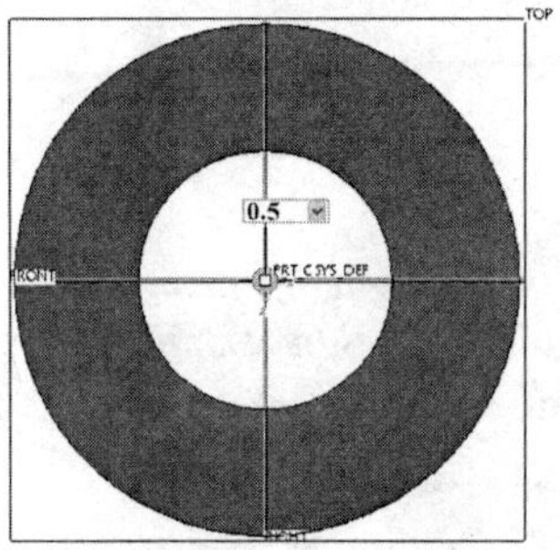

Fig. 2.13.

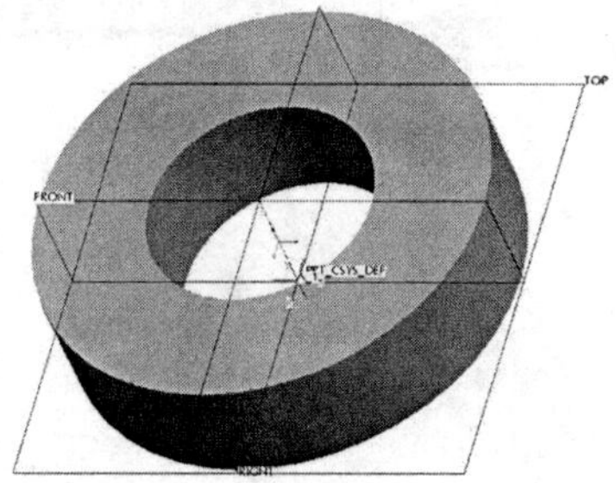
Fig. 2.14.

Fig. 2.15.

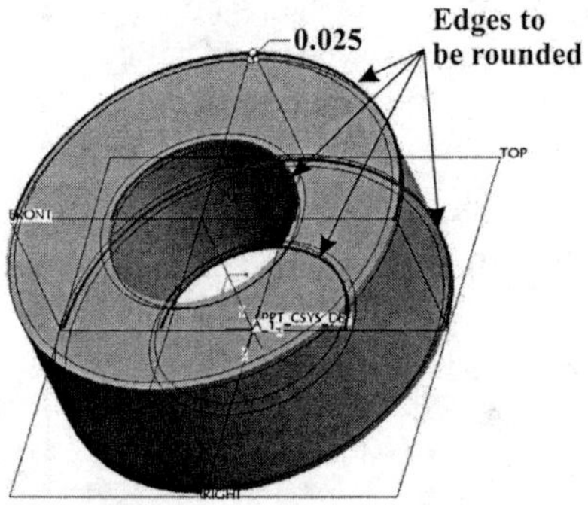

Fig. 2.16.

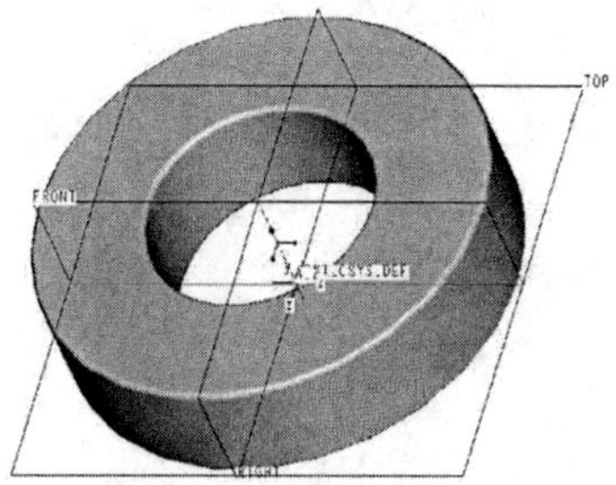
Fig. 2.17.

Goal	Step	Commands
View the model	16. Turn the datum planes off.	***Click the following icons to switch off the datum planes, axes, points, and default coordinate system.*** 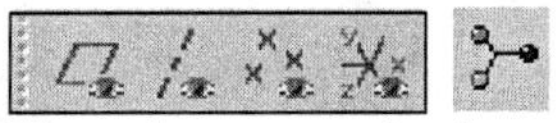 These icons turn the datum planes, axes, points, coordinate system, and spin center on/off. Refer to Fig. 2.18. Modifying the display helps in visualizing the model better. The four model display options that can be selected by clicking on the corresponding icon are: Wire-frame - Hidden line - No hidden line - Shaded - Fig. 2.19 shows the model in the four display types.

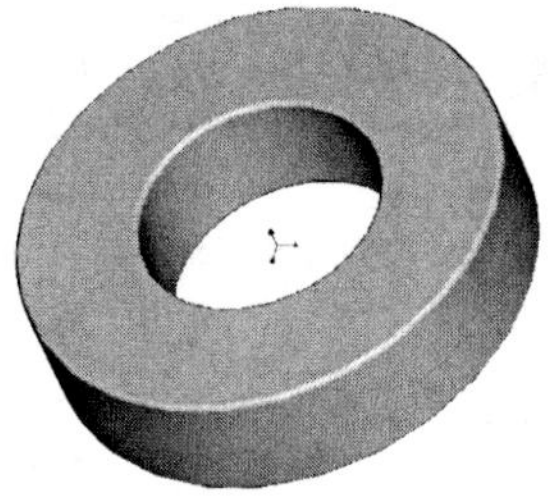

Fig. 2.18.

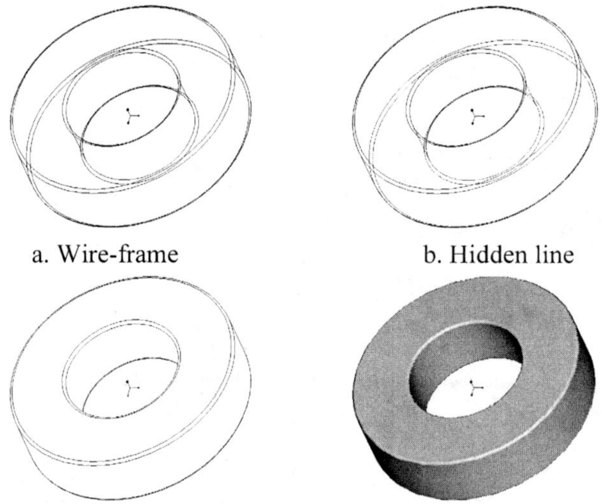

a. Wire-frame
b. Hidden line
c. No hidden line
d. Shaded

Fig. 2.19.

Goal	Step	Commands
Modify dimensions	17. Modify the dimensions.	***Select the extrusion feature in the graphics window or from the model tree → Right Mouse →* Edit →** Refer to Fig. 2.20. ***Select the 2.0 dimension →* <u>1.25</u> → *<u>ENTER</u>* → *Select the 1.0 dimension* → <u>0.6</u> → *<u>ENTER</u>* →** **EDIT → REGENERATE** (or ) Modifications take affect after regeneration. Refer to Fig. 2.21.
Use the model player	18. Use the model player to view the feature creation sequence.	**TOOLS → MODEL PLAYER →** Refer to Fig. 2.22.  →  →  →  →  →  **(till you see Feat # 5 of 6) →** **Show Dims →** Note that Pro|ENGINEER shows the final dimensions. **FINISH**
Save the file and exit Pro|ENGINEER	19. Save the file and exit Pro|ENGINEER.	**FILE → SAVE → BEARING.PRT → OK → FILE → EXIT → Yes**

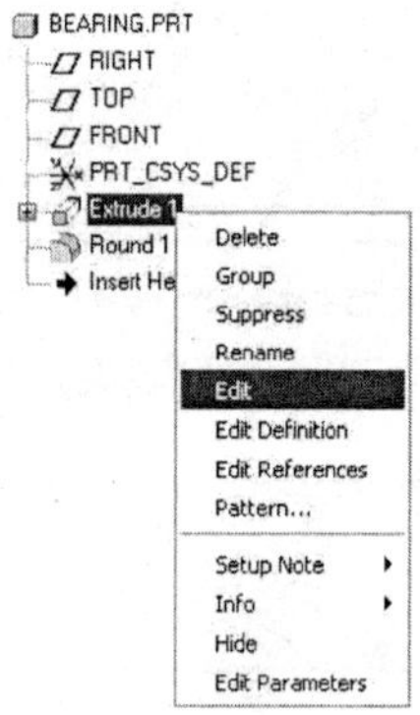

Fig. 2.20.

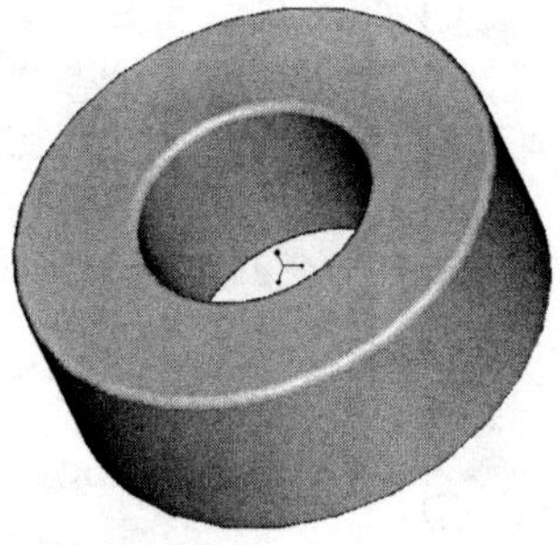

Fig. 2.21.

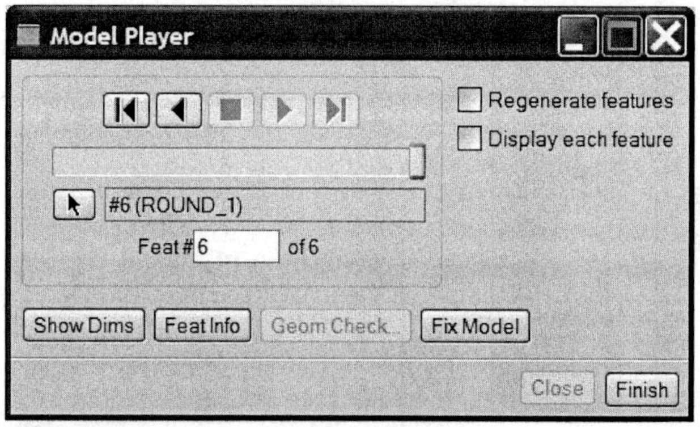

Fig. 2.22.

Goal	Step	Commands
Use trail file to recreate the session	20. Trail.txt file location depends on the configuration. Find its location by searching for trail.txt. Note that there can be several trail.txt files. Identify the correct one by checking the time it was created.	
	21. Rename the trail.txt file as bearing.txt.	
	22. Start notepad and open bearing.txt file.	
	23. Search for word "bearing" and replace it as "new_bearing". Now, when the trail file is played, it creates a part - new_bearing.	
	24. Delete the highlighted portion in the trail.txt file.	
	25. Use save as and write the file name in quotes - "bearing.txa". Now, we are changing the file extension to eliminate version number. Extension .txa is for training file. Exit notepad.	
	26. Open Pro|ENGINEER.	
	27. Play trail file.	**TOOLS → PLAY TRAIL/TRAINING FILE → Select "bearing.txa" file → OPEN** Pro|ENGINEER recreates the session. By deleting the highlighted section, Pro|ENGINEER does not exit at the end of the trail file.
Exit Pro|ENGINEER	28. Exit Pro|ENGINEER.	**FILE → EXIT → Yes**

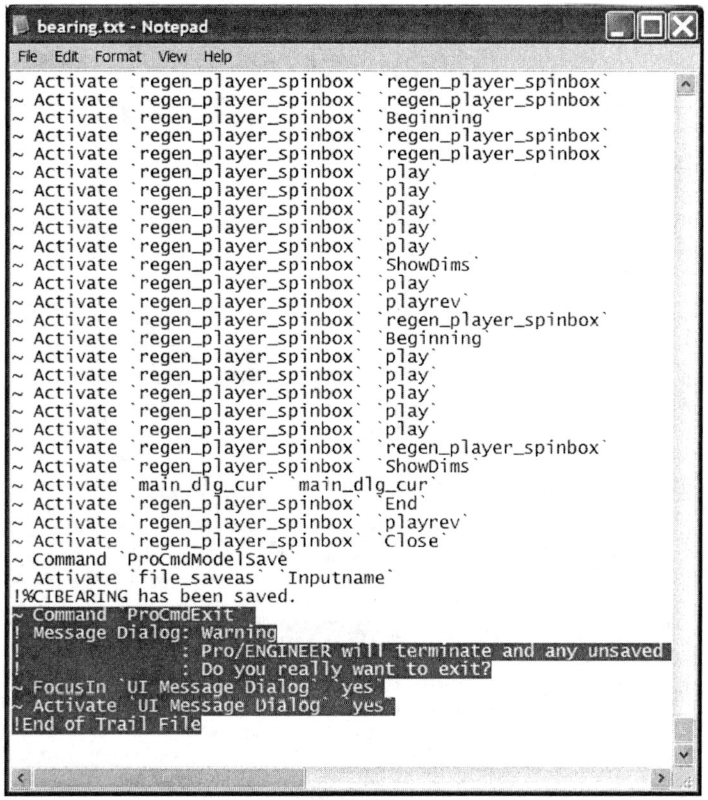

Fig. 2.23.

Step I - Extrude the base cylinder

1. Use "Extrude" feature.
2. Define the sketch plane
3. Sketch a circular section
4. Define the depth of extrusion

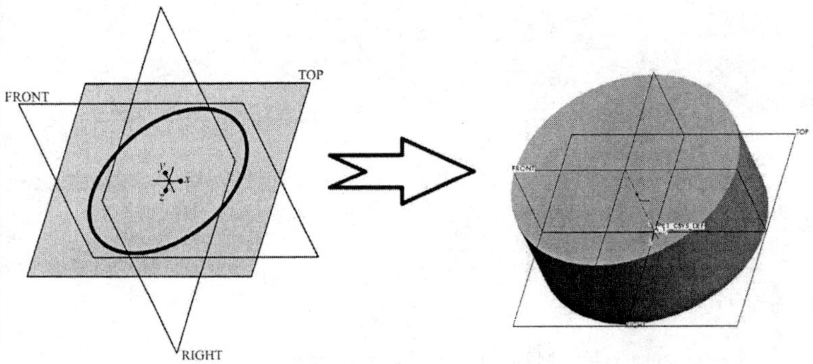

Step II - Create the circular cut

1. Use "Extrude-Cut" feature
2. Define the sketch plane
3. Sketch the inner circle
4. Define the depth of extrusion

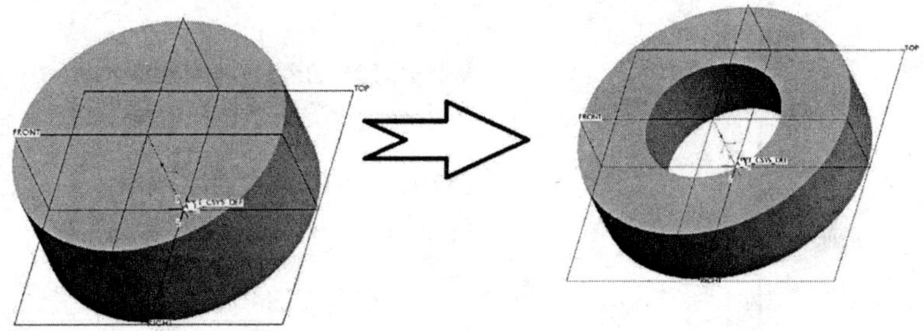

Step III - Round the edges of the base cylinder

1. Use "Round" feature
2. Specify the radius
3. Select the edges to be rounded

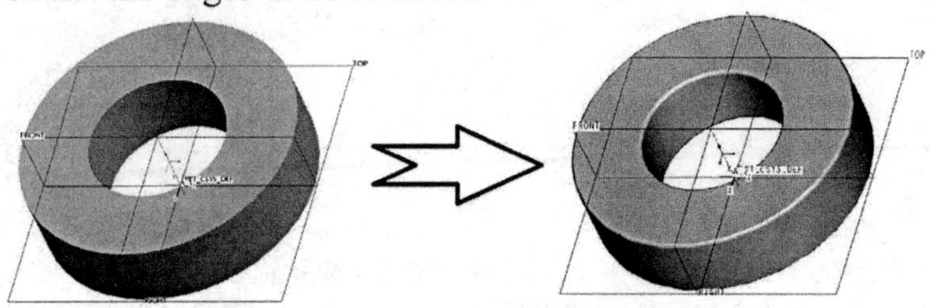

SEQUENCE OF STEPS

Goal	Step	Commands
Open a new file for the bearing part	1. Set up the working directory.	**FILE → SET WORKING DIRECTORY →** ***Select the working directory*** **→ OK**
	2. Open a new file.	We will create the bearing as a solid part. **FILE → NEW →** ***Part*** **→** ***Solid*** **→ <u>bearing1</u> → OK** Refer to Fig. 2.24. In the graphics window, Pro|ENGINEER displays the three default datum planes (FRONT, TOP, and RIGHT), and the default part coordinate system (PRT_CSYS_DEF) at the intersection of the three datum planes. Refer to Fig. 2.25.
Create the base cylinder	3. Start "Extrude" feature.	**INSERT → EXTRUDE** [Or *click* in the feature toolbar – left side]

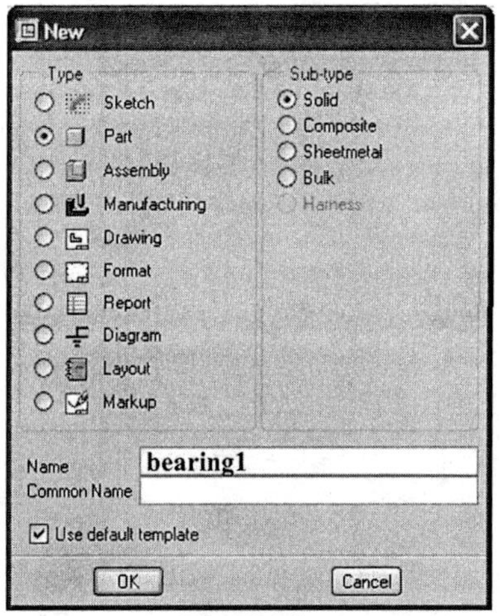

Fig. 2.24.

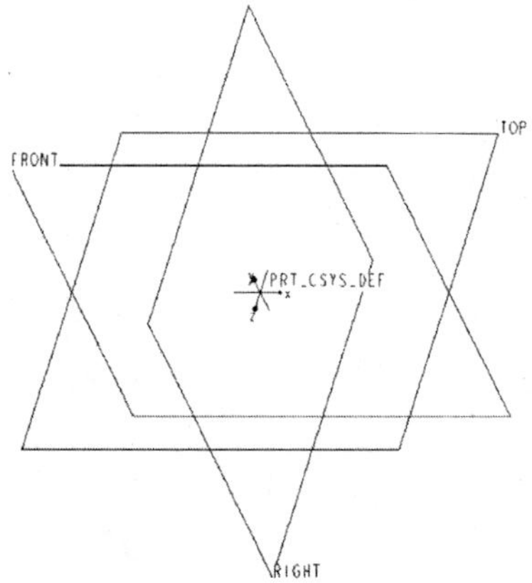

Fig. 2.25.

Goal	Step	Commands
Create the base cylinder (continued)	4. Define the sketching plane.	To select the sketch plane, ***click Placement* (in the dashboard) → Define** Refer to Fig. 2.26. Pro|ENGINEER brings up "Sketch" window where we define the sketch plane. Refer to Fig. 2.27. We are going to sketch the section on the TOP datum plane. ***Select the TOP datum plane in the graphics window or in the model tree by clicking on "TOP" →*** Refer to Fig. 2.28. **Sketch**
	5. Draw an outer circle.	O ***→ Select the center of the circle as the intersection of the FRONT and RIGHT datum planes →*** Refer to Fig. 2.29. The cursor snaps onto the intersection. ***Select a point to define the outer edge of the circle*** Refer to Fig. 2.29.

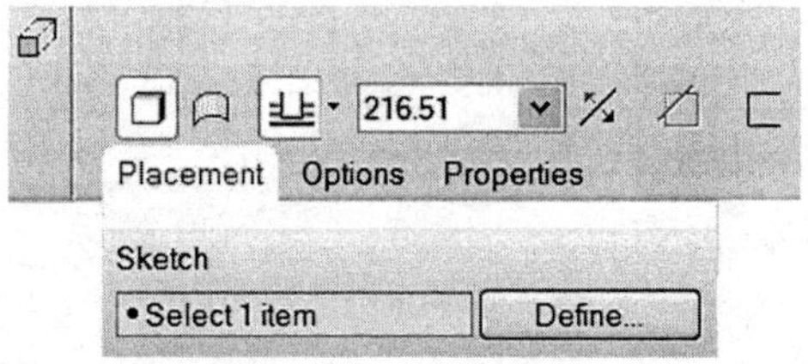

Fig. 2.26.

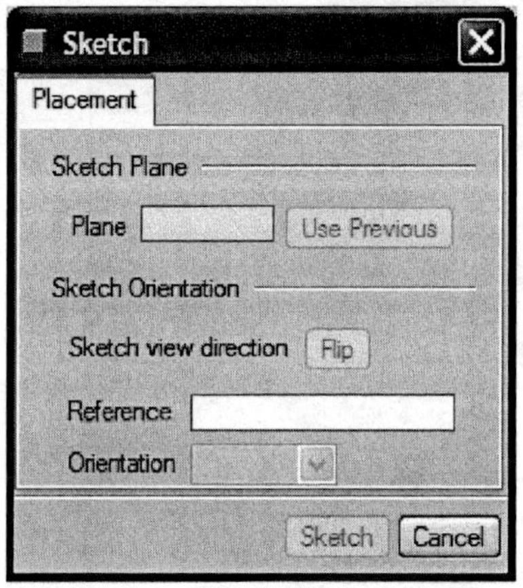

Fig. 2.27.

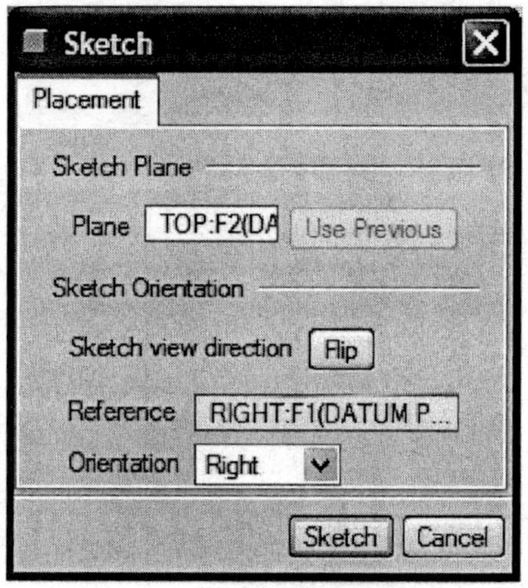

Fig. 2.28.

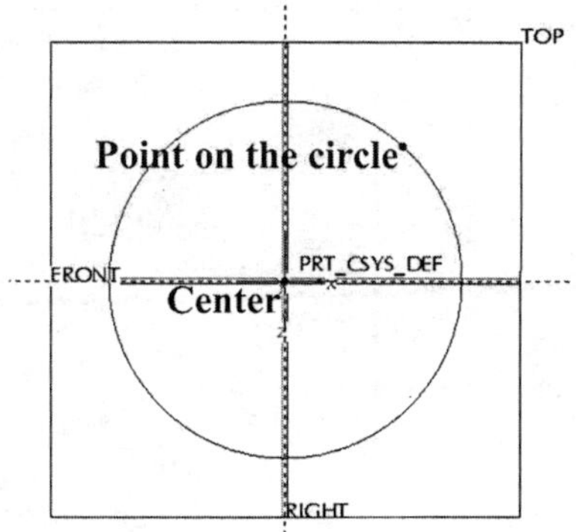

Fig. 2.29.

Goal	Step	Commands
Create the base cylinder (continued)	6. Modify the dimension.	Pro|ENGINEER automatically places dimensions for the circles. A good practice is to modify smaller dimensions first. → ***Double click the diameter dimension*** → **<u>1.25</u>** → ***<u>ENTER</u>*** Pro|ENGINEER automatically regenerates the section. Refer to Fig. 2.30.
	7. Exit sketcher.	
	8. Define the depth.	***Select the depth dimension*** → **<u>0.5</u>** → ***<u>ENTER</u>*** Refer to Fig. 2.31.
	9. Accept the feature creation.	Refer to Fig. 2.32.
Create the central hole	10. Start "Extrude – Cut" feature.	**INSERT → EXTRUDE →** Refer to Fig. 2.33.
	11. Define the sketching plane.	To select the sketch plane, ***click Placement*** **(in the dashboard) →** **Define** Pro|ENGINEER brings up "Sketch" window where we define the sketch plane. Refer to Fig. 2.33. We are going to sketch the section on the previous sketch plane - the TOP datum plane. **Use Previous**

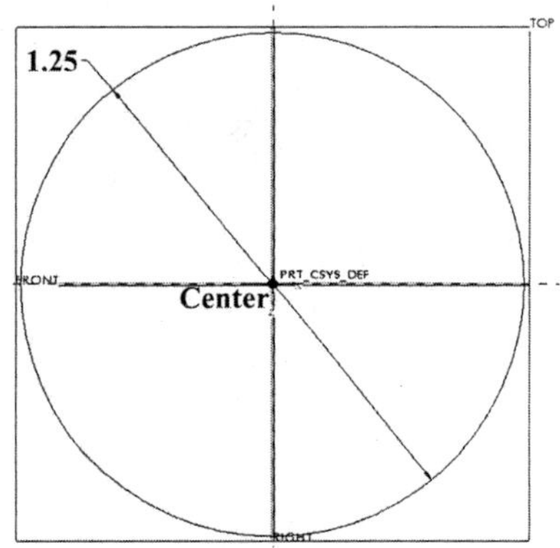

Fig. 2.30.

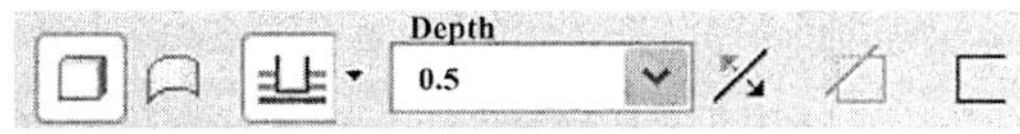

Fig. 2.31.

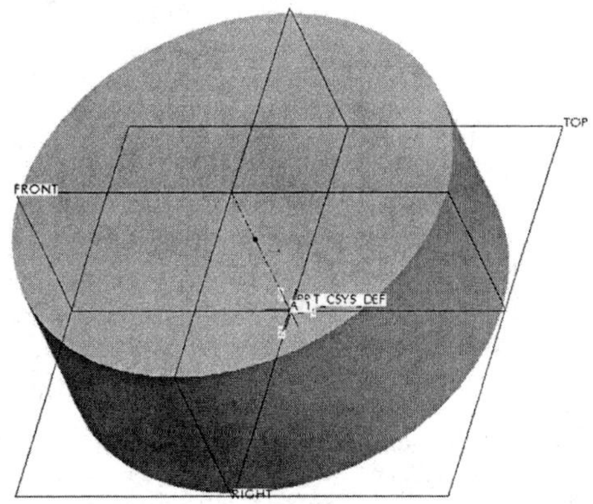

Fig. 2.32.

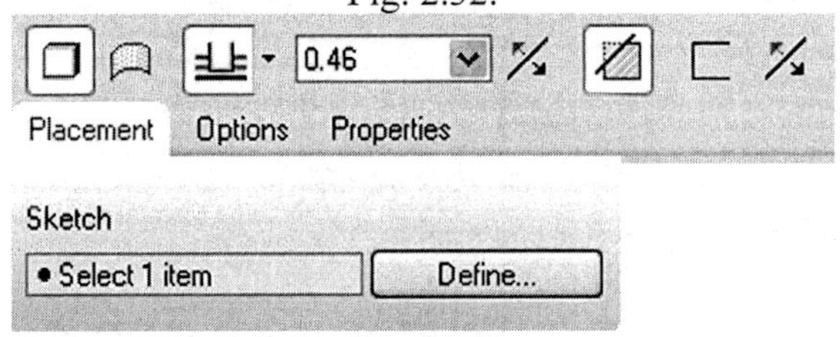

Fig. 2.33.

Goal	Step	Commands
Create the central hole (continued)	12. Draw an inner circle.	○ → ***Select the center of the circle as the intersection of the FRONT and RIGHT datum planes →*** Refer to Fig. 2.34. The cursor snaps onto the intersection. ***Select a point to define the outer edge of the circle*** Refer to Fig. 2.34.
	13. Modify the dimension.	↖ → ***Double click the diameter dimension*** → **0.60** → ***ENTER*** Pro|ENGINEER automatically regenerates the section.
	14. Exit sketcher.	✓

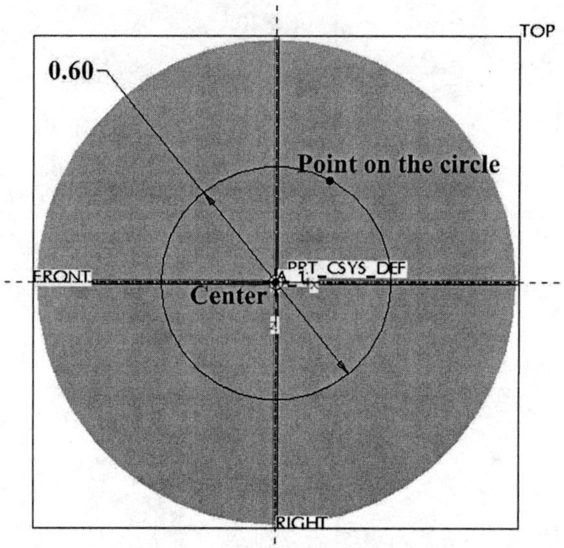

Fig. 2.34.

Goal	Step	Commands
Create the central hole (continued)	15. Define the depth.	**VIEW → ORIENTATION → DEFAULT ORIENTATION →** Notice the cut (yellow arrow) point away from the TOP datum plane. Refer to Fig. 2.35. Change the depth direction to the other side of the sketch.  (before the cut icon) Select the depth option as extrude to intersect with all surfaces.  Refer to Fig. 2.36.
	16. Accept the feature creation.	 Refer to Fig. 2.37.

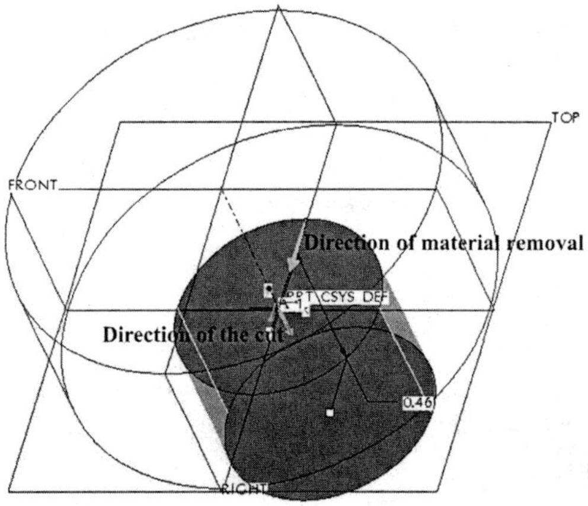

Fig. 2.35.

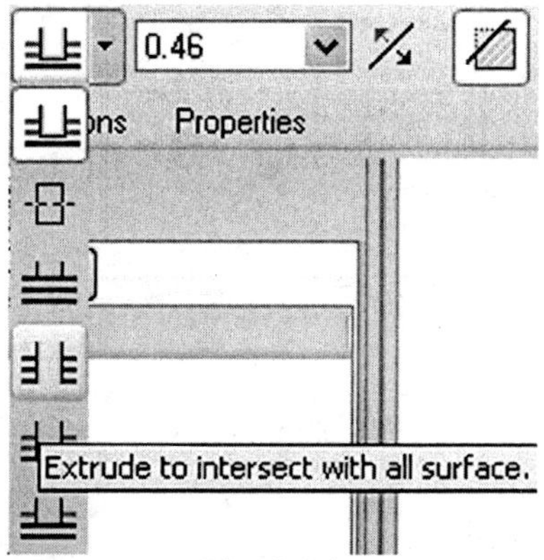

Fig. 2.36.

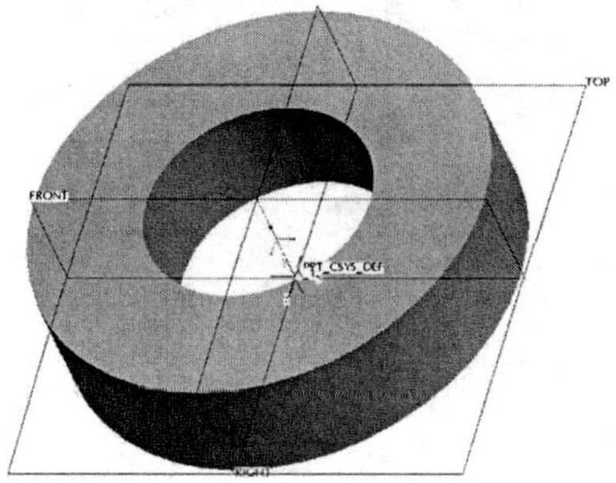
Fig. 2.37.

Goal	Step	Commands
Round the four edges	17. Round the four edges of the bearing.	**INSERT → ROUND (or) →** Specify the radius of the rounds to be 0.025. **<u>0.025</u> → *<u>ENTER</u>* →** Refer to Fig. 2.38. ***Select the four edges to be rounded while holding <u>CTRL</u>* →** Refer to Fig. 2.39. Refer to Fig. 2.40.
Save the file and exit Pro|ENGINEER	18. Save the file and exit Pro|ENGINEER .	**FILE → SAVE → <u>BEARING.PRT</u> → OK → FILE → EXIT → Yes**

Fig. 2.38.

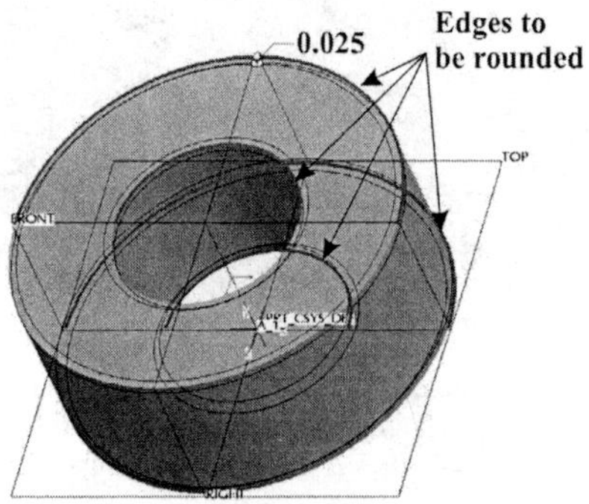

Fig. 2.39.

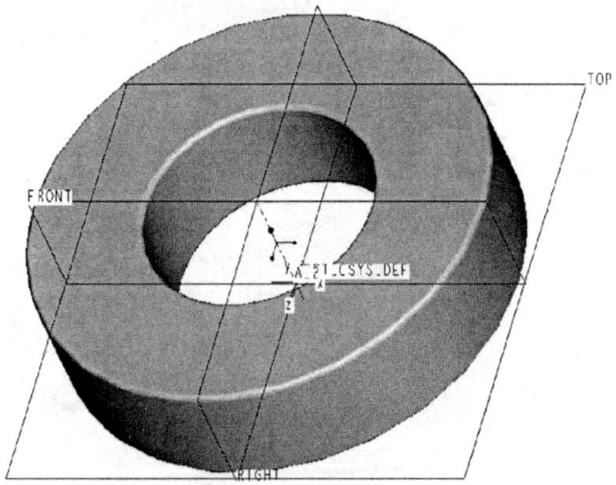

Fig. 2. 40.

Exercise

Problem 1

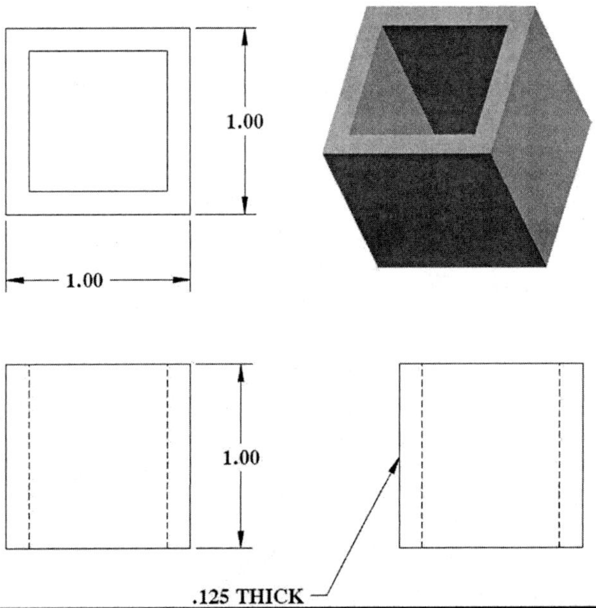

Hints:

1. Start the extrude feature. Create a rectangle (1×1) using the create rectangle tool in the sketcher.

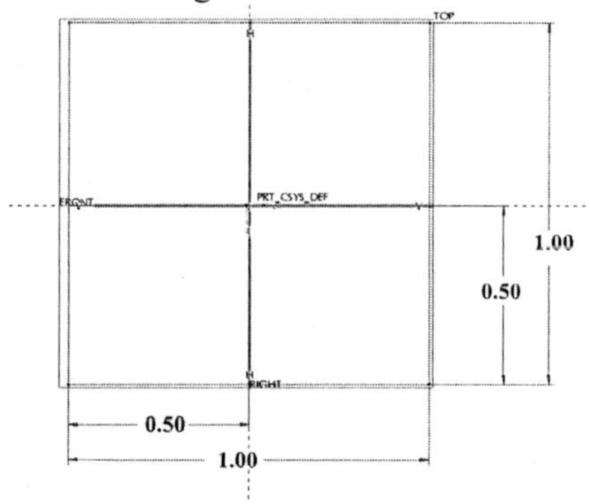

2. Select thicken option and define the thickness as 0.125. The dash is shown in the figure below.

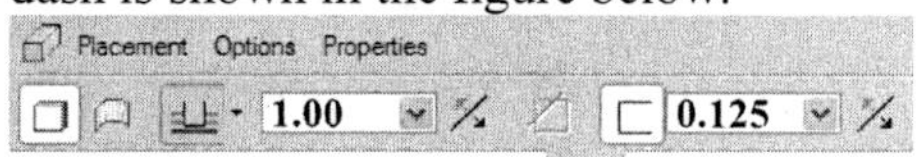

Experiment with the two icons and discover what they do.

Problem 2

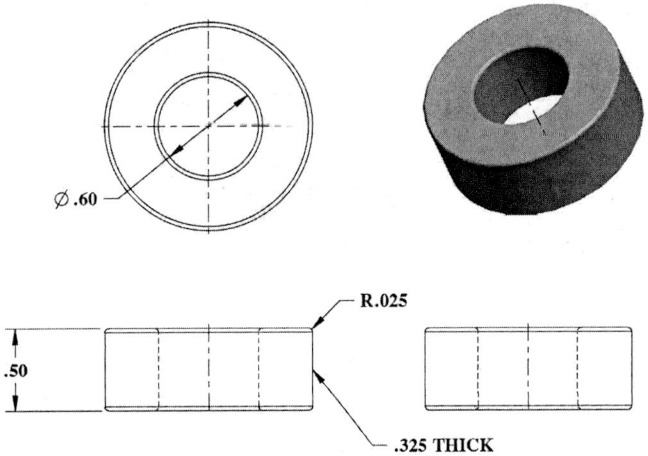

Hints:

1. Start the extrude feature.
2. Select the TOP plane as the sketching plane. Sketch a 0.6″ diameter circle. Exit sketcher.

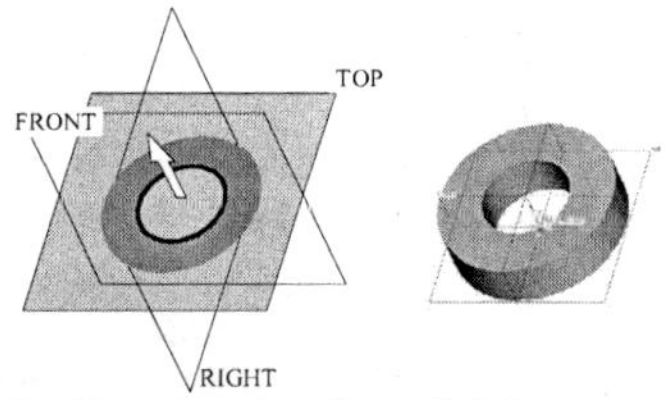

3. Define the depth as 0.5″.
4. Select thicken option and define the thickness as 0.325. Flip the direction of material addition (inside, outside, and both sides of the circle) by clicking the second . The dash is shown below.

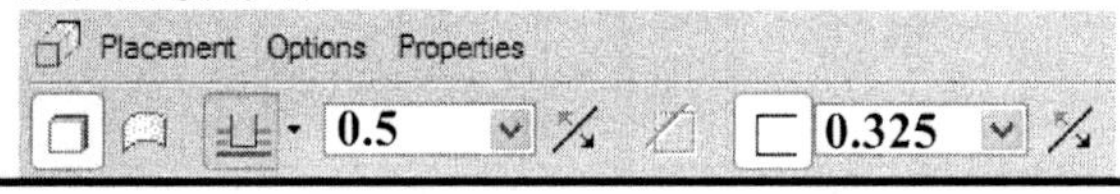

Problem 3

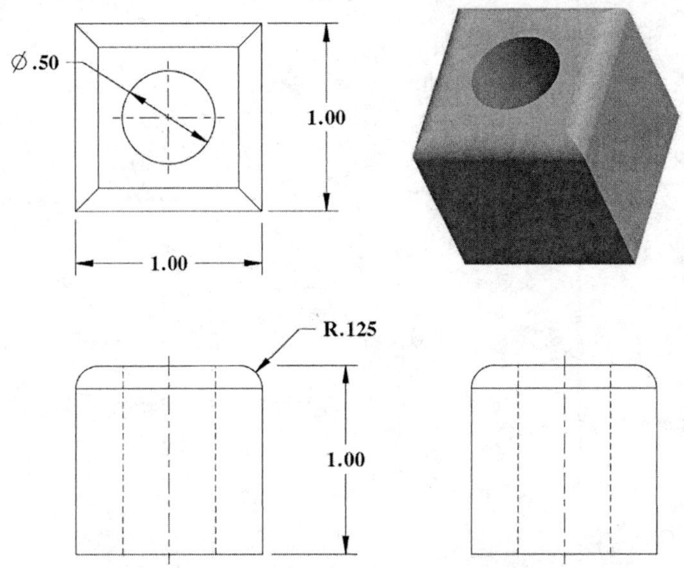

Hints:

1. Use extrude feature. The sketch is shown in the figure below.

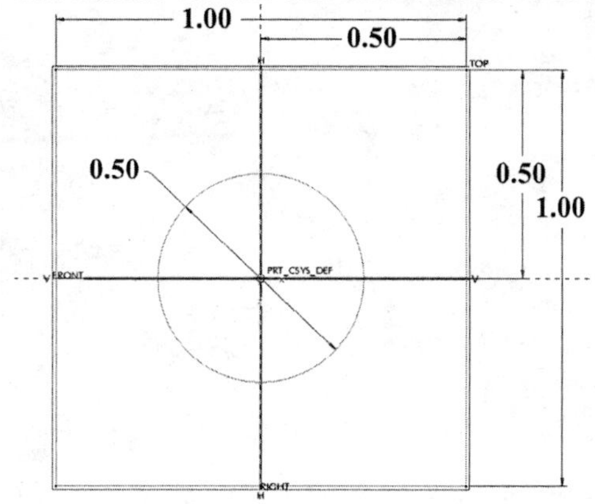

2. Use round feature.

Problem 4

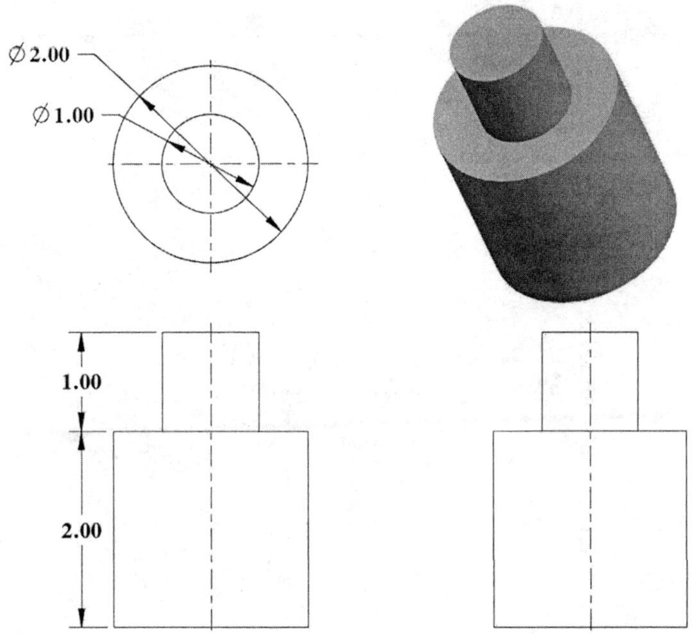

Hints:

1. Create the first cylinder.
2. Select the top of the first cylinder as the sketch plane for creating the second cylinder.

Problem 5

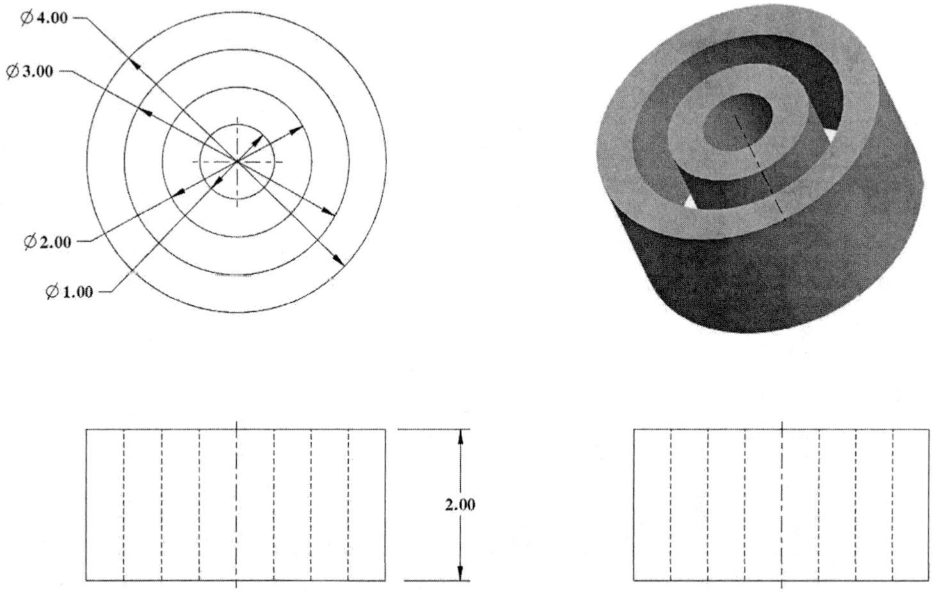

Hints:

1. Start extrude feature.
2. Create the following sketch:

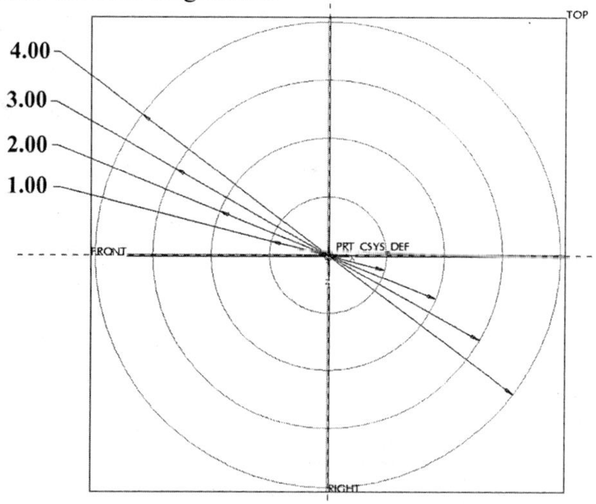

Problem 6

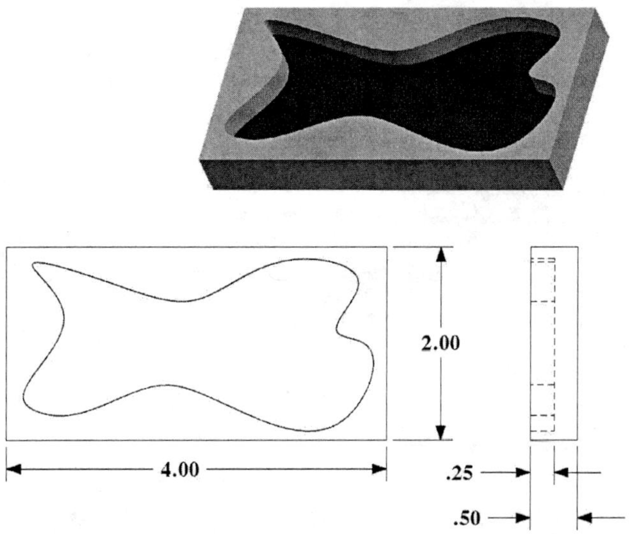

Hints:

1. Create a rectangular block.
2. Create an extrude cut. Use the spline feature ( ) in the sketcher to draw the cut profile.

OPEN-ENDED DESIGN – Explore the sketcher & create your own logo.

Hints:

1. Explore the sketcher tools.
2. Make sure that you read the message window when creating any sketches. Pro|ENGINEER prompts the next step while creating the geometry.
3. You may create several extrusions one at a time. Remember that you can not extrude intersecting geometric entities.
4. The palette [icon] has several sections which can be imported directly. Double click the section and then, click in the graphics window to drop the section.

NOTES:

LESSON 3
BEARINGS

Learning Objectives

- Learn to create macros using ***Mapkeys*** function.
- Model a part using different approaches.
- Practice ***Extrude*** and ***Round*** features.
- Learn ***Revolve*** and ***Hole*** features.

Mapkeys

Mapkeys command creates macros for frequently used command sequences. For instance, when defined, the mapkey command allows a user to change the view to the default orientation and then, shade the model with a single keystroke. The following set of commands define a Mapkey:

TOOLS → MAPKEYS

Pro|ENGINEER opens the mapkey window.

NEW →

In the record mapkey window:

(Key Sequence) **Type the keyboard key name**. For function names use prefix $. (For instance, type $F1 for F1) →

(Name) **Type a name for the macro** → (Description) **Type description** → **RECORD** → **Select the sequence of commands** (For instance, **VIEW → ORIENTATION → STANDARD ORIENTATION → VIEW → SHADE → STOP → OK → CLOSE**) → **STOP**

Mapkey can be added to the screen using the following set of commands:

TOOLS → CUSTOMIZE SCREEN → ***Select the COMMAND tab*** →

(Categories) ***Select Mapkey*** → (Mapkeys) ***Select the desired mapkey → Right Mouse → Choose button image → Double click the image → Drag the mapkey button to the desired menu and release it*** → **OK**

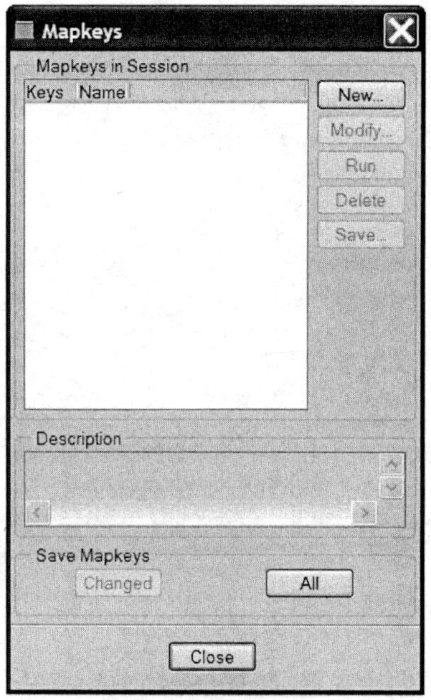

Mapkey window

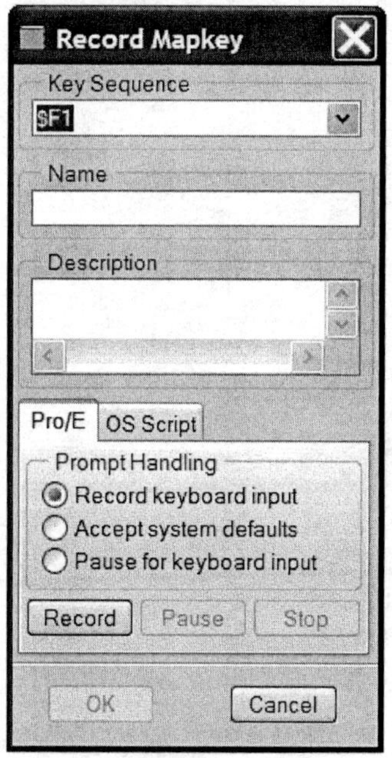

Record mapkey window

Revolve feature	
Useful for creating geometric entities such as solids, cuts, and surfaces with an axis of revolution	
Starting the feature	INSERT → REVOLVE, or
	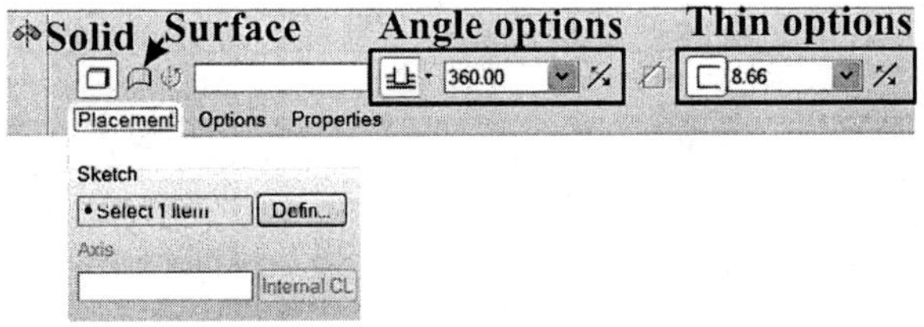
Solid	creates a solid
Surface	Creates a surface
Angle Options	variable both sides of the sketching plane by half the specified angle in each direction To a selected point, curve, plane, or surface Flips the direction of extrusion
Cut	Removes the material when the option is highlighted
Thickness Options	Create a thin feature whose thickness is specified Adds thickness to the outside/inside/either sides of the sketch
Placement	Define to create a new section or redefine the existing one
	Axis collector - Select an axis of revolution

Examples

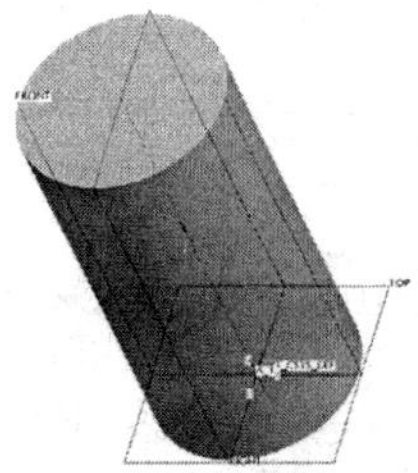
Revolve - Solid

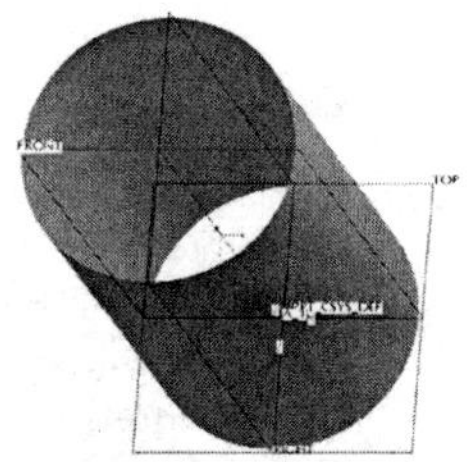
Revolve - Surface

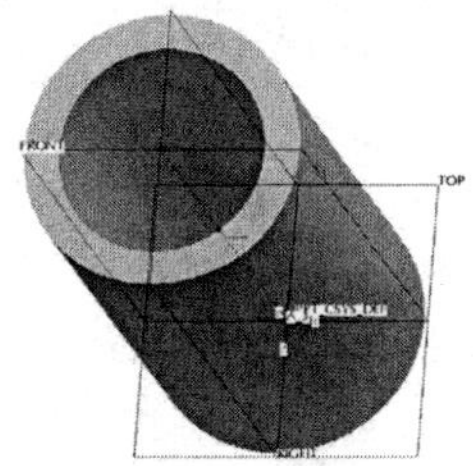
Revolve - Thin

Hole feature	
Useful for adding simple, custom, and standard holes	
Starting the feature	INSERT → HOLE, or  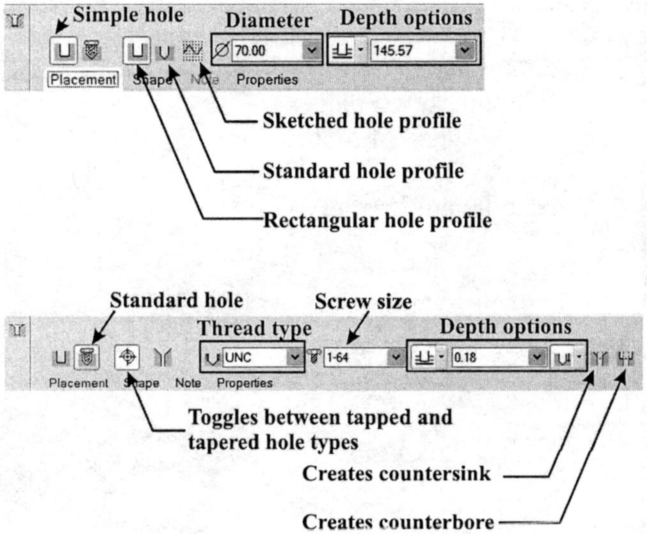
Simple hole	One-sided simple hole is the default option. Two-sided simple holes can be selected using the shape slide-up panel. Using the two-sided hole option, a user can define depth in each of the two sides. *Rectangular hole profile* – Consist of a revolved cut using a rectangular section *Standard hole profile* – The use can select standard drill sizes and specify the countersink, counterbore and tip angle options for the holes. *Sketched hole profile* — Consist of a revolved cut using a custom sketch profile.
Standard hole	The interface provides the standard dimensions for tapped and clearance holes for the fastener. Hole charts can be customized.

Depth options	 Drills the hole to a specified depth from the placement reference 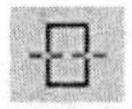 Drills on both sides of the placement reference by half the specified depth in each direction  Drills till a surface is encountered 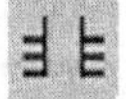 Drills the hole to intersect all surfaces  Drills the hole till it intersect a specific surface  Dills up to a selected point, curve, plane, or surface
Examples	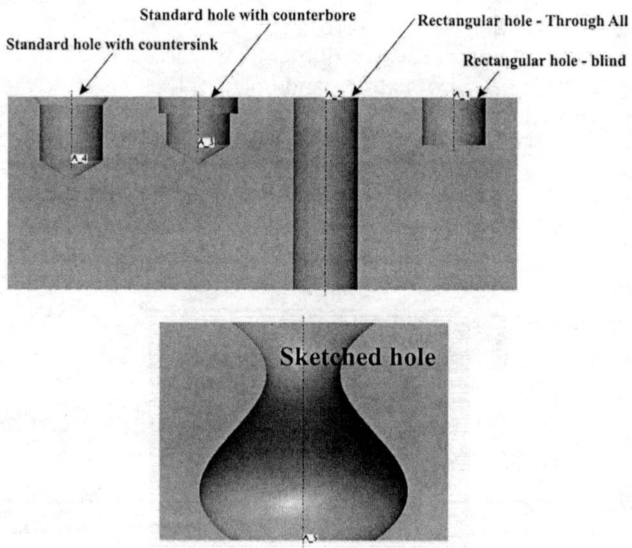

Design Information:

A designer can use a number of approaches to model a part. Some approaches are better as they:

- Are less time-intensive.
- Capture the design intent.
- Result in flexible models that require short regeneration time and are easy to modify at a later time.

The designer must carefully consider alternative approaches and then, strategically choose an appropriate approach based on the task at hand. *The strategy is the key for a successful modeling process.* One good strategy for modeling a complex part is to decompose the part into simple features that can be modeled easily. The benefits of this approach include:

- The ability to suppress individual features.
- Modify fewer dimensions at a time thereby keeping the task manageable.
- Reduce the occurrence of feature regeneration problems.

In this lesson, two additional approaches are presented for creating the bearing part.

The first approach uses the revolve feature, whereas the second approach uses a combination of extrude and hole features to create the base cylinder. For this particular task, as the part is simple, composing of simple geometry and very few features, both approaches work well.

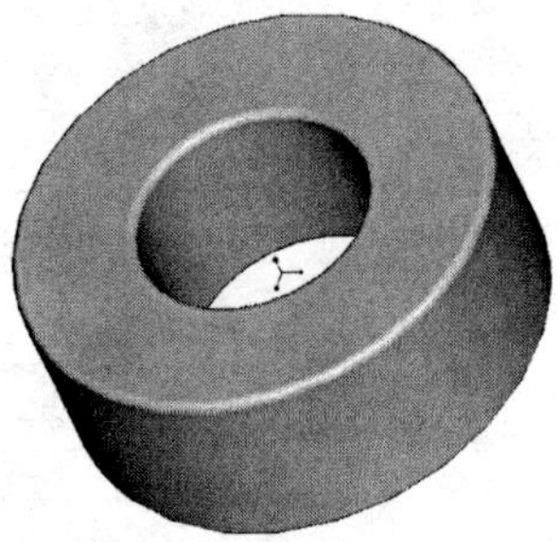

Approach #1: Create the bearing by using the revolve feature

Sequence of Steps

Step I - Revolve a rectangular section

1. Use "Revolve" feature.
2. Define the sketch plane
3. Sketch the axis of revolution
4. Sketch a rectangular section
4. Define the angle of revolution

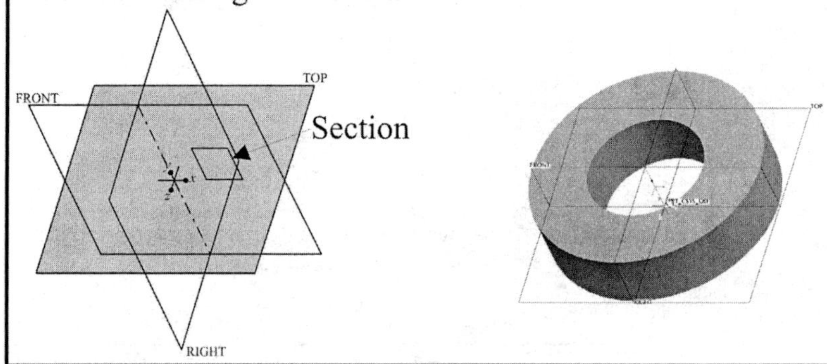

Step II - Round the edges of the base cylinder

1. Use "Round" feature
2. Specify the radius
3. Select the edges to be rounded

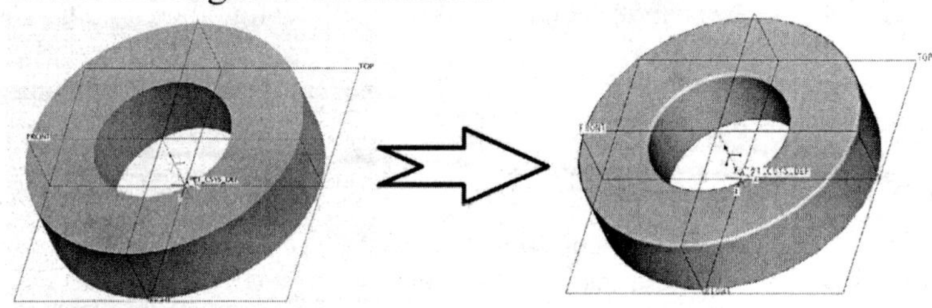

Goal	Step	Commands
Open a new file for the bearing part	1. Set up the working directory.	**FILE → SET WORKING DIRECTORY →** ***Select the working directory*** **→ OK**
	2. Open a new file.	**FILE → NEW →** ***Part*** **→** ***Solid*** **→ <u>bearing1</u> → OK**
Create the base cylinder	3. Start "Revolve" feature.	**INSERT → REVOLVE** [Or click in the feature toolbar]
	4. Define the sketching plane.	To select the sketch plane, ***click Placement*** **(in the dash) → Define** Refer to Fig. 3.1. Pro|ENGINEER brings up "Sketch" window to define the section placement. Refer to Fig. 3.2. Sketch the section on the FRONT datum plane. ***Select the FRONT datum plane in the model tree or in the graphics window by selecting the word "FRONT" →*** Pro|ENGINEER orients the sketch plane. **Sketch**
	5. Sketch the axis of revolution on the RIGHT datum plane.	**→ → *Pick points 1 and 2 on the RIGHT datum plane*** The cursor snaps onto the RIGHT datum if we move the cursor close to it.
	6. Create a rectangular section.	**→ *Pick points 3 and 4*** Refer Fig. 3.3.

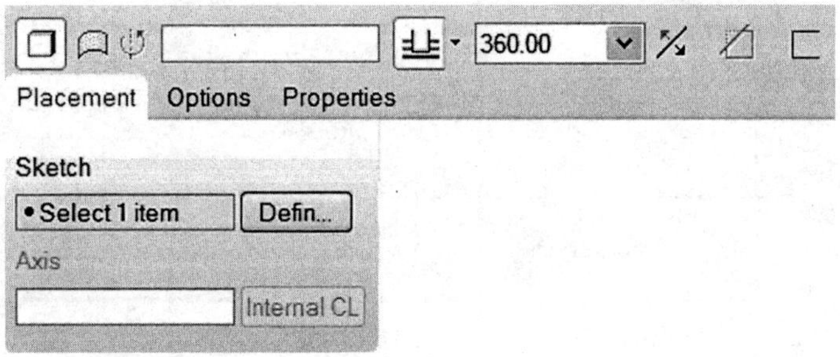

Fig. 3.1.

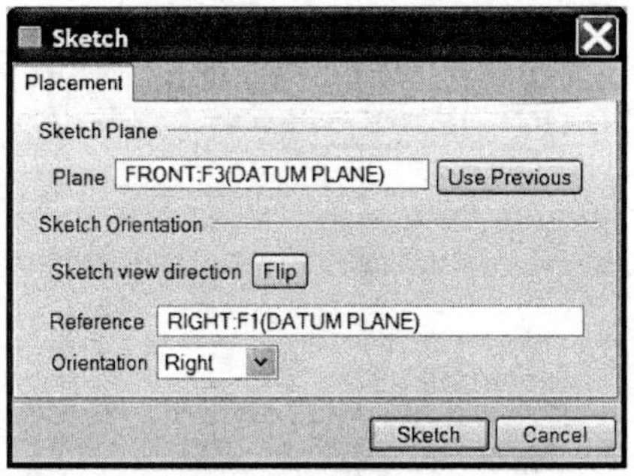

Fig. 3.2.

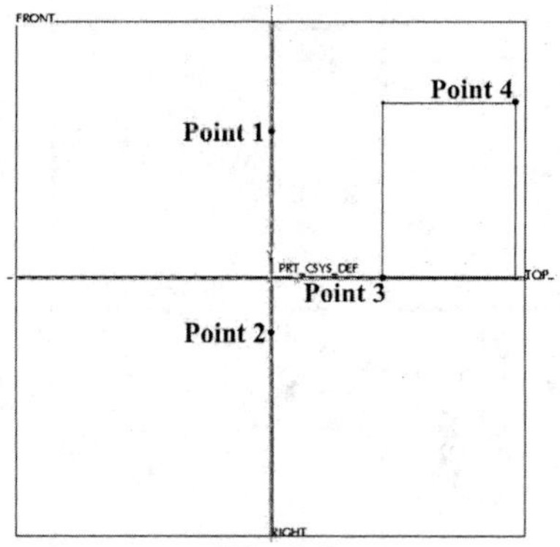

Fig. 3.3.

The revolve tool sweeps the section around the axis of revolution.

★Pro|ENGINEER uses the first centerline created in the sketcher as the axis of revolution. For the revolve feature, the entire section must lie on one side of the axis of revolution.

Goal	Step	Commands
Create the base cylinder (continued)	7. Modify the dimensions.	→ ***Double click the height dimension → <u>0.5</u> → <u>ENTER</u> → Double click the width dimension → <u>0.5</u>→ <u>ENTER</u> → Double click the horizontal placement dimension → <u>0.5</u>→ <u>ENTER</u>*** Refer Fig. 3.4.
	8. Exit sketcher.	
	9. Define the angle of revolution.	(Angle value in dash) **360**
	10. Accept the feature creation.	→ **VIEW → ORIENTATION → STANDARD ORIENTATION** Refer Fig. 3.5.
Round the edges	11. Round the four edges of the cylinder.	→ We will specify the radius of all rounds to be 0.025. (radius) **<u>0.025</u>** → ***<u>ENTER</u>*** → ***Hold <u>CRTL</u> and select the four edges to be rounded →*** Refer Fig. 3.5. Refer Fig. 3.6.

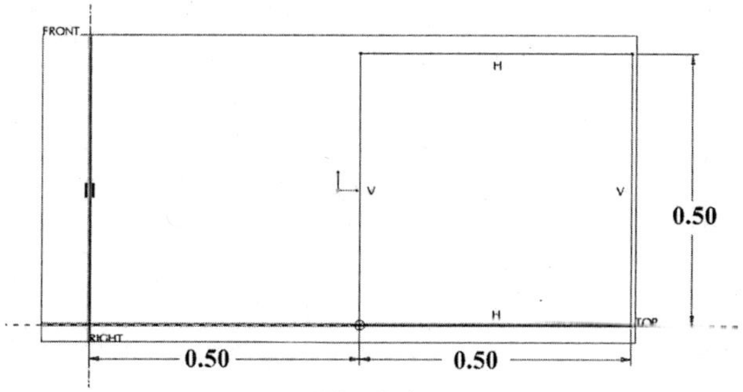

Fig. 3.4.

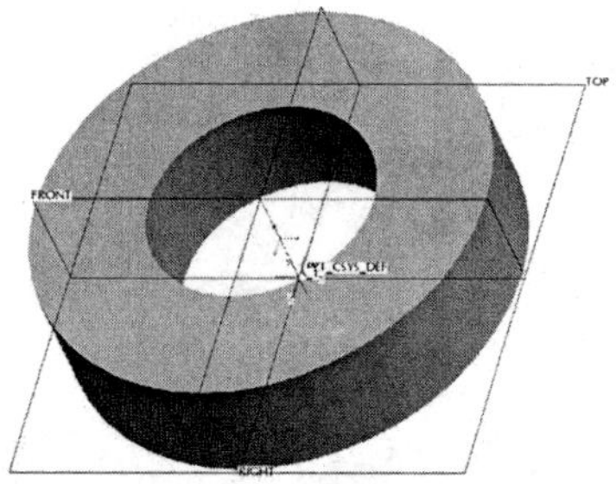

Fig. 3.6.

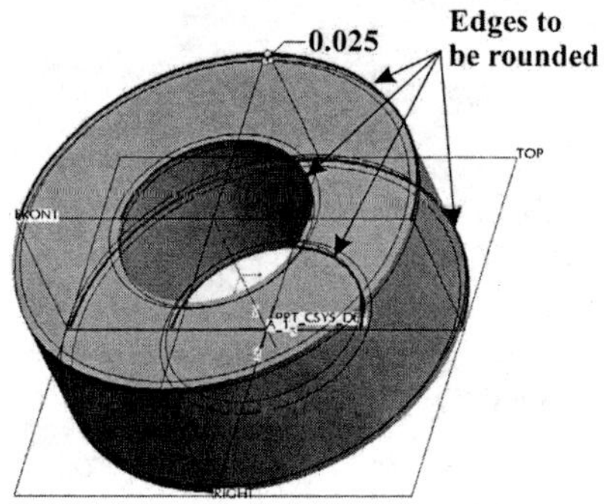

Fig. 3.7.

Goal	Step	Commands
View the model	12. View the model in the default view and turn the datum planes off.	**VIEW → ORIENTATION → STANDARD ORIENTATION →** ***Click on the following icons to switch off the datum planes, axes, points, and default coordinate system.***  Refer Fig. 3.7.
Save the file and exit Pro|ENGINEER	13. Save the file and exit Pro|ENGINEER.	**FILE → SAVE → BEARING1.PRT → OK → FILE → EXIT**

Fig. 3.7.

Approach #2: Create the base cylinder by combining extrude and hole features

Step I - Extrude the base cylinder
1. Use "Extrude" feature.
2. Define the sketch plane
3. Sketch a circular section
4. Define the depth of extrusion

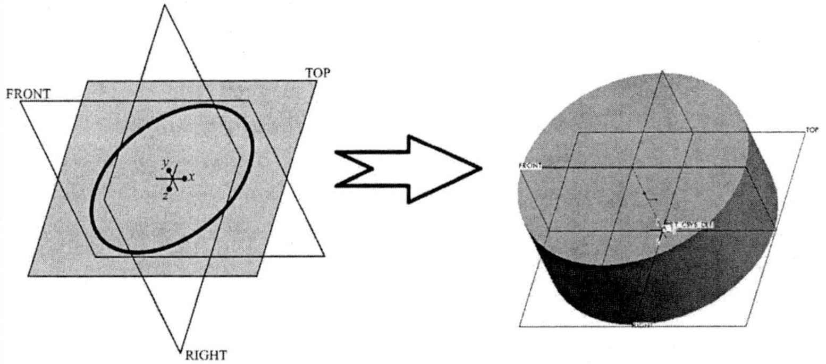

Step II - Create a hole
1. Use "Hole" feature
2. Define the primary reference surface
3. Select the secondary references (FRONT and RIGHT datum planes
4. Define the distance from the secondary references
5. Specify the diameter of the hole

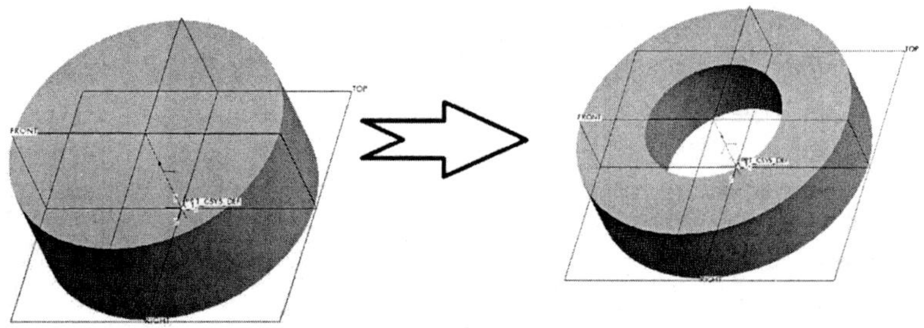

Step III - Round the edges of the base cylinder
1. Use "Round" feature
2. Specify the radius
3. Select the edges to be rounded

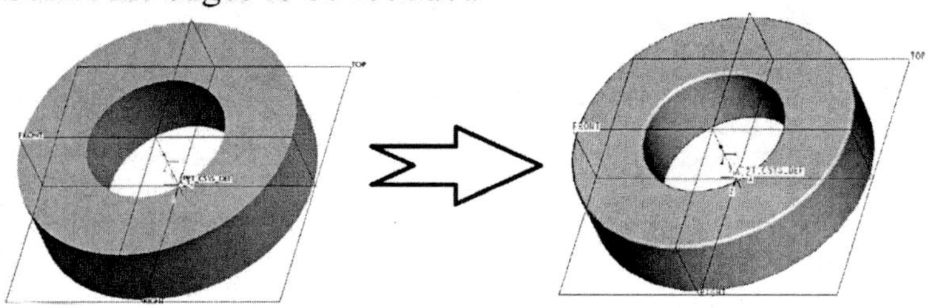

SEQUENCE OF STEPS

Goal	Step	Commands
Open a new file for the bearing part	1. Set up the working directory.	**FILE → SET WORKING DIRECTORY →** ***Select the working directory*** **→ OK**
	2. Open a new file.	FILE → NEW → *Part* → *Solid* → bearing2 → OK
Create the base cylinder	3. Start "Extrude" feature.	
	4. Define the sketching plane.	To select the sketching plane, ***Placement*** **(in the dashboard) → Define →** ***Select the TOP datum plane in the graphics window or in the model tree by clicking on the word "TOP"*** **→ Sketch**
Create the base cylinder (Continued)	5. Sketch a circle.	**→** ***Select the center of the circle as the intersection of FRONT and RIGHT datum planes →*** The cursor snaps onto the intersection. ***Select a point to define the outer edge of the circle*** Refer Fig. 3.7.
	6. Modify the dimensions.	**→** ***Double click the diameter dimension*** **→ 2 →** ***ENTER*** Refer Fig. 3.7.
	7. Exit sketcher.	✓
	8. Define the extrusion depth.	(Depth in dash) **0.5**
	9. Accept the feature creation.	✓ **→ VIEW → ORIENTATION → STANDARD ORIENTATION** Refer Fig. 3.8.

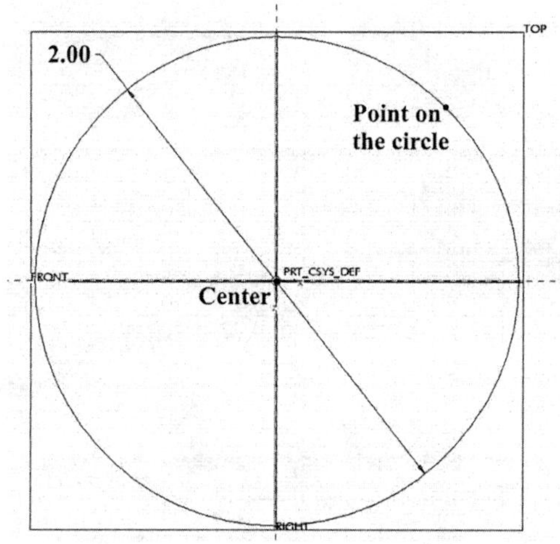

Fig. 3.7.

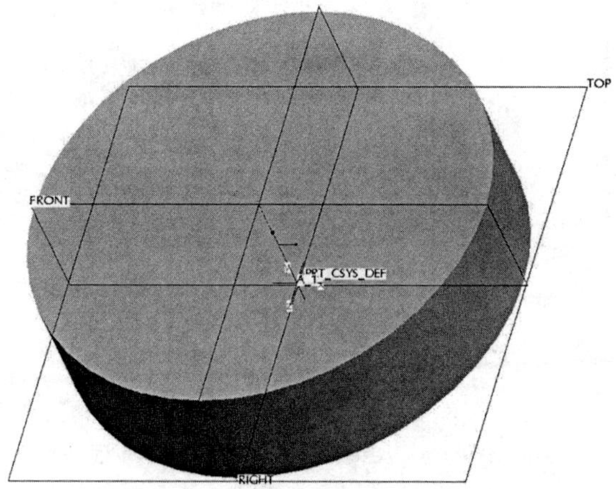

Fig. 3.8.

Goal	Step	Commands
Create a hole	10. Create a hole at the center.	(or **INSERT → HOLE**) → (Diameter) **<u>1.0</u>** → (Depth One) *(Through All)* → Refer Fig. 3.9. ***Placement (in dash) → Select the top circular surface →*** Refer Fig. 3.9. ***Click in the secondary references window → Select FRONT and RIGHT datum planes holding <u>CTRL</u> →*** ***<u>CTRL</u>*** key allows the selection of multiple entities. Refer Fig. 3.9. ***Change "offset" to "align" in "Offset References" window for both FRONT and RIGHT datum planes →***
The reader is advised to round the edges. In case of problems, refer Step 11 in the first approach.		

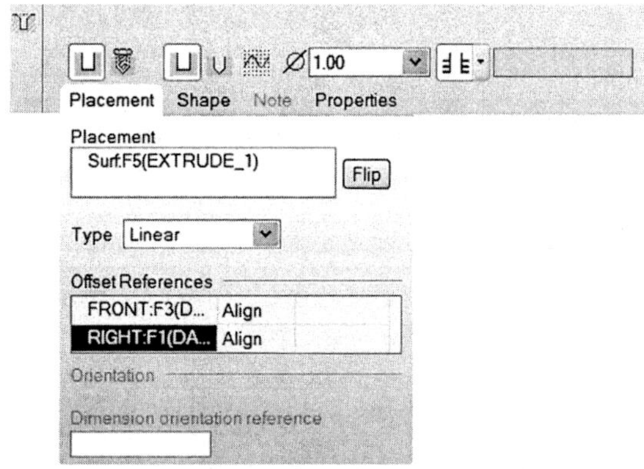

Fig. 3.9.

Primary reference refers to the plane on which the hole is placed.
The hole will be dimensioned with respect to the secondary references.

Alternative Approach:

→ ***Select the primary reference surface (top circular surface) → Drag the handles and drop the handles on the FRONT and RIGHT datums → Enter the distance dimensions*** (zero in the present case) → (Type) **Simple** → (Diameter) **<u>1.0</u>** → (Depth One) (Through All) →

Refer Fig. 3.10.

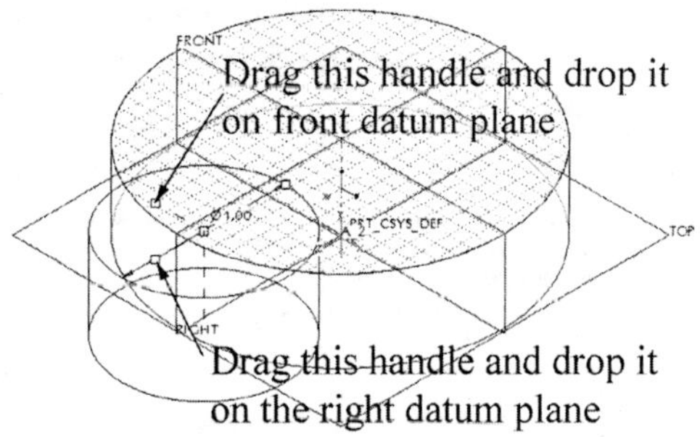

Fig. 3.10.

Exercise

Problem 1
Create the bearing part using "Revolve – Thicken" option.

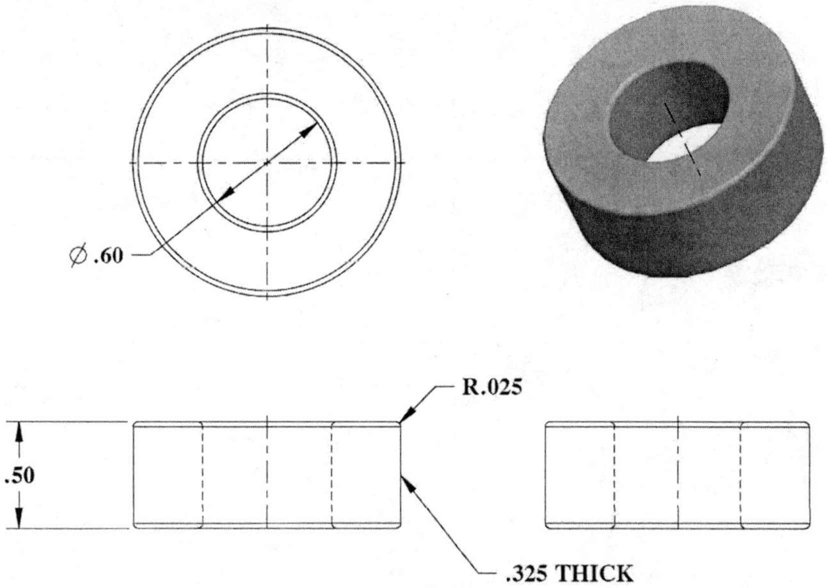

Hints:

1. Use the revolve feature – Select thicken. (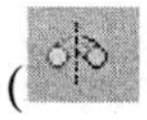 → 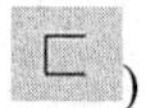)
   ★Select thicken option before sketching the section.
2. Sketch on the front datum plane.

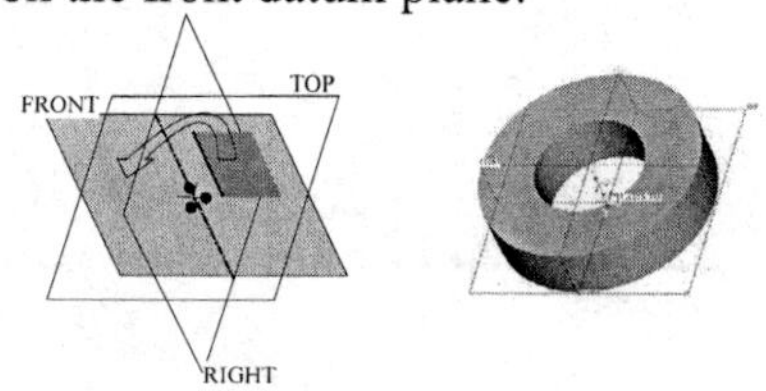

3. In the sketcher, draw a centerline and a line.

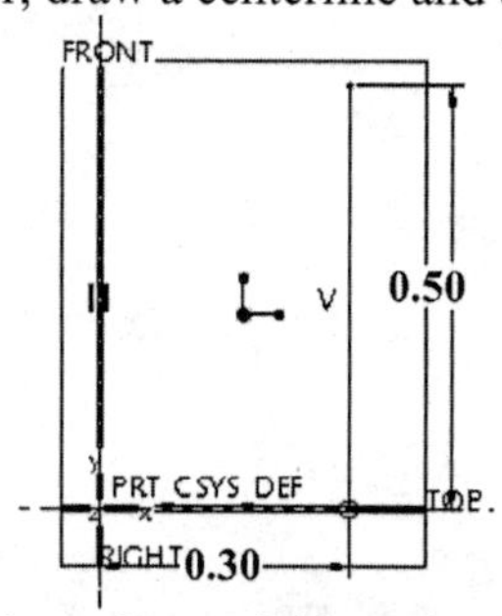

4. Flip the direction of material by selecting the second 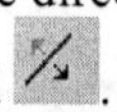.
5. Sample dash is shown in the figure below.

Problem 2

Create the part using the revolve feature. Then, round the four edges using a radius of 0.125".

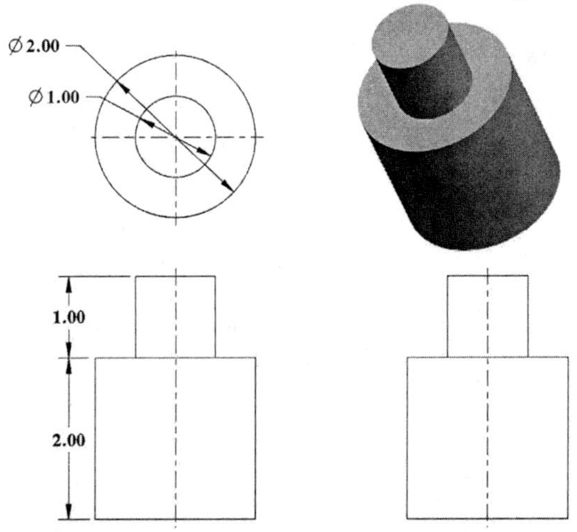

Hints:

1. Pay attention to the section required to create the part.

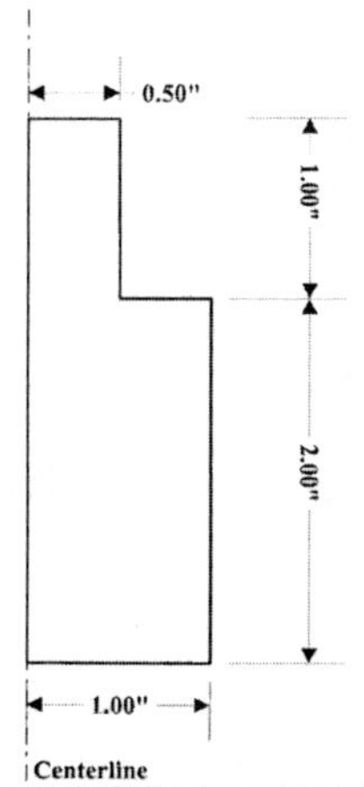

Problem 3

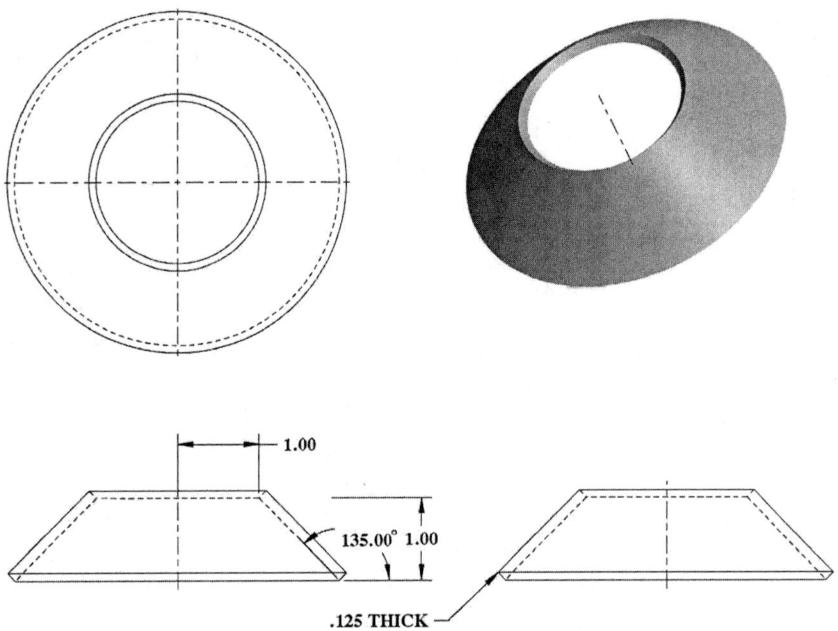

Hints:

1. Use "Revolve – Thicken" (→) feature.

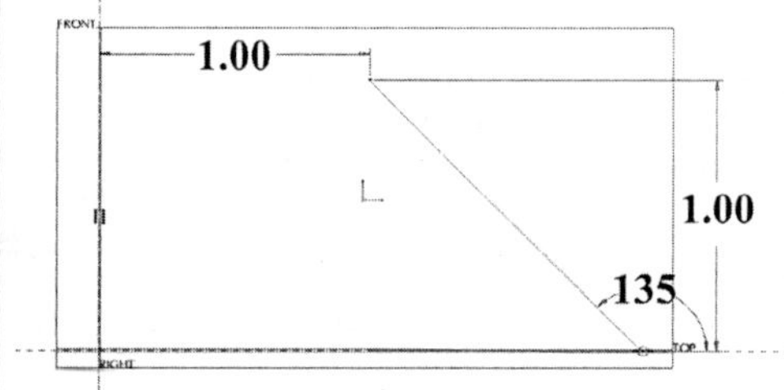

Problem 4

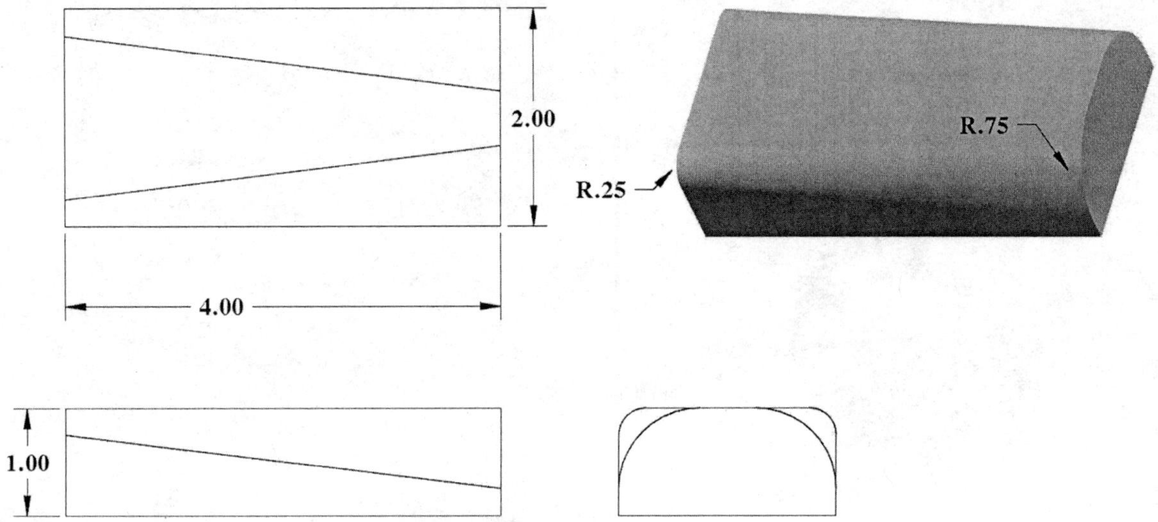

Hints:

1. Use Extrude feature to create the base block 4"x2"x1".

2. Select the round feature.
3. *Select the first edge* → *Select the center handle* → *Right Mouse* (***and hold the right mouse button***) → Add radius

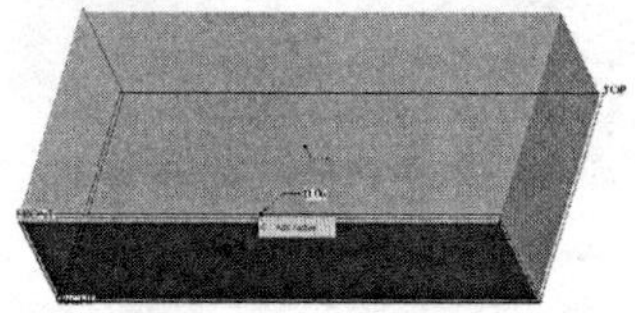

4. Modify the end radius values to 0.25" and 0.75" respectively.
5. Repeat the process for the second edge.

Problem 5

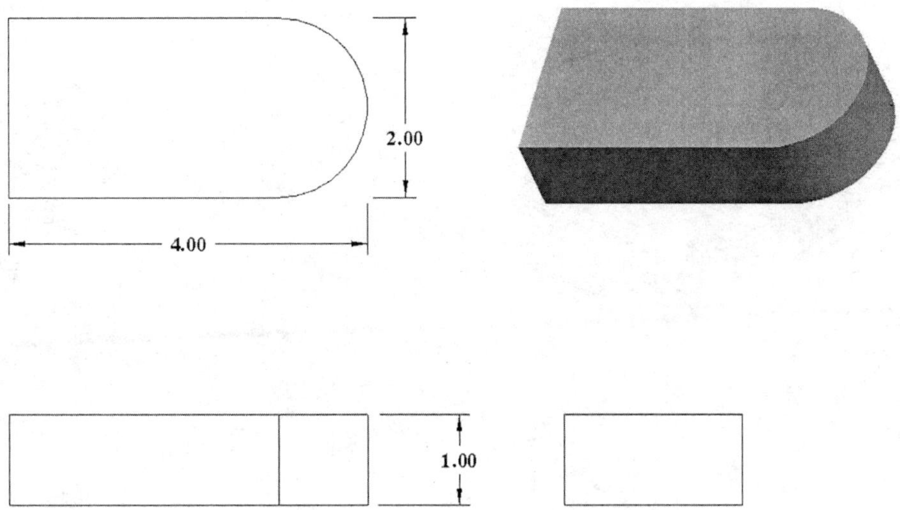

Hints:

1. Use Extrude feature to create the base block 4x2x1.
2. Select the round feature.
3. *Select the two edges*

4. Select Full round.

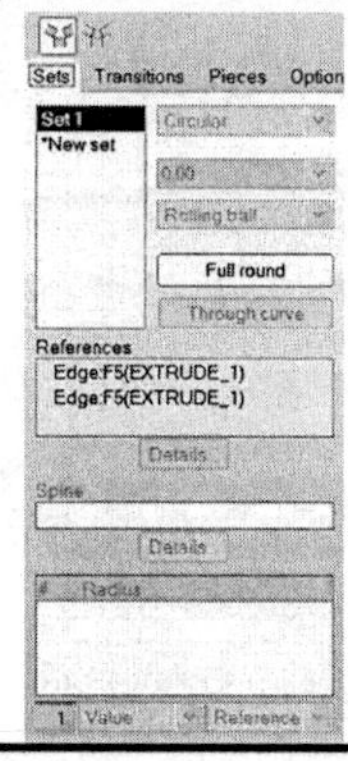

Problem 6

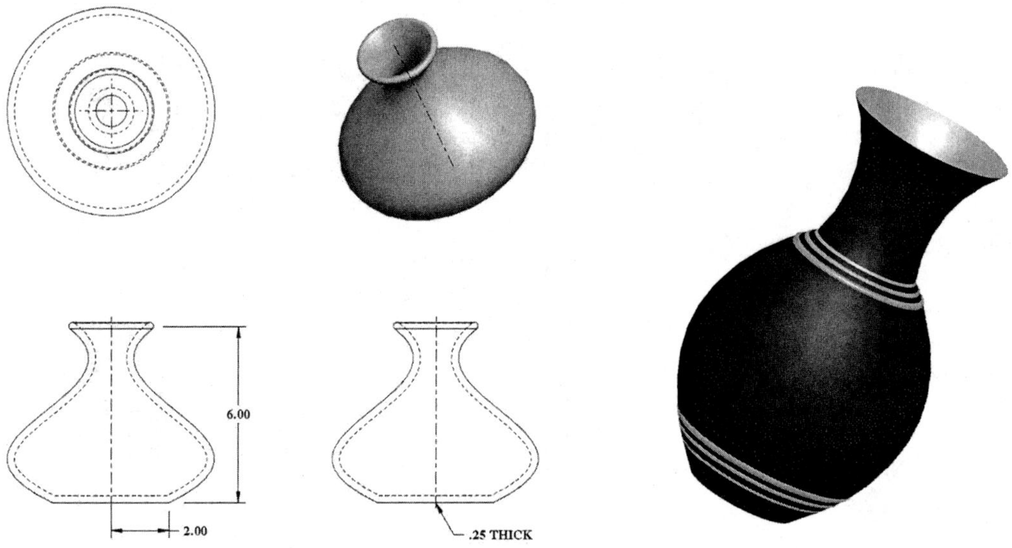

Hints:

1. Use "Revolve – Thicken" (→) feature to create the vase.
2. Pay attention to the section required to create the part.

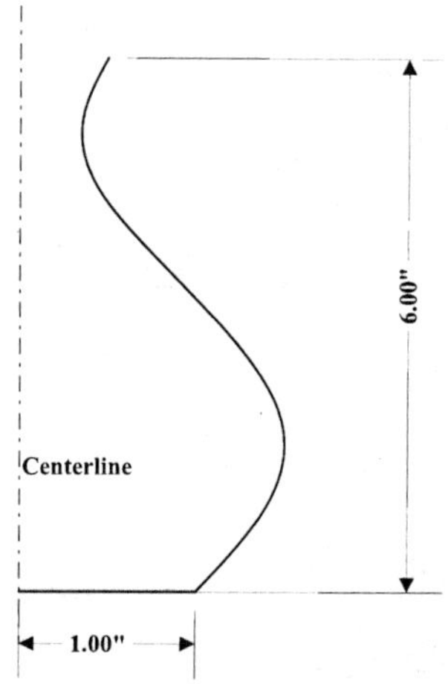

3. Create use "full round" to round the rim of the vase.

Problem 7

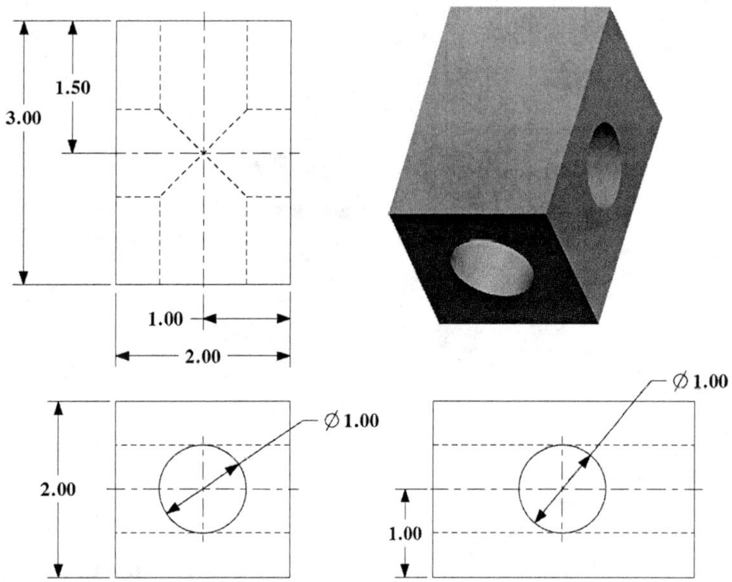

OPEN-ENDED DESIGN

Create a part with extrude, revolve, round, and hole features. There are many objects around you that can be created using these features.

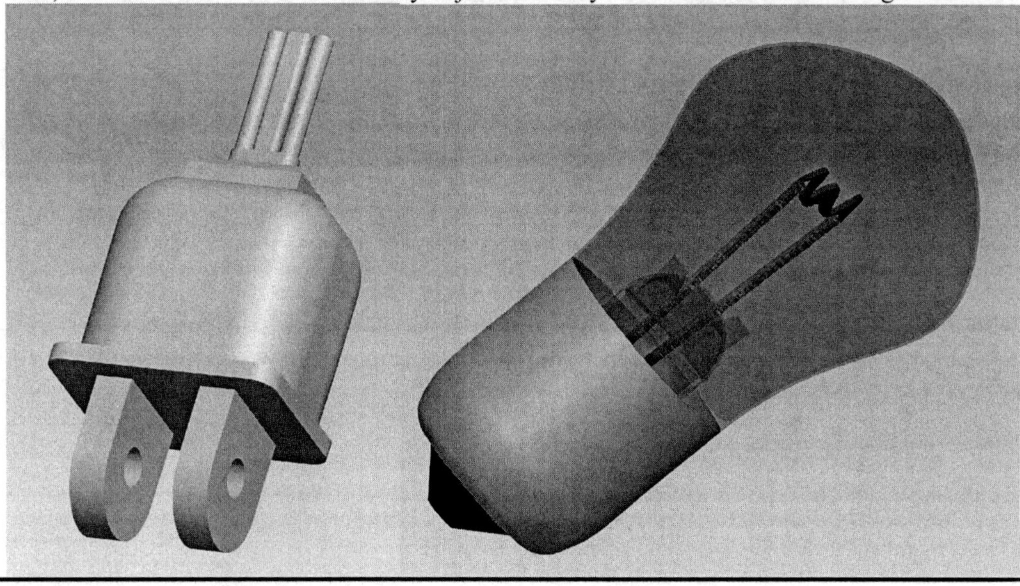

NOTES:

LESSON 4
BUSHING

Learning Objectives

- Practice Revolve and Round features.
- Create simple sketches.
- Learn Chamfer and Revolve -Cut features.
- Control the model display.

Selecting Items

The selection feature in the dash helps in selecting features or geometry. In the smart mode (default), it picks the feature first and then, geometry. The filter can be set to feature, geometry, datum or quilts. An entity gets highlighted when the cursor is placed on it. If the interested item is behind another entity, click right mouse. Entities close to the cursor get highlighted sequentially. The user can then select the appropriate entity. Another method is to right click and use "pick by list" tool.

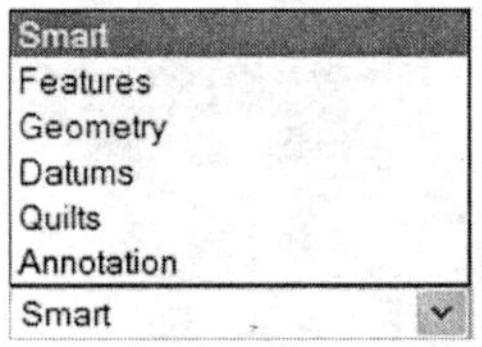

Selection feature

Pick from list

Weak and Strong Dimensions

Sketcher continually guesses the size of each feature by placing witness lines, arrows, and dimensions. These are called weak dimensions and are shown in grey color. When the user specifies true dimensions, Pro|ENGINEER shows them in yellow color. The dimensions are known as strong dimensions. The user can convert a weak dimension to strong one by selecting the weak dimension, right clicking the mouse, and choosing strong option. The sketcher regenerates the section continuously as the user enters the dimensions.

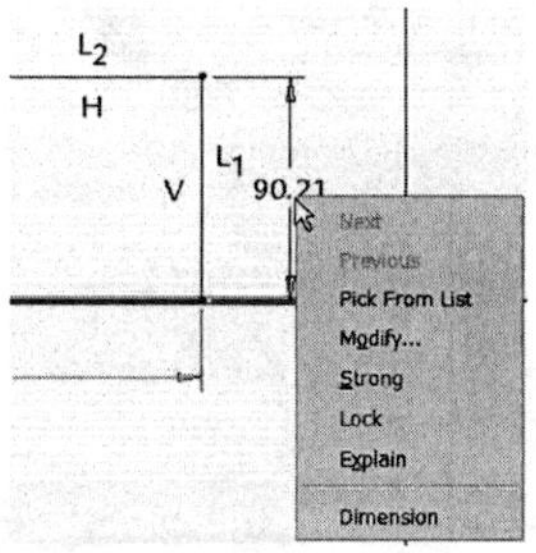

Dimensioning or constraining may over-dimension a sketch and may cause conflicts between already specified dimensions or constraints. When conflicts arise, Pro|ENGINEER lists the conflicts and lets the user delete the conflicting dimensions or constraints.

Chamfer feature		
Useful for creating a chamfer.		
Starting the feature	INSERT → CHAMFER, or 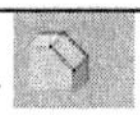 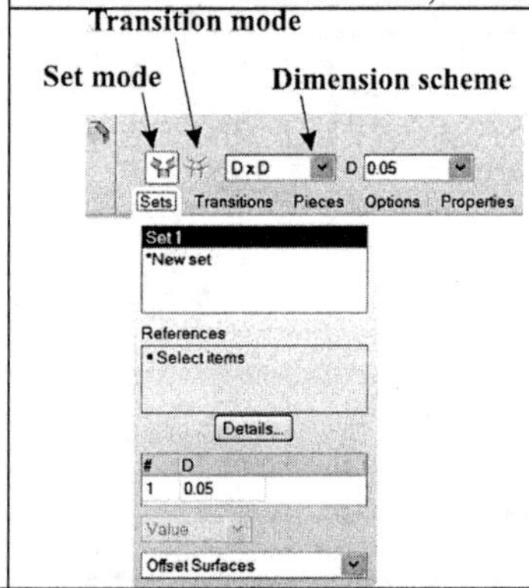	
Mode		By default, Pro|ENGINEER activates the set mode. In this mode, a user controls a set of chamfer geometry using a single chamfer dimension. When selecting a number of references (edges to be chamfered), hold ***CTRL*** to place them in a single set.
		In the transition mode, a user specifies the filler geometry to transition between chamfer geometries.
Dimension scheme	*D* x *D option* – Creates a chamfer at a distance (D) from the edge along each surface. *D1* x *D2* – Creates a chamfer from the edge at distances D1 and D2 along the two surfaces forming the edge. *Angle x D* – Creates a chamfer from the edge at a distance D along one surface and at the specified angle to the other surface. *45* x *D* – Creates a chamfer that is at 45^0 angle the two surfaces and a distance D from the edge. *O* x *O* – Creates a chamfer with an an offset distance O from the edge along each surface. O1 x O2 – Creates a chamfer with offset distances O1 and O2 along the two surfaces	

Examples	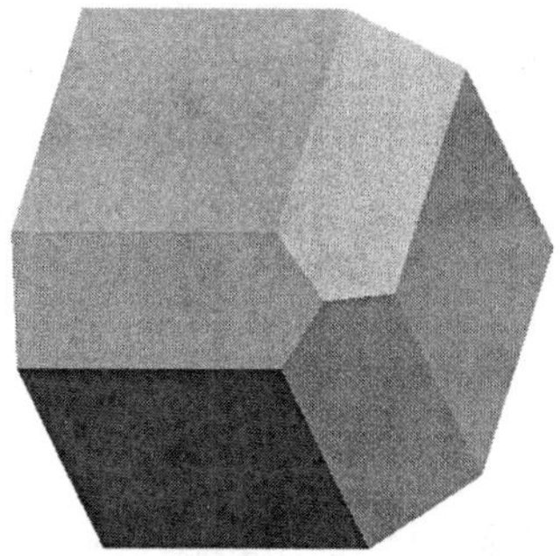 **Edge chamfer** 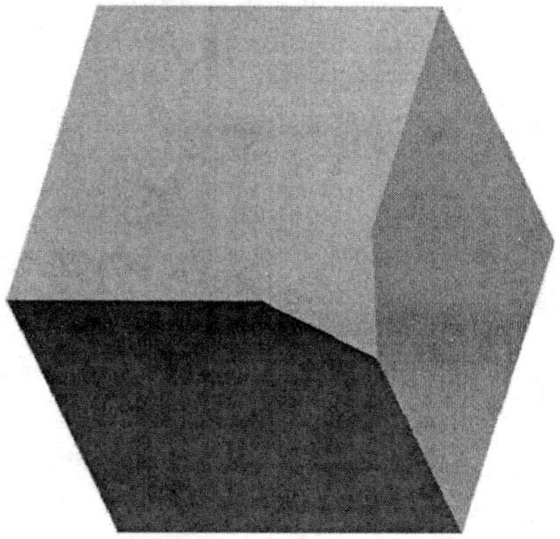 **Corner chamfer**

Sketcher Diagnostics

The sketcher provides four diagnostic tools that can be accessed by selecting SKETCH → DIAGNOSTICS or from the top tool bar.

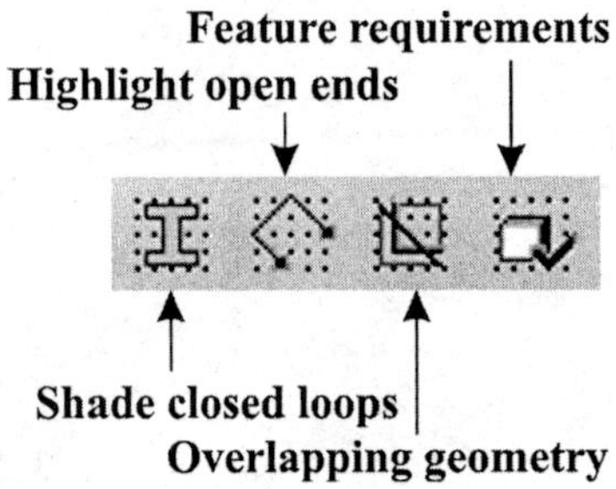

Shaded closed loops – This diagnostic tool detects and shades existing closed loops with the default color. In this mode, a new section with a closed loop will be shaded automatically. The color for closed loop can be set by selecting VIEW → DISPLAY SETTING → SYSTEM COLORS → *Select the sketcher tab → Click on the color icon before "Shaded closed loops" option and select a color.*

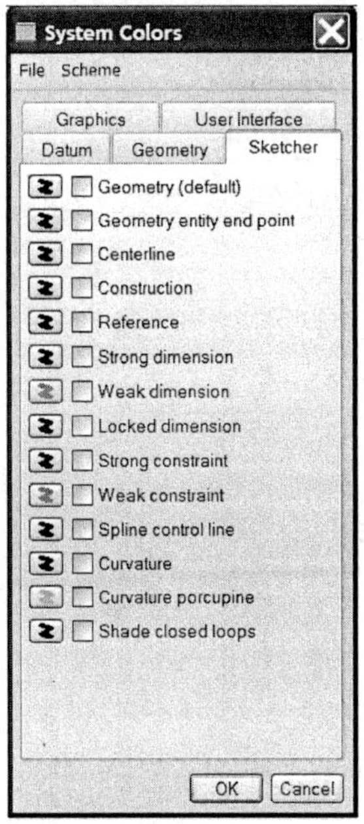

Highlight open ends– This tool highlights the open ends of existing entities in sketcher with a red circle. It also shows a portion of the entity in red. When this mode is selected, as the user sketches, Pro|ENGINEER automatically highlights the open ends.

Highlight overlapping geometry – This tool highlights geometry that overlaps other geometries. In an intelligent fashion, this feature does not highlight overlapping construction geometry.

Feature requirements – This tool determines if the sketch satisfies the requirements of the feature that it defines. When selected, Pro|ENGINEER displays the "Feature Requirements" window with a list of requirements for the feature and whether each requirement is satisfied or not. A message at the top indicates the appropriateness of the sketch for the feature.

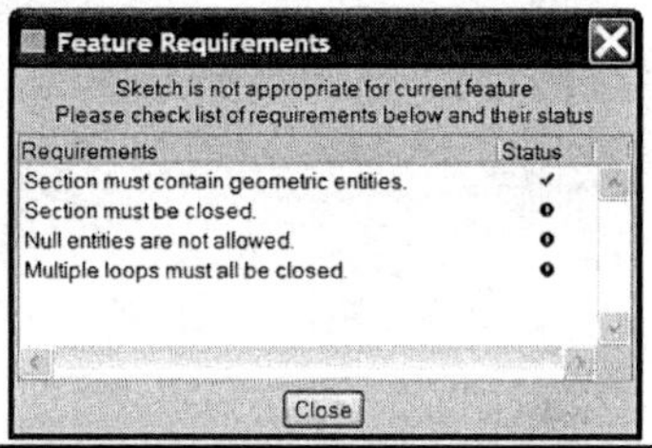

Design Information:

Bushings are the simplest form of bearings. They support rotating and translating components while using a small amount of radial space. As bushings are in direct contact with the rotating or translating elements, wear is a major problem. A tight fit between the bushing and the housing, and a running fit between the shaft and the bushing are specified. The length to diameter ratio is a key parameter that determines the performance of the bushing. Lubrication becomes a problem when the L/D ratio is less than one whereas alignment becomes a problem when the L/D ratio is greater than four.

SEQUENCE OF STEPS

Step I - Revolve the base cylinder
1. Use "Revolve" feature.
2. Define the sketch plane
3. Sketch the axis of revolution
4. Sketch the section
5. Define the angle of revolution

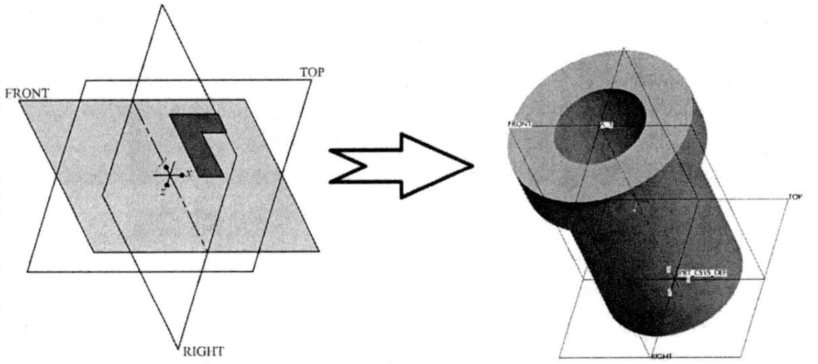

Step II - Round the edges
1. Use "Round" feature
2. Define the radius
3. Select the two edges

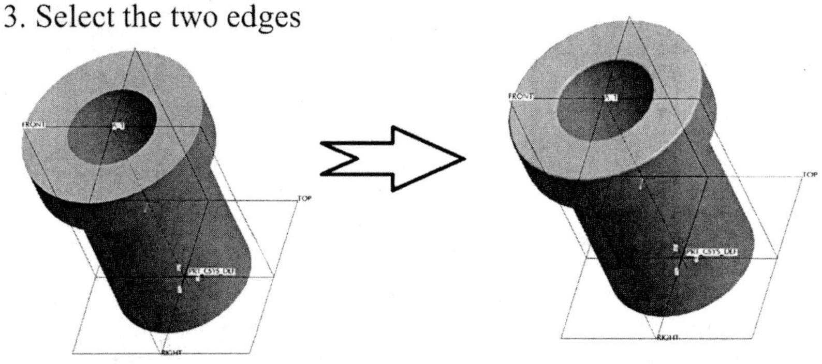

Step III - Chamfer the edge
1. Use "Chamfer" feature
2. Specify the chamfer type and dimension
3. Select the edge to be chamfered

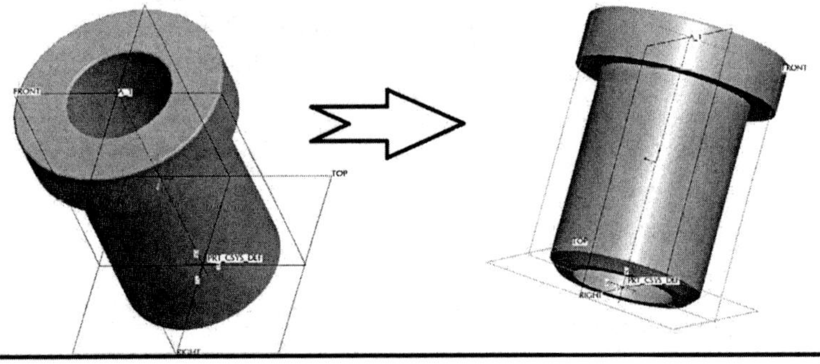

Step IV - Create the undercut
1. Use "Revolve" feature.
2. Define the sketch plane
3. Sketch the axis of revolution
4. Sketch the section
5. Define the angle of revolution

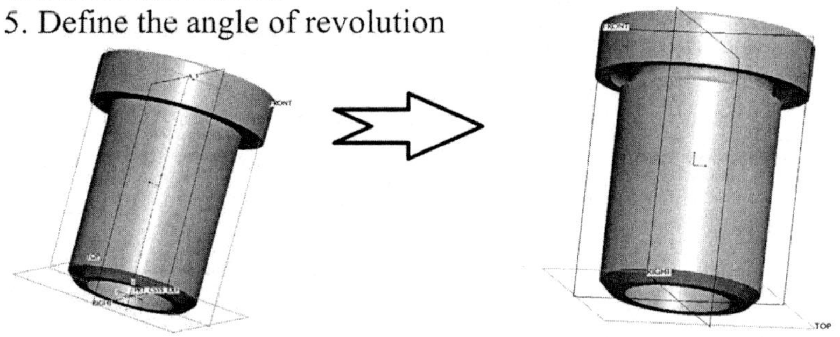

Goal	Step	Commands
Open a new file for the bushing part	1. Set up the working directory.	**FILE → SET WORKING DIRECTORY →** ***Select the working directory*** **→ OK**
	2. Open a new file.	**FILE → NEW →** ***Part*** **→** ***Solid*** **→ <u>bushing</u> → OK**
Create the base feature	3. Start "Revolve" feature.	
	4. Select the sketching plane.	***Placement*** **→ Define →** ***Select the FRONT datum plane in the graphics window or in the model tree by clicking on the word "FRONT"*** **→ Sketch**
	5. Sketch the axis of revolution on the RIGHT datum plane.	**→ → *Pick points 1 and 2 on the RIGHT datum plane***
	6. Sketch the section.	**→ → *Pick points 3, 4, 5, 6, 7, 8 and 3 → Middle Mouse* (to discontinue line creation)** Refer to Fig. 4.1.
	7. Diagnose the section using "shaded closed loops" and "feature requirements."	**SKETCH → DIAGNOSTICS → SHADE CLOSED LOOPS** Refer to Fig. 4.2. **SKETCH → DIAGNOSTICS → FEATURE REQUIREMENTS** Refer to Fig. 4.3.

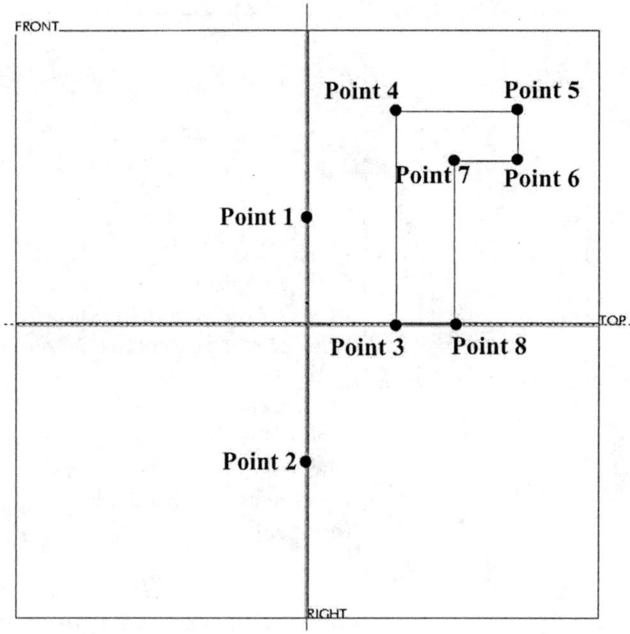

Fig. 4.1.

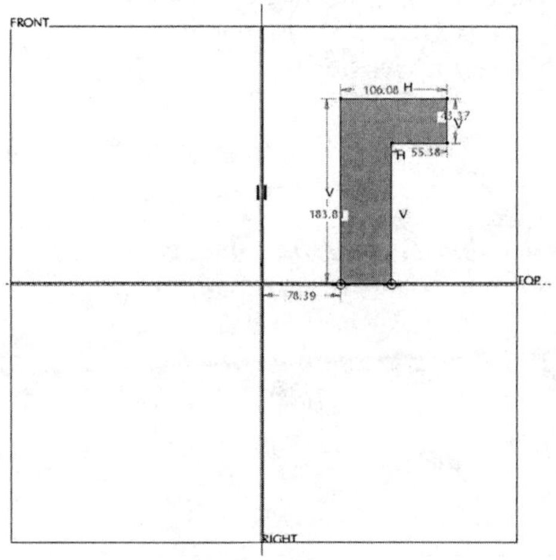

Fig. 4.2.

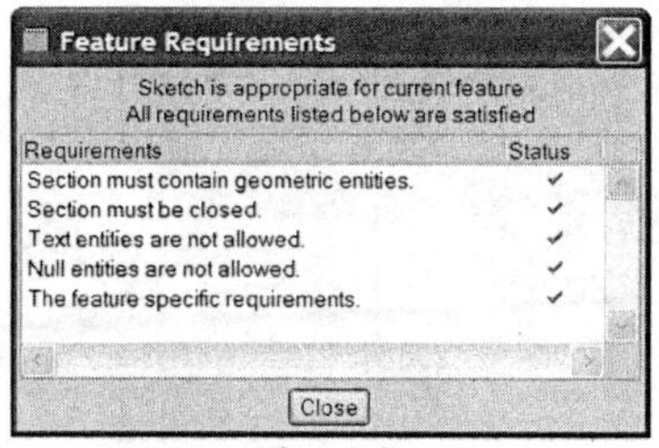

Fig. 4.3.

Goal	Step	Commands
Create the base feature (Continued)	8. Create new dimensions	★ |↔| → ***Select lines 1 and 2 → Middle Mouse at the point where the vertical dimension must be placed →*** Refer to Fig. 4.4. The position of the cursor determines the type of dimension placed (horizontal or vertical). ***Select lines 1 and 3 → Middle Mouse to place the vertical dimension →*** ***Select line 4, centerline and again on line 4 → Middle Mouse to place the diameter dimension →*** Note that Pro|ENGINEER places the diameter dimension. ***Select line 5, centerline and again on line 5 → Middle Mouse to place the diameter dimension → Select line 6, centerline and again on line 6 → Middle Mouse to place the diameter dimension***

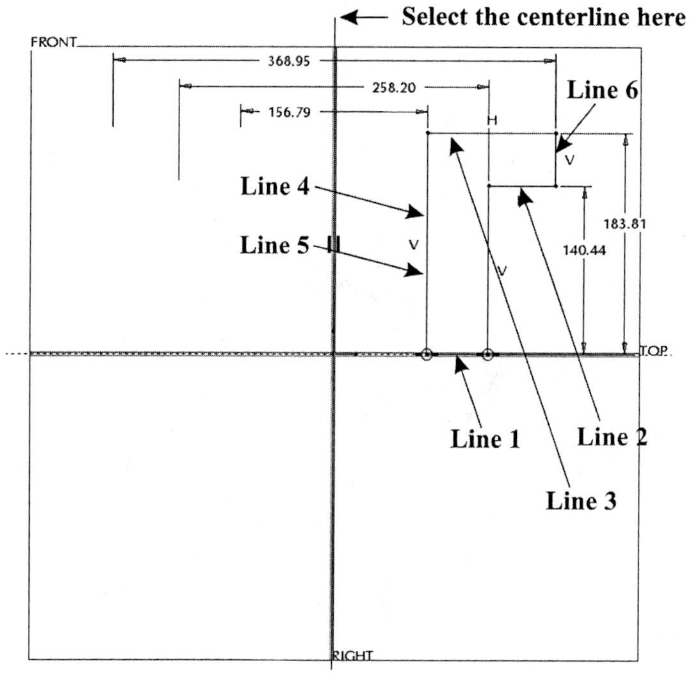

Fig. 4.4.

When an entity is created, Pro|ENGINEER automatically places weak dimensions (shown in gray color). Pro|ENGINEER erases these dimensions depending on the constraints. We can create strong dimensions (shown in yellow) by either specifying values to the weak dimensions or by creating new dimensions.

Goal	Step	Commands
Create the base feature (continued)	9. Modify the dimensions.	★ Instead of modifying one dimension at time, let us use tool. → Pro|ENGINEER opens "Modify Dimensions" window. ***Select the five dimensions that must be modified → Deselect regenerate →*** Refer to Fig. 4.5. When entering dimensions in "Modify Dimensions" window, the sketcher highlights corresponding dimension. **Enter the corresponding dimensions to reflect Fig. 4.6. → *Select regenerate →*** ✓ in "Modify Dimensions" window.
	10. Exit sketcher.	✓
	11. Define the angle of revolution.	(Angle) **360**
	12. Accept the feature creation.	✓ → **VIEW → ORIENTATION → STANDARD ORIENTATION** Refer to Fig. 4.7.

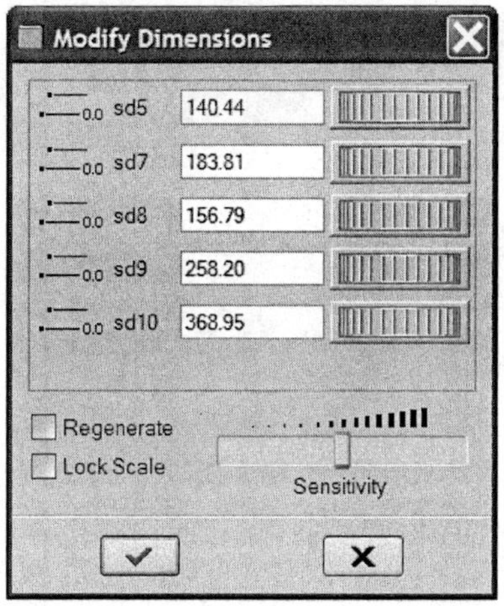

Fig. 4.5.

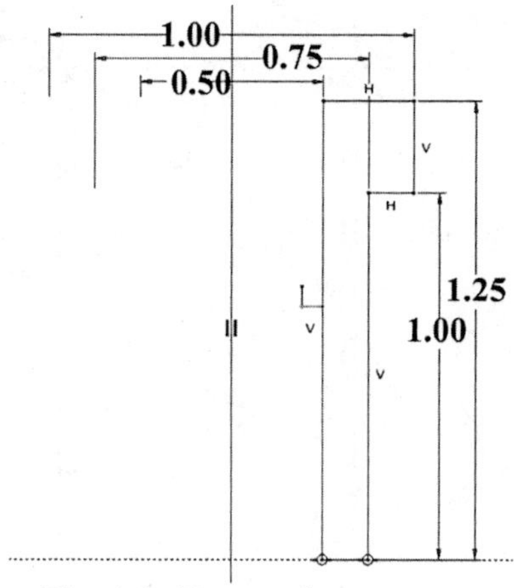

Fig. 4.6. (Datum planes are not displayed for clarity)

Fig. 4.7.

Goal	Step	Commands
Round the edges	13. Round the two outside ends of the bushing.	 **→ (Radius in the dash) <u>0.016</u> → *Select the two edges to be rounded while holding <u>CTRL</u>* →** Refer Fig. 4.8.  Refer to Fig. 4.9.
Chamfer the bottom outer edge	14. Chamfer the outer edge.	 **(or INSERT → CHAMFER→ EDGE CHAMFER) → 45 x d → <u>0.05</u> →** Refer to Fig. 4.10. ***Select the bottom edge* →** Refer to Fig. 4.11.  Refer to Fig. 4.12.
Create an undercut	15. Start "Revolve – Cut" feature.	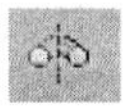 →  (in the dash)
	16. Select the sketching plane.	***Placement* → Define → Use Previous**
	17. Add new references.	**SKETCH → REFERENCES → *Select the vertical and horizontal edges* → CLOSE** Refer to Figs. 4.13 and 4.14.

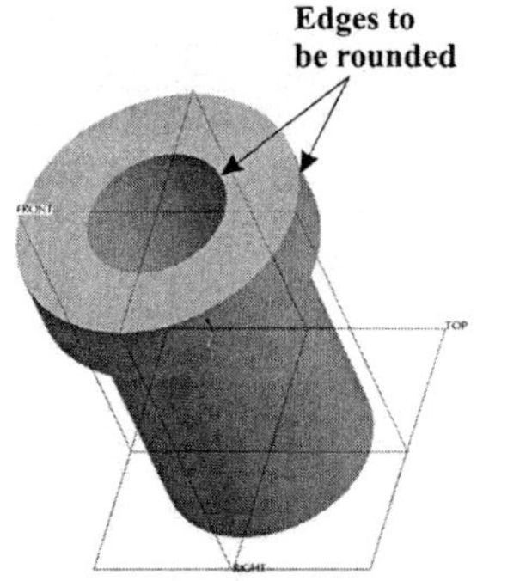

Fig. 4.8.

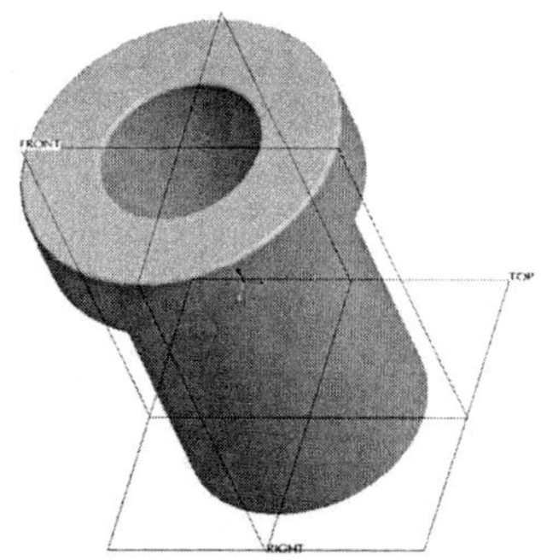
Fig. 4.9.

Fig. 4.10.

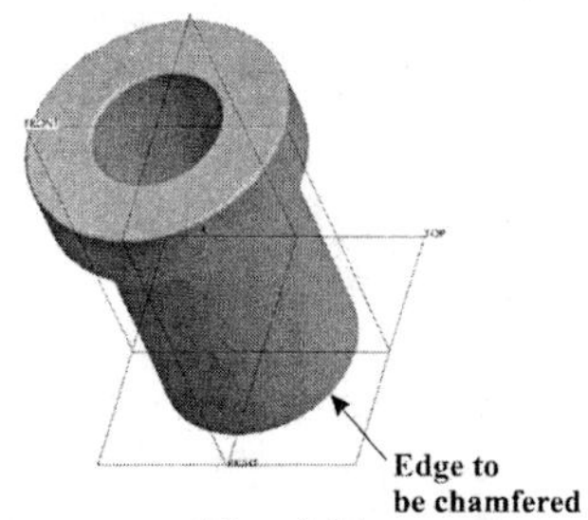

Fig. 4.11.

Fig. 4.12.

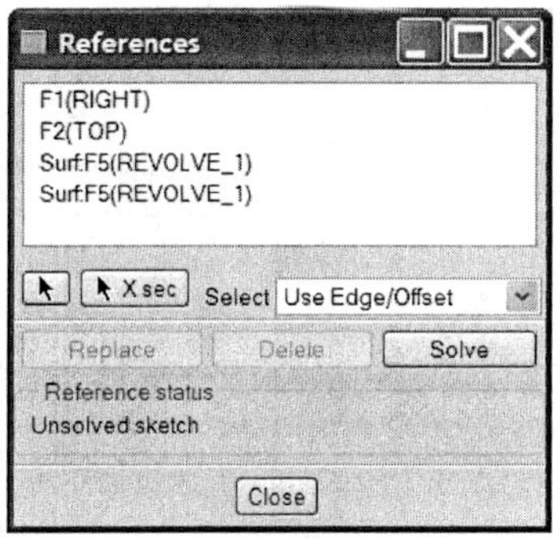

Fig. 4.13.

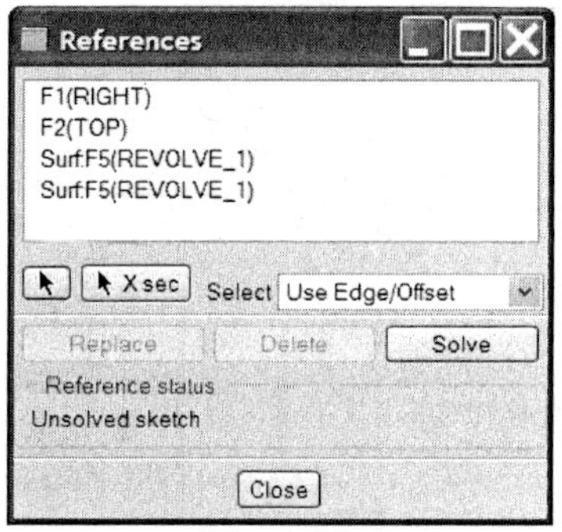

Fig. 4.14.

Goal	Step	Commands
Create an undercut (Continued)	18. Sketch an arc.	→ ***Select the center*** → Refer to Fig. 4.15. ***Pick points 1 and 2*** Refer to Fig. 4.15. A section need not be closed when making a cut.
	19. Modify the arc radius.	→ ***Double click radius*** → **0.05** → ***ENTER***
	20. Create the axis of revolution.	→ → ***Pick points 3 and 4 on the RIGHT datum plane*** Refer to Fig. 4.15.
	21. Exit sketcher.	✓
	22. Define the angle of revolution.	(Angle) **360** Refer to Fig. 4.16.
	23. Accept the feature creation.	✓ → **VIEW** → **ORIENTATION** → **STANDARD ORIENTATION** → ***Rotate the model*** Refer to Fig. 4.17.

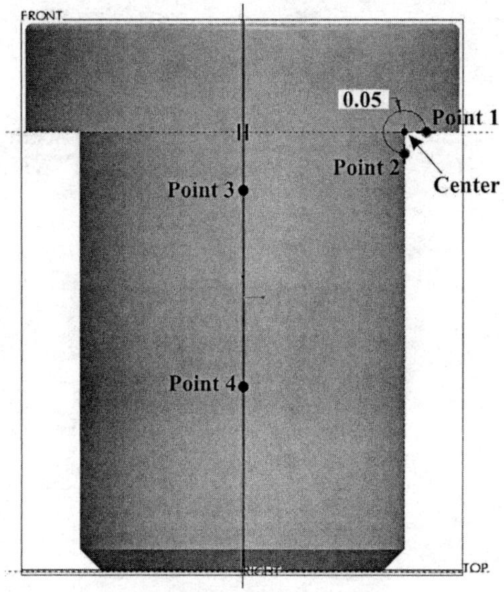

Fig. 4.15.

Fig. 4.16.

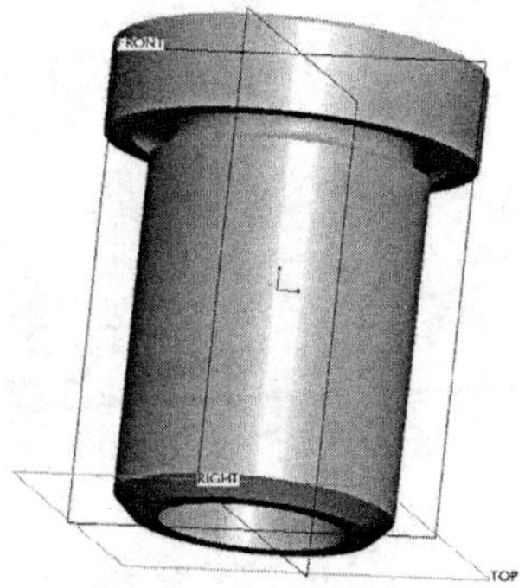
Fig. 4.17.

Goal	Step	Commands
View the model	24. Define the model color.	**VIEW → COLOR AND APPEARANCE →** Pro|ENGINEER opens the "Appearance Editor" window. **+** → Refer to Fig. 4.18. ***Click on the color →*** Refer to Fig. 4.18. Pro|ENGINEER opens the "Color Editor" window. Refer to Fig. 4.19. ***Click on Color wheel →*** Pro|ENGINEER opens the color wheel. ***Select a suitable color →* CLOSE →** ***Select the part →* APPLY → → CLOSE**
	25. View the model in the default view. Turn off the datum planes.	**VIEW → ORIENTATION → STANDARD ORIENTATION →** ***Click on the following icons to switch off the datums, axis, datum points and default coordinate system.*** → Refer to Fig. 4.20.
Save the file and exit Pro|ENGINEER	26. Save the file and exit Pro|ENGINEER.	**FILE → SAVE → BUSHING.PRT → OK → FILE → EXIT → Yes**

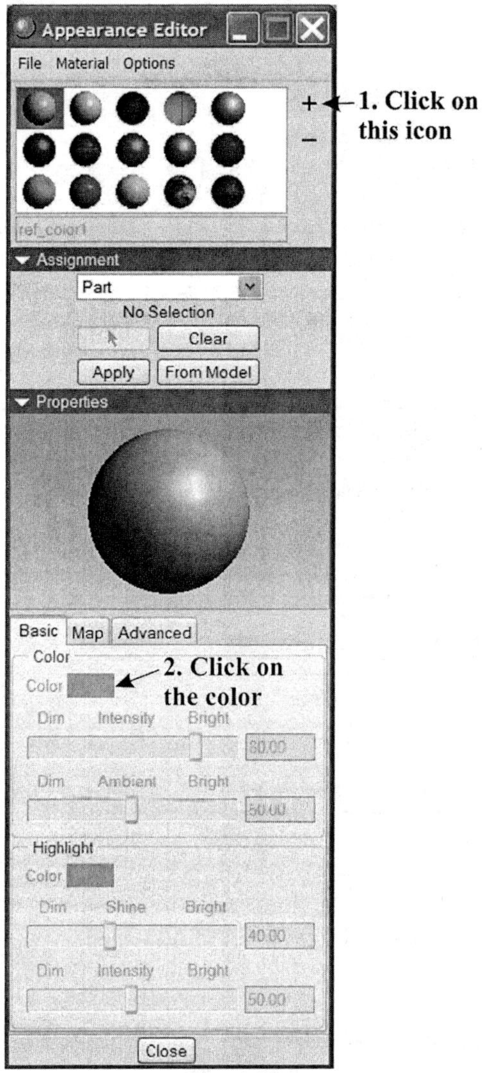

Fig. 4.18.

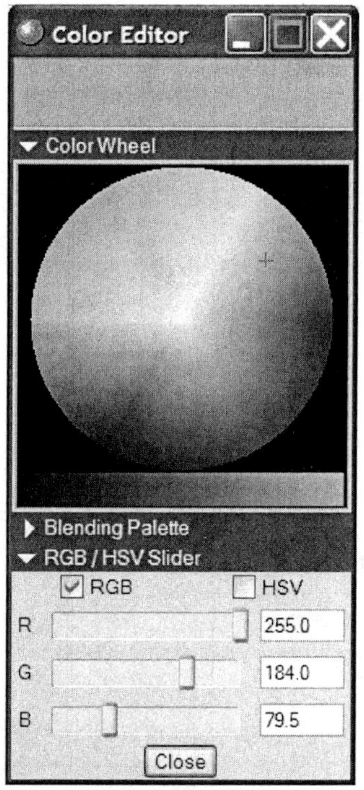

Fig. 4.19.

Fig. 4.20.

Exercise

Problem 1

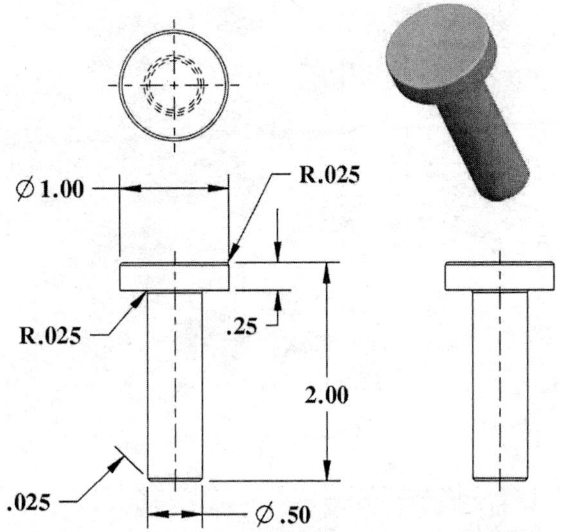

Hints:

1. Use revolve tool.
2. Draw the centerline.
3. Sketch the section (shown in the figure below)

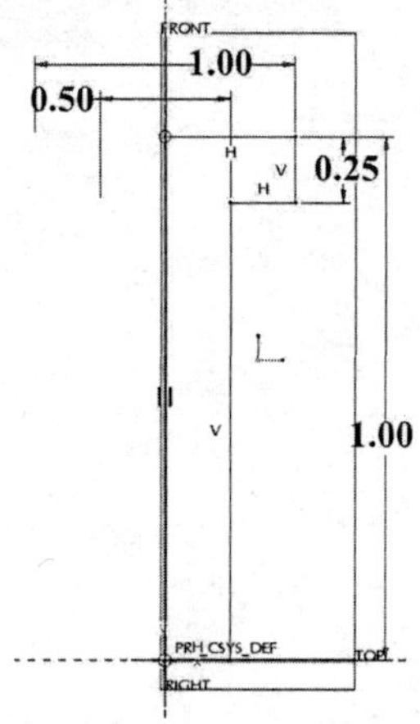

4. Chamfer the bottom edge of the shank and round the other two edges.

Problem 2

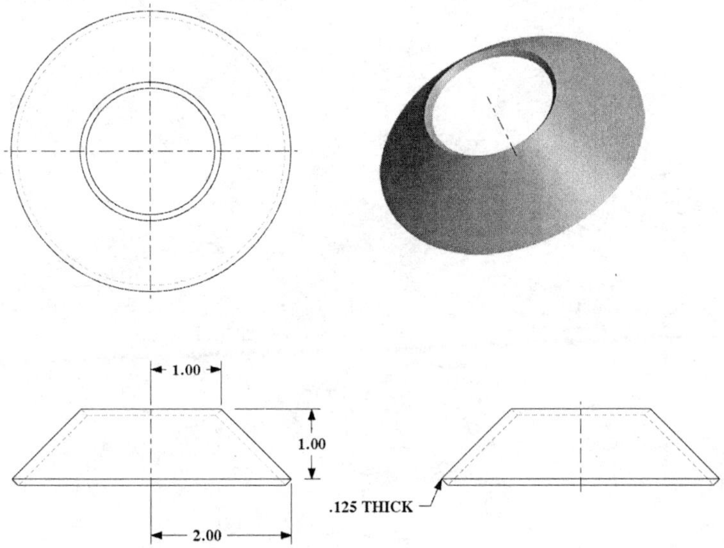

Hints:

1. Start revolve feature.
2. Select "thicken" option and specify thickness.

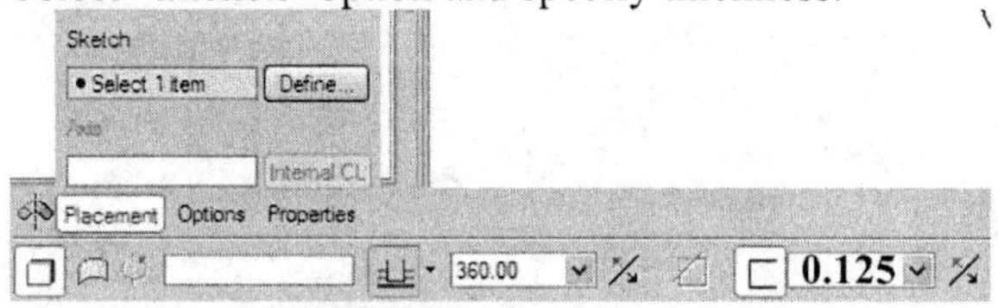

3. Sketch the section. Add additional dimensions.

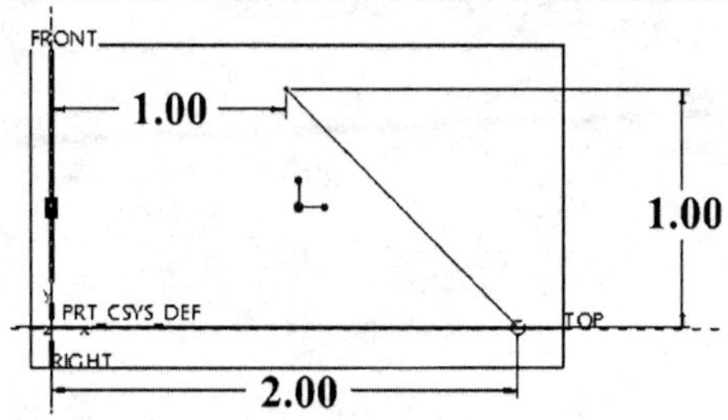

4. Exit sketcher.

Problem 3

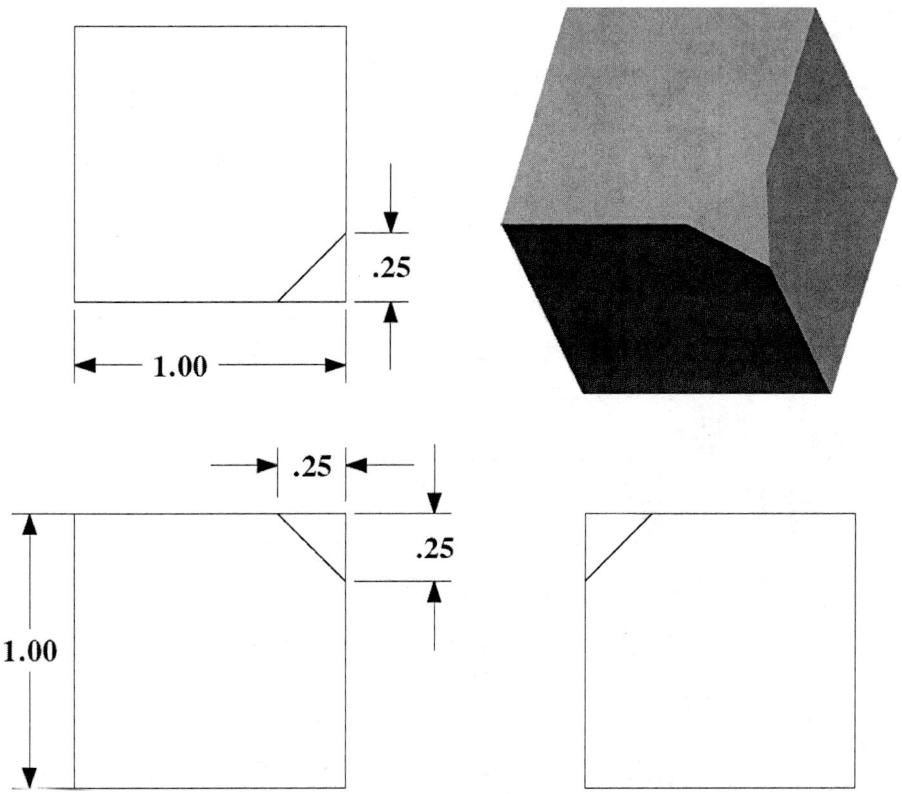

Hints:

1. Create the base feature – a block.
2. Select "INSERT → CHAMFER → CORNER CHAMFER" option.
3. Select the corner
4. Select "Enter Input" option and input .25 along each edge.

Problem 4
Create two parts.

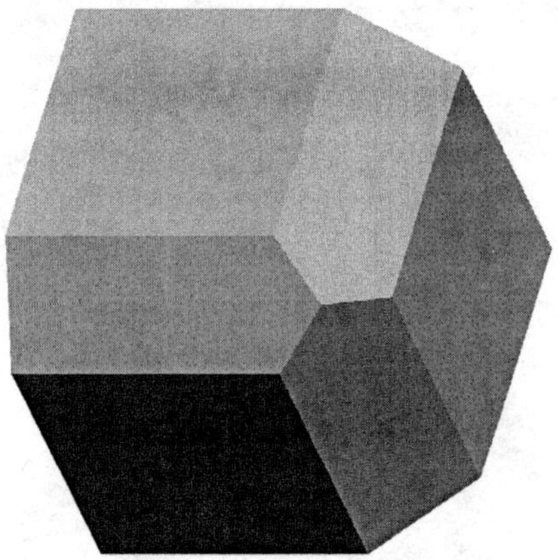

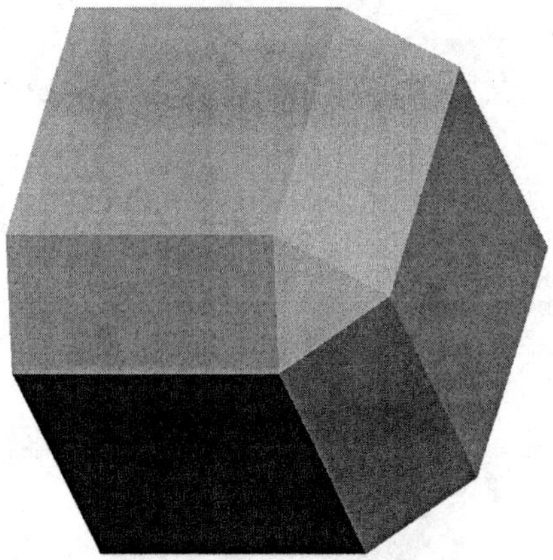

Hints:
1. Create the base feature – a block. Size 1"×1"×1".
2. Select "INSERT → CHAMFER → EDGE CHAMFER" option.
3. Select "D×D" option and enter 0.25" for D.

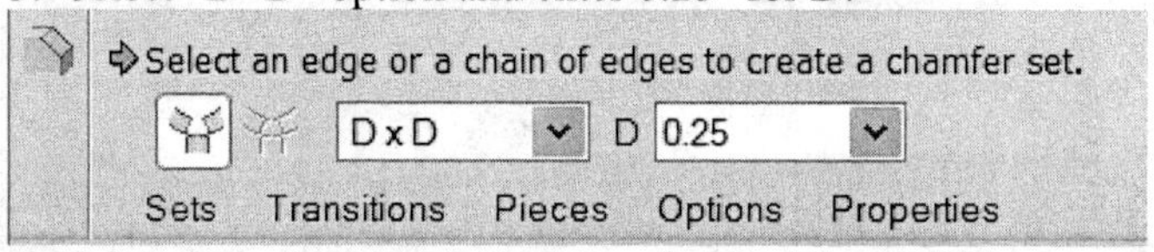

4. Select three intersecting edges while holding CTRL. Accept the feature creation.
5. You have the first part. Use "Save As" to save it as the first part file.
6. Now, select the chamfer feature in the model tree, click and hold Right Mouse and select Edit Definition.
7. Select the switch to the transition mode icon. Select the intersection of the three edges area.
8. Select patch option. Click on the triangular patch at the intersection of the three edges.

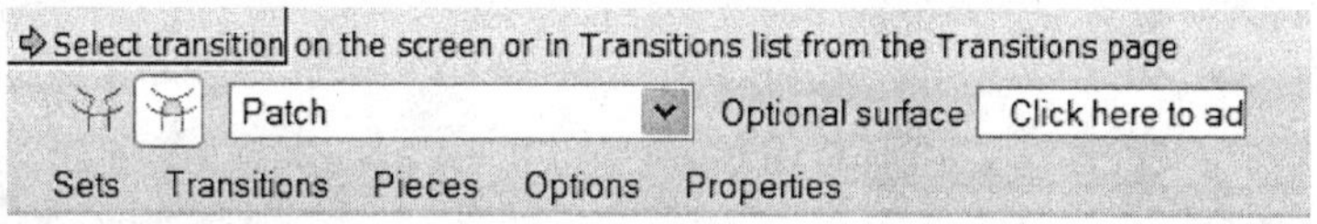

9. Accept feature creation.
10. Now, you have the second part.

Problem 5

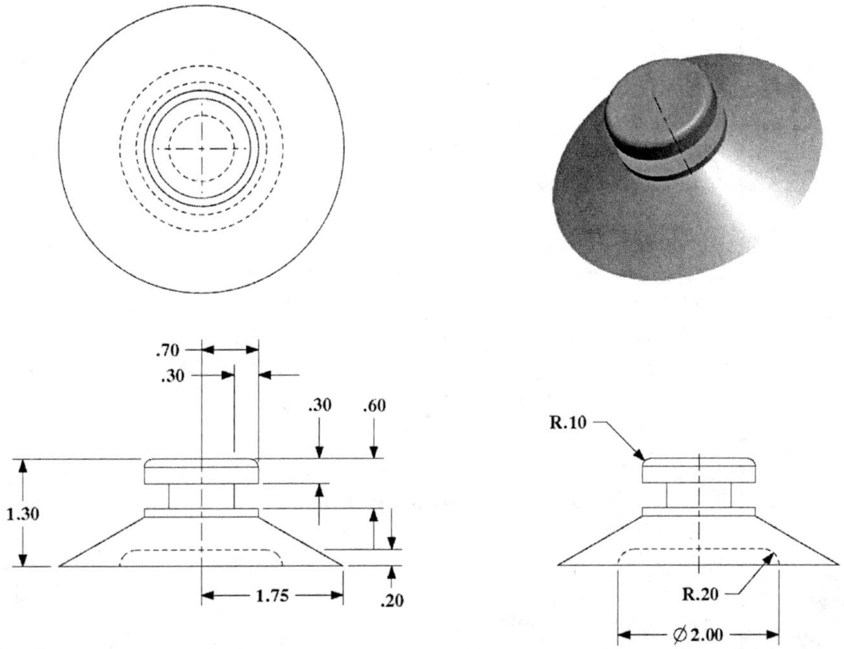

Hints:

1. Create the base feature using "Revolve".
2. Use "Revolve – Cut" to create the two cuts.
3. Use "Round" feature to round-off the edges.

Problem 6

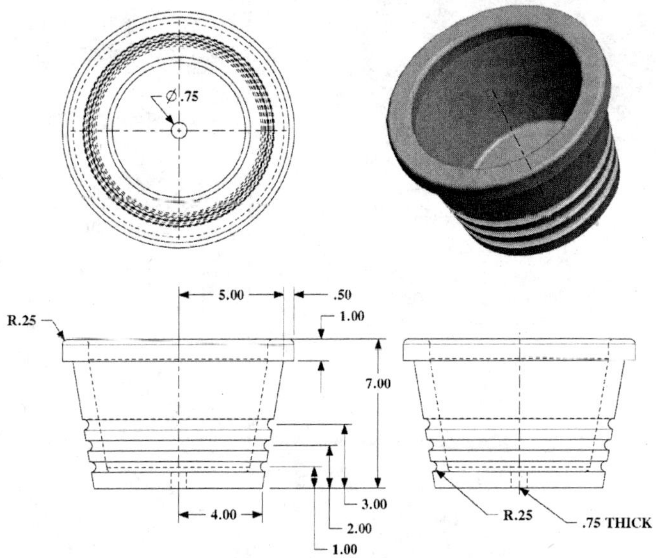

OPEN-ENDED DESIGN – Try a simple bird house. Then, a complicated one.

Hints:

1. Use extrude – thicken feature for steps 1, 2, and 3.
2. Step 3: Sketch rectangle on the floor. Extrude it till the top surface using up to surface depth option - 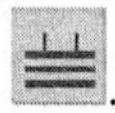.

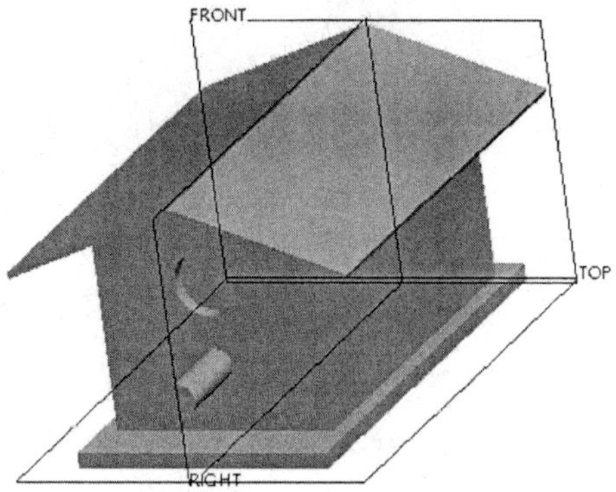

The evolution of the part is below:

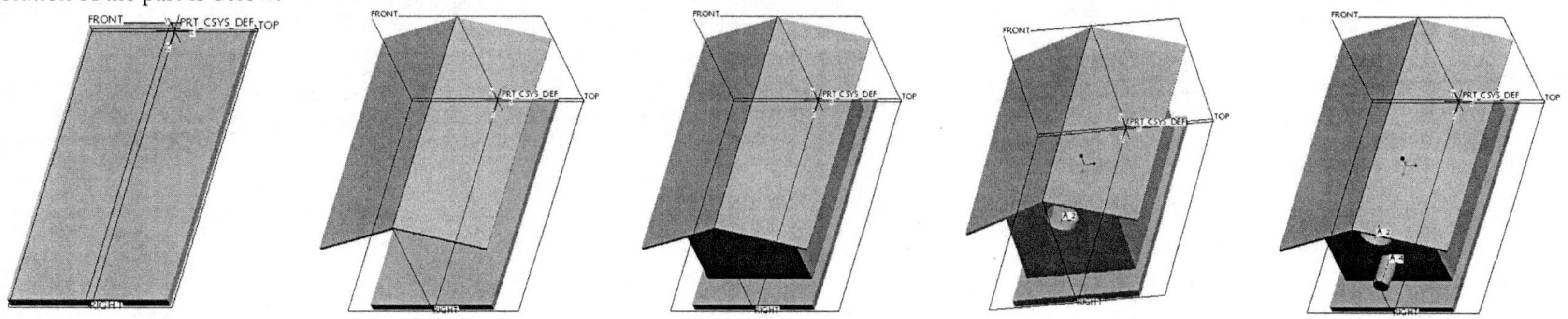

Step 1 **Step 2** **Step 3** **Step 4** **Step 5**

NOTES:

LESSON 5
RETAINING RING

Learning Objectives

- Use simple features to create a complex geometry.
- Practice Extrude, Extrude - Cut, Round and Hole features.
- Learn Mirror, Copy – Mirror and Model Analysis tools.

Sketcher Preference

The user can set the sketcher preference by selecting SKETCH → OPTIONS. Some common preferences that can be set are the turning grid on and off, setting the grid spacing, changing snap to grid, and defining the accuracy of dimensions.

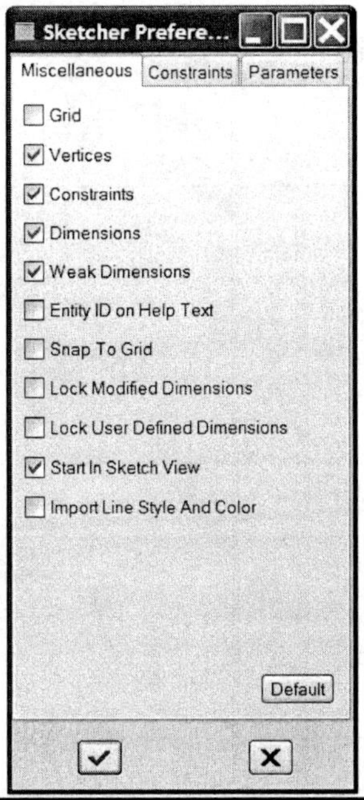

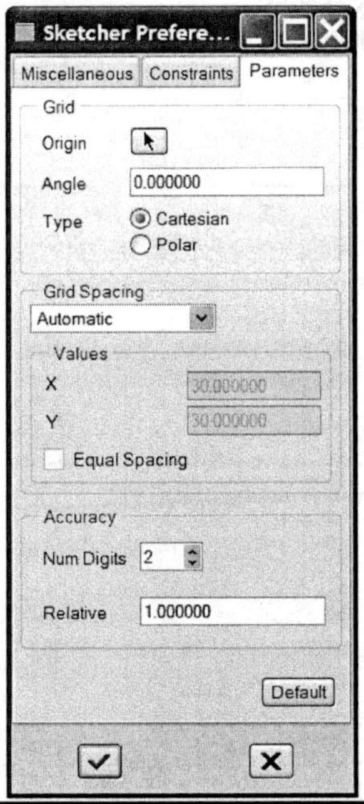

Design Information

Retaining rings are used to locate and secure machine components on a shaft by providing an accurate locating shoulder. They are placed in locating grooves machined on the shafts or in the bores. Depending on their placement, they are classified as external or internal retaining rings. Retaining rings make products easy to assemble and disassemble during production and service. They eliminate the need for expensive machining operations and shaft extensions that are required for threaded connections.

SEQUENCE OS STEPS

Step I: Create the base feature
1. Define the sketching plane
2. Sketch the section on the TOP datum plane
3, Define the extrusion depth

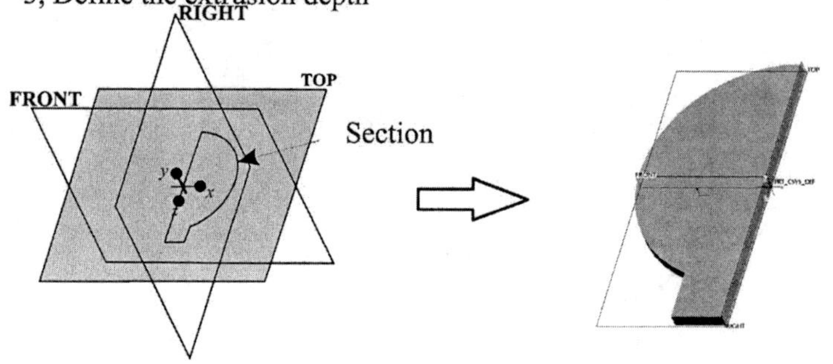

Step II: Mirror geometry
1. Mirror geometry about the RIGHT datum plane

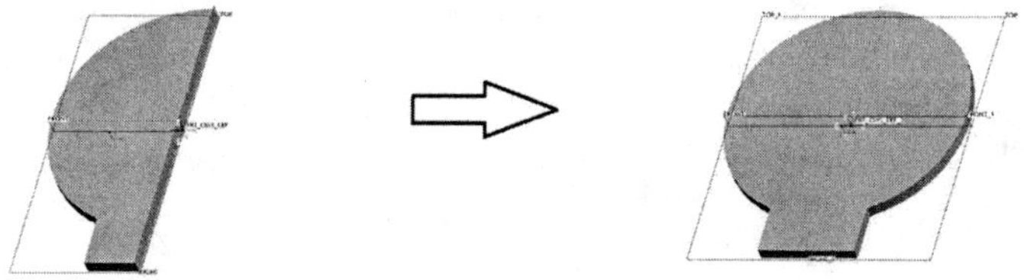

Step III: Create a hole
1. Define the diameter and depth options
2. Select the primary surface
3. Align the axis of the hole with the FRONT and RIGHT datum planes

Step IV: Create a small hole
1. Define the diameter and depth options
2. Select the primary reference
3. Select the secondary references as the FRONT and RIGHT datum planes
4. Specify the distances from the secondary references

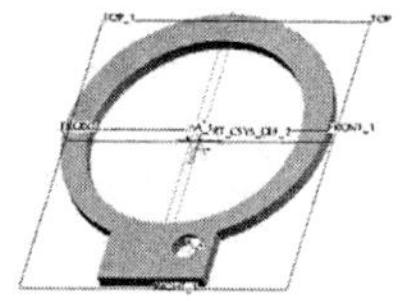

Step V: Mirror the hole feature
1. Mirror geometry about the RIGHT datum plane

Step V: Create a vertical slot
1. Sketch the cut section on the TOP datum plane
2. Specify the direction and the depth of the cut

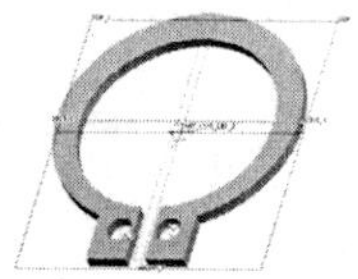

Step VI: Round the edges
1. Specify the radius of the round
2. Select the edges to be rounded

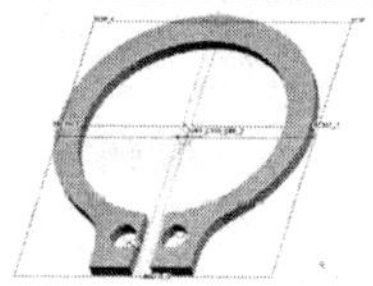

Step VII: Round the edges
1. Specify the radius of the round
2. Select the edges to be rounded

Goal	Step	Commands
Open a new file for the retaining ring part	1. Set up the working directory.	**FILE → SET WORKING DIRECTORY →** ***Select the working directory* → OK**
	2. Open a new file.	**FILE → NEW →** ***Part* → *Solid* → ring → OK**
Create the base feature	3. Start "Extrude" feature.	
	4. Define the sketching plane.	***Placement* → Define → *Select the TOP datum plane* → Sketch**
	5. Create an arc.	→ → ***Pick center on the RIGHT datum plane → Pick points 1 and 2*** Refer to Fig. 5.1.
	6. Create three lines.	***→ Pick points 2, 3, 4, and 1 → Middle Mouse*** (to discontinue line creation) Refer to Fig. 5.2.
	7. Add dimensions.	***→ Select the arc center and then the PRT_CSYS_DEF → Middle Mouse at the point where the vertical dimension must be placed → Select line 1 → Middle Mouse to place the vertical dimension → Select line 2 → Middle Mouse to place the horizontal dimension*** Refer to Fig. 5.3.
	8. Modify dimensions.	★ Modify linear dimensions first and then, the radius. ***→ Double click on each dimension and enter the corresponding value*** [Or ***→ Select each dimension to be modified and then modify it***] Refer to Fig. 5.3.

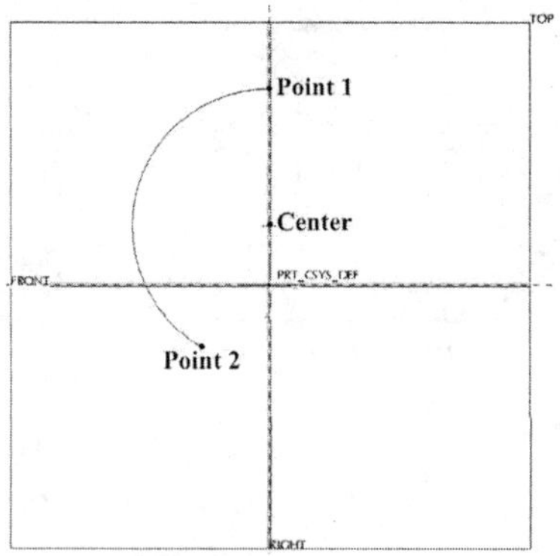

Fig. 5.1.

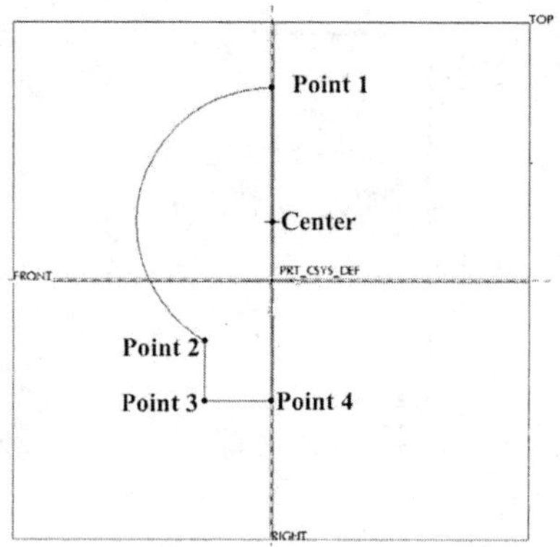

Fig. 5.2.

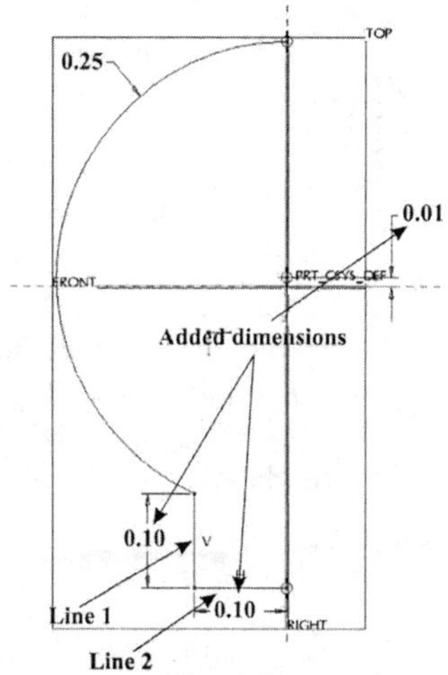

Fig. 5.3.

Goal	Step	Commands
Create the base feature (Continued)	9. Exit sketcher.	✓
	10. Define the extrusion depth.	(Depth) **0.025** → ***ENTER***
	11. Accept the feature creation.	→ **VIEW → ORIENTATION → STANDARD ORIENTATION** Refer to Fig. 5.4.
Mirror the extrude feature	12. Mirror the geometry.	***Select the part name from the model tree*** → → ***Select the RIGHT datum plane*** → Refer to Fig. 5.5.
Create a large hole	13. Create a hole at the center.	→ (Hole Type) **Simple** → (Diameter) **0.4** → (Depth One) ***Thru All*** → ***Placement*** *(in dash)* → ***Select the top surface → Drag the handles and drop on the front and right datum planes*** (Hole will be dimensioned with respect to these two planes) → Refer to Figs. 5.6 and 5.7. ***Select align option for the offset reference*** → Refer to Fig. 5.8.

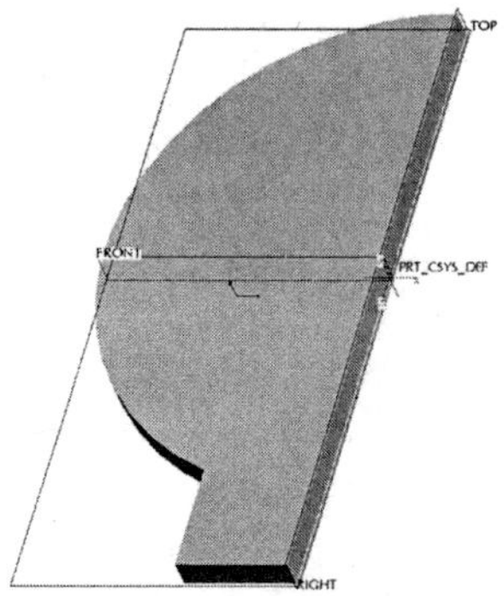
Fig. 5.4.

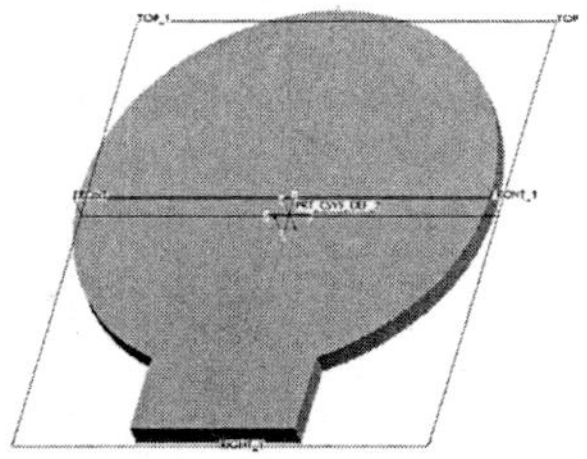
Fig. 5.5.

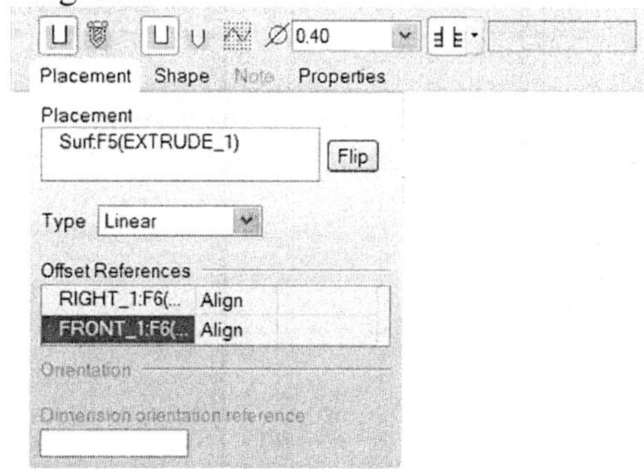

Fig. 5.6.

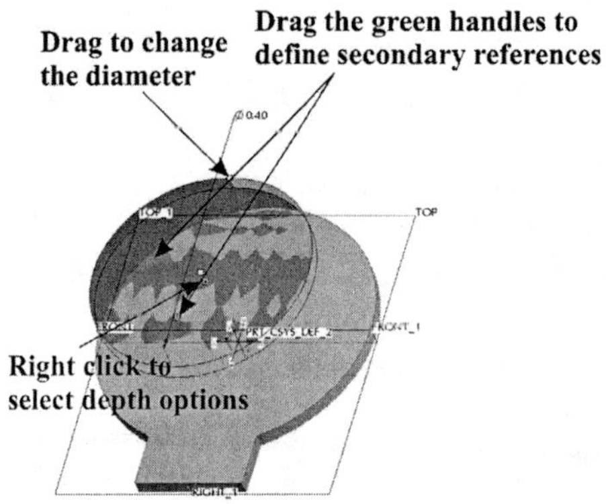

Fig. 5.7.

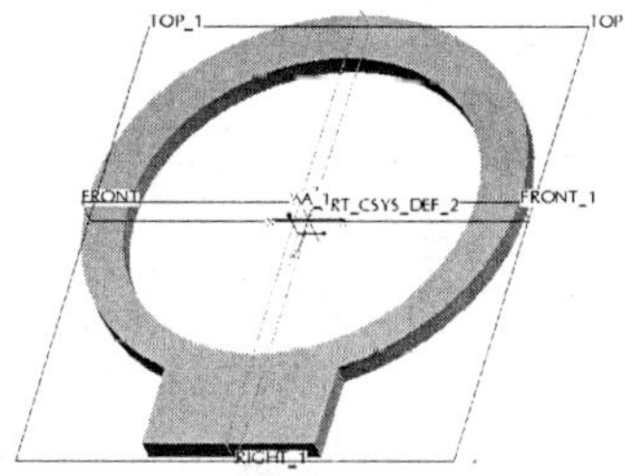
Fig. 5.8

Goal	Step	Commands
Create a small hole	14. Create a small hole.	 → **(Hole Type) Simple → (Diameter) <u>0.05</u> →** **(Depth One) *Thru All* →** ***Placement (in dash) → Select the top surface →*** ***Drag the green handles and drop them on the FRONT and RIGHT datum planes*** **(Hole will be dimensioned with respect to these two datum planes) →** Refer to Fig. 5.9. ***Select the distance from the FRONT datum plane → <u>0.25</u> → <u>ENTER</u> → Select the distance from the RIGHT datum plane → <u>ENTER</u> → <u>0.05</u> →***  Refer to Fig. 5.10.
Mirror the small hole	15. Start "Copy – Mirror" command.	**EDIT → FEATURE OPERATIONS → Copy → Mirror → Select → Dependent → Done**
	16. Pick the feature to be mirrored.	***Select the small hole (last feature)* → OK**
	17. Pick the mirror plane.	**Plane → *Select the RIGHT datum plane* → Done** Refer to Fig. 5.11.

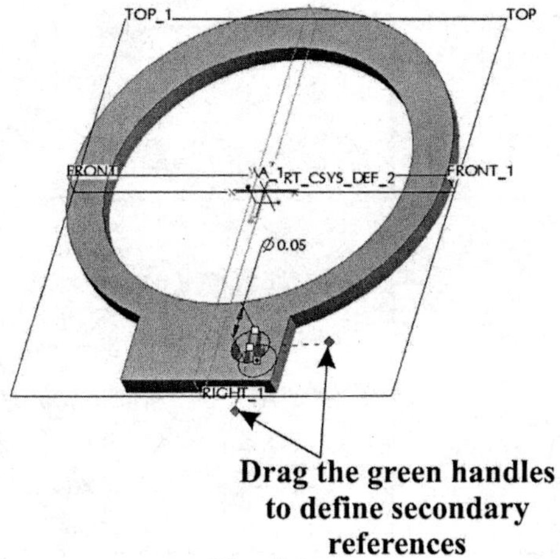

Fig. 5.9.

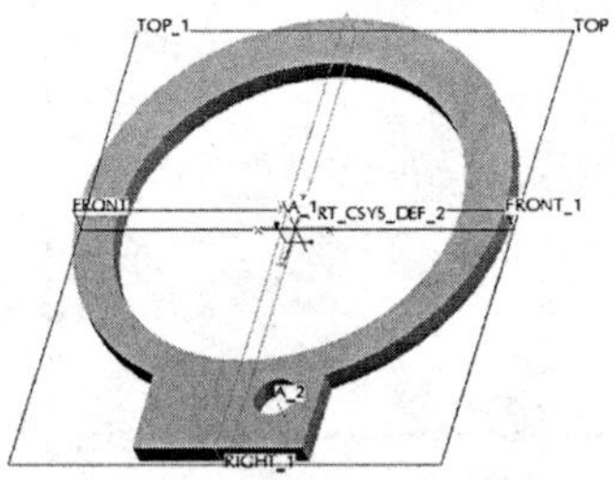
Fig. 5.10.

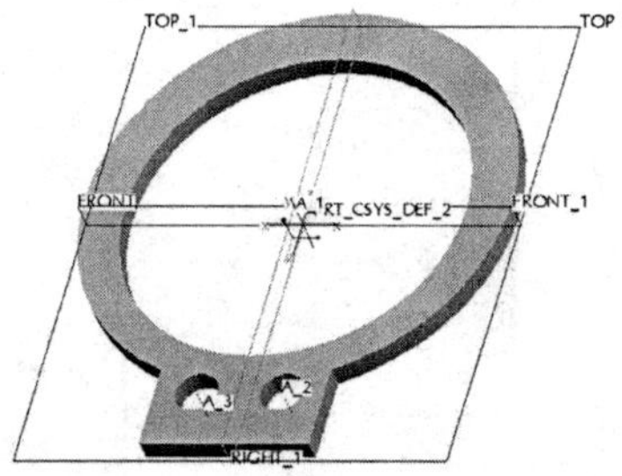
Fig. 5.11.

By selecting "Dependent" option using "Copy" command, the parent feature (the original hole) and dependent feature (the mirrored hole) will have same dimensions. Changes to the parent propagates automatically to the child.

Goal	Step	Commands
Create the vertical cut	18. Start "Extrude – Cut" feature.	 → 
	19. Use the previous sketcher plane.	**Placement** → **Define** → **Use Prev** The "Use Prev" command uses the previous sketching plane.
	20. Add additional references.	**SKETCH** → **REFERENCES** → Refer to Fig. 5.12. ***Select inner circle*** → ***Select the lower edge*** → **CLOSE** Refer to Fig. 5.13.
	21. Sketch the cut section.	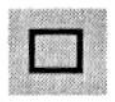 → ***Pick points 1 and 2*** Refer to Fig. 5.13.

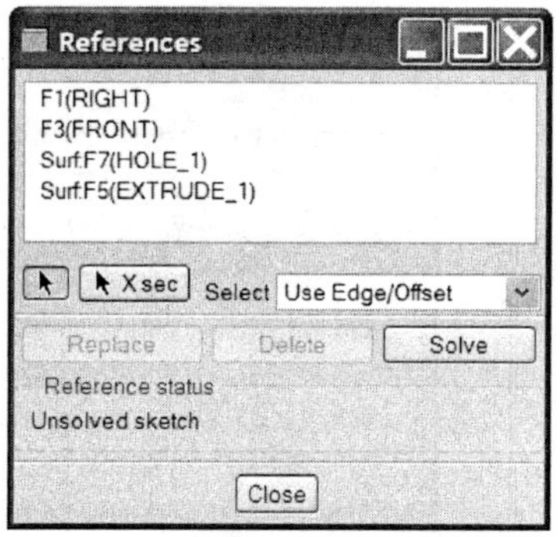

Fig. 5.12.

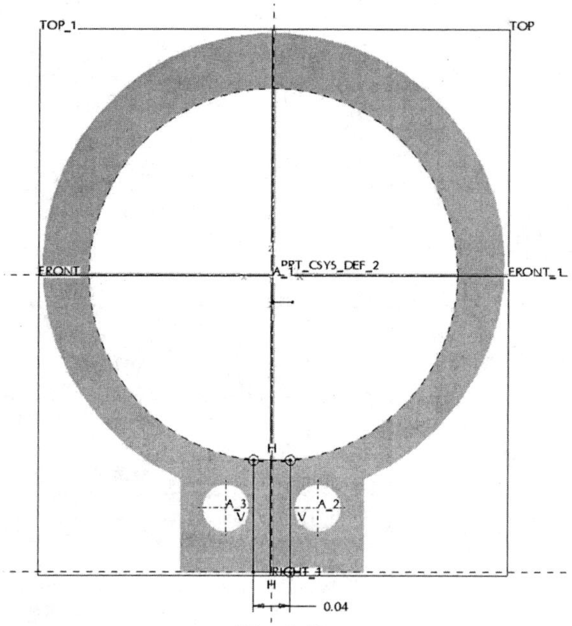

Fig. 5.13.

Goal	Step	Commands
Create the vertical cut (Continued)	22. Modify the width dimension.	→ ***Double click on the width dimension*** → **0.04** → ***ENTER***
	23. Exit sketcher.	
	24. Define the cut properties.	**VIEW** → **ORIENTATION** → **STANDARD ORIENTATION** → (Depth) (ThruAll) →
	25. Accept the feature creation.	Refer to Fig. 5.14.
Round the edges	26. Round the two inner edges.	→ (Radius in the dash) **0.1** → ***Select the two edges to be rounded*** (Selecting the hidden edge may require you to move the mouse over it until it gets highlighted or Right mouse till it gets highlighted) → Refer to Fig. 5.14. Refer to Fig. 5.15.

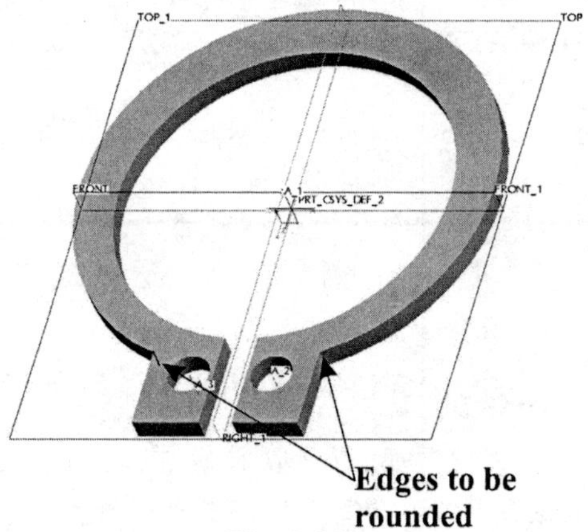

Fig. 5.14.

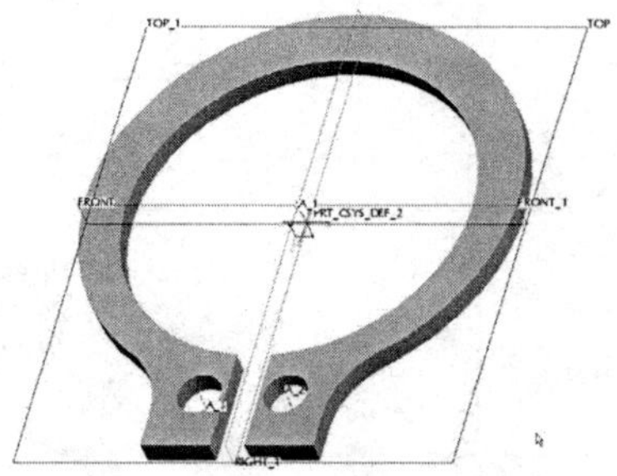
Fig. 5.15.

Goal	Step	Commands
Round the edges (Continued)	27. Round the two outer edges.	→ (Radius in the dash) **0.05** → ***Select the edges 1 and 2*** → Refer to Fig. 5.16. Refer to Fig. 5.17.
View the model	28. View the model in the default view. Turn off the datum planes.	**VIEW → ORIENTATION → STANDARD ORIENTATION →** ***Click on the following icons to switch off the datums, axis, datum points and default coordinate system*** →
Setup units	29. Setup units.	**EDIT → SETUP → Units →** ***Select IPS system*** → Set... → **OK** → **CLOSE**
Setup material properties	30. Define the material properties.	**Material →** ***Select steel*** → → **OK → Done** Refer to Fig. 5.19.

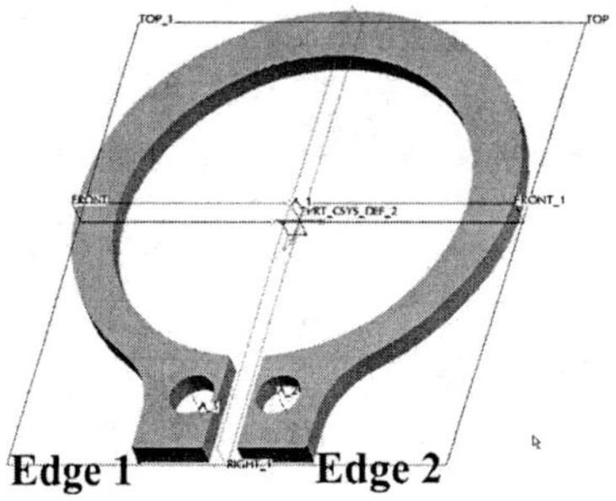

Fig. 5.16.

Fig. 5.17.

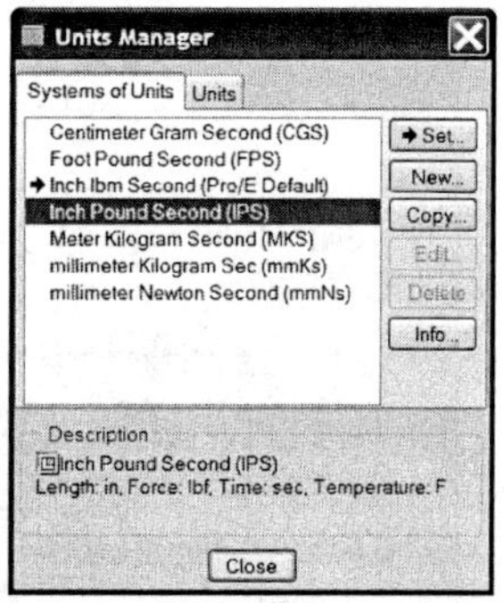

Fig. 5.18.

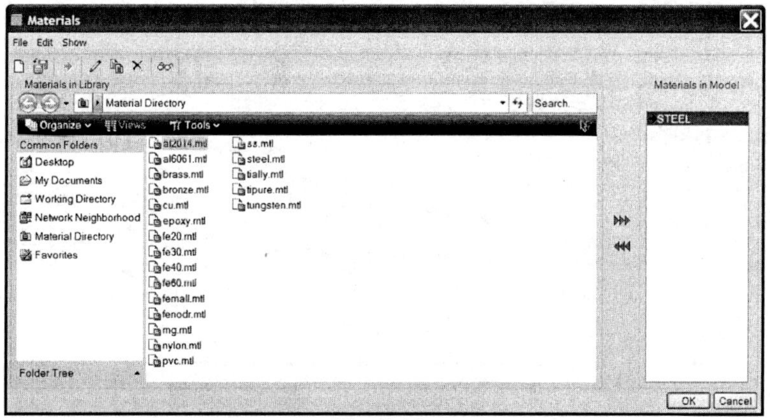

Fig. 5.19.

Goal	Step	Commands
Determine the weight	31. Determine the weight.	**ANALYSIS → MODEL → MASS PROPERTIES →** [glasses icon] **→** Refer to Fig. 5.20. [X icon]
Save the file and exit ProE	32. Save the file and exit ProE.	**FILE → SAVE → RING.PRT →** [✓] **→ FILE → EXIT → Yes**

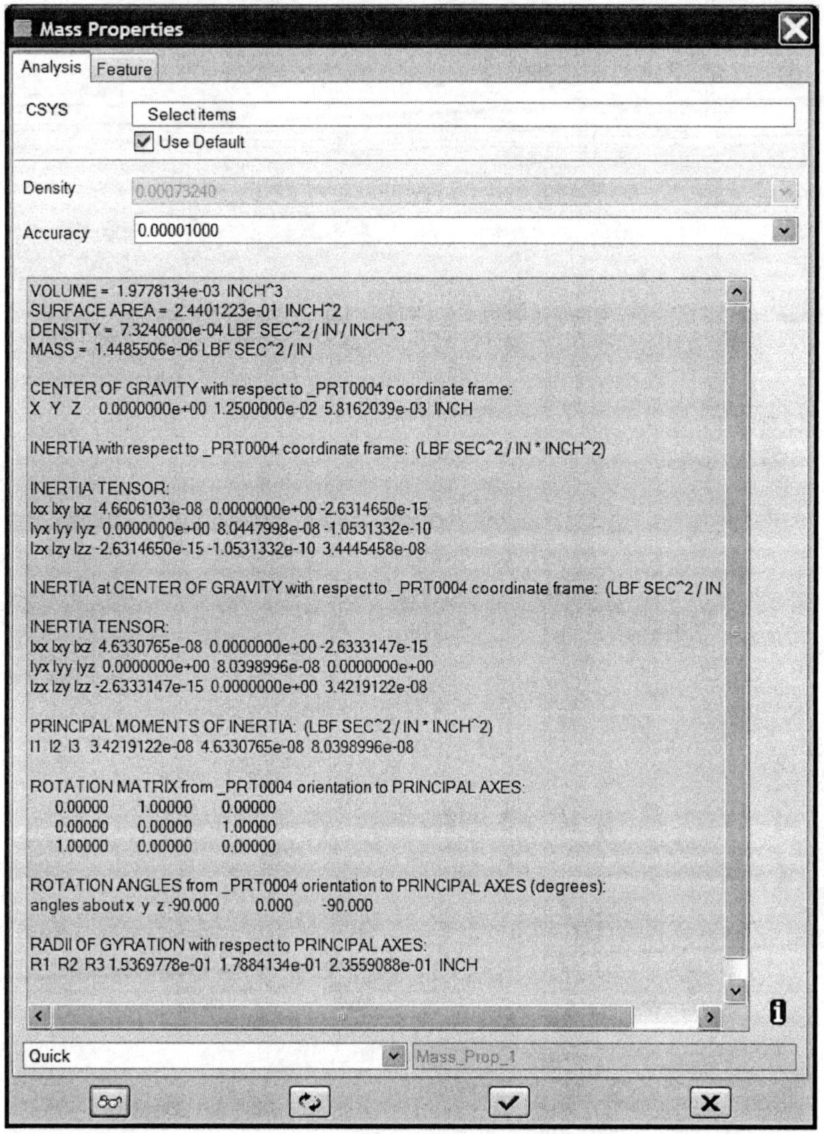

Fig. 5.20.

Exercise

Problem 1

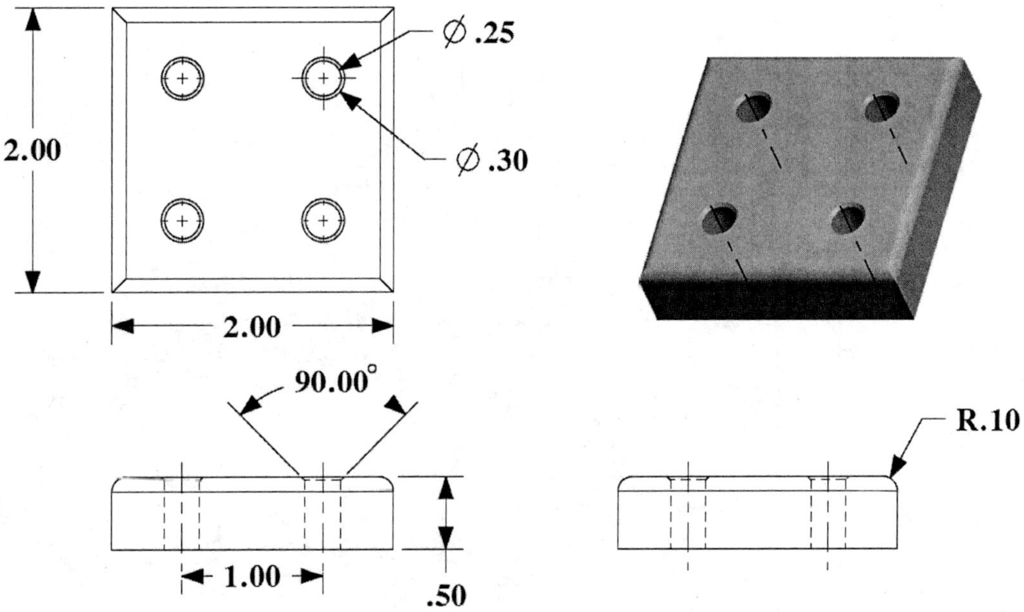

Hints:

1. Create quarter model (extrusion + hole + 2 rounds). The quarter model is shown in the figure below.

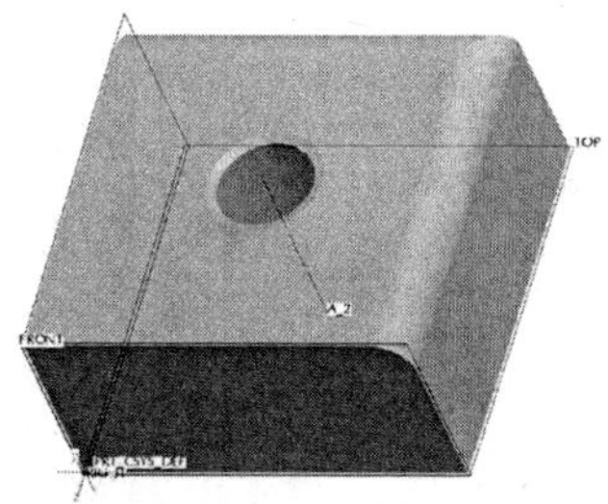

2. Hole properties:

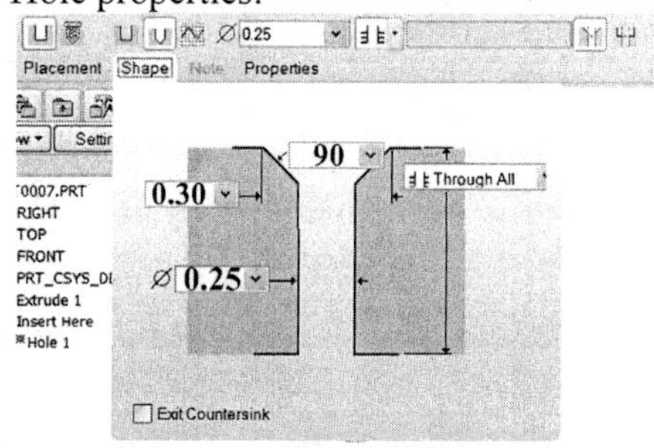

1. Select the model in the model tree. Mirror the entire model. The tool can be accessed either from EDIT → FEATURE OPERATIONS → MIRROR or by using the mirror button:

Problem 2

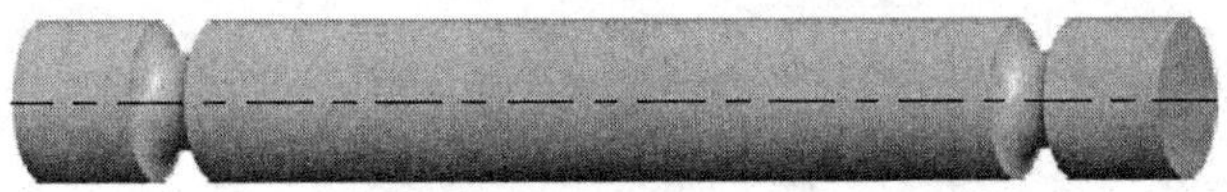

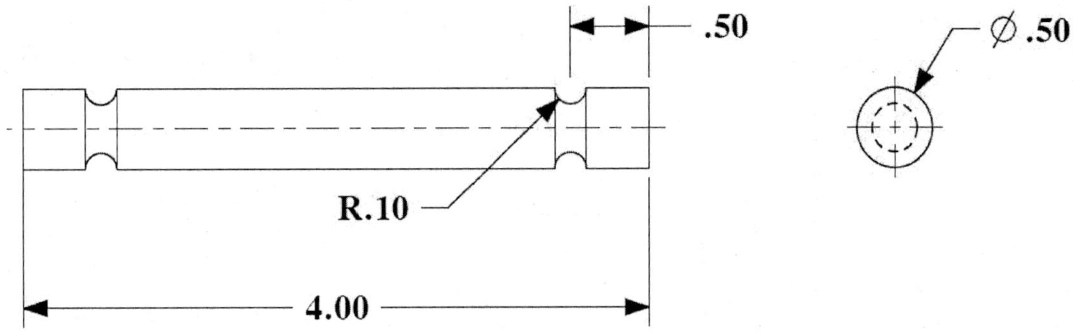

Hints:

1. Create a cylinder (Length 2″ & diameter .5″).

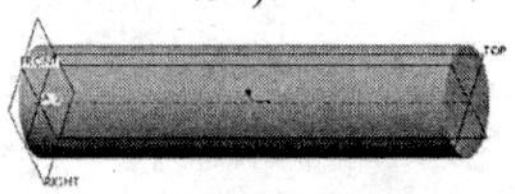

2. Create a groove. For the groove, use revolve cut feature. The section for the cut is shown in the figure below.

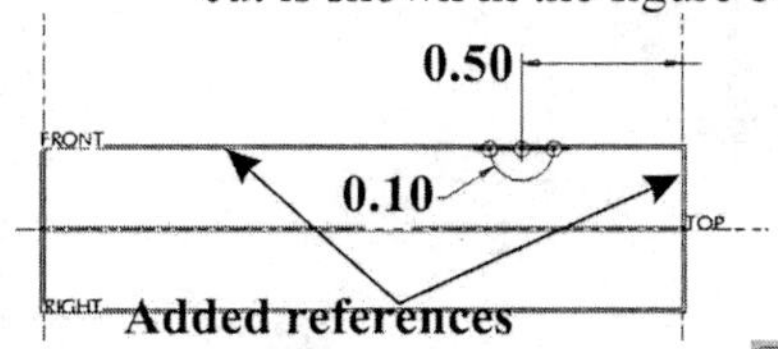

3. Make sure that you select .
4. If you get an error message, then 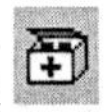 → Quick Fix → Delete → Confirm. Read hint 3.
5. Select the model in the model tree. **EDIT → MIRROR →** ***Select the mirror plane.***

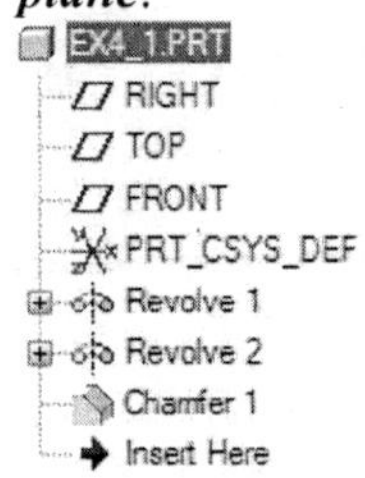

Problem 3

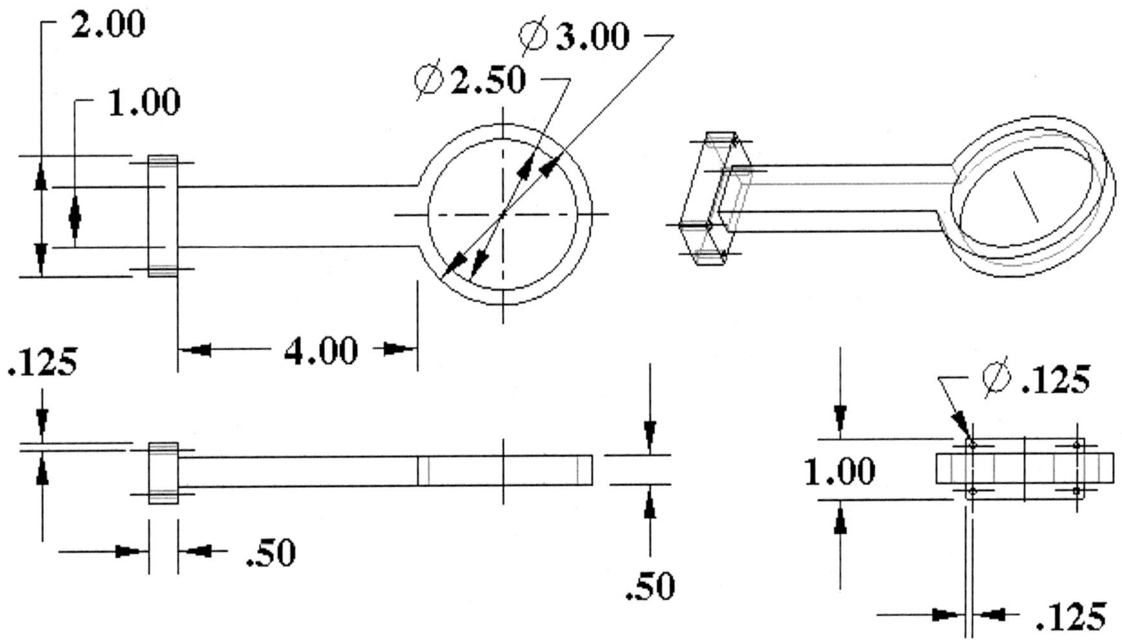

Hints:

1. Create the extrusions in three steps as shown in the figures below. Use both sides option: 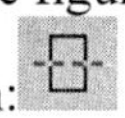

2. Create one hole and reference it with respect to datum planes.
3. The copy – mirror feature to create the four holes.

Problem 4

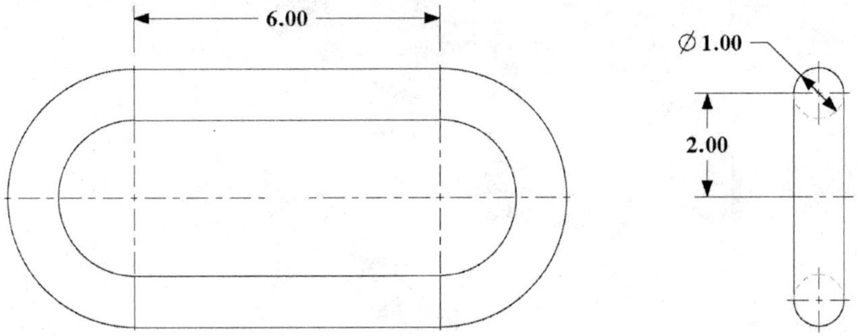

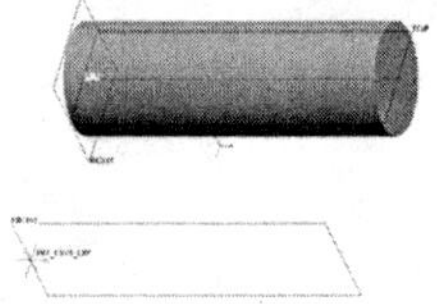

Step 1

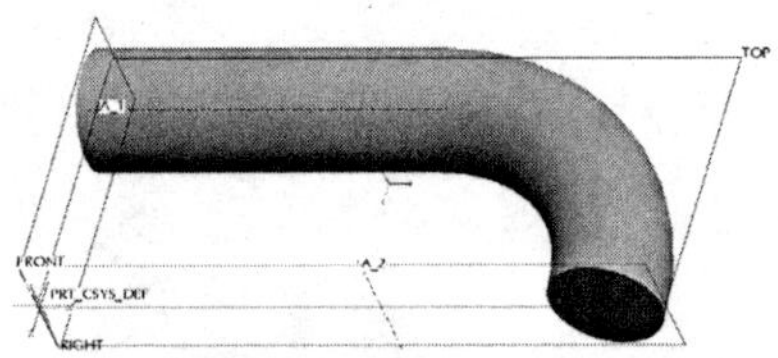

Step 2

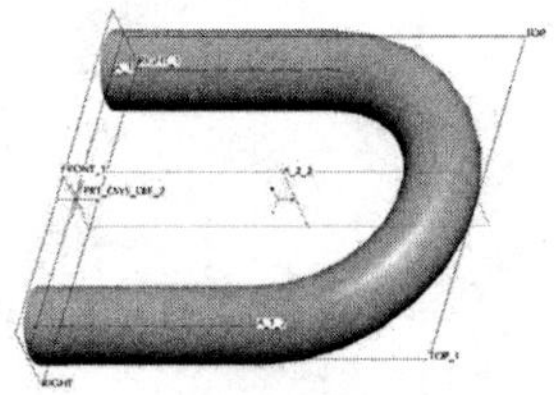

Step 3

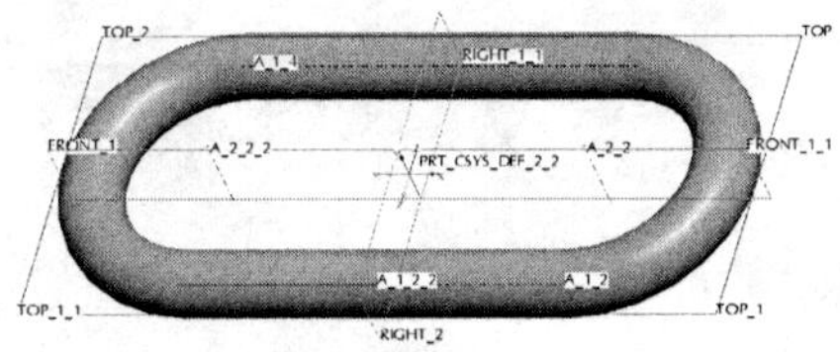

Step 4

Hints:

1. Step 1: Extrude base cylinder.
2. Step 2: Use revolve feature. In the sketcher, select edge tool -  and select the edges of the cylinder. Revolve 90^0.
3. Mirror twice to get the final model.

Problem 5

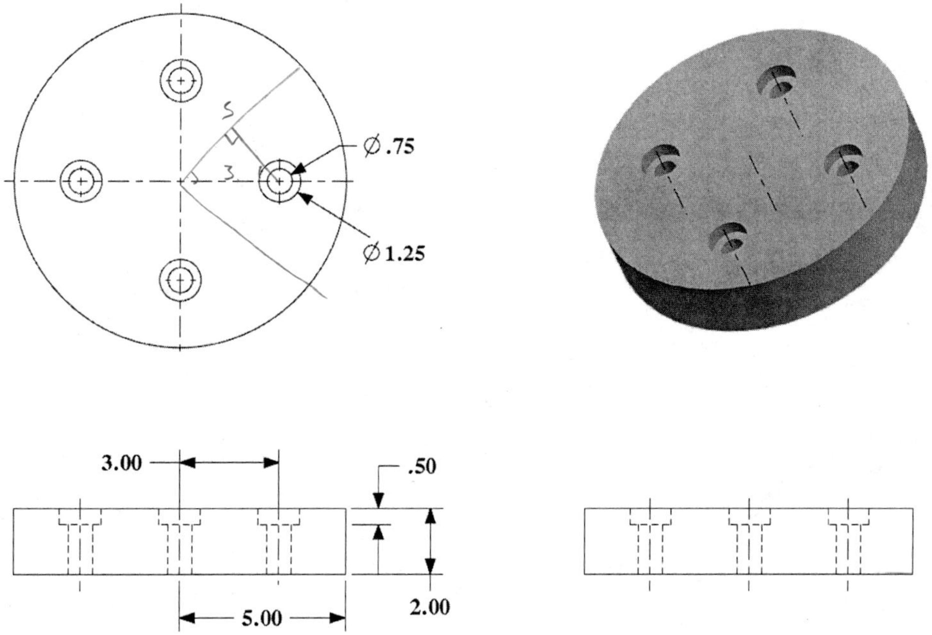

Hints:

1. Extrude a quarter of the base cylinder. Use both sides option.

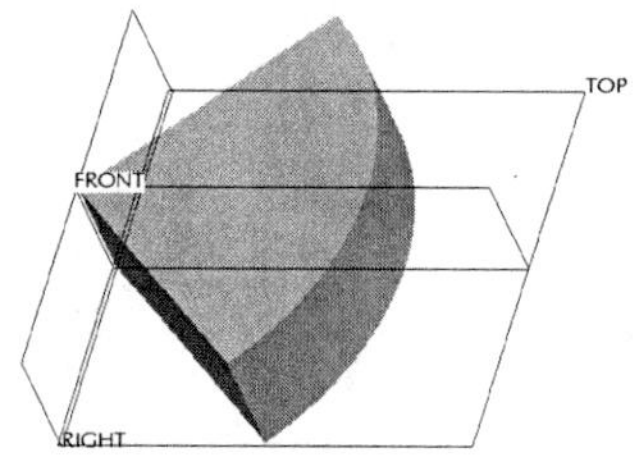

2. Create a countersunk hole.

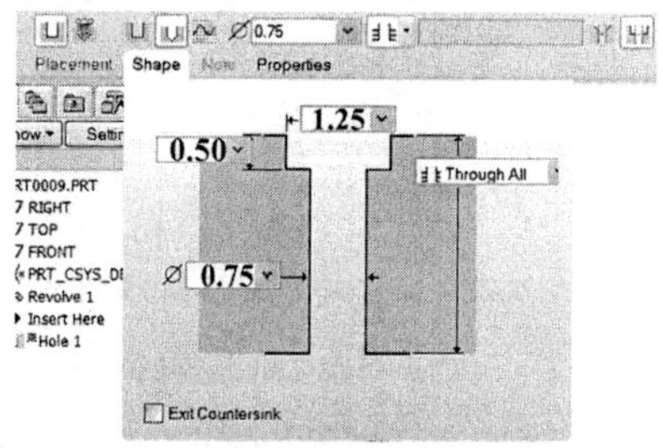

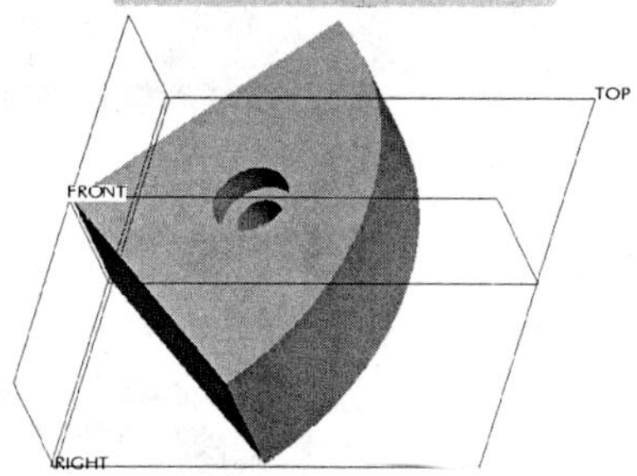

3. Mirror geometry twice to get the final model.

Problem 6

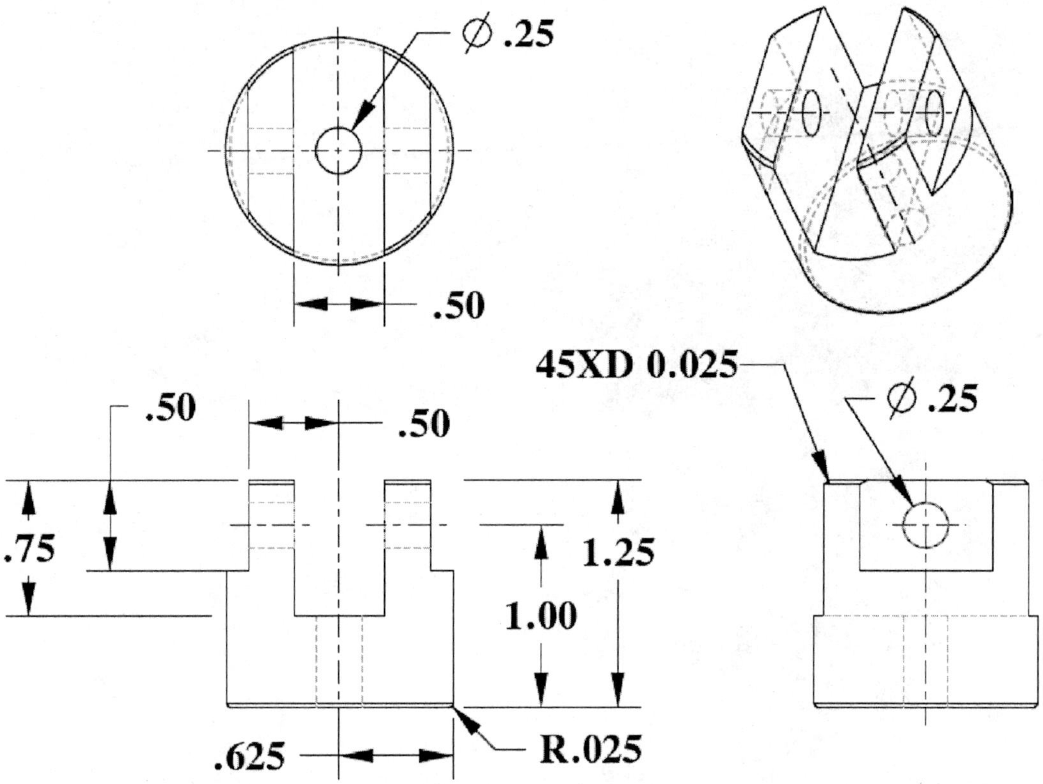

The evolution of the part is below:

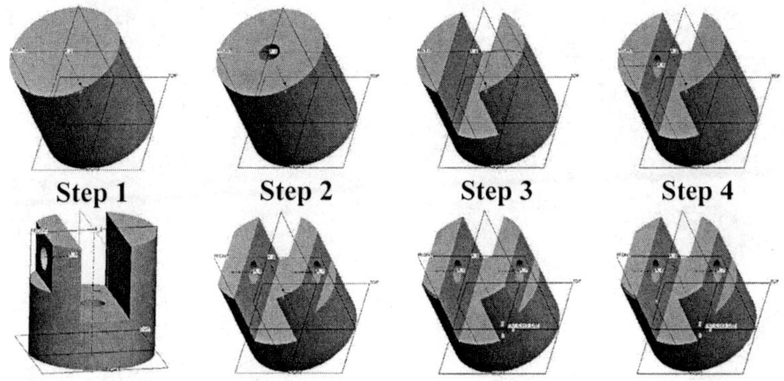

Step 1 Step 2 Step 3 Step 4

Step 5 Step 6 Step 7 Step 8

Hints:

1. In step 2, select the axis of the cylinder as the primary reference. Select Coaxial and top surface as the secondary reference.

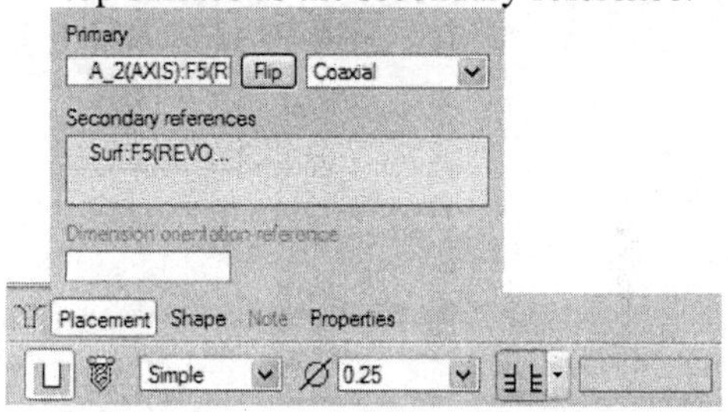

2. In step 3, use extrude cut feature. Sketch a rectangle on the front datum. Select "through all" option for both sides.

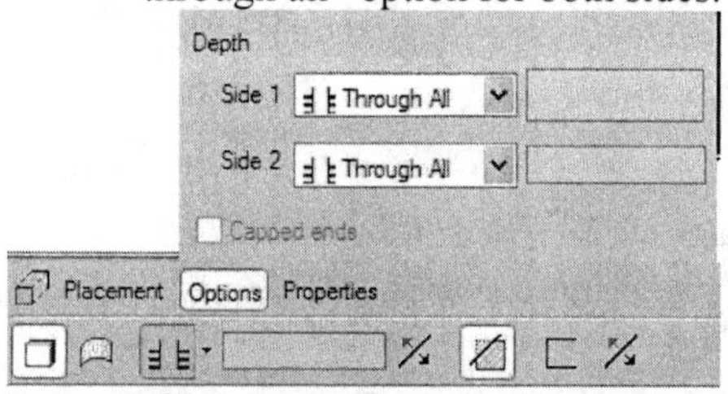

3. After step 5, group the hole and extrude cut features: *Select both features in the model tree* → *Right Mouse* → Group.
4. Mirror the group.

OPEN-ENDED DESIGN

Model an everyday object that uses extrude, revolve, round, cut, and hole features.

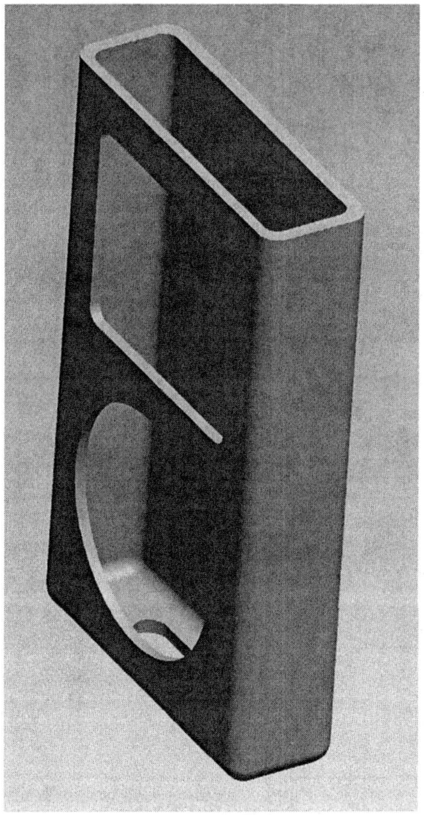

LESSON 6
NUTS AND BOLTS

Learning Objectives

- Use sketches in part creation.
- Learn ***Mirror*** tool to mirror features.
- Create ***Cosmetic Threads***.
- Practice ***Make Datum*** command.
- Practice ***Extrude, Extrude – Cut***, ***Revolve – Cut***, ***Chamfer***, and ***Hole*** features.
- Understand the use of ***Constraints***, ***Relations***, and ***Dependent Features***.

Cosmetic Threads

A common modeling practice is the use of cosmetic threads feature to model threads. The cosmetic thread feature reduces the regeneration time at the same time allows easy to access to the thread specification. In ProE, helical sweep can be used to create threads. However, this feature is memory intensive and also, time consuming to regenerate.

Cosmetic thread is used to represent the diameter of a thread and is displayed in purple color in the wire-frame display. The cosmetic thread feature can be specified for cylinders, cones, and splines. When defining cosmetic threads, specify the minor diameter for external threads and major diameter for internal threads. The thread definition has the following parameters

- Major diameter
- Thread height (for conic surfaces)
- Threads per inch
- Form
- Class
- Placement (A for external and B for internal)
- Metric (True or False)

Constraints

While sketching, the sketcher continually displays constraints to locate and size the entity. For instance, when the cursor is close to the midpoint of a line, the sketcher assumes that you want to align the new entity with the midpoint. If you design intent is the same, you can just pick the point with left mouse. However, you can disable/enable the constraint by clicking the right mouse button. Weak constraints are shown in grey color. The user can strengthen a weak constraint by selecting it, clicking right mouse, and choosing strong option. Additional constraints can be specified by: SKETCH → CONSTRAIN or clicking . The constraints that can be imposed are:

Makes line or vertices vertical	Makes line or vertices horizontal	Makes two entities perpendicular
Makes two entities tangential	Places a point in the middle of the line	Creates coincident points or collinear constraint
Makes two points or vertices symmetric about the centerline	Makes the lengths, radii or curvatures equal	Makes two lines parallel

Configuration File

The configuration files specify how ProE handles the modeling tasks, and also the display. The file allows the user to specify the display options like color, and modeling options such as the number of significant digits and tolerances. The configuration file (config.sys) can be accessed by: TOOLS → OPTIONS. ProE opens the preferences window. The user can search for the desired option using FIND. The user may create a custom configuration file, and open and save it from this window. ProE, when initiated, looks at the system configuration file, config.sup, and then, the configuration files in the ProE load point, user login and working directories. A ProE session uses the last value of the configuration option.

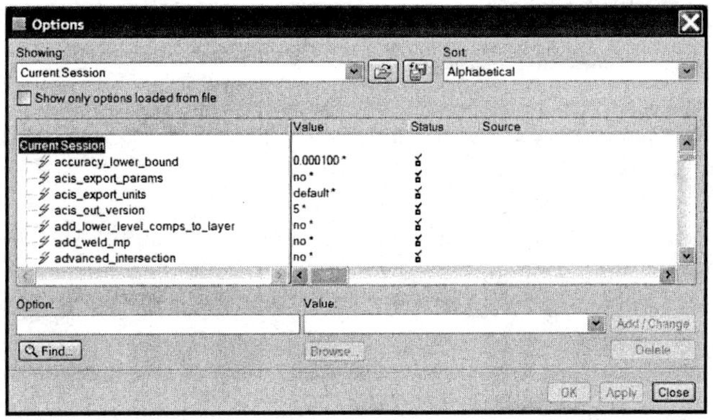

Design Information

Bolts are used to fasten two or more components. Depending on the application, a designer can choose from a variety of bolts. For instance, a socket head applies large torque using Allen wrenches. When inserted in a countersunk hole, a socket head bolt will be flush with the surface. Nuts incorporate internal threads to engage with bolts. To avoid loosening, they are normally torqued to a high value. Also, special nuts are available with cotter pins, chemical thread locking systems, and lock washers to prevent loosening.

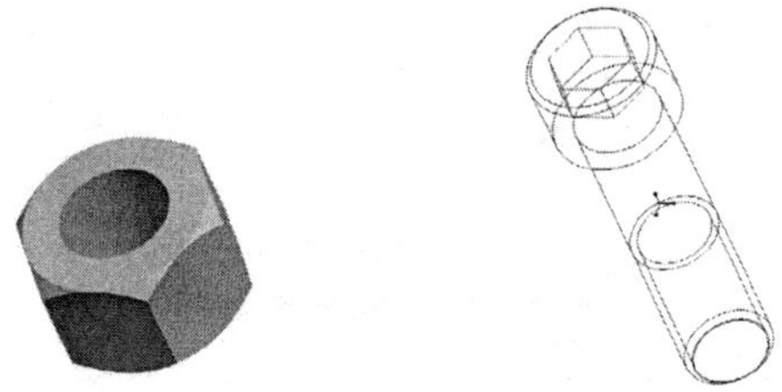

SEQUENCE OF STEPS

Step I - Create a hexagonal section
1. Create a construction circle
2. Create the hexagon

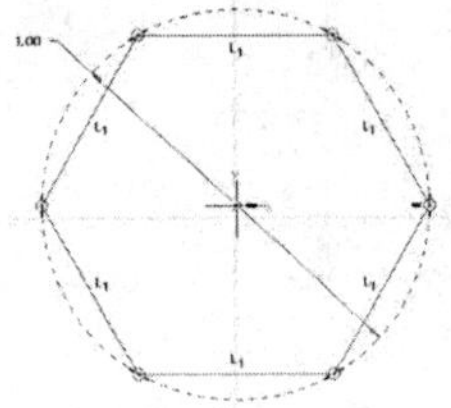

Step II - Create the base feature
1. Import the hexagon section
2. Define the depth of extrusion

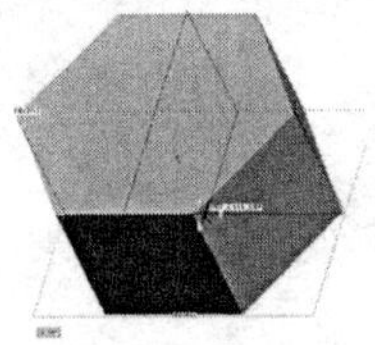

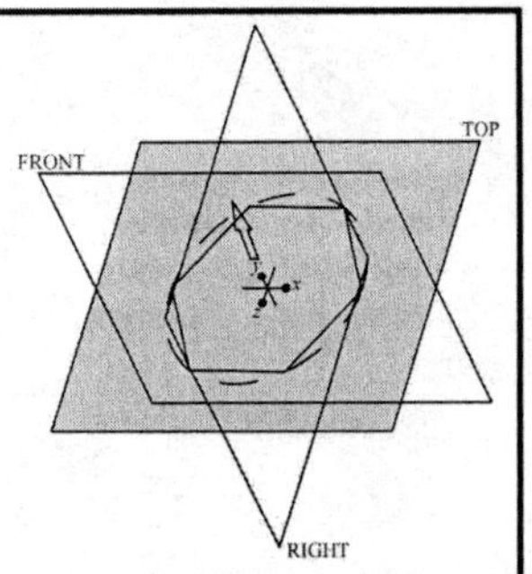

Step III - Create a threaded hole
1. Use "Hole" feature
2. Specify the primary and secondary references
3. Specify the thread parameters

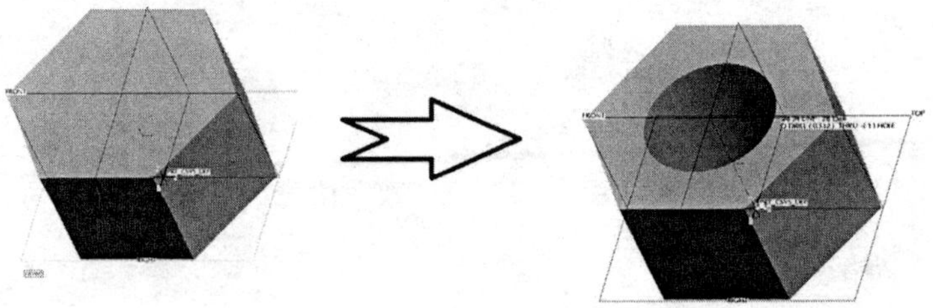

Step V - Create the cut
1. Use "Revolve - Cut" feature
2. Sketch the cutting line
3. Select the axis of revolution
4. Define the angle of revolution

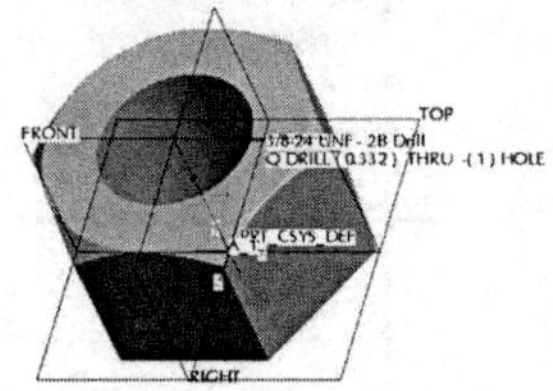

Step VI - Mirror the cut
1. Create a datum plane in the middle of the nut parallel to the TOP datum plane
2. Mirror the cut feature
3. Add a relation to center the datum plane

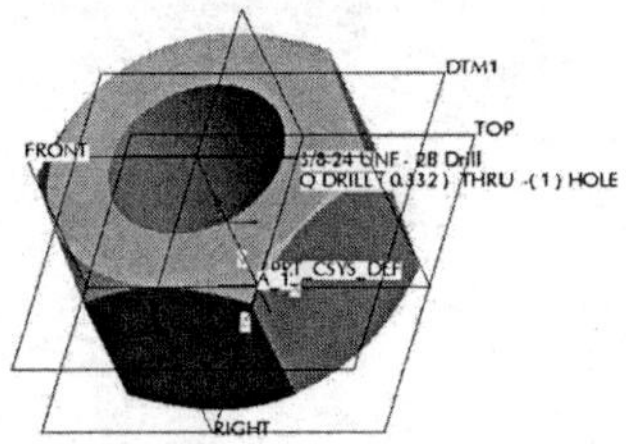

Step VII - Check the model
1. Check the validity of the relations and dependancy

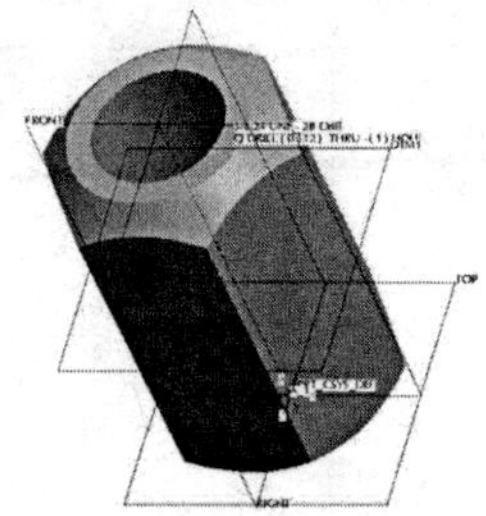

Goal	Step	Commands
Open a new file for the nut section	1. Set up the working directory.	**FILE → SET WORKING DIRECTORY →** ***Select the working directory*** **→ OK**
	2. Open a new file.	**FILE → NEW →** ***Sketch*** **→ <u>hexagon</u> → OK**
Create the reference coordinate system	3. Create a reference coordinate system.	(to display grid) → → → ***Pick a point in the center of the graphics window*** Refer to Fig. 6.1. The reference coordinate system aids in dimensioning the section.
Create a hexagon	4. Create a construction circle.	→ ***Select the origin of the reference coordinate system → Select a point to define the outer edges of the circle →*** → ***Double click on the diameter dimension*** **→** ***<u>1</u>*** **→** ***<u>ENTER</u>*** **→** → ***Select the circle*** **→ EDIT → TOGGLE CONSTRUCTION** Refer to Fig. 6.2. "Toggle Construction" changes a regular geometric entity into a construction entity.
	5. Create the sides of the hexagon.	→ ***Pick points 1, 2, 3, 4, 5 and 6 → Middle Mouse*** (to discontinue) Refer to Fig. 6.3.
	6. Delete constraints.	→ ***Select each constraint → <u>DELETE</u>*** Delete all constraints (parallel, equal, horizontal…). Refer to Fig. 6.3.

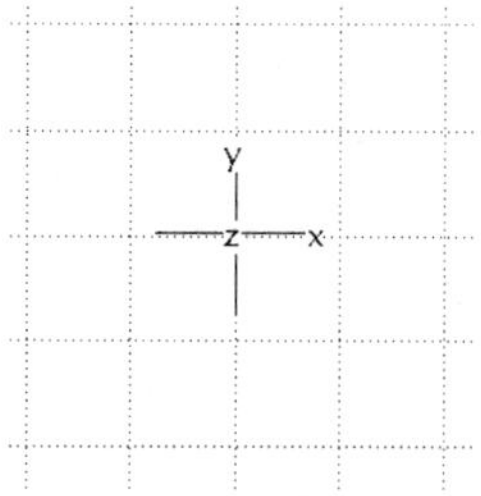

Fig. 6.1.

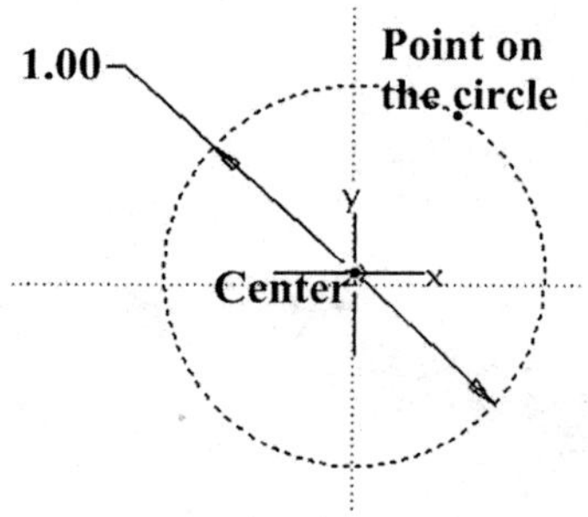

Fig. 6.2.

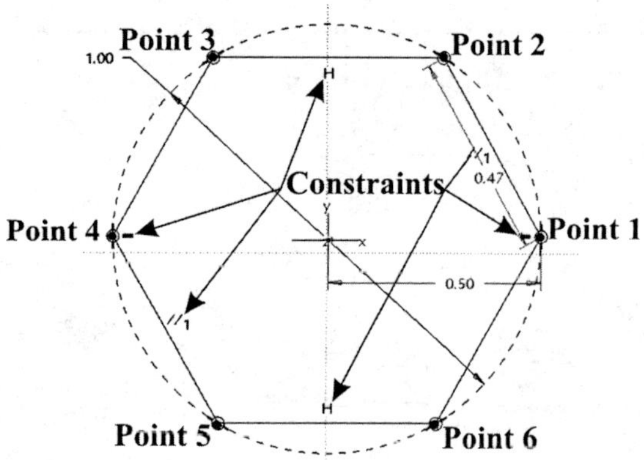

Fig. 6.3.

Goal	Step	Commands
Create a hexagon (continued)	7. Add equal to and horizontal constraints.	→ → *Select lines 1 and 2 → Select lines 2 and 3 → Select lines 3 and 4 → Select lines 4 and 5 → Select lines 5 and 6 →* → *Select line 5* Refer to Fig. 6.4 and 6.5.
Save the section and exit sketcher	8. Save the section and exit sketcher.	**FILE → SAVE → hexagon.sec → OK → FILE → CLOSE WINDOW**
Open a new file for the nut part	9. Open a new file.	**FILE → NEW →** ***Part*** **→** ***Solid*** **→ Nut → OK**
Create the base feature	10. Start "Extrude" feature.	
	11. Set up the sketching plane.	**PLACEMENT → DEFINE →** ***Select the TOP datum plane*** **→ Sketch**
	12. Open the hexagonal section.	**SKETCH → DATA FROM FILE → FILE SYSTEM→*****Select hexagon.sec file*** **→ OPEN**
	13. Center the section.	***Click in the graphics window → Drag and drop the handle on the intersection of the FRONT and RIGHT datum plans →*** **(scale) 0.65 → (rotate) 0 →** **→** Refer to Figs. 6.6, 6.7 and 6.8.
	14. Exit sketcher.	
	15. Define the depth.	(Depth) **0.35**
	16. Accept the feature creation.	**→ VIEW → ORIENTATION → STANDARD ORIENTATION** Refer to Fig. 6.9.

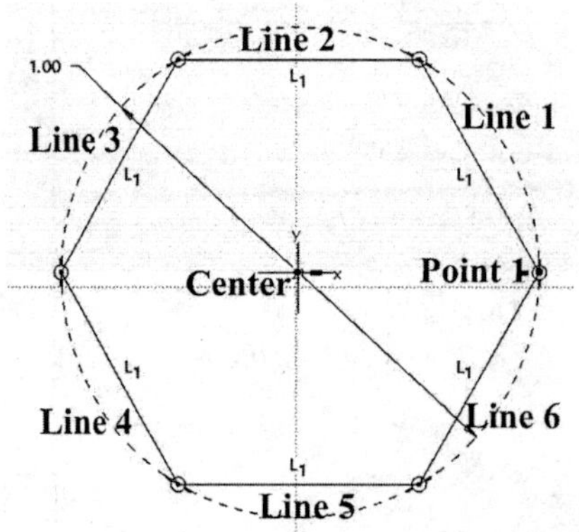

Fig. 6.4.

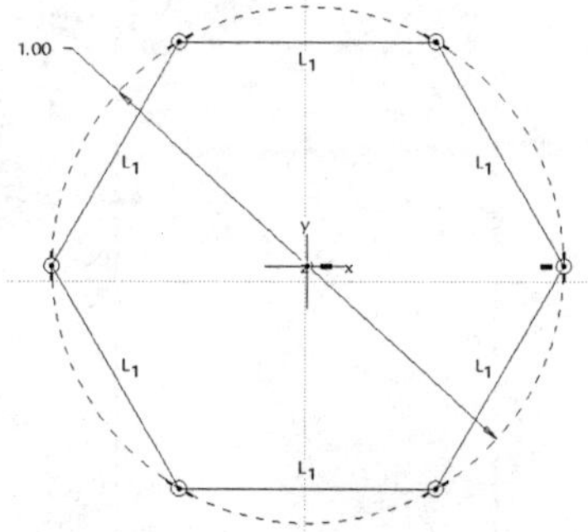

Fig. 6.5.

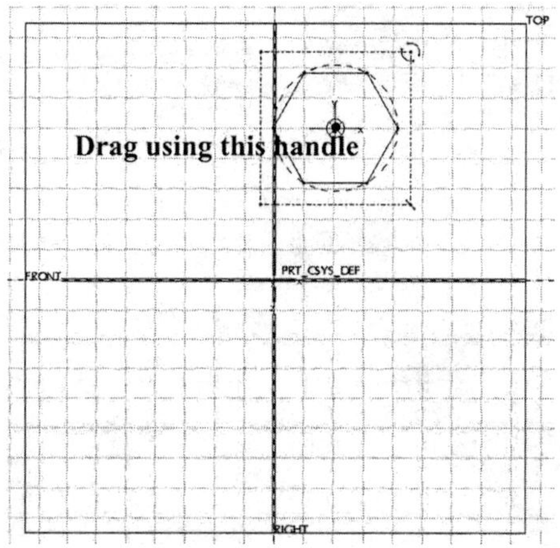

Fig. 6.6.

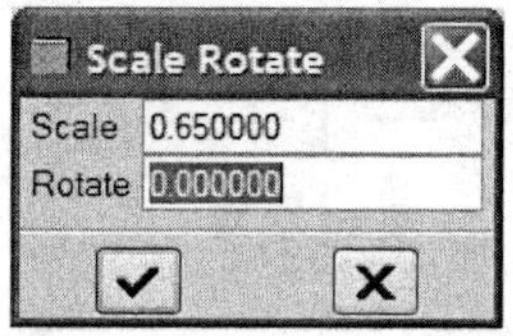

Fig. 6.7.

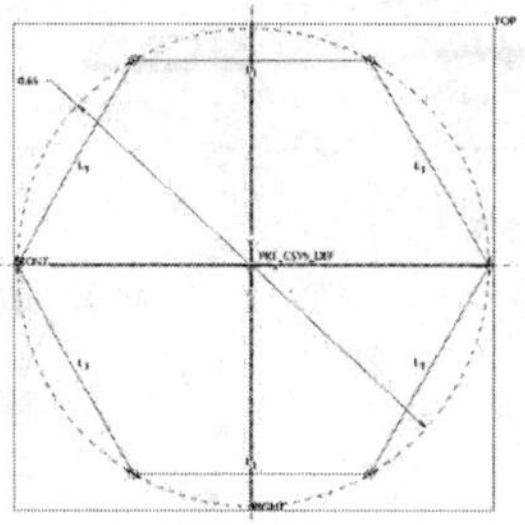
Fig. 6.8.

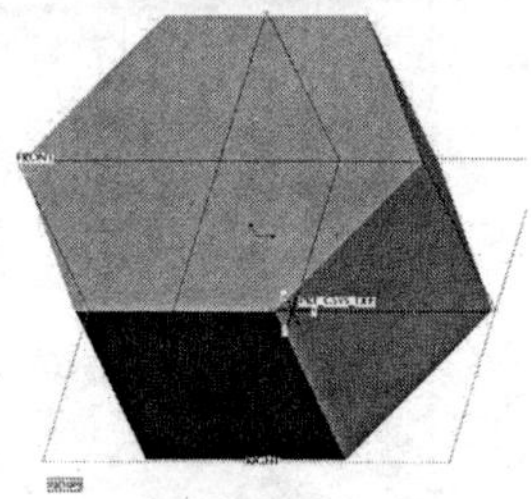
Fig. 6.9.

Goal	Step	Commands
Create a standard hole	17. Create a standard hole.	 → (Hole Type)  → **UNF** → (Diameter and threads per inch) **3/8 – 24** → (Depth One) ***Thru All*** → ***Placement*** *(in dash)* → ***Select the top surface*** → Refer to Fig. 6.10. ***Click in the secondary references window → Select FRONT DATUM PLANE from the model tree → Align → Hold <u>CNTRL</u> (to select multiple items) and select RIGHT DATUM PLANE → Align →*** Refer to Fig. 6.10.  Refer to Fig. 6.11.
Cut top corners	18. Start "Revolve – Cut" feature.	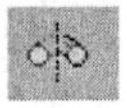 → 
	19. Define and orient the sketcher.	**PLACEMENT** → **DEFINE** → ***Select the FRONT datum plane*** → **Sketch**
	20. Add new references.	**SKETCH** → **REFERENCES** → ***Select the top surface → Select the right edge of the nut*** → **CLOSE** Refer to Figs. 6.12 and 6.13.

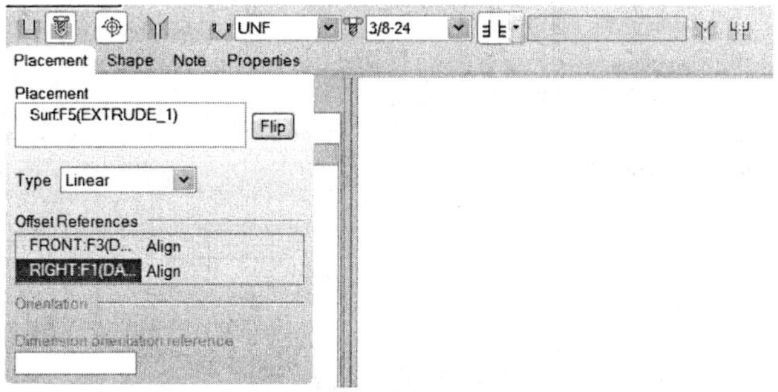

Fig. 6.10.

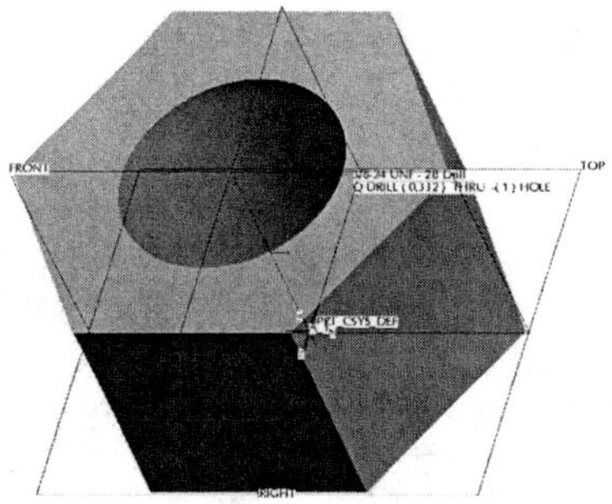

Fig. 6.11.

In ProE, helical sweep can be used to create threads. However, this feature is memory intensive and also, time consuming to regenerate. Therefore, it is a common practice to use a standard hole to create threaded holes. Even though this feature does not show the actual threads, it allows the specification of (and easy access to) various thread parameters.

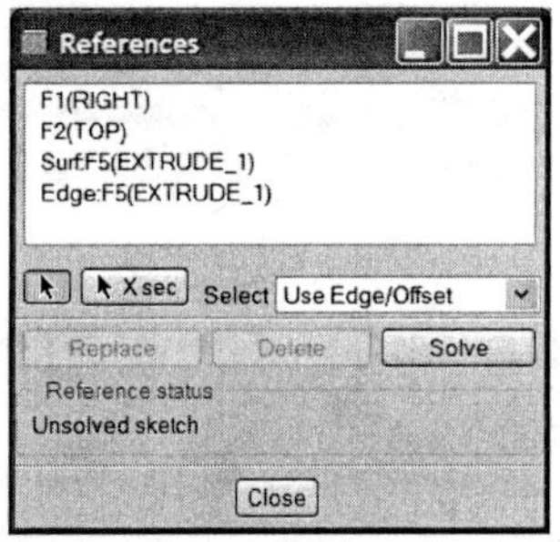

Fig. 6.12.

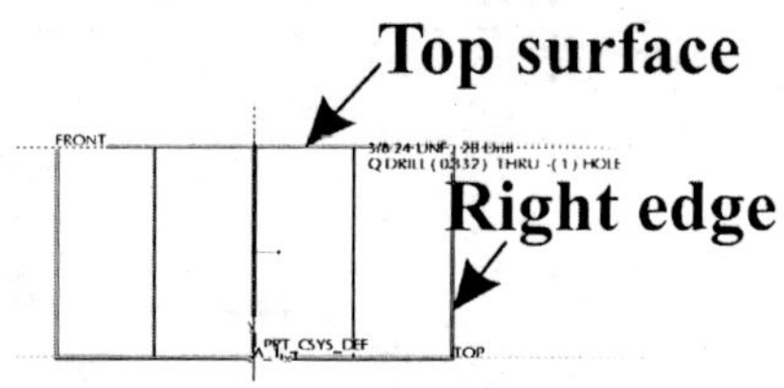

Fig. 6.13.

Goal	Step	Commands
Cut top corners (continued)	21. Sketch the cutting line.	→ ***Pick points 1 and 2*** → ***Middle Mouse*** Refer to Fig. 6.14.
	22. Dimension the line.	→ ***Double click on the distance dimension*** → **0.045** → ***ENTER*** → ***Double click on the angular dimension*** → **45** → ***ENTER*** Refer to Fig. 6.14.
	23. Exit sketcher.	
	24. Select the axis of revolution.	**PLACEMENT** → ***Click the Axis selection box*** → ***Select the axis***
	25. Define the direction of material removal.	The arrow should point away from the nut. If it is pointed towards the nut, flip the direction using (next to thin option)
	26. Define the angle of revolution.	(Angle) **360**
	27. Accept the feature creation.	→ **VIEW** → **ORIENTATION** → **STANDARD ORIENTATION** Refer to Fig. 6.15.
Mirror the cut geometry	28. Select the feature to be mirrored.	**EDIT** → **FEATURE OPERATIONS** → **Copy** → **Mirror** → **Select** → **Dependent** → **Done** → ***Select the revolve cut feature (last feature) from the model tree*** → **OK**
	29. Create a datum plane for mirroring.	**Make Datum** → **Offset** → **Plane** → **Coor Sys** → **FacetFace** → ***Select the TOP datum plane*** → **Enter Value** → **0.175** → → **Done** → **Done** Refer to Fig. 6.16.

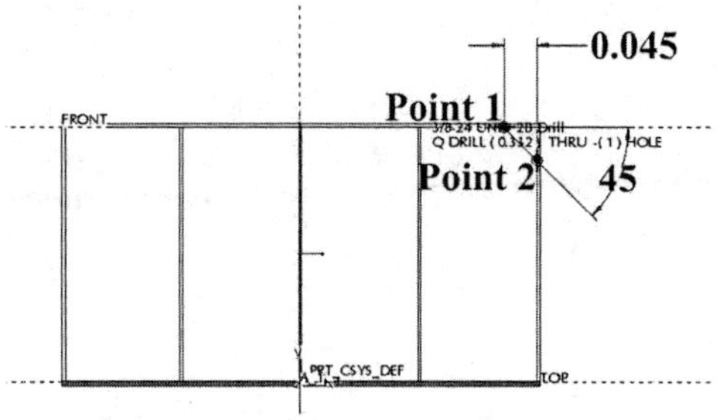

Fig. 6.14.

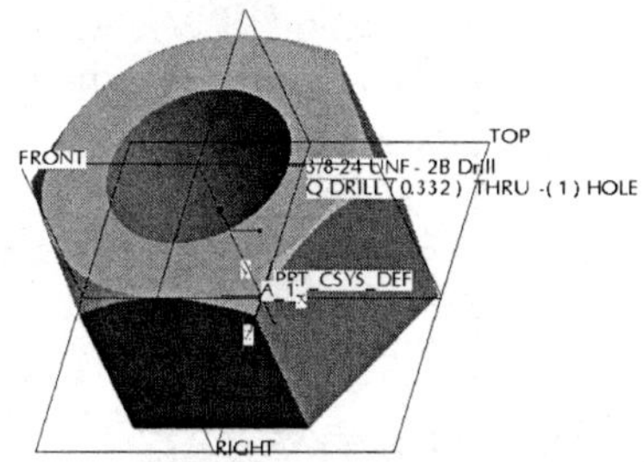

Fig. 6.15.

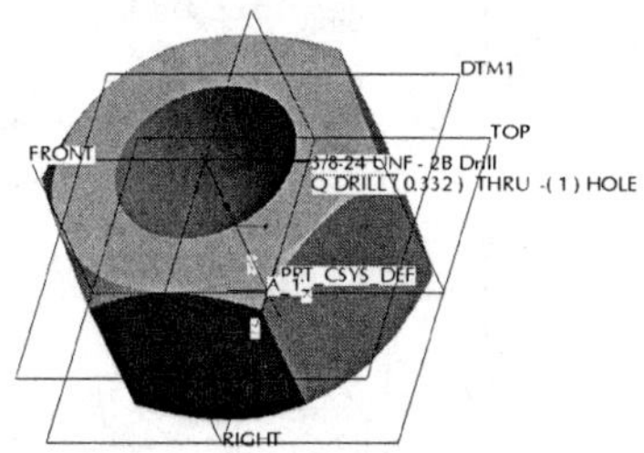

Fig. 6.16.

Goal	Step	Commands
Check the model	30. Add a relation between the height and the datum position.	**TOOLS → RELATIONS →** ***Select DTM 1 → Select the base extrusion (first feature) from the model tree →*** Refer to Fig. 6.17. **d14 = 0.5 * d0 → OK**
	31. Check the validity of the relationship and dependent features.	***Select the first extrusion → Right Mouse →*** **Edit →** ***Double click on the height dimension of the nut →*** **1 →** ***ENTER →*** **EDIT → REGENERATE →** By adding the relationship (d17 = 0.5 * d0), the mirror feature regenerates without problems. ***Select the revolve cut → Right Mouse →*** **Edit →** ***Double click on the height dimension of the cut dimension →*** **0.1 →** ***ENTER →*** **EDIT → REGENERATE →** By making the bottom cut dependent, the two cuts remain identical mirror images. Refer to Fig. 6.18. ***Select the first extrusion → Right Mouse →*** **Edit →** ***Double click on the height dimension of the nut →*** **0.375 →** ***ENTER →*** **EDIT → REGENERATE →** ***Select the cut → Right Mouse →*** **Edit →** ***Double click on the height dimension of the cut →*** **0.045 →** ***ENTER →*** **EDIT → REGENERATE**
Save the file and close the window	32. Save the file and close window.	**FILE → SAVE → NUT.PRT → OK →** **FILE → ERASE → CURRENT**

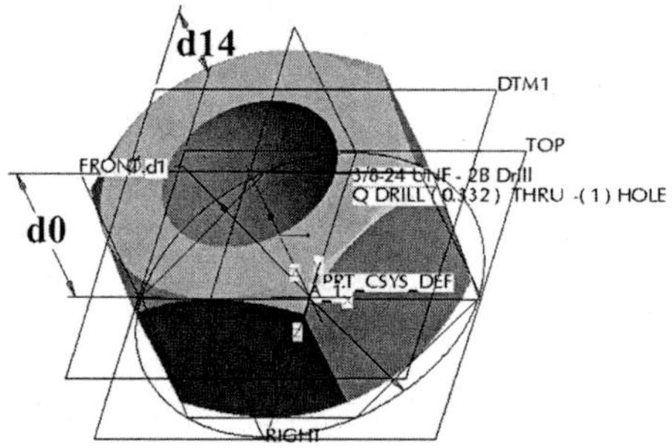

Fig. 6.17.

★ ProE displays the parameter names. The names vary depending on the order of feature creation. These variables (d0 and d14) may have slightly different names in your model.

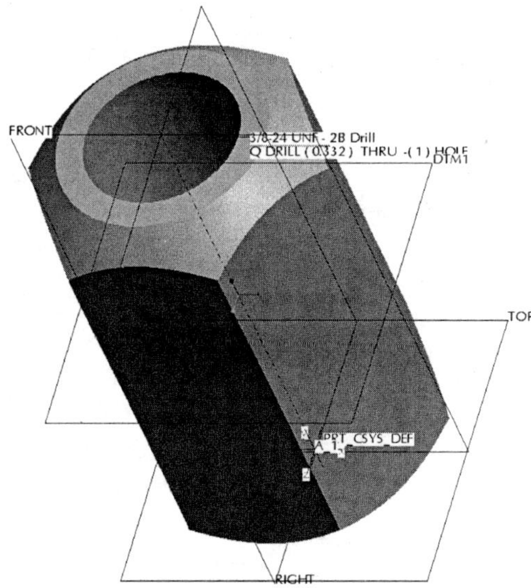

Fig. 6.18.

Step I - Create the bolt head
1. Use "Extrude" feature
2. Sketch a circle on the TOP datum plane
3. Define the depth of extrusion

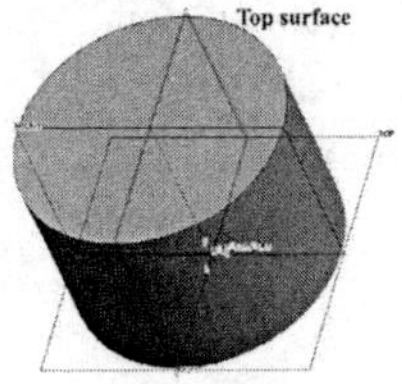

Step II - Create a hexagonal socket
1. Use "Extrude - Cut" feature
2. Import the hexagon section
2. Define the depth of extrusion

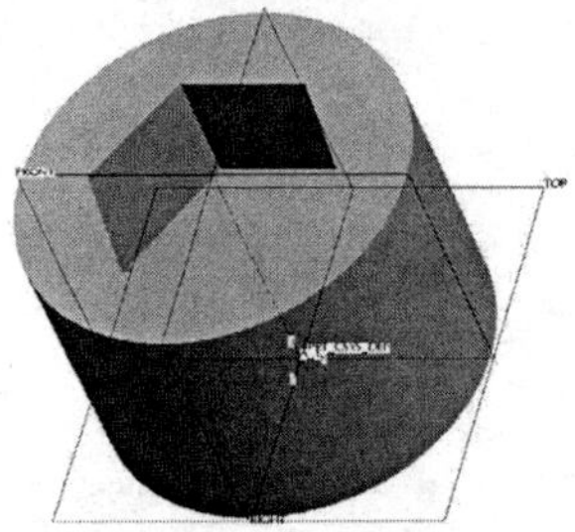

Step III - Create the shank
1. Use "Extrude" feature
2. Define the section (a circle)
3. Define the direction and depth of extrusion

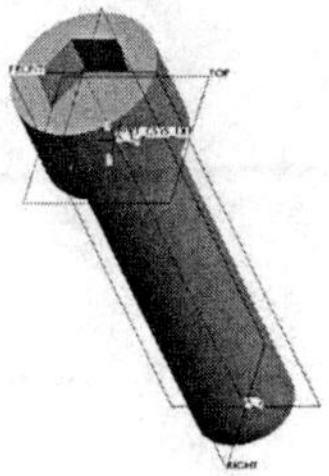

Step V - Chamfer the edges
1. Use "Chamfer" feature
2. Select the edges to be chamfered
3. Specify the chamfer dimension

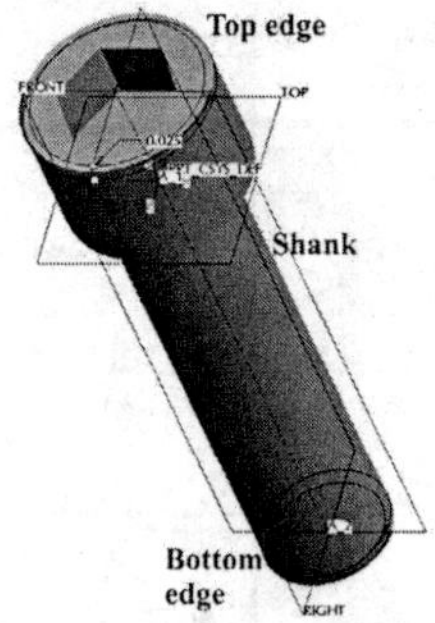

Step VI - Create cosmetic threads
1. Start "Cosmetic Threads" feature
2. Select the thread surface, the start surface, and the depth
3. Define the thread parameters

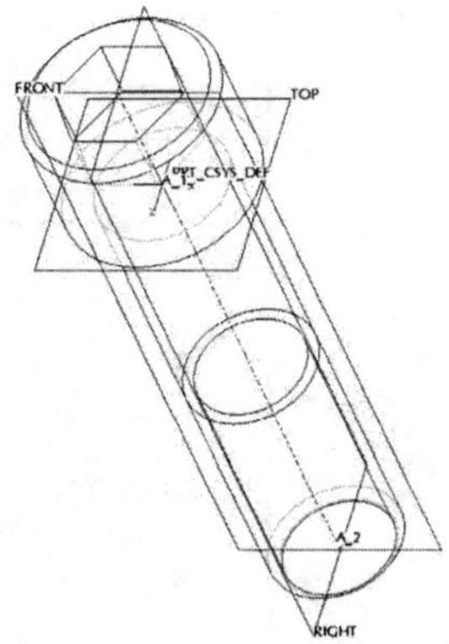

SEQUENCE OF STEPS

Goal	Step	Commands
Open a new file for the bolt part	1. Open a new file.	**FILE → NEW → *Part* → *Solid* →** **<u>Bolt</u> → OK**
Create the bolt head	2. Start "Extrude" feature.	
	3. Set up the sketching plane.	**PLACEMENT → DEFINE → → *Select the TOP datum plane* → Sketch**
	4. Create a circular section.	 **→ *Select the center and then, a point to define the outer edge of the circle***
	5. Modify the dimensions.	 **→ *Double click on the diameter dimension* → <u>0.55</u> → *<u>ENTER</u>*** Refer to Fig. 6.19.
	6. Exit sketcher.	
	7. Define the depth.	(Depth) **<u>0.375</u> → *<u>ENTER</u>***
	8. Accept the feature creation.	 **→ VIEW → ORIENTATION → STANDARD ORIENTATION** Refer to Fig. 6.20.
Create a hexagonal socket in the head	8. Start "Extrude – Cut" feature.	 → 
	10. Set up sketching plane.	**PLACEMENT → DEFINE → *Select the top surface of the cylinder* → Sketch** Refer to Fig. 6.20.

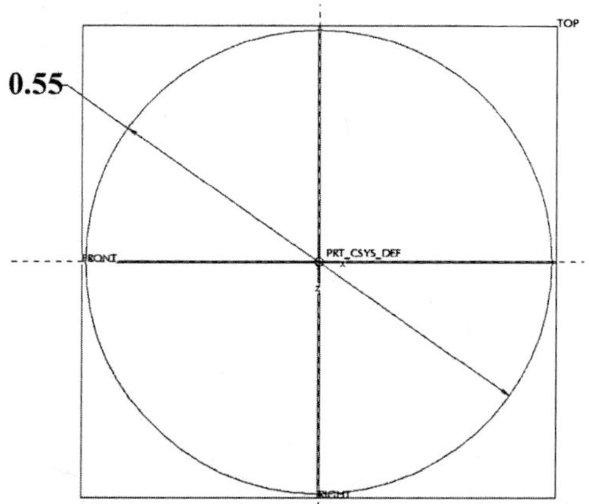

Fig. 6.19.

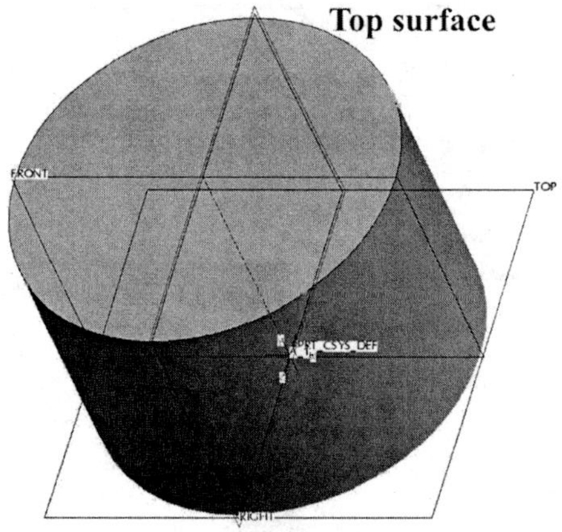

Fig. 6.20.

Goal	Step	Commands
Create a hexagonal socket in the head (Continued)	11. Insert the hexagonal section.	**SKETCH → DATA FROM FILE → FILE SYSTEM →** ***Select hexgon.sec file*** **→ OPEN**
	12. Center the section.	***Click in the graphics window → Drag and drop the section on the PRT_CSYS_DEF (The section coordinate system must lie on the PRT_CSYS_DEF)*** **→ (scale) <u>0.25</u> → (rotate) <u>0</u> →** ✓ Refer to Fig. 6.21.
	13. Delete the diameter dimension.	**→** ***Select the diameter dimension → <u>DELETE</u>*** Refer to Fig. 6.22.
	14. Add new constraints and the distance dimension (distance between two parallel sides).	**→** ***Select th top line and then, bottom line → Middle Mouse to place the dimension*** Refer to Fig. 6.22.
	15. Modify the width.	**→** ***Double click on the width dimension*** **→ <u>5/16</u> →** ***<u>ENTER</u>***
	16. Exit sketcher.	✓ **→ VIEW → ORIENTATION → STANDARD ORIENTATION**
	17. Define the cut.	**(Depth) <u>0.182</u> →** ***<u>ENTER</u>*** Refer to Fig. 6.23.
	18. Accept the feature creation.	✓ **→ VIEW → ORIENTATION → STANDARD ORIENTATION** Refer to Fig. 6.24.

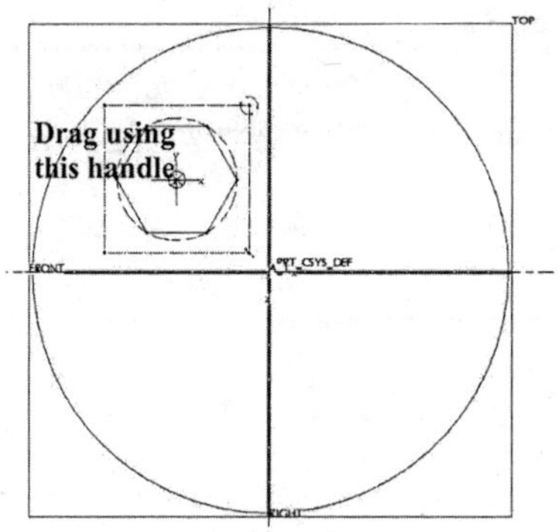

Fig. 6.21.

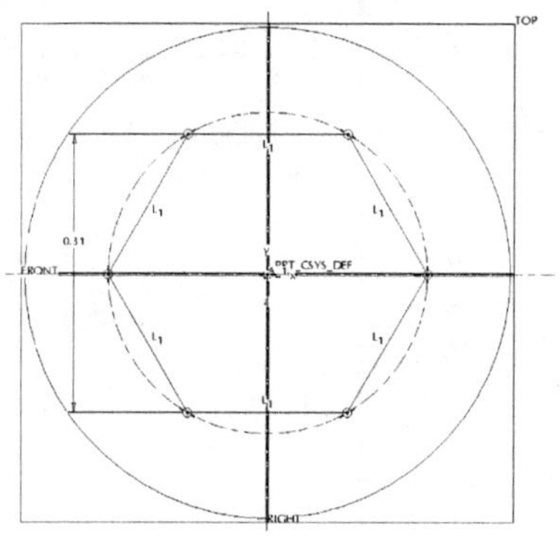
Fig. 6.22.

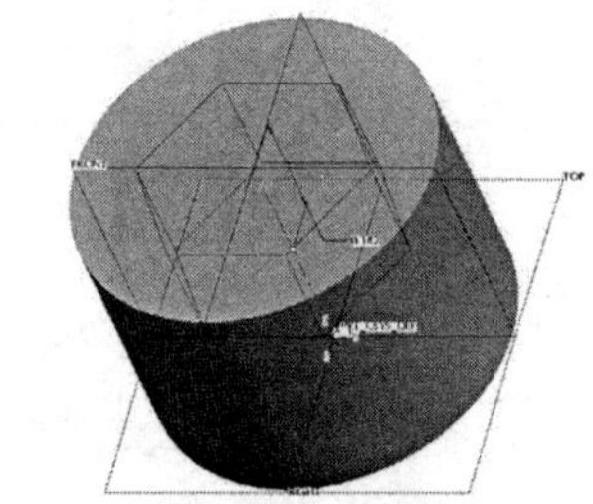
Fig. 6.23.

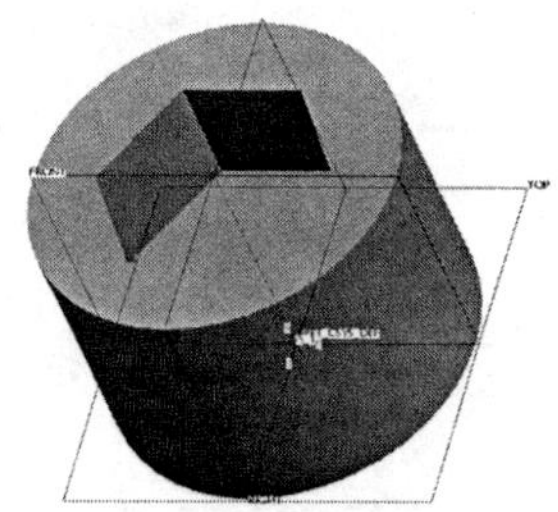
Fig. 6.24.

Goal	Step	Commands
Create the shank	19. Start "Extrude" feature.	
	20. Set up the sketching plane.	**PLACEMENT → DEFINE →** ***Select the TOP datum plane →*** **Sketch**
	21. Create a circular section.	***→ Select the center and then, a point to define the circle***
	22. Modify the dimensions.	***→ Double click on the diameter dimension → 0.375 → ENTER*** Refer to Fig. 6.25.
	23. Exit sketcher.	
	24. Define the depth.	(Depth) **1.5** → (to flip the direction of extrusion)
	25. Accept the feature creation.	**→ VIEW → ORIENTATION → STANDARD ORIENTATION** Refer to Fig. 6.26.
Chamfer the edges	26. Chamfer the top and bottom edges of the bolt.	**→ 45 X D → 0.025 →** ***ENTER→ Select the top edge of the head and the bottom end of the shank while holding CTRL →*** Refer to Fig. 6.27.
Create a cosmetic thread	27. Create cosmetic threads.	**INSERT → CONSMETIC → THREAD→** ***Select the outer surface of the shank → Select the bottom surface of the bolt (End of the bolt) →*** **Okay → Blind → Done → 0.75 → → 5/16 →** Refer to Fig. 6.27.

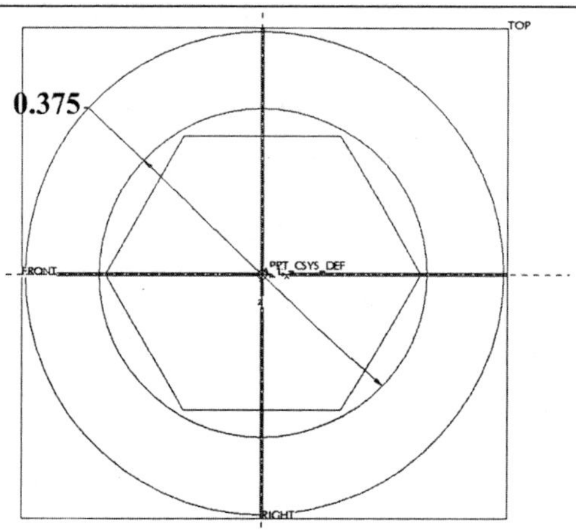

Fig. 6.25.

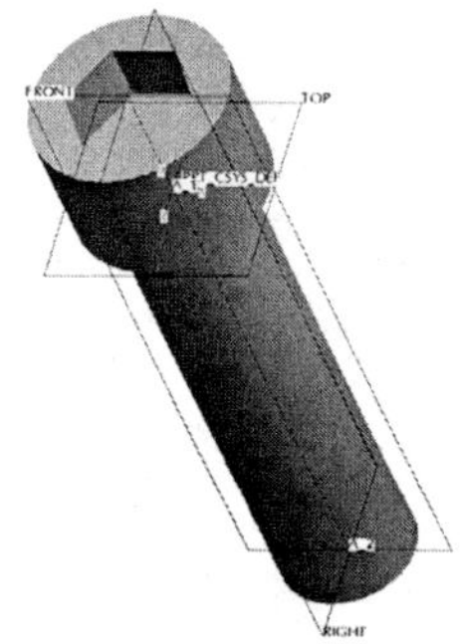
Fig. 6.26.

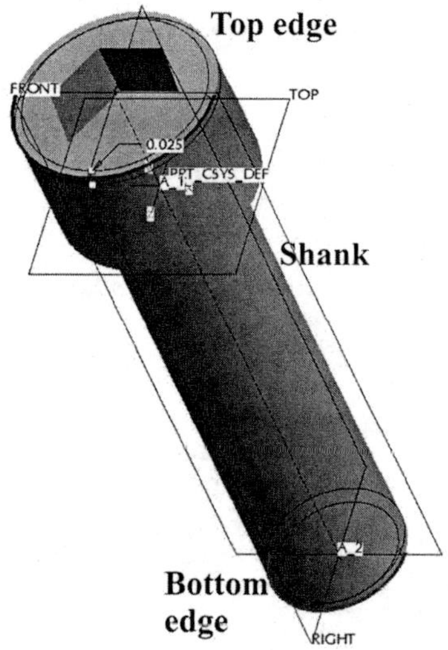

Fig. 6.27.

Goal	Step	Commands
Create a cosmetic thread (continued)	28. Specify thread parameters.	**Mod Params → Enter the parameter values shown in Fig. 6.28 →** Refer to Fig. 6.28. **FILE → SAVE → FILE → EXIT → Done/Return**
	29. Create the threaded surface.	**OK**
	30. View the threaded surface.	**VIEW → ORIENTATION → STANDARD ORIENTATION →** Refer to Fig. 6.29.
Save the file and exit ProE	31. Save the file and exit ProE.	**FILE → SAVE → BOLT.PRT → OK → FILE → EXIT → YES**

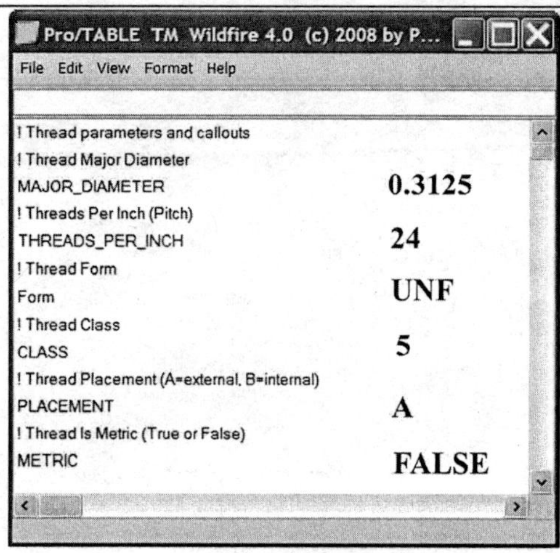

Fig. 6.28.

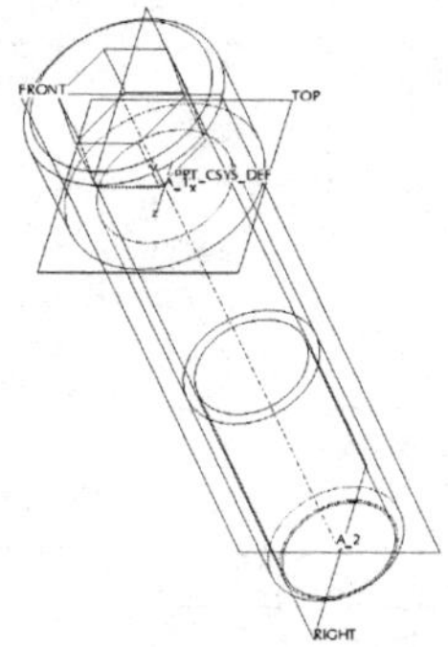

Fig. 6.29.

Exercise

Problem 1

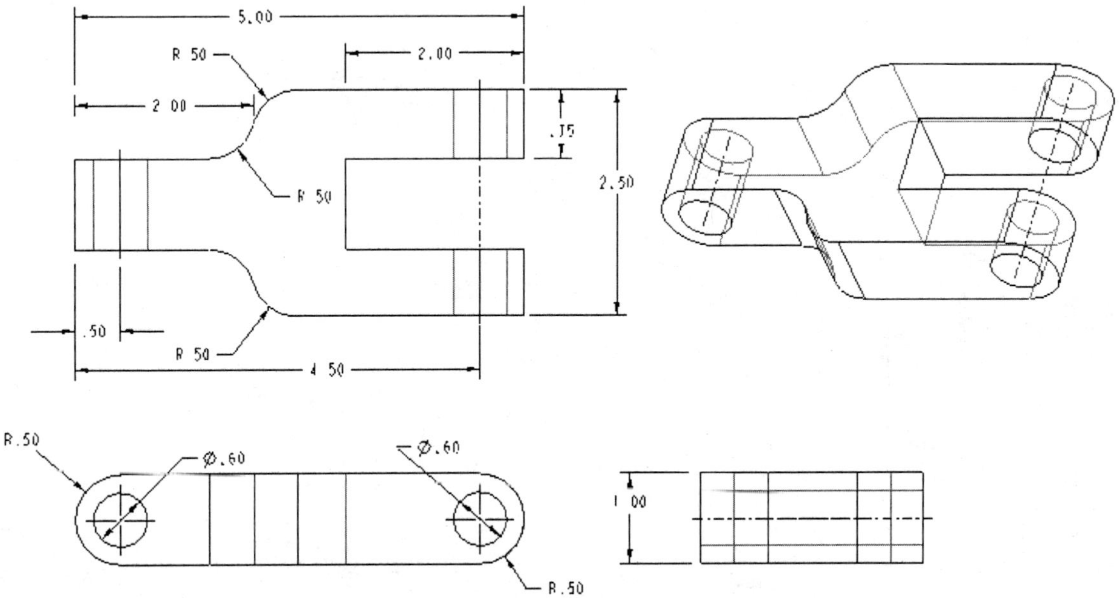

Hints:
The part progression is shown in the figures below.

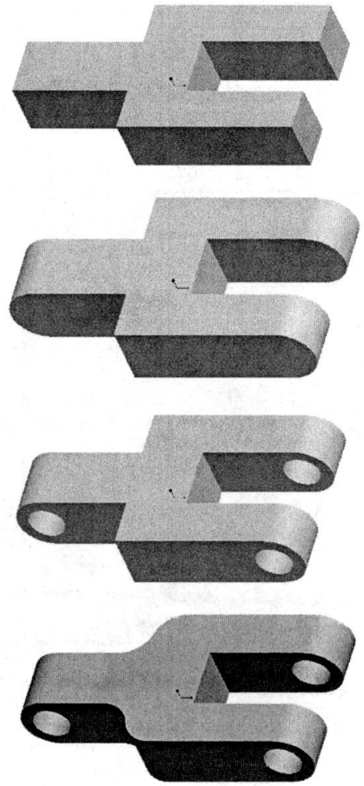

Problem 2

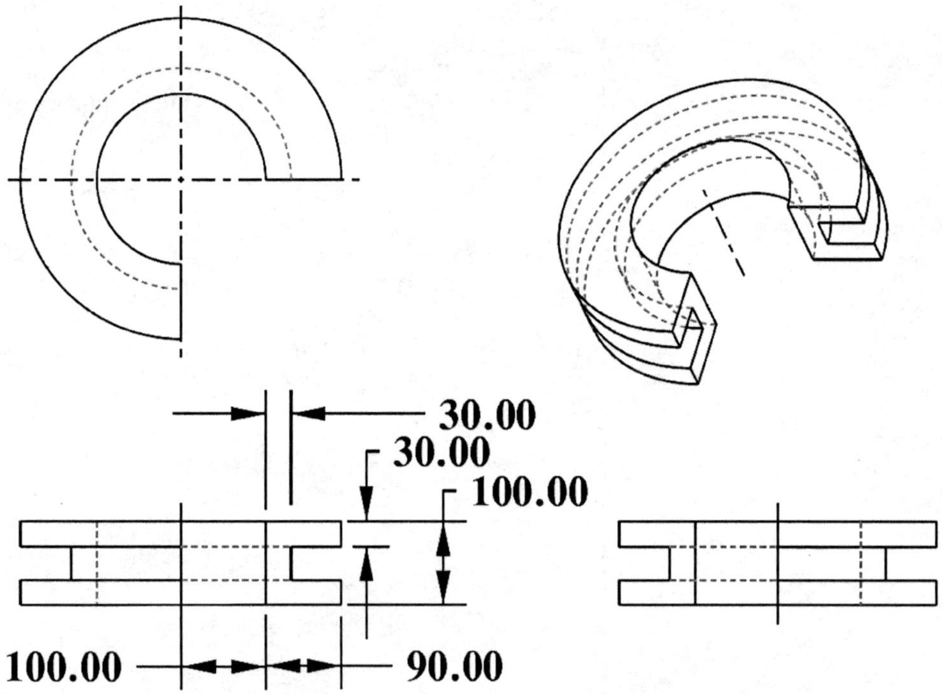

Hints:

1. Use the revolve feature.
2. Sketch on the front datum plane.
3. In the sketcher, draw a centerline on the right datum plane.
4. Select the sketcher pallet 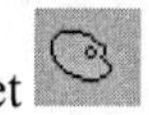 (or SKETCH → DATA FROM FILE → PALETTE). Select the profiles tab.

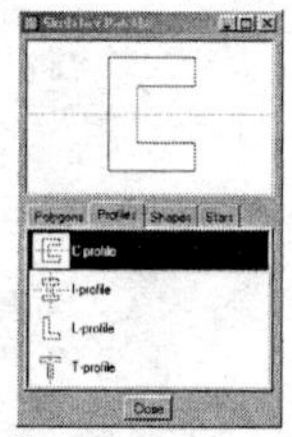

5. Double click on C-section to select the section. Click on the top datum to place the section. Leave the scale at the default value.

6. Exit sketcher.
7. Define the angle of rotation.
8. Accept feature creation.
9. Modify the key dimensions and then, regenerate the model (EDIT → REGENERATE).

Problem 3

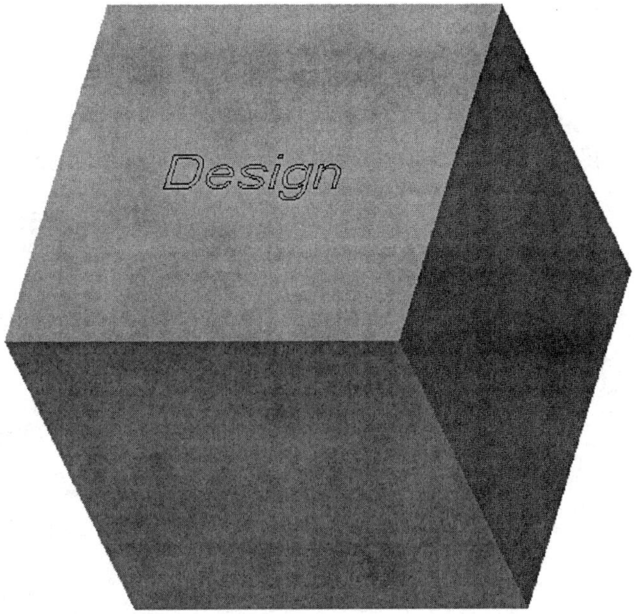

Designers use sketched cosmetic features to include company name, part number and other manufacturing information. Also, they are useful in creating regions so that loads can be applied later in ProMechanica. The procedure for creating cosmetic features is:

INSERT → COSMETIC → SKETCH →

Regular Sec/Proj Sec →
Projected section projects the section drawn onto a surface.

Xhatch/No Xhatch
This option allows hatching of the cosmetic feature.

Select the sketching plane → Okay → TOP → Select the top surface to orient the sketching plane →

SKETCH → TEXT → ***Select the start point of the text → Select another point to determine the text height and orientation →***

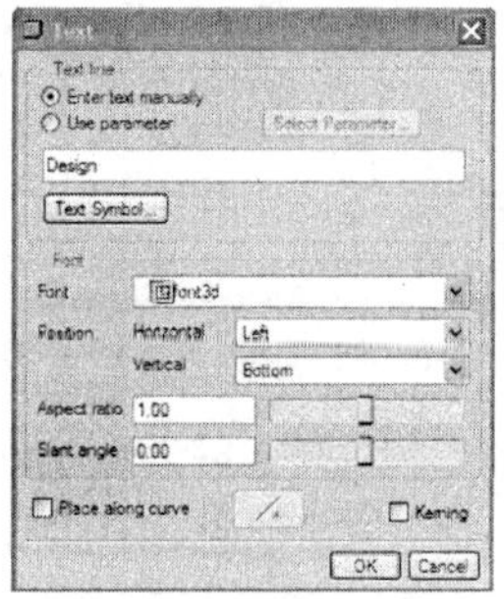

(Text line) **<u>Enter Text</u>** **→** ***Select the font, aspect ratio and slant angle →*** **→**

→ ***Modify the dimensions →*** **→ Done**

OPEN-ENDED DESIGN – Finger grip ruler
Create the grip ruler and add marking (cosmetic)

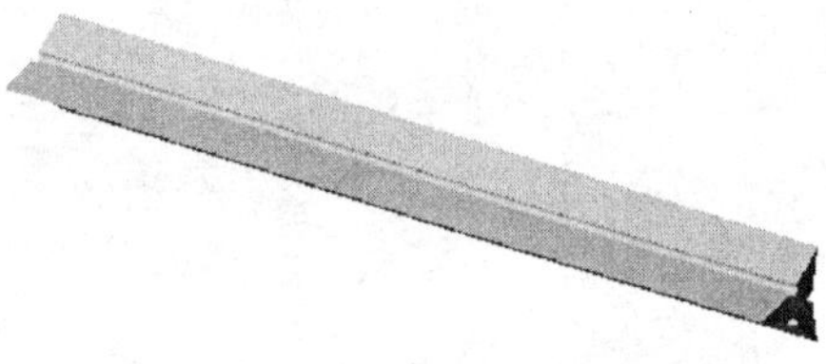

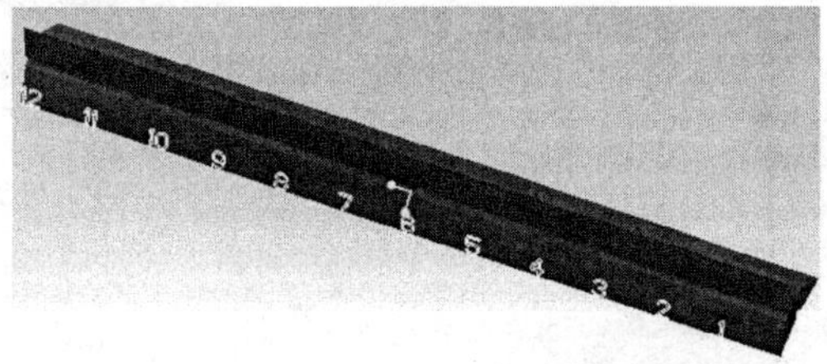

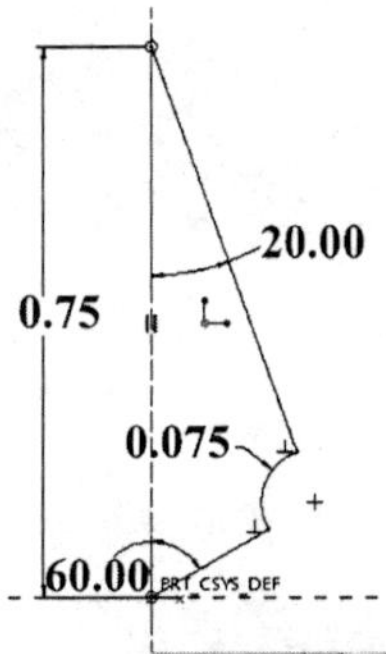

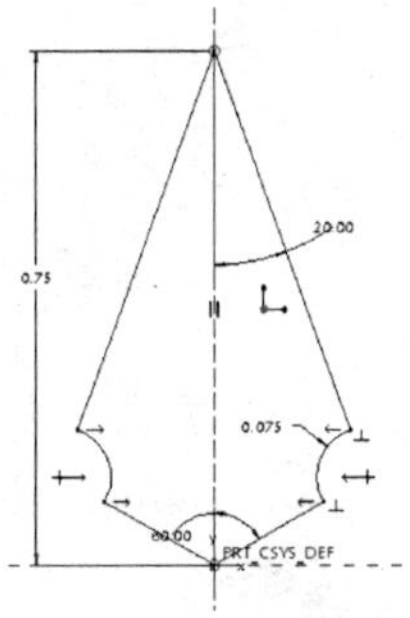

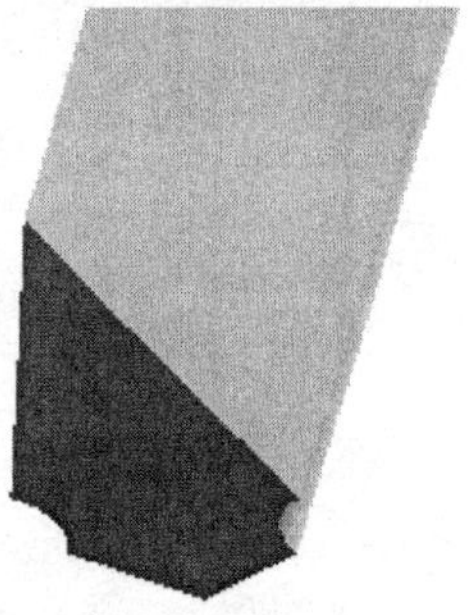

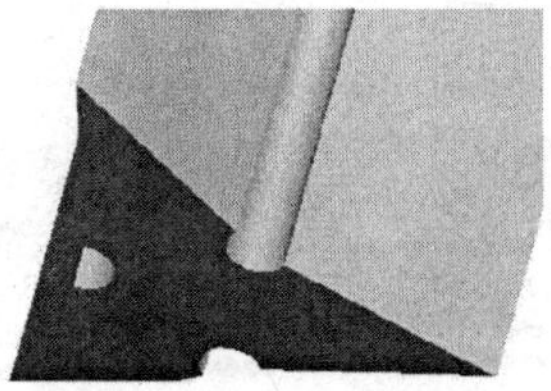

Hints:

1. Use extrude feature.
2. Sketch two lines and an arc. Use trim to get to the first sketch.
3. Mirror the sketch.
4. Use feature operations to mirror the feature twice.

NOTES:

LESSON 7
SHAFT

Learning Objectives

- Practice ***Revolve***, ***Extrude - Cut***, ***Hole***, ***Chamfer***, and ***Round*** features.
- Practice ***Mirror*** tool in the sketcher.
- Learn ***Make Datum*** and ***Pattern*** commands.
- Learn the use of ***Layers***.

Layers

Layers are useful for organizing the model i.e., deleting, reordering, suppressing or resuming features. A feature can be assigned to multiple layers. The display status of a layer can be set to:

Show – Selected layers are displayed.

Blank – Selected layers are blanked. Only datum features, feature axes, cosmetic features and quilts can be blanked.

Isolate – Only the selected layers are displayed. All other layers are blanked.

Hidden –Components in the hidden layers blanked in accordance with the Environment for the hidden-line display. A hide status of a layer does not affect the solid geometry. However, suppressing a layer suppresses the geometric features contained in that layer.

Design Information

Shafts transmit rotational energy (rotary motion and torque). They are stepped for easy mounting of machine components such as cams and bearings. These steps act as stress concentrations. To reduce the stress concentration, the steps are rounded. The radius of the round is a key parameter as an inappropriate value results in the premature failure, or prevents the assembly of machine components. The torque transfers from the shaft to the machine components through keys. The shape of the keyway depends on the geometry of the key and also, the manufacturing process (edge- or end-milling). Setscrews often hold the keys.

SEQUENCE OF STEPS

STEP I: Create the base feature

1. Use "Revolve" feature
2. Define the sketch plane
3. Sketch the section on the FRONT datum plane
4. Define the angle of revolution

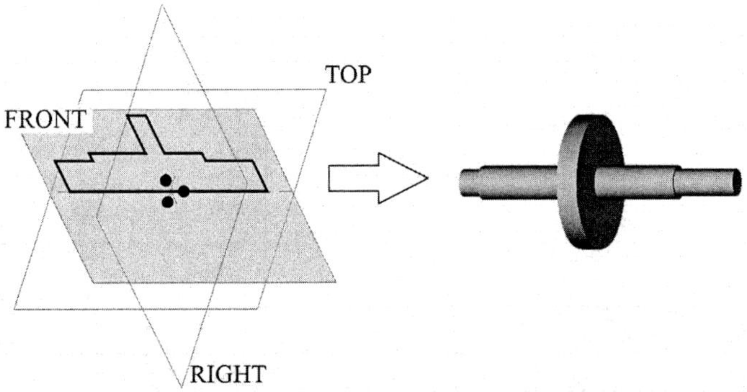

STEP II: Round edges

1. Round the four edges

STEP III: Chamfer the edges

1. Chamfer the outer edges

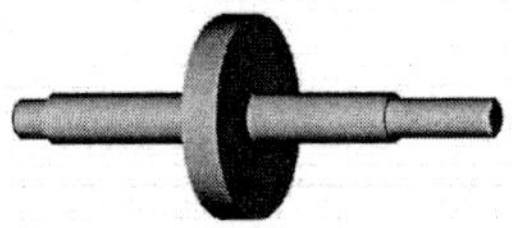

STEP IV: Suppress the round and chamfer features

1. Create a new layer and move the two features
2. Suppress the layer

STEP V: Create the keyway

1. Use "Extrude - Cut" feature
2. Define the sketch plane using the "Make datum" command
3. Define the section
4. Specify the depth

STEP VI: Create a hole

1. Use "Hole" feature
2. Define the hole parameters
3. Define the primary reference surface
4. Define the axial reference and distance
5. Define the angular reference and angle

STEP VII: Pattern the hole

1. Define the dimensional increment
2. Define the total number of instances

STEP VIII: Resume all features

Goal	Step	Commands
Open a new file for the shaft part	1. Set up the working directory.	**FILE → SET WORKING DIRECTORY →** ***Select the working directory*** **→ OK**
	2. Open a new file.	**FILE → NEW →** ***Part*** **→** ***Solid*** **→ <u>shaft</u> → OK**
Create the base feature	3. Start "Revolve" feature.	
	4. Select the sketching plane.	***Placement*** **→ Define** ***→ Select the FRONT datum plane →*** **Sketch**
	5. Sketch the axis of revolution on the RIGHT datum plane.	***→ Pick points 1 and 2 on the TOP datum***
	6. Sketch the section.	***→ Pick points 3, 4, 5, 6, 7, 8, 9, 10, 11, 12, 13, 14 and 3 → Middle Mouse*** Refer to Fig. 7.1.
	7. Align points 7 and 10, and 5 and 12.	(or **SKECTCH → CONSTRAIN**) ProE opens "Constraints" window. Refer to Fig. 7.2. ***→ Select points 7 and 10 → Select points 5 and 12***

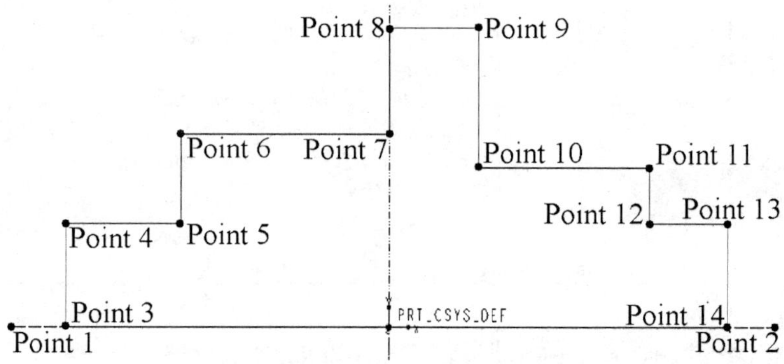

Fig. 7.1. SELECT AND DELETE ANY EQUAL LENGTH CONSTRAINTS (L1, L2,… SYMBOLS NEXT TO THE LINES).

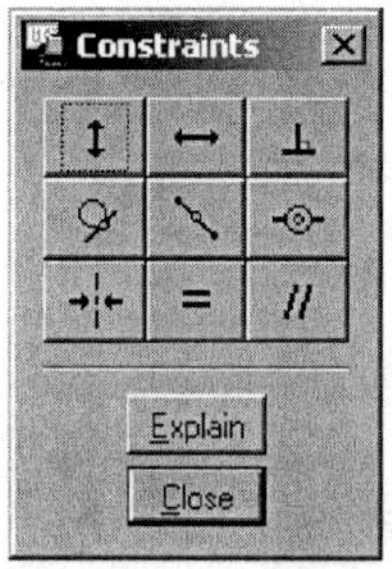

Fig. 7.2.

Makes line or vertices vertical	Makes line or vertices horizontal	Makes two entities perpendicular
Makes two entities tangential	Places a point in the middle of the line	Creates coincident points or collinear constraint
Makes two points or vertices symmetric about the centerline	Makes the lengths, radii or curvatures equal	Makes two lines parallel

Goal	Step	Commands
Create the base feature (continued)	8. Create the horizontal dimensions.	→ ***Select the RIGHT datum and line 1 → Middle Mouse → Select the RIGHT datum and line 2 → Middle Mouse→ Select the RIGHT datum and line 3 → Middle Mouse→ Select the RIGHT datum and line 4 → Middle Mouse → Select the RIGHT datum and line 5 → Middle Mouse*** Refer to Fig. 7.3.
	9. Create diameter dimensions.	→ ***Select line 6, centerline and again line 6 → Middle Mouse to place the diameter dimension → Select line 7, centerline and again line 7 → Middle Mouse → Select line 8, centerline and again line 8 → Middle Mouse*** Refer to Fig. 7.3.
	10. Modify the dimensions.	★First modify the smaller dimensions. → ***Double click each dimension and enter the corresponding value*** [Or → Select each dimension to be modified and then modify it in the "Modify Dimensions" window] Refer to Fig. 7.4.
	11. Exit sketcher.	✓
	12. Define the angle of revolution.	<u>(Angle)</u> **<u>360</u>**

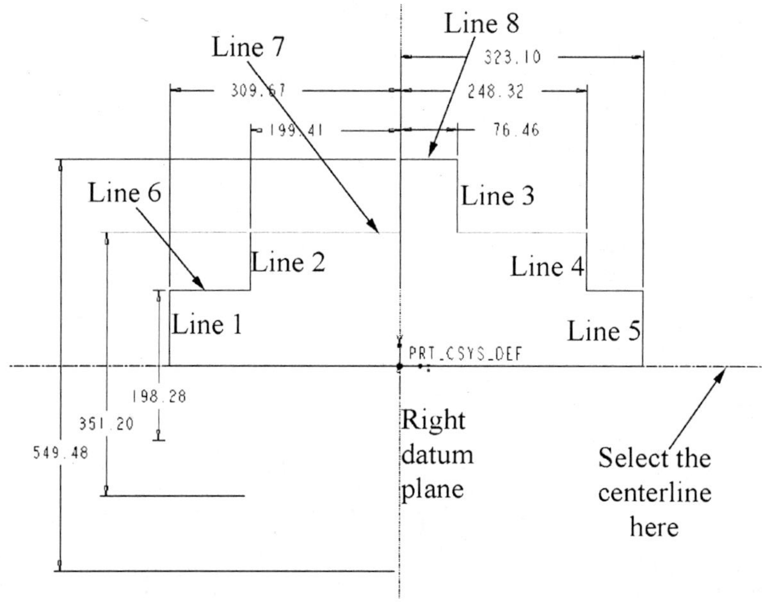

Fig. 7.3.

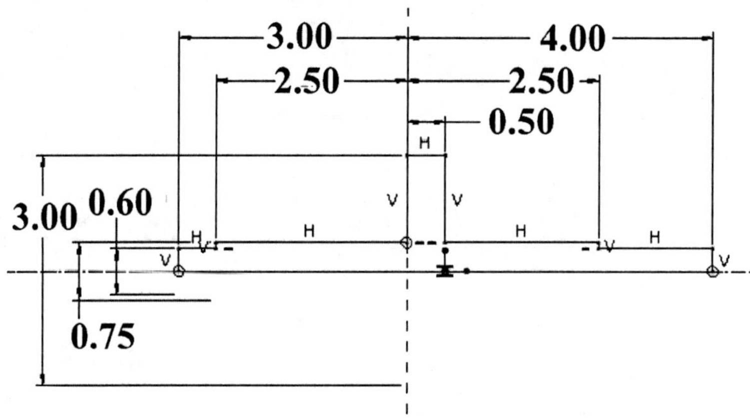

Fig. 7.4.

Goal	Step	Commands
Create the base feature (continued)	13. Accept the feature creation.	→ **VIEW** → **ORIENTATION** → **STANDARD ORIENTATION** REFER TO Fig. 7.5.
Round the edges	14. Round the four edges.	→ (Radius in the dash) **<u>0.02</u>** → ***Select the edges to be rounded (take the cursor on the edge – edge gets highlighted – select the edge – repeat the process for each edge)*** → Refer to Fig. 7.6. Refer to Fig. 7.7.

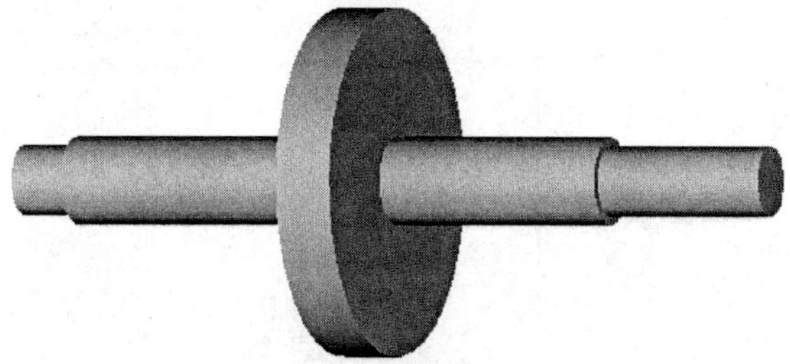
Fig. 7.5.

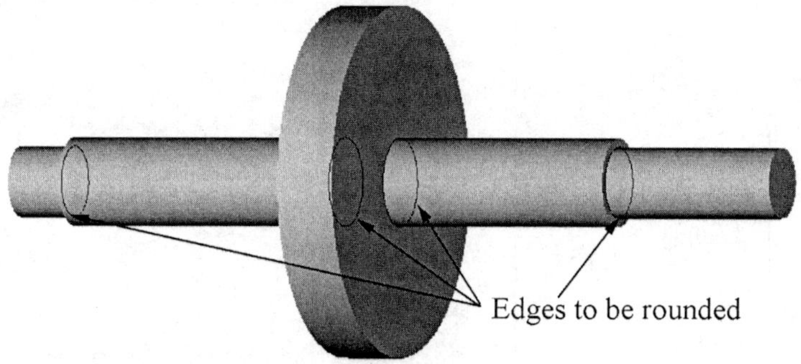

Fig. 7.6.

Fig. 7.7.

Goal	Step	Commands
Chamfer the outer edges	15. Chamfer the outer edges.	→ **45 x d** → **<u>0.05</u>** → ***Select the outer edges***→ Refer to Fig. 7.8. Refer to Fig. 7.9.
Move the round and chamfer features into a new layer	16. Create a new layer.	**Show** → **Layer Tree** Refer to Fig. 7.10. ProE opens the layer tree. **Layer** (next to the show icon) → **New Layer** → (Name) **<u>Rounds_Chamfers</u>**
	17. Move the round and chamfer features to the new layer.	***Click in the contents window*** → Refer to Fig. 7.11. **Show** → **Model Tree** → ***Select the round and chamfer features from the model tree*** → → **OK** → **Show** → **Layer Tree**

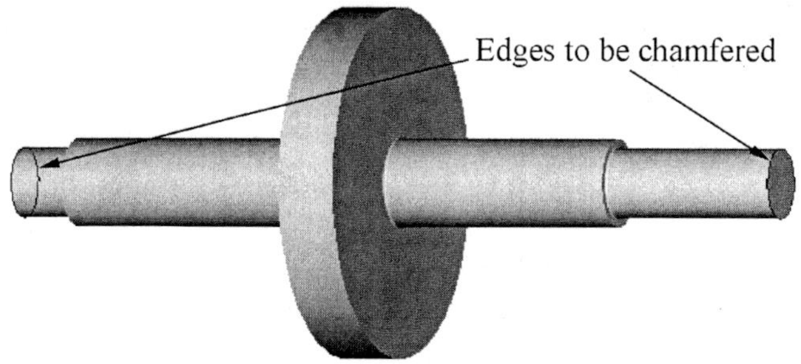

Fig. 7.8.

Fig. 7.9.

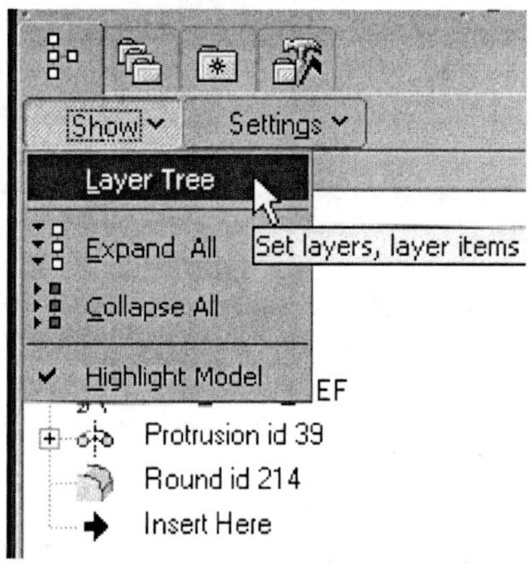

Fig. 7.10.

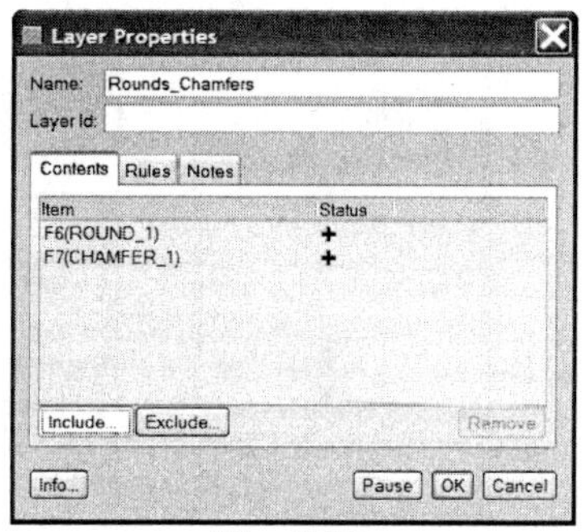

Fig. 7.11.

Goal	Step	Commands
Suppress the rounds and the chamfers	18. Suppress the rounds_chamfers layer.	***Select the round_chamfer layer* → *Right Mouse* → Hide →** A hide status of a layer does not affect the solid geometry. However, suppressing a layer suppresses the geometric features contained in that layer. ***Right Mouse* → Unhide → *Select the round_chamfer layer* → *Right Mouse* → *Select Items* → EDIT → SUPRESS → OK**
Create the keyway	19. Start "Extrude – Cut" feature.	→
	20. Set up the sketching plane.	(in the right tool bar) → ***Select the TOP datum plane*** → (Translation) **0.3** → **OK** → Refer to Fig. 7.12. **→ Placement → Define → *Select the DTM 1 datum plane* → Sketch**
	21. Add additional references.	**SKETCH → REFERENCES →** ***Add the right edge of the shaft to the existing references*** **→ CLOSE** Refer to Fig. 7.13.

Layers are useful for organizing the model i.e., deleting, reordering, suppressing or resuming features. A feature can be assigned to multiple layers. The display status of a layer can be set to:
Show – Selected layers are displayed.
Blank – Selected layers are blanked. Only datum features, feature axes, cosmetic features and quilts can be blanked.
Isolate – Only the selected layers are displayed. All other layers are blanked.
Hidden –Components in the hidden layers blanked in accordance with the Environment for the hidden-line display.

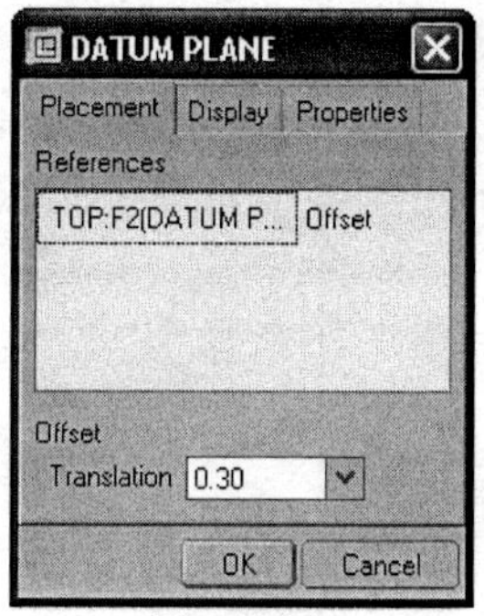

Fig. 7.12.

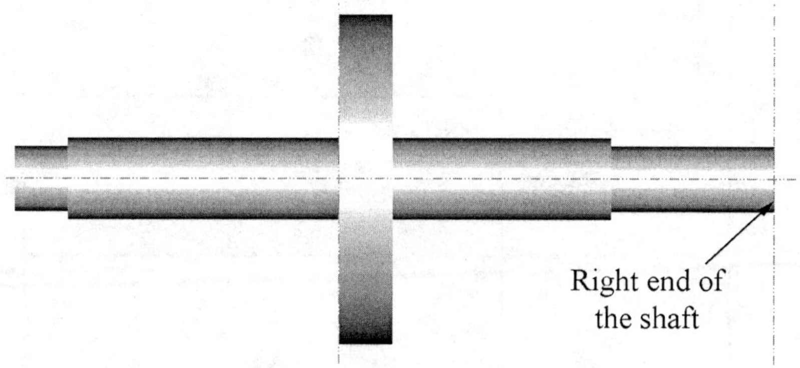

Fig. 7.13.

Goal	Step	Commands
Create the keyway (continued)	22. Sketch the key section.	**Zoom in on the right end →** → ***Pick points 1, 2 (Do not select the middle point shown by constraint "M"), 3 → Middle Mouse →*** → ***Pick points 3 and 4 (Point 4 and the center should be on the TOP datum) →*** → → ***Pick points 5 and 6 on the TOP datum →*** → ***Select the two straight lines and the arc (by drawing a box around them)* → EDIT → MIRROR →** ***Select the centerline*** Refer to Fig. 7.14.
	23. Modify the dimensions.	→ ***Double click each dimension and enter the corresponding value*** Refer to Fig. 7.14.
	24. Exit sketcher.	
	25. Define the cut direction and the depth.	(depth) **<u>0.10</u>**
	26. Accept the feature creation.	**→ VIEW → ORIENTATION → STANDARD ORIENTATION** REFER TO Fig. 7.15.

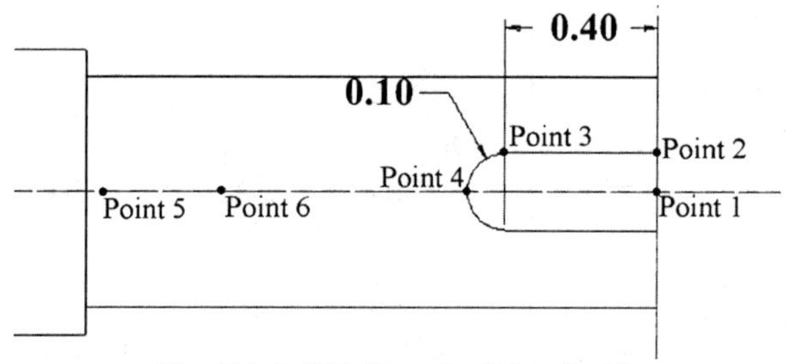

Fig. 7.14. (Right end of the shaft)

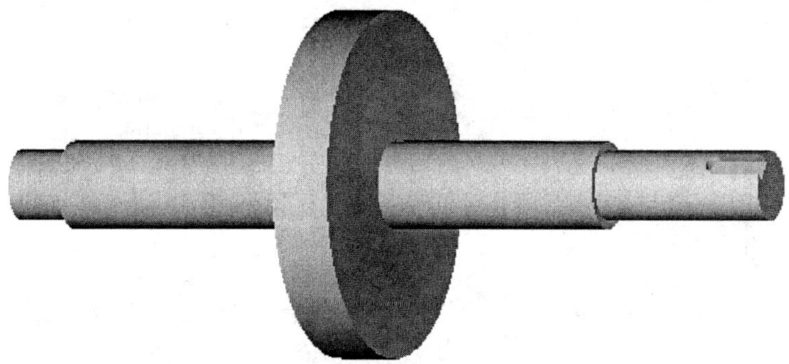
Fig. 7.15.

Goal	Step	Commands
Create a hole	27. Start "Hole" feature.	
	28. Define the parameters.	(Diameter) **<u>0.375</u>** → (Depth One) → **Placement** → (Primary Reference) ***Select the surface shown in Fig. 7.16.*** → (Placement Type) ***Radial*** → (SecondaryReference) ***Select the shaft axis*** → (Radius) **<u>1</u>** → ***<u>CNTRL</u>*** + ***Select the TOP datum plane*** → (Angle) **<u>45</u>** Refer to Fig. 7.17.
	29. Create the feature.	
Pattern the hole	30. Start "Pattern" command.	***Select the hole*** →
	31. Define the pattern parameters.	***Select the 45° angle*** → **<u>90</u>** → ***<u>ENTER</u>*** → **<u>4</u>** → Refer to Figs. 7.18 and 7.19.
Resume all features	32. Resume all features.	**EDIT → RESUME → RESUME ALL** Refer to Fig. 7.20.
Save the file and exit ProE	33. Save the file and exit ProE.	**FILE → SAVE → <u>SHAFT.PRT</u> → OK → FILE → EXIT → YES**

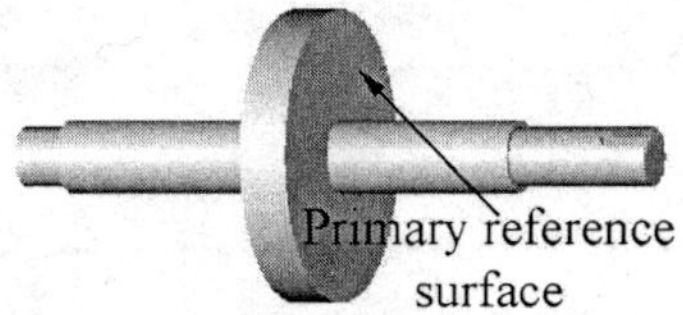

Fig. 7.16.

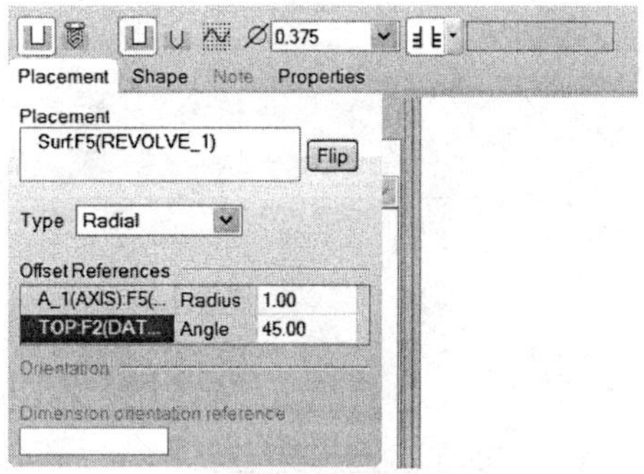

Fig. 7.17.

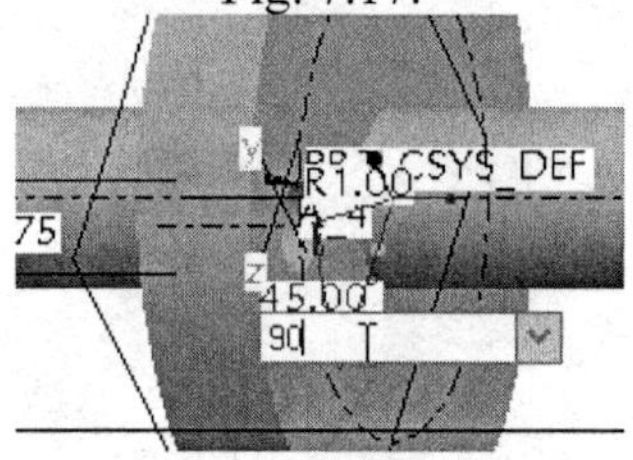

Fig. 7.18.

Fig. 7.19.

Fig. 7.20.

Exercise

Problem 1

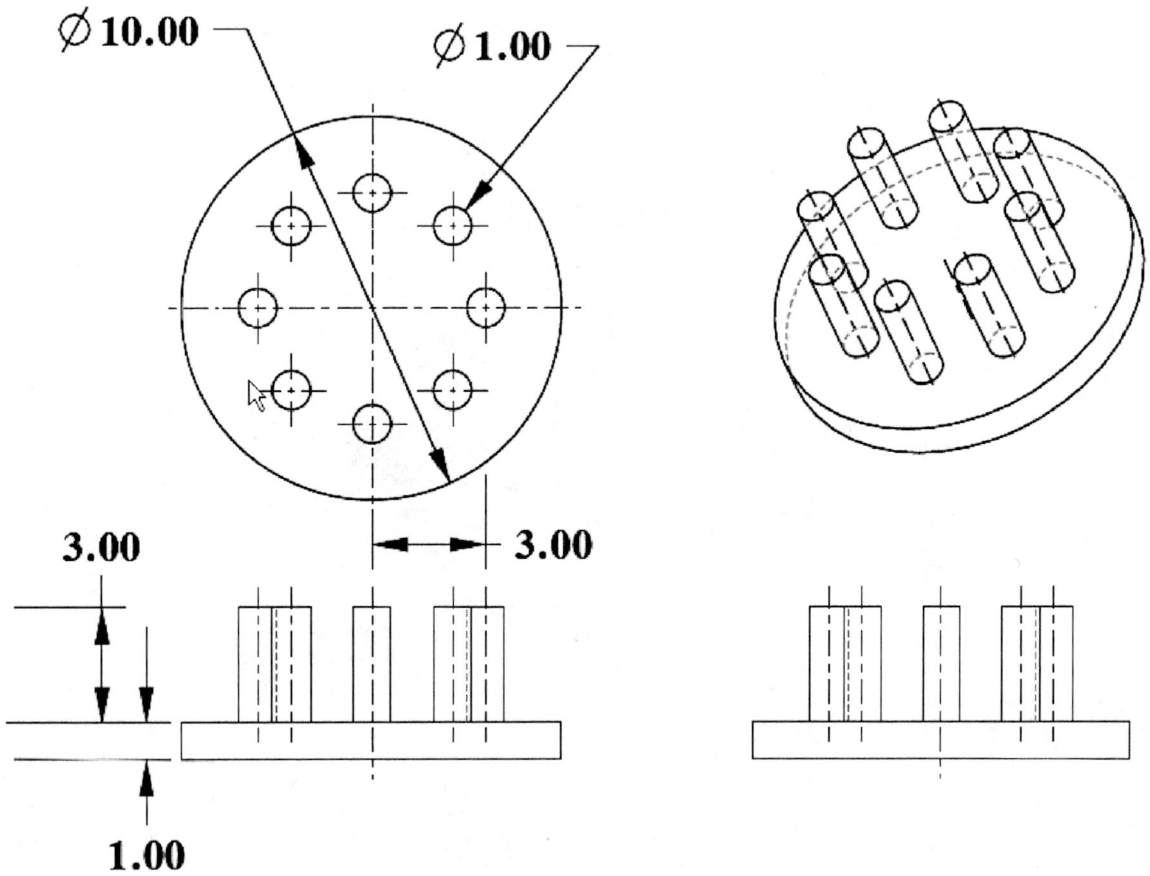

Hints:

1. Create the base protrusion.
2. Create another extrusion. The section is shown below.

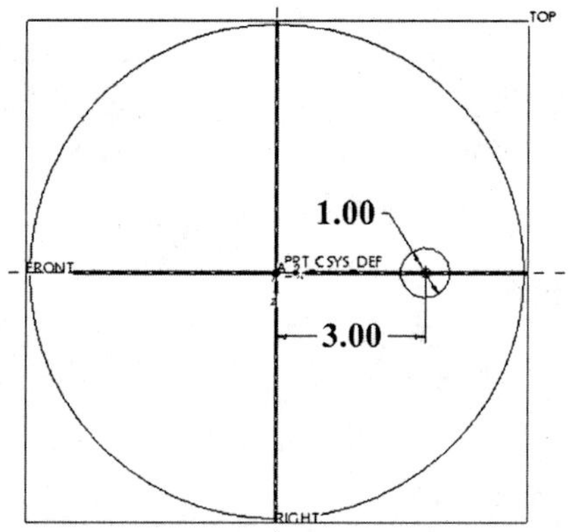

3. Pattern the new extrusion. Specify "Axis" option and select the axis of the shaft. Specify eight instances and 45 degrees (default options).

Problem 2

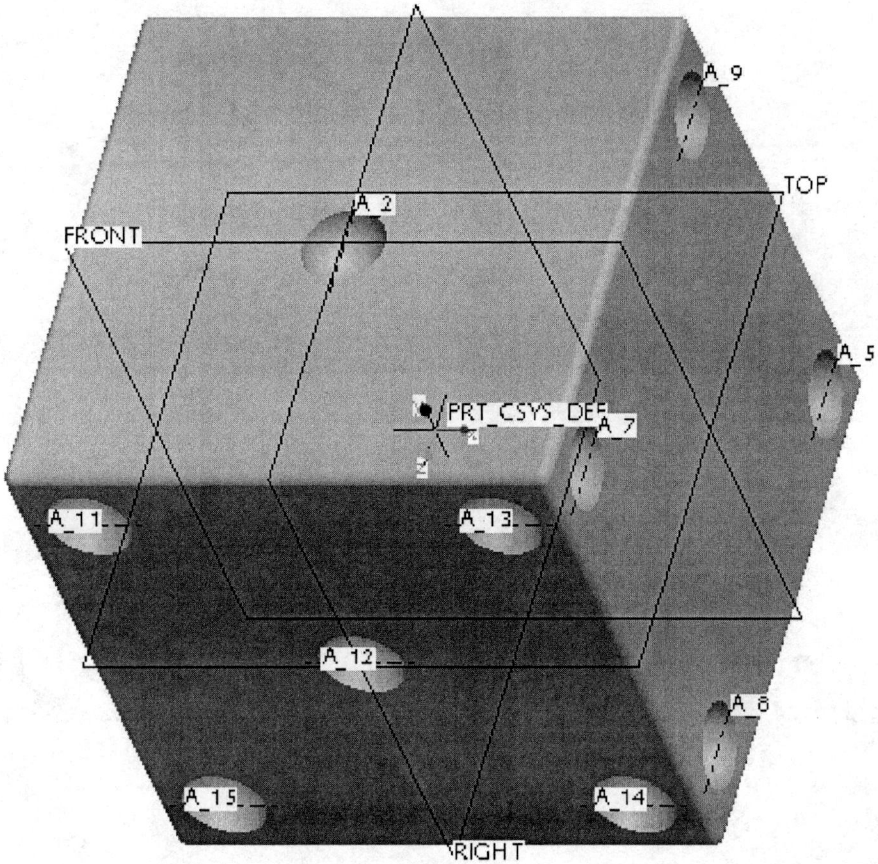

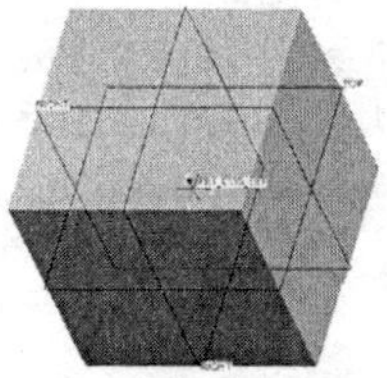

Step 1

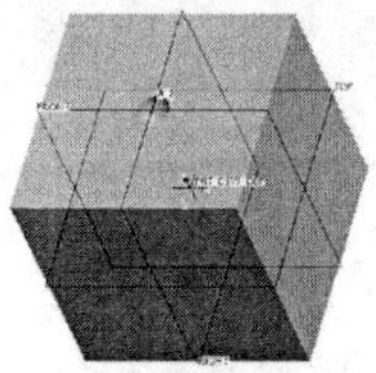

Step 2

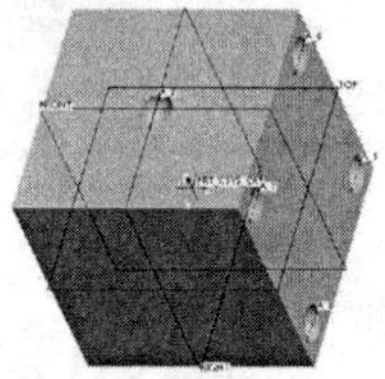

Step 3

Hints:

1. Step 1: Create the base protrusion (1X1X1).
2. Step 2: Create a pip using a revolve cut on face 1 at the center.
3. Step 3: Create a pip near the edge.

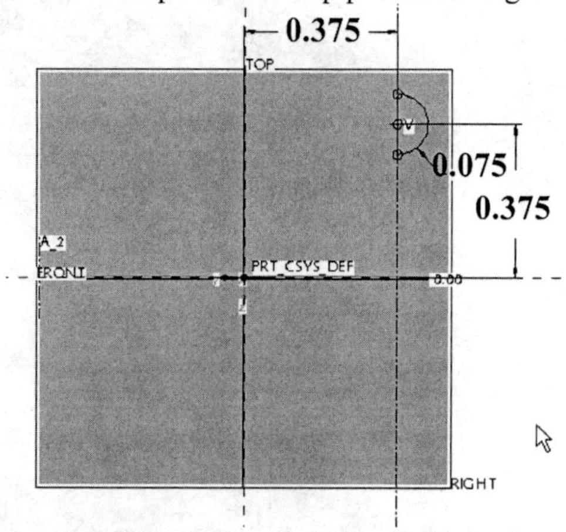

4. Pattern the cut. Select Table option and two placement dimensions. Then, edit the table.

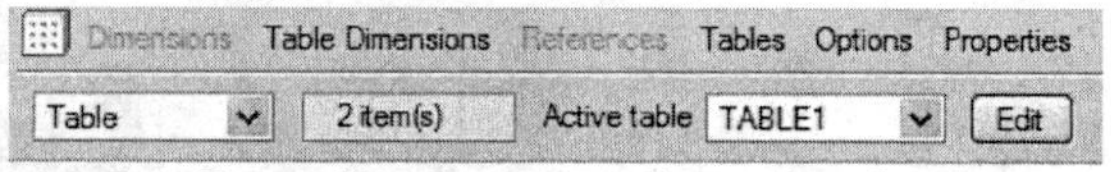

5. Enter the placement dimension for the other cuts.

!idx	d12(0.375)	d10(0.375)
1	-0.375	-0.375
2	-0.375	0.375
3	0.375	-0.375

6. Repeat the process to create other faces.
7. Round the edges (radius 0.02).
8. Color the dice and also, the cuts.

Problem 3 – Dice – Alternative Approach

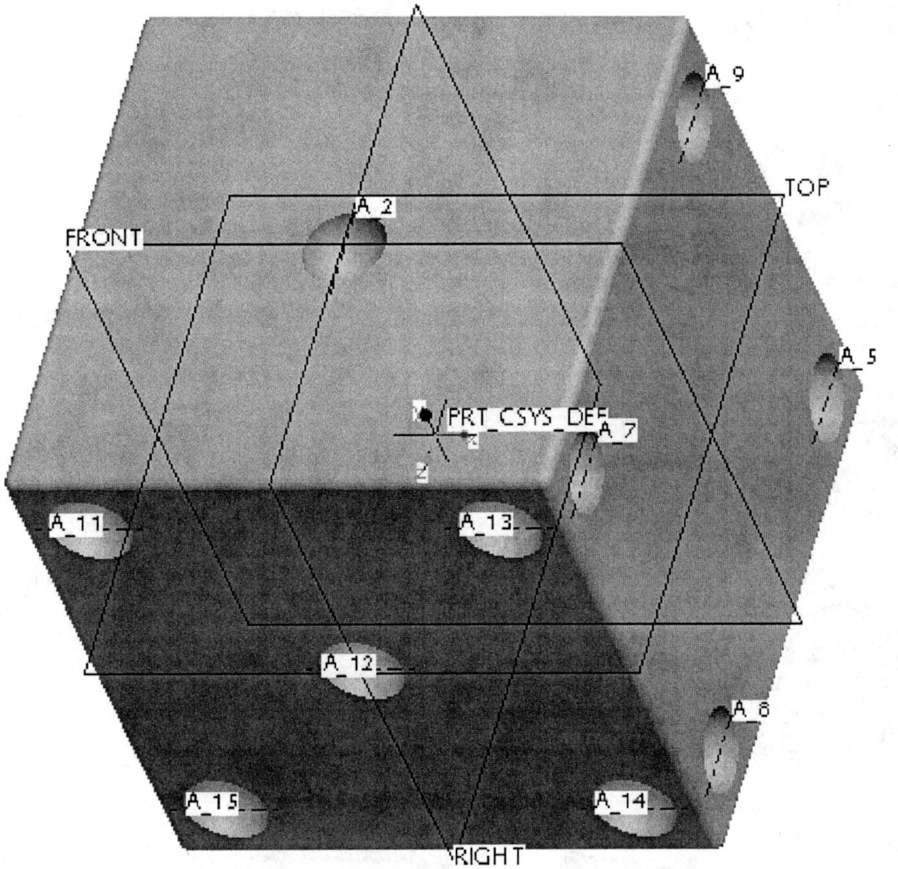

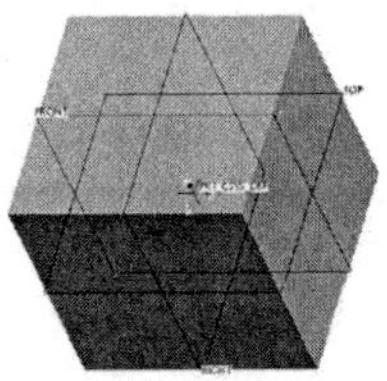
Step 1

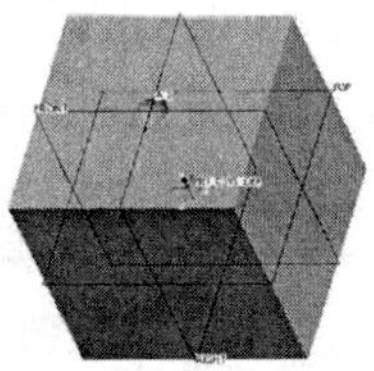
Step 2

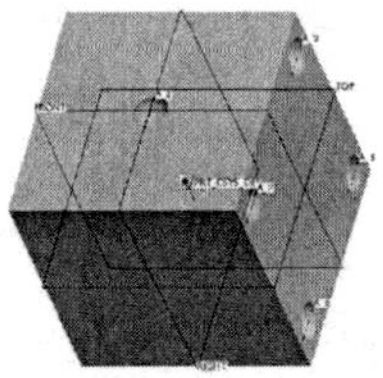
Step 3

Hints:

1. Step 1: Create the base protrusion (1X1X1).
2. Step 2: Create a pip using a revolve cut on face 1 at the center.
3. Step 3: Create a pip near the edge.

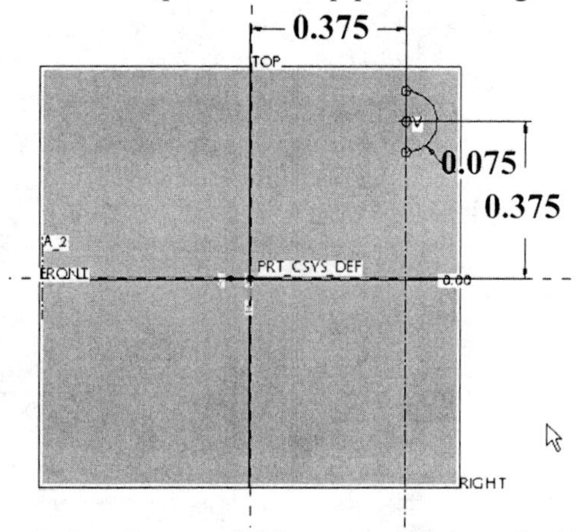

4. Create a 3X3 pattern. Click on the black circles to turn off the unwanted pips.

Problem 4

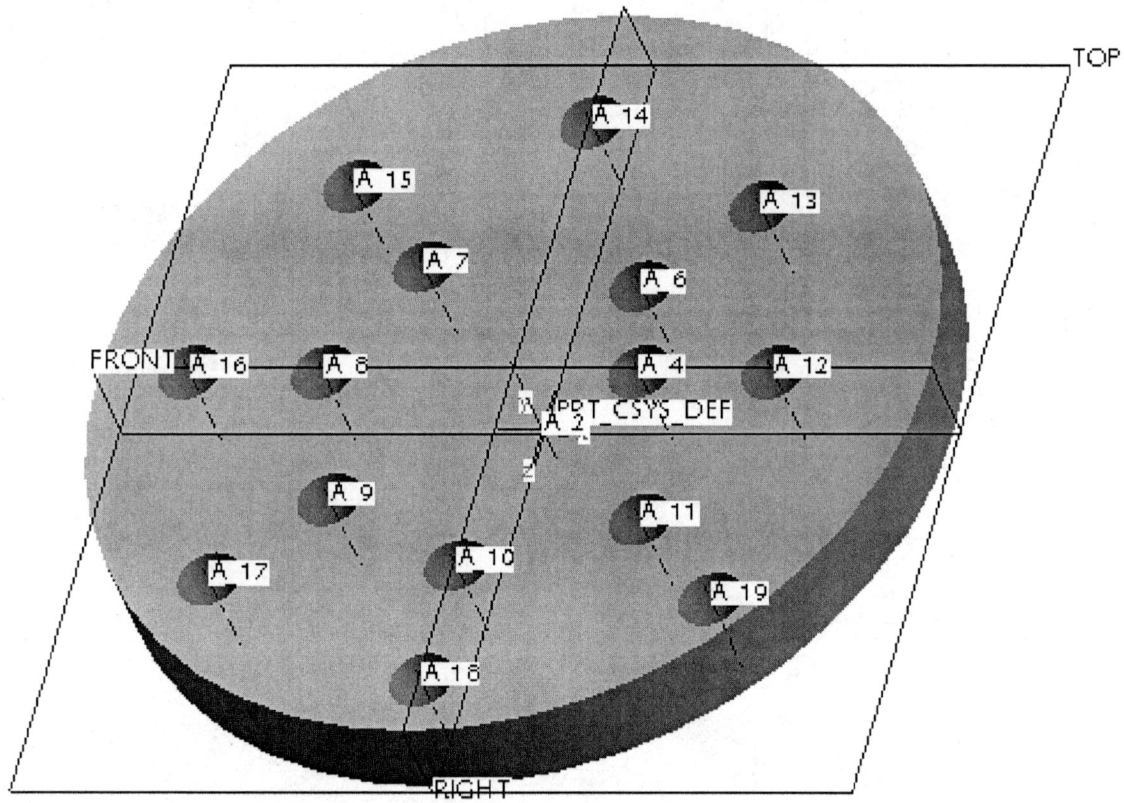

Hints:

1. Create the base cylinder (diameter 10; depth 1).

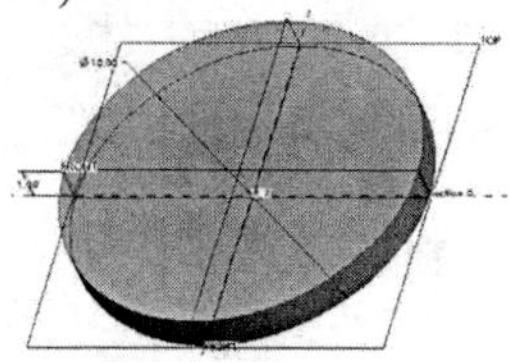

2. Create a hole.

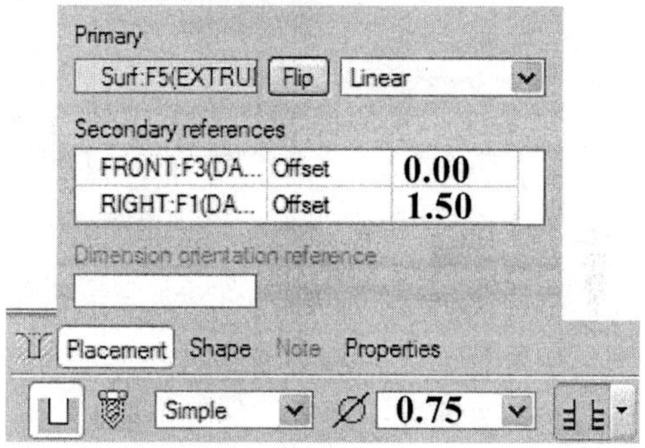

3. Pattern the hole. Select axis option and then, the axis of the cylinder. Specify 16 instances – 45 degrees option. Select the 1.50 placement dimension. Specify 0.20 increment and accept feature creation.

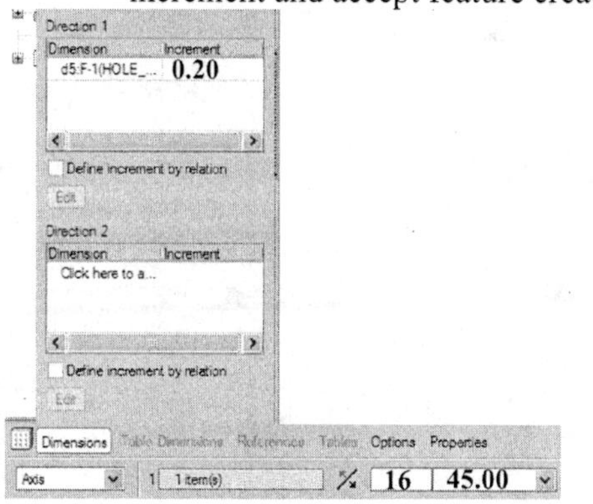

Problem 5

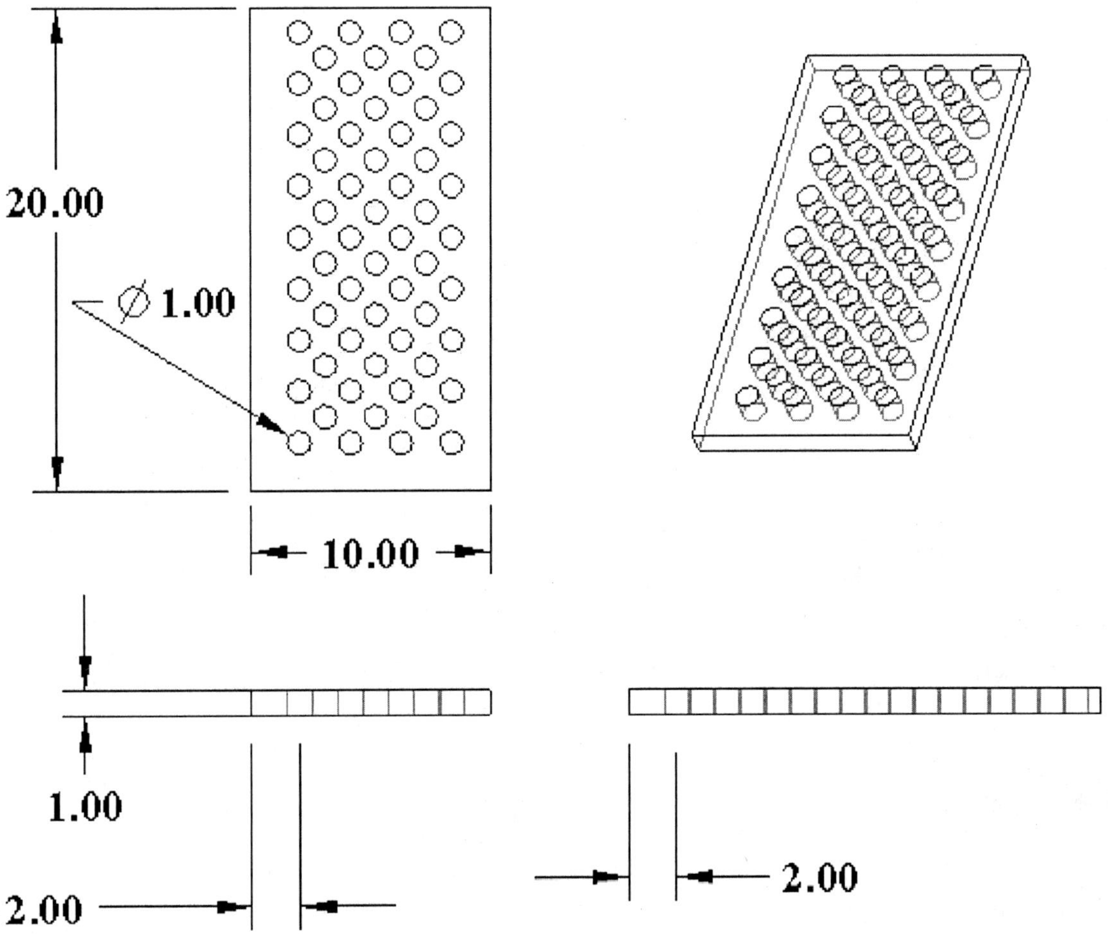

Hints:

1. Create a block and then, a hole.

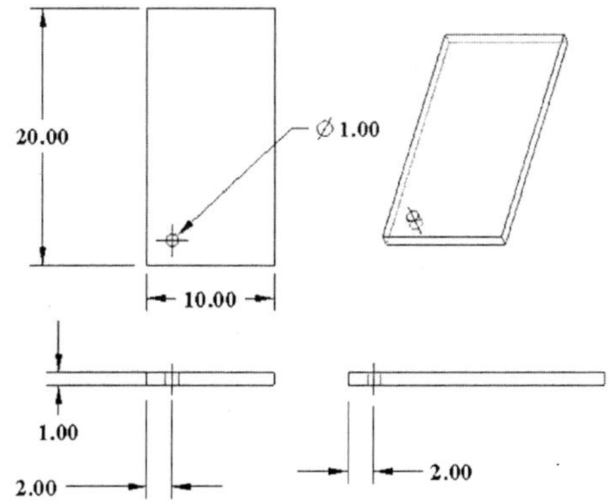

2. Pattern the hole. Select fill option. Select References – Define in the dash. Sketch a rectangle on the top surface.

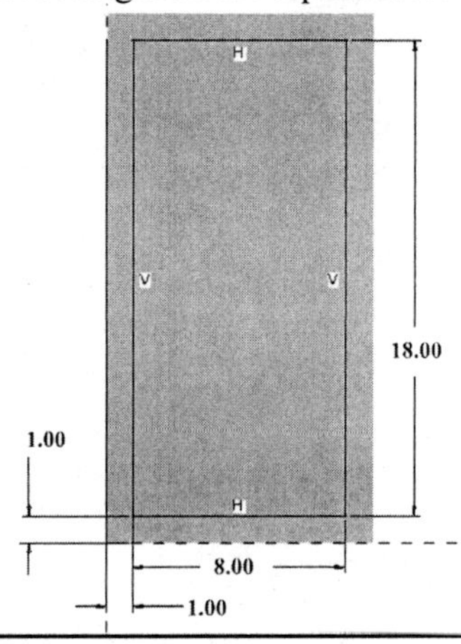

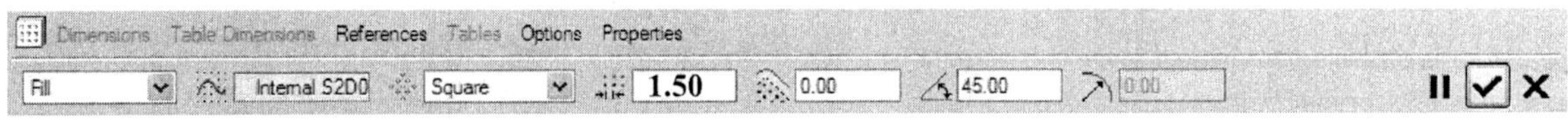

Problem 6

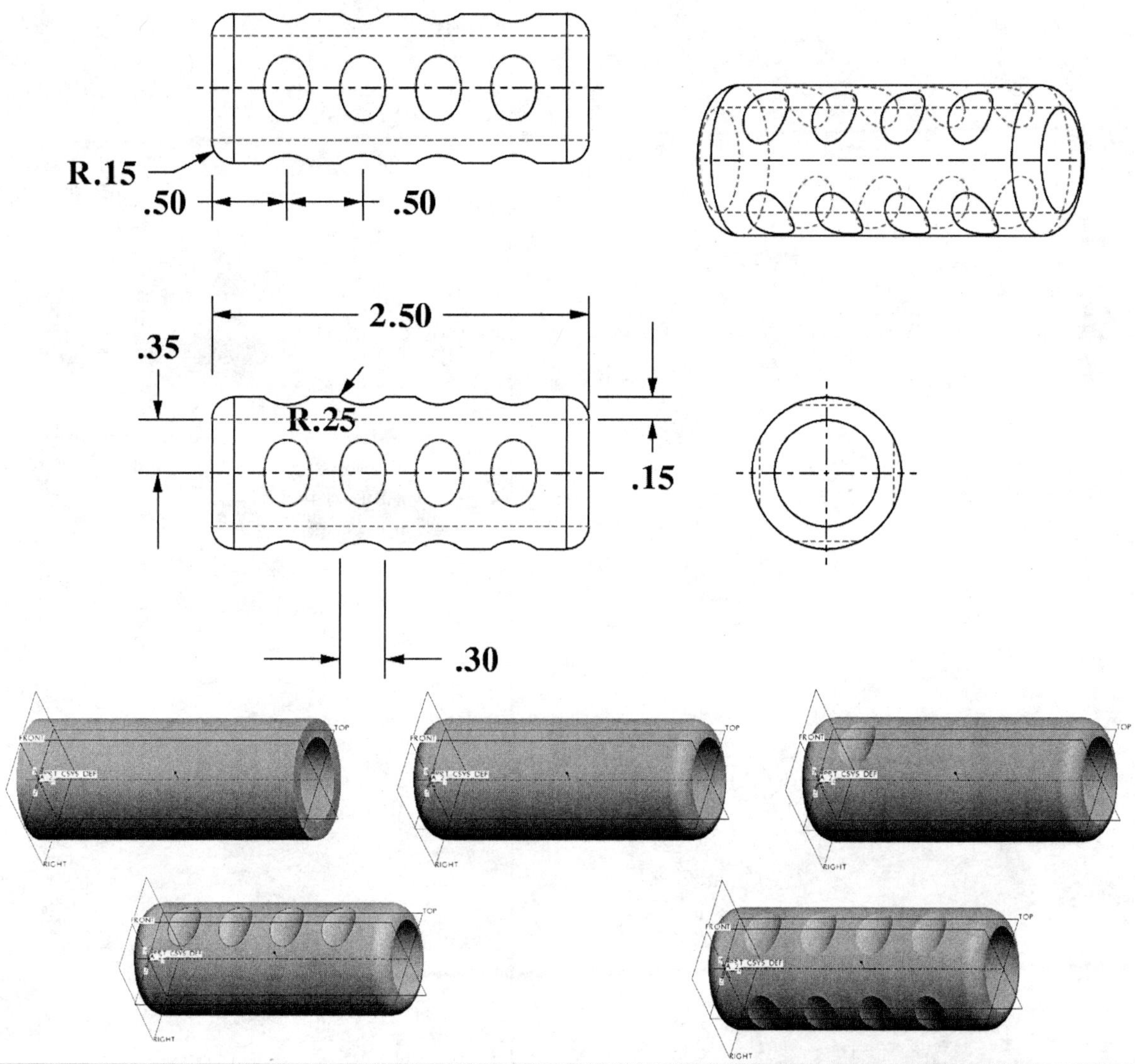

Hints:

1. Create a cylinder. The sketch is shown below.

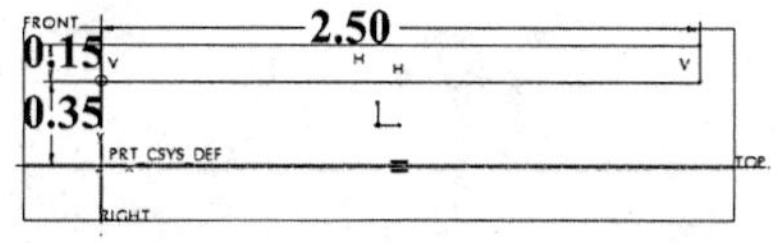

2. Round the edges using 0.15 radius round.
3. Start an extrude cut. Add the outer edge of the cylinder as a reference. Sketch an arc (select points 1, 2 and 3). Draw a line to close the arc. Select options, and specify depth 1 and 2 as through all.

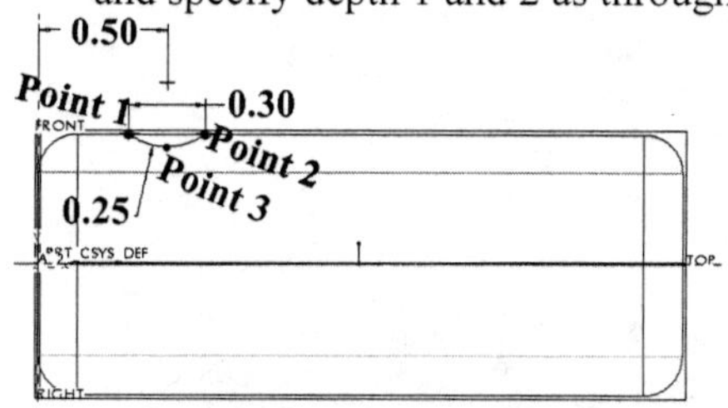

4. Pattern the cut. Select the placement dimension 0.5. Increment it by 0.5. Specify four instances.
5. Select the pattern feature and pattern it again. This time specify the axis and four instances. Dash shown below:

Problem 7

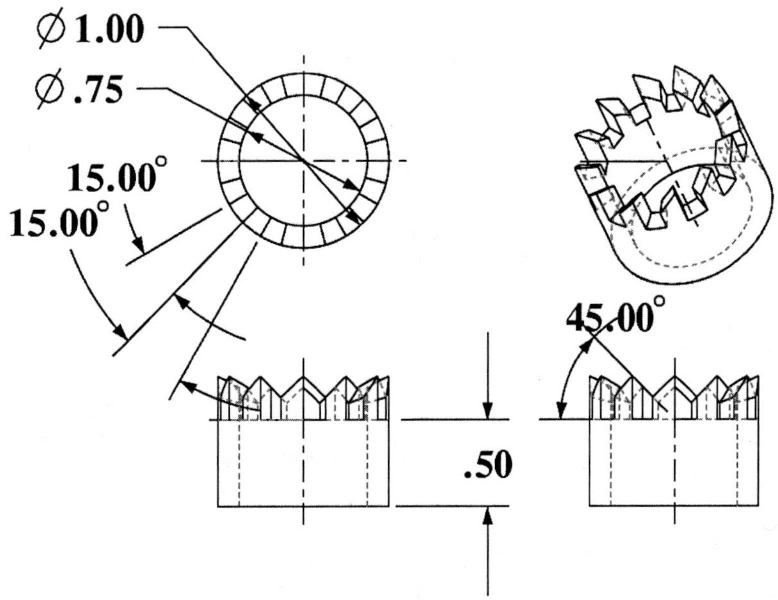

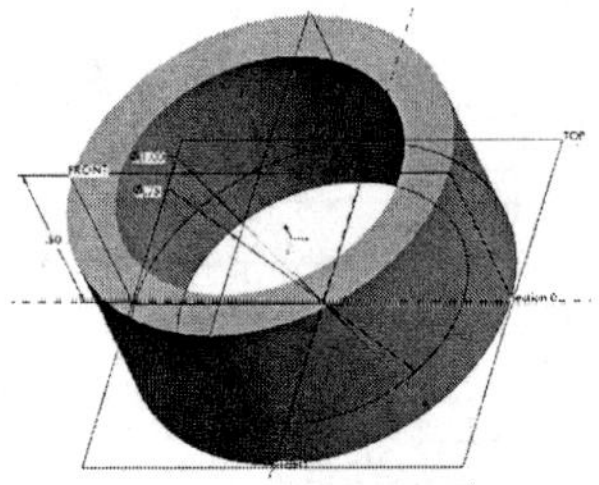

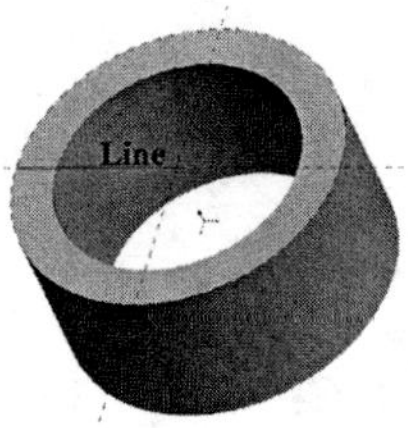

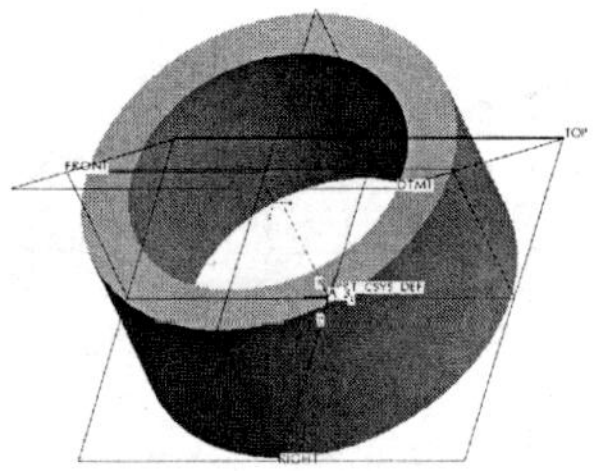

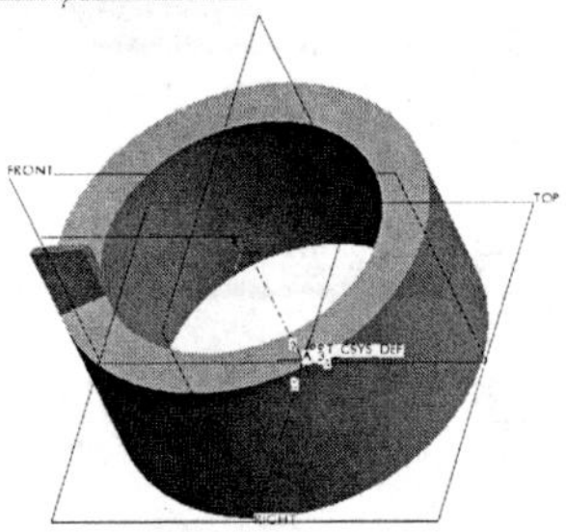

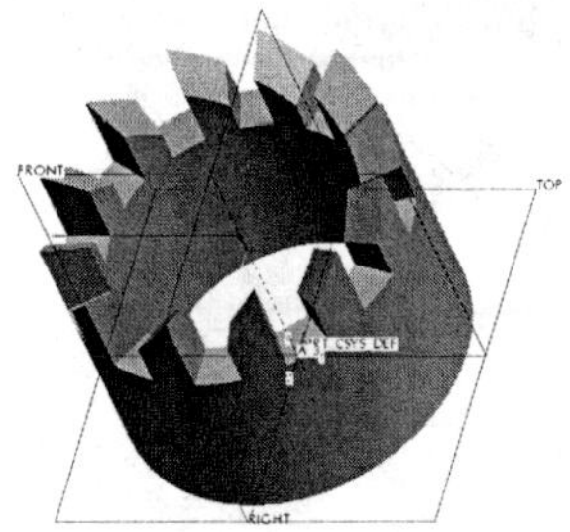

Hints:

1. Create a cylinder (1″ OD, 0.75″ ID 0.5″ Length).
2. Start extrude feature. Click on 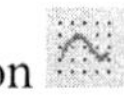 icon. Sketch a line at the intersection of the top surface and the FRONT datum.

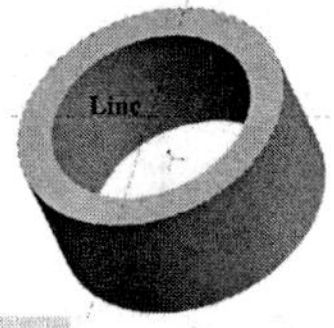

3. Click on . Select the line and then the top surface while holding ***CTRL***. Enter offset as 45.

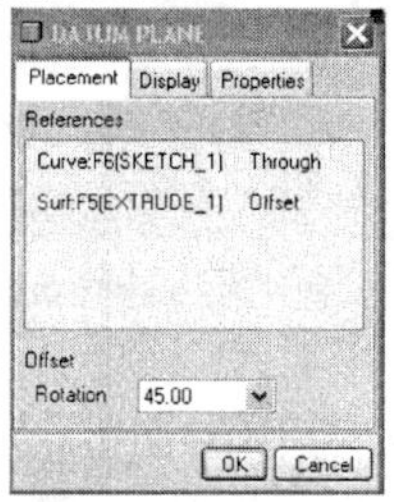

4.  (resume) extrude feature. Sketch on the top surface of the cylinder.

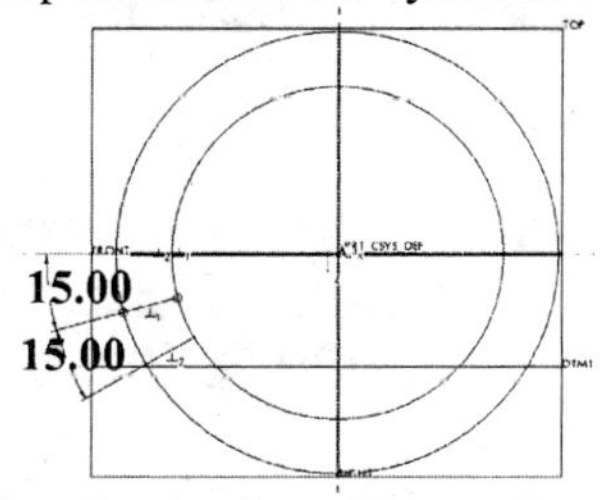

5. Define the depth as Up to selected surface and select the datum plane.
6. Pattern the extrusion around the axis. Pattern parameters – instances: 12 and angle: 30.

Problem 8

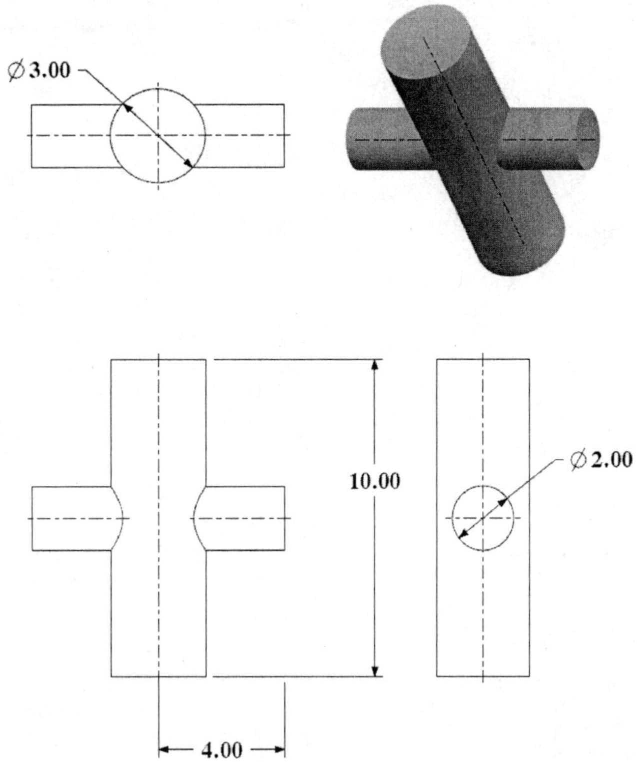

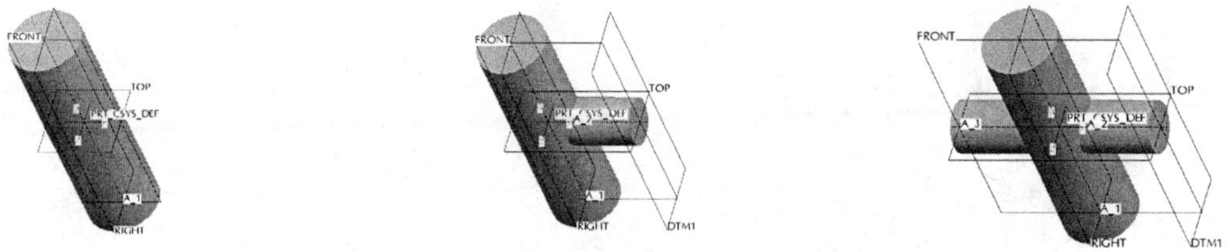

Hints:

1. Use Extrude – "Both Sides" depth option.

2. Create an offset datum plane (INSERT → MODEL DATUM → PLANE → Select the RIGHT datum plane → 4.00 → ***ENTER***).

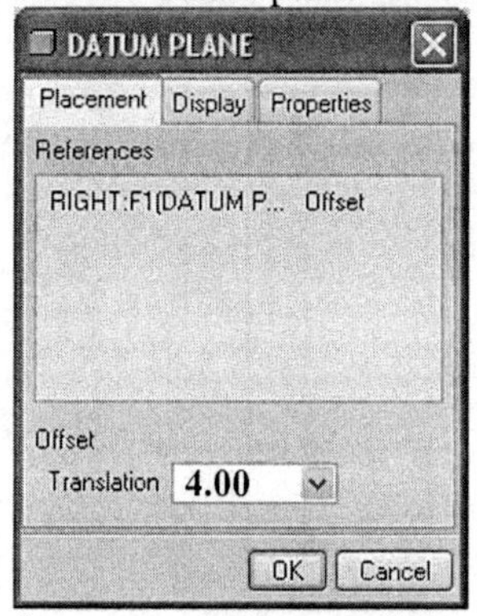

3. Start extrude feature. Select the new datum as the sketching plane. Sketch the section on this offset datum. View the model in the default orientation. It may be necessary to flip the direction of extrusion. Then, extrude the sketch up surface.

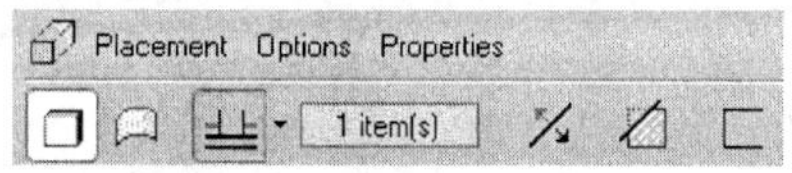

4. Mirror the last feature.

Problem 9

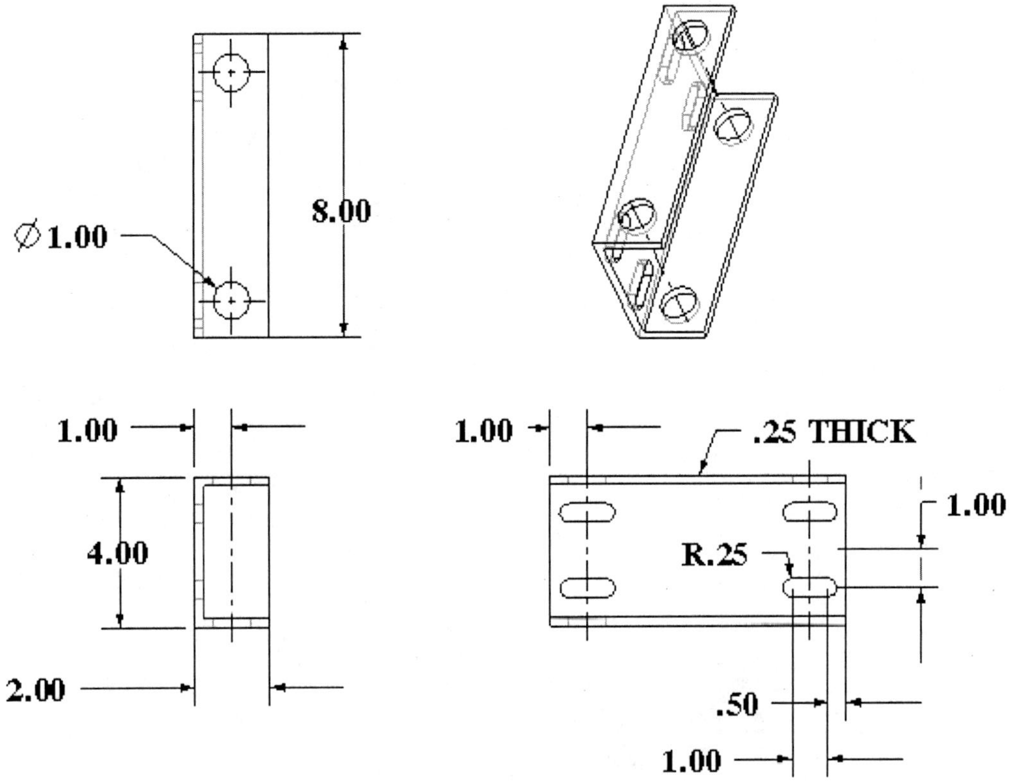

Hints:

1. Use "Extrude - Thicken - Both sides" option.
2. Use the MIRROR tool to minimize the number of cuts made. The tool can be accessed either from EDIT → FEATURE OPERATIONS → MIRROR or by using the mirror button:

3. If you need to create datum planes across which to mirror features, use the CREATE DATUM PLANE tool either using INSTERT → MODEL DATUM → PLANE, or use the create datum plane button: 

However, this step should be unnecessary with sufficient planning.

OPEN-ENDED DESIGN – Try some thing that uses patterns. Objects that use pattern are everywhere around you.

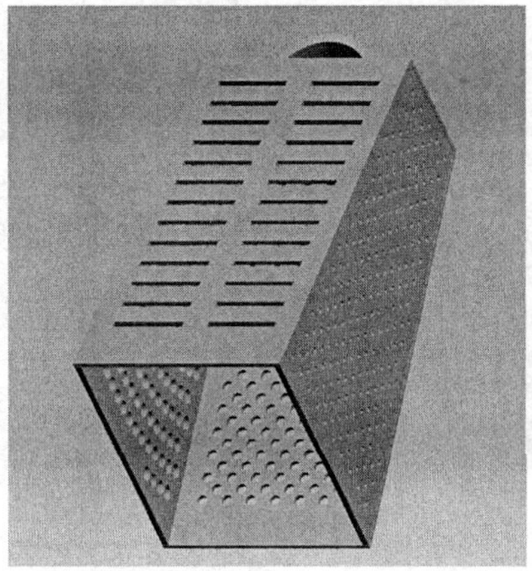
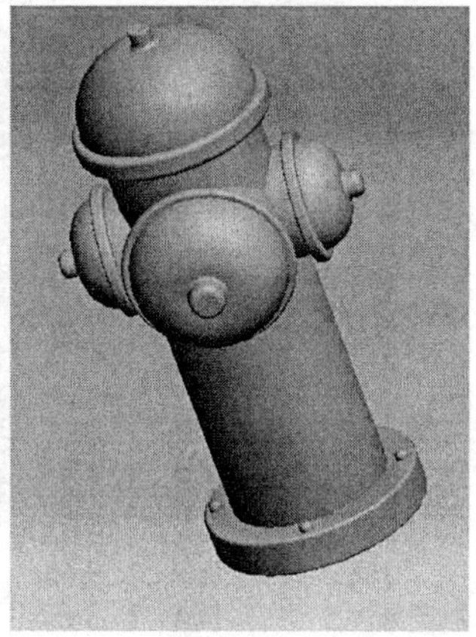
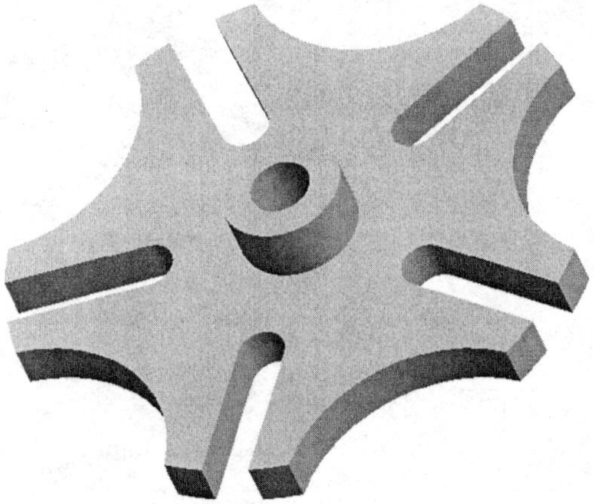
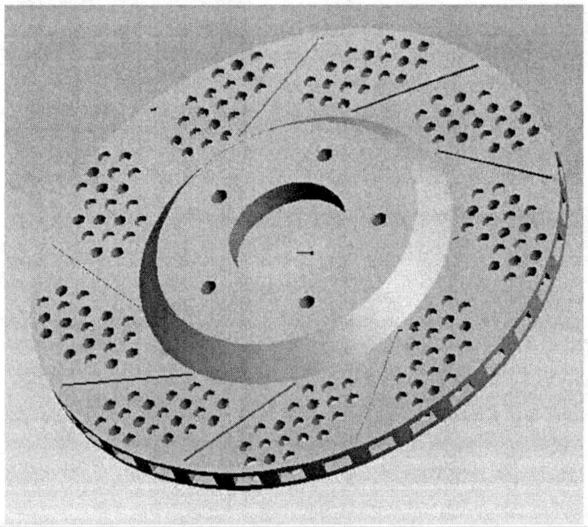

NOTES:

LESSON 8
SHAFT DRAWING

Learning Objectives

- Learn to create ***Drawing Format Sheets***.
- Learn to create ***Orthographic*** and ***Trimetric Views*** for a part.
- Learn to ***Dimension*** and ***Tolerance*** a part drawing.

Design Information

An engineering drawing is the primary document exchanged between designers and manufacturing engineers. A drawing defines the overall geometry, all the dimensions, and the required tolerances for producing the part. A good drawing which accurately and unambiguously represents a part, avoid unexpected manufacturing delays and disputes. Manufacturing engineers follow these guidelines to manufacture the part. To facilitate easy manufacturing, it is important to include additional views to accurately represent the part and increase clarity by properly arranging the dimensions and tolerances.

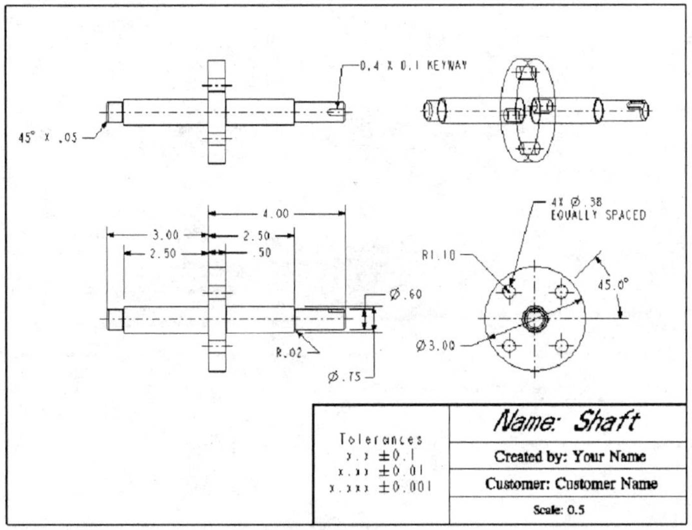

Standard Drawing Sheet Size

Standard drawing sheet sizes facilitate the ease of readability and folding. A standard drawing sheet is sized based on ANSI/ASME or ISO metric system. In the ANSI/ASME system, the sheet sizes are:

A	8.5" × 11"
B	11" × 17"
C	17" × 22"
D	22" × 34"

In the ISO system, the area of drawing sheet A0 is 1 square meter. The sizes are:

A0	841 mm × 1189 mm	33.1" × 46.8"
A1	594 mm × 841 mm	23.4" × 33.1"
A2	420 mm × 594 mm	16.5" × 23.4"
A3	297 mm × 420 mm	11.7" × 16.5"
A4	210 mm × 297 mm	8.3" × 11.7"

Note that the paper sizes follow the golden ratio where the ratio of length to width is same for any paper and is equal to $\sqrt{2}$.

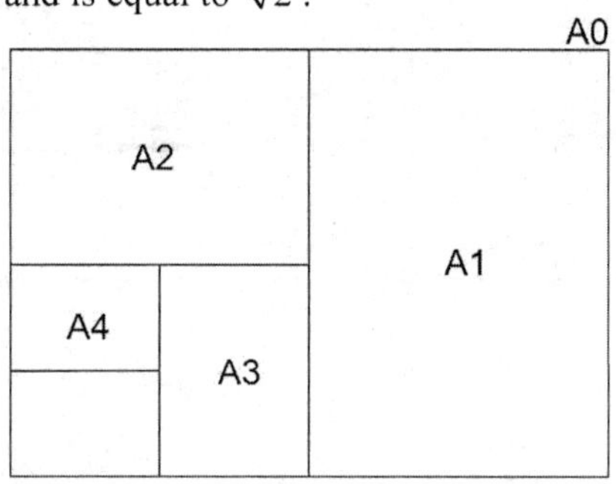

SEQUENCE OF STEPS

STEP I: Create a drawing format

1. Create borders
2. Create the title box
3. Enter text in the title box
4. Format the text in the title box
5. Save the format sheet

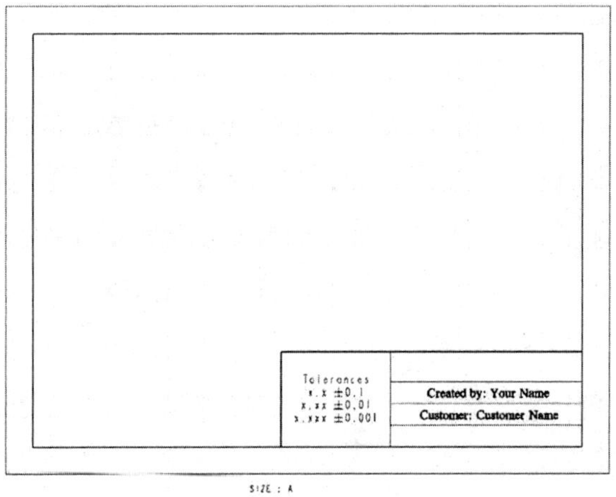

STEP II: Create a drawing for the casing part

1. Add the front view
2. Add the top view
3. Add the side view
4. Create a trimetric view
5. Move views
6. Display centerlines
7. Dimension all features
8. Clean up the drawing by moving the dimensions\
9. Add name and scale to the title box

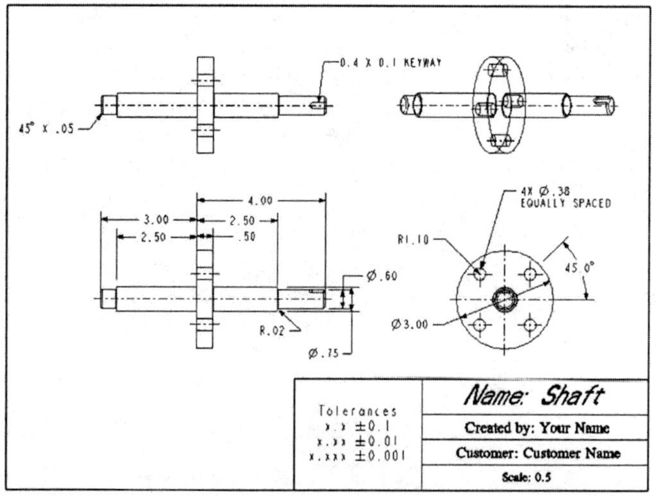

Goal	Step	Commands
Open a drawing file for the shaft part	1. Set up the working directory.	**FILE → SET WORKING DIRECTORY →** ***Select the working directory*** **→ OK**
	2. Open a drawing file for the shaft part.	**FILE → NEW → FORMAT → <u>format A</u>→ OK→ (Specify Templete)** ***Empty*** **→ (Orientation) Landscape → (Standard Size) A → OK**
Create borders	3. Create line 1.	**SKETCH → SKETCHER PREFERENCES →** ***Check chain sketching*** **→ CLOSE** Refer Fig. 8.1. **SKETCH → LINE → LINE → SKETCH → SPECIFY → ABSOLUTE COORDINATES →** (x) **<u>0.5</u>** → (Y) **<u>0.5</u>** → ✓ **→ SKETCH → SPECIFY → ABSOLUTE COORDINATES COORDS →** (x) **<u>10.5</u>** → (y) **<u>0.5</u>** → ✓
	4. Create line 2.	(x) **<u>10.5</u>** → (y) **<u>8</u>** → ✓
	5. Create line 3.	(x) **<u>0.5</u>** → (y) **<u>8</u>** → ✓
	6. Create line 4.	(x) **<u>0.5</u>** → (y) **<u>0.5</u>** → ✓ → ✗ Refer Fig. 8.2.

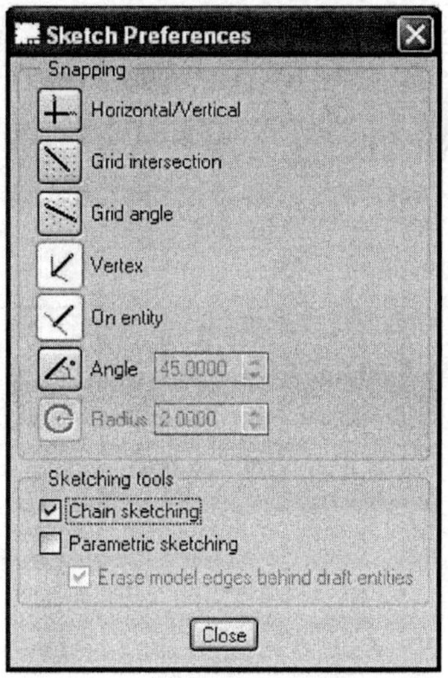

Fig. 8.1.

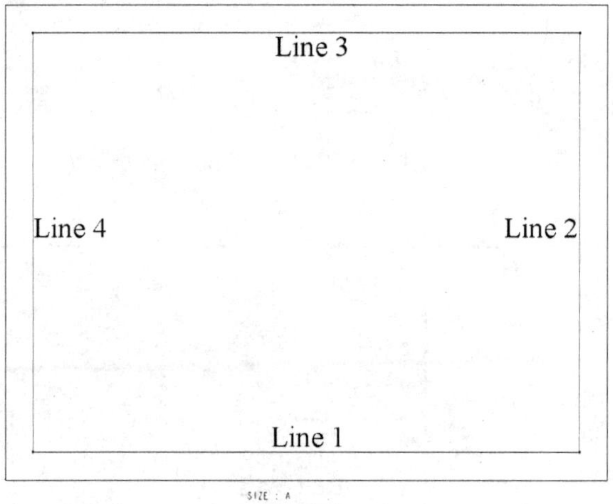

Fig. 8.2.

Goal	Step	Commands
Create the title box	7. Create line 5.	**SKETCH → SPECIFY → ABSOLUTE COORDINATES →** (x) **<u>10.5</u>** → (y) **<u>2.25</u>** → → **SKETCH → SPECIFY → ABSOLUTE COORDINATES →** (x) **<u>5</u>** → (y) **<u>2.25</u>** →
	8. Create line 6.	(x) **<u>5</u>** → (y) **<u>0.5</u>** → →
	9. If lines are created by mistake, then delete them.	→ ***Select the items*** → ***<u>DELETE</u>***
	10. Modify the line thickness.	**FORMAT → LINE STYLE → Modify Lines →** ***Draw a box to select the six lines*** **→ OK →** (Width) **0.03 → Apply → Close → Done/Return** Refer Figs. 7.3 and 7.4.
	11. Create the inside vertical line.	**SKETCH → LINE → LINE → SKETCH → SPECIFY ABS COORDS** → (x) **<u>7</u>** → (y) **<u>0.5</u>** → → **SKETCH → SPECIFY → ABSOLUTE COORDINATES** → (x) **<u>7</u>** → (y) **<u>2.25</u>** → → ***Middle Mouse***

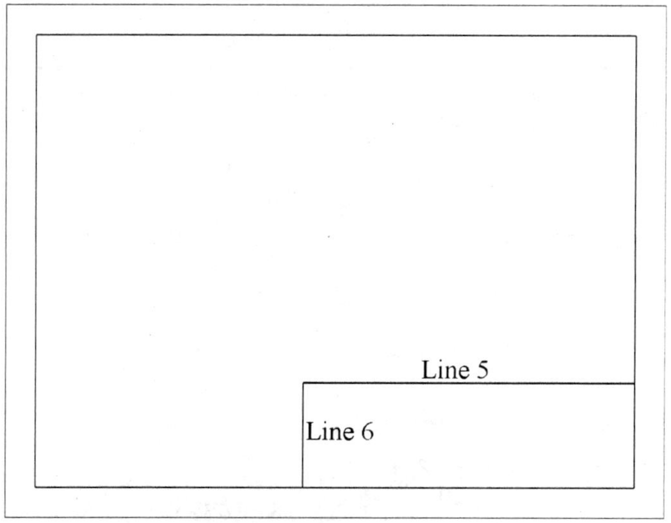

Fig. 8.3.

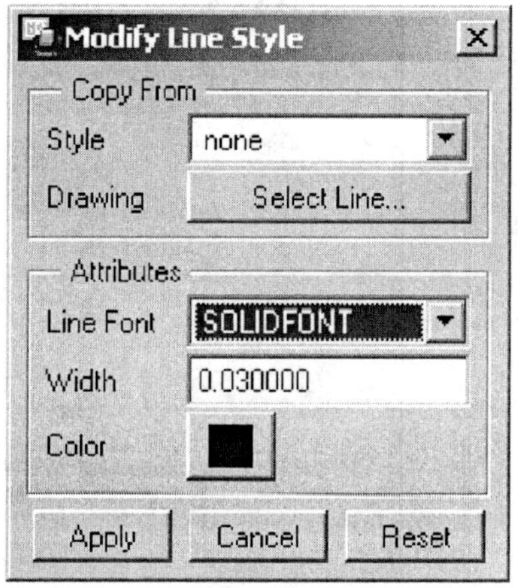

Fig. 8.4.

Goal	Step	Commands
Create the title box (Continued)	12. Create horizontal line 1.	**SKETCH → SPECIFY → ABSOLUTE COORDINATES →** (x) **7** → (y) **0.9** → ✓ → **SKETCH → SPECIFY → ABSOLUTE COORDINATES →** (x) **10.5** → (y) **0.9** → ✓ → ***Middle Mouse***
	13. Create horizontal line 2.	**SKETCH → SPECIFY → ABSOLUTE COORDINATES →** (x) **7** → (y) **1.3** → ✓ → **SPECIFY → ABSOLUTE COORDINATES →** (x) **10.5** → (y) **1.3** → ✓ → ***Middle Mouse***
	14. Create horizontal line 3.	**SKETCH → LINE → SKETCH → SPECIFY ABS COORDS →** (x) **7** → (y) **1.7** → ✓ → **SKETCH → SPECIFY ABS COORDS →** (x) **10.5** → (y) **1.7** → ✓ → ***Middle Mouse*** Refer Fig. 8.5.
Enter text in the title box	15. Create the text in the title box.	**INSERT → NOTE → No Leader → Enter → Horizontal → Standard → Default → Make Note → Pick Pnt →** ***Select a point in the second column, second row*** → **Created by: Name** → ✓ → ✓ → **Make Note → Pick Pnt →** ***Select a point in the second column, third row*** → **Customer: Customer Name** → ✓ → ✓ → **Make Note → Pick Pnt →** ***Select a point in the first column*** → **Tolerances** → ✓ → **x.x ±0.1** → ✓ → **x.xx ±0.01** → ✓ → **x.xxx ±0.001** → ✓ → ✓ → **Done/Return** ± symbol is available in the symbol palette. (arrow icon) → ***Select the text, move it to the desired location and then, click again to place the text*** Refer Fig. 8.6.

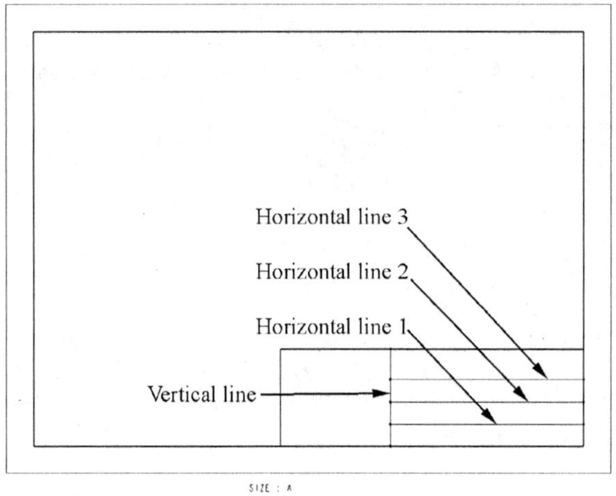

Fig. 8.5.

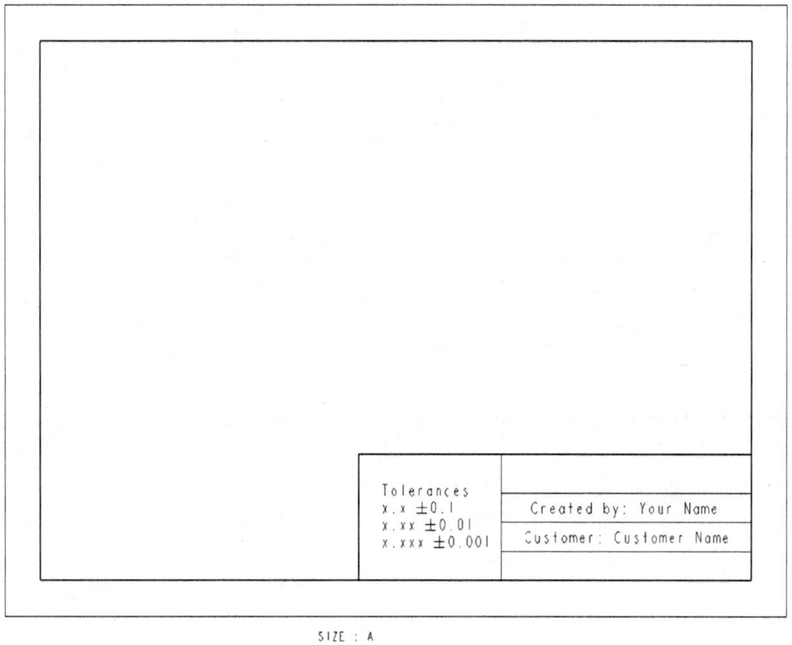

Fig. 8.6.

Goal	Step	Commands
Enter text in the title box (Continued)	16. Justify the tolerance text to the center.	**FORMAT → TEXT STYLE →** ***Select the four tolerance text lines while holding CTRL*** **→ OK →** (Note/Dimension - Horizontal) ***Center*** **→ Apply → OK** Refer Fig. 8.7.
	17. Move the text to the desired location.	↖ → ***Select the text, move it to the desired location and then, click again to place the text*** Refer Fig. 8.8.
Change the font	18. Change the font.	**FORMAT → TEXT STYLE →** ***Select the text lines*** **→ OK →** (Font) ***CG Times Bold*** **→ Apply → OK** Refer Fig. 8.8.
Save drawing format & erase the current session	19. Save the drawing format.	**FILE → SAVE → FormatA.FRM → OK**
	20. Erase the current session.	**FILE → ERASE → CURRENT → YES**

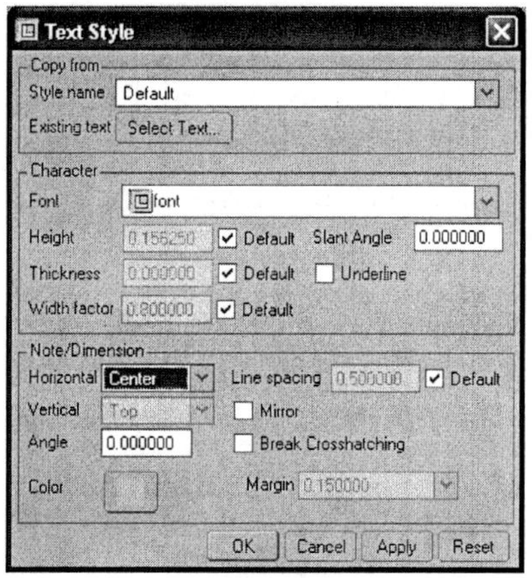

Fig. 8.7.

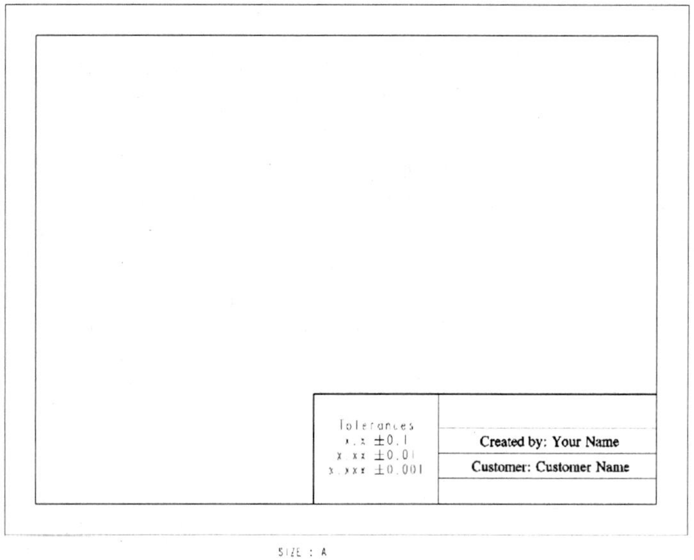

Fig. 8.8.

Goal	Step	Commands
Open a new file for the drawing	21. Open a new drawing file with the format created earlier.	**FILE → NEW → DRAWING → SHAFT → OK → (Default Model)** ***Browse and select the shaft.prt file → Empty with format → Browse and select formatA.frm → OK*** Refer Fig. 8.9.
Create the front view	22. Create the front view.	 → ***Click in the lower left quadrant*** → (View Name) **Front view** → (Model view names) **FRONT → APPLY** Refer Figs. 7.10 and 7.11.
	23. Set the scale and display state.	***Select scale under categories → Check custom scale → 0.5 → APPLY → Select view display →*** (Display style) ***Hidden→*** **OK** Refer Figs. 7.12, 7.13 and 7.14.
Create the top view	24. Create the top view.	**INSERT → DRAWING VIEW → PROJECTION →** ***Click in the top left quadrant → Double click on the view → View display → (Display style) Hidden*** **→ OK**
Create the side view	25. Create the side view.	**INSERT → DRAWING VIEW → PROJECTION →** ***Click in the bottom right quadrant → Double click on the view → View display →*** (Display style) ***Hidden →*** **OK**

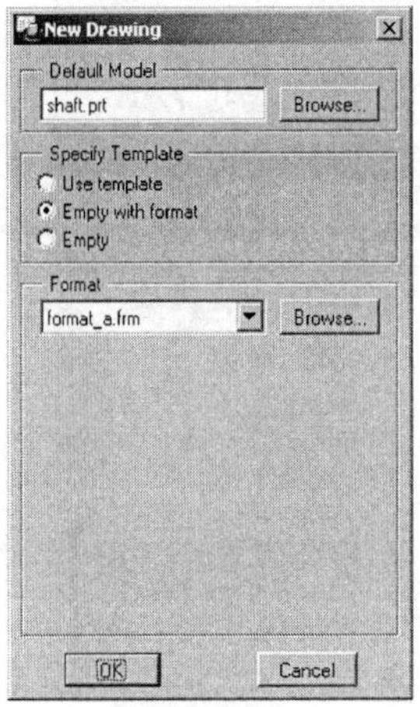

Fig. 8.9.

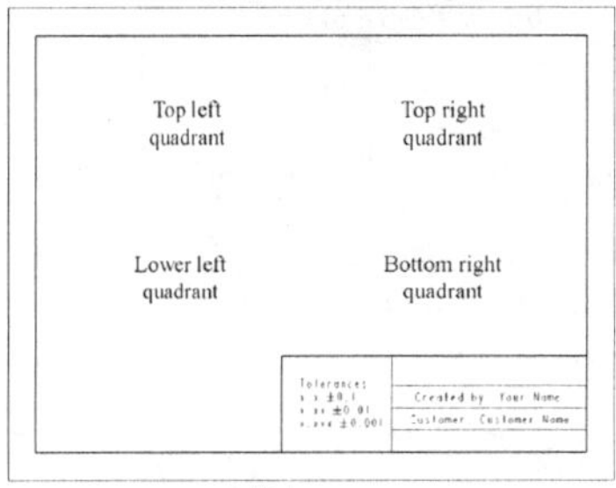

Fig. 8.10.

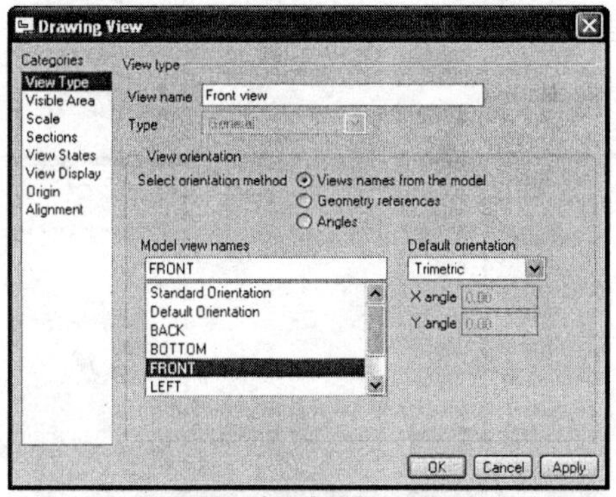

Fig. 8.11.

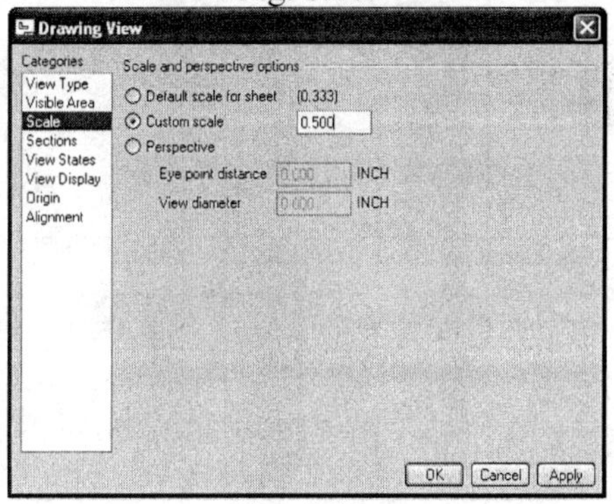

Fig. 8.12.

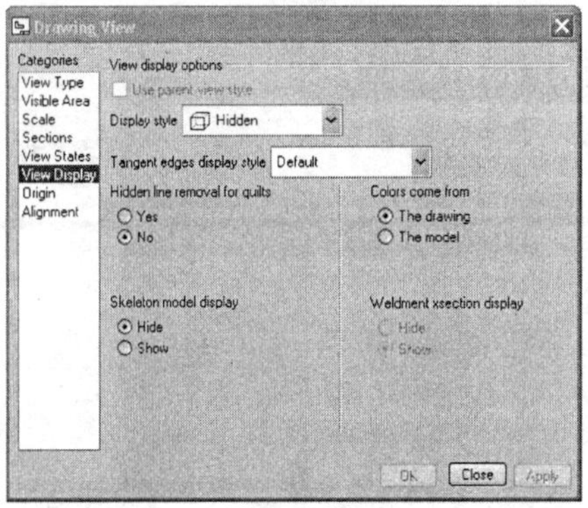

Fig. 8.13

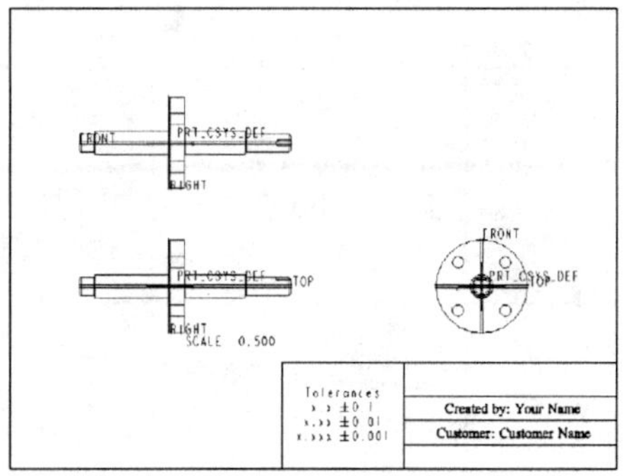

Fig. 8.14

Goal	Step	Commands
Create a trimetric view	26. Create a trimetric view for visualization.	→ *Click in the top right quadrant of the drawing sheet* → **(View name)** **<u>Trimetric</u>** → **Model view names)** ***Default Orientation*** → **(Default Orientation)** ***Trimetric*** → **APPLY** → ***Select scale under categories*** → ***Select custom scale*** → **<u>0.5</u>** → **APPLY** → **CLOSE** Refer Fig. 8.15.
Move views	27. Move the views to create an appropriate layout.	**(allows/disallows the motion of the views)** → → ***Select and move each view*** →
Turn off datums	28. Turn off datum features.	***(Turn off datum planes and coordinate system)*** → **VIEW** → **REPAINT**
Display centerlines	29. Show all centerlines.	**VIEW** → **SHOW AND ERASE** → **SHOW** → ----A_1 → **Show All** → **Yes** → **ACCEPT ALL**
Dimension all features	30. Show all dimensions.	**SHOW** → ⟵1.2⟶ → **SHOW ALL** → **YES** → **ACCEPT ALL** → **CLOSE**
Clean up the drawing	31. Change the display type to the hidden view.	As we have not set the display type, the trimetric view follows the environment. Refer Fig. 8.16.

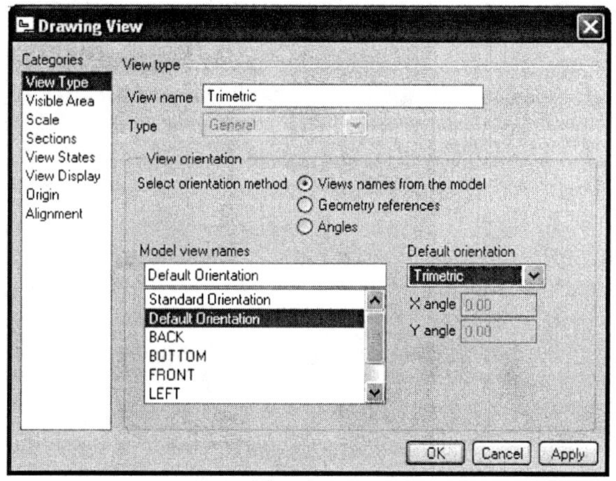

Fig. 8.15.

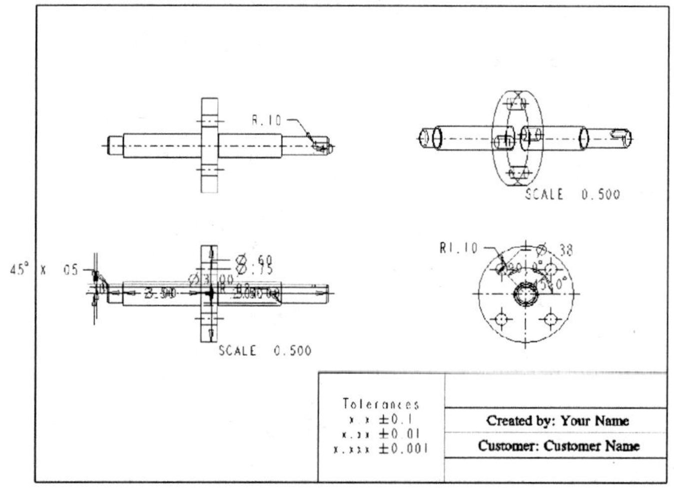

Fig. 8.16.

Reader can avoid the cluttering of dimensions by picking one feature at a time, and then showing its dimensions.

Goal	Step	Commands
REFER FIG. 8.21 before proceeding with the following steps. *Clean up the drawing (Continued)*	32. Set drawing parameters.	**FILE → PROPERTIES → Drawing Options → (Option) <u>draw_arrow_length</u> → (Value) <u>0.1</u> → ADD/CHANGE → (Option) <u>draw_arrow_style</u> → (Value) <u>Filled</u> → ADD/CHANGE → <u>drawing_text_height</u> → (Value) <u>0.125</u> → ADD/CHANGE → APPLY → CLOSE → Done/Return → VIEW → REPAINT** Refer Fig. 8.18. These preferences can be saved as a drawing set up file (.DTL).
	33. Move the dimensions so that they do not overlap with each other.	***→ Select and move each dimension***
	34. Flip arrows if the space between them is too narrow.	***→ Select the dimension → Right Mouse → Flip Arrow***
	35. Switch dimensions across views. Try to place dimensions between the views as far as possible.	***→ Select the dimension → Right Mouse → Move Item to View → Click on the view to which the dimensions should be switched***
	36. Provide a gap between the witness lines and the geometry.	***→ Select the dimension → Select the witness line end and move it***

The goal is to create a drawing similar to Fig. 8.17.
Steps 32-40 help in organizing the drawing.

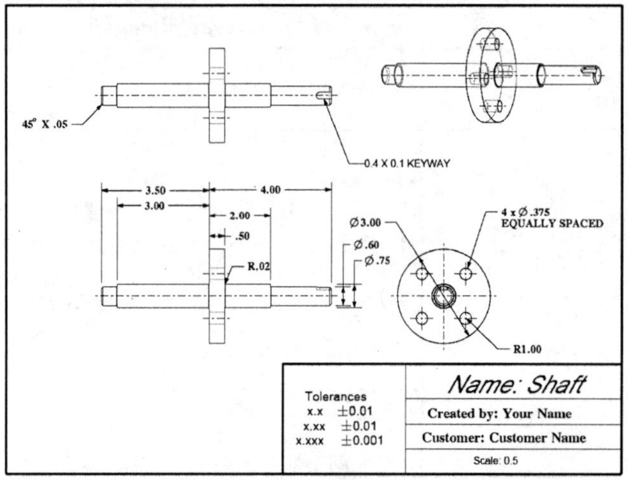

Fig. 8.17.

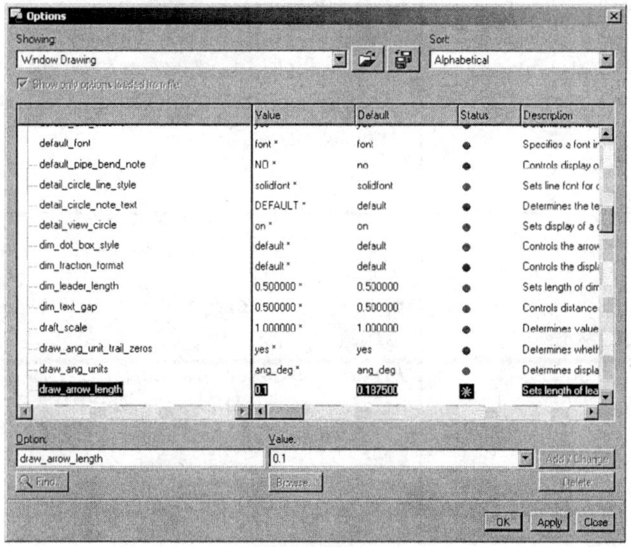

Fig. 8.18.

Goal	Step	Commands
Clean up the drawing (Continued)	37. Erase the unnecessary dimensions.	***Select 45 and 90 dimension while holding <u>CTRL</u> → Right Mouse → Erase → Select the keyway dimensions of the keyway → Right Mouse → Erase →*** **VIEW → REPAINT**
	38. Make note describing the keyway.	**INSERT → NOTE → With Leader → Enter → Horizontal → Standard → Default → Make Note → On Entity → Arrow Head →** ***Select the keyway edge*** **→ Done →** ***Select location for the note*** **→ <u>0.4 X 0.1 KEYWAY</u> → ✓ → ✓**
Add part name and the scale	39. Add part name and scale in the title box.	**No Leader → Enter → Horizontal → Standard → Default → Make Note → Pick Pnt →** ***Select location for the note*** **→ <u>Name: Shaft</u> → ✓ → ✓ → Make Note → Pick Pnt →** ***Select location for the note*** **→ <u>Scale: 0.5</u> → ✓ → ✓ → Done/Return**
	40. Change the font.	**FORMAT → TEXT STYLE →** ***Select the text "Name: Shaft" →*** **OK → (Font)** ***Filled → Deselect two defaults next to height and thickness →*** **(Height) <u>0.3</u> → (Thickness) <u>0.02</u> → (Slant Angle) <u>30</u> → OK** Refer Fig. 8.19.

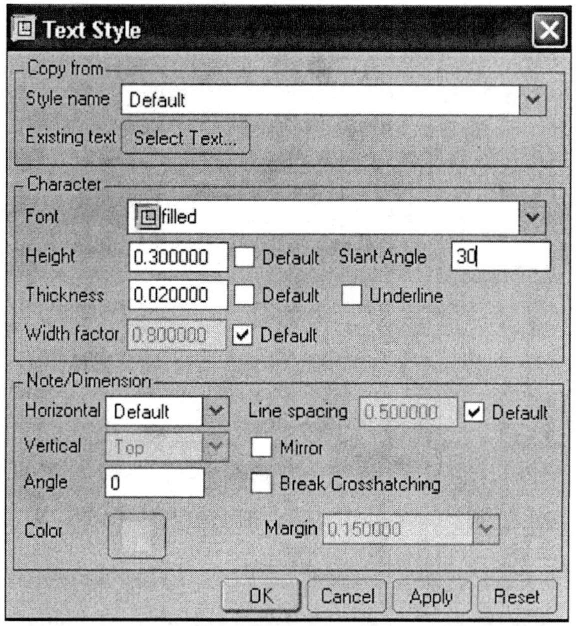

Fig. 8.19.

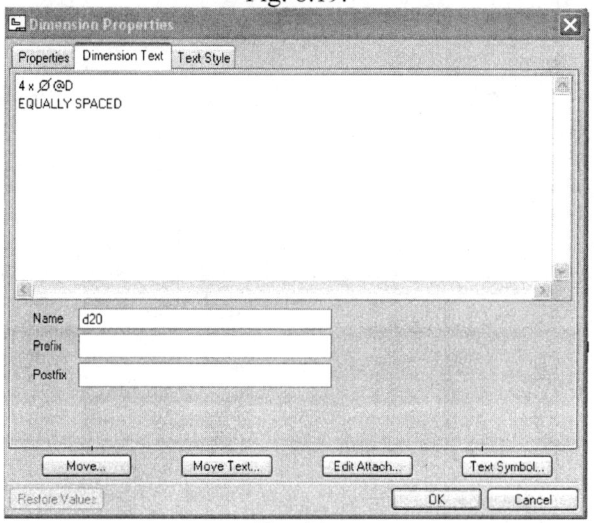

Fig. 20.

Goal	Step	Commands
Open the shaft part	41. Open the shaft part file.	**FILE → OPEN → *Select shaft.prt file* → OPEN**
Modify dimensions	42. Modify the dimensions.	***Select the first revolve feature from the model tree → Right Mouse →* Edit Definition → Placement → Edit → Sketch →** → ***Modify the three length dimensions as shown in Fig. 8.20. →*** **→ OK →** Refer Fig. 8.20.
	43. Save the changes.	**FILE → SAVE → SHAFT.PRT → OK**
Switch to the drawing window	44. Switch to the drawing window.	**WINDOW → SHAFT.DRW** The drawing reflects the changes made in the part mode. Refer Fig. 8.21.
Save the file and exit ProE	45. Save the file and exit ProE.	**FILE → SAVE → SHAFT.DRW → OK → FILE → EXIT → Yes**

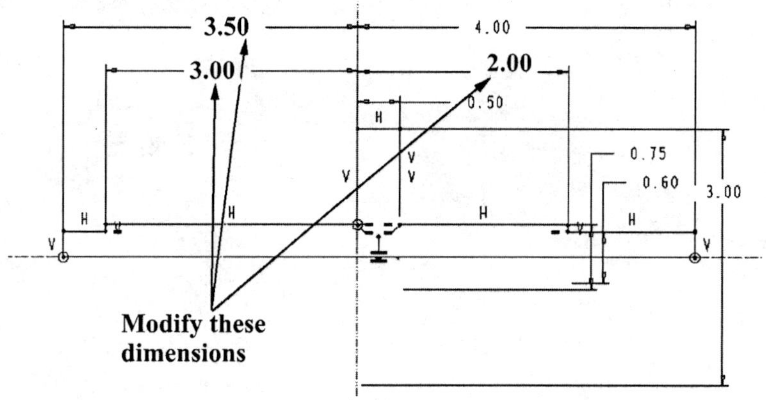

Fig. 8.20.

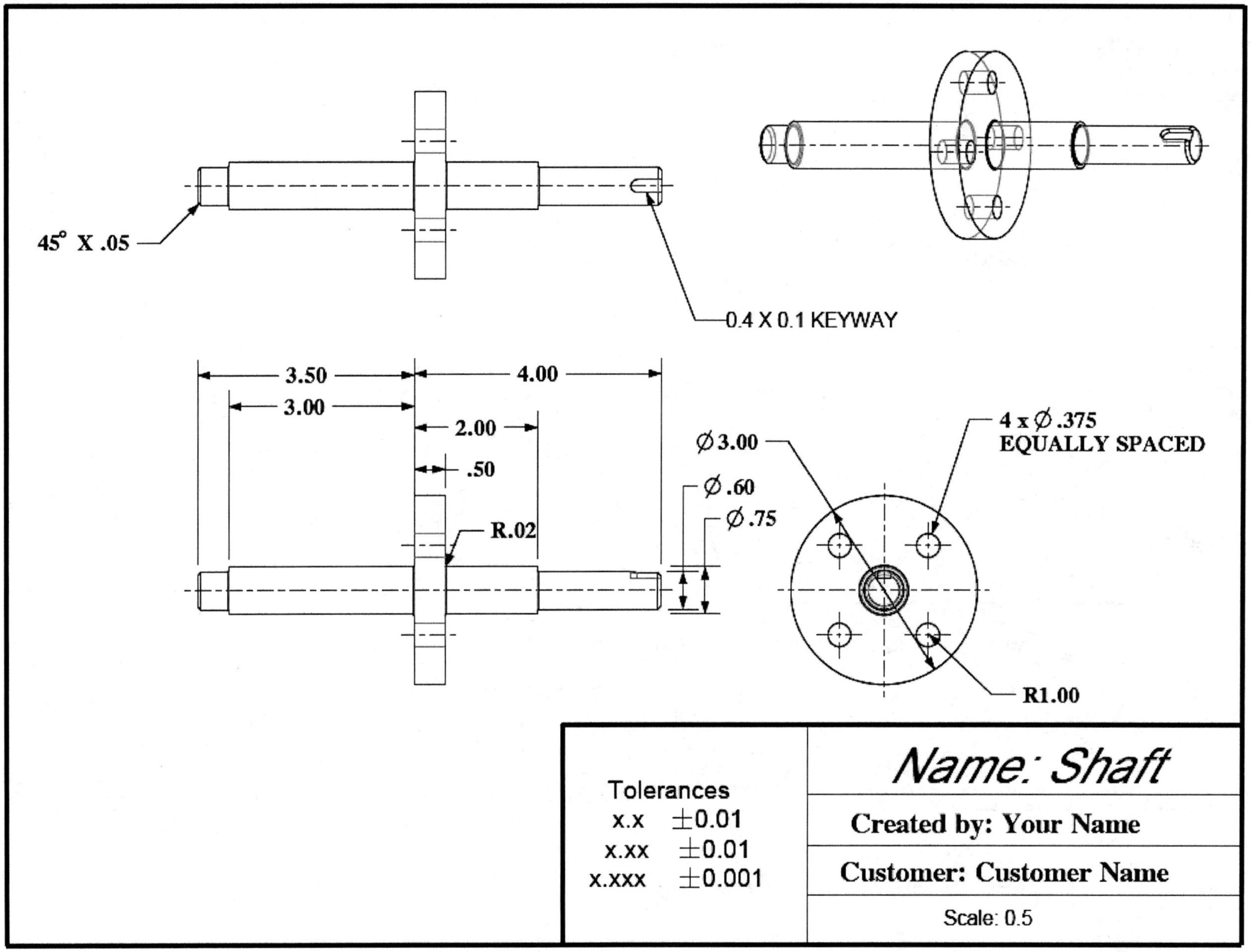

45° X .05
0.4 X 0.1 KEYWAY
3.50
4.00
3.00
2.00
.50
R.02
Ø3.00
Ø.60
Ø.75
4 x Ø.375
EQUALLY SPACED
R1.00
Tolerances
x.x ±0.01
x.xx ±0.01
x.xxx ±0.001
Name: Shaft
Created by: Your Name
Customer: Customer Name
Scale: 0.5

Fig. 8.21.

Exercise

Create the following drawings.

Problem 1

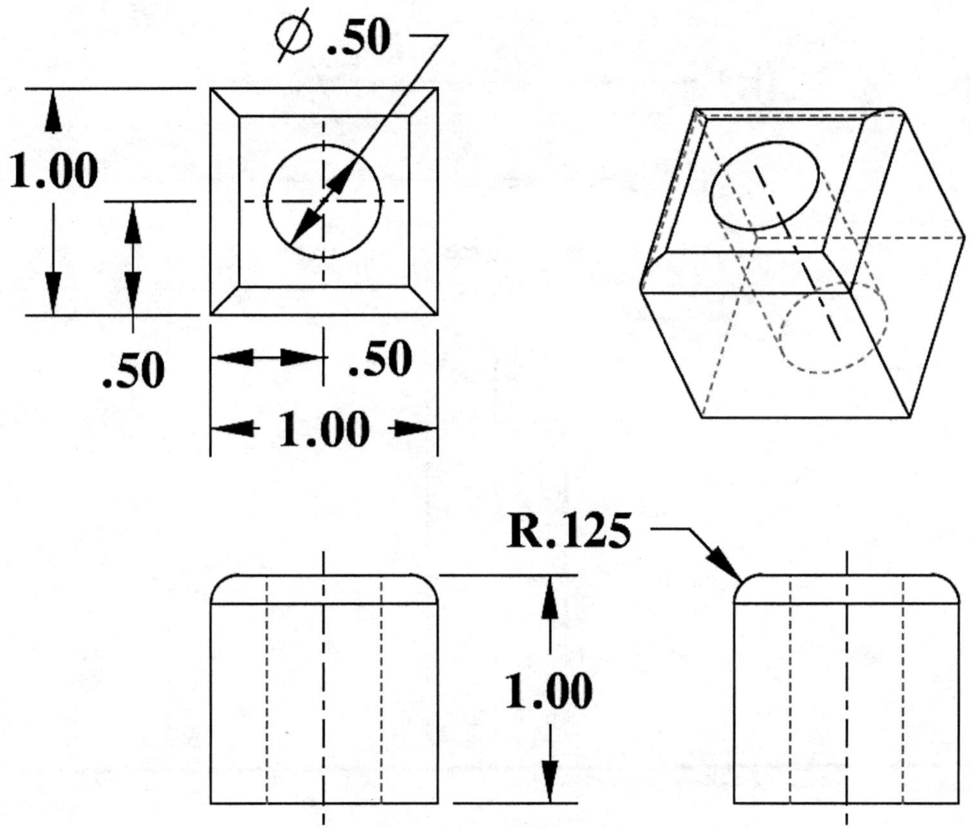

Problem 2

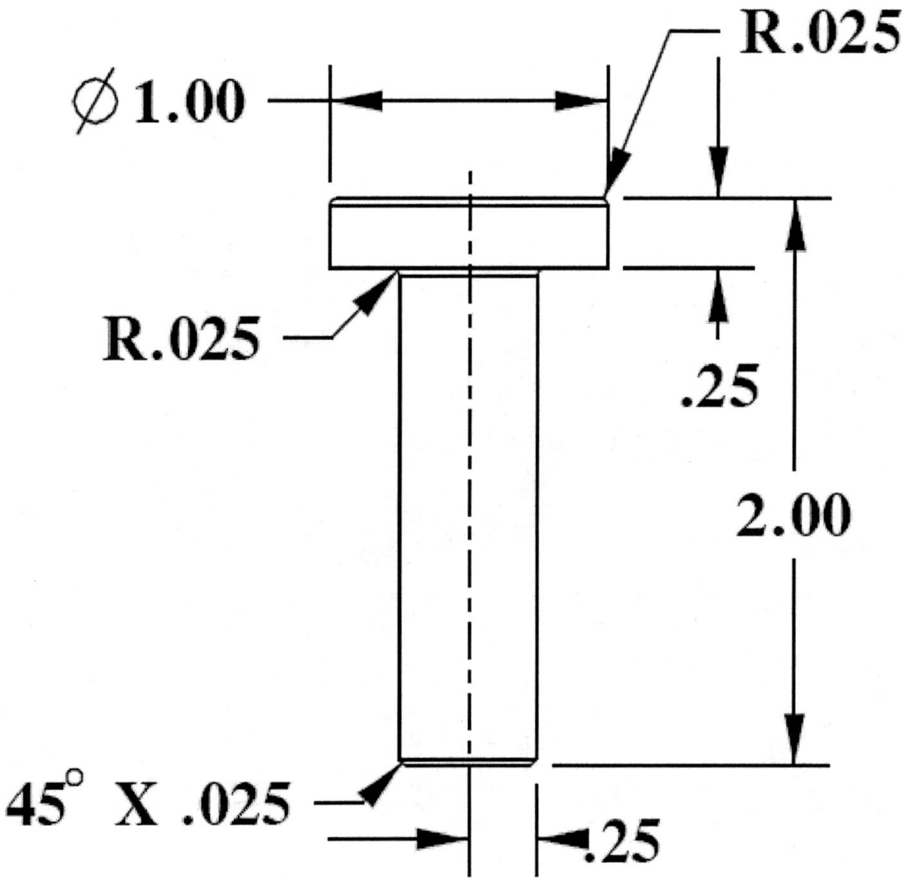

Problem 3

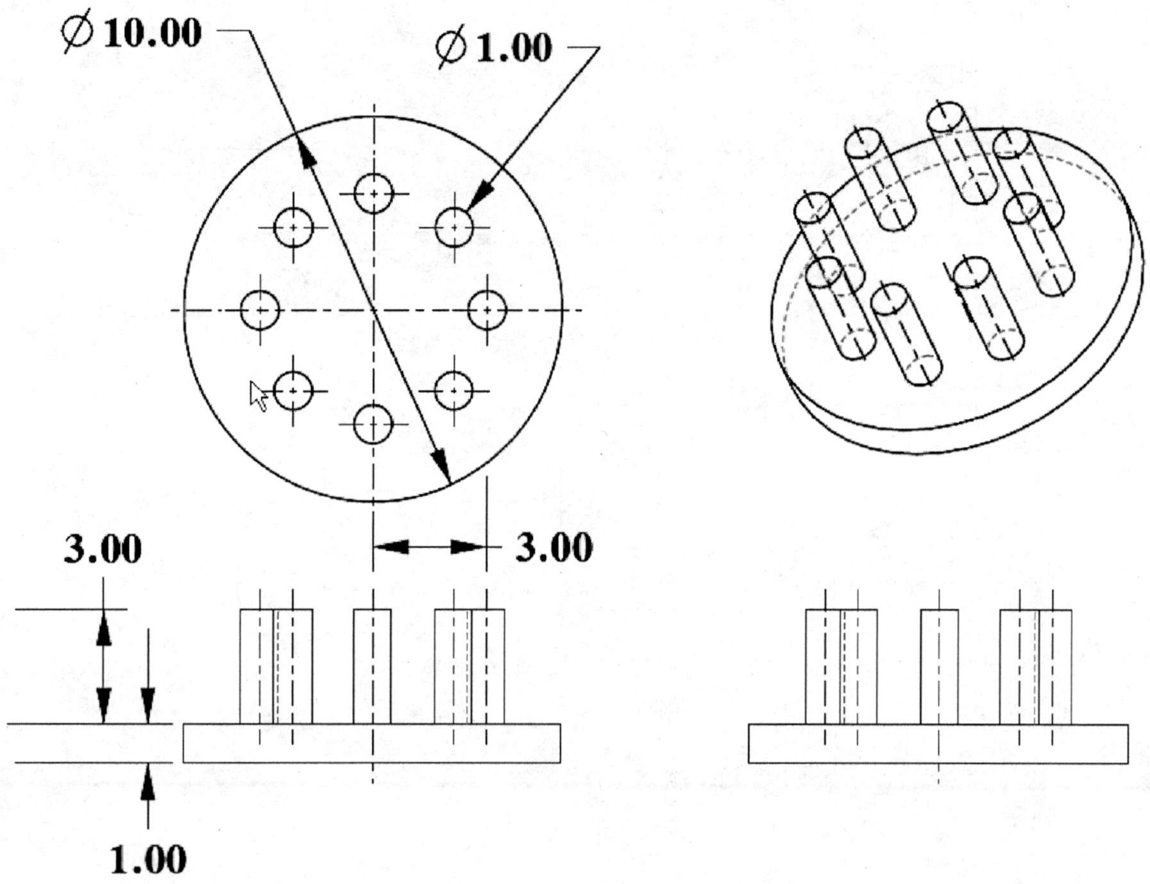

Problem 4

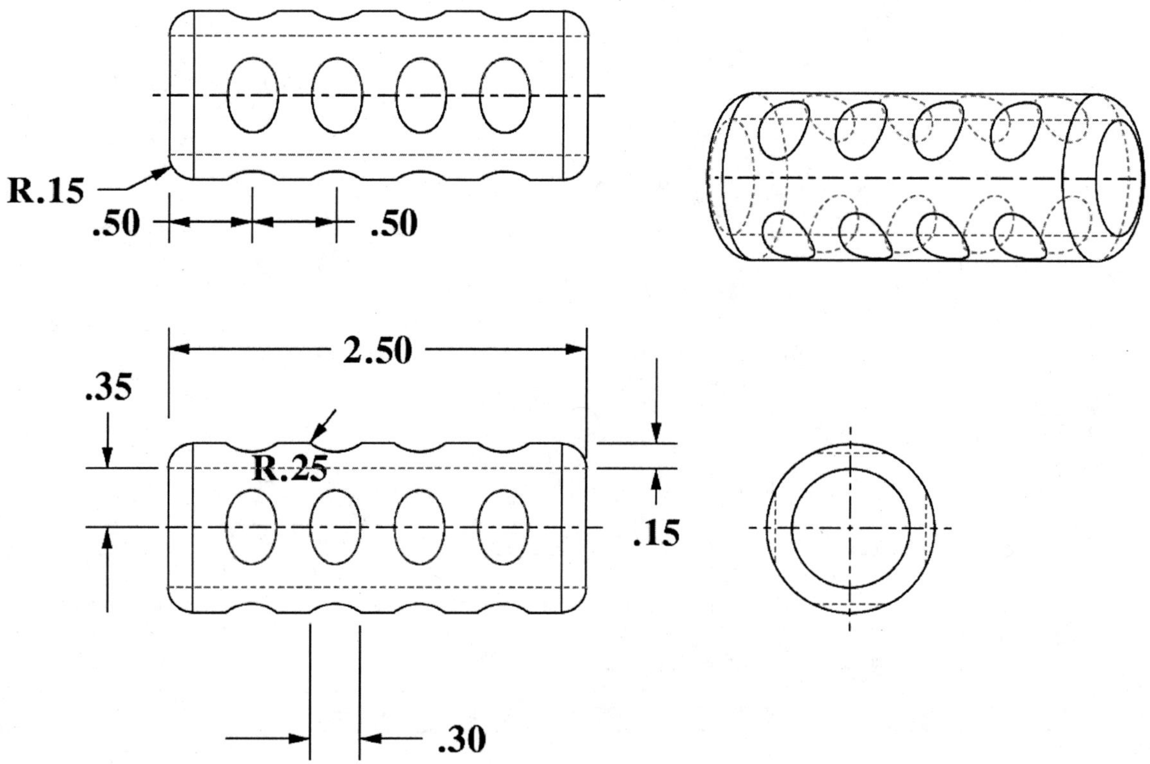

LESSON 9
RADIAL PLATE CAM

Learning Objectives

- Learn ***Datum – Curves – From Equations, Sketched Hole,*** and ***Pattern – Radial*** features.
- Practice ***Extrude, Hole,*** and ***Datum – Curves – Sketch*** features.
- Learn ***Suppress*** and ***Resume*** commands.

Datum Curves from Equation

In ProE, the a datum curve can be constructed based on an equation. The definition includes the coordinate system, coordinate system type (Cartesian, cylindrical, or spherical), and the equation. The equation is written in the parametric form in terms of variable *t*. ProE automatically varies *t* between 0 and 1 and evaluates the value of x, y, and z (or r, θ, and z) for various values of t. For instance, the following set of equations:

x = 10 * t
y = t^2
z = 0

varies x from 0 to 10. The corresponding values of y range from 0 to 1. The value of z remains constant (zero).

Background Information

Cam-follower systems are commonly used for precise motion generation. Radial cams move the follower in the radial direction. In a radial plate cam, an external force is required to keep the contact between the follower and the cam. Therefore, the open cams are known as force-closed cams. The cam profiles are shaped to minimize both jerk and peak velocity. The commonly used profiles are modified trapezoidal acceleration profile, modified sinusoidal acceleration profile and cycloidal displacement profile. As the cycloidal displacement profile creates the least amount of jerk, it is commonly used in cam design. While we create a cycloidal plate cam in this lesson, the procedure for creating other cam profiles from equations is identical.

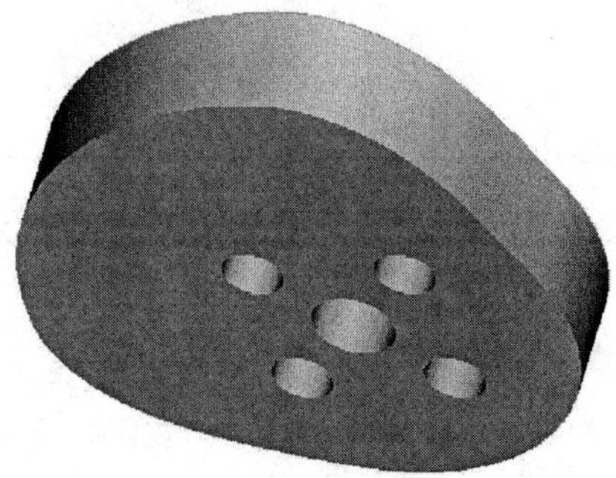

SEQUENCE OF STEPS

STEP I: Create the datum curves defining the profile

1. Create the rise profile
2. Create the fall profile
3. Create the dwell profile

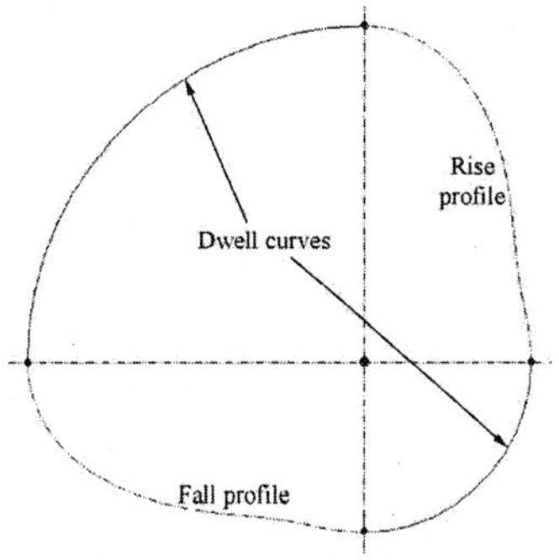

STEP II: Create the cam

1. Use “Extrude” feature
2. Create the cam using the "Use Edge" command

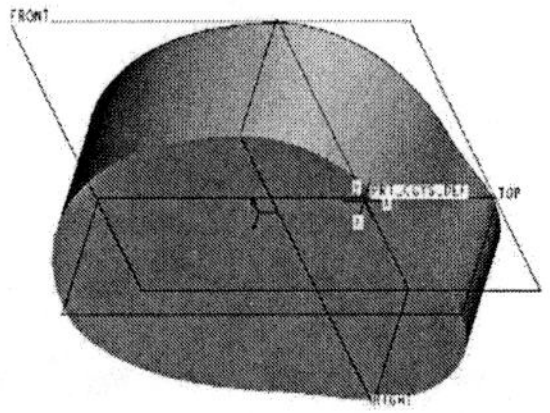

STEP III: Create a central hole

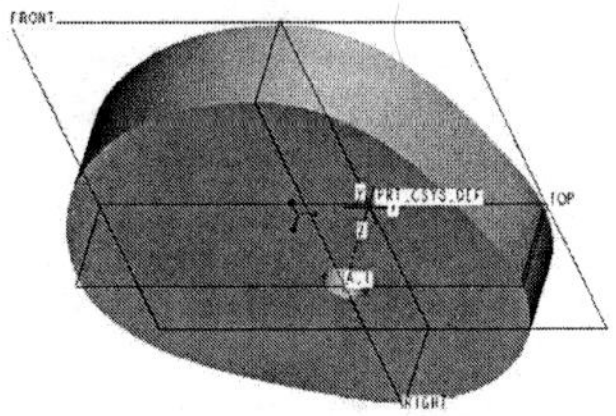

STEP IV: Create a sketched radial hole

1. Define the placement parameters for the hole
2. Sketch the shape of the hole

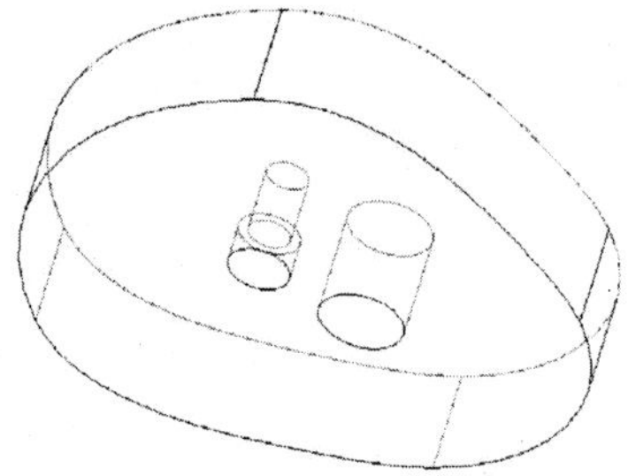

STEP V: Pattern the hole

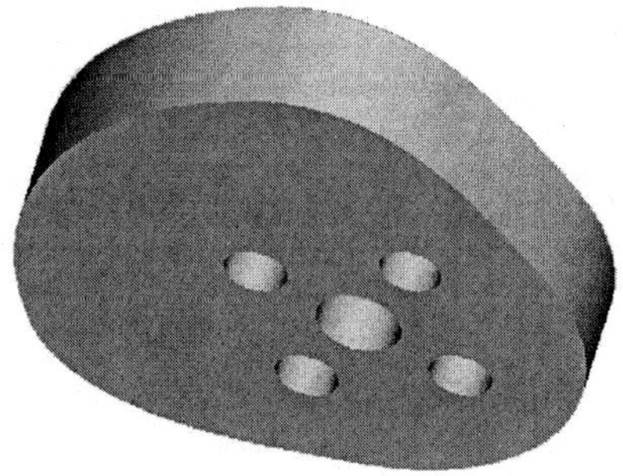

Goal	Step	Commands
Open a new file for the bearing part	1. Set up the working directory.	**FILE → SET WORKING DIRECTORY → *Select the working directory* → OK**
	2. Open a new file.	**FILE → NEW → *Part* → *Solid* → <u>platecam</u> → OK**
Create a datum curve for the rise	3. Start creating the datum curve.	[curve icon] **→ From Equation → Done**
	4. Select a cylindrical coordinate system.	**Select → *Select the default coordinate system PRT_CSYS_DEF* → Cylindrical** ProE opens equation editor.
	5. Enter the equations of cycloidal rise.	**<u>Input the equations shown in Fig. 9.2.</u>** Refer to Figs. 9.1 and 9.2.
	6. Exit equation editor.	In the equation editor window: **FILE → SAVE → FILE → EXIT**

The equation for cycloidal rise is:

$$r = r_i + \frac{h}{2}\left\{\left[1-\cos\left(180\frac{\theta}{\beta}\right)\right] - \frac{1}{4}\left[1-\cos\left(360\frac{\theta}{\beta}\right)\right]\right\}$$

where

r is the radius at angle θ.

r_i is the base radius. Assumed to be 1″ for this design task.

h is the rise. Assumed to be 1″.

β is the angle during which the rise occurs. Assumed to be 90^0.

In ProE, the equations is written in the parametric form in terms of variable t. ProE automatically varies t between 0 and 1 and evaluates the value of r, θ, and z for various values of t. As θ varies between 0 and 90, we can write θ as:

$$\theta = 90 \times t$$

By rearranging the terms in the equation for r, we get

$$r = r_i + \frac{h}{2}\left\{\left[1-\cos(180t)\right] - \frac{1}{4}\left[1-\cos(360t)\right]\right\}$$

Fig. 9.1.

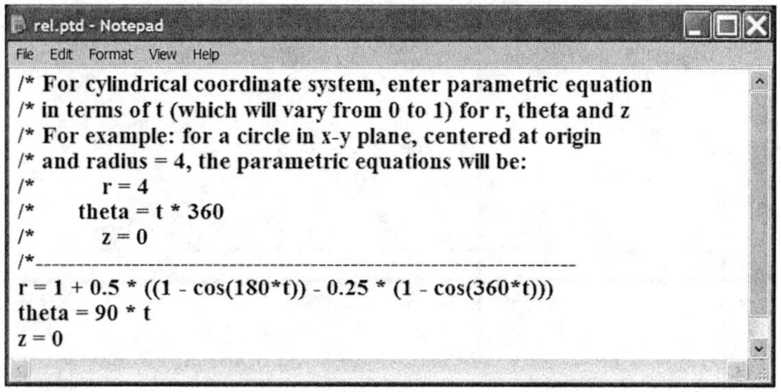

```
/* For cylindrical coordinate system, enter parametric equation
/* in terms of t (which will vary from 0 to 1) for r, theta and z
/* For example: for a circle in x-y plane, centered at origin
/* and radius = 4, the parametric equations will be:
/*        r = 4
/*     theta = t * 360
/*        z = 0
/*------------------------------------------------------------
r = 1 + 0.5 * ((1 - cos(180*t)) - 0.25 * (1 - cos(360*t)))
theta = 90 * t
z = 0
```


Fig. 9.2.

Goal	Step	Commands
Create a datum curve for the rise (Continued)	7. Accept the datum curve.	**Preview** → **OK** Refer Fig. 9.3.
Create a datum for the fall	8. Start creating the datum curve.	 → **From Equation** → **Done**
	9. Select a cylindrical coordinate system.	**Select** → ***Select the default coordinate system PRT_CSYS_DEF*** → **Cylindrical** ProE opens equation editor.
	10. Enter the equations of cycloidal fall. **Refer Fig. 9.4. for the equations.**	**<u>Input the equations shown in Fig. 9.5.</u>** Note that the fall occurs between 180^0 and 270^0. Refer Fig. 9.5.
	11. Exit equation editor.	In the equation editor window: **FILE → SAVE → FILE → EXIT**

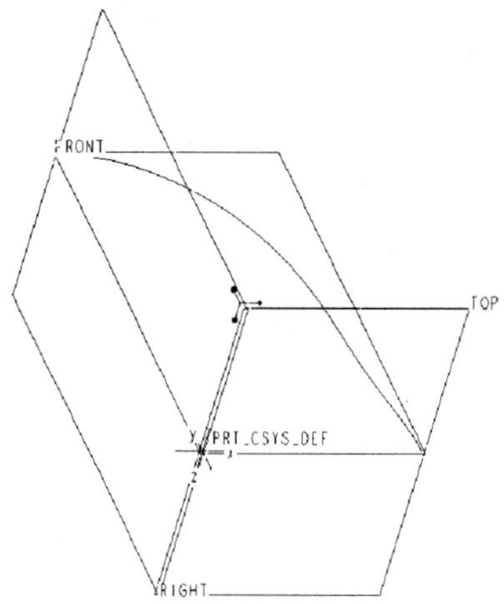

Fig. 9.3.

The equation for cycloidal fall is:

$$r = r_i + \frac{h}{2}\left\{\left[1+\cos\left(180\frac{\theta}{\beta}\right)\right] - \frac{1}{4}\left[1-\cos\left(360\frac{\theta}{\beta}\right)\right]\right\}$$

Fig. 9.4.

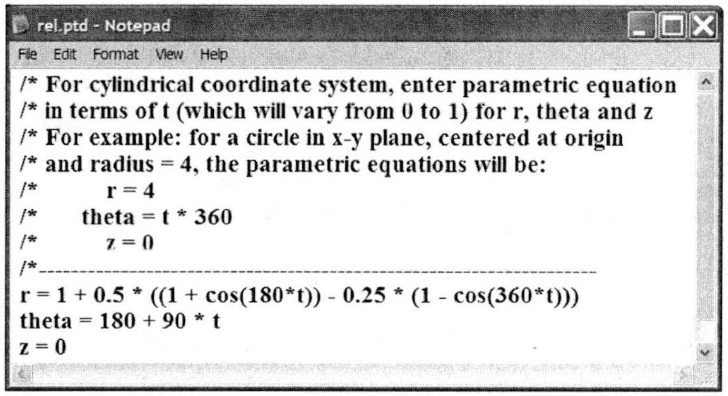

```
/* For cylindrical coordinate system, enter parametric equation
/* in terms of t (which will vary from 0 to 1) for r, theta and z
/* For example: for a circle in x-y plane, centered at origin
/* and radius = 4, the parametric equations will be:
/*       r = 4
/*    theta = t * 360
/*       z = 0
/*-----------------------------------------------------------
r = 1 + 0.5 * ((1 + cos(180*t)) - 0.25 * (1 - cos(360*t)))
theta = 180 + 90 * t
z = 0
```

Fig. 9.5.

Goal	Step	Commands
Create a datum for the fall (Continued)	12. Accept the datum curve.	**Preview** → **OK** Refer Fig. 9.6.
Create datum curves for the dwell	13. Start creating the dwell datum curves.	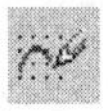
	14. Select the sketch plane.	***Select the FRONT datum plane*** → **Sketch**
	15. Add references.	**SKETCH** → **REFERENCES** → ***Select datum curves (rise and fall)*** → **Close** Refer Fig. 9.7.
	16. Draw the two dwell curves.	 →  → ***Select the center and points 1 and 2*** → ***Select the center and points 3 and 4*** ★Make sure that points 1, 2, 3 and 4 are coincide with the corresponding points on the datum planes. In other words, there should not be any dimensions in this sketch. If you see dimensions, delete the curves and repeat this step. Refer Fig. 9.8.
	17. Exit sketcher.	

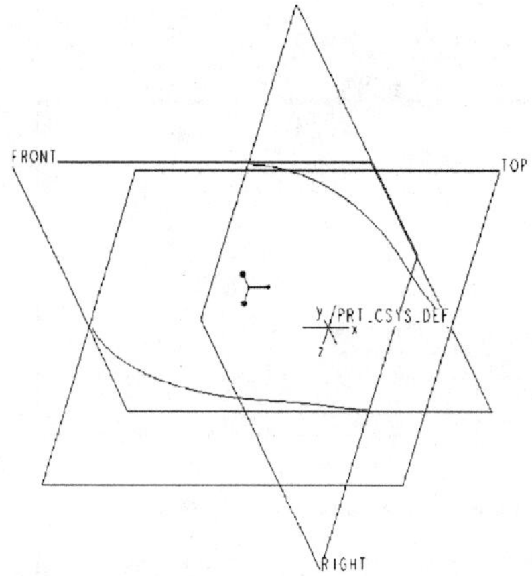

Fig. 9.6.

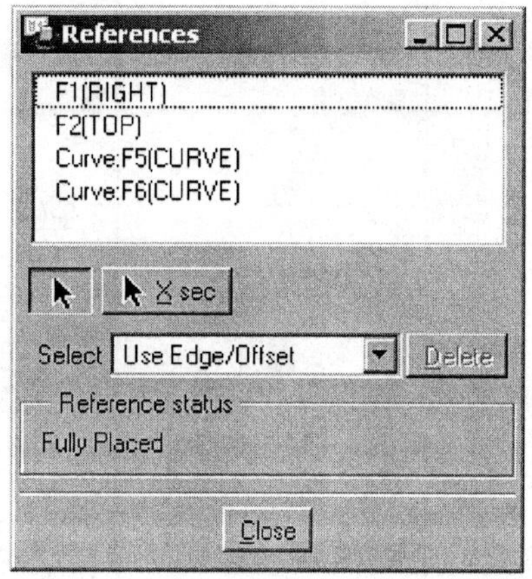

Fig. 9.7.

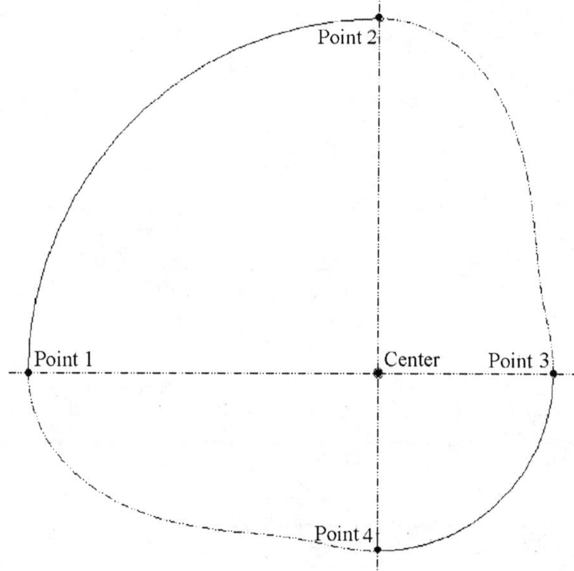

Fig. 9.8.

Goal	Step	Commands
Create datum curves for the dwell (Continued)	18. View the feature.	**VIEW → ORIENTATION → STANDARD ORIENTATION**
Create the cam	19. Start "Extrude" feature.	
	20. Set up the sketch plane.	**Placement → Define → Use Previous**
	21. Outline the cam profiles using the datum curves.	**→ Single →** ***Select the four datum curves*** **→ Close**
	22. Exit sketcher.	★ If ProE prompts the message "the section is not closed," then delete the dwell datum curves and repeat steps 13-17. Points 1, 2, 3 and 4 must be aligned with the corresponding points on the fall and rise datum curves.
	23. Define the depth.	(Depth) → **1**
	24. Accept the feature creation.	**→ VIEW → ORIENTATION → STANDARD ORIETATION** Refer Fig. 9.9.

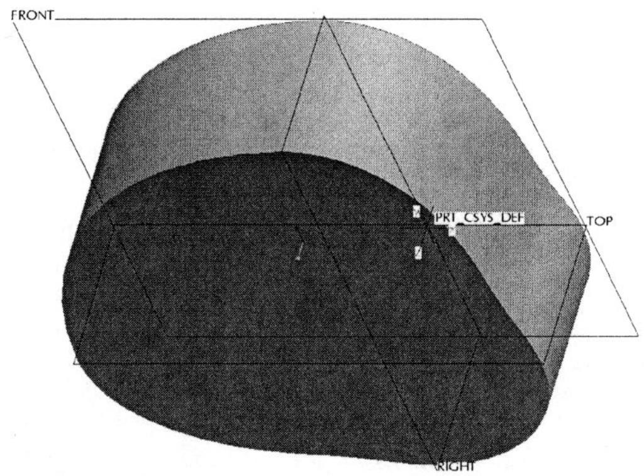

Fig. 9.9.

Goal	Step	Commands
Create a hole	25. Create a hole at the center.	 → (Diameter) **<u>0.5</u>** → (Depth) ***Thru All*** → ***Placement*** *(in dash)* → ***Select the flat surface of the cam parallel to the FRONT datum plane*** → Refer Fig. 9.10. ***Click in the secondary references window*** → ***Select the TOP and RIGHT datum planes while holding <u>CTRL</u>*** → Refer Fig. 9.11. ***Select the distance from the TOP datum plane*** → **<u>0</u>** → ***<u>ENTER</u>*** → ***Select the distance from the RIGHT datum plane*** → **<u>0</u>** → ***<u>ENTER</u>*** →  Refer Fig. 9.12.

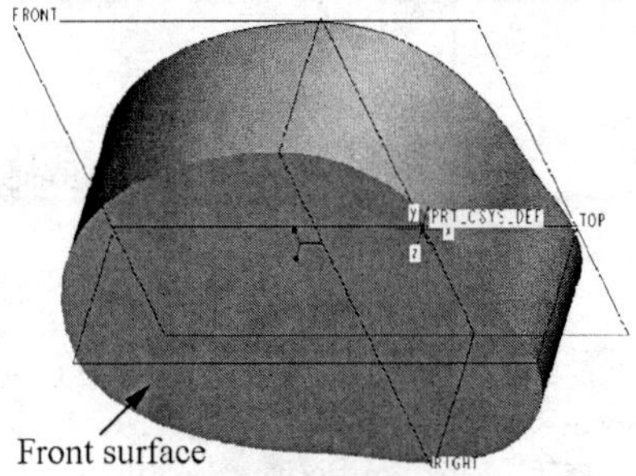

Fig. 9.10.

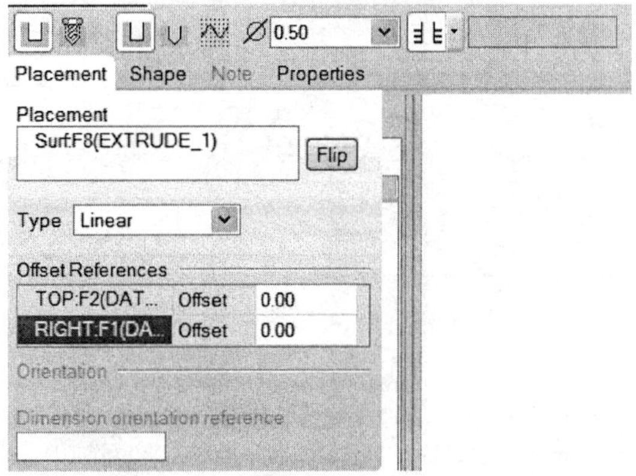

Fig. 9.11.

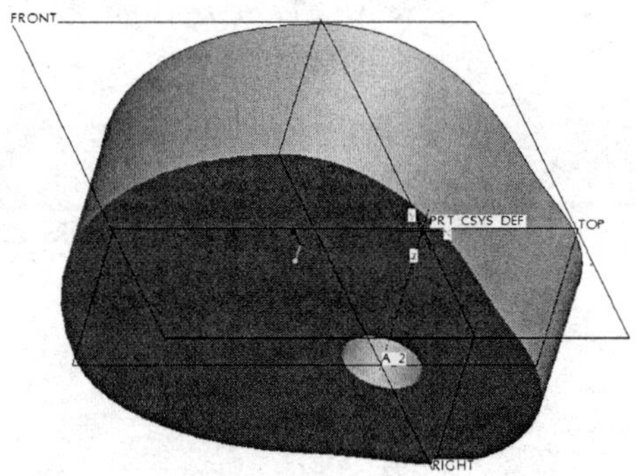

Fig. 9.12.

Goal	Step	Commands
Suppress protrusion and hole features	26. Suppress protrusion and hole features.	As there is not enough space between the hole and outer edge of the cam to place radial holes, the base radius of the cam must be increased. This involves modifying one datum curve at a time. To prevent feature failure errors, we must suppress dwell curves, protrusion and hole features. ***Select the dwell curves, extrusion and hole in the model tree → Right Mouse → Suppress →*** **OK** Refer Fig. 9.13.
Modify the datum curves	27. Redefine the rise curve.	***Select the first datum curve → Right Mouse → Edit definition →*** Refer Fig. 9.14. ***Select Equation from the CURVE window →*** **Define** **→** Refer Fig. 9.15. **Change the value of base radius (highlighted in Fig. 8.16) from 1 to 2 →** **FILE → SAVE → FILE → EXIT → OK** Refer Fig. 9.16.

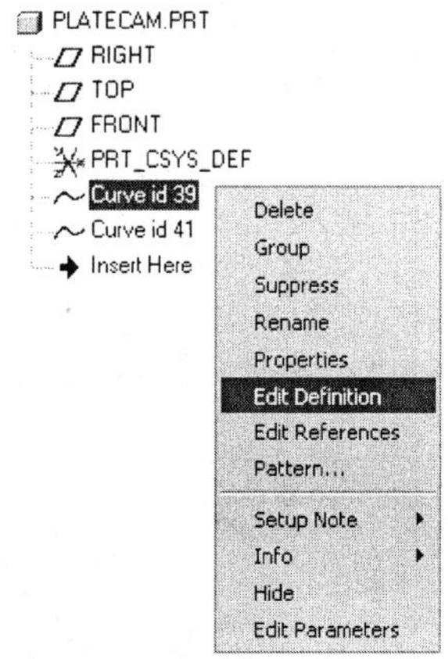

Fig. 9.14.

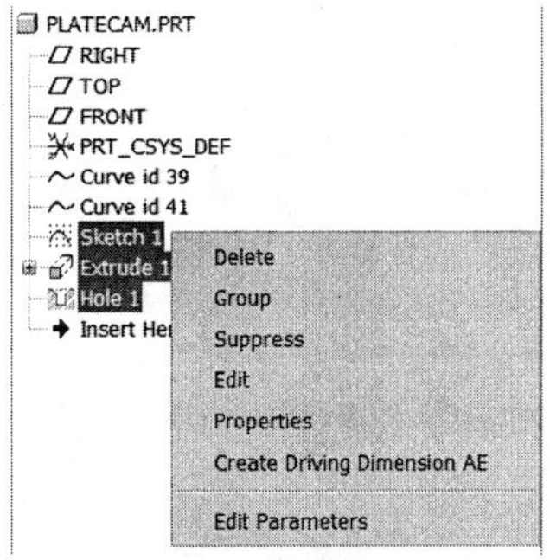

Fig. 9.13.

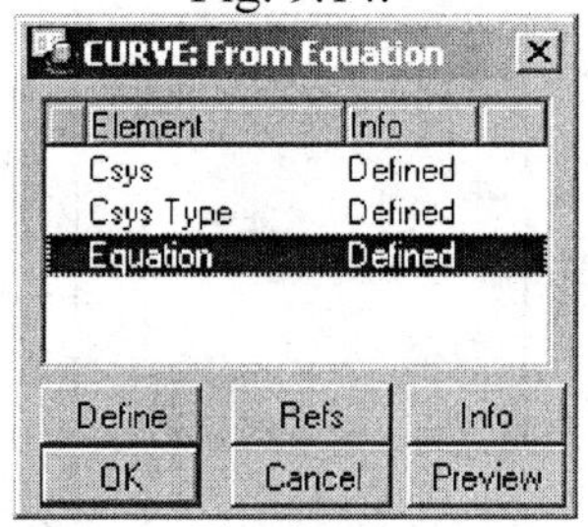

Fig. 9.15.

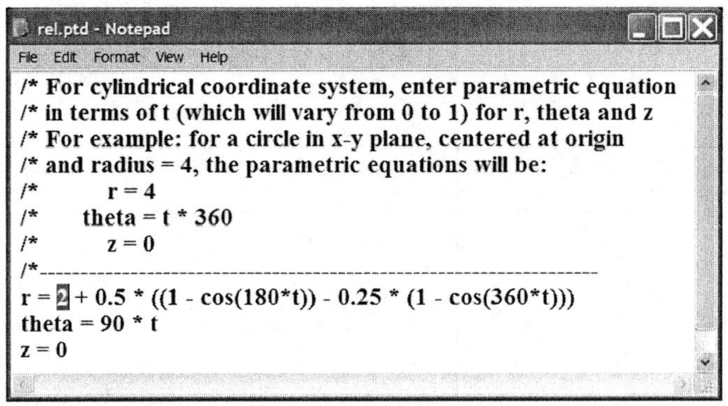

Fig.9.16.

Goal	Step	Commands
Modify the datum curves (continued)	28. Redefine the fall datum curve.	***Select the second datum curve → Right Mouse → Edit definition →*** ***Select equation from the CURVE window* → Define →** **<u>Change the value of base radius (highlighted in Fig. 9.17) from 1 to 2</u> →** **FILE → SAVE → FILE → EXIT → OK** Refer Fig. 9.17.
Resume suppressed features	29. Resume the protrusion and hole features.	**EDIT→ RESUME→ ALL** Refer Fig. 9.18.
	30. Modify the dwell datum curves.	Optional step: Dwell datum curves automatically align themselves with the first two datum curves. Otherwise, modify the radius of the datum curves to 2.
Modify the hole size	31. Change the hole diameter.	***Select the hole from the model tree → Right Mouse* → Edit → *Select the diameter* → <u>0.75</u> → *<u>ENTER</u>* → EDIT → REGENERATE**
Create a radial hole	32. Start a sketched hole.	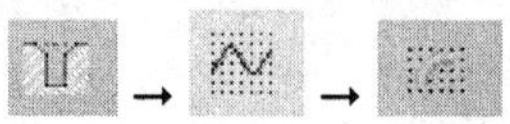 ProE opens sketcher. Refer Fig. 9.19.

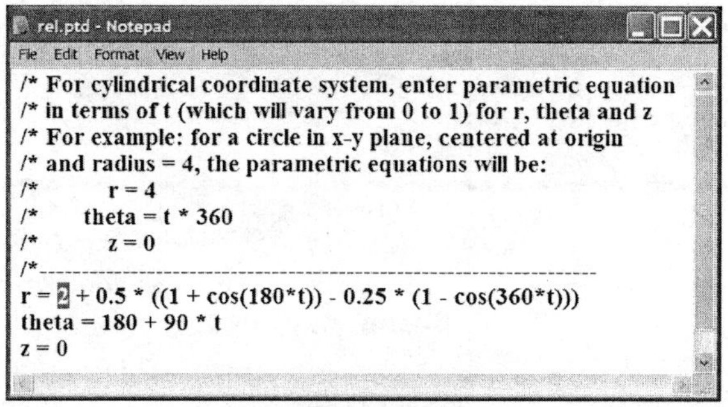

Fig. 9.17.

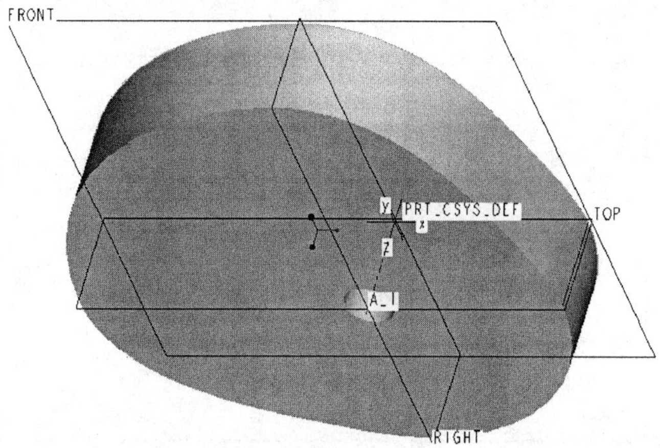

Fig. 9.18.

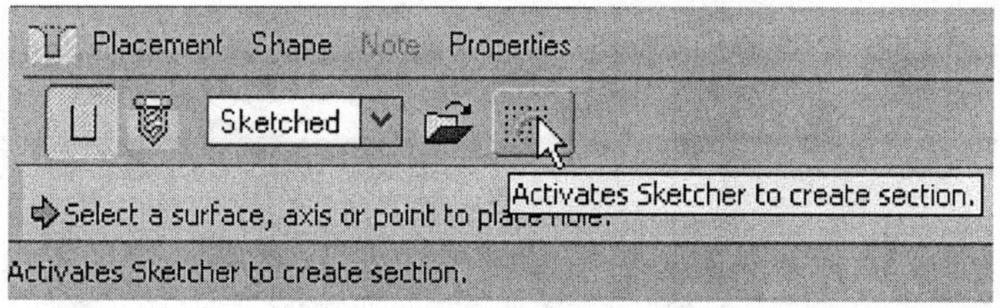

Fig. 9.19.

Goal	Step	Commands
	33. Sketch the axis of revolution.	→ → *Pick points 1 and 2*
	34. Draw the section	→ → ***Pick points 3, 4, 5, 6, 7, 8 and 3*** **→** ***Middle Mouse*** **(to discontinue line creation)** Refer Fig. 9.20.
Create a radial hole (continued)	35. Dimension the section.	→ ***Select line 1*** → ***Select the centerline*** (★ SELECT THE CENTERLINE AT POINT 1) → ***Select line 1*** (again) → ***Middle Mouse to place the diameter dimension*** → ***Select line 2*** → ***Select the centerline*** → ***Select line 2*** (again) → ***Middle Mouse to place the diameter dimension*** Refer Fig. 9.20.
	36. Add dimensions.	Optional step: If necessary add dimensions.
	37. Modify dimensions.	→ ***Double click each dimension and enter the corresponding value*** Refer Fig. 9.20.
	38. Exit sketcher.	

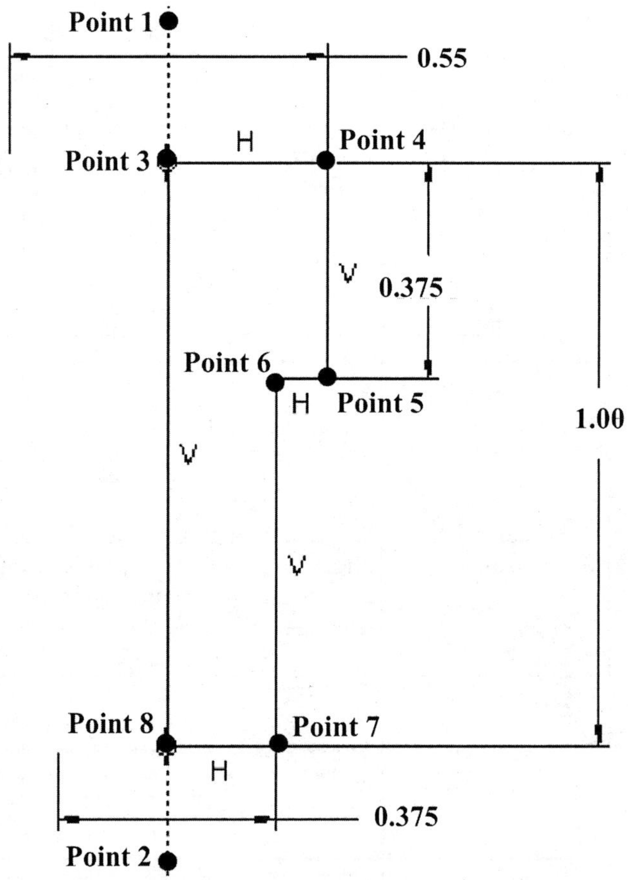

Fig. 9.20.

Pro|ENGINEER automatically aligns the top edge of the sketched hole with the placement plane and the axis of the hole with the placement point.

Goal	Step	Commands
Create a radial hole (continued)	39. Specify the hole placement.	Placement → *Select the front surface of the cam*→ (Reference Type) *Radial* → **Refer Fig. 9.21.** (Secondary References) → *Select the axis of the central hole and the TOP datum plane while holding* ***CTRL*** → *Select the distance from the axis* → 1 → ***ENTER*** → *Select the angle from the TOP datum plane* → 45→ ***ENTER*** → **Refer Figs. 9.21 and 9.22.**

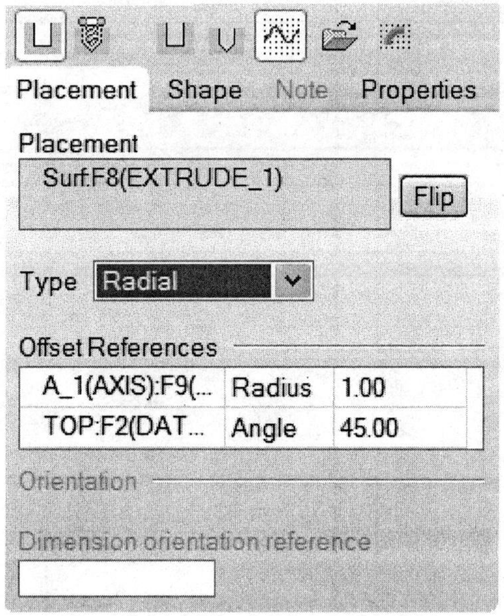

Fig. 9.21.

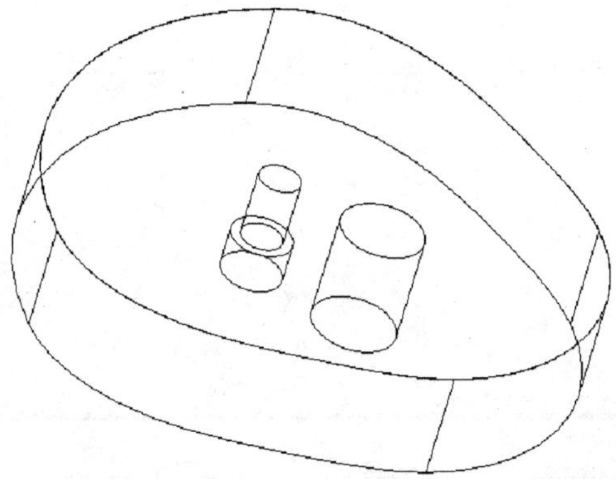
Fig. 9.22.

Goal	Step	Commands
Pattern the radial hole	40. Start pattern command.	***Select the last hole*** **→**
	41. Specify the pattern parameters.	***Select the 45° angle*** **→** **<u>90</u>** **→** ***<u>ENTER</u>*** **→** Refer Fig. 9.23. **<u>4</u>** **→** Refer Figs. 9.24 and 9.25.
Save and exit ProE	42. Save the file and exit ProE.	**FILE → SAVE → <u>PLATECAM.PRT</u> → OK → FILE → EXIT → Yes**

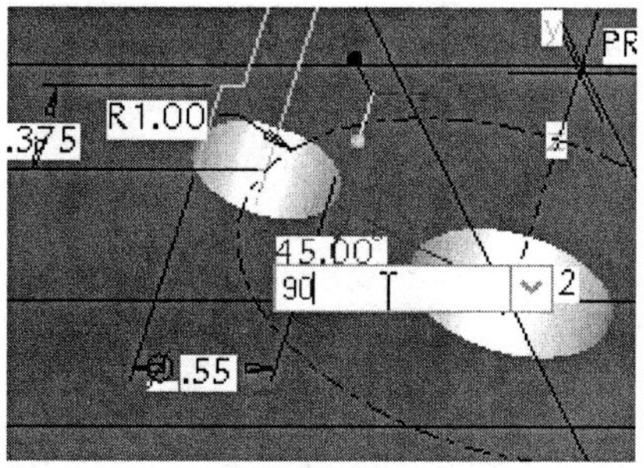

Fig. 9.23.

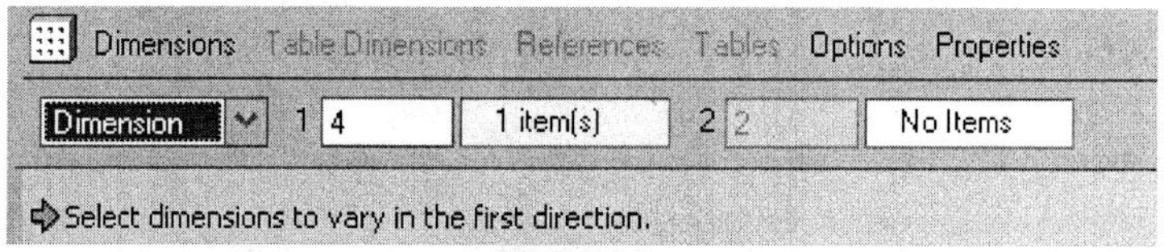

Fig. 9.24.

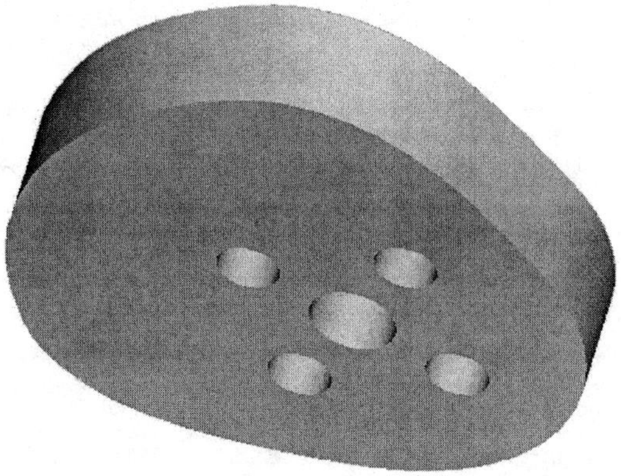

Fig. 9.25.

Exercise

Problem 1

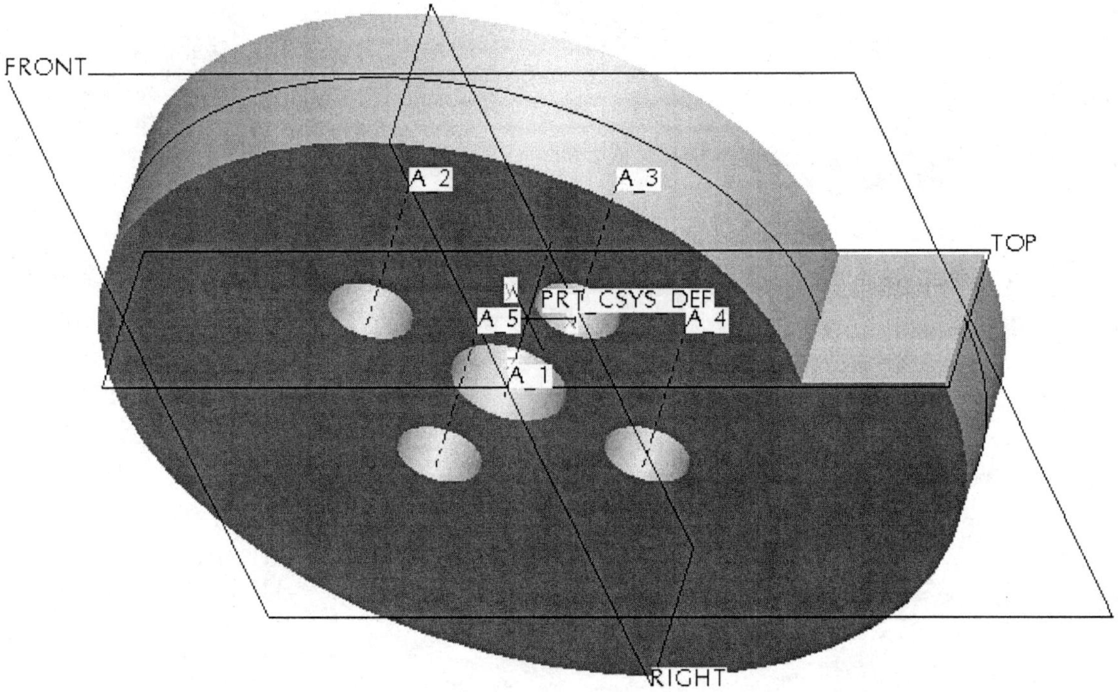

Hints:

1. Equation for the datum curve:
   r = 2 + sin(90 *t)
   theta = 360 * t
   z = 0
2. The hole pattern is identical to the cam in the lesson.

Open ended design

Create the satellite dish (parabolic* shape).

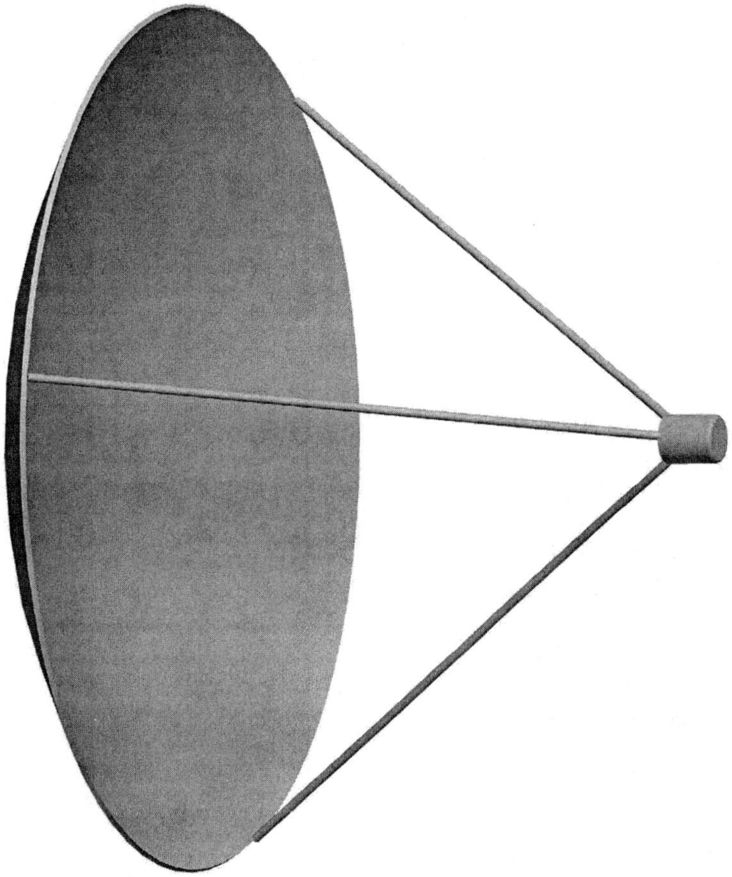

Hints:

1. Create a parabolic datum curve. You need the equation for the parabola in the parametric form.

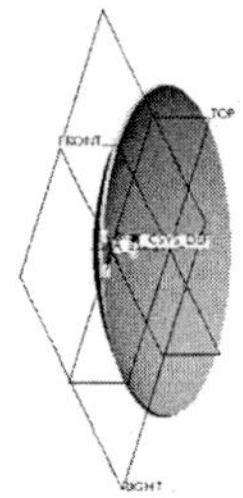

2. Use revolve – thicken – use edge to create the parabolic dish.
3. Create a support using revolve feature.

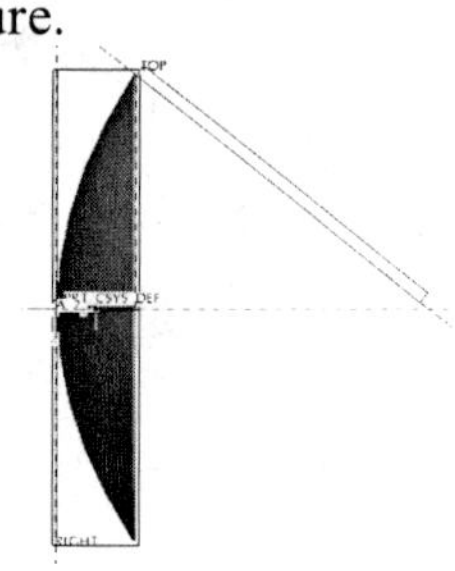

4. Pattern the support rod around the axis.

*Parabolic reflectors are also used for a variety of applications such as headlights and heat reflectors.

Lesson 10
Housing

Learning Objectives

- Practice ***Extrude*** and ***Hole*** features.
- Learn ***Shell*** feature.
- Learn to create ***General***, ***Sectional***, and ***Detailed Views***.
- Practice ***Show/Erase*** and ***Pattern*** tools.

Shell

The Shell feature removes or hollows out the inside of a solid object from the specified surfaces, leaving a shell of a specified wall thickness. Note that if no surfaces are specified, it shells out inside of the object creating a hollow solid or "closed" shell. The non-default thickness collector lets you specify the surfaces where you want to assign a different thickness. The exclude surface collector specifies the surfaces that have to be excluded from the shell.

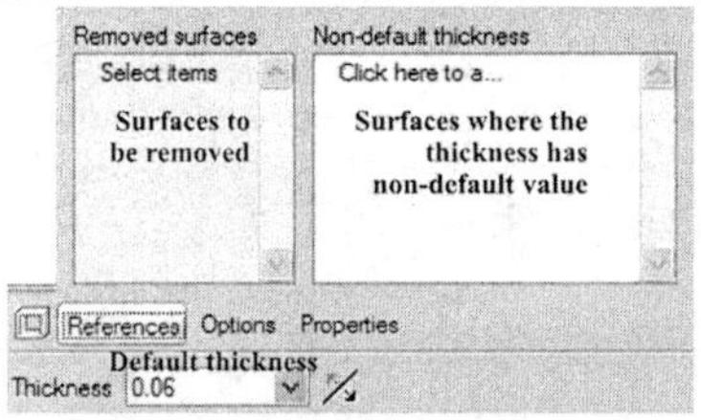

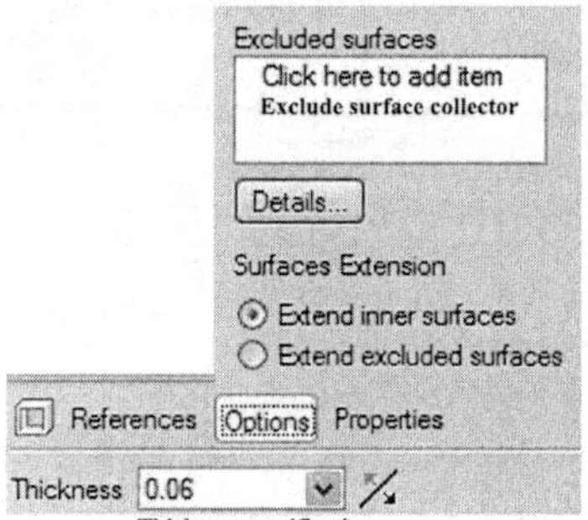

Thickness specification

Background Information:

In this lesson, we will create the housing for the cam assembly. We will then attempt to create an engineering drawing. To this end, we will start with defining the front and top views. Then, we will search for a proper sectional side view that shows maximum details in one view. During this quest, we will explore and learn full-, half- and offset-sectional views. We will add a detailed view to enlarge small details. The lesson ends with a detailed discussion on how to create other types of views.

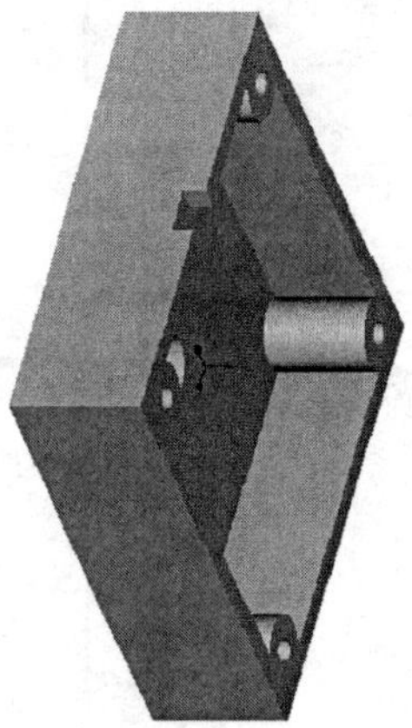

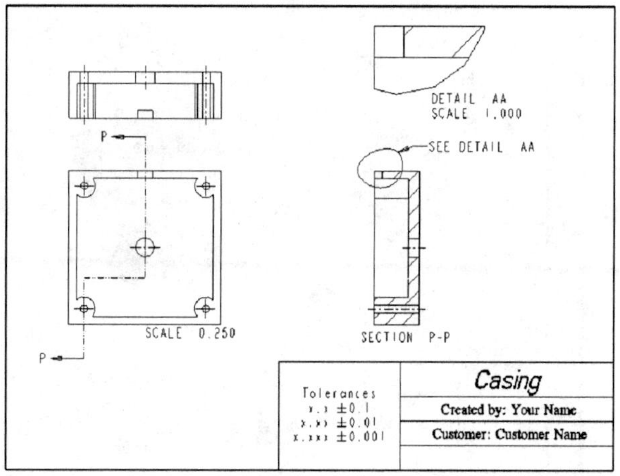

SEQUENCE OF STEPS

STEP I: Create the housing part

1. Create the base feature

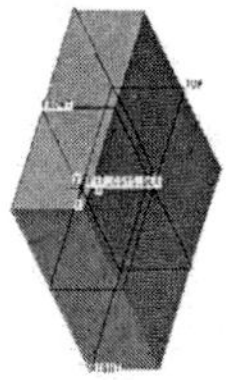

2. Create the bolt holes

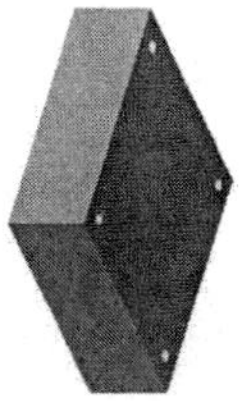

3. Shell the inside surface

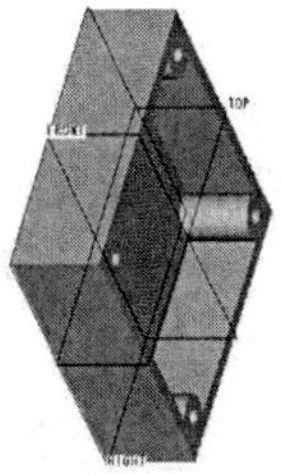

4. Create a cut

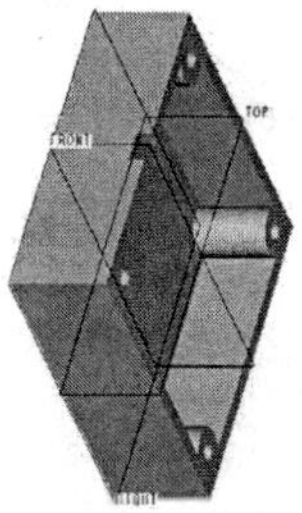

5. Create a central hole

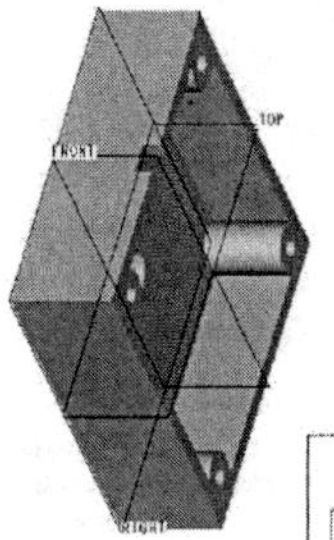

6. Create an offset section

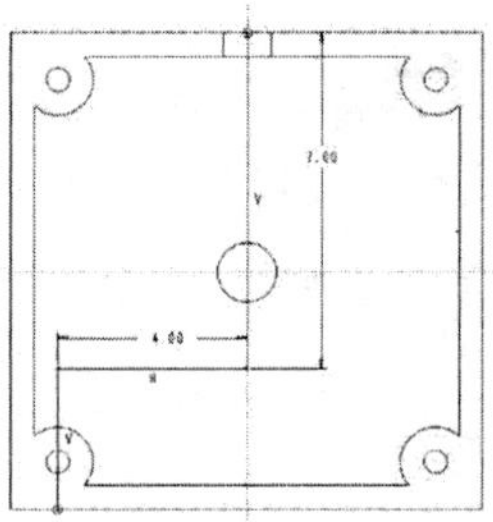

STEP II: Create a drawing for the housing part

1. Add the front view

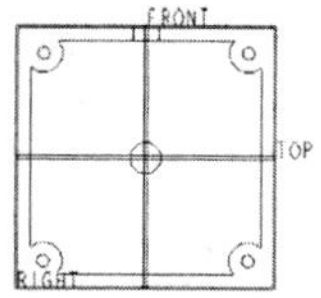

2. Add the top view

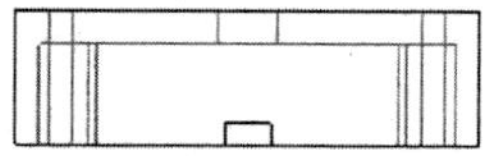

3. Add the full sectional view

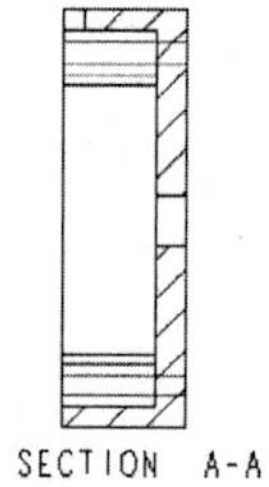

4. Add the half-sectional view

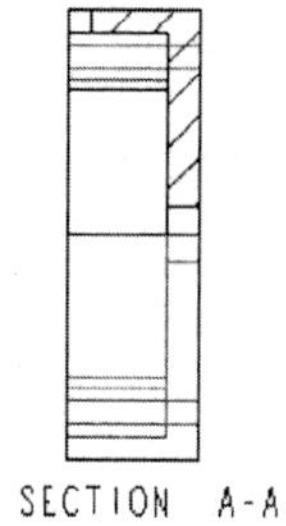

5. Add the offset sectional view

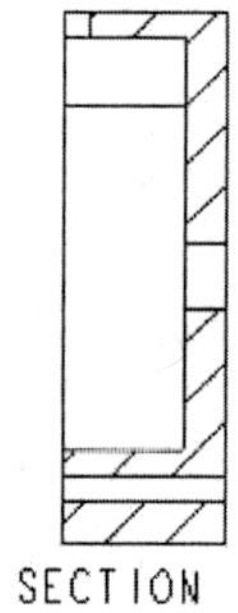

6. Add the detailed view

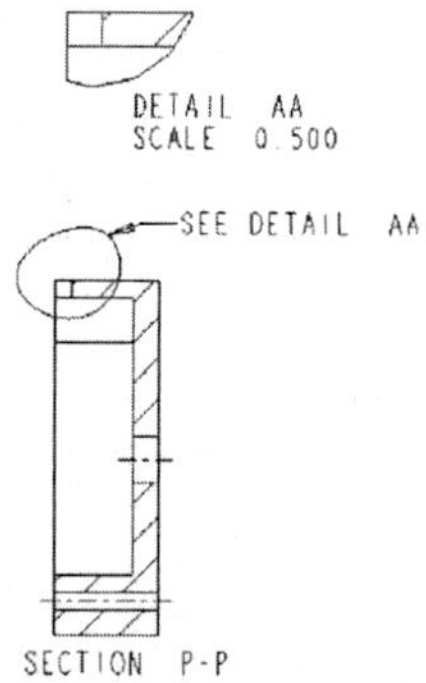

Goal	Step	Commands
Open a new file for the housing part	1. Set up the working directory.	**FILE → SET WORKING DIRECTORY →** ***Select the working directory*** **→ OK**
	2. Open a new file for the housing part	**FILE → NEW →** ***Part*** **→** ***Solid*** **→ housing → OK**
Create the base feature	3. Start "Extrude" feature.	
	4. Define the sketch plane.	**Placement → DEFINE →** ***Select the RIGHT datum plane*** **→ Sketch**
	5. Sketch the section.	**→** ***Select points 1 and 2*** Refer Fig. 10.1.
	6. Modify the dimensions.	**→** ***Double click each dimension and enter the corresponding value*** Refer Fig. 10.1.
	7. Add relations to center the section.	**TOOLS → RELATIONS → Type the relations shown in Fig. 10.2.**
	8. Sort relations	**UTILITIES → REORDER RELATIONS → OK → OK**
	9. Exit sketcher.	✓
	10. Define the depth.	(Depth) 3 → ***ENTER***
	11. Accept the feature creation.	**→ → DEFAULT ORIENTATION** Refer Fig. 10.3.

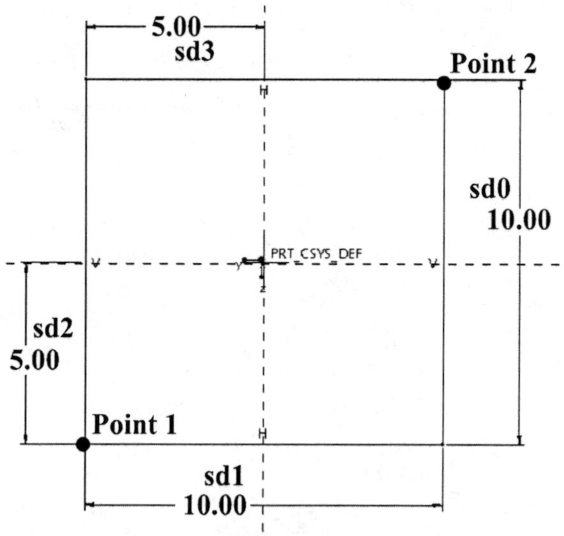

Fig. 10.1.

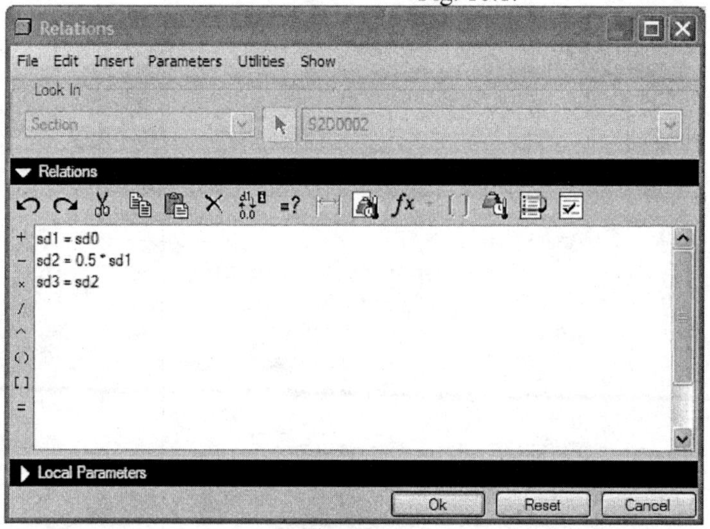

Fig. 10.2.

Note that sd#s may be slightly different in your model. The "reorder" command sorts the relations in the order of precedence.

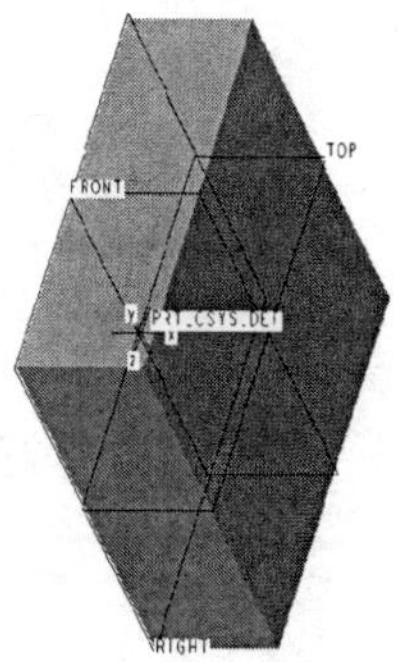

Fig. 10.3.

Goal	Step	Commands
Create the bolt holes	12. Create a corner hole.	→ (Diameter) **<u>0.5</u>** → (Depth) ***Thru All → Placement → Select the surface parallel to the RIGHT datum → Click in the secondary references window → Select the top and front surfaces of the base feature while holding <u>CTRL</u> →*** Refer Fig. 10.4. ***Select the distance from the top surface → <u>1</u> → <u>ENTER</u> → Select the distance from the front surface → <u>1</u> → <u>ENTER</u> →*** Refer Figs. 10.4 and 10.5.
	13. Pattern the hole.	***Select the hole from the model tree →*** → **Dimensions** → ***Click in the direction 1 window → Select the horizontal dimension (1.0) → <u>8</u> → <u>ENTER</u> → Click in the direction 2 window → Select the vertical dimension (1.0) → <u>8</u> → <u>ENTER</u> →*** Refer Figs. 10.6 and 10.7.

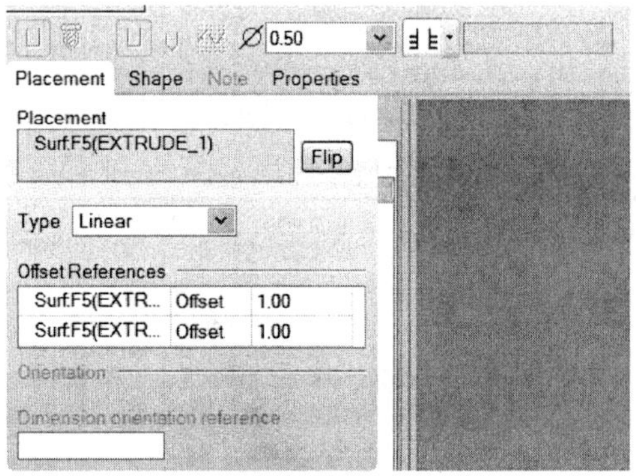

Fig. 10.4.

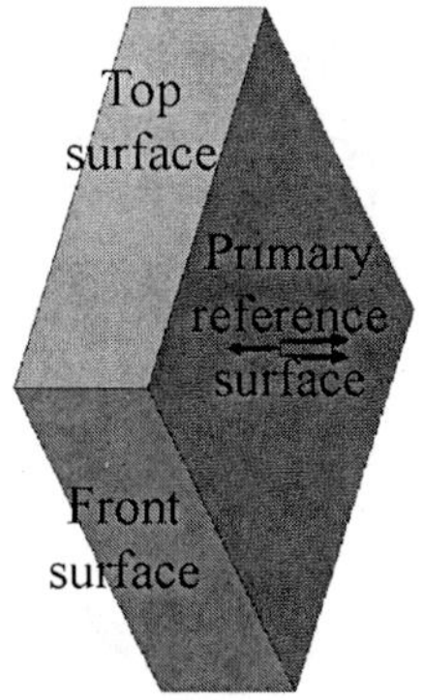

Fig. 10.5.

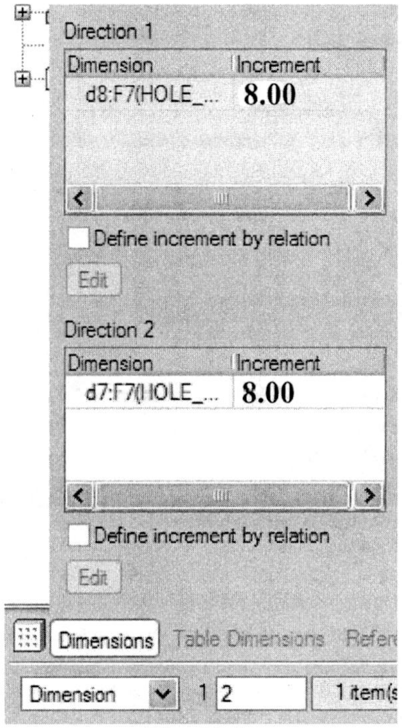

Fig. 10.6.

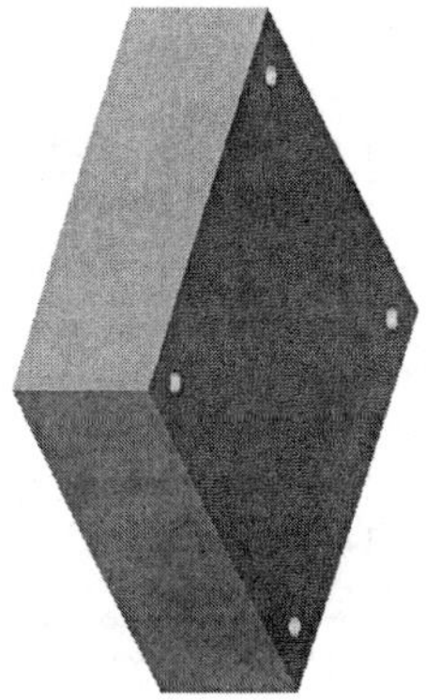
Fig. 10.7.

Goal	Step	Commands
Remove the inside material	14. Apply shell command.	→ (Thickness) **0.5** → **References** → ***Click in the removed surfaces window → Select surface 1(Refer Fig. 10.7.) → Click in the non-default thickness window → Select surface 2 (Surface that is lying on the RIGHT datum plane)*** → **0.75** → Refer Figs. 10.8 and 10.9.
Create a cut	15. Start "Extrude - Cut" feature.	→
	16. Select the sketching plane.	**Placement** → **DEFINE** → ***Select surface 3*** → **Sketch** Refer Fig. 10.10.
	17. Add a new reference.	**SKETCH → REFERENCES** ***Select the right edge of the protrusion*** → **CLOSE**
	18. Sketch the section.	→ ***Select points 1 and 2*** Refer Fig. 10.11.
	19. Modify the dimensions.	→ ***Double click each the dimension and enter the corresponding value*** Refer Fig. 10.11.
	20. Add relations.	**TOOLS → RELATIONS → sd4 = 0.5*sd3 → OK** sd4 refers to 0.5 and sd3 refers to 1.00 dimension.

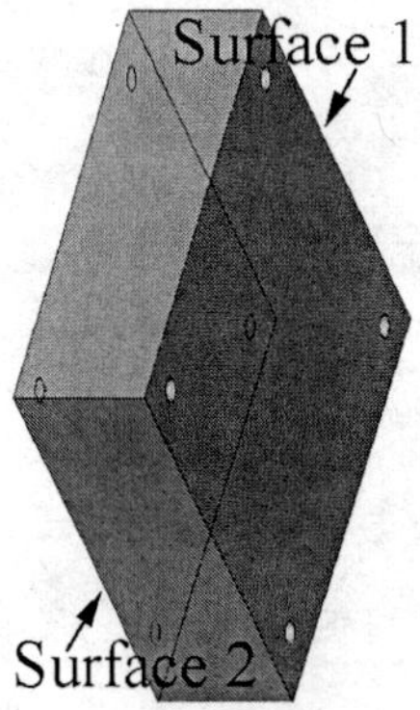

Fig. 10.8.

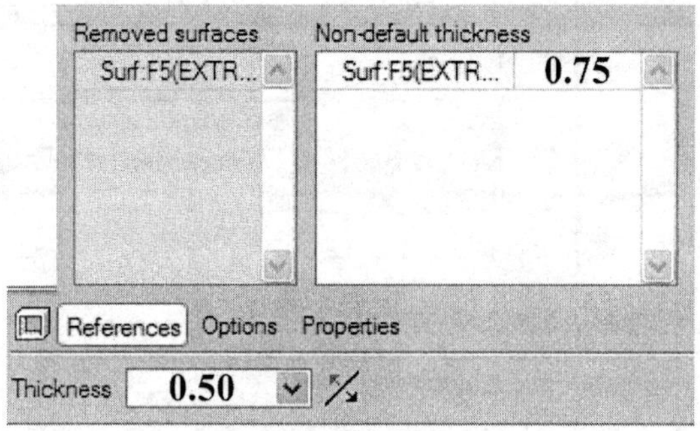

Fig. 10.9.

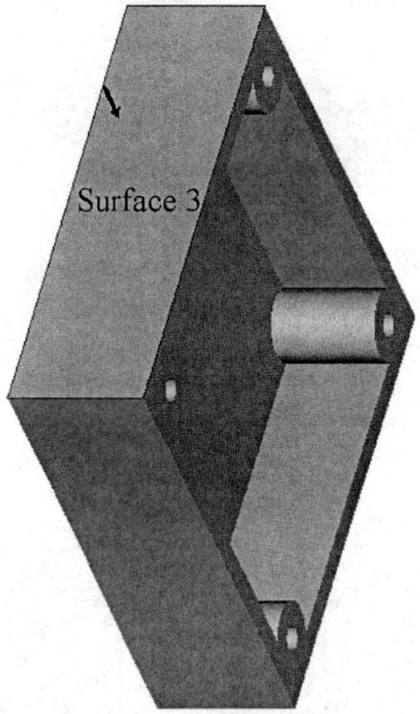

Fig. 10.10.

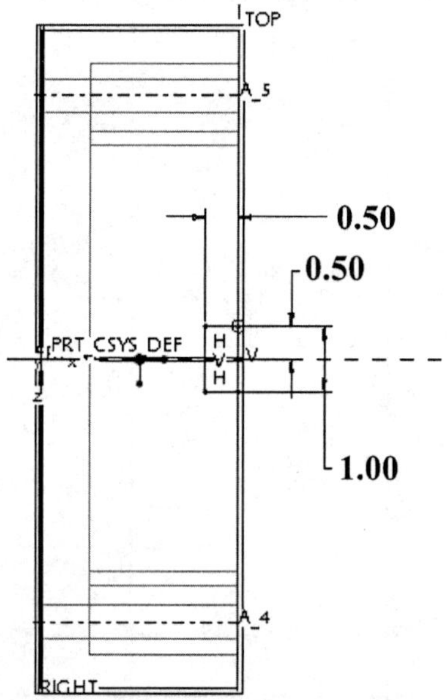

Fig. 10.11.

Goal	Step	Commands
Create a cut (continued)	21. Exit sketcher.	✔
	22. Define the depth.	(Depth) Thru next
	23. Accept the feature creation.	✔ → → **DEFAULT ORIENTATION** Refer Fig. 10.12.
Create a central hole	24. Create a central hole.	→ **(Diameter) <u>1.25</u> → (Depth)** ***Thru All → Placement (in dash) → Select surface 1 (Refer Fig. 10.13) → Click in the secondary references window → Select the TOP and FRONT datum planes by holding the <u>CTRL</u> key → Select the distance from the TOP datum plane → <u>0</u> → <u>ENTER</u> → Select the distance from the FRONT datum plane → <u>0</u> → <u>ENTER</u> →*** ✔ Refer Figs. 10.14 and 10.15.
Create an offset section	25. Create an offset section.	**VIEW → VIEW MANAGER →** ***Click on Xsec tab →*** **New → (Name)** ***<u>P</u> → <u>ENTER</u>*** **→ Offset → Both Sides → Single → Done**

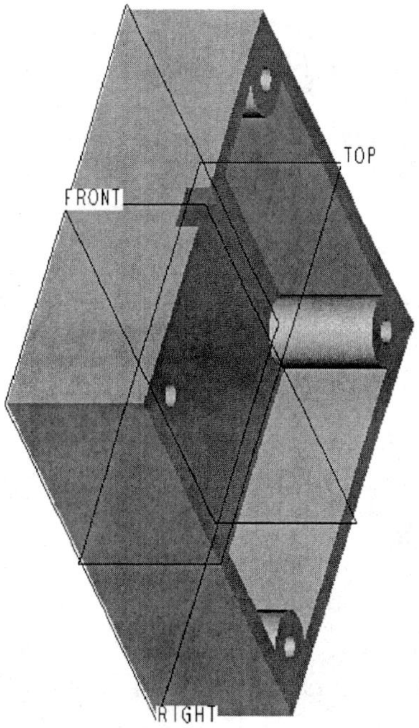

Fig. 10.12.

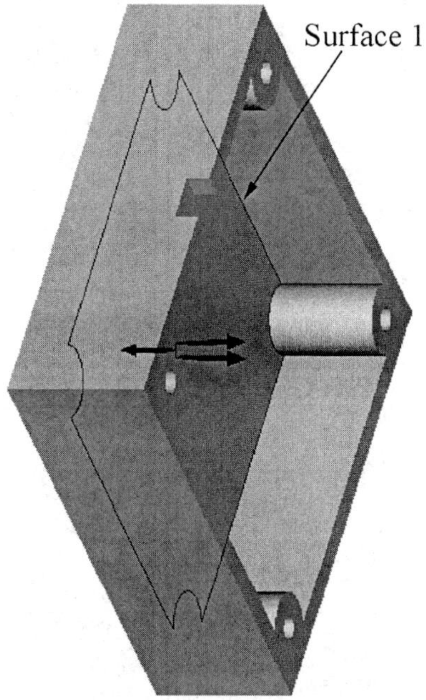

Fig. 10.12.

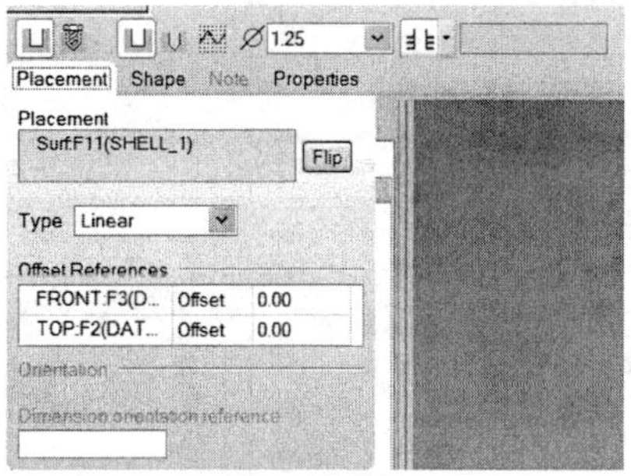

Fig. 10.13.

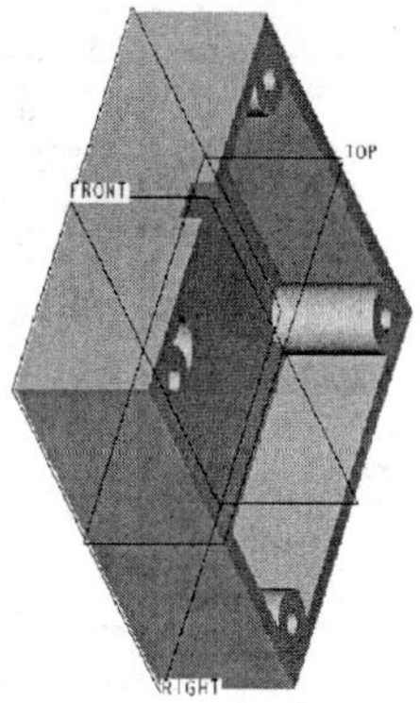

Fig. 10.14.

Goal	Step	Commands
	26. Set up and orient the sketch plane.	**Setup New** → **Plane** → ***Select the RIGHT datum plane*** → **Okay** → **Default**
	27. Add references.	**SKETCH** → **REFERENCES** → ***Select the right and left edges*** → **CLOSE** Refer Fig. 10.15.
Create an offset section (continued)	28. Sketch the cutting plane.	[line icon] → **Select points 1, 2, 3, and 4** → ***Middle Mouse*** Refer Fig. 10.15.
	29. Modify the dimensions.	[select icon] → ***Double click each dimension and enter the corresponding value*** Refer Fig. 10.15.
	30. Exit sketcher.	[✓] → **CLOSE**
Save the part	31. Save the part.	**FILE** → **SAVE** → **HOUSING.PRT** → **OK**
Open a drawing file for the housing part	32. Open a new drawing file with the format created in the shaft drawing chapter.	**FILE** → **NEW** → **DRAWING** → **HOUSING** → **OK** → **(Default Model)** ***housing.prt*** → ***Empty with format*** → ***Format_A.frm*** → **OK**

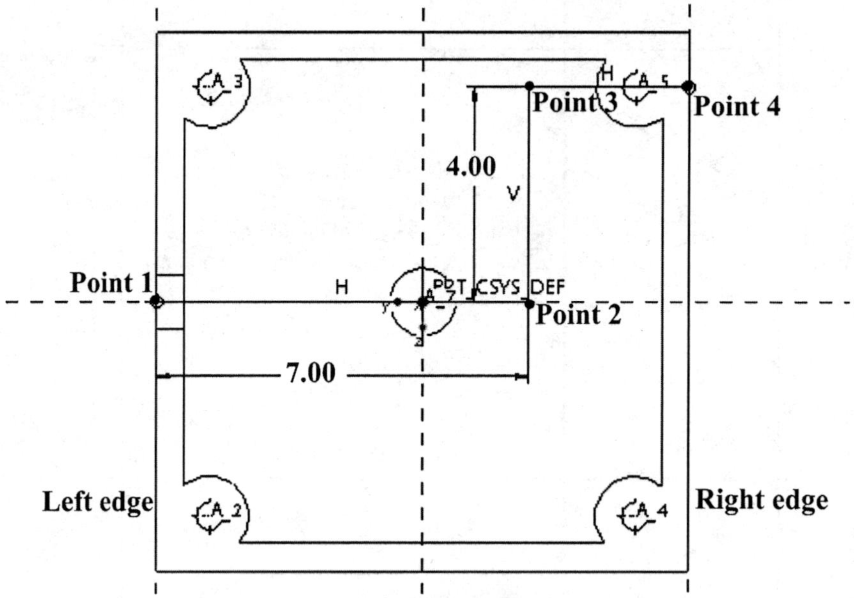

Fig. 10.15.

Goal	Step	Commands
Create the front view	33. Start creating the front view.	→ ***Click in the lower left quadrant*** → **(View Name)** **<u>Front view</u>** → **(Model view names) RIGHT** → **APPLY** Refer Figs. 10.16 and 10.17.
Create the front view (continued)	34. Setup the scale and display type.	***Select scale under categories*** → ***Check custom scale*** → **<u>0.25</u>** → **APPLY** → ***Select view display under categories*** → ***View display*** → ***(Display style) Hidden*** → **OK** Refer Fig. 10.17.
Create the top view	35. Create the top view.	**INSERT** → **DRAWING VIEW** → **PROJECTION** → ***Click in the top left quadrant*** → ***Double click on the view*** → ***View display*** → ***(Display style) Hidden*** → **OK** Refer Fig. 10.18.

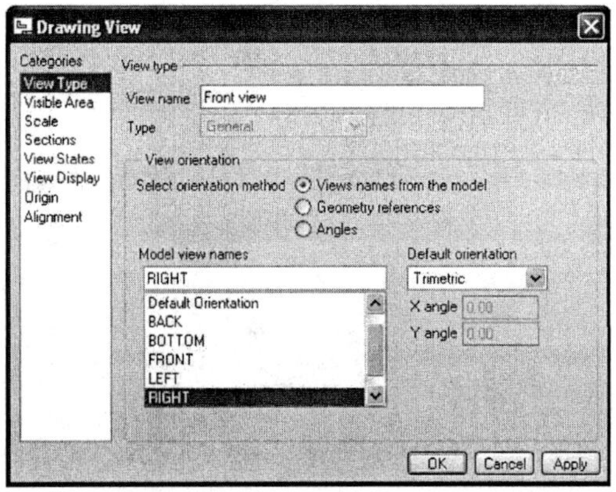

Fig. 10.16.

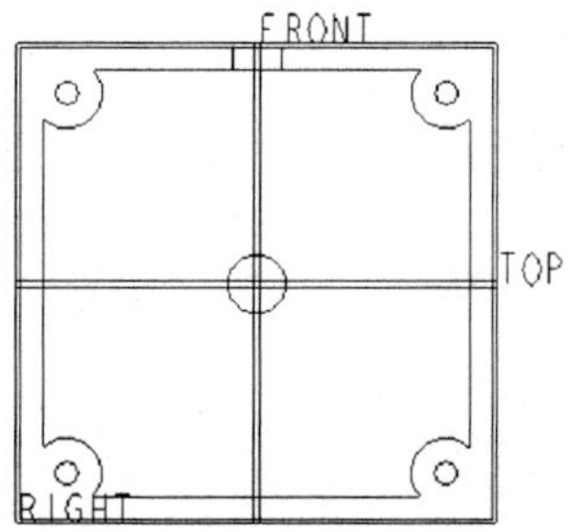

Fig. 10.17.

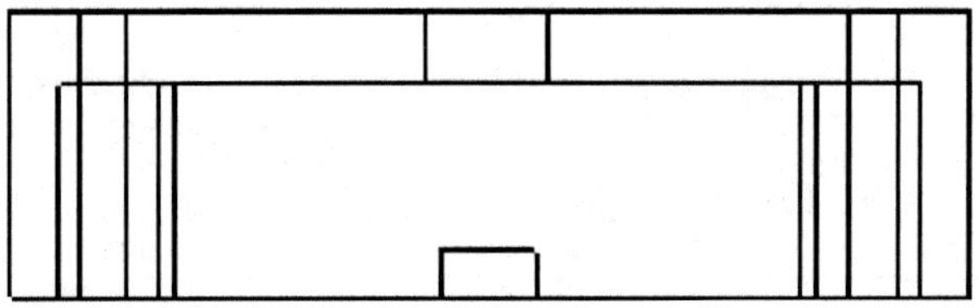
Fig. 10.18.

Goal	Step	Commands
Create the right section view	36. Create the right section view.	***Select the front view* → INSERT → DRAWING VIEW → PROJECTION → *Click in the bottom right quadrant* (Side view position) → *Double click the view* → *Select sections under categories* → *2D cross-section* → → Create New →** Refer Fig. 10.19. **Planar → Single → Done → AA→ → Plane → *Select the FRONT datum plane in the front view* (Fig. 10.17) → OK** Refer Fig. 10.20.
	37. Change the display type.	***Double click on the view* → *View display* → *(Display style) Hidden* → OK**

ProE associates the sections with the part file. Therefore, the sections can be created, deleted, viewed, modified or erased in the part mode. "X-section" command in the part mode provides the access to the sections.

The full sectional view in this particular example is not efficient as the top half is identical to the bottom half. On the other hand, a half sectional view can provide both internal and external details.

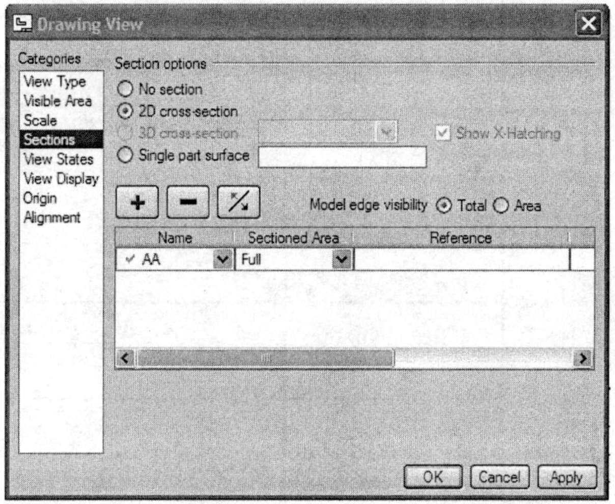

Fig. 10.19.

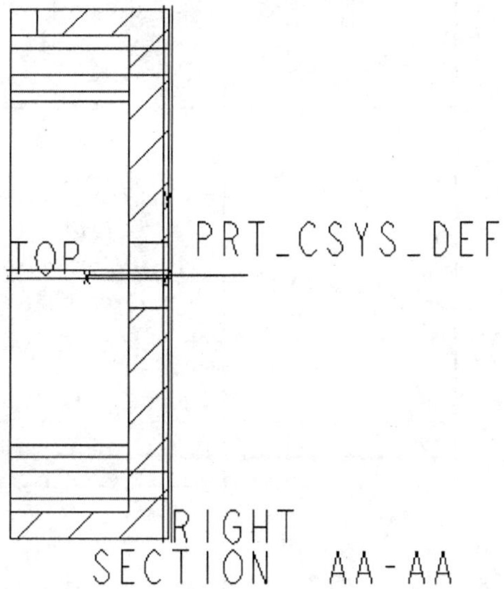

Fig. 10.20.

Goal	Step	Commands
Create the right section view (continued)	38. Change the view to a half-section view.	***Double click the view → Select sections under categories → Half → Select the TOP datum plane in the front view →*** **OK** Refer Figs. 10.21 and 10.22.
	39. Insert another drawing sheet.	**INSERT → SHEET**
	40. Start creating the front view.	→ ***Click in the lower left quadrant of the drawing →*** **(View Name) Front view → (Model view names) RIGHT → APPLY**
	41. Setup scale and display type.	***Select scale under categories → Check custom scale →*** **0.25** ***→*** **APPLY** ***→ Select view display under categories → View display → (Display style) Hidden →*** **OK** Refer Fig. 10.23.
	42. Turn off the datum planes, axes, points and coordinate system.	**Click on the following icons**

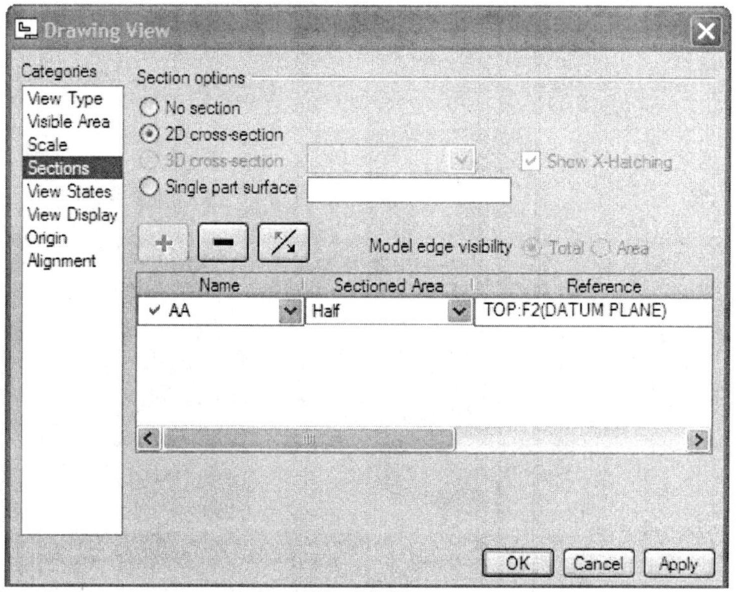

Fig. 10.21.

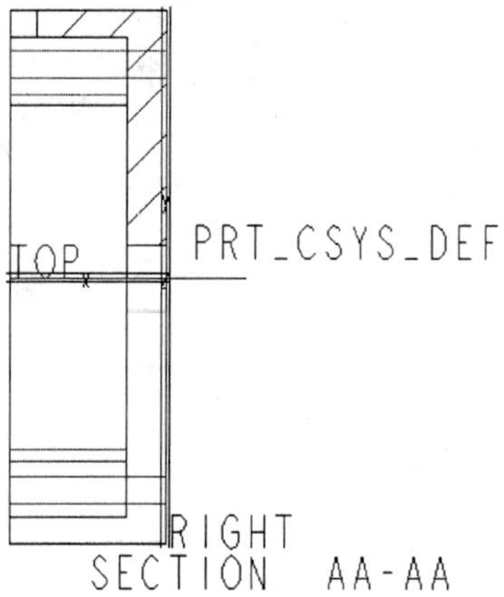

Fig. 10.22.

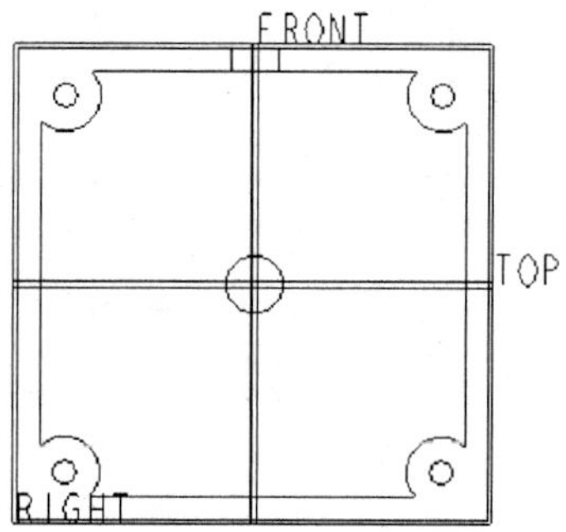

Fig. 10.23.

Goal	Step	Commands
Create the right section view (continued)	43. Create an offset section.	**INSERT → DRAWING VIEW → PROJECTION →** ***Click in the bottom right quadrant*** **(Side view position) →** ***Double click on the view → Select view display under categories → View display → (Display style) No hidden →*** **APPLY →** ***Select sections under categories →***  **→ (Name) P → (Sectioned area) Full → OK →** ***Select the offset section view → Right Mouse → Add Arrows → Select the front view*** Refer Figs. 10.24, 10.25, and 10.26.

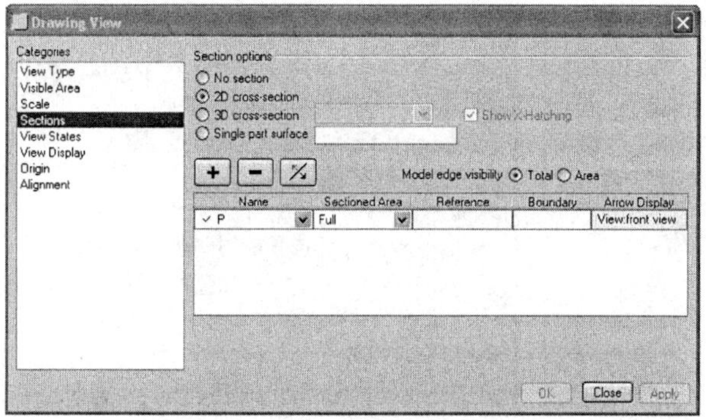

Fig. 10.24.

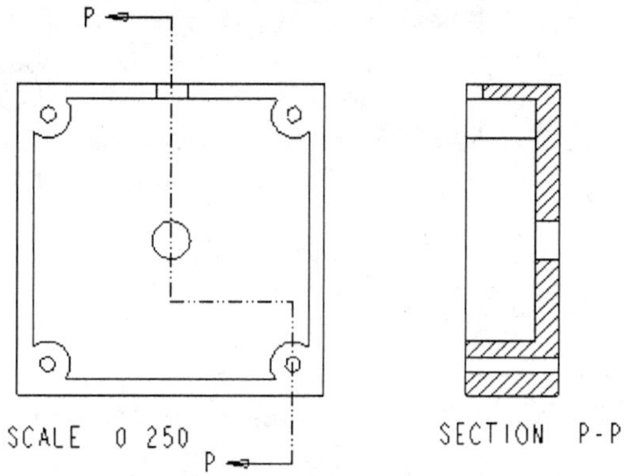

Fig. 10.25.

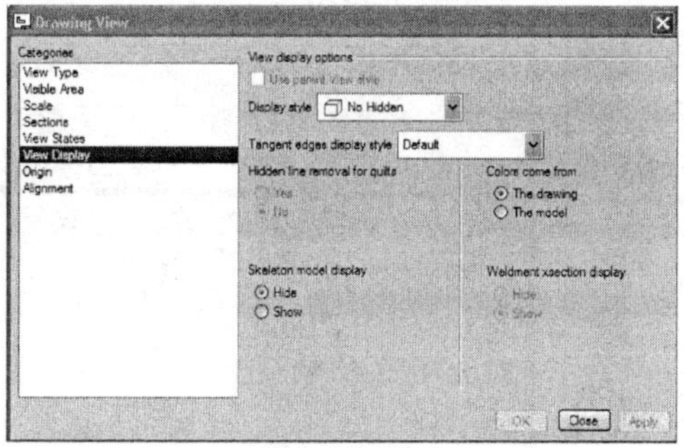

Fig. 10.26.

Goal	Step	Commands
Create the right section view (continued)	44. Show centerlines.	**VIEW → SHOW AND ERASE →** **Show** → ----A_1 → **Show All** → **YES** → **Accept All** → **CLOSE** → ***Select unnecessary axes* → *Right Mouse* → *Erase* → VIEW → REPAINT** Refer Fig. 10.28.
Create a detailed view	45. Create a detailed view to increase the visibility of the notch.	**INSERT → DRAWING VIEW → DETAILED VIEW → *Select point 1 (Refer Fig. 10.29.)* → *Sketch a spline (Middle Mouse to discontinue the spline creation)* → *Select the top right quadrant*** Refer Figs. 10.29 and 10.30.
Modify scale	46. Modify the scale.	***Double click the detailed view* → Scale → *Check custom scale* → <u>1</u> → OK** Refer Fig. 10.30.
Save the file and exit ProE	47. Save the file and exit ProE.	**FILE → SAVE → HOUSING.DRW → OK → FILE → EXIT → Yes**

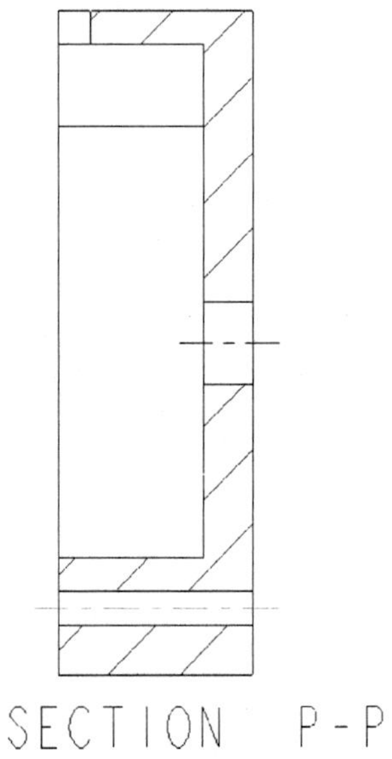

Fig. 10.28.

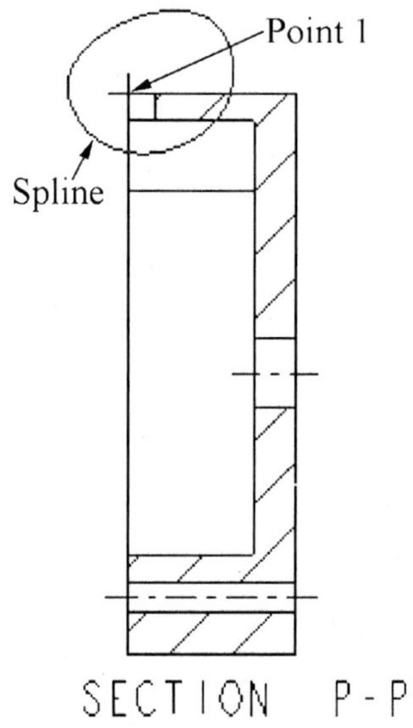

Fig. 10.29.

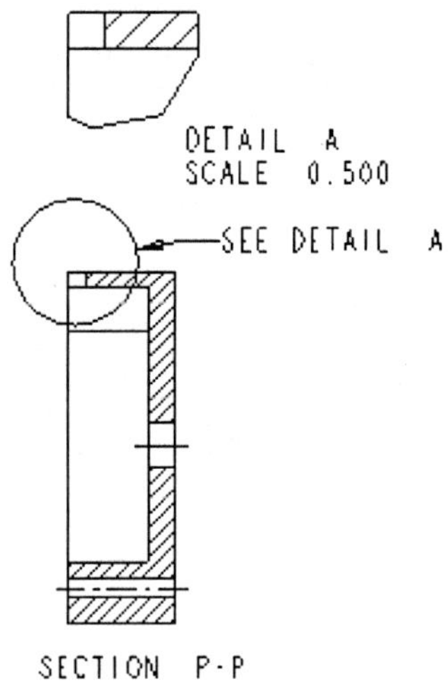

Fig. 10.30.

Exercise

Problem 1. Auxiliary View for C-channel
Auxiliary views are used to show the true geometry and dimensions of a geometric entity that is not parallel to any of the principle planes (Front, Top and Side). For instance, if we need to show the true geometry of the C-channel at the incline, we need to add an auxiliary view.

Create a part which may require an auxiliary view and then, create drawing.

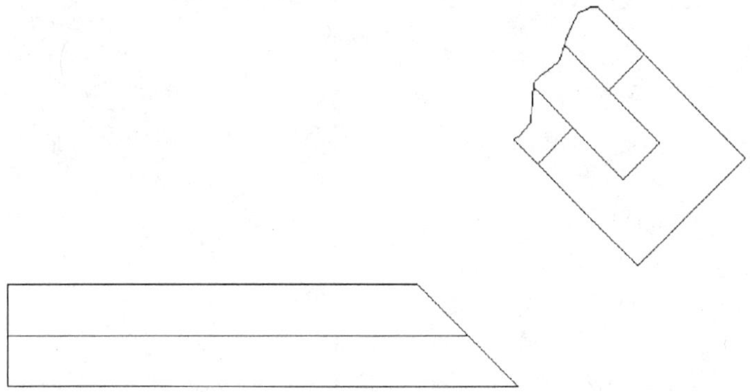

Example of an auxiliary view.

Hints:

1. Add an auxiliary view:
   INSERT → DRAWING VIEW → AUXILARY
2. *Select an edge or an axis through, edge of or datum plane from which to project the view → Select the center point for the auxiliary view*
3. Setup properties. Add dimensions.

Problem 2. Broken View

When the aspect ratio (overall length to section width) of a part is very large, the broken view is the most effective drawing technique. For instance, only parts of the long channel can be shown without sacrificing any design details.

Create a part which may require a broken view and then, create drawing.

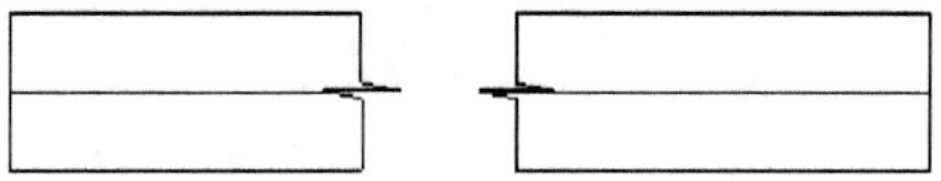

Example of a broken view.

Hints:

1. Add a broken view:
   → *Click the point of view insertion* → *Set view type* → *Select visible area* → (View visibilities) *select Broken View*
   →
   Sketch two points to define the broken view → APPLY

2. Add dimensions.

Problem 3. Revolved Section

Revolved sections are used to show the cross section of bar or beam.

Create a part which may require a revolved view and then, create drawing.

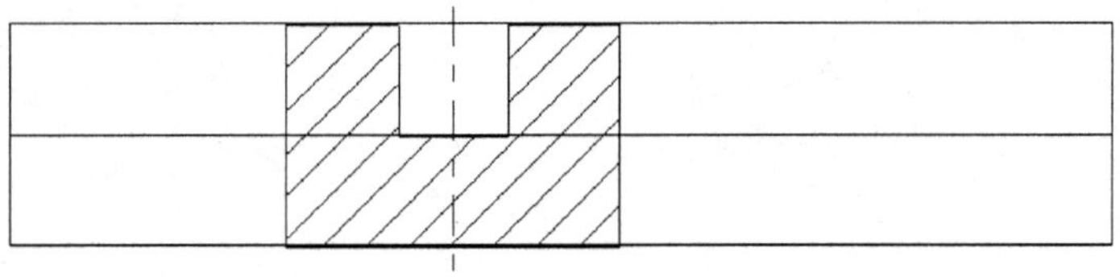

Example of a revolved view.

Hints:

1. Add an revolved view:
   INSERT → DRAWING VIEW → Revolved
2. *Select the parent view for the revolved view* → *Select the center point of the drawing view* → Define the properties if necessary → APPLY
3. Add dimensions.

NOTES:

LESSON 11
CAM ASSEMBLY

Learning Objectives

- Explore the basic assembly operations.
- Learn advanced features such as ***Repeat*** and ***Pattern***.

Constraints

Constraints position the parts in the assembly. Some common constraints are:

ALIGN: Lines up the selected surfaces or axes. In other words, the constraint makes the surfaces coplanar and the axes collinear.

MATE: Makes the surfaces coincident facing each other.

Variations of these constraints include Mate Offset and Align Offset wherein the surfaces are offset by a specified distance.

DEFAULT: Automatically aligns the default part coordinate system with that of the assembly.

INSERT: Makes the axes of two revolved surfaces (example: bolt and bolt hole) coincident.

Background Information

The components created in the previous lessons (shaft, bearing, nuts and bolts, and radial cam) fit together to form the cam assembly. Bolts can be assembled easily by referencing to the hole pattern. The pattern command in assembly reduces the modeling time. Also, a change in the number of bolt holes automatically reflects in the number of bolts and therefore, captures the true design intent. This assembly is then assembled into the cam follower assembly.

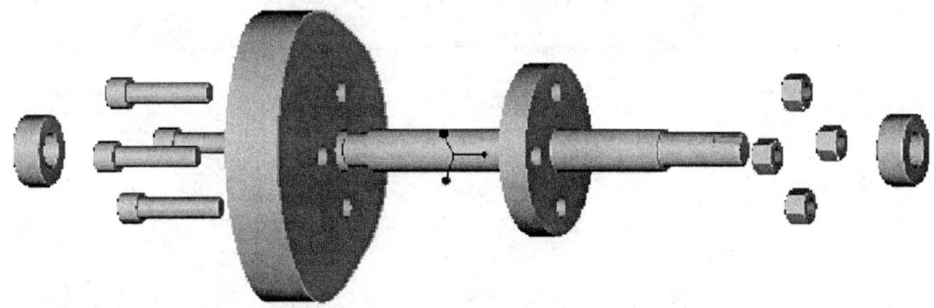

SEQUENCE OF STEPS

STEP I: Assemble the shaft

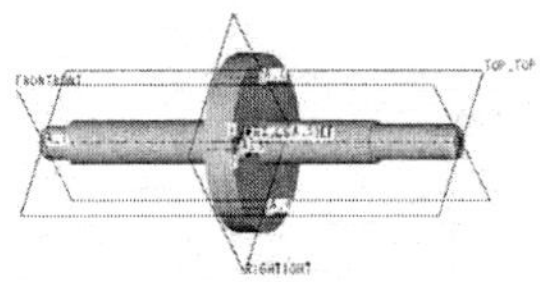

STEP II: Assemble the bearings

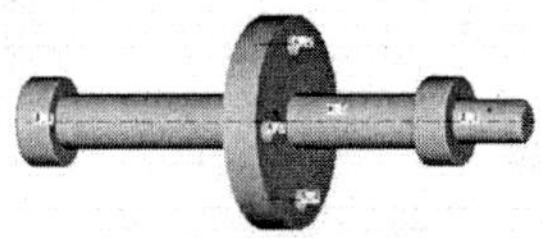

STEP III: Assemble the cam

STEP IV: Assemble the bolts

STEPV: Assemble the nuts

STEPVI: Create an exploded view

STEP VII: Set colors

Goal	Step	Commands
Open a new file for the cam subassembly	1. Set up the working directory.	FILE → SET WORKING DIRECTORY → *Select the working directory* → OK
	2. Open a new file for the cam assembly.	FILE → NEW → Assembly → Design → Cam → OK
Assemble the shaft	3. Start assembling the shaft part.	INSERT → COMPONENT → ASSEMBLE → (or) *Select shaft.prt* → Open
	4. Establish constraints.	Placement → (Constraint type) *Default* **Refer Fig. 11.1.** **The placement status should indicate "fully constrained."**
	5. Place the shaft part.	**Refer Fig. 11.2.**

Fig. 11.1.

Constraint types

Constraints position the parts in the assembly. Some common constraints are:

ALIGN: Lines up the selected surfaces or axes. In other words, the constraint makes the surfaces coplanar and the axes collinear.

MATE: Makes the surfaces coincident facing each other.

Variations of these constraints include Mate Offset and Align Offset wherein the surfaces are offset by a specified distance.

DEFAULT: Automatically aligns the default part coordinate system with that of the assembly.

INSERT: Makes the axes of two revolved surfaces (example: bolt and bolt hole) coincident.

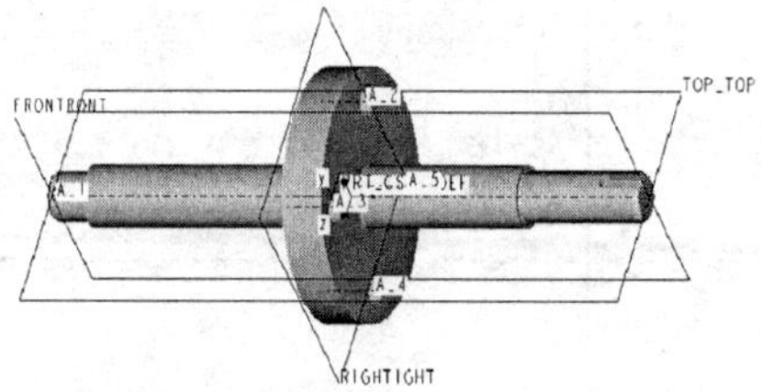
Fig. 11.2.

Goal	Step	Commands
Assemble the left bearing	6. Start assembling the bearing part.	→ *Select bearing.prt* → Open
	7. Turn off datum planes and coordinate systems.	→
	8. Align the axes.	Placement → (Constraint type) Align → *Select the bearing axis* → *Select the shaft axis* **Refer Figs. 11.3.**
	9. Mate the bearing surface with the shoulder.	*New Constraint* → (Constraint Type) Mate → *Select the right flat face of the bearing* → *Select the left bearing shoulder* (Rotate the model if necessary) **Refer Figs. 11.4 and 11.5.**
	10. Place the bearing part.	Refer Fig. 11.6.

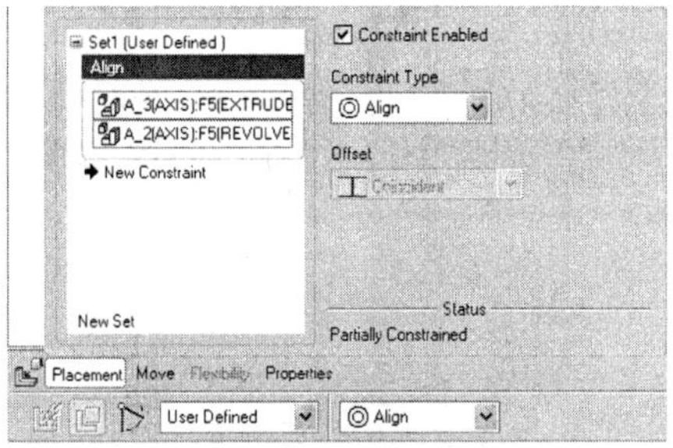
Fig. 11.3.

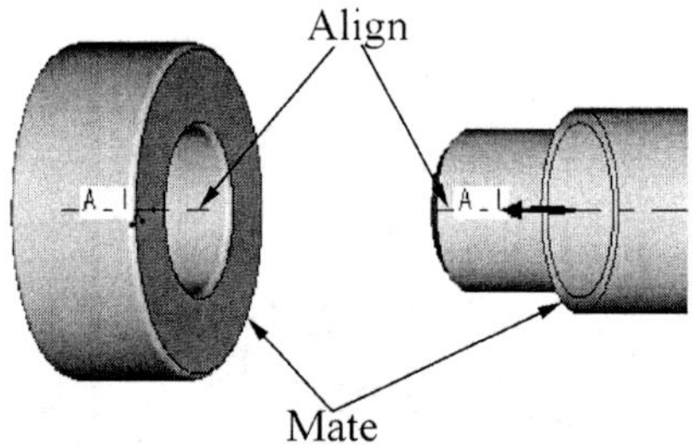

Fig. 11.5.

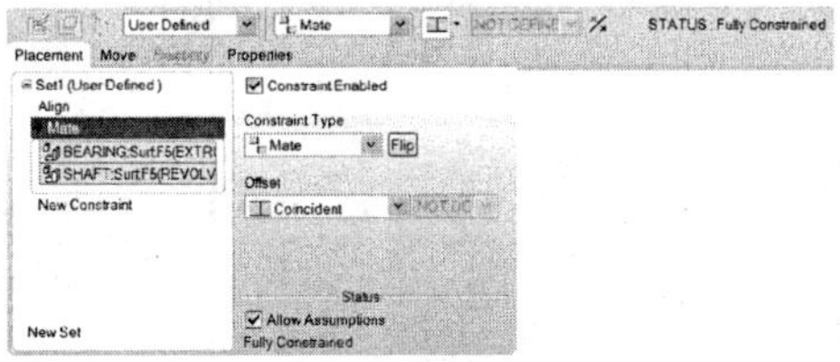
Fig. 11.4.

Fig. 11.6.

Display component Options

SEPARATE WINDOW: Opens the component in a separate window. The constraint type automatic is not available in this option.

ASSEMBLY: Displays the component is the assembly window. The component placement is updated with each additional constraint.

Goal	Step	Commands
Assemble the right bearing	11. Repeat the previous bearing.	***Select the bearing part from the model tree* → EDIT → REPEAT → *Select the mate constraint as it has to be changed in the "Variable Assemble Refs" box* → ADD → *Select the right bearing shoulder* → CONFIRM** **Refer Figs. 11.7, 11.8 and 11.9.**
	12. Start assembling the cam part.	→ *Select platecam.prt* → Open
	13. Align the axes.	Placement → (Constraint type) Align → *Select the cam central hole axis* → *Select the shaft axis*
Assemble the plate cam	14. Mate the cam surface with its shoulder.	→ *New Constraint* → (Constraint type) Mate → ★*Select the cam surface where the countersunk hole is ending* → *Select the left surface of the shoulder* → **Refer Fig. 11.10.**
	15. Place the cam part.	**Refer Fig. 11.11.**

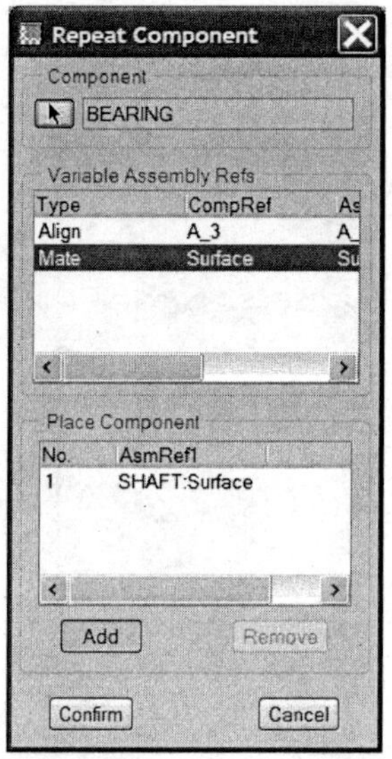

Fig. 11.7.

Repeat

Repeat allows the user to assemble a component at multiple locations. The command simplifies the assembly process changing few constraints rather than defining all the constraints.

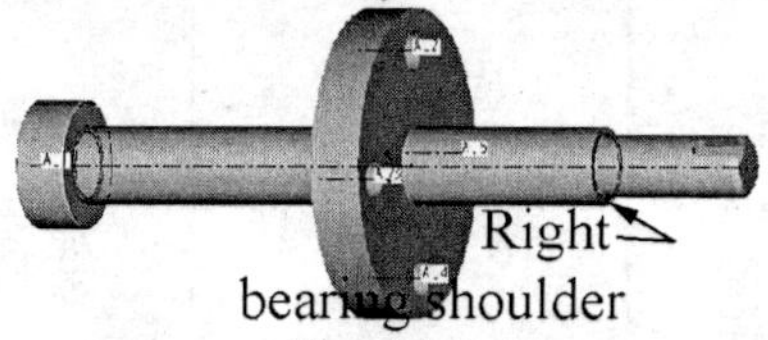

Fig. 11.8.

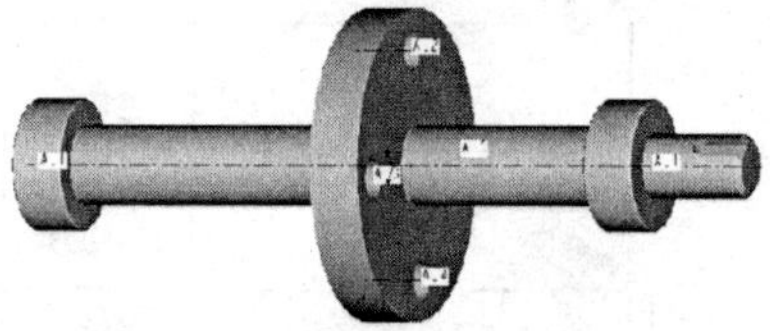
Fig. 11.9.

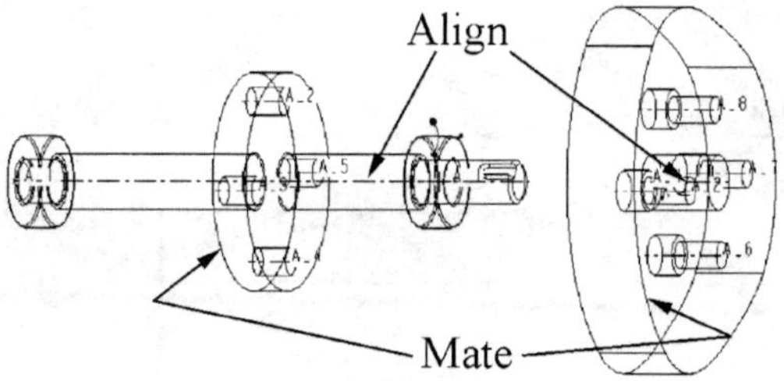

Fig. 11.10.

Fig. 11.11.

Goal	Step	Commands
	16. Start assembling the bolt part.	→ *Select bolt.prt* → Open
	17. Insert the bolt.	Placement → (Constraint type) Insert → *Select the shank surface* → *Select the surface of the bolt hole in the shaft part*
Assemble the bolts	18. Mate the bottom surface of the bolt head with the bottom surface of the countersunk hole.	*New Constraint* → (Constraint type) Mate → *Select the bottom surface of the bolt head* → *Select the bottom surface of the countersunk hole* **Refer Figs. 11.12 and 11.13.**
	19. Place the bolt part.	**Refer Fig. 11.14.**
	20. Pattern the bolt.	*Select the bolt part from the model tree* → *Right Mouse* → Pattern → Reference → **Refer Fig. 11.15.**
	21. Start assembling the nut part.	→ *Select nut.prt* → Open
Assemble the nuts	22. Align the axis of the nut with that of the bolt.	Placement → (Constraint type) Align → *Select the axis of the nut* → *Select the axis of the bolt*

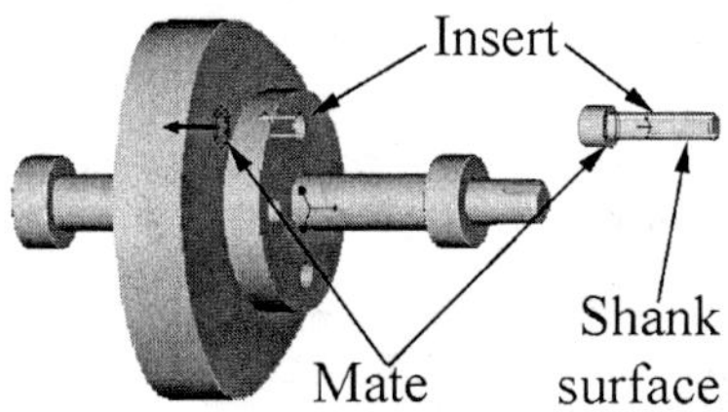

Fig. 11.12.

Fig. 11.13.

Fig. 11.14.

Fig. 11.15.

Goal	Step	Commands
Assemble the nuts (continued)	23. Mate the left surface of the nut with the right surface of the shaft shoulder.	New Constraint → (Type) Mate → *Select a nut face* → *Select the right surface of the shoulder*
	24. Place the nut part.	 **Refer Fig. 11.16.**
	25. Pattern the nut.	*Select the nut part from the model tree* → *Right Mouse* → Pattern → Reference →  **Refer Fig. 11.17.**
Create an exploded view	26. Check the current exploded view.	VIEW → EXPLODE → EXPLODE VIEW → VIEW → EXPLODE → UNEXPLODE VIEW **Refer Fig. 11.18.**
	27. Start creating a custom exploded view.	VIEW → VIEW MANAGER → *Click on explode tab* → NEW → EXP0001 → ***ENTER***
	28. Select the axis for the reference motion.	Properties >> →  → *(Motion Reference) Select the shaft axis* **Refer Fig. 11.19.**
	29. Select each part and translate it along the axis.	*Select each part and move it along the axis* → OK → CLOSE **Refer Fig. 11.20.**

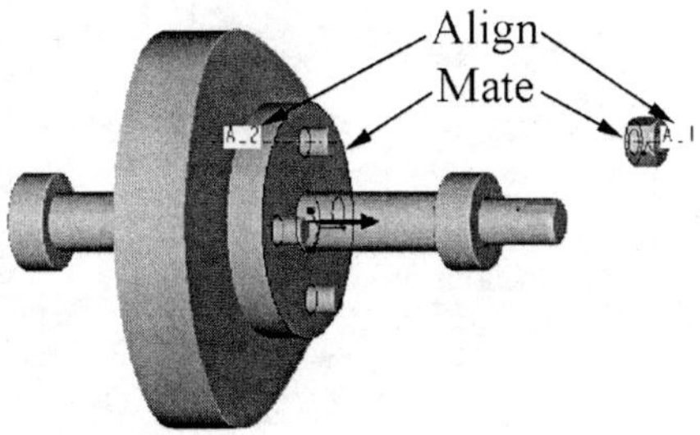

Fig. 11.16.

Fig. 11.17.

Fig. 11.18.

Fig. 11.20.

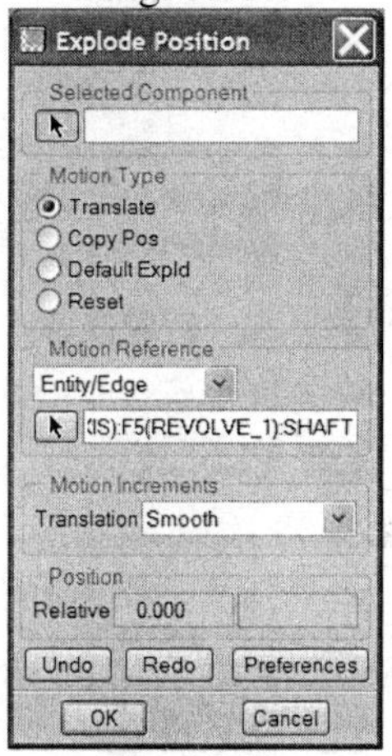

Fig. 11.19.

Goal	Step	Commands
Set up color	30. Define the model colors.	VIEW → COLOR AND APPEARANCE → **ProE opens the "Appearance Editor" window.** **+** → **Refer Fig. 11.21.** *Click on the color* → **Refer Fig. 11.20.** **ProE opens the "Color Editor" window.** **Refer Fig.11.21.** *Click on Color wheel* → **ProE opens the color wheel.** *Select a suitable color* → CLOSE → **ProE closes the "Color Editor."** Repeat the process to add five colors

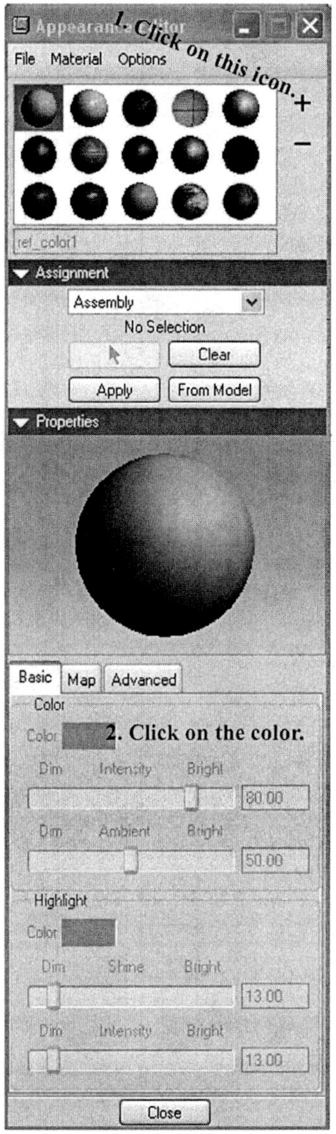

Fig. 11.21.

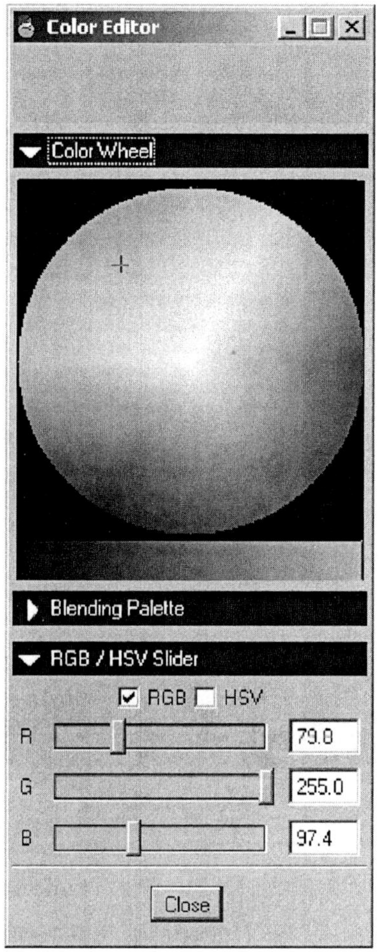

Fig. 11.22.

Goal	Step	Commands
Set up color (continued)	31. Define the colors of the components.	*In the assignment drop-down menu, select components* → **Refer Fig. 11.22.** *Select a color* →  → *Select a component* → OK → Apply → Repeat the process and apply different colors → CLOSE
Save the subassembly file	32. Save the file.	FILE → SAVE → <u>CAM.ASM</u> → OK

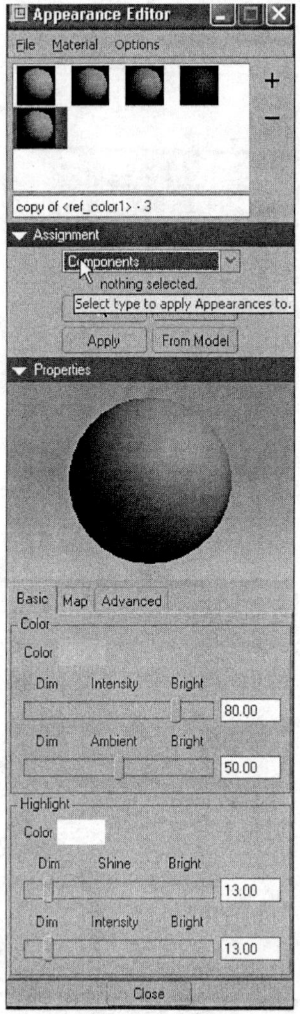

Fig. 11.22.

Problem 1

Wheel Base:
Create the wheel base using the "Revolve" operation and the following cross section.

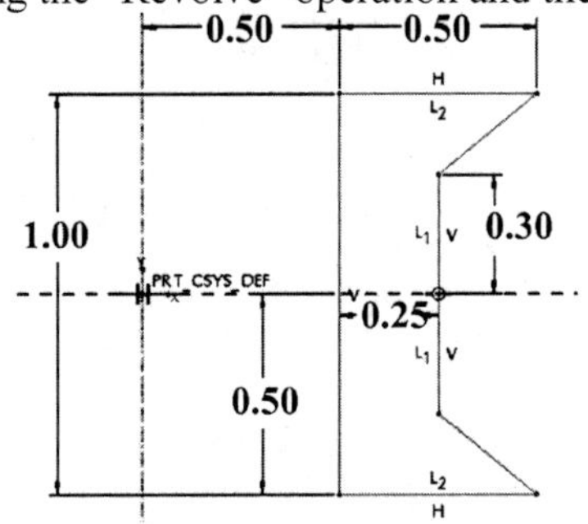

Wheel:
Create the wheel using the "Revolve" operation and the following cross section.

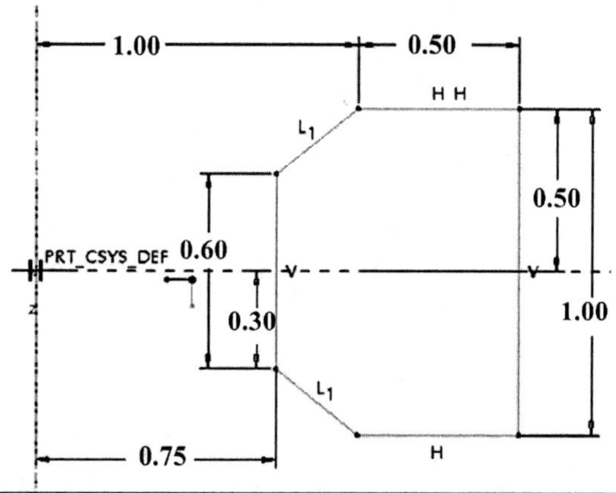

Axle:
The axle will be a cylinder of diameter 1 and length 15.

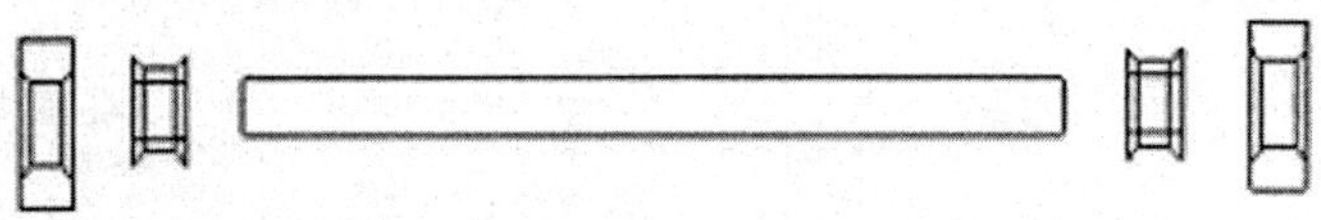

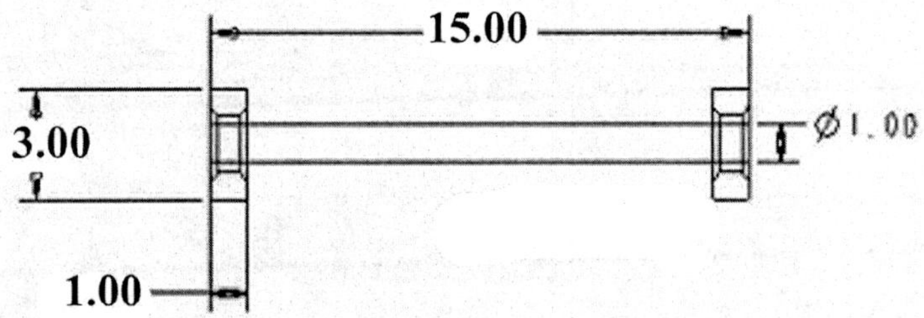

OPEN-ENDED DESIGN

1.) Create a lego block shown in the figure below:

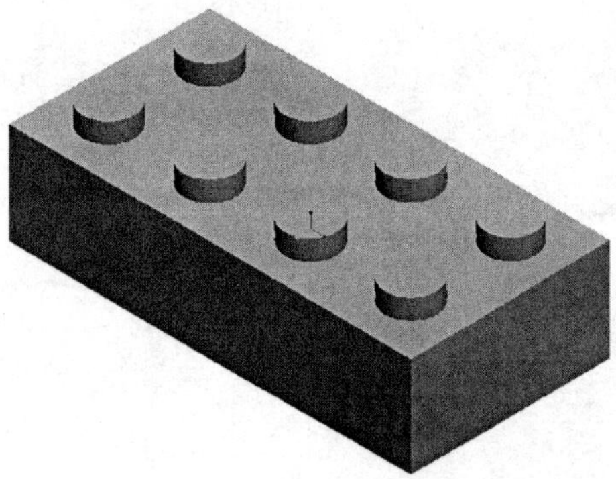

2.) Assemble at least ten of these blocks into a new structure of your choice and create a drawing of your result.

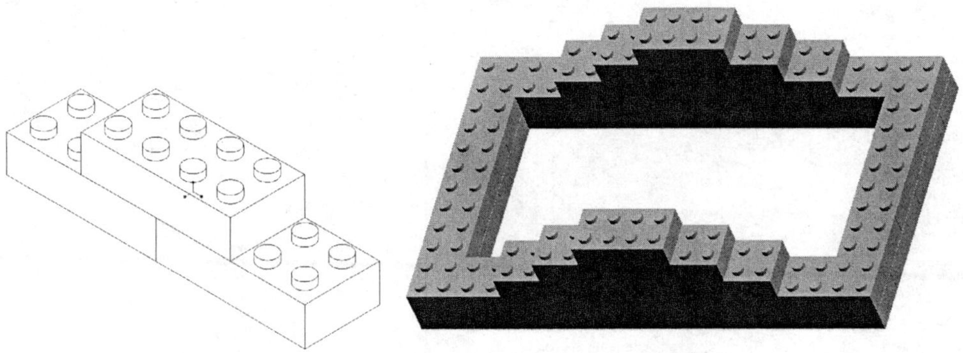

Hints:

1. Lego's are not solid, but hollow. A sound procedure for creating the block is to create the base rectangular prism, add a cylinder, pattern the cylinder, and then to use the "shell" tool to remove material to a specified thickness.
2. Assembling the Lego's will require a lot of repetition. Use "repeat" function for assembly.

OPEN-ENDED DESIGN

Tetrahedron and octahedron are the most stable three-dimensional shapes. They offer more stability than a cube. Note that a tetrahedron and an octahedron are in fact an assemblage of triangles.

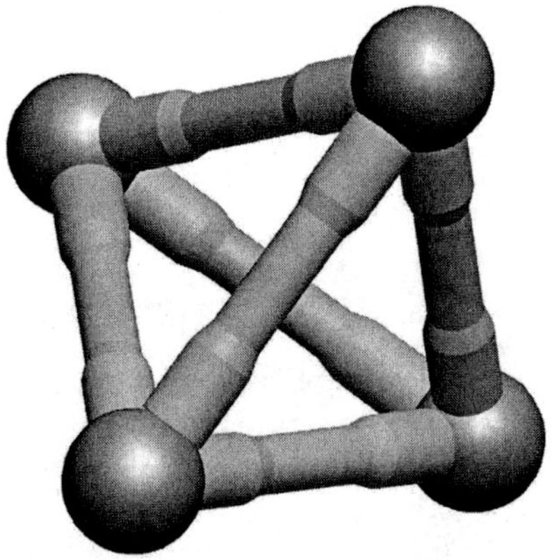

Tetrahedron

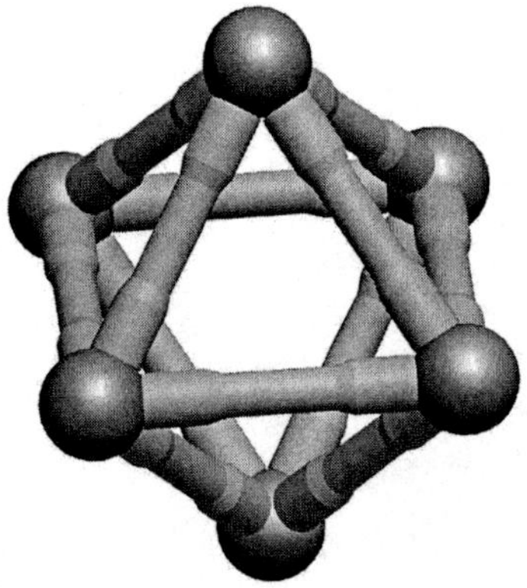

Octahedron

A sample tetrahedron.

Hints:

1. Create the connector part with datum points at the location where the sphere would be assembled. Use these datum points in the assembly.

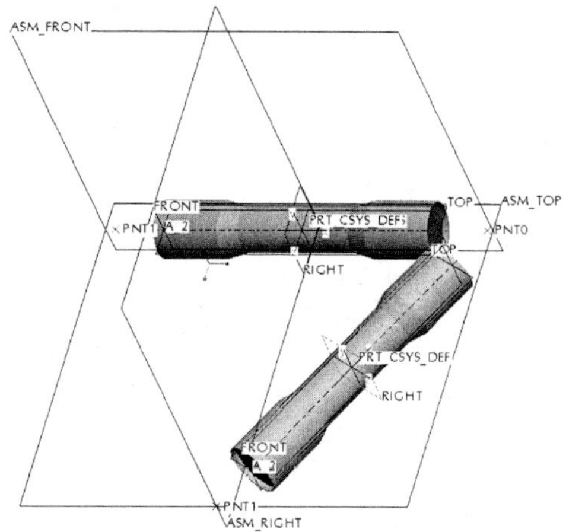

OPEN-ENDED DESIGN

Create a model of your watch.

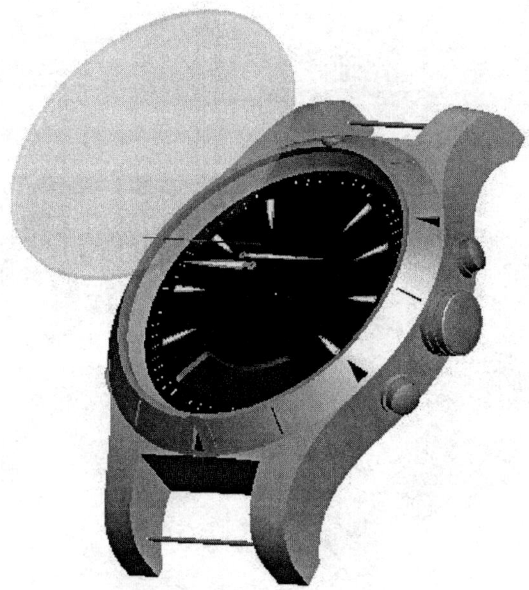

OPEN-ENDED DESIGN
Create a model of the globe.

OPEN-ENDED DESIGN

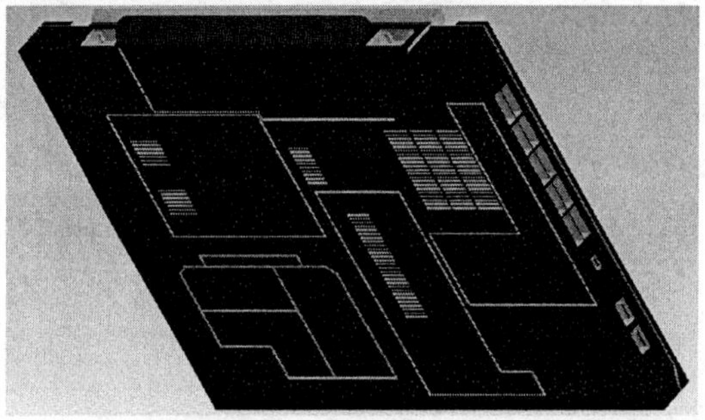

NOTES:

LESSON 12
CAM FOLLOWER ASSEMBLY

Learning Objectives

- Practice the basic assembly tools.
- ***Suppress*** and ***Resume*** components in assembly,
- ***Animate*** components in the assembly mode.
- Create parts in the assembly mode.

Background Information

The housing (Lesson 10) and the cam subassembly (Lesson 11) fit together to form the cam follower assembly. First, the cam assembly is inserted. By creating a datum plane at an angle to the TOP datum plane, and setting appropriate relationships, the cam assembly can be rotated dynamically. Regenerate evaluates all the relations and, therefore, it increments the angle between the datum and the TOP datum plane. If the cam subassembly is assembled to this datum, then it will also rotate with the datum plane. The housing part is then assembled. The follower part is created in the assembly mode. The follower constraints ensure that it translates up and down when the cam assembly rotates. These simple motion checks ensure that there is no motion interference in the final assembly.

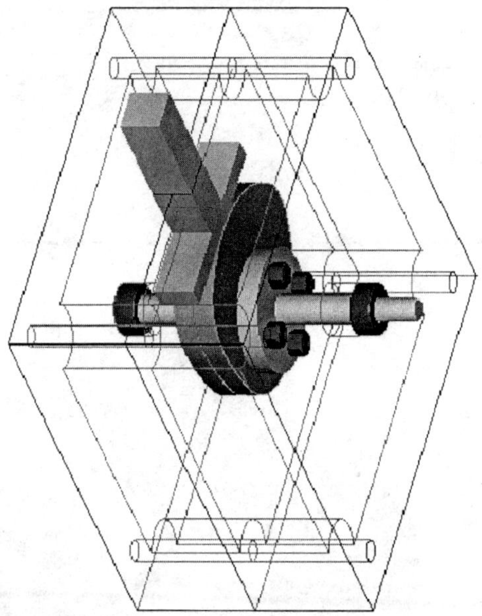

SEQUENCE OF STEPS

Step I - Create a dynamic datum plane
1. Create a datum axis
2. Create a plane through the axis
3. Add relations to allow the motion of the datum plane

Step II - Assemble the cam subassembly
1. Insert the cam assembly
2. Verify the assembly motion
3. Suppress the cam assembly

Step III - Assemble the housing

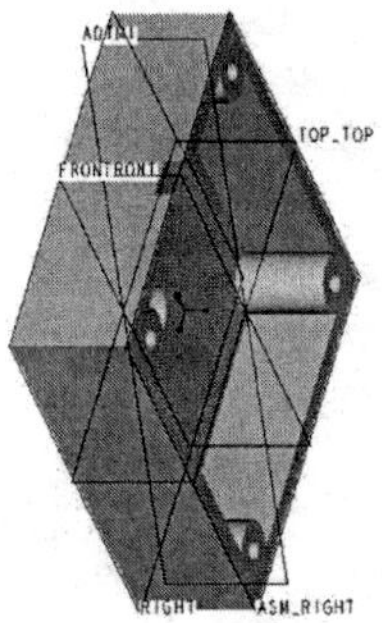

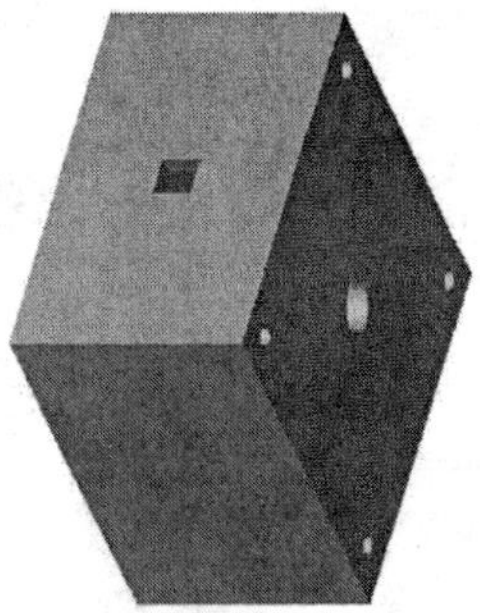

Step IV - Setup the model display

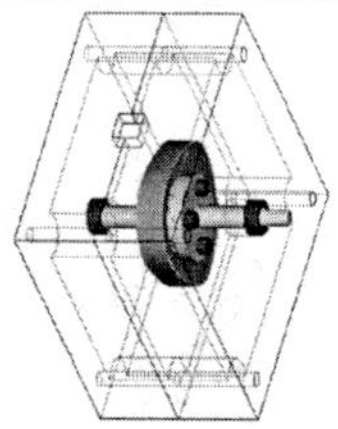

Step V - Create the follower part
1. Create a datum point at the apex of the cam
2. Create the follower part

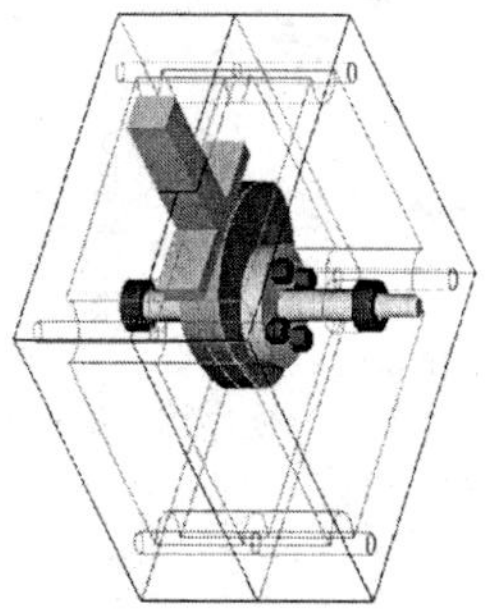

Step VI - Verify the cam motion

Goal	Step	Commands
Open a new file for the cam follower assembly	1. Set up the working directory.	**FILE → SET WORKING DIRECTORY →** ***Select the working directory*** **→ OK**
	2. Open a new file for the cam follower assembly.	**FILE → NEW → Assembly → Design → CamFollower → OK**
Create a datum axis	3. Create a datum axis.	**→** ***Select ASM_TOP and ASM_FRONT datum planes while holding CTRL*** **→ OK →** ***Deselect the axis*** Refer Fig. 12.1.
Create a datum plane	4. Create a datum plane.	**→** ***Select the datum axis created in the previous step and ASM_TOP datum plane while holding CTRL*** **→ (Rotation) 30 →** ***ENTER*** **→ OK** Refer Figs. 12.2 and 12.3.
	5. Modify the angular dimension name.	***Select ADTM1*** **→** ***Right Mouse*** **→ Edit →** ***Select the angular dimension*** **→** ***Right Mouse*** **→ Properties →** ***Select the Dimension Text Tab*** **→ (Name)CamAngle → OK** Refer Fig. 12.4.

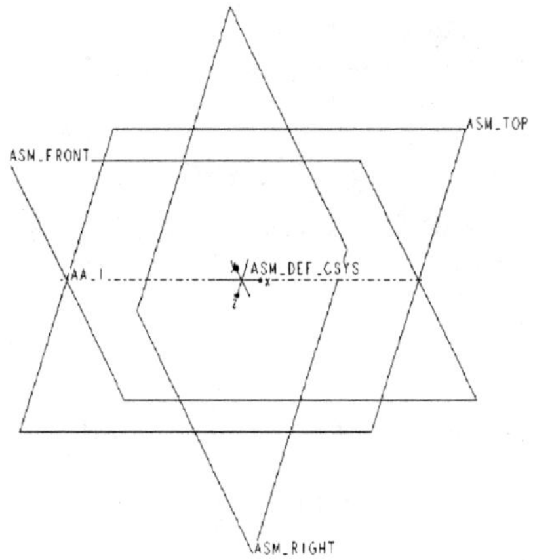

Fig. 12.1.

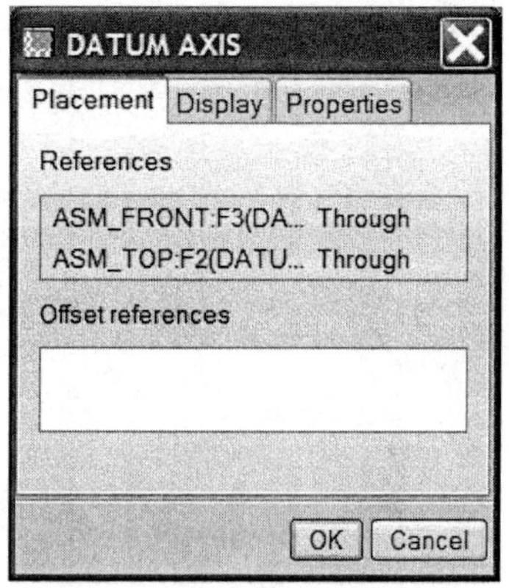

Fig, 12. 2.

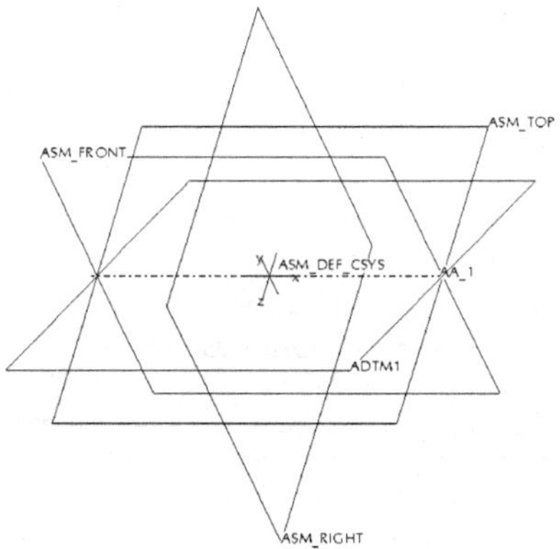

Fig. 12.3.

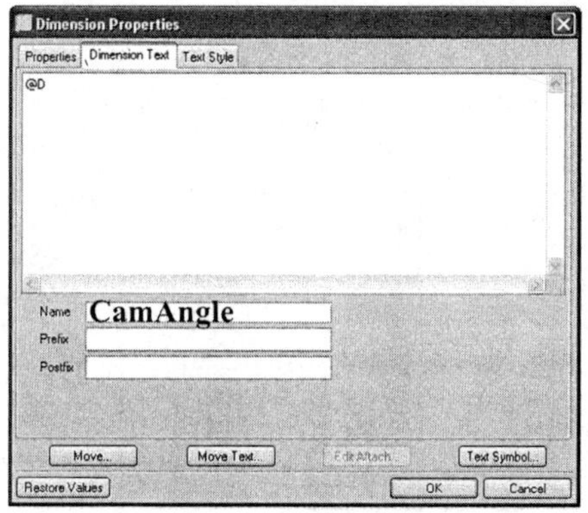

Fig. 12.4.

Goal	Step	Commands
Add relations to animate this datum plane	6. Add relations.	**TOOLS → RELATIONS → <u>Add relations as shown in Fig. 12.5</u> → OK** Refer Fig. 12.5.
Verify the relationship	7. Verify the relationship.	**(or EDIT → REGENERATE) → Repeat the regenerate command till the datum comes back to the original position.**
Assemble the cam subassembly	8. Start inserting the cam assembly.	→ ***Select cam.asm*** → **Open**
	9. Move the assembly.	***Move*** **(in the dash)** → ***Select the subassembly and move it*** Refer Fig. 12.6.
	10. Align the axis of the shaft to the assembly datum axis.	***Placement*** **→ (Constraint type) Align → (Component reference)** ***Select the axis of the shaft*** **→ (Assembly reference)** ***Select the assembly datum axis***
	11. Align the subassembly TOP datum with the datum created in the step 33.	**New Constraint → (Constraint type) Align → (Component reference)** ***Select the subassembly ASM_TOP datum plane*** **→ (Assembly reference)** ***Select the assembly ADTM1*** **→ 0 →** ***<u>ENTER</u>***

Regenerate evaluates all the relations and, therefore, it increments the angle. If the cam subassembly is assembled to this datum, then it will also rotate with the datum plane.

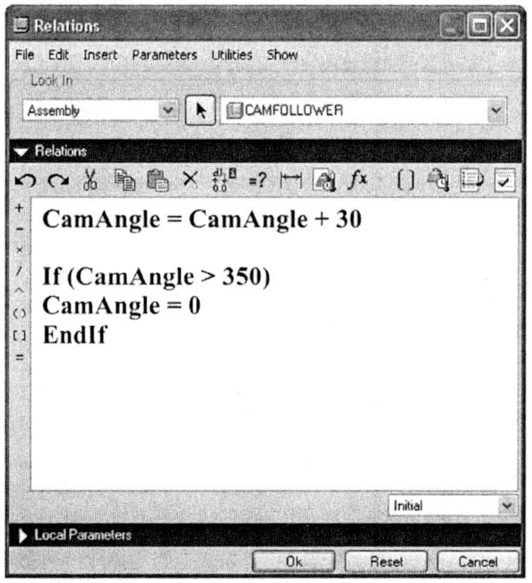

Fig. 12.5.

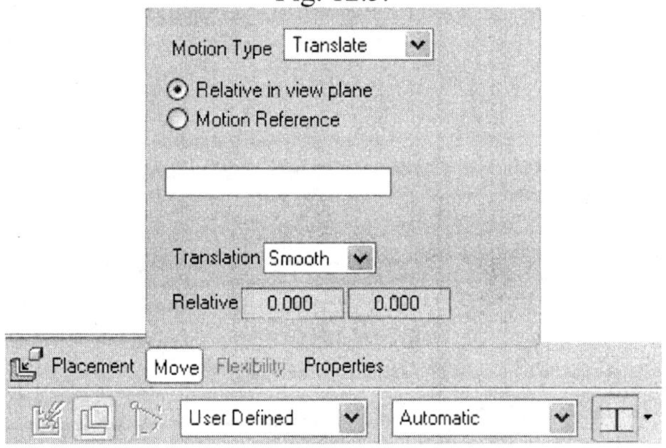

Fig. 12.6.

Goal	Step	Commands
Assemble the cam subassembly (Continued)	12. Align the subassembly RIGHT datum with the assembly RIGHT datum plane.	**New Constraint → (Constraint type) Align → (Component reference)** ***Select the subassembly ASM_RIGHT datum plane*** **→ (Assembly reference)** ***Select the assembly ASM_RIGHT datum plane → Offset →*** **0.5** ***→ ENTER*** At this point, the main assembly right datum plane should lie in the middle of the plate cam.
	13. Place the cam subassembly.	Refer Fig. 12.7.
Verify the motion	14. Verify the motion.	**EDIT → REGENERATE**
Suppress the cam subassembly	15. Suppress the cam subassembly.	***Select the cam subassembly from the model tree → Right Mouse →*** **Suppress → OK**
Assemble the left housing	16. Start assembling the housing part.	→ ***Select housing.prt →*** **Open**
	17. Align the TOP datum with the assembly TOP datum plane.	***Placement*** **→ (Constraint type) Align → (Component reference)** ***Select the TOP datum*** **→ (Assembly reference)** ***Select the assembly TOP datum plane***
	18. Align the FRONT datum with the assembly FRONT datum plane.	**New Constraint → (Constraint type) Align → (Component reference)** ***Select the FRONT datum*** **→ (Assembly reference)** ***Select the assembly FRONT datum plane***

Fig. 12.7.

Goal	Step	Commands
Assemble the left housing (continued)	19. Align the housing right (shelled) surface with the assembly RIGHT datum plane.	**New Constraint → (Constraint type) Align → (Component reference) *Select the housing right surface* → (Assembly reference) *Select the assembly RIGHT datum plane***
	20. Place the housing part.	✓ Refer Fig. 12.8.
Assemble the right housing	21. Start assembling the housing part.	→ ***Select housing.prt*** → **Open**
	22. Align the TOP datum with the assembly TOP datum plane.	***Placement* → (Constraint type) Align → (Component reference) *Select the TOP datum plane* → (Assembly reference) *Select the assembly TOP datum plane***
	23. Mating the two-shelled surfaces of the housings.	**New Constraint → (Constraint type) Mate → (Component reference) *Select the shelled surface of the right housing* → (Assembly reference) *Select the shelled surface of the left housing*** Refer Fig. 12.9.
	24. Mate the FRONT datum with the assembly FRONT datum plane.	**New Constraint → (Constraint type) MATE → (Component reference) *Select the FRONT datum plane* → (Assembly reference) *Select the assembly FRONT datum plane***
	25. Place the housing part.	✓ Refer Fig. 12.10.

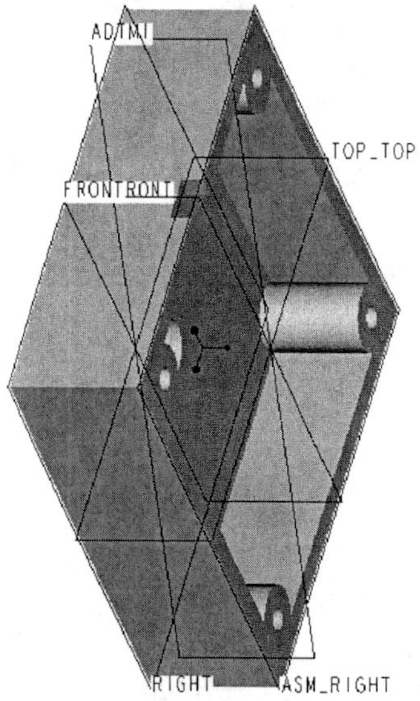

Fig. 12.8.

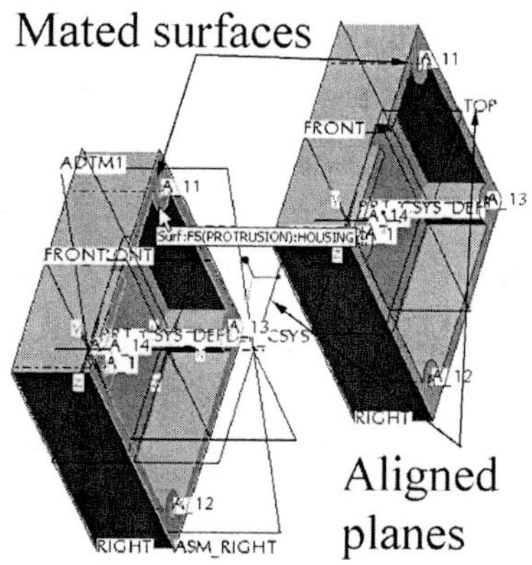

Fig. 12.9.

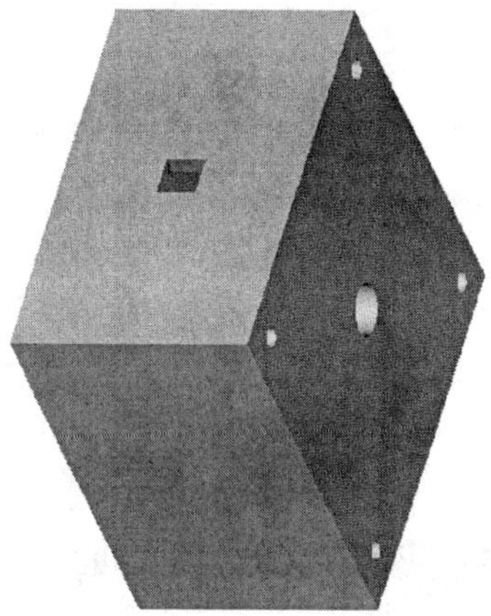
Fig. 12.10.

Goal	Step	Commands
Resume all features	26. Resume all features.	**EDIT → RESUME → ALL**
Set up model display	27. Set up model display.	***Select the housings in the model tree while holding <u>CTRL</u>*** **→ VIEW → DISPLAY STYLE → HIDDEN LINE** Refer Fig. 12.11.
Suppress the housings	28. Suppress the housing.	***Select both housings from the model tree while holding <u>CTRL</u> → Right Mouse*** **→ Suppress → OK**
Sketch a datum curve	29. Start "Datum Curve" feature.	***→ Select the assembly RIGHT datum plane (centered on the plate cam)*** **→ (Orientation) Top → Sketch** Refer Fig. 12.12.
	30. Sketch the datum curve.	***→ Pick points 1 and 2 → Middle Mouse*** Refer Fig. 12.13.
	31. Modify the dimensions.	***→ Double click each dimension and enter the corresponding value*** Refer Fig. 12.13.

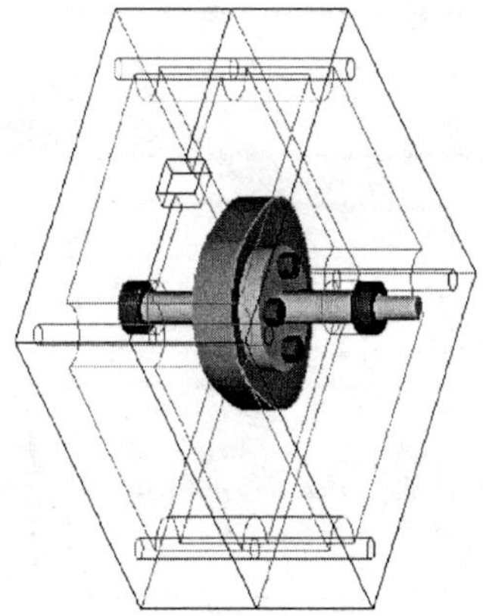

Fig. 12.11.

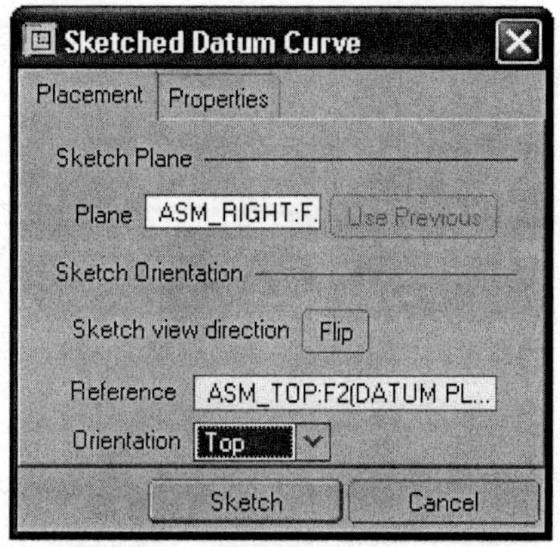

Fig. 12.12.

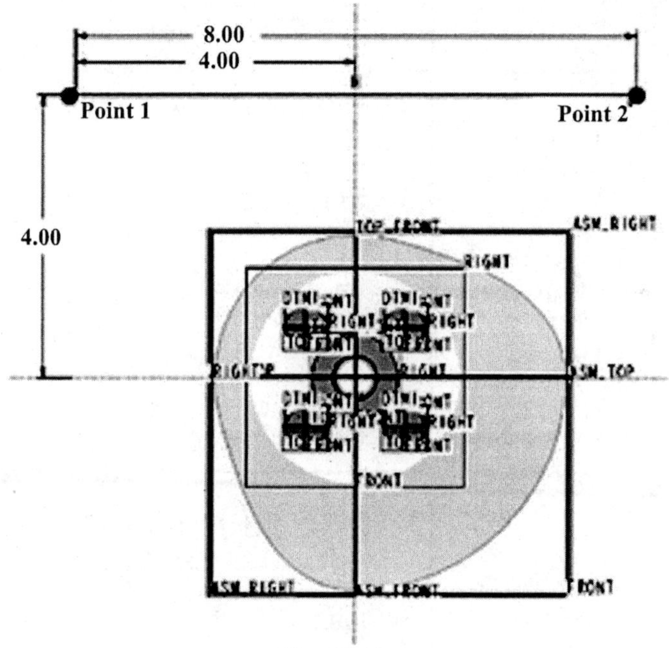

Fig. 12.13.

Goal	Step	Commands
	32. Exit sketcher.	✔
Sketch a datum curve (continued)	33. Start "Datum Curve" feature.	→ **Use Previous**
	34. Sketch the datum curve.	→ ***Loop*** → ***Select the four datum curves defining the cam profile***
	35. Exit sketcher.	✔ → **VIEW** → **ORIENTATION** → **STANDARD ORIENTATION** Refer Fig. 12.14.
Create a datum point	36. Create a datum point. **As the two curves do not intersect, the datum point will be created at the highest point on the datum curve (in step 35).**	***Select the datum curve created in the step 35*** → **Refer Fig. 12.15.** → ***while holding <u>CTRL</u>, select the straight line datum curve*** → **OK** → → Refer Fig. 12.15.
Start creating the follower component	37. Start creating the follower component.	**INSERT** → **COMPONENT** → **CREATE** → **<u>Follower</u>** → **OK** → Refer Fig. 12.16. **Locate default datums** → **Three planes** → **OK**

Fig. 12.14.

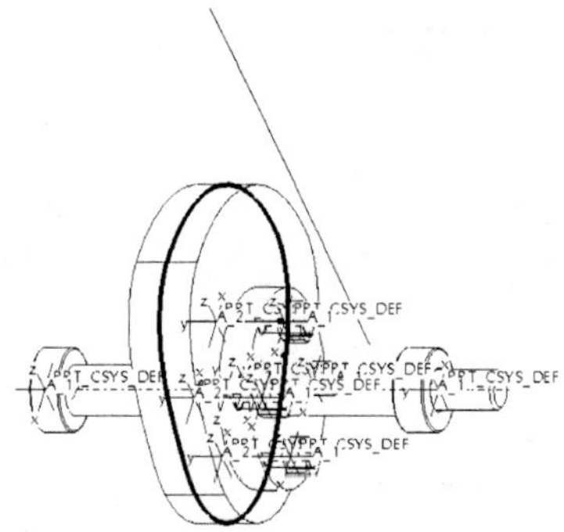

Fig. 12.15.

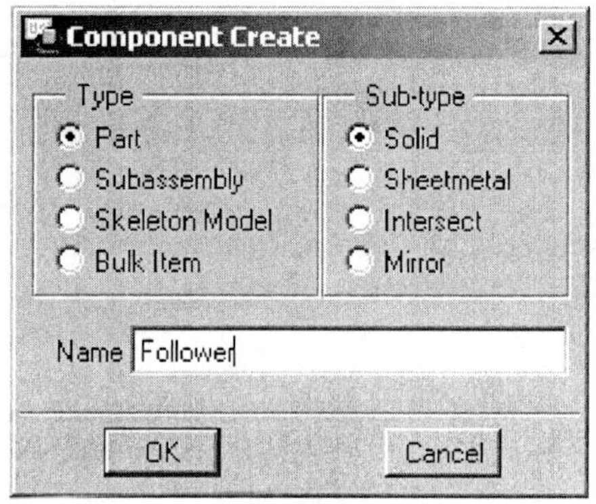

Fig. 12.16.

Goal	Step	Commands
Start creating the follower component (continued)	38. Set up the datum planes.	***Select assembly RIGHT datum plane → Select assembly TOP datum plane → Select assembly FRONT datum plane***
	39. Start "Extrude" feature.	**→ Placement → DEFINE →** ***Select the ASM_RIGHT → Click in the reference window →*** **(Reference)** ***Select ASM_TOP datum plane →*** **(Orientation) TOP → Sketch** Refer Fig. 12.17.
	40. Add a new reference.	***Select the datum point (APNT0) as a new reference***
	41. Sketch the section.	**→** ***Click to create the section shown in Fig. 12.17.***
	42. Add dimensions.	**→** ***Create the horizontal dimensions*** Refer Fig. 12.18.
	43. Modify the dimensions.	**→** ***Double click each dimension and enter the corresponding value*** Refer Fig. 12.18.
	44. Exit sketcher.	✓
	45. Define the depth and accept the feature creation.	**(Depth)** **1** **→** ***ENTER*** **→ (Icon before depth - Both Sides) →**

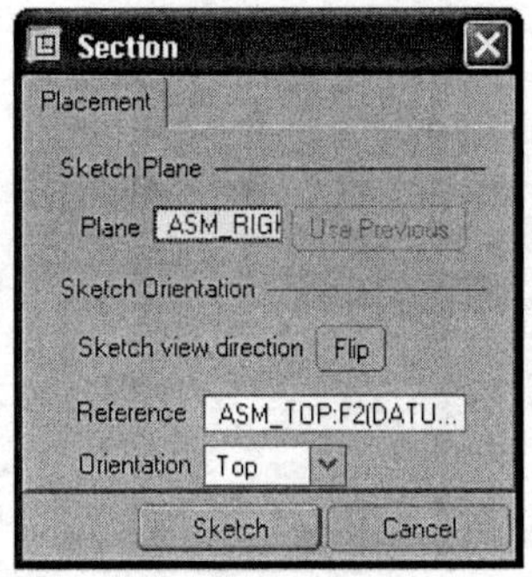

Fig. 12.17.

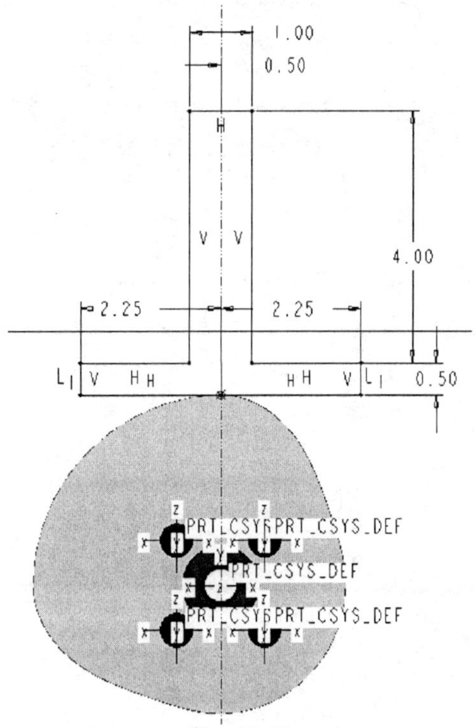

Fig. 12.18.

Goal	Step	Commands
Resume all features	46. **OPTIONAL STEP:** Resume all features.	**WINDOWS → ACTIVATE → Click in the assembly window → EDIT → RESUME → ALL** Refer Fig.12.19.
Verify the motion	47. Verify the motion.	**EDIT → REGENERATE** Repeat the process to identify any motion interference. You may get a better grasp if you view from the side.
Save the file and exit ProE	48. Save the file and exit ProE.	**FILE → SAVE → CAMFOLLOWER.PRT → OK → FILE → EXIT → YES**

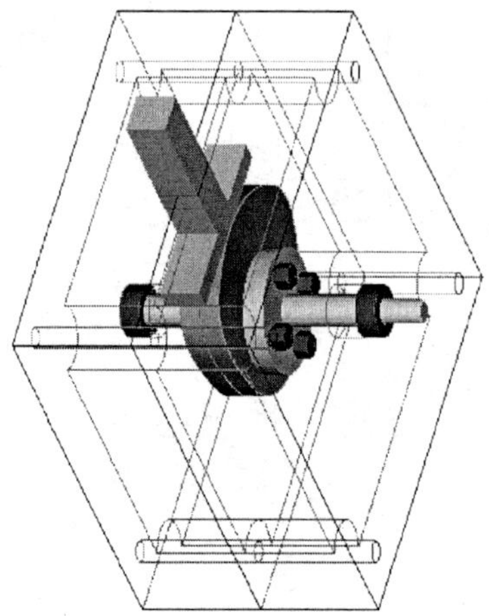

Fig. 12.19.

OPEN-ENDED DESIGN

Create parts for a pen and assemble them.

OPEN-ENDED DESIGN

Create a Swiss Army knife. There are many varieties with varying degrees of complexity.

OPEN-ENDED DESIGN

Create an object of that uses several parts and assembly features.

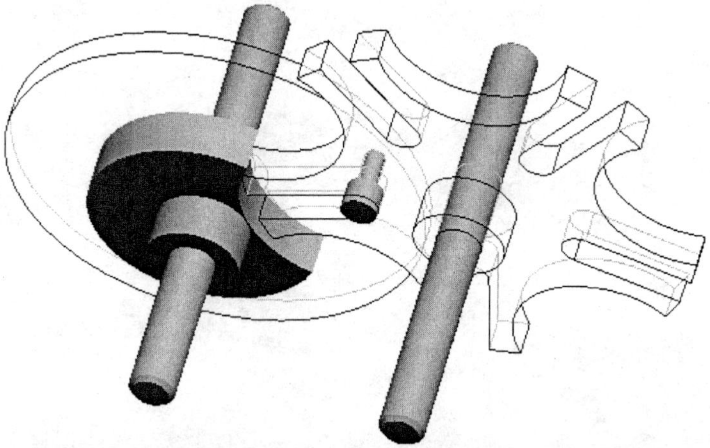

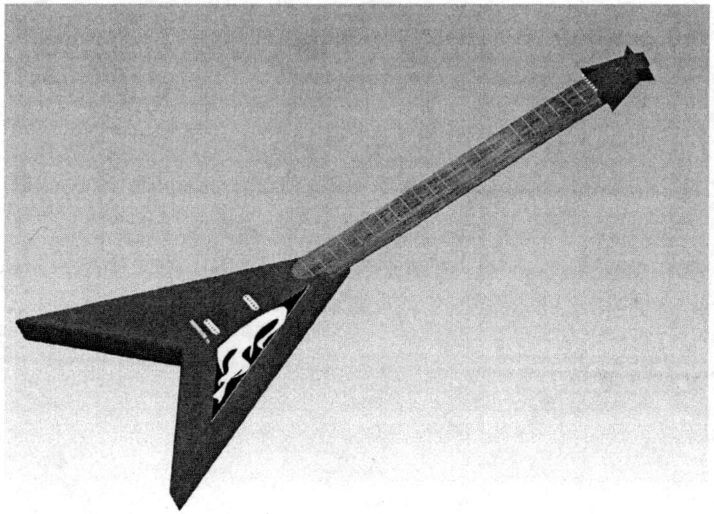

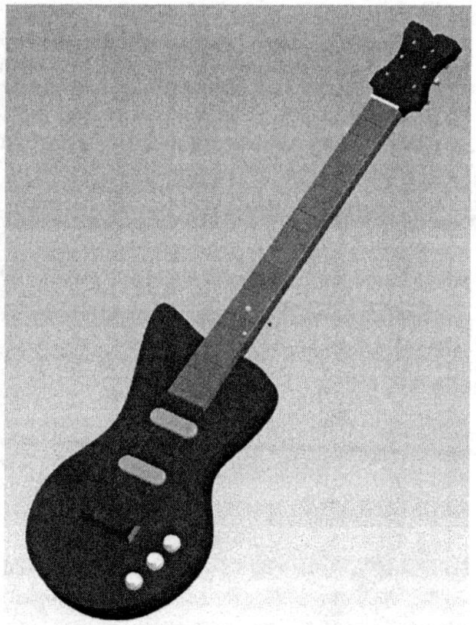

NOTES:

LESSON 13
WASHINGTON MONUMENT AND WING

Learning Objectives

- Learn ***Blend*** feature.
- Practice ***Relations*** and ***Mirror*** commands
- Practice importing sketches.

Blend

Blend feature merges two or more sections. There are two types of blends – parallel and rotational blends. In parallel blend, the sections that are blended are parallel and the depth is specified. On the other hand, in the rotational blend option, the sections are separated by specified angle. In the rotational blend, the sections rotate about a common axis (specified in terms of a coordinate system) and the rotational angle should not exceed 120^0. The blend connects the starting point of each section with the corresponding point on the next section. Then, the corresponding vertices of the sections are connected. Note that for this connection to work, the number of vertices should be equal. An exception is when a section has only one vertex, the blend feature connects the vertices of the other section to this vertex. all the vertices of one section join to one vertex (the next section). The start point can be changed to create or avoid twisting. The start point can be varied by "Selecting the start point → SKETCH → FEATURE TOOLS → START POINT" command. We can move from one section to another by using "SKETCH → FEATURE TOOLS → TOGGLE SECTION" command. The straight option connects vertices of one section to the corresponding vertices of the next section using straight lines. The smooth option is used with three or more sections and connects the corresponding vertices of sections using smooth curve instead of straight line.

Background Information:

Washington Monument was designed by Robert Mills to pay tribute to George Washington's achievements. Shaped in the form of an obelisk, with a height of 550 ft. and a weight of 90,000 tons, it is the world's largest masonry structure. In 30-mile wind gusts, it sways less than 0.125 inches. In this lesson, the monument will be modeled by using the blend feature.

Wings are designed to maximize the lift created due to the airflow. Several factors such as the air density, speed and wing area affect the forces on the wing: lift and drag. Based on these factors, the wing sections are determined at regular intervals along the length of the wing. The sections are often defined by a set of data points. These sections are then joined using straight blend feature.

SEQUENCE OF STEPS

STEP I: Setup units

1. Set the units to the FPS system.

STEP II: Create protrusion blend feature

1. Define the blend parameters as parallel and regular sections.
2. Select the type of transition surface as straight.
3. Define and orient the sketching plane.
4. Sketch the ground section (section #1) of the obelisk.
5. Toggle section.
6. Sketch the second section (section #2) of the obelisk.
7. Toggle section.
8. Define the tip of the obelisk (section #3)
9. Define the distance between the sections.

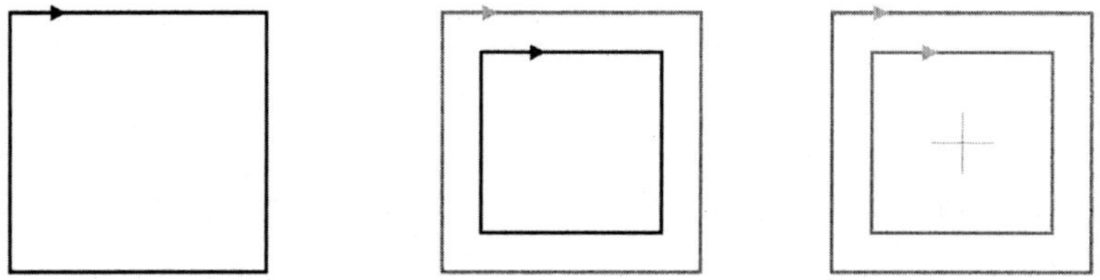

Section #1 Section #2 Section #3

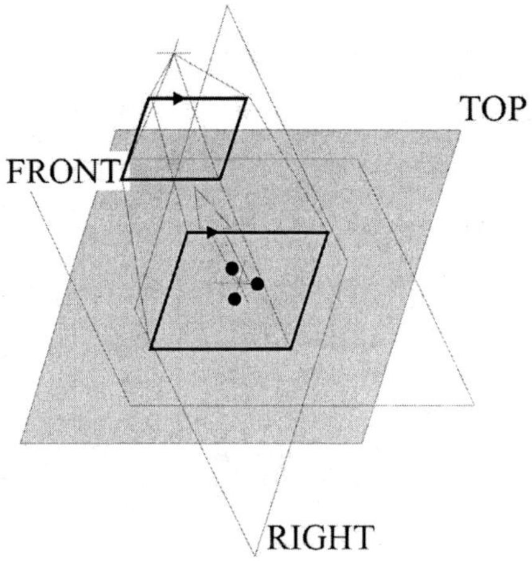

Goal	Step	Commands
Open a new file for the monument part	1. Set up the working directory.	**FILE → SET WORKING DIRECTORY → *Select the working directory* → OK**
	2. Open a new file.	**FILE → NEW → *Part* → *Solid* → <u>monument</u> → OK**
Set up units	3. Set the units to the FPS system.	**EDIT → SET UP → Units → *Select Foot Pound Second (FPS)* →** Set... **→** **Refer Fig. 13.1.** **OK →** Refer Fig. 13.2. **CLOSE → Done**
Create the obelisk	4. Start "Blend" feature.	**INSERT → BLEND → PROTRUSION**
	5. Select the sketch option.	**Parallel → Regular Sec → Sketch Sec→ Done**
	6. Select the type of transition surface.	**Straight → Done** Straight option connects the vertices of various sections using straight lines whereas smooth connects the vertices with curves.
	7. Select the sketching plane.	**Setup New → Plane → *Select the TOP datum plane***
	8. Define the direction of material extrusion.	**Okay**
	9. Orient the sketcher.	**Default**

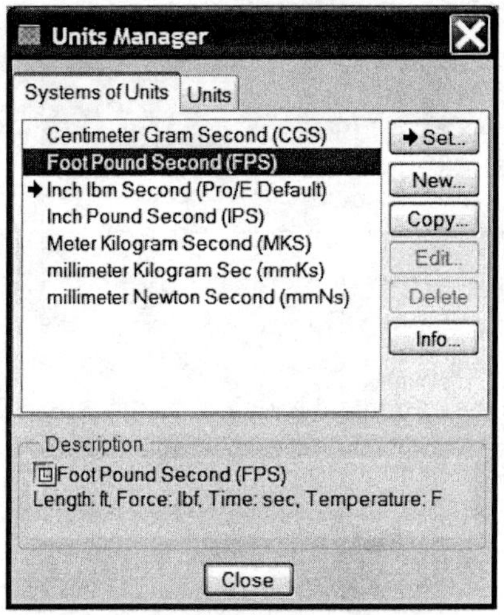

Fig. 13.1.

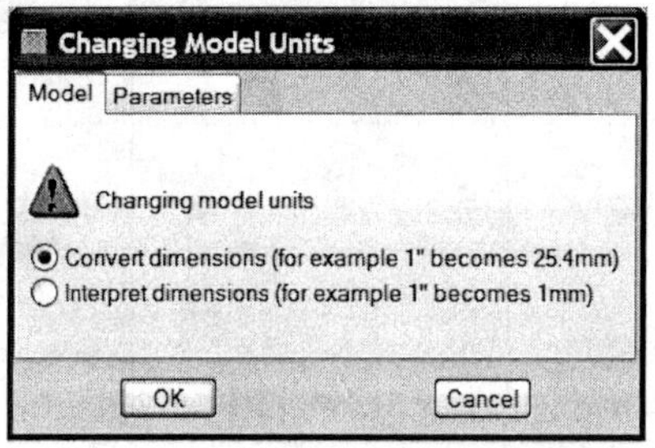

Fig.13.2.

In parallel blend, the sections that are blended are parallel and the depth is specified. On the other hand, in the rotational blend option, the sections are separated by specified angle.

Goal	Step	Commands
	10. Sketch a rectangle.	→ *Pick points 1 and 2* Refer Fig. 13.3.
	11. Add relations to center the section.	Note that the dimension names (sd#s) may be different in your model. **TOOLS → RELATIONS → <u>Type the relations shown in Fig. 13.4.</u>**
Create the obelisk (continued)	12. Sort relations.	**UTILITIES → REORDER RELATIONS → OK → OK** The "reorder" command sorts the relations in the order of precedence.
	13. Modify the side dimension.	→ ***Double click the side sd2 dimension*** (you will not be able to edit other dimensions which are governed by relations) → **<u>55</u>** → ***<u>ENTER</u>*** Refer Fig. 13.5.
	14. Toggle the section to construct a new section.	**SKETCH → FEATURE TOOLS → TOGGLE SECTION**

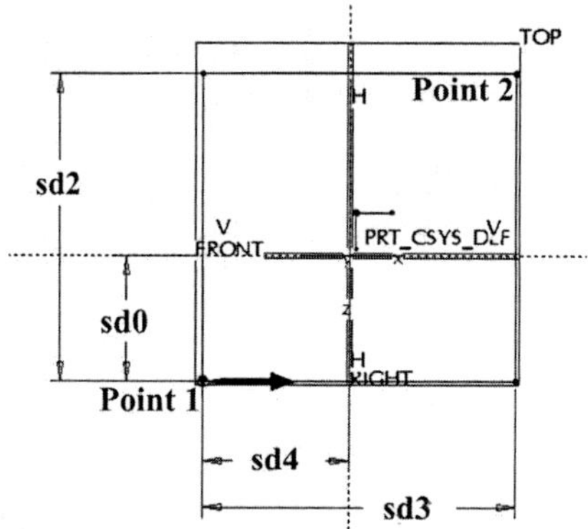

Fig. 13.3.

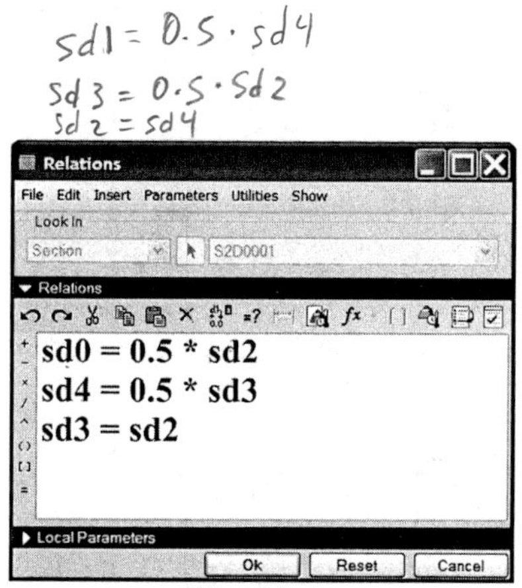

Fig. 13.4.

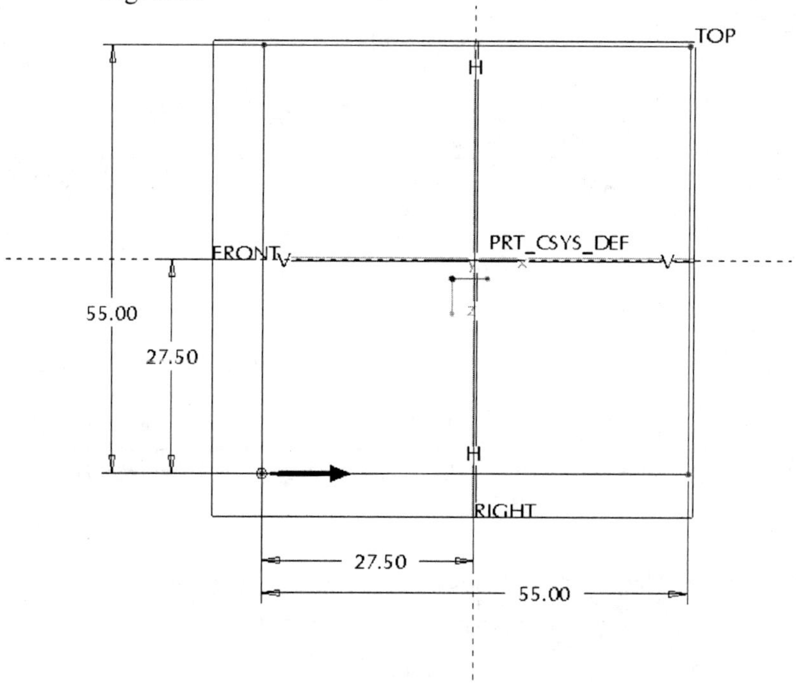

Fig. 13.5.

Goal	Step	Commands
Create the obelisk (continued)	15. Sketch a rectangle.	→ *Pick points 3 and 4* Make sure that Point 3 is close to point 1. Refer Fig. 13.6.
	16. Add dimensions.	→ ***Select the bottom edge → Middle Mouse to place the horizontal dimension →*** ***Select the right edge → Middle Mouse to place the vertical dimension →*** ***Select the bottom edge → Select the FRONT datum plane → Middle Mouse to place the vertical placement dimension →*** ***Select the right edge → Select the RIGHT datum plane → Middle Mouse to place the horizontal placement dimension*** Refer Fig. 13.6.
	17. Add relations to center the section.	Note that sd#s may be slightly different in your model. **TOOLS → RELATIONS → <u>Type the relations shown in Fig. 13.7.</u>** Refer Fig. 13.7.
	18. Sort relations.	**UTILITIES → REORDER RELATIONS → OK → OK**
	19. Modify the side dimension.	→ ***Double click the sd11 dimension →*** ***<u>34.5</u> → <u>ENTER</u>*** Refer Fig. 13.8.
	20. Toggle the section to construct new section.	**SKETCH → FEATURE TOOLS → TOGGLE SECTION**

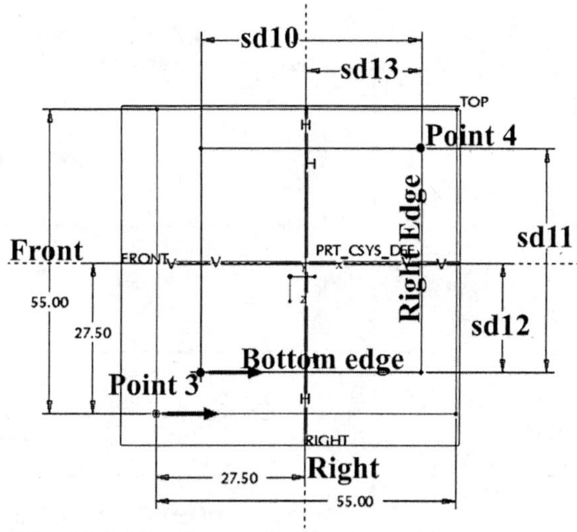

Fig. 13.6. The first section is shown in gray color.

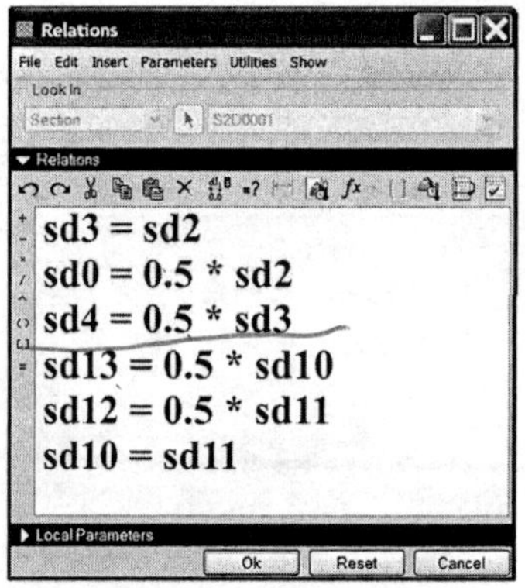

Fig. 13.7.

Sd14 = 0.5 · sd11
Sd13 = 0.5 · Sd12
sd11 = sd12

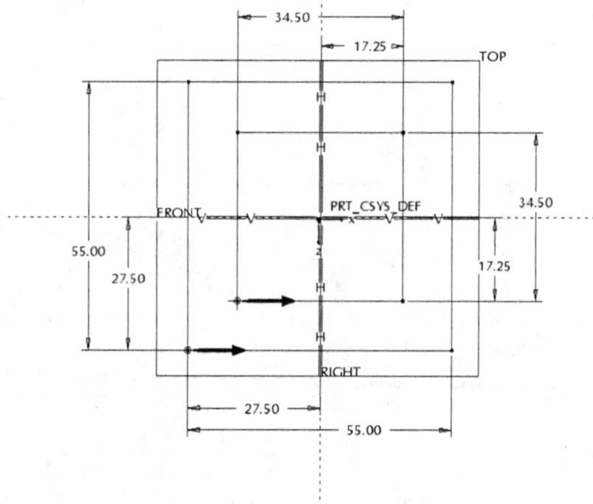

Fig. 13.8.

Goal	Step	Commands
Create the obelisk (continued)	21. Sketch a data point.	→ ***Pick point 5 at the intersection of the FRONT and RIGHT datum planes*** Refer Fig. 13.9.
	22. Exit sketcher.	
	23. Define the depths.	**500** → → **55** →
	24. Accept the feature creation.	**OK** → **VIEW** → **STANDARD ORIENTATION** Refer Fig. 13.9.
Save the file	25. Save the file.	**FILE** → **SAVE** → **MONUMENT.PRT** → **OK**
Play with the monument	26. Redefine the attributes.	***Select the protrusion feature from the model tree*** → ***Right Mouse*** → **Edit Definition** → **Attributes** → **Define** → Refer Fig. 13.10. **Smooth** → **Done** → **OK** Refer Fig. 13.11.

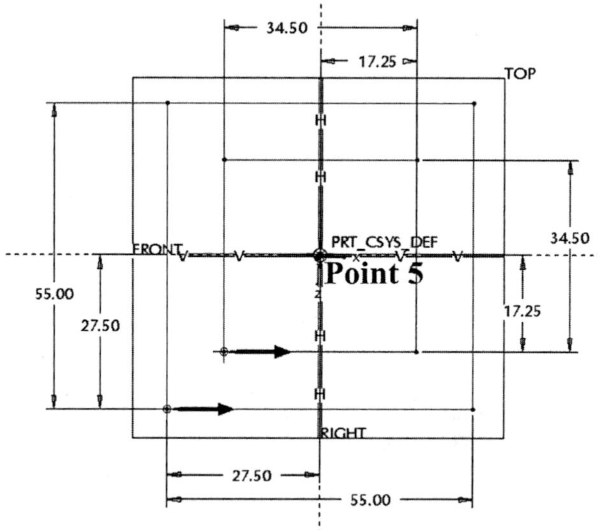

Fig. 13.8.

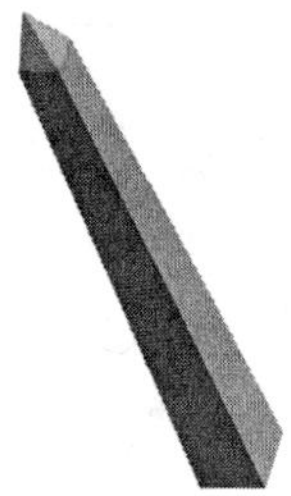
Fig. 13.9.

ProE connects the corresponding vertices of the two sections starting with the start points. The start point can be varied by "Selecting the start point → SKETCH → FEATURE TOOLS → START POINT" command. We can move from one section to another by using "SKETCH → FEATURE TOOLS → TOGGLE SECTION" command.

Fig. 13.10.

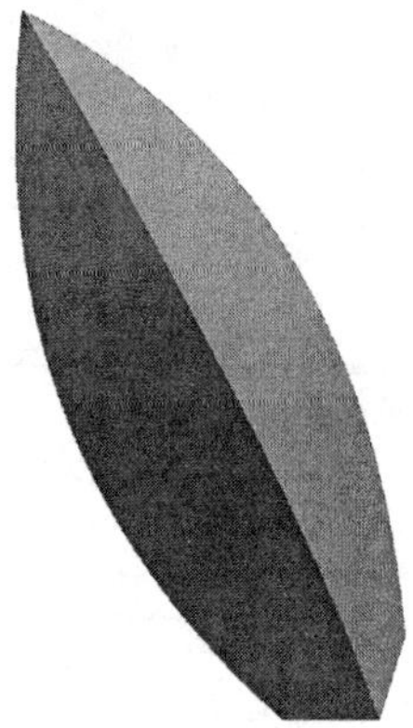
Fig. 13.11.

Goal	Step	Commands
	27. Redefine the start points.	***Select the protrusion feature from the model tree* → *Right Mouse* → Edit Definition →** **Section → Define →** Refer Fig. 13.12. **Sketch → SKETCH → FEATURE TOOLS → TOGGLE SECTION (the small square should get highlighted) → Select a new start point →** ***Right Mouse*** **→ Start Point →** Refer Fig. 13.13. ✓ → **OK** Refer Fig. 13.14.
Exit ProE	28. Exit ProE ***without*** saving.	**FILE → EXIT → YES**

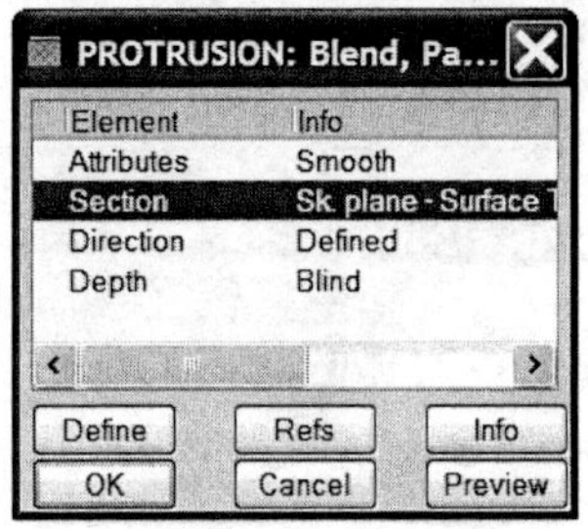

Fig. 13.12.

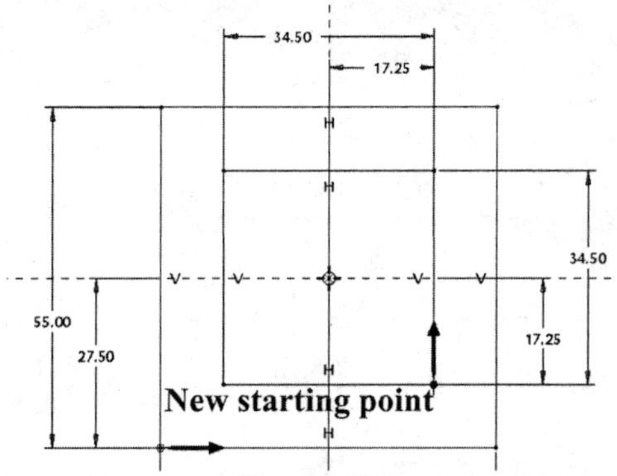

Fig. 13.13.

Fig. 13.14.

SEQUENCE OF STEPS

STEP I: Create the data points

1. Create the data points in Notepad or Excel.

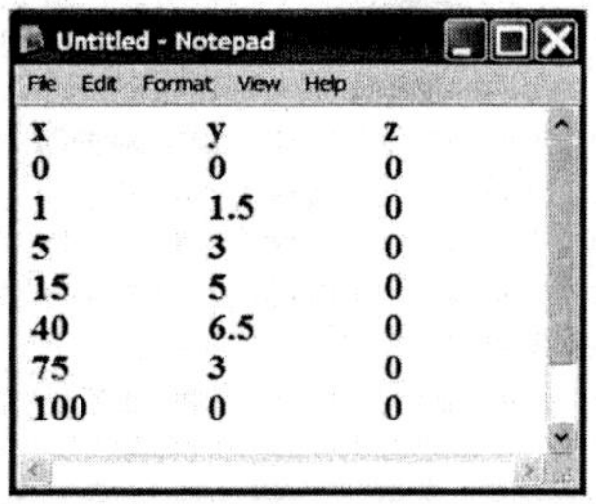
Untitled - Notepad
File Edit Format View Help

x	y	z
0	0	0
1	1.5	0
5	3	0
15	5	0
40	6.5	0
75	3	0
100	0	0

STEP II: Create the airfoil section

1. Create a coordinate system.
2. Create a spline.
3. Assign the coordinate system to the spline.
4. Read data points

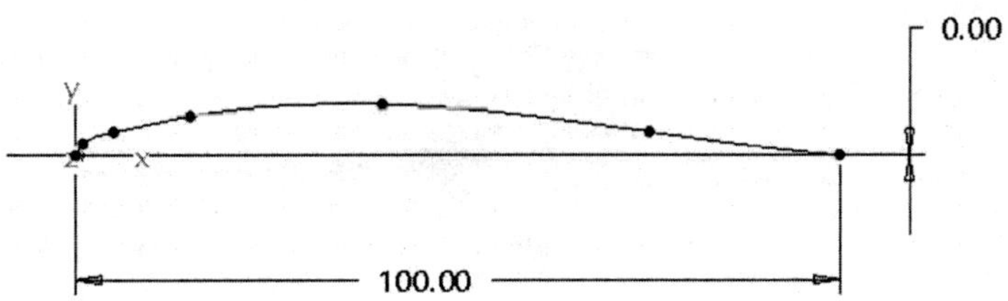

STEP III: Create the airfoil

1. Define the blend parameters as parallel and regular sections.
2. Select the type of transition surface as straight.
3. Define and orient the sketching plane.
4. Insert the base section of the wing.
5. Toggle section.
6. Insert the tip section of the wing.

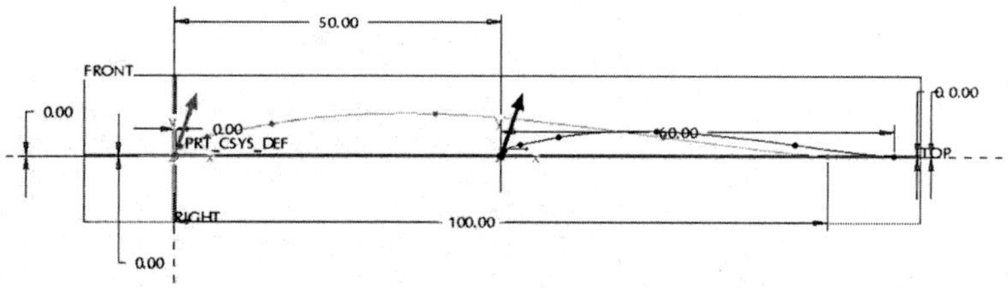

7. Mirror the surface.

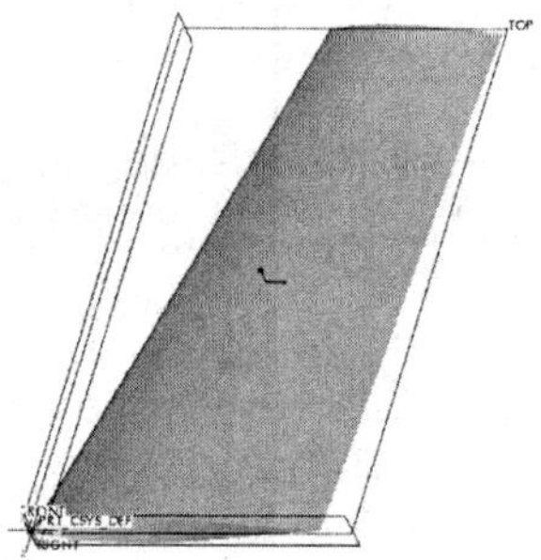

Goal	Step	Commands
IN NOTEPAD OR EXCEL		
Create the airfoil data points	1. Open notepad or Excel.	
	2. Enter the surface data points.	**Enter data points** Refer Fig. 13.15.
	3. Save the data file.	**FILE → SAVE AS →** ***Select the working directory*** → (File name) **"spline.pts"** (If the name is enclosed in quotes, then Windows will not attach any extension to the file name.) → (Save as type) **Text document** → (Encoding – if prompted) **ANSI → Save** **FILE → EXI** Refer Fig. 13.16.
IN PROE		
Open a new file for the airfoil section	4. Setup the working directory.	**FILE → SET WORKING DIRECTORY →** ***Select the working directory*** **→ OK**
	5. Open a new file.	**FILE → NEW → Sketch → airfoil → OK**
Create the airfoil section	6. Create a coordinate system.	→ → ***Select a point in the graphics window***
	7. Create a spline.	→ ***Pick points 1, 2 and 3 → Middle Mouse*** Refer Fig. 13.17.
	8. Modify the dimensions.	→ ***Double click each dimension and enter the corresponding value*** Refer Fig. 13.17.

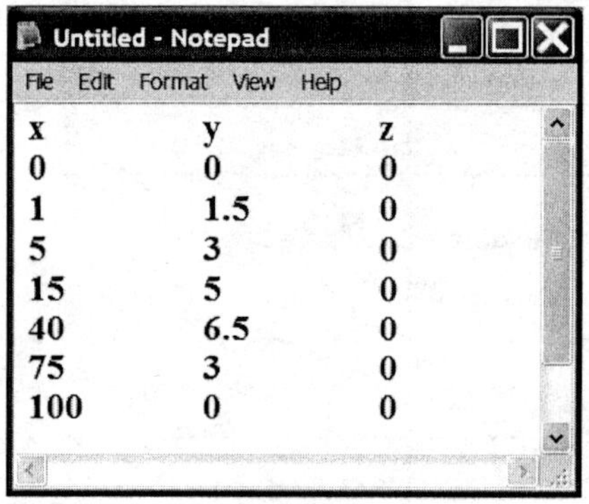

Fig. 13.15.

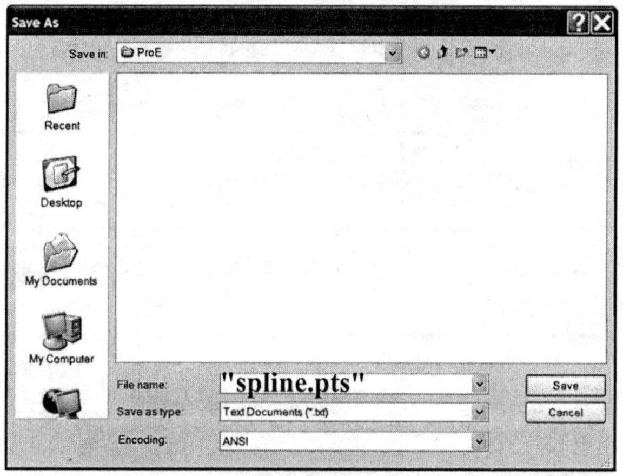

Fig. 13.16.

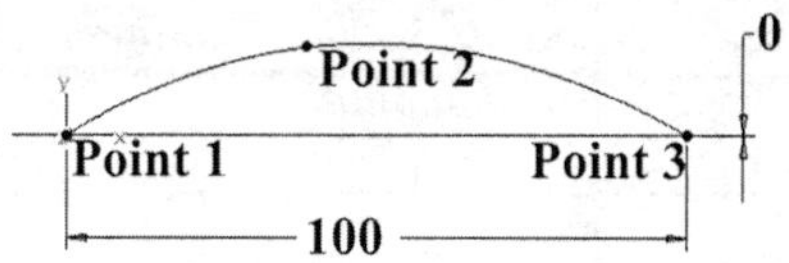

Fig. 13.17.

Goal	Step	Commands
Create the airfoil section (continued)	9. Select the Cartesian coordinate system.	***Select the spline*** → → ***In the dash - Click file*** → ***(in the popup window)*** → ***Select the Cartesian coordinate system created in step 6*** Refer Fig. 13.18.
	10. Open the data file.	→ ***Select "spline.pts" file*** → **OPEN** → **Yes** → **Yes**
	11. Accept the spline creation.	
	13. Save the section file.	**FILE** → **SAVE** → **AIRFOIL.SEC** → **OK** → **FILE** → **CLOSE WINDOW**
Open a new file for the wing part	14. Open a new file.	**FILE** → **NEW** → **Part** → **Solid** → **wing** → **OK**
Create the wing part	15. Start "Blend - Surface" feature.	**INSERT** → **BLEND** → **SURFACE**
	16. Select the sketch option.	**Parallel** → **Regular Sec** → **Sketch Sec** → **Done**
	17. Select the type of transition surface.	**Straight** → **Open Ends** → **Done**
	18. Select the sketching plane.	**Setup New** → **Plane** → ***Select the FRONT datum plane***
	19. Define the direction of material extrusion.	**Okay**
	20. Orient the sketcher.	**Default**

Fig. 13.18.

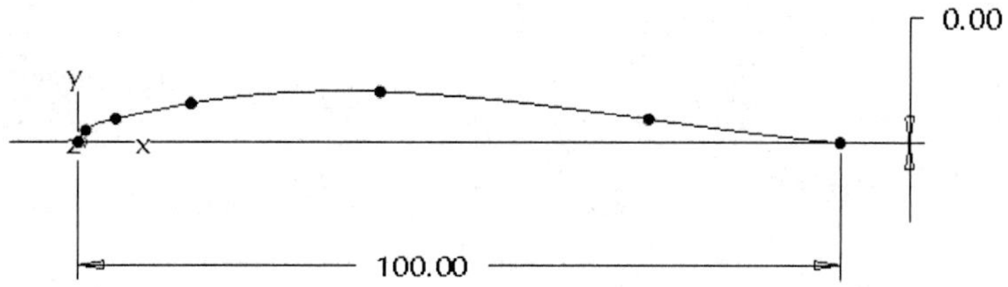

Fig. 13.19.

Goal	Step	Commands
Create the wing part (continued)	21. Import the airfoil section.	**SKETCH → DATA FROM FILE →** ***Select "airfoil.sec" file → Click in the graphics window*** Refer Fig. 13.20. (Scale) **1** → (Angle) **0** → →
	22. Modify the distance between the coordinate systems.	→ ***Double click on the horizontal distance dimension → 0 → ENTER → Double click on the vertical distance dimension → 0 → ENTER*** Refer Figs. 13.20 and 13.21.
	23. Toggle the section.	**SKETCH → FEATURE TOOLS → TOGGLE SECTION**
	24. Import the airfoil section.	**SKETCH → DATA FROM FILE →** ***Select "airfoil.sec" file →Click in the graphics window*** Refer Fig. 13.22. (Scale) **0.6** → (Angle) **0** →
	25. Modify the placement dimensions.	→ ***Double click on the horizontal distance dimension → 0 → ENTER → Double click on the vertical distance dimension → 50 → ENTER*** Refer Figs. 13.22 and 13.23.
	26. Exit sketcher.	✓

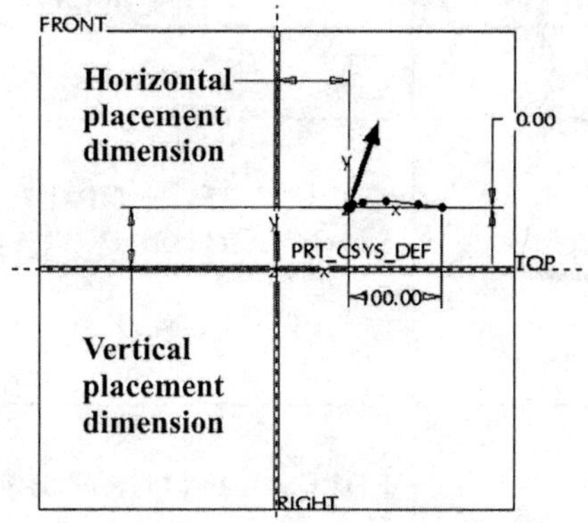

Fig. 13.20.

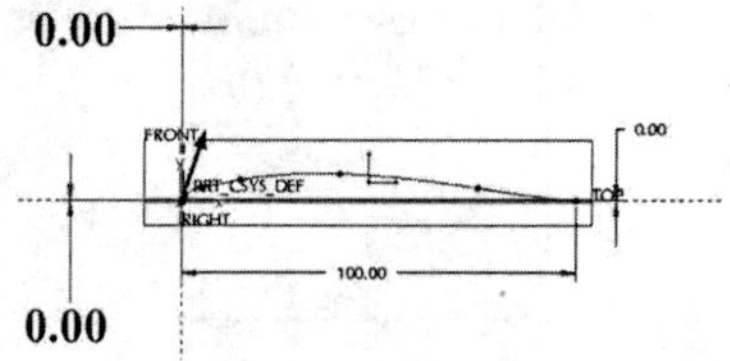

Fig. 13.21.

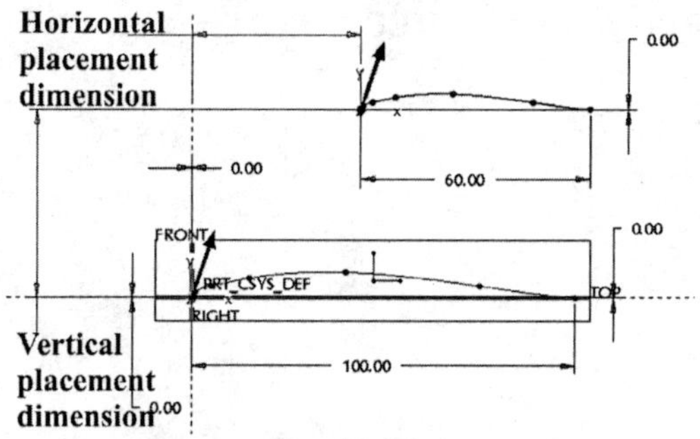

Fig. 13.22.

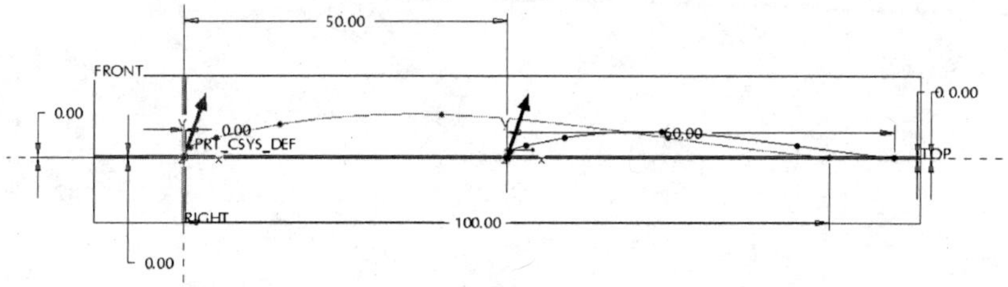

Fig. 13.23.

Goal	Step	Commands
Create the wing part (continued)	27. Define the depths.	**200** → 
	28. Accept the feature creation.	**OK → VIEW → ORIENTATION → STANDARD ORIENTATION** Refer Fig. 13.24.
	29. Mirror the feature.	**EDIT → FEATURE OPERATIONS → Copy → Mirror → Select → Dependent → Done →** ***Select the surface*** **→ OK → Done → Plane →** ***Select the TOP datum plane*** **→ Done** Refer Fig. 13.25.
Save the file and exit ProE	30. Save the file and exit ProE.	**FILE → SAVE → WING.PRT→ OK → FILE → EXIT→ YES**

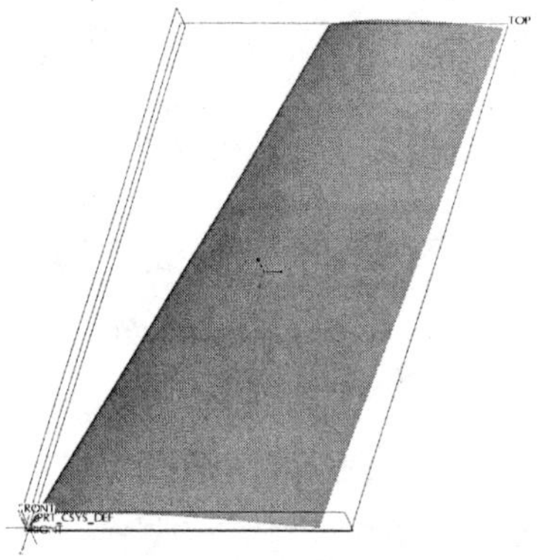

Fig. 13.24.

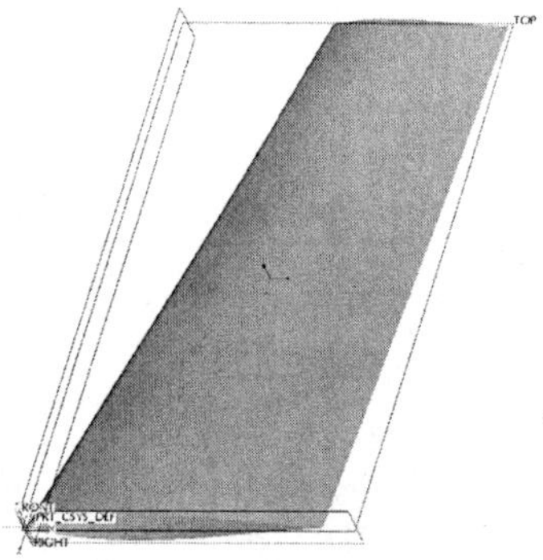

Fig. 13.25.

Exercise

Problem 1

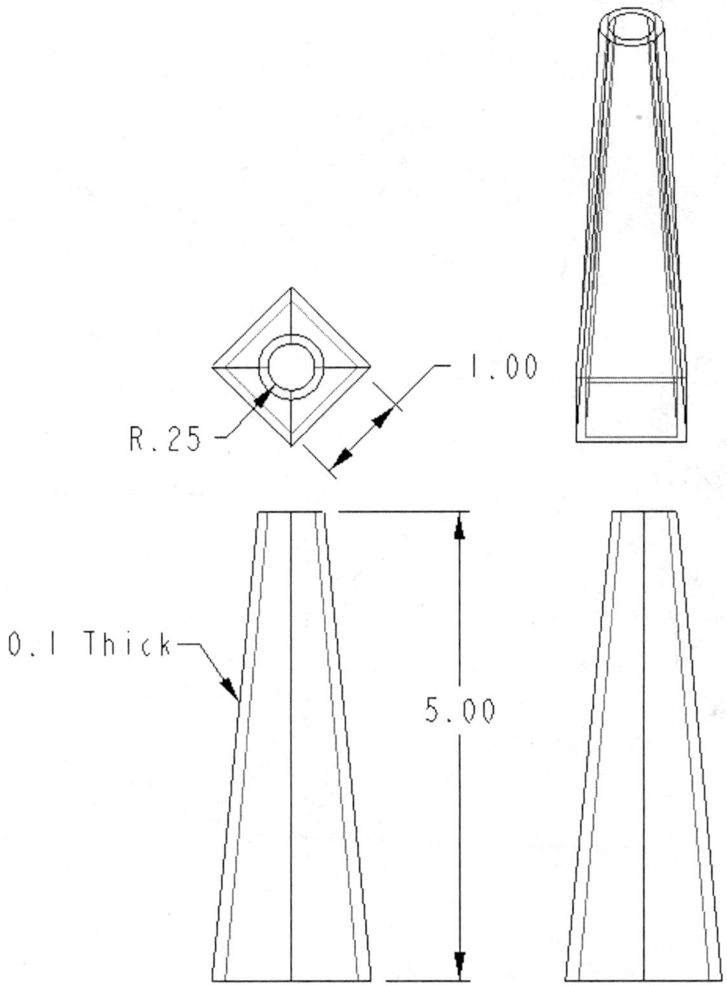

Hints

1. Use Blend – Thicken feature.
2. Draw a square using line tool. Add three normal constraints (→). Then, toggle the section.
3. Draw a circle and divide it into four segments → .
4. Change the start point if necessary by selecting the start point, right mouse and clicking "start point" in the menu (shown in the figure below). Selecting the start point a second time changes the direction of the arrow.

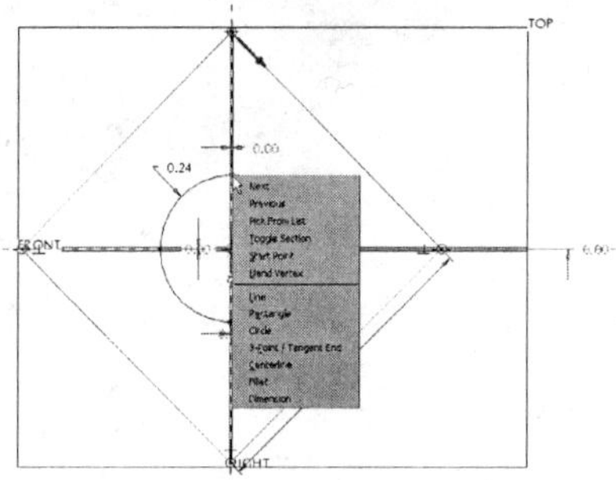

5. Sketch is shown in the figure below :

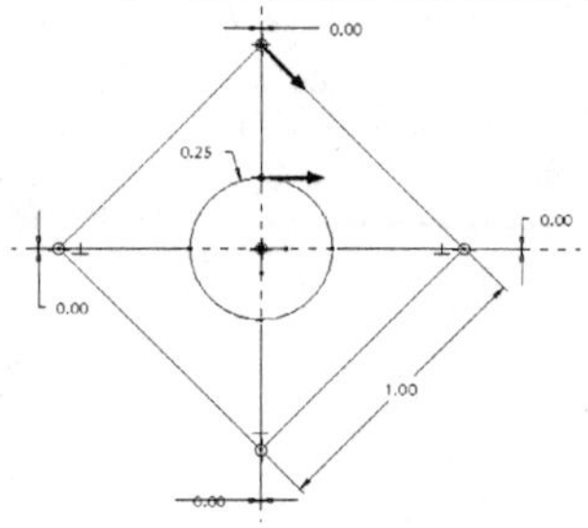

Problem 2

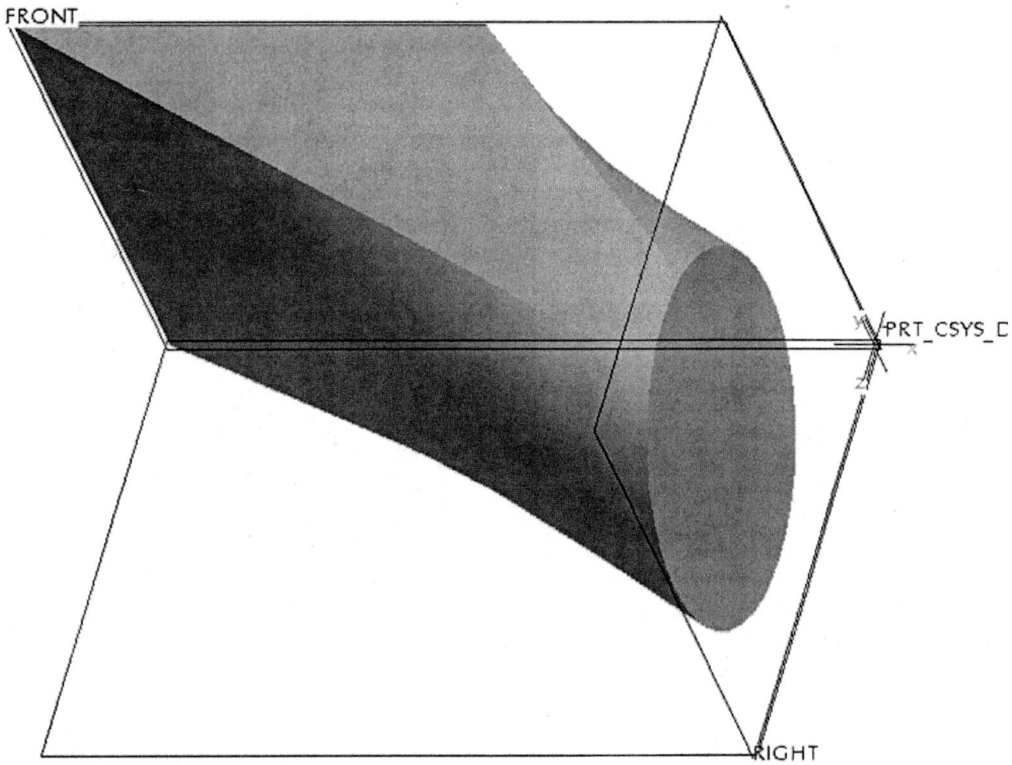

Hints

1. Use Blend – Rotational feature.
2. Select the front datum plane.
3. Insert a coordinate system and then, sketch section 1 (square). Dimension the section with respect to the coordinate system. Exit sketch.
4. Define the angle as 90 degrees.
5. Insert a coordinate system and then section 2 (circle). Divide it into four segments 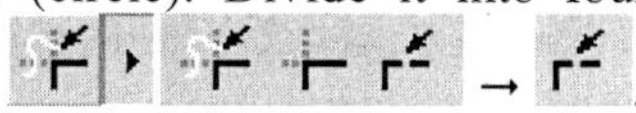.

OPEN-ENDED DESIGN

Create an aircraft carrier.

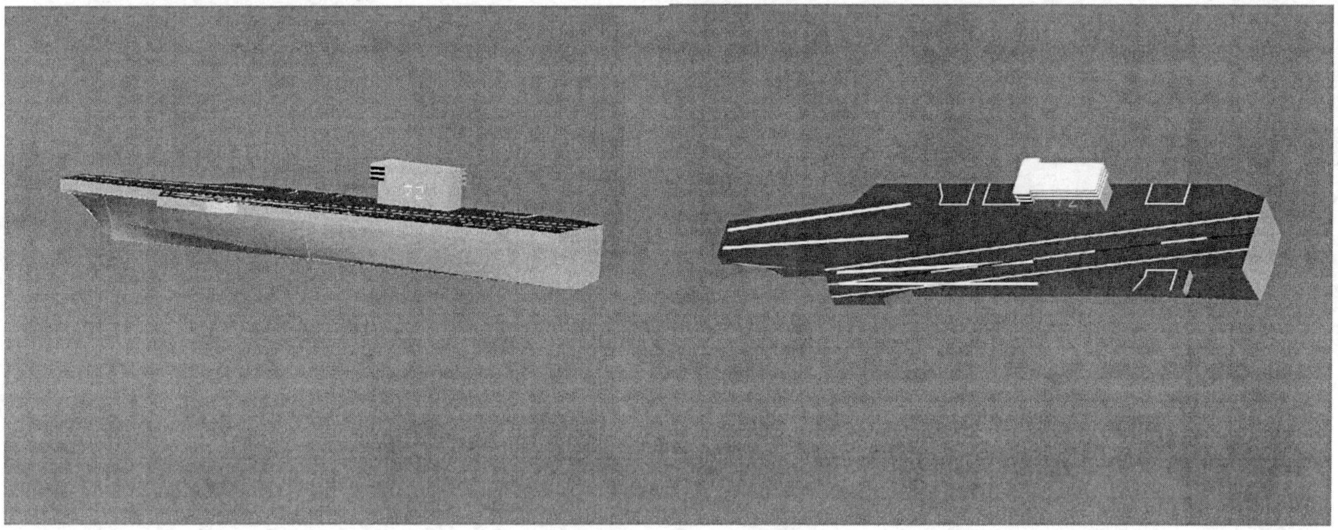

NOTES:

LESSON 14
GATEWAY ARCH

Learning Objectives

- Learn ***Swept – Blend*** feature.
- Practice Setup – Units.
- Learn PhotoRender.
- Practice the Use of Sections and Mirror commands.
- Practice Datum Curve – From Equation feature.

SWEPT BLEND

A swept blend feature is the generic version of the blend feature. It blends two or more sections while sweeping them along a specified trajectory.

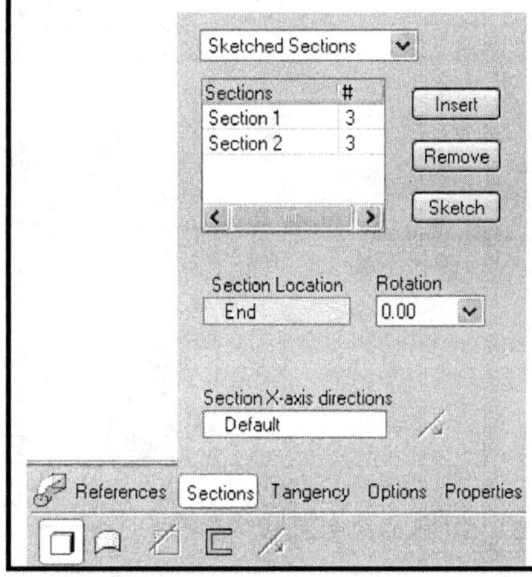

Allows the user to select or sketch sections.

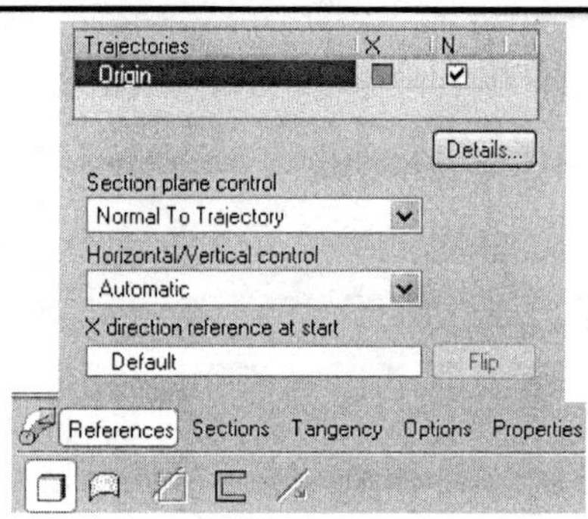

Allows the user to specify origin trajectory and a secondary trajectory. The user can orient the section xy specifying the orientation of the sketch plane. The default option for a swept blend feature is normal to trajectory. In this option, the section remains normal to the origin trajectory. Other options are constant normal direction and normal to projection.

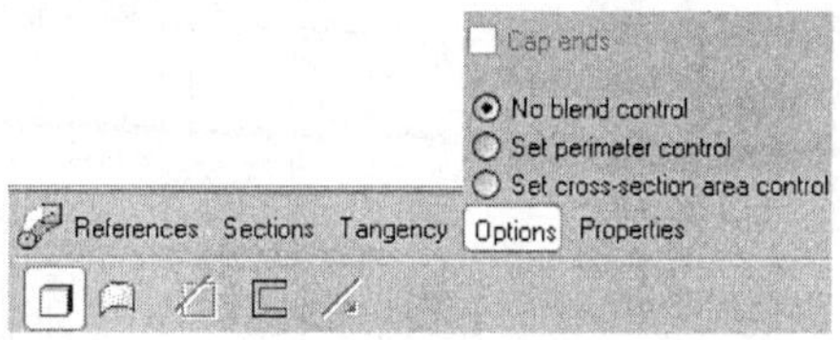

Capped ends option is available when creating surfaces. The default option is no blend control. The perimeter control option linearly varies the perimeter of the blend. Cross-section area control allows the specification of the cross-sectional area at specific locations.

Background Information

Architect Eero Saarinen conceived the Gateway Arch to commemorate the westward expansion of the United States. It was completed in 1965 on the banks of the River Mississippi, in St. Louis. The stainless steel arch spans 630 ft. between its legs. At 630 ft., it is the tallest memorial in the United States. Each leg of the arch is an equilateral triangle with its sides measuring 54 ft. at the ground level and tapering to 17 ft. at the top. Saarinen used an inverted catenary curve shape for the arch. Catenary curve is the shape assumed by a flexible cable hanging under its own weight between two supports. Even though it looks like a parabola, the equations are quite different from that of a parabola.

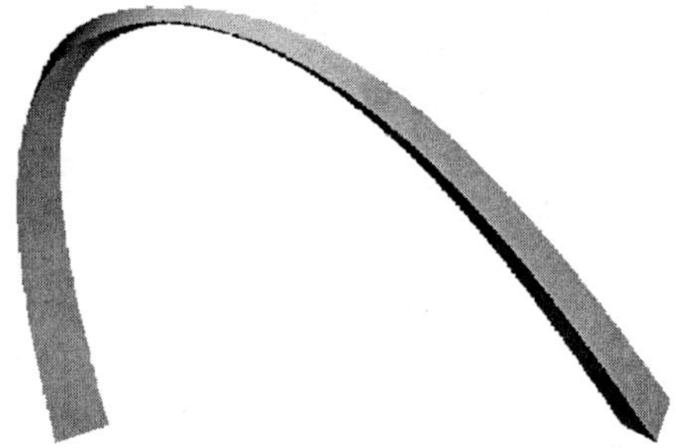

SEQUENCE OF STEPS

STEP I: Create an equilateral triangle (arch section)

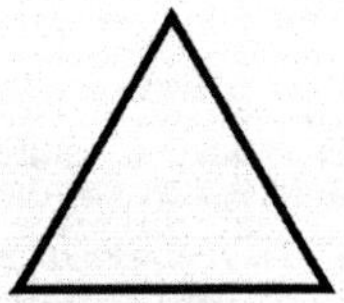

STEP II: Set up units

STEP III: Create a datum curve using catenary curve equations

1. Set up the coordinate system.

2. Define the equations.

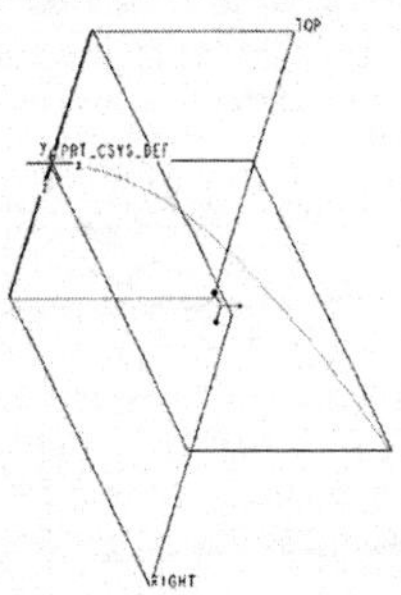

STEP IV: Create half-arch

1. Start "Swept - Blend" feature.

2. Specify the sweep trajectory.

3. Specify the sweep section at the top and bottom of the arch.

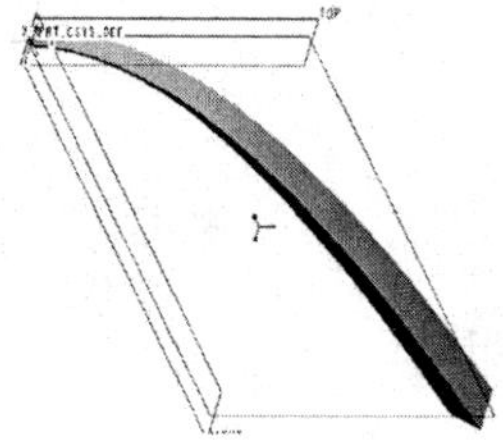

STEP V: Mirror the half-arch

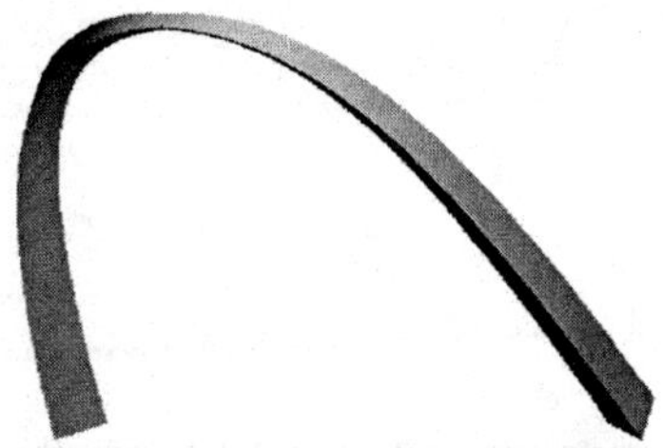

Goal	Step	Commands
Open a new file for the arch section	1. Set up the working directory.	**FILE → SET WORKING DIRECTORY →** ***Select the working directory*** **→ OK**
	2. Open a new file.	**FILE → NEW →** ***Sketch*** **→ archsection → OK**
Create the arch section (equilateral triangle)	3. Establish a reference coordinate system.	→ → → ***Click in the graphics window*** Refer to Fig. 14.1.
	4. Draw a triangle.	→ ***Pick points 1, 2, 3 and 1 to create a triangle → Middle Mouse to discontinue line creation*** Refer to Fig. 14.2.
	5. Dimension the triangle.	→ → ***Select lines 1 and 2 → Select lines 2 and 3 →*** → → ***Select the coordinate system → Select the apex*** **→ CLOSE** **INFO → SWITCH DIMS →** ***Double click the placement dimension between the reference coordinate system and the right side (sd6)*** **→ sd2/(2*sqrt(3))** **→** ***ENTER*** **→ YES →** Refer to Fig. 14.3. sd2 dimension refers to base dimension and may be differentin your model. ***Double click the base dimension → 1 → ENTER*** Refer to Fig. 14.4.
Save the section and	6. Save the section.	**FILE → SAVE → ARCHSECTION.SEC → OK**

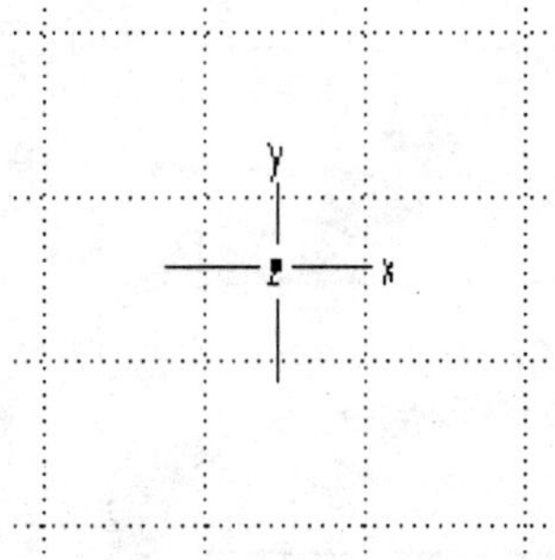

Fig. 14.1.

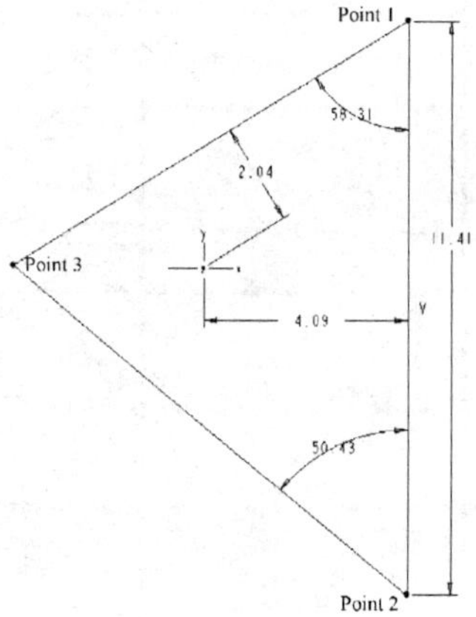

Fig. 14.2.

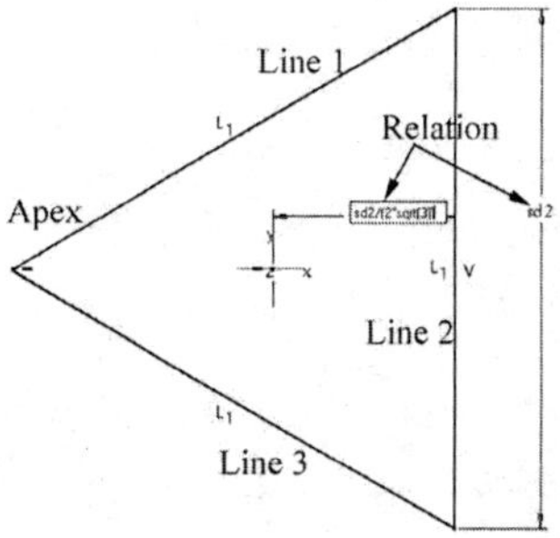

Fig. 14.3.

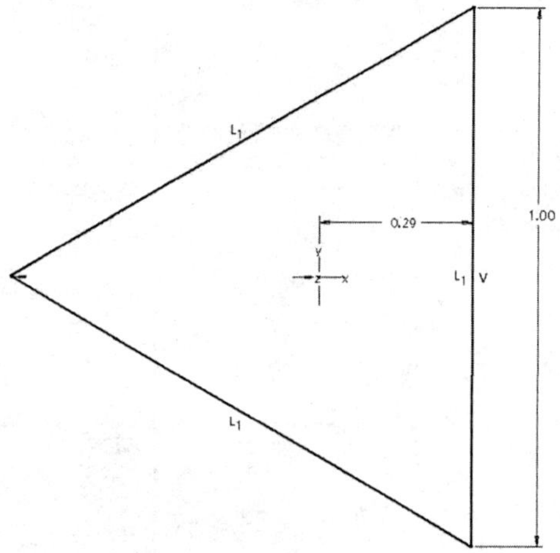

Fig. 14.4.

Goal	Step	Commands
exit sketcher	7. Exit sketcher.	**FILE → CLOSE WINDOW**
Open a new file for the arch part	8. Open a new file.	**FILE → NEW → Part → Solid → <u>Arch</u> → OK**
Set up units	9. Change the units to FPS system.	**EDIT → SETUP → Units → *Select Foot Pound Second (FPS) system* → *Set* → OK → Close → Done**
Create a datum curve	10. Establish the coordinate system.	**→ From Equation → Done → Select → *Select the default coordinate system PRT_CSYS_DEF from the model tree* → Cartesian** ProE opens the equation editor.
	11. Input equations in the equation editor.	**<u>Input the equations shown in Fig. 14.5.</u>** **FILE → SAVE → FILE → EXIT** ProE automatically varies t from 0 to 1.
	12. Create the datum curve.	**OK** Refer to Fig. 14.6.
Create half-arch	13. Start "Swept Blend" feature.	**INSERT → SWEPT BLEND →**
	14. Specify the sweep trajectory.	**References → *Select the datum curve*** Refer to Fig. 14.7.

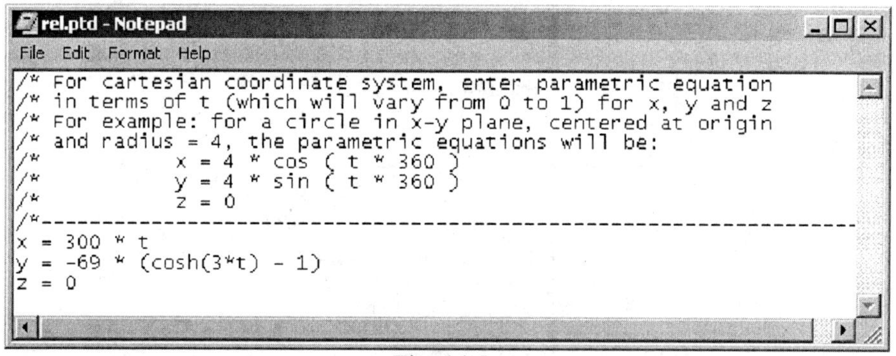

Fig. 14.5.

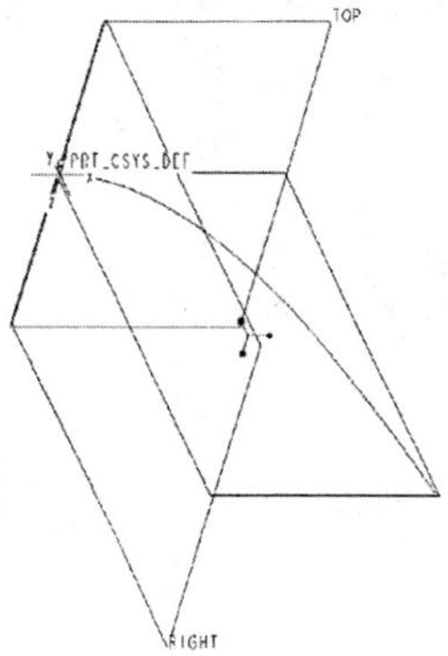

Fig. 14.6.

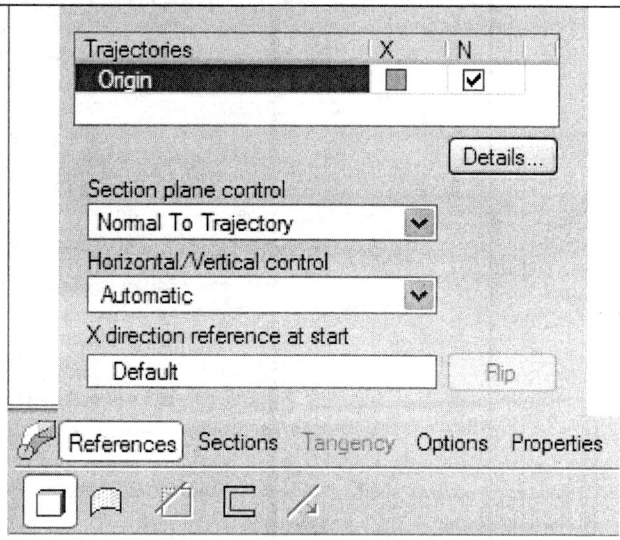

Fig. 14.7.

Goal	Step	Commands
Create half-arch (continued)	15. Specify the sweep section orientation and the section at the top of the arch.	***Sections* → *Select the curve start point at the part coordinate system* →** **SKETCH → DATA FROM FILE → FILE SYSTEM → *Select archsection.sec* → *Click in the graphics window* → OPEN → NO → Drag the section using the handle and drop it on the FRONT datum plane →** Refer Fig. 14.9 and 14.10. **(Scale) <u>17</u> → (Rotation) <u>0</u> → ✓ →** ***→ Select the sketcher coordinate system → Select the section coordinate system in the triangle →*** ***Middle Mouse to place horizontal dimension →*** ***→ Double click the horizontal placement dimension → <u>0</u> → <u>ENTER</u> → ✓*** ***Double click the vertical placement dimension → <u>0</u> → <u>ENTER</u> → ✓*** Refer to Fig. 14.10.

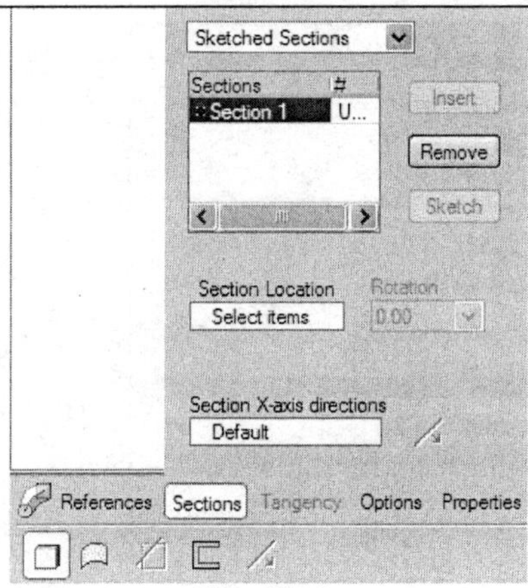

Fig. 14. 8.

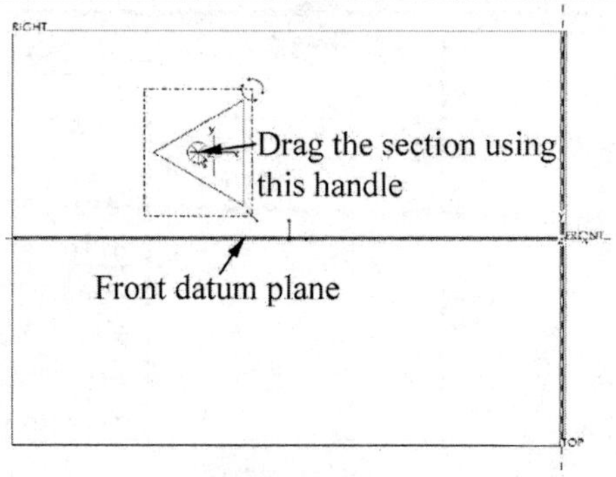

Fig. 14.9.

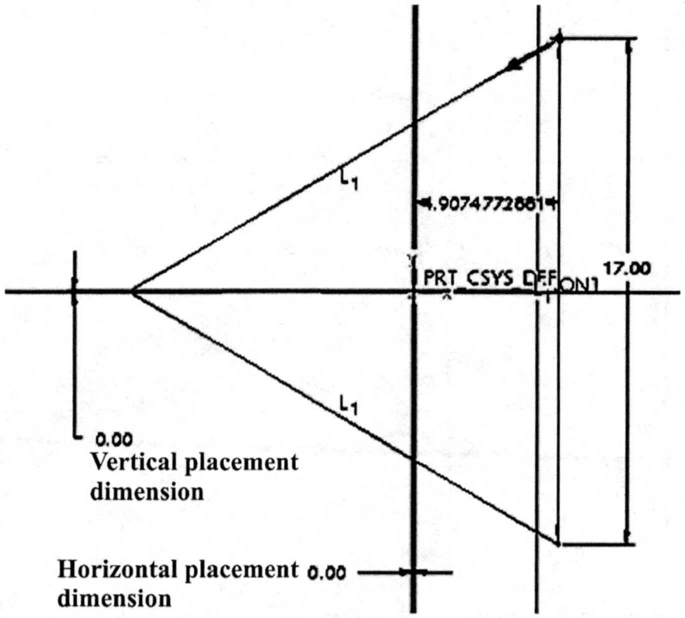

Fig. 14.10.

Goal	Step	Commands
Create half-arch (continued)	16. Specify section orientation and section at the bottom of the arch.	**Insert** → ***Select the curve start point at the part coordinate system*** → **Sketch** → **DATA FROM FILE** → **FILE SYSTEM** → ***Select archsection.sec*** → ***Click in the graphics window*** → **OPEN** → **NO** → → **Drag the section using the handle and drop it on the FRONT datum plane** → **(Scale) <u>54</u>** → **(Rotation) <u>0</u>** → → → ***Select the sketcher coordinate system (CtrPnt:SectEnt) (Refer Fig. 14.9.)*** → ***Select the section coordinate system CtrPnt:SectEnt in the triangle (Easier to pick the section coordinate from the list by "right mouse in the imported triangle*** → ***Pick from list*** → ***select CtrPnt:SectEnt")*** → ***Middle Mouse to place horizontal dimension*** → → ***Double click the horizontal placement dimension*** → **<u>0</u>** → ***<u>ENTER</u>*** → Refer Fig. 14. 10.

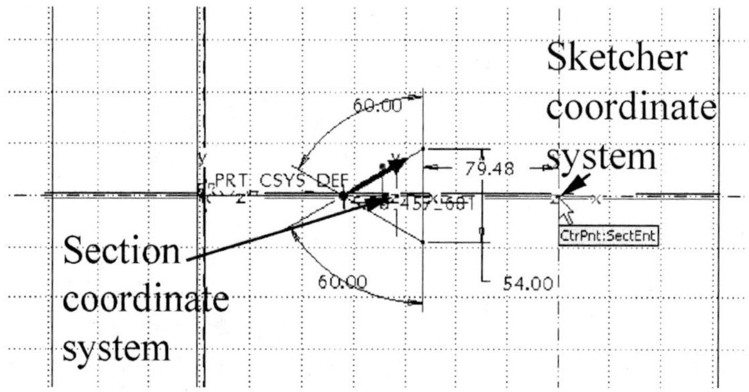

Fig. 14. 9.

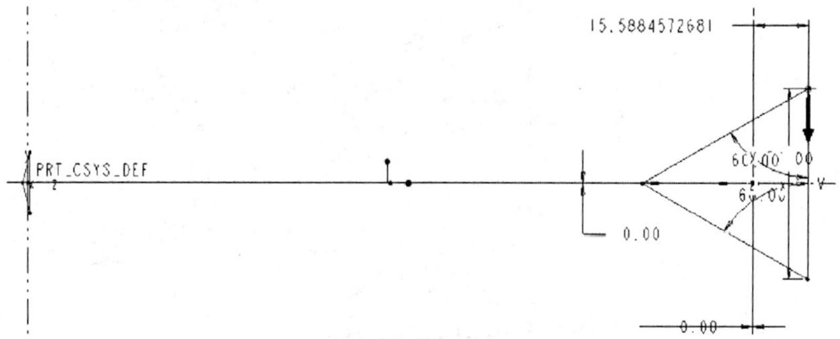

Fig. 14.10.

Goal	Step	Commands
Create half-arch (continued)	17. Create the arch leg.	 Refer Fig. 14.11.
Create the arch	18. Mirror protrusion feature.	**EDIT → FEATURE OPERATIONS → Copy → Mirror → Select → Dependent → Done → Select →** ***Select the arch leg*** **→ Done → Plane →** ***Select RIGHT datum plane*** **→ Done** Refer Fig. 14. 12.
View the arch	19. View the model in the default orientation.	***Click on the following icons to switch off the datums, axes, datum points and default coordinate system.*** 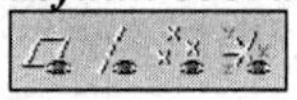 Refer Fig. 14.13.
Save the part	20. Save the part.	**FILE → SAVE → ARCH.PRT → OK**

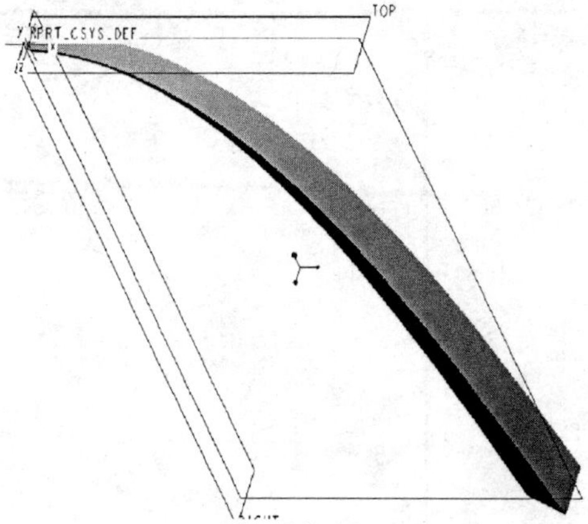

Fig. 14. 11.

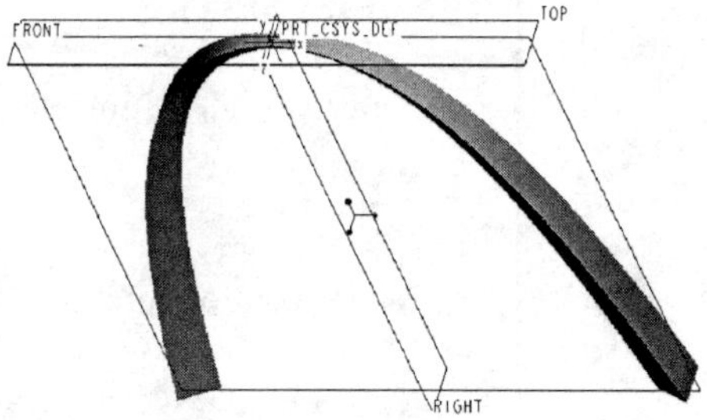

Fig. 14.12.

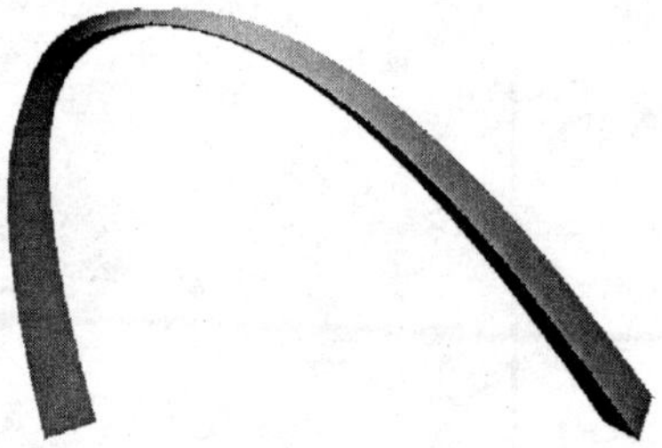
Fig. 14.13.

Goal	Step	Commands
Open PhotoRender	21. Open PhotoRender module.	**VIEW → MODEL SETUP → RENDER CONTROL** ProE opens Render Control menu bar. Refer Fig. 14.14. The render control options are described in Fig. 14.15.

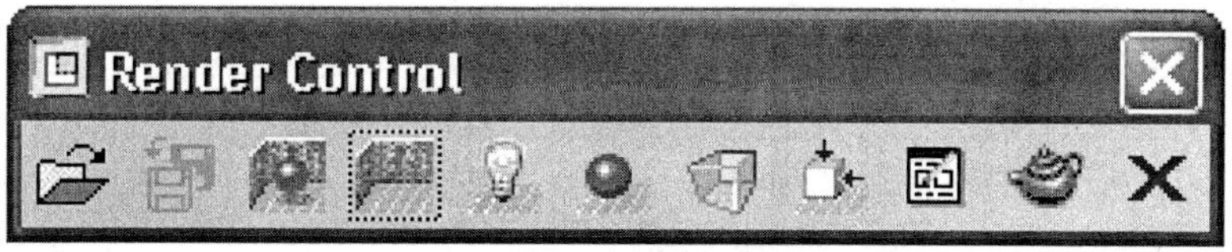

Fig. 14.14.

Option	Description
	Open an image.
	Save the image.
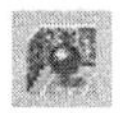	Modify render settings.
	Modify room settings, including the texture and size.
	Setup lights.
	Assign colors and appearances.
	Modify perspective.
	Reorient the view.
	Image editor.
	Render image.
	Close.

Fig. 14.15.

Goal	Step	Commands
Render the object	22. Define the room.	→ *Click on any wall* → Refer Fig. 14.16. **+ →** ***Click on the Map tab in the room appearance editor window → Click on the image shown in Fig. 14.17 to open appearance placement window →*** **FILE → OPEN →** ***Select a texture for wall (ANY JPEG OR GIF FILE) →*** **OPEN** ***→ Select the texture for wall (ANY JPEG OR GIF FILE) →*** **Close** **→ Close** Refer Fig. 14.17. **→ Follow the above process to assign different jpeg files for the remaining sides of the room →** **CLOSE**
	23. Render the model.	
Save the image	24. Save the image.	→ **Arch** → **OK** → **X**
Save the file and exit ProE	25. Save the file and exit ProE.	**FILE → SAVE → ARCH.PRT → OK → FILE → EXIT → Yes**

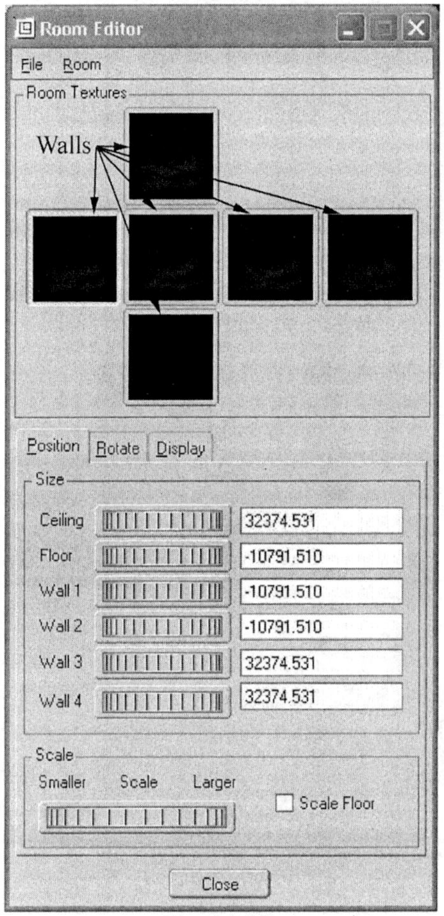

Fig. 14.16.

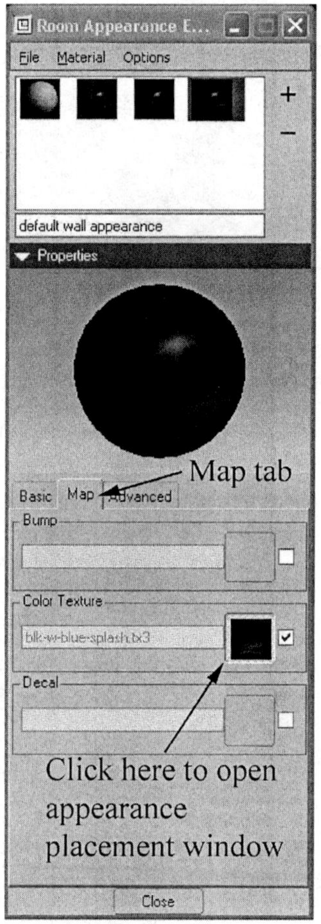

Fig. 14.17.

Exercise

Problem 1

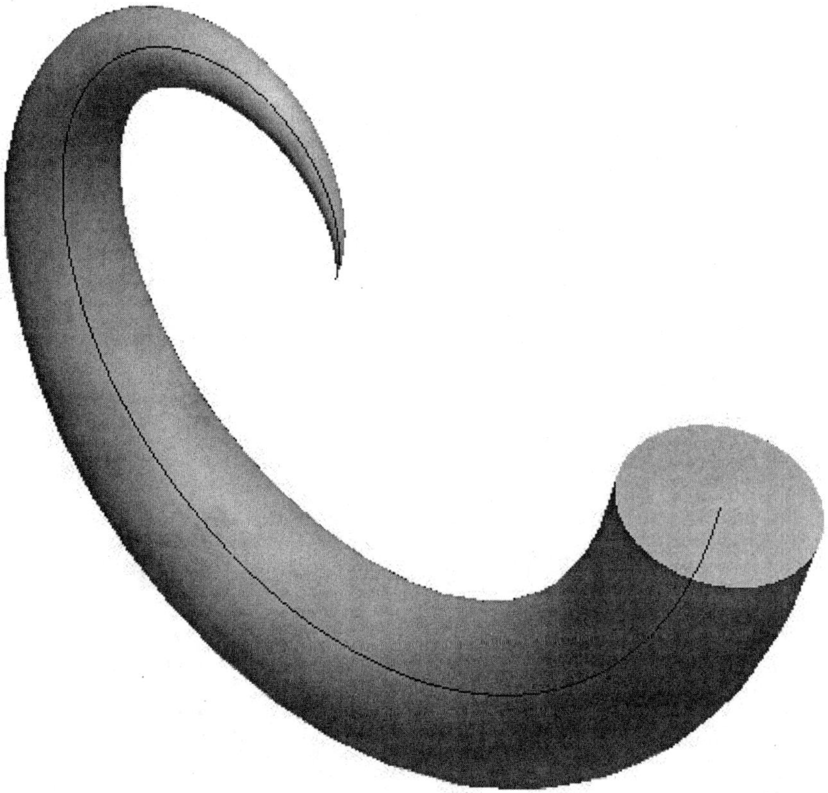

Background Information:

The equations of a plane spiral are:

$$R = k \times e^{\frac{\ln 2}{\alpha}\theta}$$

where R is the radius at an angle θ, k is the starting radius and α is the angle over which the spiral doubles.

Use the following values:

k =1
α = 2.42
θ goes from 0 to 360 degrees
Diameter of the circle at the end is 2".

Hints:

1. Create a datum curve with the following equations.

rel.ptd - Notepad

```
/* For cylindrical coordina
/* in terms of t (which wil
/* For example: for a circl
/* and radius = 4, the para
/*          r = 4
/*       theta = t * 360
/*          z = 0
/*-------------------------
r = exp(0.005*theta)
theta = t * 360
z = 0
```

2. Create the start section (circle of diameter 2) and the end section (a point) in the variable section sweep feature.

Problem 2

Background Information:
The equiangular spiral describes a family of spirals. It is a monotonic curve that cuts all radii vectors at a constant angle. Nautilus shells, arrangement of sunflower seeds in the sunflower and many other natural phenomena follow this spiral. The equations of the spiral are:

$$R = r\_initial \times k^{\theta}$$

where R is the radius at an angle θ, r_initial is the starting radius and k is any number.
Use the following values:

r_initial = 0.5”
k =1.2
θ goes from 0 to 1080 degrees
Diameter of the small circle is 0.125”
Diameter of the large circle is 5”

Hint:
Create a datum curve with the following equations.

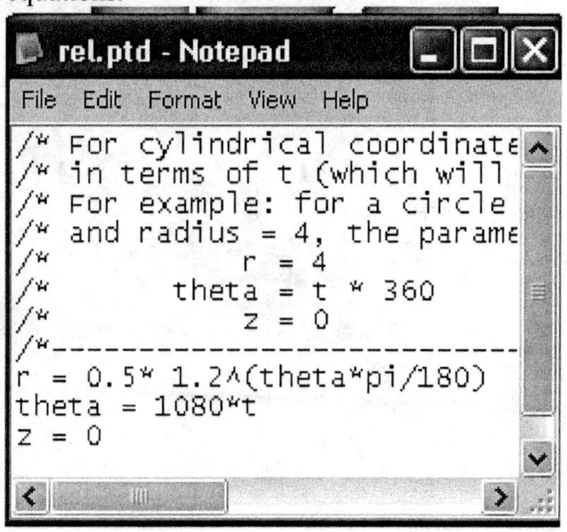

Problem 3 – Moebius Strip
The Moebius Strip is a three-dimensional shape with only one surface. You can create a Moebius Strip by gluing the ends of a long strip of paper. But remember to turn one end of the strip before connecting. For this surface, there is only one edge and no top or bottom.

Create the Moebius strip using swept blend.

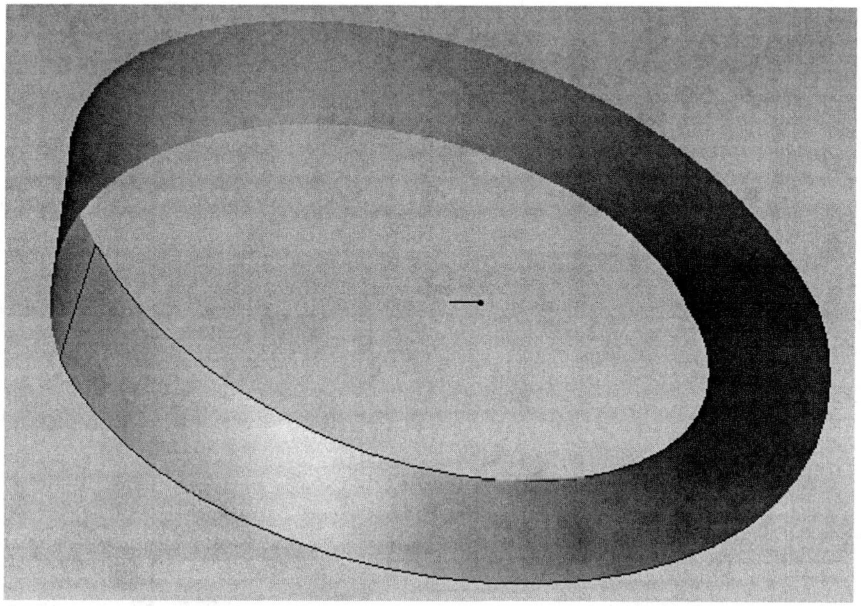

Hints:

1. Create the strip using two swept blends.
2. For the first swept blend:

Trajectory:

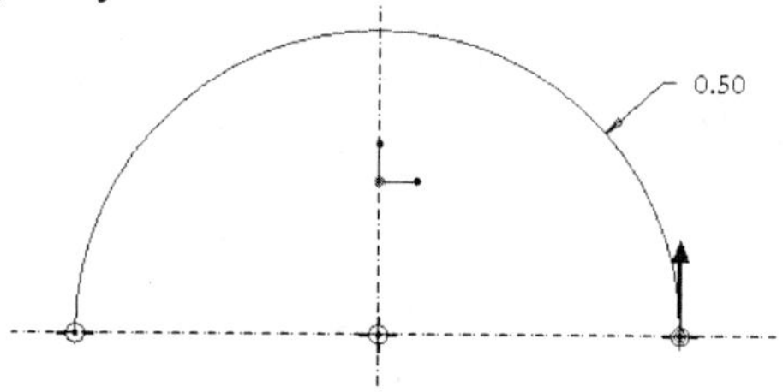

Start section

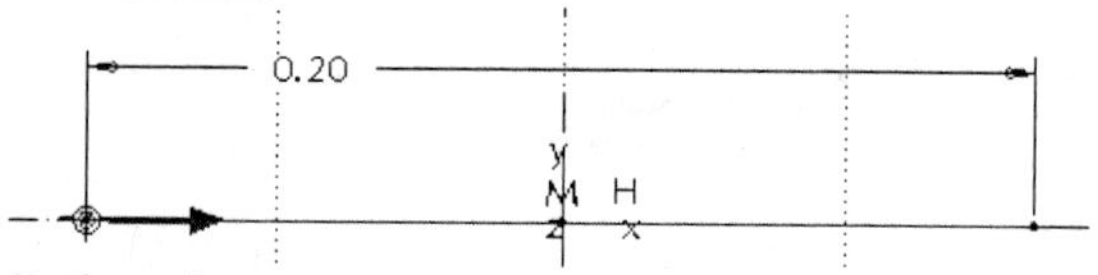

End section

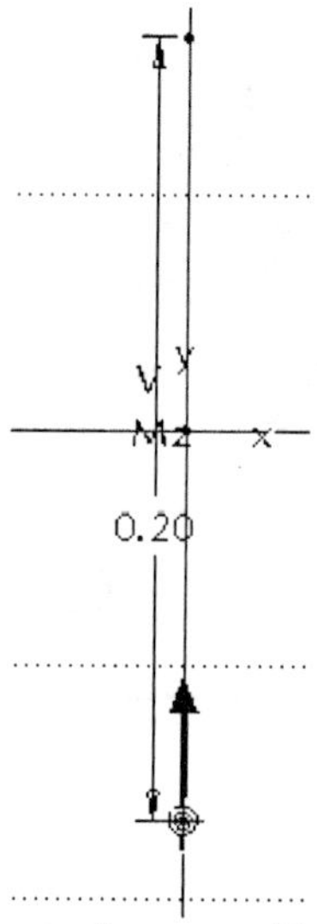

3. Now, create the second half following the same procedure.

OPEN-ENDED DESIGN

Create a model of the Golden Gate bridge.

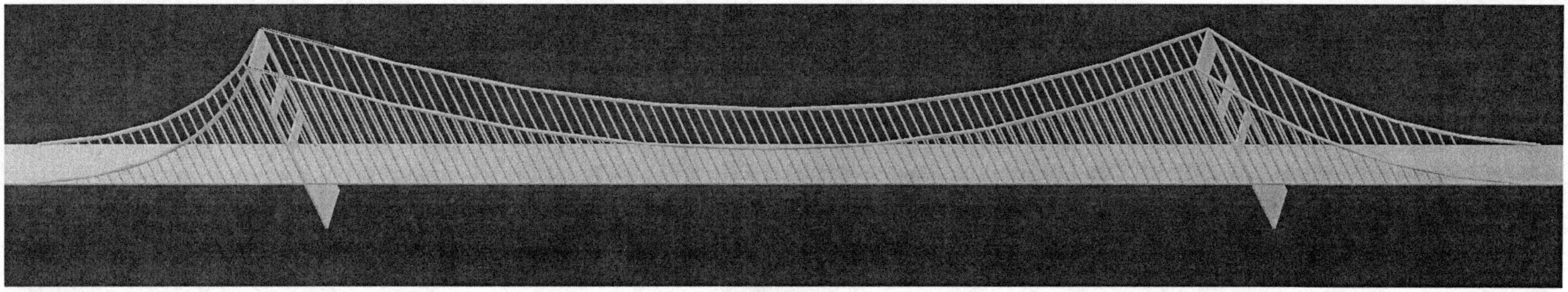

Hints:

1. Create the four main parts (main cable, support towers, stringers, and deck). You need the equations for the main cable.
2. Note that if the first stringer is extruded up to the main cable, then, it can be patterned easily.

OPEN-ENDED DESIGN

Create a model of the Canada's National tower (the world's tallest building 1,815 ft or 553 m)

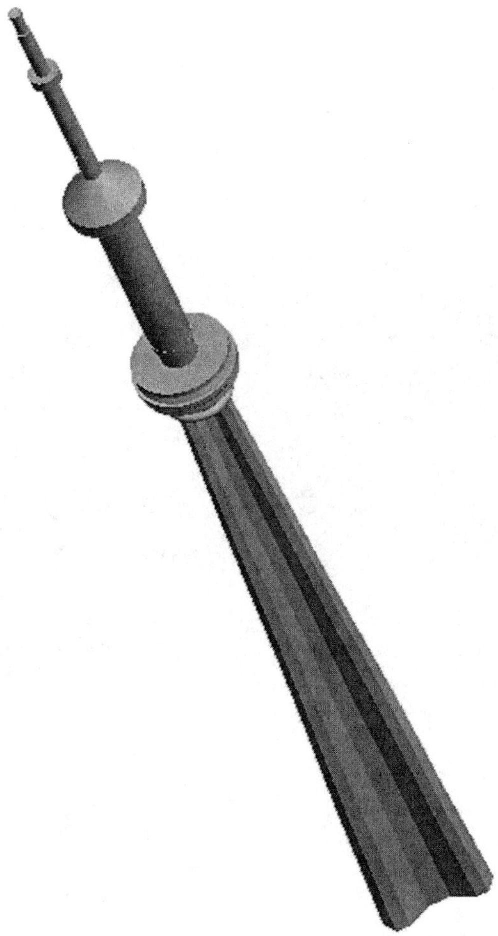

LESSON 15
SPRINGS

Learning Objectives

- Learn ***Sweep*** and ***Helical Sweep*** features.

Helical Sweep

A helical sweep feature can be used to create springs and threads. It requires the specification of:

a. the axis of revolution
b. a profile line defining the profile of the spring
c. pitch – the distance between the centers of two adjacent wires – can be constant or variable and defined in the pitch definition window,
d. section, and
e. right- or left-handed helix

Note that typically for a protrusion, the section is sketched at the start point. On the other hand, for a cut, the section is below the profile line. This helps to cut the

Background Information

A spring is a flexible element used to:

- Store energy;
- Exert a force or torque over specified distance; and
- Isolate vibrations.

Several different geometries can be used for a spring.

Helical springs are the most commonly used in engineering applications. Sometimes the pitch of the helical coils is varied to avoid resonant surging. The primary advantage of conical springs is the nesting of coils in the fully compressed position. It results in the smallest shut height. Conical springs have a nonlinear spring rate. However, the spring rate can be made constant by adjusting the pitch.

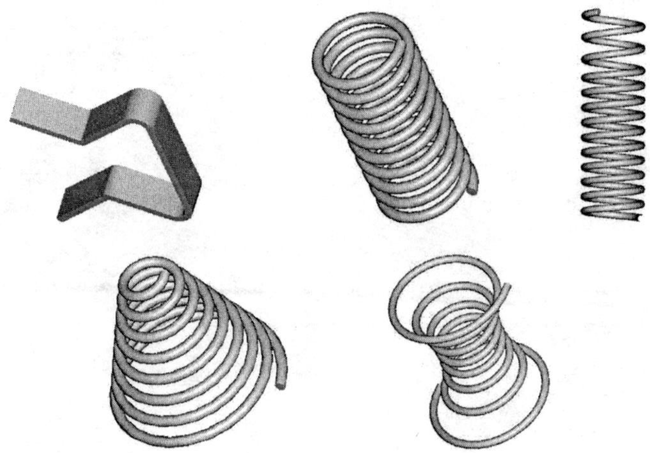

SEQUENCE OF STEPS

STEP I: Create a sweep feature

1. Sketch the rough sweep profile.
2. Modify dimensions.

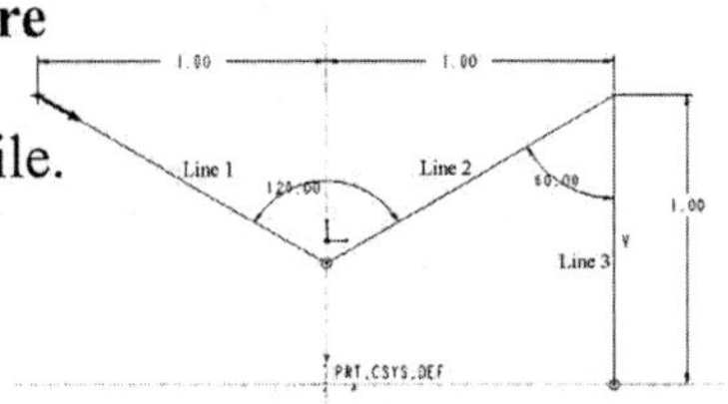

3. Add two fillets.

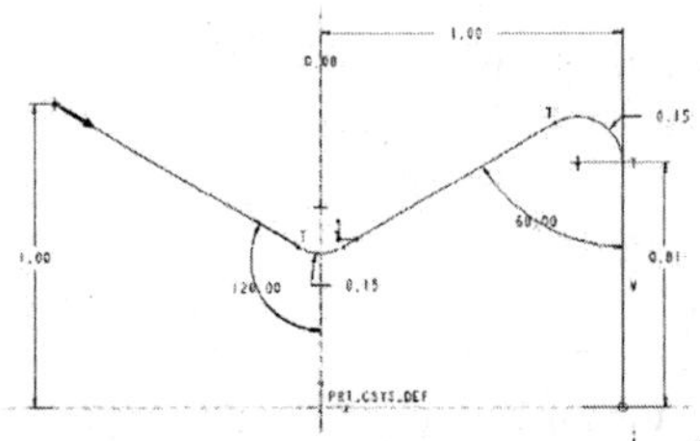

4. Create the sweep section.

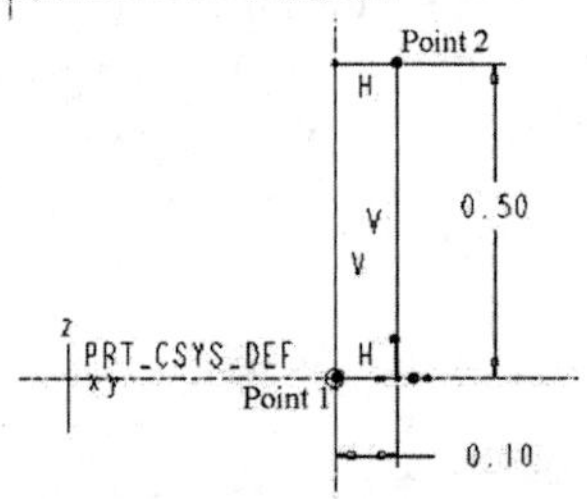

5. Accept the feature creation.

STEP II: Mirror the sweep feature.

1. Select the sweep feature.
2. Define the mirror plane.

Goal	Step	Commands
Open a new file for the spring part	1. Set up the working directory.	**FILE → SET WORKING DIRECTORY →** ***Select the working directory*** **→ OK**
	2. Open a new file.	**FILE → NEW →** ***Part*** **→** ***Solid*** **→ <u>spring1</u> → OK**
Create a sweep	3. Start "Sweep" feature.	**INSERT → SWEEP → PROTRUSION**
	4. Define the sketching plane.	**Sketch Traj → Setup New → Plane →** ***Select the FRONT datum plane*** **→ Okay → Default**
	5. Draw a rough section.	**→** ***Pick points 1, 2, 3, and 4*** **→** ***Middle Mouse*** Refer Fig. 15.1.
	6. Modify the dimensions.	**Add dimensions if necessary** Refer Fig. 15.1. **→** ***Double click each dimension and enter the corresponding value*** Refer Fig. 15.2.
	7. Add two fillets.	**→** ***Select lines 1 and 2*** **→** ***Select lines 2 and 3***
	8. Modify the dimensions of the fillets.	**→** ***Double click each fillet dimension and enter 0.15*** **Add dimensions if necessary → Select each weak dimension shown in gray →** ***Right Mouse*** **→ Strong** Refer Fig. 15.3.
	9. Exit sketcher.	✓
	10. Draw the sweep section.	**→** ***Select points 1 and 2*** Refer Fig. 15.4.

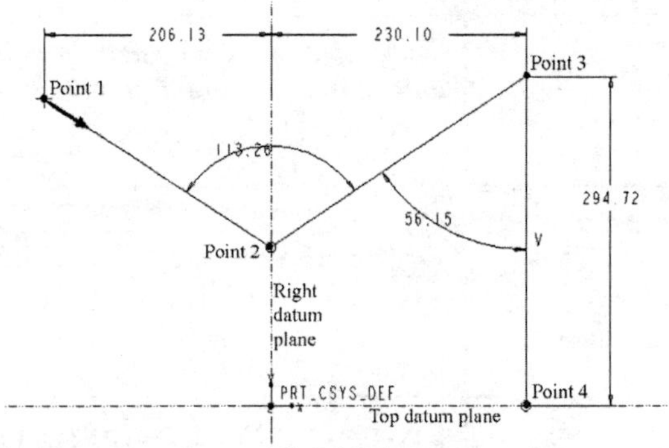

Fig. 15.1.

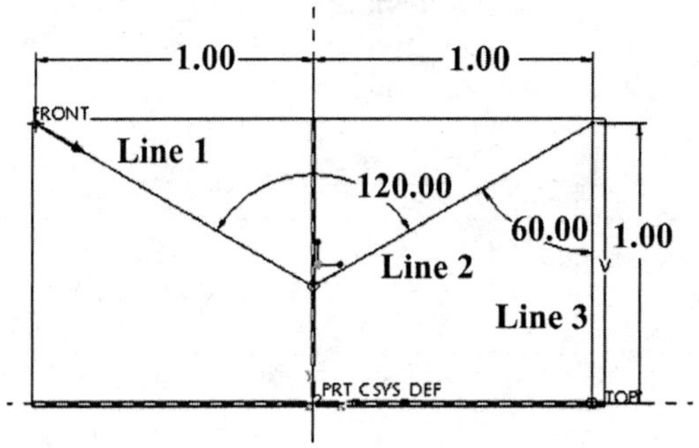

Fig. 15.2.

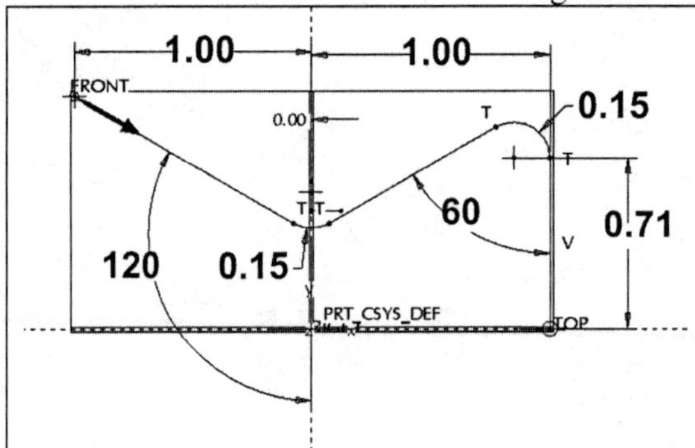

Fig. 15.3.

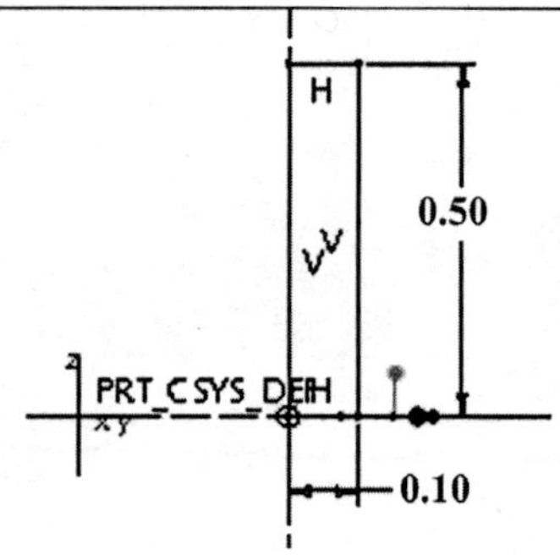

Fig. 15.4.

Goal	Step	Commands
Create a sweep (Continued)	11. Modify the dimensions.	[pointer icon] → ***Double click each dimension and enter the corresponding value*** Refer Fig. 15.4.
	12. Exit sketcher.	✓
	13. Accept the feature creation.	**OK → VIEW → ORIENTATION →** STANDARD ORIENTATION Refer Fig. 15.5.
Mirror the protrusion feature	14. Mirror the feature.	**EDIT → FEATURE OPERATIONS → Copy → Mirror → Select → Dependent → Done →** ***Select the protrusion*** **→ OK → Done →** ***Select the TOP datum plane*** **→ Done** Refer Fig. 15.6.
Save the file and exit ProE	15. Save the file and exit ProE.	**FILE → SAVE → SPRING1.PRT → OK → FILE → EXIT → YES**

Fig. 15.5.

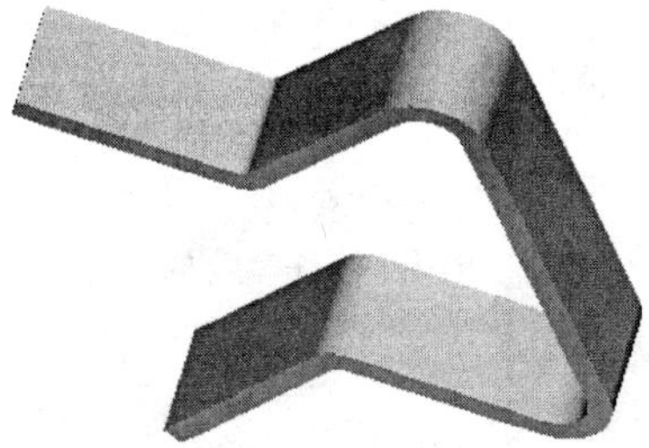

Fig. 15.6.

SEQUENCE OF STEPS

STEP I: Create the helical sweep feature

1. Start the helical feature.

2. Define the helical sweep properties.

3. Sketch the axis.

4. Sketch the sweep profile.

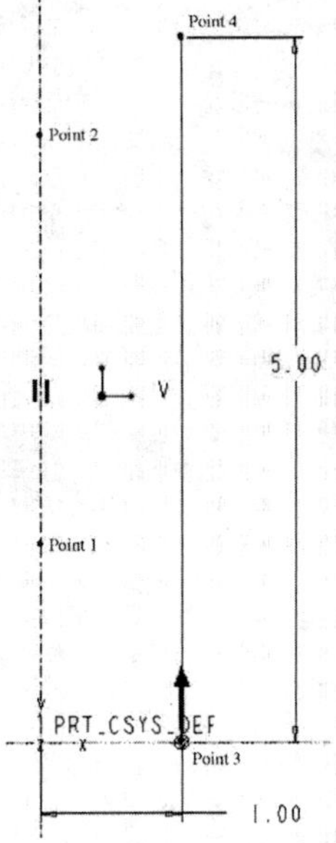

5. Sketch the sweep section.

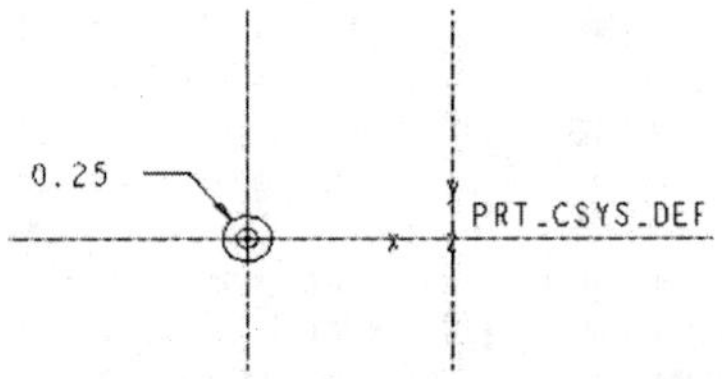

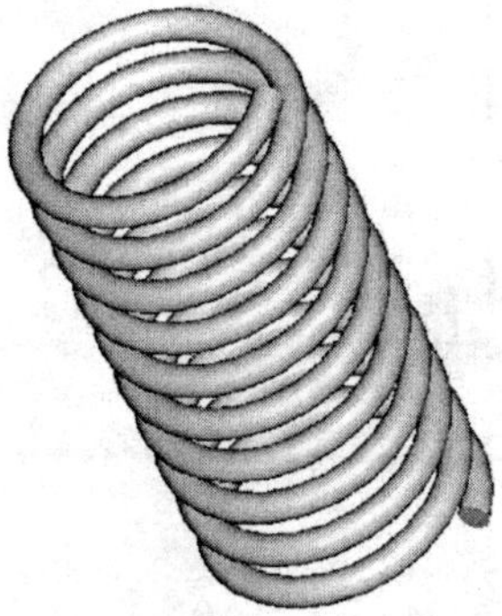

STEP II: Add coils

1. Start the helical sweep feature.

2. Define the helical sweep properties.

3. Select the sketching plane as the previous coil end.

4. Sketch the axis.

5. Sketch the sweep profile.

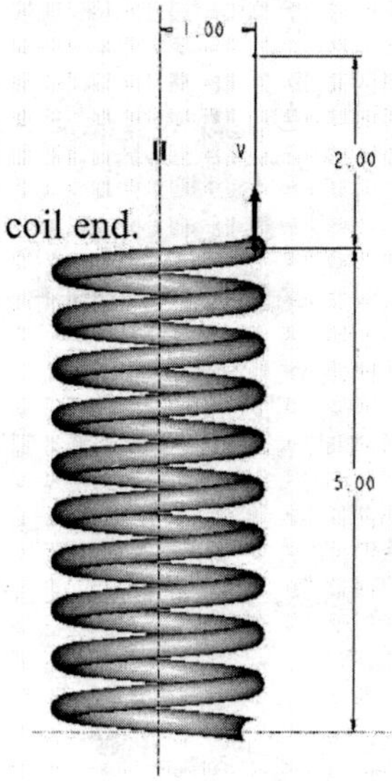

6. Sketch the sweep section.

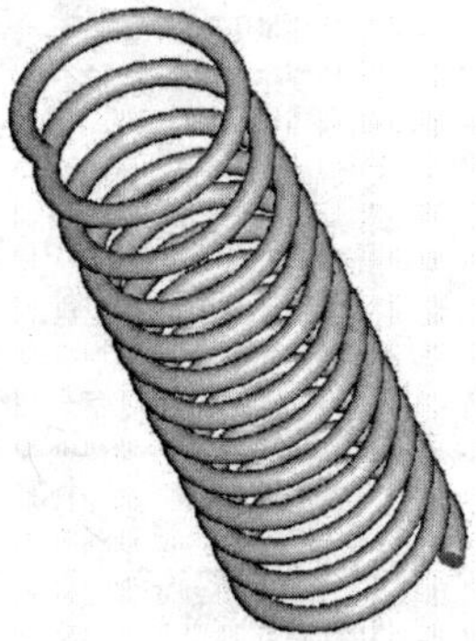

Goal	Step	Commands
Open a new file for the spring part	1. Set up the working directory.	**FILE → SET WORKING DIRECTORY →** ***Select the working directory*** **→ OK**
	2. Open a new file.	**FILE → NEW →** ***Part*** **→** ***Solid*** **→ <u>Spring2</u> → OK**
Create the close coiled spring	3. Start "Helical Sweep" feature.	**INSERT → HELICAL SWEEP → PROTRUSION**
	4. Define the helical sweep properties.	**Constant → Thru Axis → Right Handed → Done**
	5. Select the sketching plane.	**Setup New → Plane →** ***Select FRONT datum plane*** **→ Okay**
	6. Orient the sketching plane.	**Default**
	7. Sketch the axis.	**→ → *Pick points 1 and 2 on the RIGHT datum plane***
	8. Sketch the sweep profile.	**→ → *Pick points 3 and 4 → Middle Mouse*** Refer Fig. 15.7.
	9. Modify the dimensions.	***→ Double click the height dimension → <u>5</u> → <u>ENTER</u> → Double click the horizontal placement dimension → <u>1</u> → <u>ENTER</u>*** Refer Fig. 15.7.
	10. Exit sketcher.	
	11. Enter pitch value.	**<u>0.5</u> →** Pitch defines the distance between two adjacent coils.

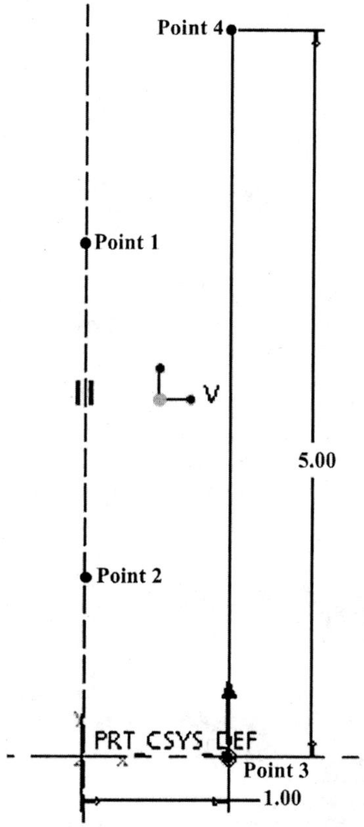

Fig. 15.7.

Goal	Step	Commands
Create the close coiled spring (continued)	12. Sketch the sweep section.	→ ***Select the center of the circle at the intersection of the cross-hairs*** → ***Select a point to define the circle*** → → ***Double click the diameter dimension*** → **<u>0.25</u>** → ***<u>ENTER</u>*** Refer Fig. 15.8. The term sweep section refers to the section that is swept along the helix. The axis of the helix and the radius of revolution are defined in steps 7 and 8.
	13. Exit sketcher.	
	14. Accept the feature creation.	**OK → VIEW → ORIENTATION → STANDARD ORIENTATION** Refer Fig. 15.9.
Add coils to the spring	15. Start "Helical Sweep" feature.	**INSERT → HELICAL SWEEP → PROTRUSION**
	16. Define the helical sweep properties.	**Constant → Thru Axis → Right Handed → Done**
	17. Select the sketching plane.	**Setup New → Plane →** ***Select the flat face of the spring (Right mouse until the sketching plane is highlighted, left mouse to select)*** **→ Okay → Default** Refer Figs. 15.10 and 15.11.

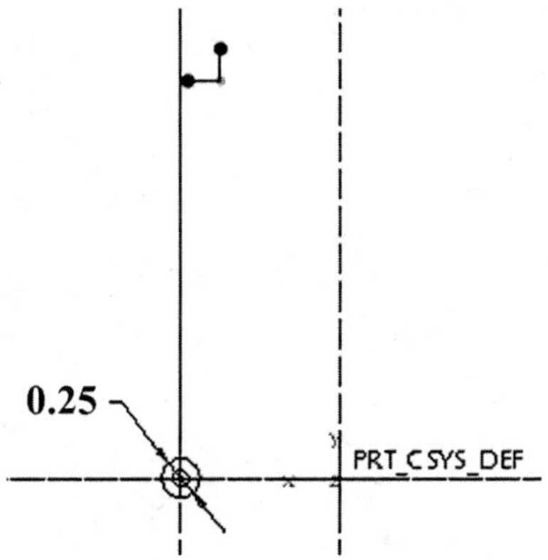

Fig. 15.8.

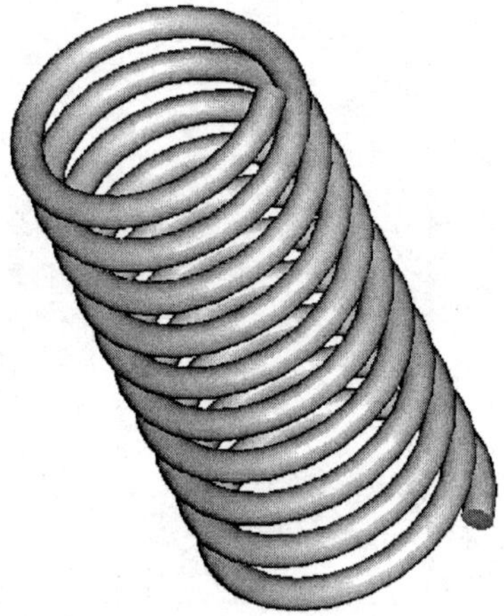

Fig. 15.9.

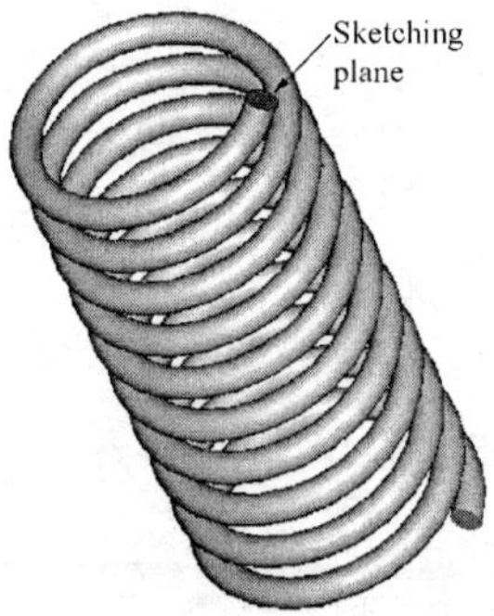

Fig. 15.10.

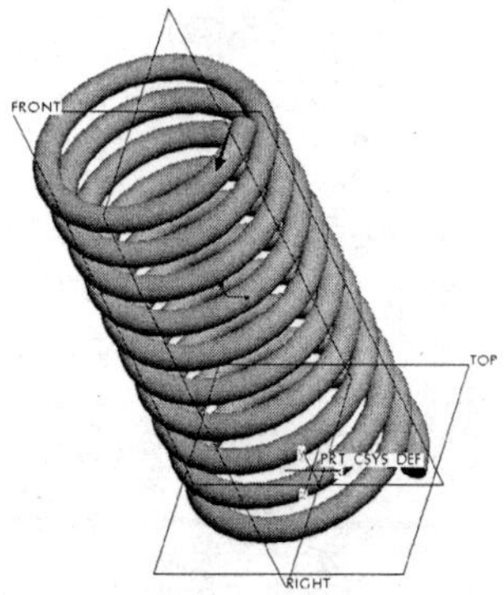

Fig. 15.11.

Goal	Step	Commands
Add coils to the spring (continued)	18. Select references.	***Select the TOP and RIGHT datum planes*** → **CLOSE** Refer Figs. 15.12 and 15.13.
	19. Sketch the axis.	→ → ***Pick points 1 and 2 on the RIGHT datum plane*** Refer Fig. 15.13.
	20. Sketch the sweep profile.	→ → ***Pick points 3 and 4*** → ***Middle Mouse*** Refer Fig. 15.13.
	21. Modify the dimensions.	→ ***Double click each dimension and enter the corresponding values*** Refer Fig. 15.14.
	22. Exit sketcher.	✓
	23. Enter pitch value.	**0.75** → ✓
	24. Sketch the sweep section.	→ *Select the center of the circle at the intersection of the cross-lines* → *Select a point to define the circle* → → *Double click on the diameter dimension* → 0.25 → ***ENTER*** Refer Fig. 15.15.
	25. Exit sketcher.	✓
	26. Accept the feature creation.	OK → VIEW → ORIENTATION → STANDARD ORIENTATION Refer Fig. 15.16.
Save the file and exit ProE	27. Save the file and exit ProE.	FILE → SAVE → SPRING2.PRT → OK → FILE → EXIT → YES

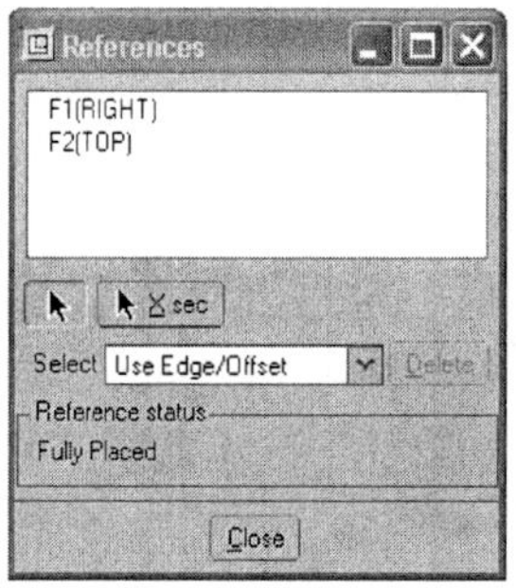

Fig. 15.12.

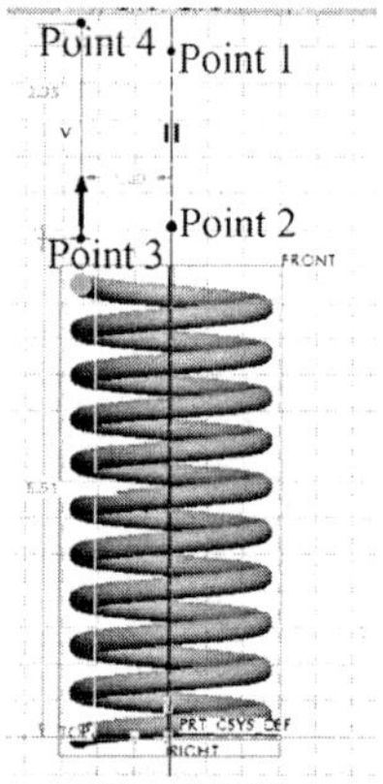

Fig. 15.13.

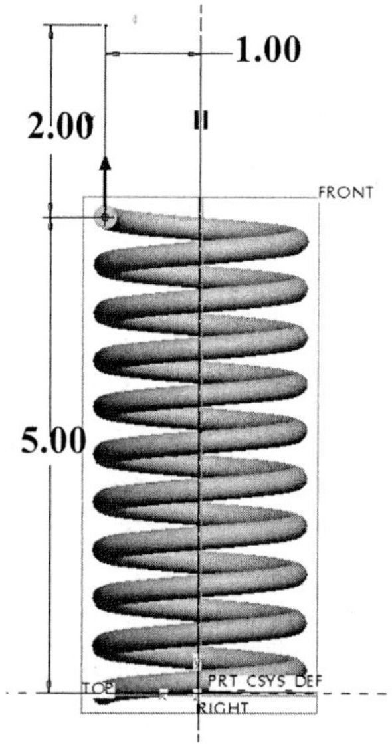

Fig. 15.14.

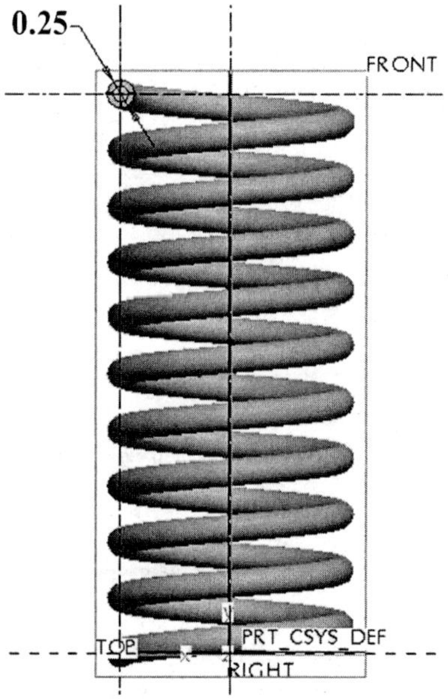

Fig. 15.15.

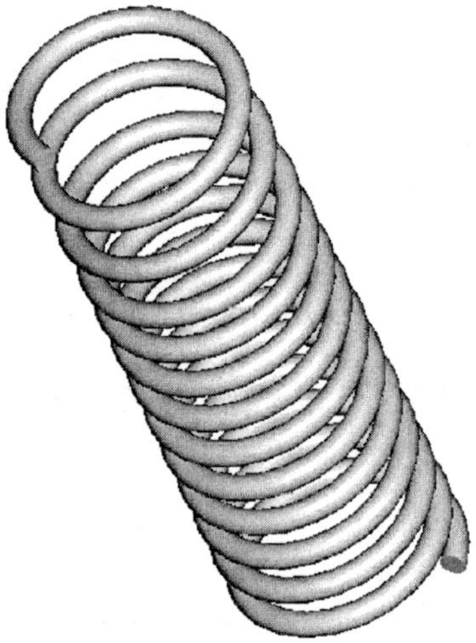
Fig. 15.16.

SEQUENCE OF STEPS

Create the helical sweep feature

1. Start the helical feature.

2. Define the helical sweep properties (variable pitch).

3. Sketch the axis.

4. Sketch the sweep profile.

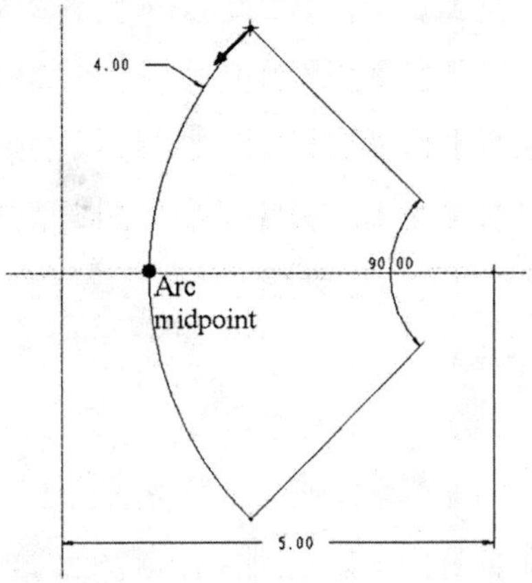

5. Divide the arc at the midpoint.

6. Define the pitch values at the intermediate locations.

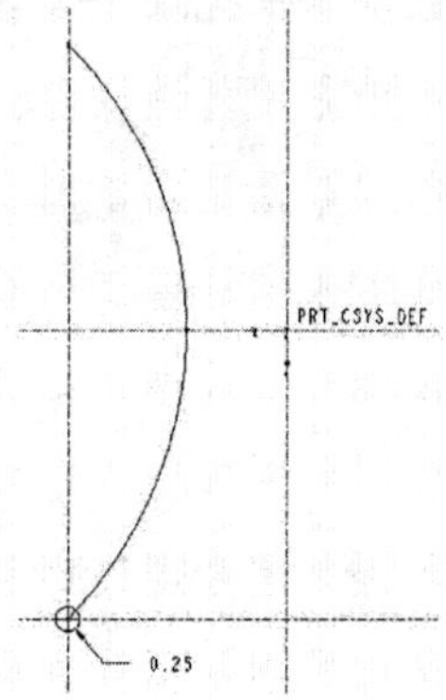

7. Sketch the sweep section.

8. Accept the feature creation.

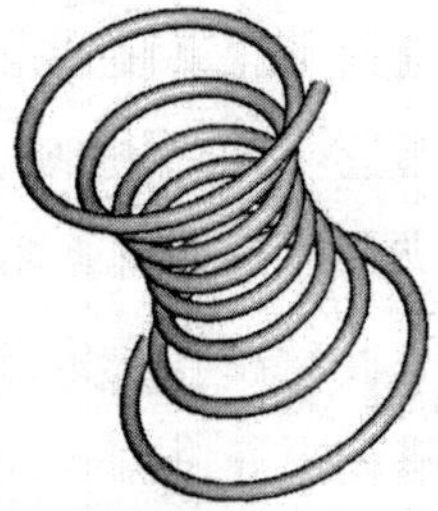

Goal	Step	Commands
Open a new file for the spring part	1. Set up working directory.	**FILE → WORKING DIRECTORY →** ***Select working directory*** **→ OK**
	2. Open a new file.	**FILE → NEW →** ***Part*** **→** ***Solid*** **→ hourglassspring → OK**
Create the conical spring	3. Start "Helical Sweep" feature.	**INSERT → HELICAL SWEEP → PROTRUSION**
	4. Define the helical sweep properties.	**Variable → Thru Axis → Right Handed → Done**
	5. Select the sketching plane.	**Setup New → Plane →** ***Select the FRONT datum plane →*** **Okay**
	6. Orient the sketching plane.	**Default**
	7. Sketch the axis.	 →  → ***Pick points 1 and 2 on the RIGHT datum plane → Pick points 3 and 4 on the TOP datum plane*** Refer Fig. 15.17.
	8. Sketch the sweep profile.	 →  → ***Pick points 5 (Center of the arc), 6 and 7*** **(start and end points of the arc)** Refer Fig. 15.17.
	9. Dimension the arc.	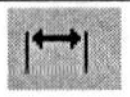 → ***Select the two end points of the arc (points 6 and 7), then the arc → Middle Mouse to place the angular dimension*** Refer Fig. 15.18.
	10. Modify the dimensions.	 → ***Double click each dimension and enter the corresponding value (Start with the placement dimensions and then the radius)*** Refer Fig. 15.19.

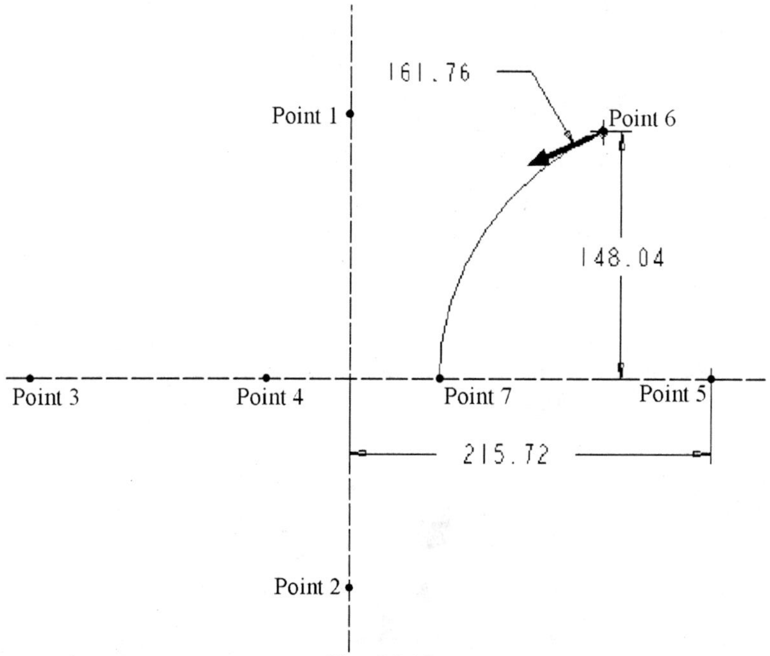

Fig. 15.17.

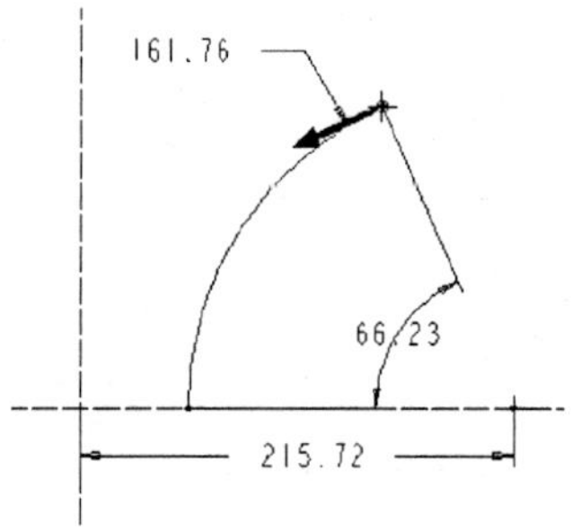

Fig. 15.18.

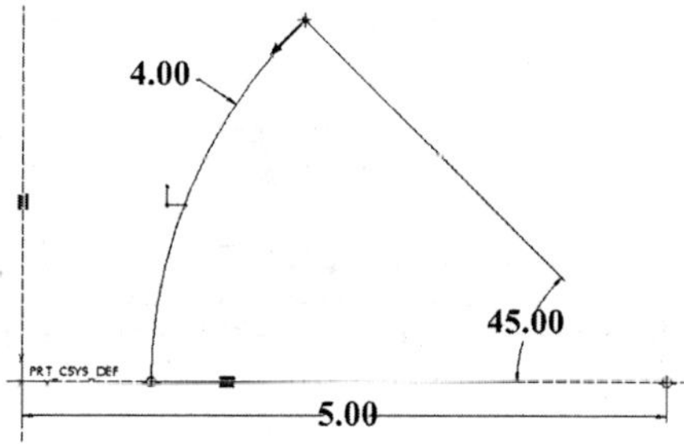

Fig. 15.19.

Goal	Step	Commands
Create the conical spring (continued)	11. Mirror the entities.	→ ***Select the arc*** → **EDIT** → **MIRROR** → ***Select the horizontal centerline*** Refer Fig. 15.20.
	12. Divide the arc.	→ → ***Select the intersection of the arc and the TOP datum plane*** Refer Fig. 15.20.
	13. Exit sketcher.	✓
	14. Enter pitch value.	**(Pitch value at the start) 1** → → **(Pitch value at the end) 1** →
	15. Define the pitch values at the intermediate locations.	**Define** → **Add Point** → **Refer Fig. 15.21.** ***Select midpoint on the arc*** → **(Pitch) 0.5** → → **Done/Return** → **Done** Refer Fig. 15.22.
	16. Sketch the sweep section.	→ ***Select the center of the circle at the intersection of the cross-lines*** → ***Select a point to define the circle*** → → ***Double click the diameter dimension*** → **0.25** → ***ENTER*** Refer Fig. 15.23.
	17. Exit sketcher.	✓
	18. Accept the feature creation.	**OK** → **VIEW** → **ORIENTATION** → **STANDARD ORIENTATION** Refer Fig. 15.24.
Save the file and exit ProE	19. Save the file and exit ProE.	**FILE** → **SAVE** → **HOURGLASSSPRING.PRT** → **OK** → **FILE** → **EXIT** → **YES**

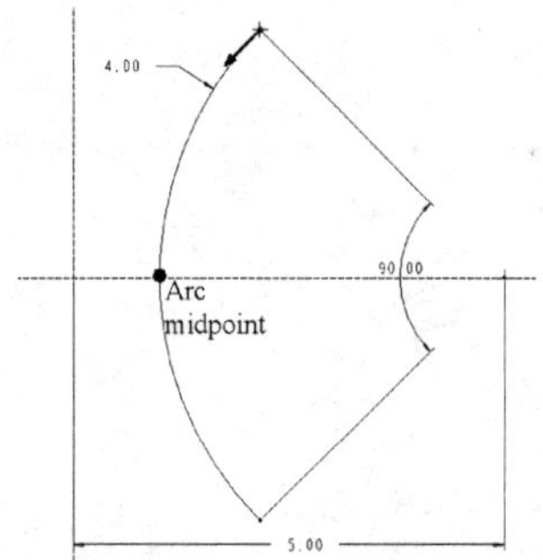

Fig. 15.20.

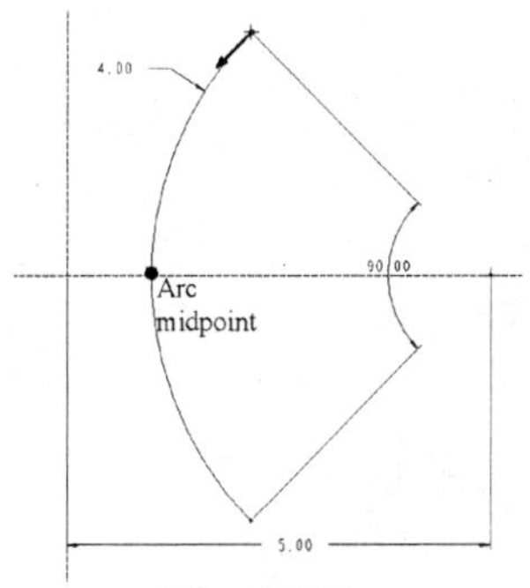

Fig. 15.21.

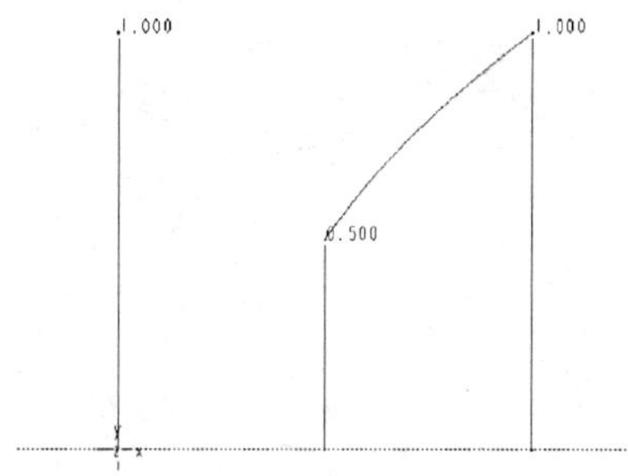

Fig. 15.22.

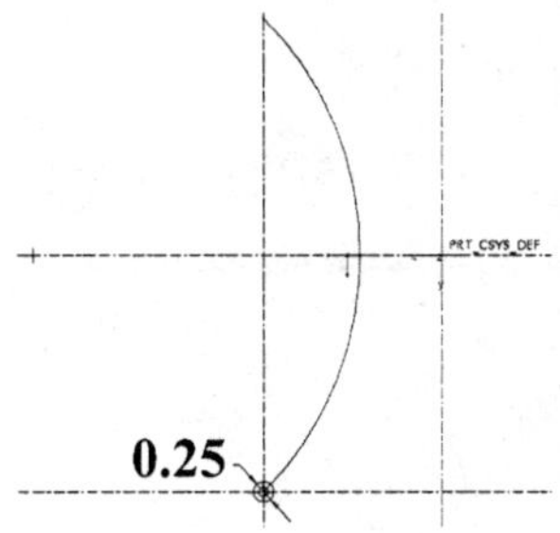

Fig. 15.23.

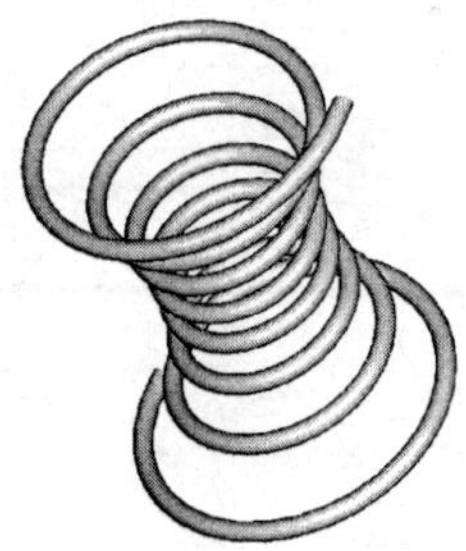

Fig. 15.24.

Exercise

Problem 1

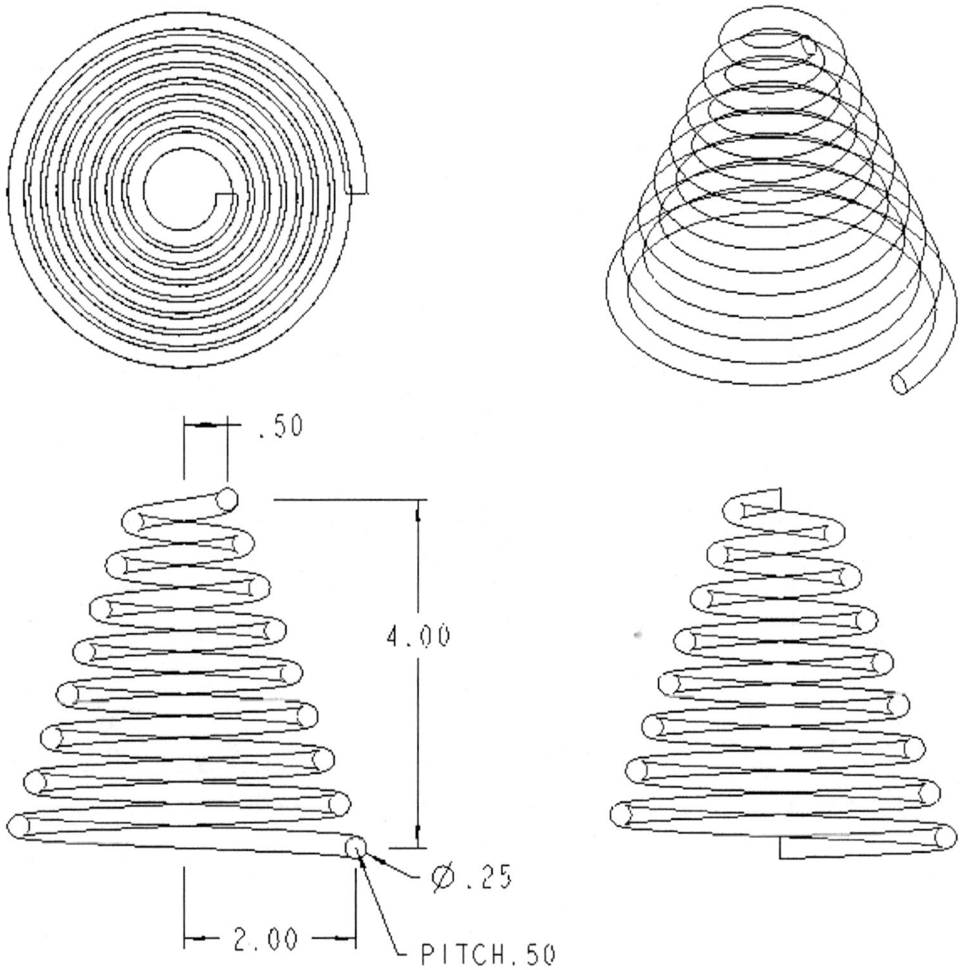

Hints:

1. Use helical sweep feature.
2. The trajectory is shown in the figure below.

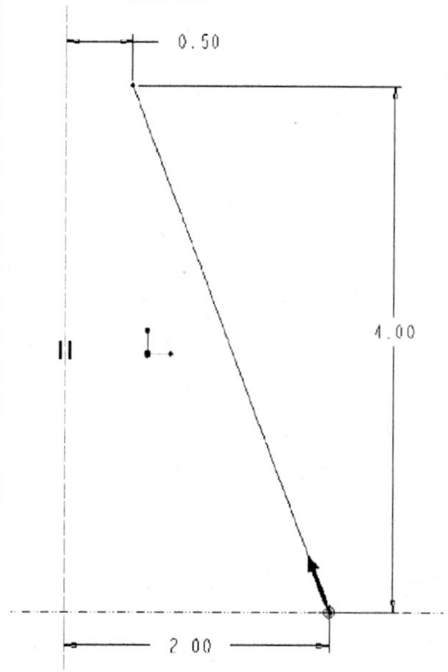

Problem 2

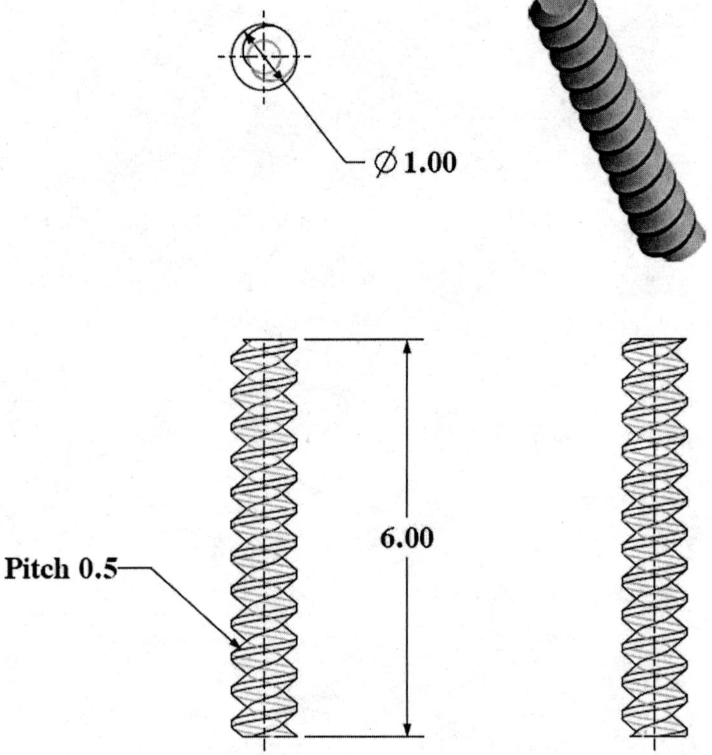

Hints:

1. Use "Helical Sweep Cut" feature.
2. Sketch trajectory and the cut section.

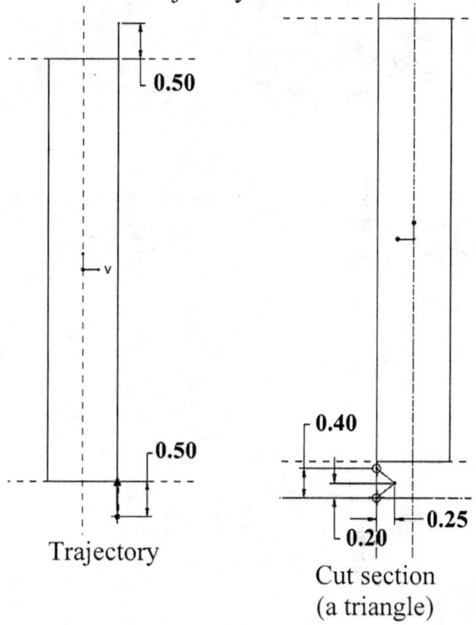

NOTES:

LESSON 16
SPUR AND HELICAL GEARS

Learning Objectives

- Learn to ***Set Up Parameters***
- Learn **Variable Section Sweep** feature
- Learn ***Surface*** operations
- Practice ***Relations***, ***Group***, and ***Pattern*** commands

Variable Section Sweep

The Variable Section Sweep feature is a powerful tool that can be used to create complex solid/surface geometry. The feature is used to sweep a section along a predefined trajectory. Further, the section geometry, and orientation can be controlled by additional trajectories. In the constant section option, the sketch remains same in size and shape and is swept along the trajectory. Its orientation can change along the path. On the other hand, a section can be made to change the shape/size by constraining the sketch to trajectories or relations. The primary trajectory is the Origin trajectory – the frame containing the sketch is swept along the origin trajectory. The orientation of the frame is specified by using Normal to Trajectory, Normal to Projection, or Constant Normal.

Background Information

Gears provide an effective means of transferring power from one shaft to another without slippage. Typically, the teeth are shaped in the form of an involute profile to maintain a fixed angular velocity ratio between the gears. The involute profile can be obtained by tracing the end of a string, as it is unwrapped from a base cylinder while keeping the string tangential to the cylinder. The pitch circle is used for calculating the velocity ratio. Addendum is the amount of tooth that extends above the pitch circle. The dedendum circle represents the bottom of the tooth. Typically, the dedendum circle is bigger than the base circle from which the involute profile originates. Spur gear has straight teeth. Helical gear teeth are shaped in the form a helix and, therefore, share the load between multiple teeth.

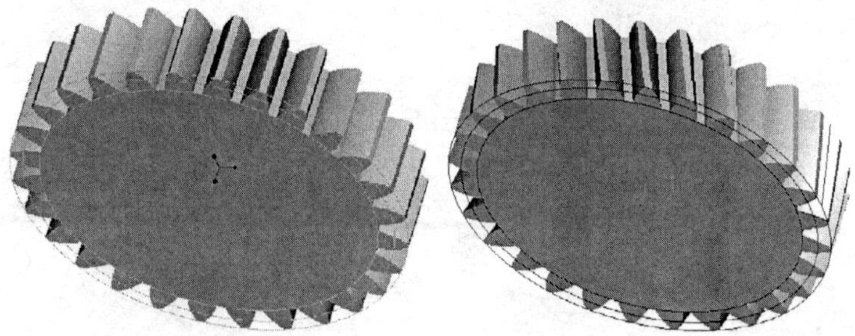

SEQUENCE OF STEPS

STEP I: Set up design parameter

1. Set up the design parameter (names and the initial values).

STEP II: Add relations

STEP III: Create datum circles

1. Create the addendum, dedendum, and pitch circles.

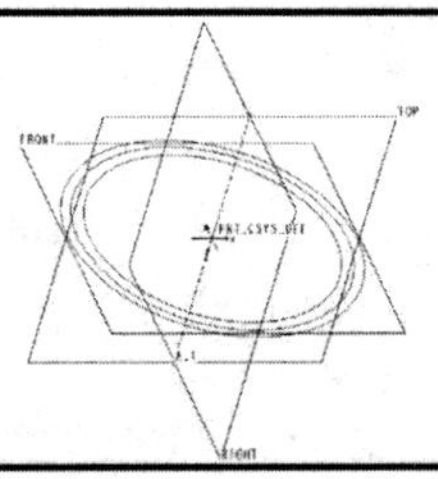

STEP IV: Create the involute profile

1. Define the datum coordinate system.
2. Enter involute profile equations.
3. Create the pitch point.
4. Mirror the involute profile.

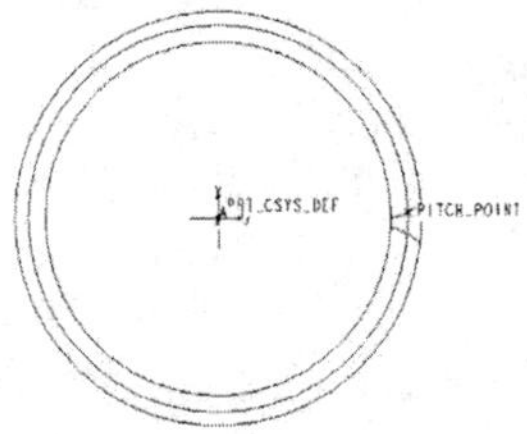

STEP V: Create a profile for cutting the teeth

1. Establish new references.
2. Sketch the profile using the existing involute profiles.
3. Trim the excess lines.

STEP VI: Create a profile for cutting the teeth

1. Start "Extrude - Surface" feature.
2. Select the cutting profile.
3. Define the depth of extrusion.

STEP VII: Create the base cylinder

1. Define the circle.
2. Define the depth of extrusion.

STEP VIII: Create the teeth

1. Copy the cutting surface.
2. Create a cut using the cutting surface.
3. Pattern the cut.

Goal	Step	Commands
Open a new file for the gear part	1. Set up the working directory.	**FILE → SET WORKING DIRECTORY →** ***Select the working directory*** **→ OK**
	2. Open a new file.	**FILE → NEW →** ***Part*** **→** ***Solid*** **→ spurgear → OK**
Set up design parameters	3. Set up design parameters.	**TOOLS → PARAMETERS →**  **→** ***Add the parameter name, type and value as shown in Fig. 16.1. Note the value of F is 1.*** **OK** Refer Fig. 16.1. N – Number of teeth P – Diametral pitch Phi – Pressure angle A – Addendum B – Dedendum Dp – Pitch diameter Dd – Dedendum diameter Db – Base diameter Da – Addendum diameter F – Face width The values defined by the parameter is nonassociative. In other words, changing the model parameter does not change the value of the user-defined parameter.

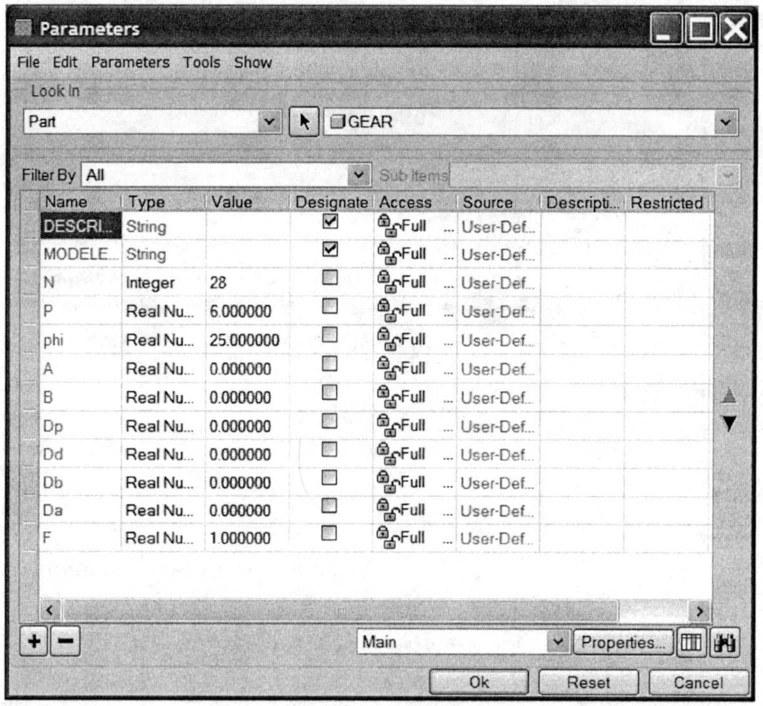

Fig. 16.1.

Goal	Step	Commands
Add relations	4. Add relations.	**TOOLS → RELATIONS →** **Type the relations as shown in Fig. 16.2.** **→** **UTILITIES → REORDER RELATIONS → OK → OK → TOOLS → PARAMETERS → Note that the values of some of the parameters have changes → OK**
Create the datum circles	5. Create a datum axis.	***→ Click in the references window → Select the TOP and RIGHT datum planes while holding CTRL → OK*** Refer Fig. 16.3.
	6. Create the addendum datum circle.	***→ Select the FRONT datum plane → Sketch → → Select the intersection of the RIGHT and TOP datum planes → Select a point to define the circle → → Double click the diameter dimension → Da → ENTER → Yes → ✓ → VIEW → ORIENTATION → STANDARD ORIENTATION*** Refer Fig. 16.4.

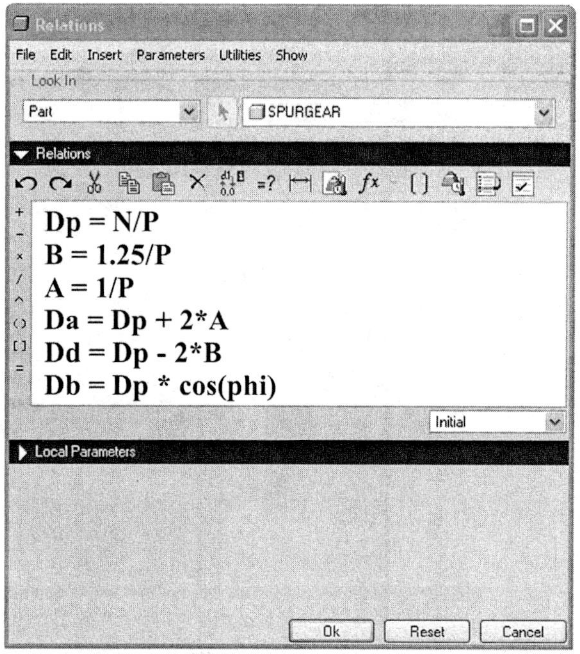

Fig. 16.2.

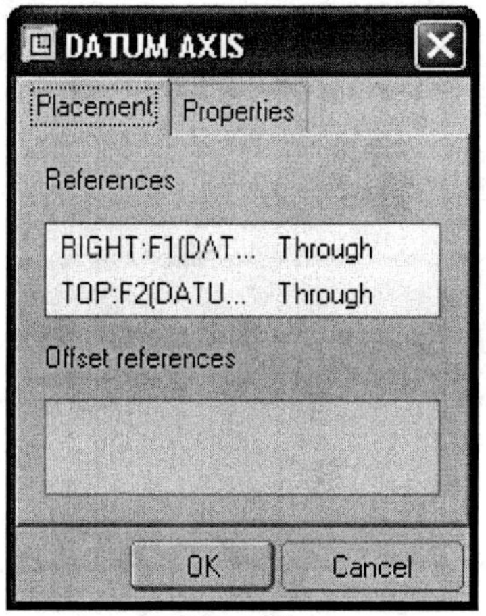

Fig. 16.3.

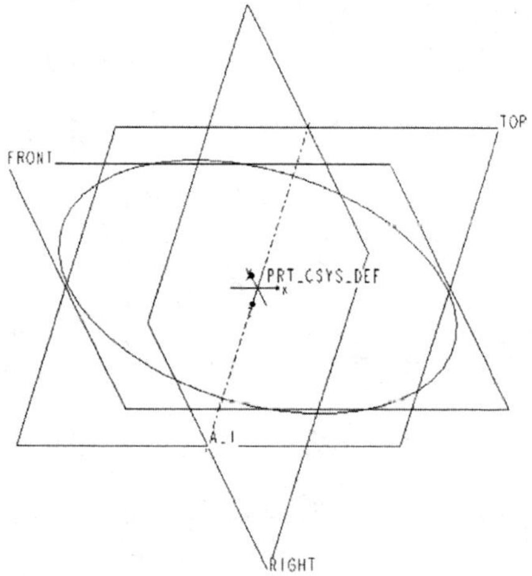

Fig. 16.4.

Goal	Step	Commands
Create the datum circles (Continued)	7. Create the dedendum datum circle.	→ ***Use Previous*** → → ***Select the intersection of the RIGHT and TOP datum planes → Select a point to define the circle*** → → ***Double click the diameter dimension*** → **Dd** → ***ENTER*** → **Yes** → → **VIEW → ORIENTATION → STANDARD ORIENTATION** Refer Fig. 16.5.
	8. Create the pitch datum circle.	→ ***Use Previous*** → → ***Select the intersection of the RIGHT and TOP datum planes → Select a point to define the circle*** → → ***Double click the diameter dimension*** → **Dp** → ***ENTER*** → **Yes** → → **VIEW → ORIENTATION → STANDARD ORIENTATION** Refer Fig. 16.6.
	9. Name the circles.	***Double click each circle name in the model tree and enter the corresponding name*** Refer Fig. 16.7.

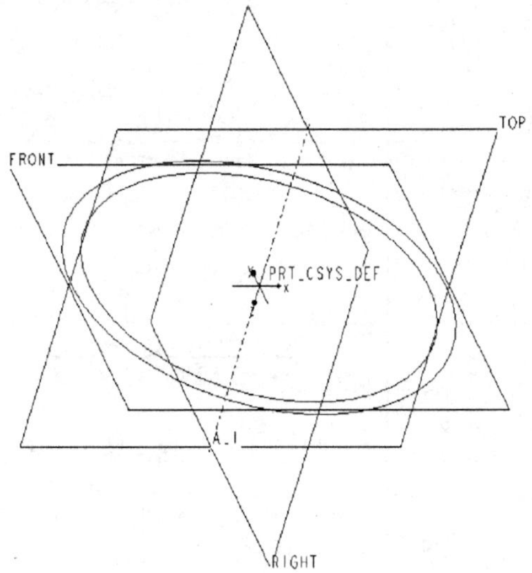

Fig. 16.5.

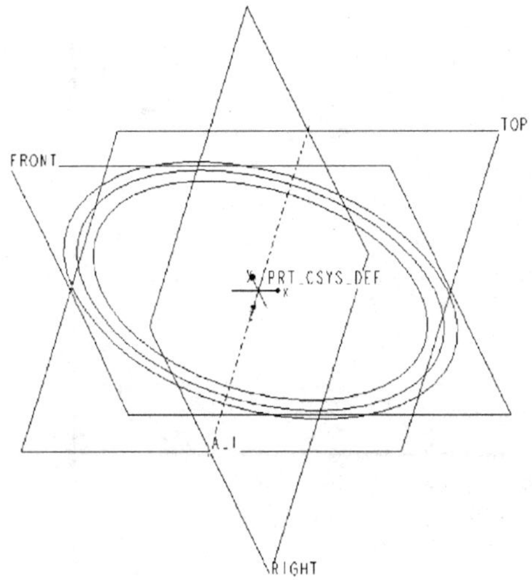

Fig. 16.6.

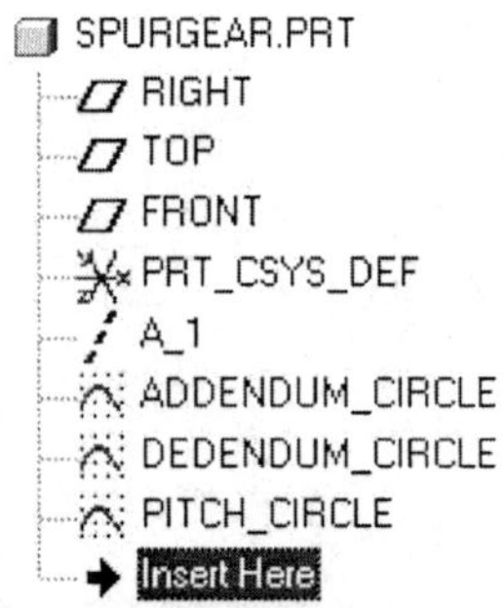

Fig. 16.7.

Goal	Step	Commands
Create an involute profile datum curve	10. Start "Datum Curve – From Equation" command.	→ **From equation** → **Done**
	11. Define the coordinate system.	**Select** → ***Select the default coordinate system PRT_CSYS_DEF from the model tree*** → **Cylindrical**
	12. Enter the equations for the involute profile.	**<u>Type the equations in the equation editor</u> (Refer Fig. 16.8.)** **FILE → SAVE → FILE → EXIT**
	13. Accept the feature creation after previewing.	**OK** → **VIEW** → **ORIENTATION** → **STANDARD ORIENTATION**
Create a datum through the pitch point	14. Define the pitch point.	→ ***Click in the references window*** → ***Select the involute profile and the pitch circle while holding <u>CTRL</u>*** → **OK** Refer Figs. 16.9, 16.10 and 16.11.
	15. Create a datum plane through the pitch point.	→ ***Click in the references window*** → ***Select the datum axis from the model tree*** **and** ***PNT0 while holding <u>CTRL</u>*** → **OK** → → **FRONT** Refer Fig. 16.12.

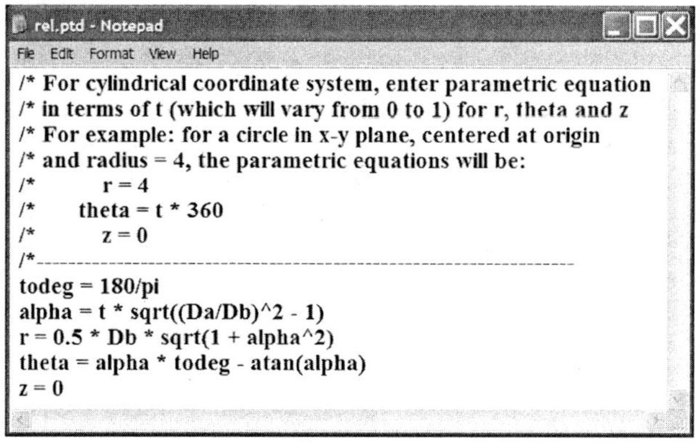

Fig. 16.8.

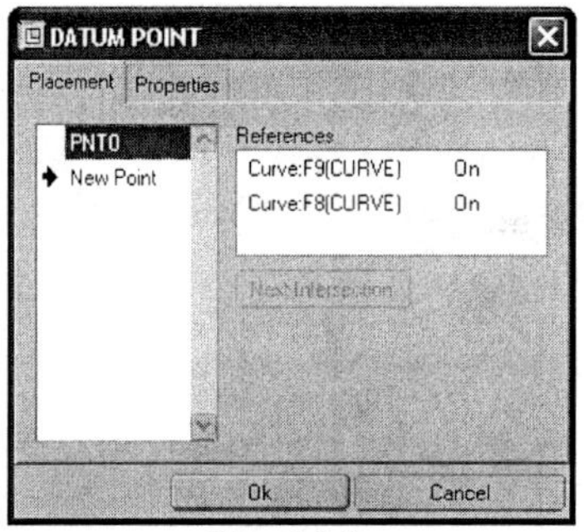

Fig. 16.9.

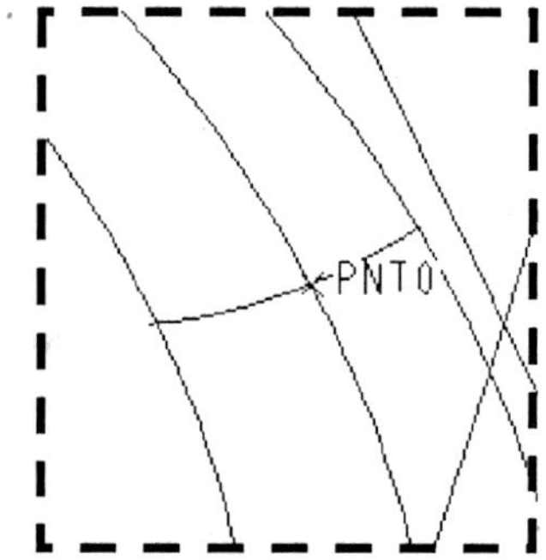

Fig. 16.11.

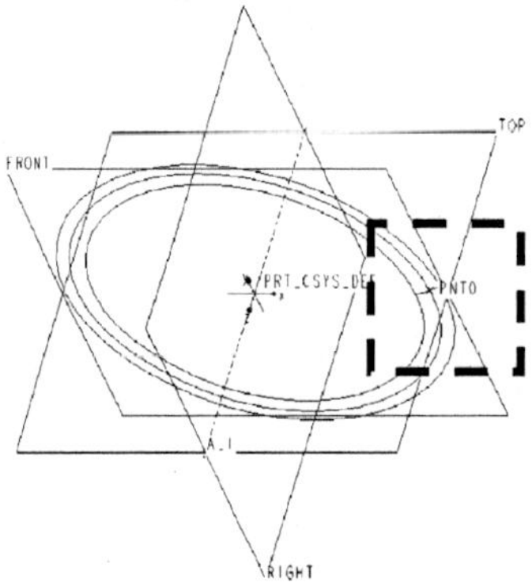

Fig. 16.10.

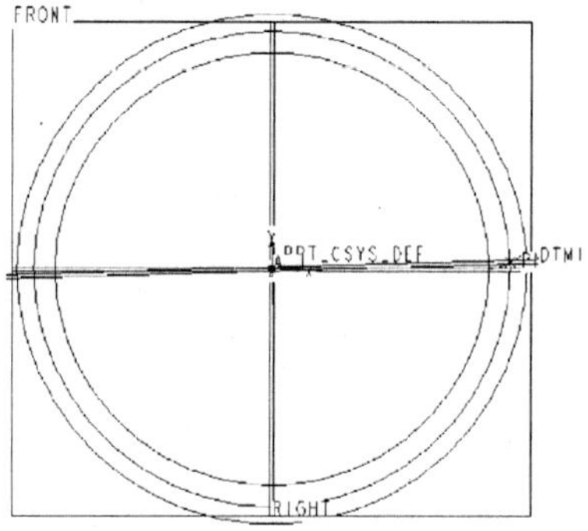

Fig. 16.12.

Goal	Step	Commands
Name the involute profile and the pitch point	16. Name the involute profile and the pitch point.	***Double click the involute profile and pitch point features and enter the corresponding name*** Refer Fig. 16.13.
Mirror the involute profile	17. Mirror the involute profile.	**EDIT → FEATURE OPERATIONS → Copy → Mirror → Select → Dependent → Done →** ***Select the involute profile from the model tree*** **→ OK → Make Datum → Through →** ***Select the datum axis (A_1) from the model tree*** **→ Angle → Plane → FacetFace →** ***Select DTM1 from the model tree*** **→ Done → Enter Value → 90/N → ✓ → Done** Refer Fig. 16.14.
Create a profile for cutting the teeth	18. Start "Datum – Curve" feature.	→ ***Use Previous***

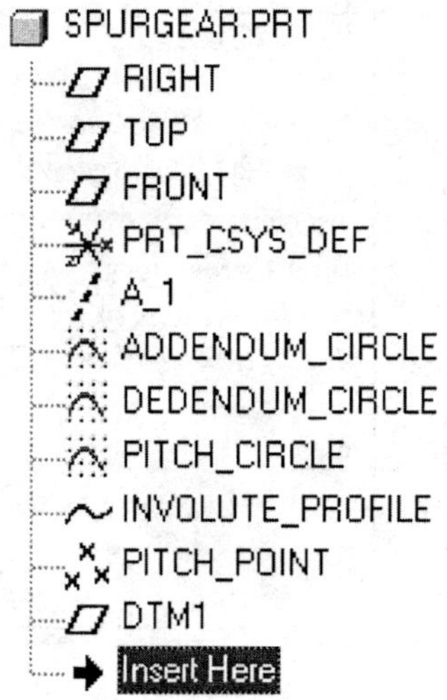

Fig. 16.13.

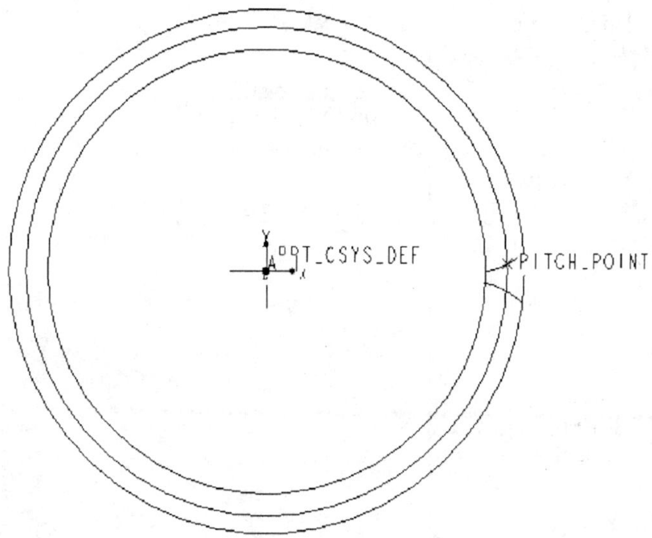

Fig. 16.14.

Goal	Step	Commands
Create a profile for cutting the teeth (Continued)	19. Establish new references.	**SKETCH → REFERENCES →** ***Select F2 (TOP) in the reference window* → Delete → *Select F3(RIGHT) in the reference window* → Delete → (in the "References" window) → *Select the two involute profiles, and addendum and dedendum circles* → CLOSE** Refer Fig. 16.15.
	20. Sketch the profile.	**→ Single → *Select the two involute profiles* → Loop → *Select the dedundum circle* (inner most circle)**
	21. Trim the additional lines from the dedendum circle.	**EDIT → TRIM → DELETE SEGMENT (or) → *Click on the top half of the circle away from the involute profile* → *Click on the bottom half of the circle away from the involute profile*** **Refer Fig. 16.16.**
	22. Trim the additional lines from the involute profile.	**Zoom in → *Remove the involute profile below the dedendum circle*** **Refer Figs. 16.17 and 16.18.**
	23. Exit sketcher.	✓

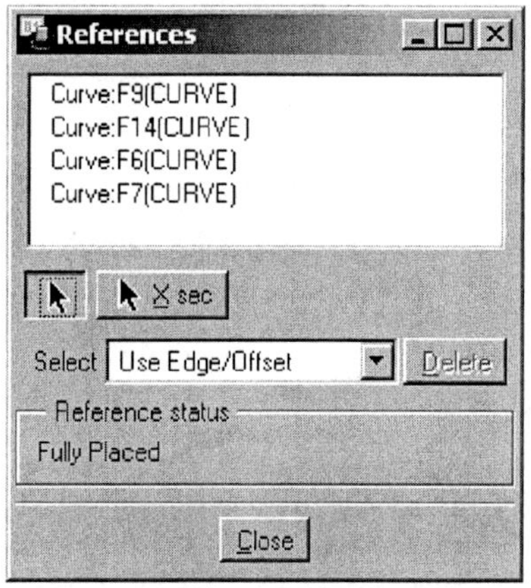

Fig. 16.15.

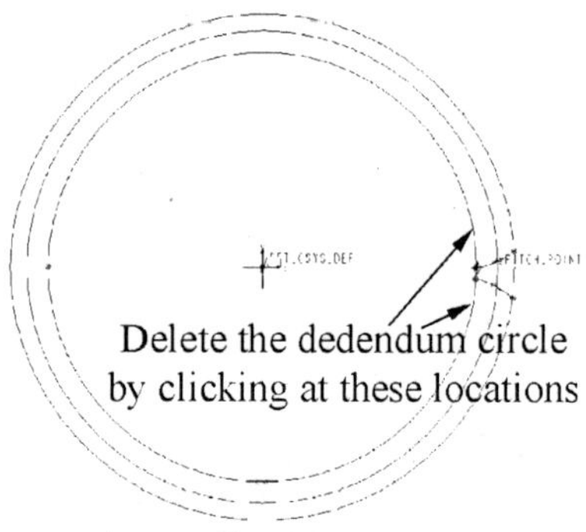

Fig. 16.16.

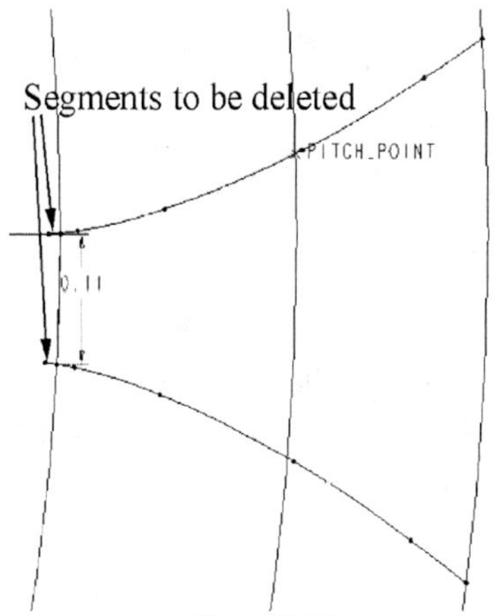

Fig. 16.17.

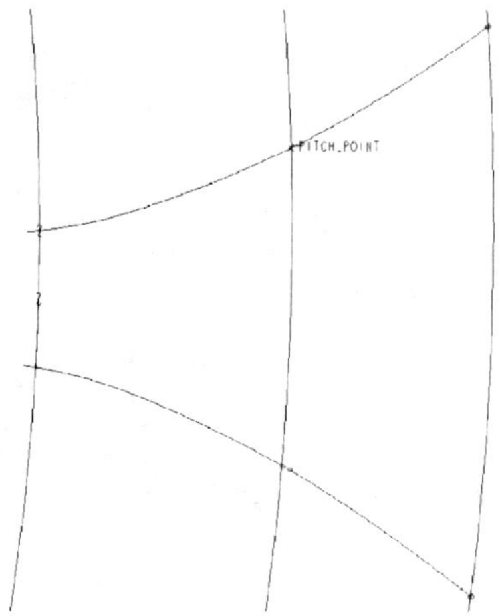

Fig. 16.18.

Goal	Step	Commands
Create a cutting surface	24. Start "Extrude - Surface" feature.	→
	25. Establish the sketching plane.	**Placement → Define →** ***Use Previous***
	26. Sketch the profile.	**→ Loop →** ***Select the profile of the cut (the previous datum curve)***
	27. Exit sketcher.	✓
	28. Define the depth.	**(Depth) F →** ***ENTER*** **→ YES**
	29. Accept the feature creation.	**VIEW → ORIENTATION → STANDARD ORIENTATION →** ✓ Refer Fig. 16.19.
Create a base cylinder	30. Start "Extrude" feature.	
	31. Define the sketching plane.	**Placement → Define →** ***Use Previous***
	32. Create the outer circle.	***→ Loop → Select the addendum circle (outermost circle)***
	33. Exit sketcher.	✓
	34. Define the depth.	**(Depth) F →** ***ENTER*** **→ YES**
	35. Accept the feature creation.	✓ **→ VIEW → ORIENTATION → STANDARD ORIENTATION** Refer Fig. 16.20.

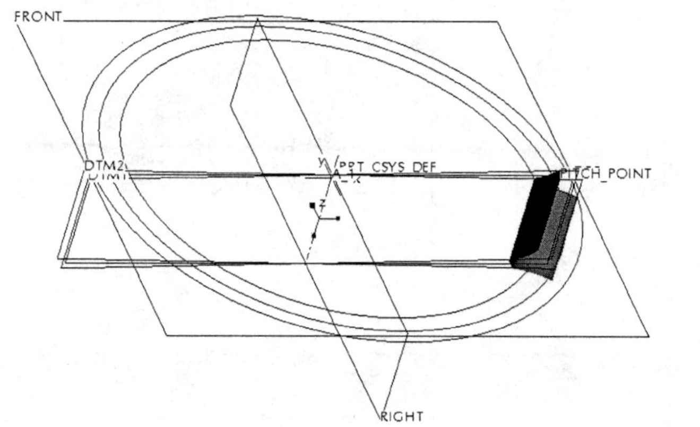

Fig. 16.19.

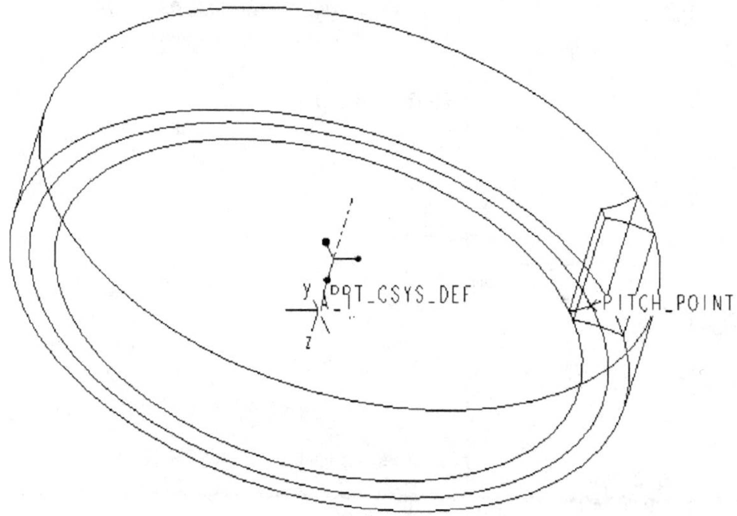

Fig. 16.20.

Goal	Step	Commands
Name the new features	36. Name the two new features.	*Double click cut_profile, cutting surface and base cylinder features and enter the corresponding name* **Refer Fig. 16.21.**
Reorder the features	37. Reorder features.	*Select cutting_surface feature and drop it after the base_cylinder in the model tree* **Refer Fig. 16.22.**
Create the cut	38. Create the initial cut.	*Select cutting_surface feature from the model tree* → EDIT → SOLIDIFY →  →  **Refer Fig. 16.23.**

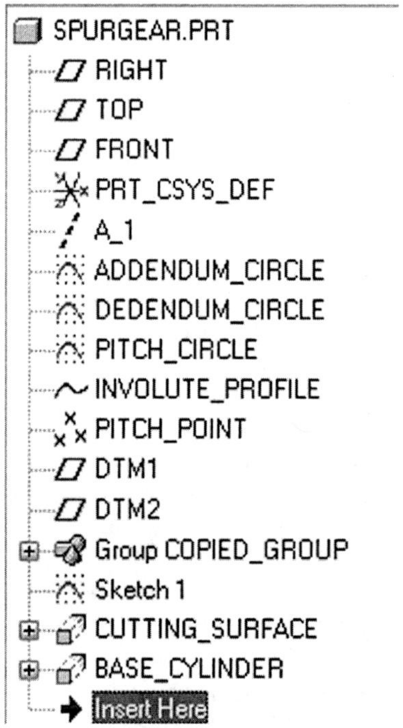

Fig. 16.21.

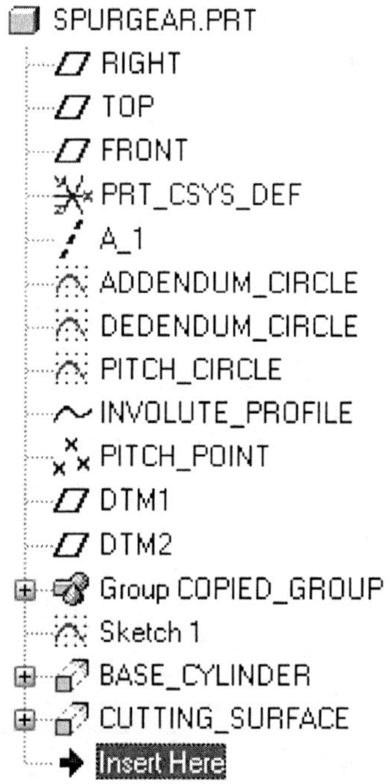

Fig. 16.22.

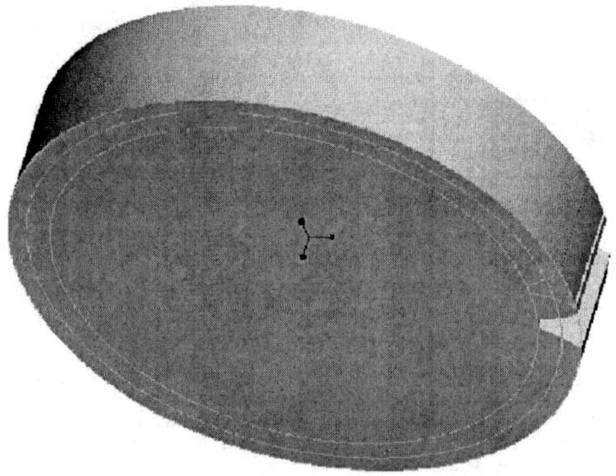
Fig. 16.23.

Goal	Step	Commands
Create the teeth	39. Group the cutting surface and the cut.	*Select the last two features (cutting_surface and solidify) from the model tree →Right Mouse →* Group → *Double click on the Group Name* → CUT → ***ENTER***
	40. Pattern the cut.	*Select the Group CUT from the model tree* → EDIT → PATTERN → *Axis* → *Select axis*→ (Number of instances) 28 → (Enter the increment) 360/N → ***ENTER*** → YES → ✓ **Refer Figs. 16.24 and 16.25**
Save the file and exit ProE	41. Save the file and exit ProE.	FILE → SAVE → SPURGEAR.PRT → OK → FILE → EXIT → YES

Fig. 16.24.

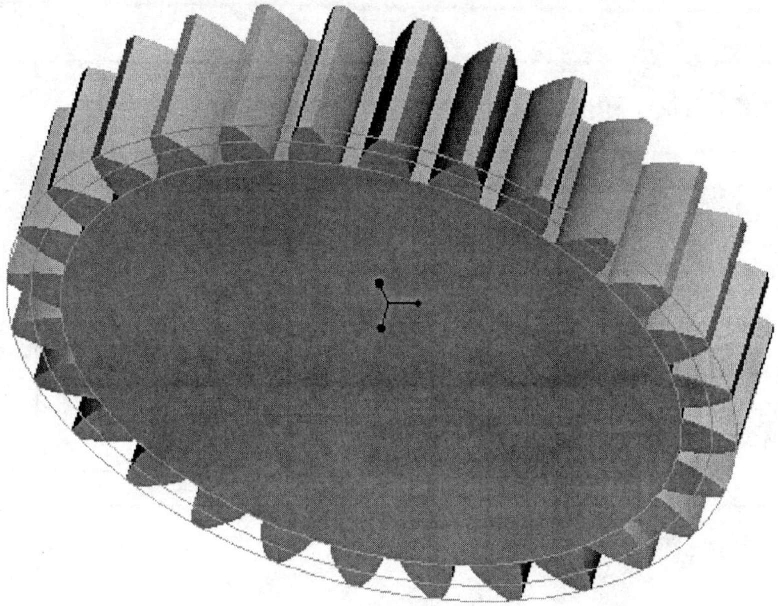

Fig. 16.25.

SEQUENCE OF STEPS

STEP I: Copy spur gear file

STEP II: Delete unnecessary features

STEP III: Add new parameters

1. Add helix angle as a new parameter.

STEP IV: Create the sweep trajectory

1. Define the datum coordinate system.

2. Enter helical sweep trajectory equations.

STEP V: Create the normal trajectory

1. Sketch a straight line on the datum axis.

STEP VI: Create a profile for cutting the teeth

1. Start "Variable Section Sweep - Surface" feature.

2. Define the origin trajectory.

3. Define the normal trajectory.

4. Sketch the sweep section.

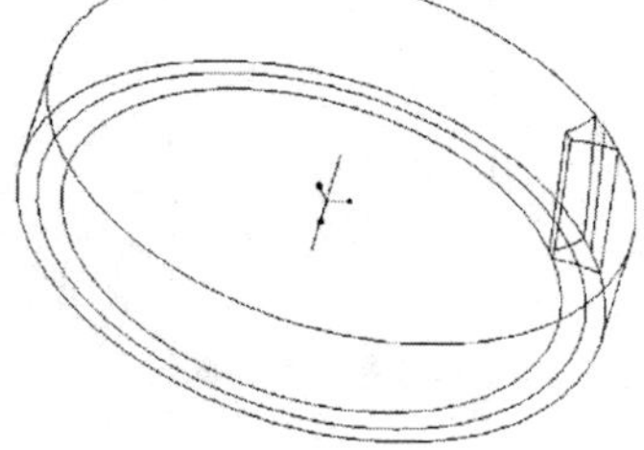

STEP VII: Create the teeth

1. Copy the cutting surface.

2. Create a cut using the cutting surface.

3. Pattern the cut.

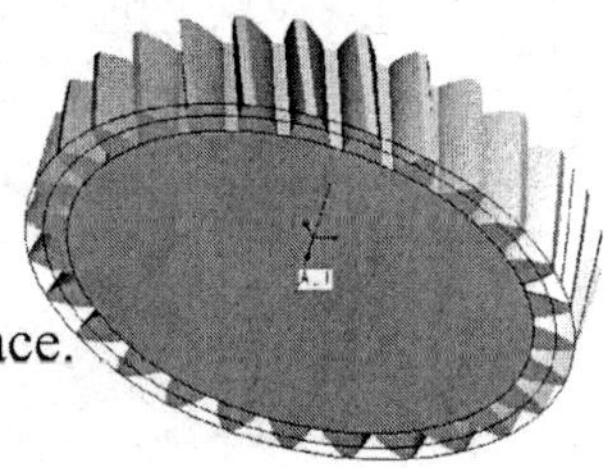

Goal	Step	Commands
Open a new file for the helical gear part	1. Set up the working directory.	**FILE → SET WORKING DIRECTORY →** ***Select the working directory*** **→ OK**
	2. Open spur gear part.	**FILE → OPEN → <u>spurgear</u> → OPEN**
	3. Save the part as the helical gear part.	**FILE → SAVE A COPY → (New Name) <u>HelicalGear</u> → OK**
	4. Open the helical gear part.	**FILE → ERASE → CURRENT → YES → FILE → OPEN →** ***Select the HELICALGEAR.PRT*** **→ OPEN**
	5. Delete the cutting surface and the patterned cuts.	***Select the last feature (Refer Fig. 16.26) → Right Mouse → Delete →*** **OK** Refer Figs. 16.26.
Add new parameter	6. Add helix angle as a new parameter.	**TOOLS → PARAMETERS → [+] → <u>beta</u> (for helix angle) → Real Number → <u>20</u> → OK**

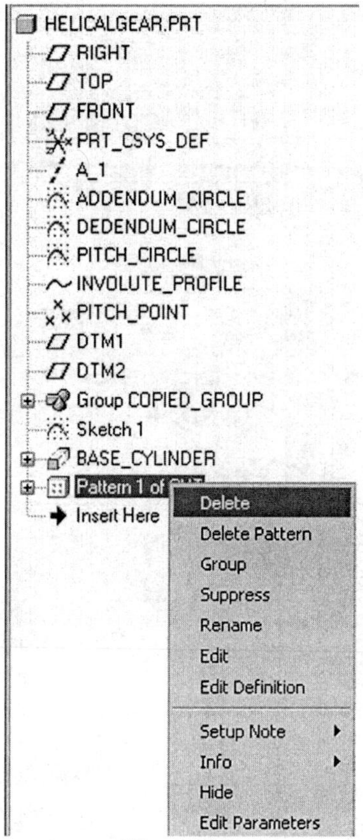

Fig. 16.26.

Goal	Step	Commands
Create the sweep trajectory	7. Create the sweep trajectory curve.	→ **From Equation** → **Done** → **Select** → ***Select the default coordinate system*** → **Cylindrical**
	8. Enter the equations for the helical sweep trajectory.	**Type the equations in the equation editor** → Refer Fig. 16.27. **FILE** → **EXIT** → **YES** → **OK**
	9. View the feature creation.	**VIEW** → **ORIENTATION** → **STANDARD ORIENTATION** Refer Fig. 16.28.
Create a normal trajectory	10. Start "Datum – Curve" feature.	
	11. Define the sketcher plane.	***Select the RIGHT datum plane*** → → **Sketch**
	12. Add new reference.	**SKETCH** → **REFERENCES** → ***Select the face of the base cylinder*** → **CLOSE**
	13. Sketch a straight line on the datum axis.	→ ***Select points 1 and 2*** → ***Middle Mouse*** Refer Fig. 16.29.
	14. Exit sketcher.	
	15. View the feature.	**VIEW** → **ORIENTATION** → **STANDARD ORIENTATION**

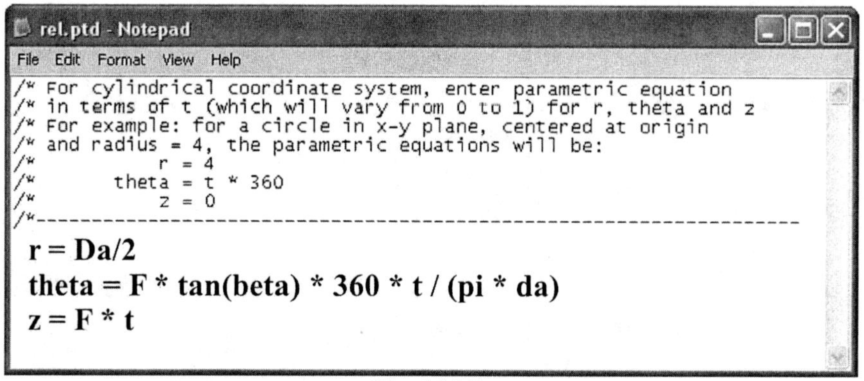
rel.ptd - Notepad
File Edit Format View Help

```
/* For cylindrical coordinate system, enter parametric equation
/* in terms of t (which will vary from 0 to 1) for r, theta and z
/* For example: for a circle in x-y plane, centered at origin
/* and radius = 4, the parametric equations will be:
/*          r = 4
/*      theta = t * 360
/*          z = 0
/*-------------------------------------------------------------------
r = Da/2
theta = F * tan(beta) * 360 * t / (pi * da)
z = F * t
```

Fig. 16.27.

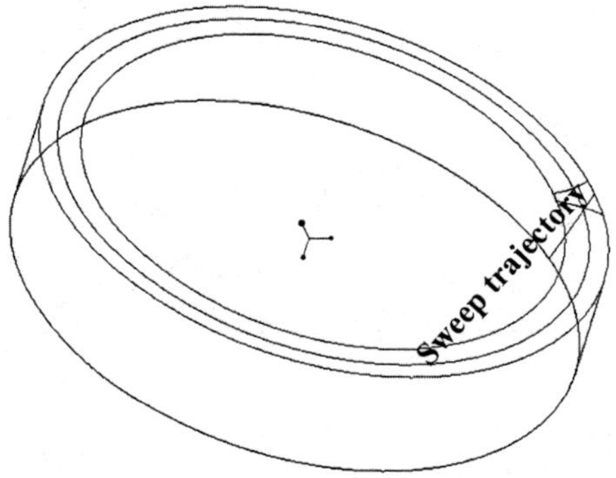

Fig. 16.28.

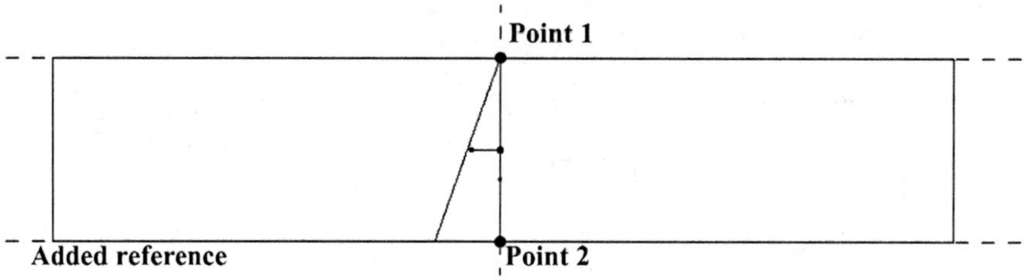

Fig. 16.29.

Goal	Step	Commands
	16. Start "Variable Section Sweep – Surface" feature.	→
	17. Define the origin trajectory.	**References** → ***Click in the trajectories window*** → ***Select the helical sweep trajectory curve*** Refer Fig. 16.30.
	18. Define the normal trajectory.	***While holding <u>CTRL</u>, Select the normal trajectory curve*** → ***Check X and N boxes next to chain 1*** Refer Figs. 16.30 and 16.31.
Create a cutting surface	19. Sketch the sweep section using use edge.	→ → ***Loop*** → ***Select the cut profile datum curve in the graphics window***
	20. Delete all references.	**SKETCH** → **REFERENCES** → ***Select the curves references only*** → **DELETE** → **CLOSE** Refer Fig. 16.32. New dimensions defining the curve should appear in the graphics window.
	21. Exit sketcher.	
	22. Accept the feature creation.	→ **VIEW** → **ORIENTATION** → **STANDARD ORIENTATION** → Refer Fig. 16.33.

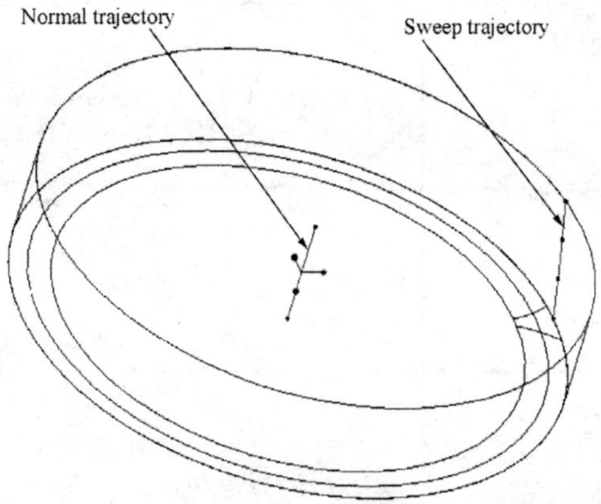

Fig. 16.30.

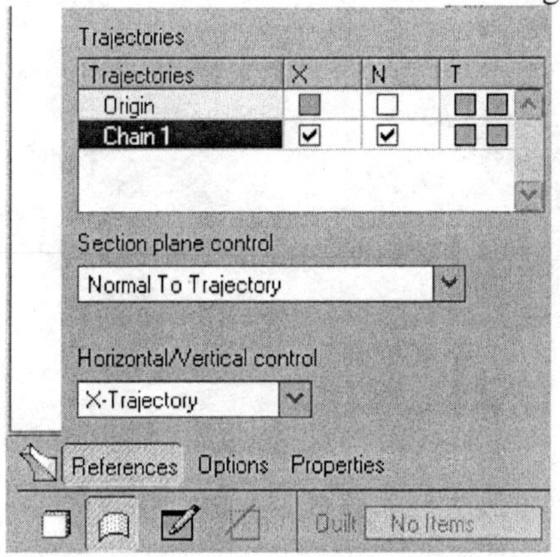

Fig. 16.31

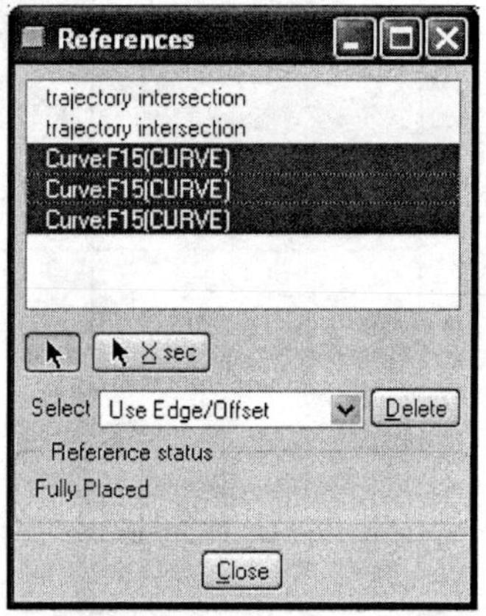

Fig. 16.32.

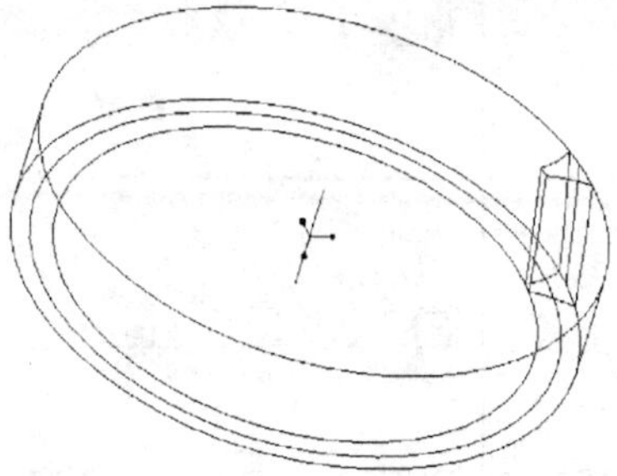
Fig. 16.33.

Goal	Step	Commands
Create the teeth	23. Create the initial cut.	***Select the last cutting surface from the model tree*** → **EDIT** → **SOLIDIFY** → → Refer Fig. 16.35.
Create the teeth (Continued)	24. Group the cutting surface and the cut.	***Select the last two features (Variable section sweep and Solidify) from the model tree*** → ***Right Mouse*** → **Group** → ***Double click on the Group Name*** → **<u>CUT</u>** → ***<u>ENTER</u>***
	25. Pattern the cut.	***Select the Group CUT from the model tree*** → **EDIT** → **PATTERN** → ***Axis*** → ***Select axis*** → **(Number of instances) <u>28</u>** → **(Enter the increment) <u>360/N</u>** → ***<u>ENTER</u>*** → YES → Refer Figs. 16.36 and 16.37.
Save the file and exit ProE	26. Save the file and exit ProE.	**FILE** → **SAVE** → **<u>HELICALGEAR.PRT</u>** → **OK** → **FILE** → **EXIT** → **YES**

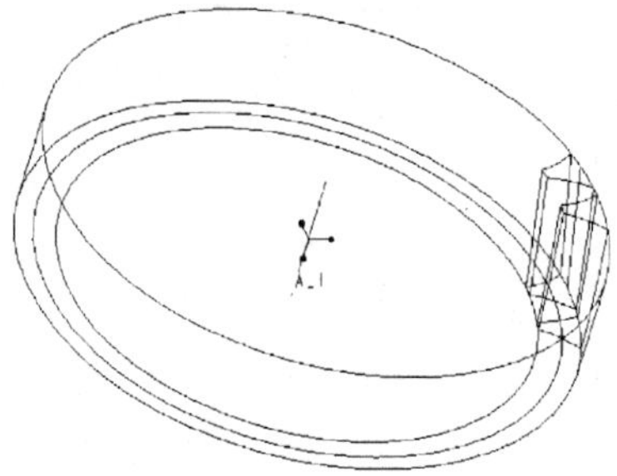

Fig. 16.34.

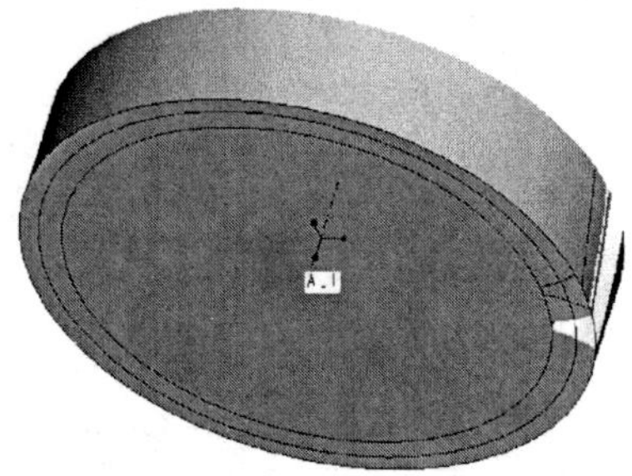

Fig. 16.35.

Fig. 16.36

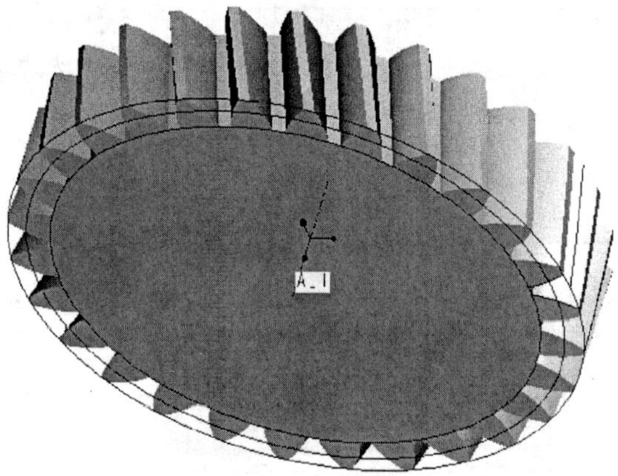

Fig. 16.37.

Exercise

Problem 1. Vase

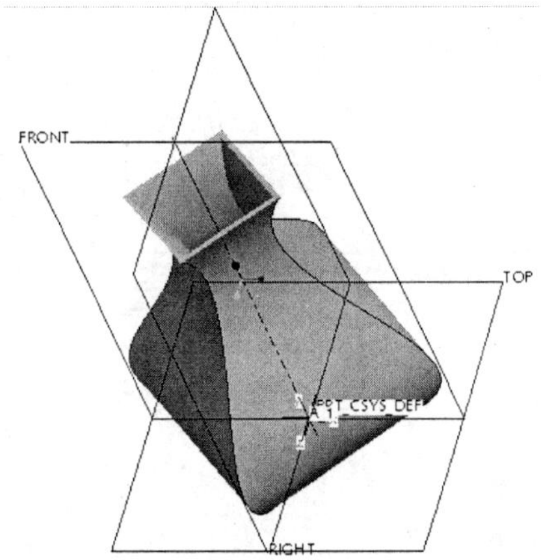

You can create complex geometries like these using the warp tool. You can create a simple geometry (like a square extrusion) and then, select INSERT WARP and then, modify the geometry to create organic structures.

Hints:

1. Create a datum axis at the intersection of the FRONT and RIGHT datums.
2. Sketch a spline on the right datum plane.
3. Create a pattern (four trajectories) using the axis

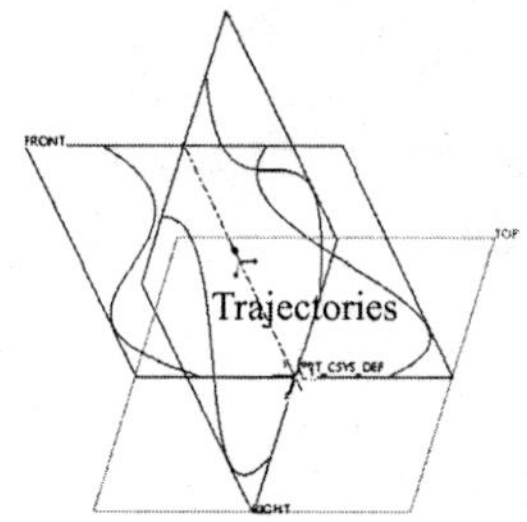

4. Sketch a datum line on top of the datum axis.

5. Start a variable section sweep. Select the four trajectories and direction reference as the datum line.

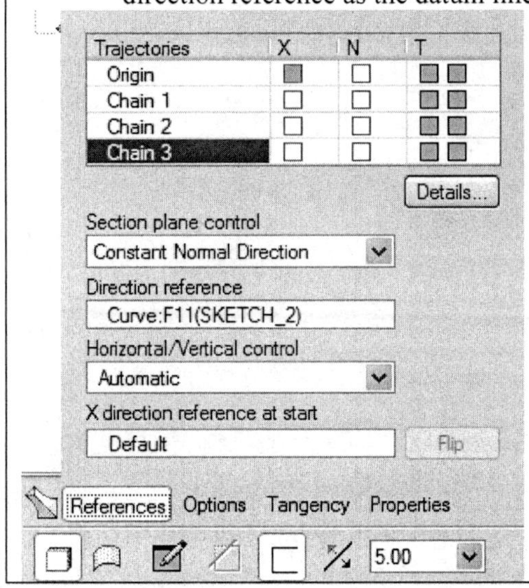

6. Sketch the section. Note that the corners of the square are exactly at the ends of the datum curves.

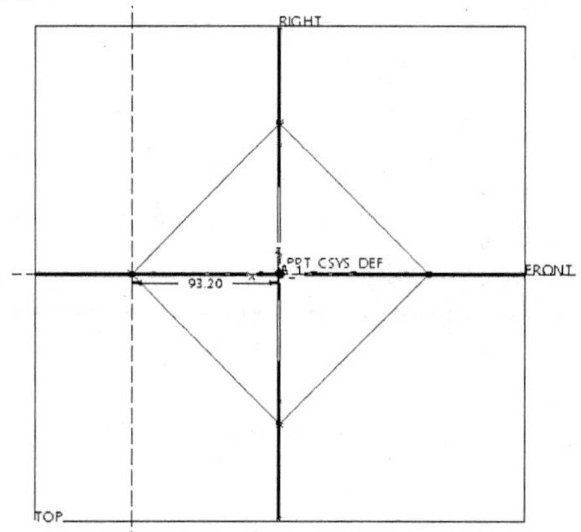

NOTES:

LESSON 17
AXIAL CAM

Learning Objectives

- Learn ***Variable Section Sweep*** and ***Datum – Graph*** features
- Practice ***Protrusion – Extrude*** and Relations, ***Datum – Curves*** features
- Learn ***Suppress*** command

Design Information

Cam-follower systems are commonly used for precise motion generation. The term "axial cam" refers to cams whose follower motion is in the axial direction (parallel to the axis of the cam rotation). The follower can ride either in a track or on a rib. Cam design involves plotting the rise, dwell and fall periods of the follower as a displacement graph. The follower experiences motion only during the rise and fall periods. The displacement graph can be constructed by connecting the desired extreme positions of the follower using straight lines. This simplistic approach leads to infinite acceleration and jerk and therefore, is highly undesirable. This lesson shows the steps in creating this naive axial cam. The same procedure is used in designing sophisticated cams.

Variable Section Sweep using Graph

Variable section sweep is the most powerful feature creation tool in ProE. At minimum, it requires two curves – the first curve defines the path of the sweep and the second curve defines the orientation. Origin trajectory defines the path of the sweep. The origin of the swept section (cross-hairs) is located on the origin trajectory. Often, several errors occur due to overlapping of the section as it sweeps the origin trajectory. The option "Normal to origin trajectory" specifies that the section is always normal to the origin trajectory. When using graph to guide the path, the X-Trajectory specifies the positive x-axis of the swept section's coordinate system. The section always points towards the x-trajectory.
Evalgraph function evaluates a graph to determine the location of the section at along the origin trajectory. The form of the equation is:
Sd# = evalgraph("Graph Name", trajpar * Width of the graph * Horizontal Scale) * Vertical Scale.
Sd# is the dimension defining the distance from the origin trajectory to the origin of the section. Trajpar is a normalized variable (varies between 0 and 1). If the horizontal scale is 1, then the x-axis of the graph is scaled to fit the length of the origin trajectory. The vertical scale scales the y-value of the graph.

SEQUENCE OF STEPS

STEP I: Create the base cylinder

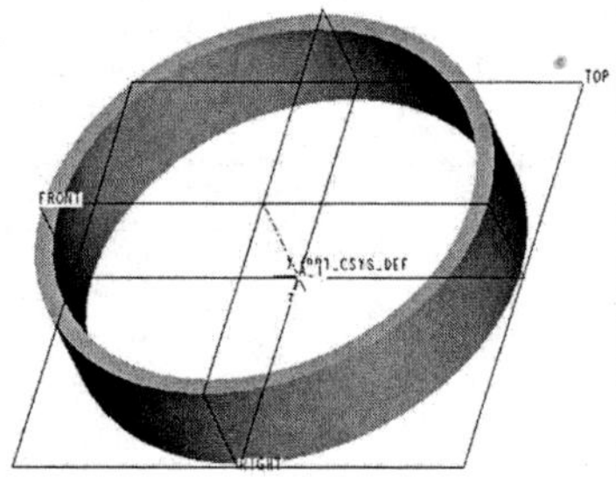

STEP II: Create the displacement graph

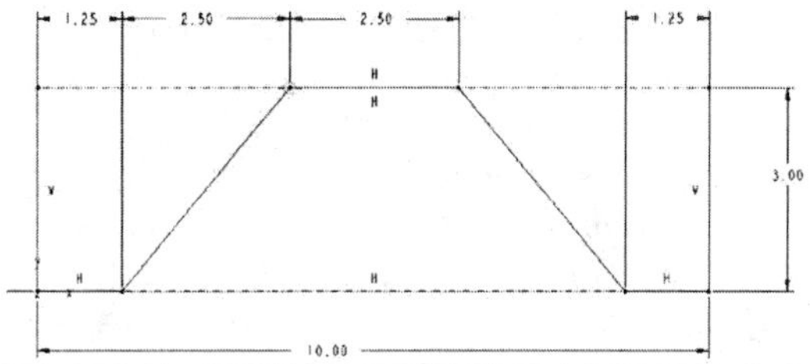

STEP III: Create two datum circles on the outer surface

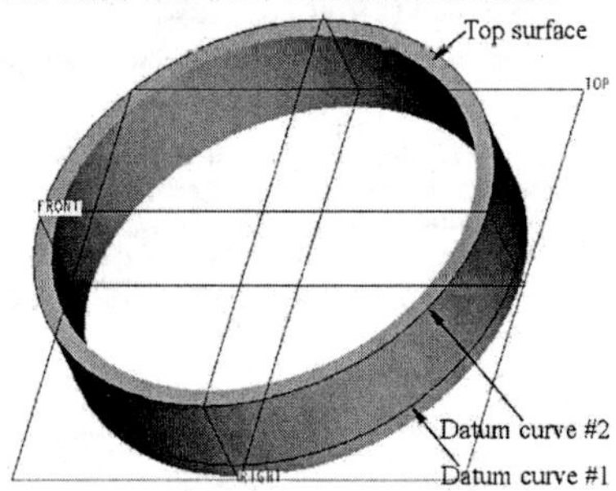

STEP IV: Create a track

1. Start "Variable Section Sweep - Cut" feature.

2. Select the origin- and x-trajectories.

3. Draw the track section.

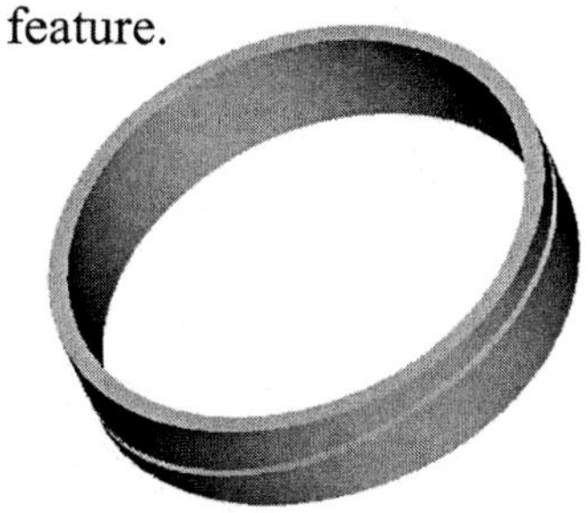

STEP V: Create a rib

1. Start "Variable Section Sweep - Protrusion" feature.

2. Select the origin- and x-trajectories.

3. Draw the rib section.

Goal	Step	Commands
Open a new file for the axial cam part	1. Set up the working directory.	**FILE → SET WORKING DIRECTORY →** ***Select the working directory*** **→ OK**
	2. Open a new file.	**FILE → NEW →** ***Part*** **→** ***Solid*** **→ axialcam → OK**
Create the base cylinder	3. Start "Extrude" feature.	
	4. Define the sketching plane.	**Placement → Define →** ***Select the TOP datum plane*** **→ Sketch**
	5. Draw a circle.	**→** ***Select the center of the circle at the intersection of the FRONT and RIGHT planes → Select a point to define the outer edge of the circle*** Refer to Fig. 17.1.
	6. Modify the diameter.	**→** ***Double click the diameter dimension*** **→ 48 →** ***ENTER***
	7. Exit sketcher.	
	8. Define the direction and thickness of material creation.	**(Depth) 12 → →(Thickness) 2 → (Fig. 17.2 – click only once - changes the direction of extrusion to outside.)** Refer to Fig. 17.2.
	9. Accept the feature creation.	**→ VIEW → ORIENTATION → STANDARD ORIENTATION** Refer to Fig. 17.3.

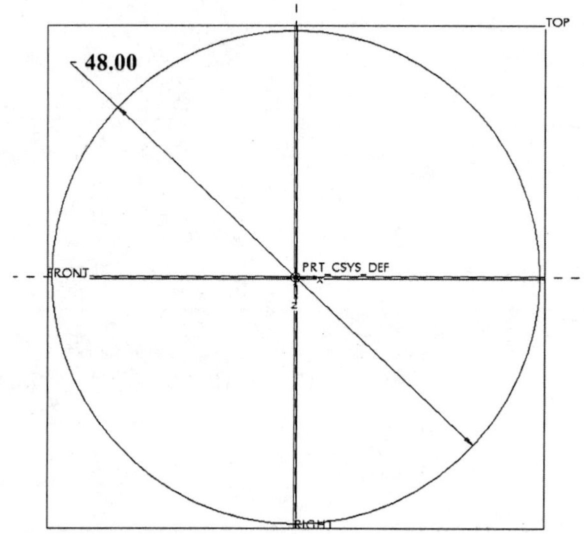

Fig. 17.1.

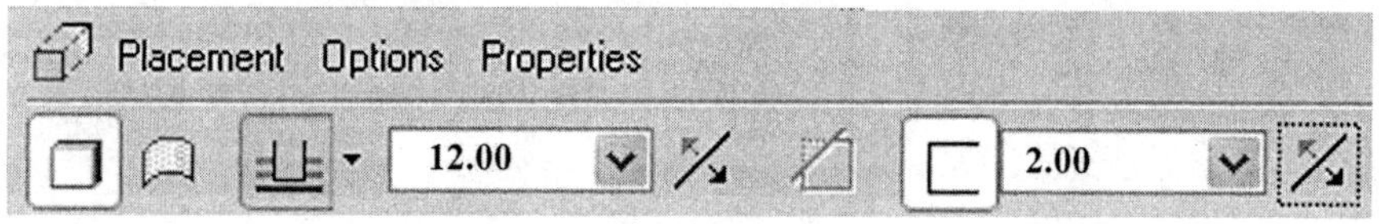

Fig. 17.2.

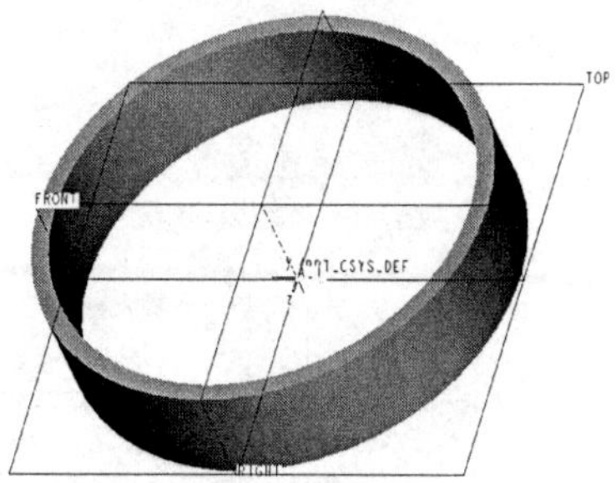
Fig. 17.3.

Goal	Step	Commands
Create datum graph	10. Start "Datum – Graph" feature.	**INSERT → MODEL DATUM → GRAPH → <u>Profile</u> →** ✓ ProE opens the sketcher.
	11. Define a coordinate system.	→ ***Select a point in the graphics window***
	12. Draw a rectangle.	→ ***Pick points 1 and 2*** Refer to Fig. 17.4.
	13. Modify the dimensions.	→ ***Double click the horizontal dimension → <u>10</u> → <u>ENTER</u> → Double click the height dimension → <u>3</u>→ <u>ENTER</u>*** Refer to Fig. 17.4.
	14. Change the rectangle into a construction entity.	→ ***Select the four sides*** **(Hold *<u>CNTRL</u>* key while selecting multiple entities) → EDIT → TOGGLE CONSTRUCTION** Refer to Fig. 17.5.
	15. Create the displacement profile.	→ ***Pick points 3, 4, 5, 6, 7 and 8 → Middle Mouse*** Refer to Fig. 17.5.
	16. Add dimensions.	→ ***Select points 4 and 5 → Middle Mouse to place the horizontal dimension*** Refer to Fig. 17.6. Add additional dimensions if necessary
	17. Modify dimensions.	→ ***Double click each dimension and enter the corresponding values*** Refer to Fig. 17.6.
	18. Exit sketcher.	✓

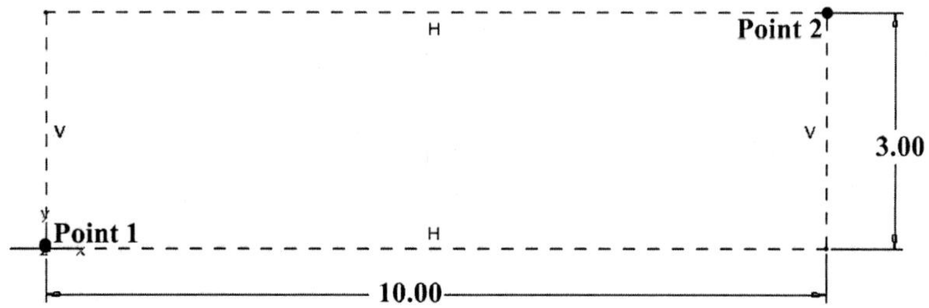

Fig. 17.4.

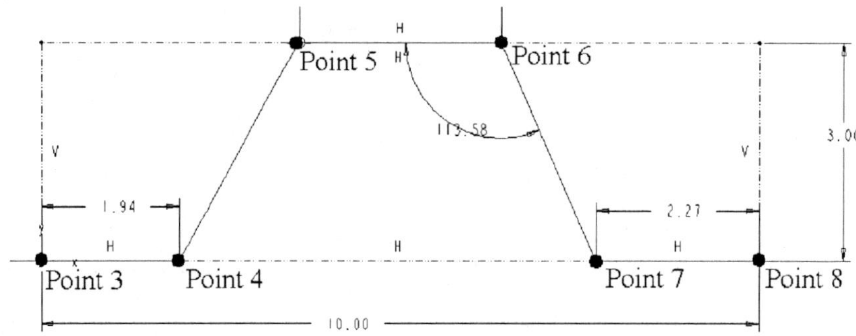

Fig. 17.5.

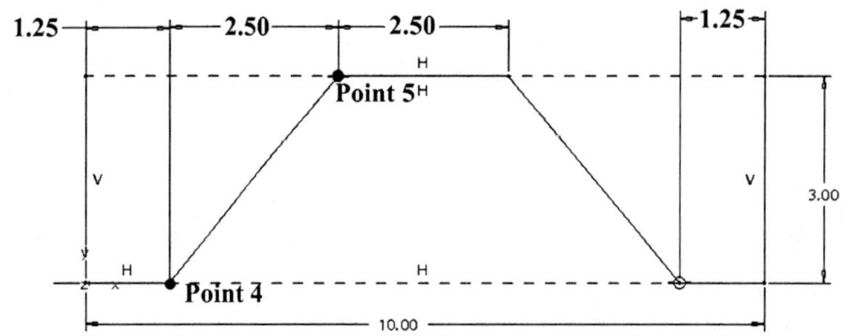

Fig. 17.6.

Goal	Step	Commands
Create datum curves	19. Start "Datum – Curve" command.	
	20. Set up a sketching plane that is 2″ above the bottom surface of the cylinder.	→ ***Select the TOP datum plane*** → **(Translation) <u>2.0</u>** → **OK** → **Sketch** Refer to Fig. 17.7.
	21. Create a datum circle.	→ ***Single (in the Type window)*** → ***Select the top half of the outer circle*** → ***Select the bottom half of the outer circle*** Refer to Fig. 17.8.
	22. Exit sketcher.	✔
	23. View the datum curve.	**VIEW → ORIENTATION → STANDARD ORIENTATION** Refer to Fig. 17.9.
	24. Start "Datum Curve" command.	
	25. Setup a sketching plane.	***Select the top surface of the cylinder*** → **Sketch** Refer to Fig. 17.10.
	26. Create a datum circle.	→ ***Select the top half of the outer circle*** → ***Select the bottom half of the outer circle***
	27. Exit sketcher.	✔
	28. View the datum curve.	**VIEW → ORIENTATION → STANDARD ORIENTATION** Refer to Fig. 17.10.

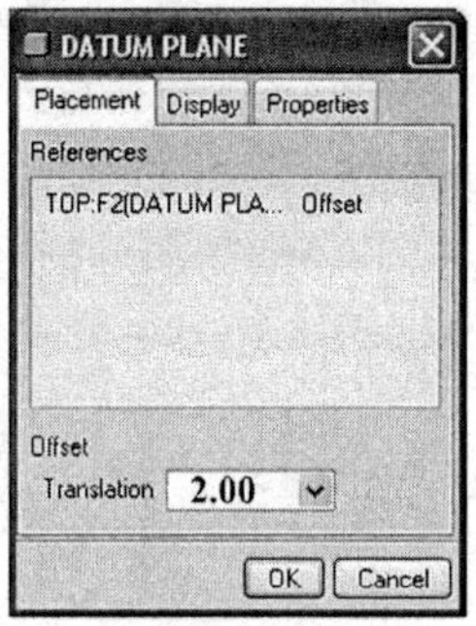

Fig. 17.7.

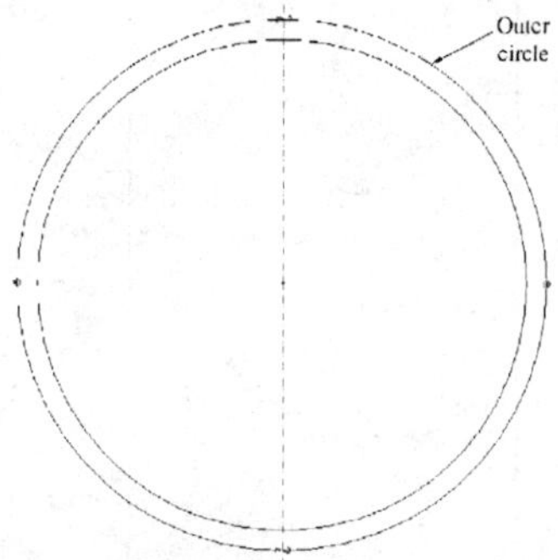

Fig. 17.8.

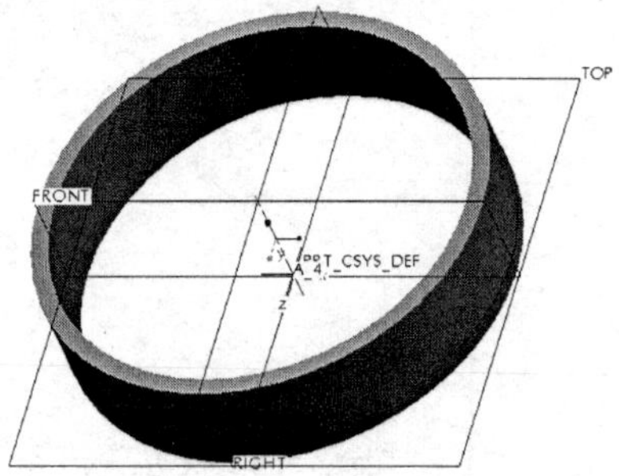

Fig. 17.9.

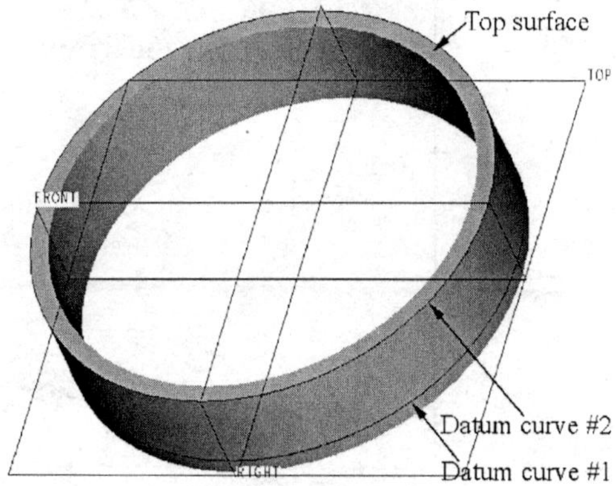

Fig. 17.10.

Goal	Step	Commands
Create a track	29. Start "Variable Section Sweep - Cut" feature.	**(or INSERT → VARIABLE SECTION SWEEP) → →**
	30. Select the origin- and x-trajectories.	**References →** ***Click in the trajectories window → Select the datum curve 1 and then, curve 2*** **(holding <u>*CNTRL*</u> key) →** ***Select X for chain 1 in the trajectory window*** **to define the datum curve 2 as the X-trajectory** Refer to Fig. 17.11.

Origin Trajectory – The origin of the swept section (cross-hairs) is located on the origin trajectory. The option "Normal to origin trajectory" specifies that the section is always normal to the origin trajectory.

X-Trajectory – The positive x-axis of the swept section's coordinate system points towards the x-trajectory.

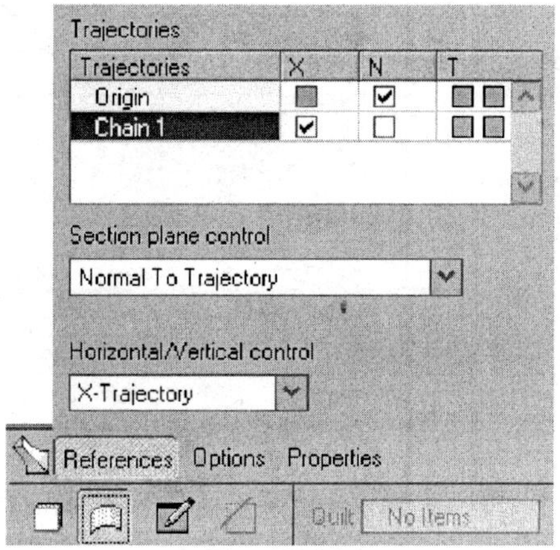

Fig. 17.11.

Goal	Step	Commands
Create a track (continued)	31. Draw a rectangle.	→ → ***Pick points 1 and 2*** Refer to Fig. 17.12. If ProE prompts whether to align the highlighted points with the inner edge of the cylinder, then select NO.
	32. Modify the dimensions of the rectangle.	→ ***Double click the side dimensions and enter 1*** Refer to Fig. 17.12.
	33. Add relationship.	**TOOLS → RELATIONS → <u>sd5 = evalgraph ("profile",trajpar*10) * 2</u> → OK** Refer to Figs. 17.12(b) and 17.13. Sd5 (the distance of the section from the origin) may be different in your model.
	34. Exit sketcher.	✓
	35. Accept the feature creation.	✓ → **VIEW → ORIENTATION → STANDARD ORIENTATION** Refer to Fig. 17.14.

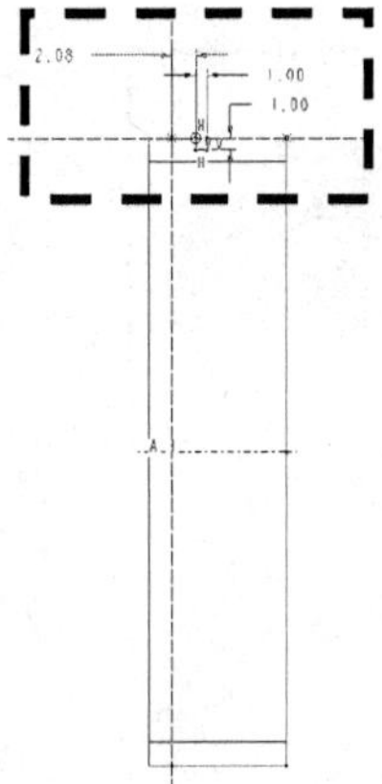

(a)

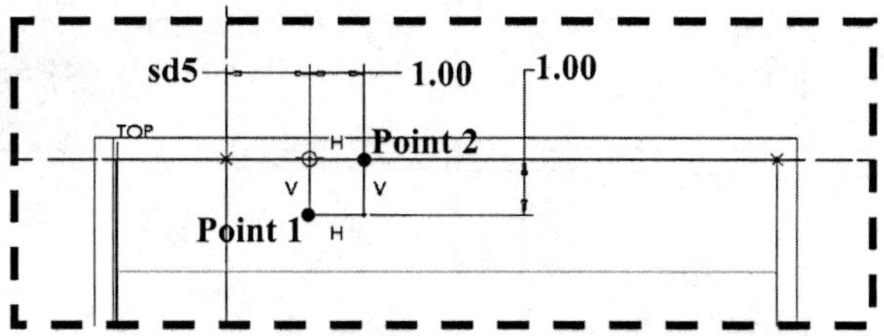

(b) Detailed view of the top portion of Fig. 17.12(a).

Fig. 17.12.

Common form of the equation is: <u>Sd# = evalgraph("Graph Name", trajpar * Width of the graph * Horizontal Scale) * Vertical Scale</u>
Trajpar is a normalized variable (varies between 0 and 1). If the horizontal scale is 1, then the x-axis of the graph is scaled to fit the length of the origin trajectory. The vertical scale scales the y-value of the graph.

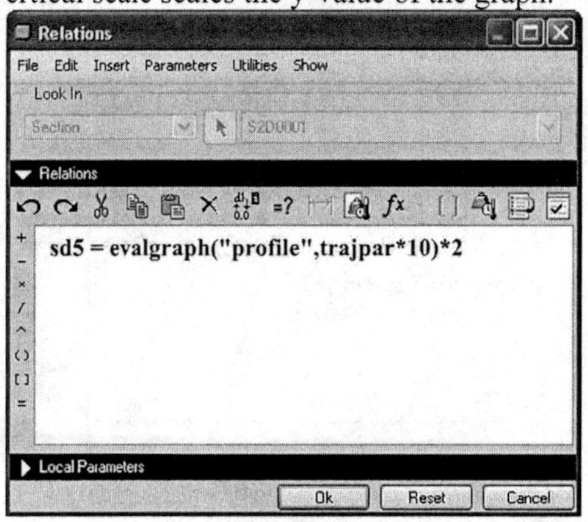

Fig. 17.13.

Fig. 17.14.

Goal	Step	Commands
Suppress the track feature	36. Suppress the feature.	***Select the cut feature from the model tree* → EDIT → SUPRESS → OK**
Create a rib	37. Start "Variable Section Sweep" feature.	→
	38. Select the origin- and x-trajectories.	**References → *Click in the trajectories window* → *Select the datum curve 1 and then, curve 2* (holding <u>CNTRL</u> key) → *Select X for chain 1 in the trajectory window* to define the datum curve 2 as the X-trajectory**
	39. Draw a rectangle.	→ → ***Pick points 1 and 2*** Refer to Fig. 17.15.
	40. Modify the dimensions of the rectangle.	→ ***Double click the dimensions of the rectangle and enter 1*** Refer to Fig. 17.15.
	41. Add relationship.	**TOOLS → RELATIONS → <u>sd7 = evalgraph ("profile",trajpar*10) * 2</u> → OK**
	42. Exit sketcher.	✓

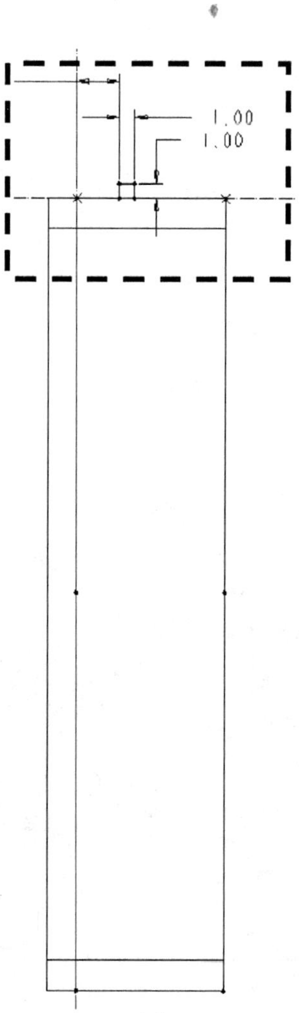

(a)

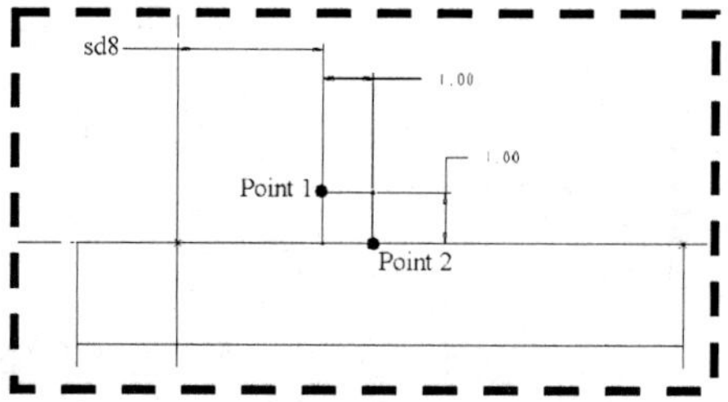

(b) Detailed view of the top portion of Fig. 17.15(a).

Fig. 17.15.

Goal	Step	Commands
Create a rib (continued)	43. Finish the feature creation.	 → **VIEW → ORIENTATION → STANDARD ORIENTATION** Refer to Fig. 17.16.
	44. Turn off datum curves.	**VIEW → DISPLAY SETTINGS → MODEL DISPLAY →** ***Click on the "Shade" tab*** **→ Unselect "With datum curves" → OK**
Save the file and exit ProE	45. Save the file and exit ProE.	**FILE → SAVE → AXIALCAM.PRT → OK → FILE → EXIT → Yes**

Fig. 17.16.

Exercise

Problem 1

1. The datum curves are shown in the figure.
2. All the dimensions are same as in the chapter.
3. Cut the cam using the graph created.

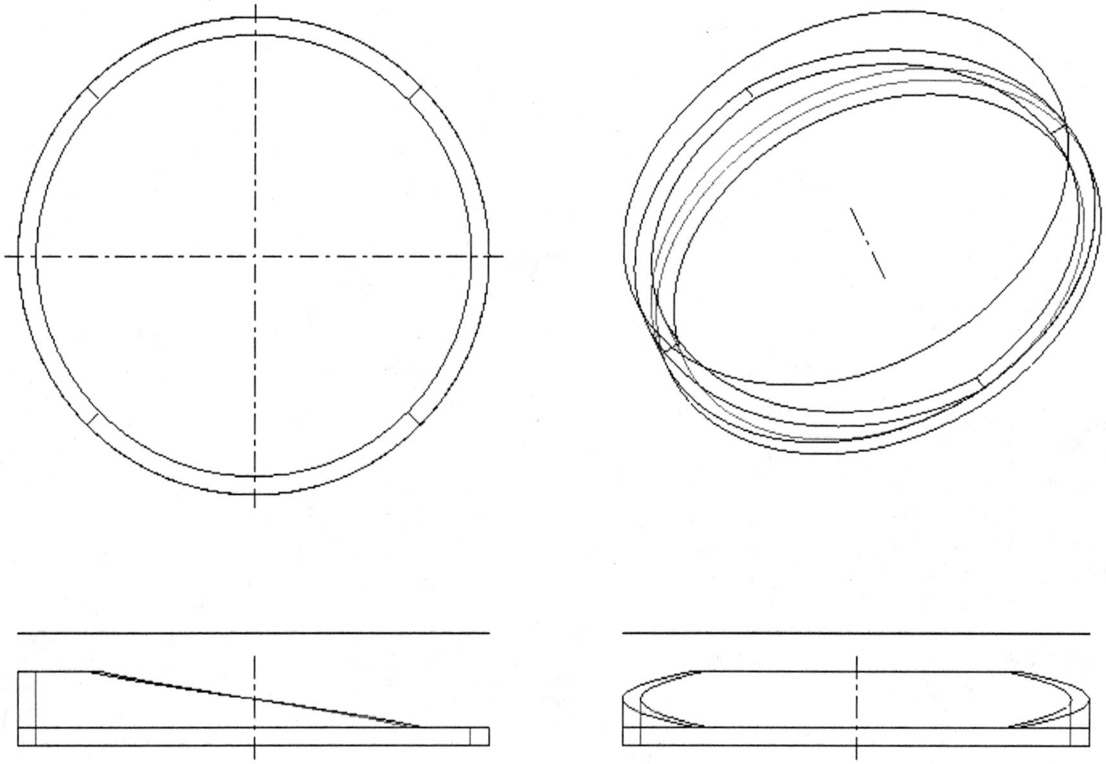

Hints:

1. Suppress the cut and protrusion features created.
2. Create another cut.

LESSON 18
GROOVED CAM

Learning Objectives

- Create ***Spline*** from data points.
- Learn the use of ***User Define Features***.
- Practice ***Extrude*** and ***Extrude – Cut*** features.

User Define Feature

Using a User Defined Feature (UDF), a user can define a set of features as a UDF and insert this UDF in any part/assembly. It provides an accurate and fast method to reproduce geometry. Further, flexibility can be incorporated by defining the UDF parameters which can be varied while placing it. When a UDF is defined, Pro|ENGINEER creates a file with ".gph" extension.

A UDF can be subordinate or standalone. A subordinate UDF is linked to the original model where the UDF is defined, and gets its dimensions directly from the original model at the run time. Dimensional changes in the original model automatically propagate to the UDF. In the Standalone mode, the feature information is copied during the UDF creation. The changes in the original model do not reflect in the UDF. Even though the original referenced part is not required in the standalone mode, including the reference part helps in identifying the references correctly while placing the UDF.

UDF provides the ability to define variable dimensions which are specified at the time of creating the part, and table-driven dimensions where the dimensions are driven by the family table. Invariable dimensions are held constant during the creation of UDF. A UDF can also be used to specify feature elements such as section that can be defined while placing the UDF

Background Information

Grooved cams use form closure (closes the joint by geometry) and require no external forces to keep the cam and follower in contact. Grooved cams are in fact two cam surfaces (upper and lower surfaces of the track) making the follower move in the groove. These cams can push and pull the follower. When equations defining the displacement profile become complicated, it is easier to define a cam in terms of data points. The data points can be created outside Pro|ENGINEER environment and then imported into Pro|ENGINEER to define the profile. The lesson also describes the use of User Defined Features (UDF), which can be a collection of features that are used repeatedly. For instance, bolt hole pattern can be an UDF and can be inserted into any part.

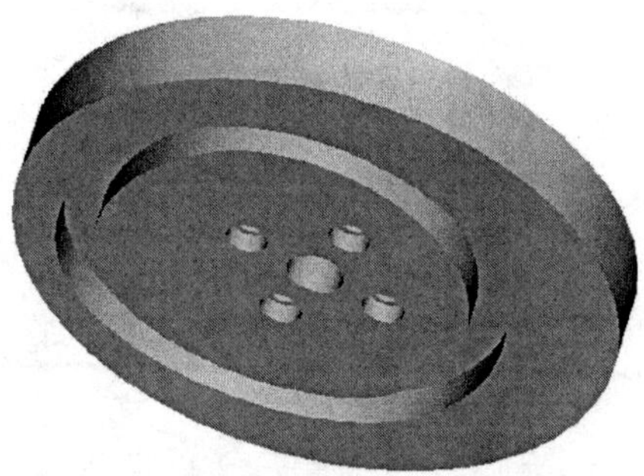

STEP I: Create the base cylinder

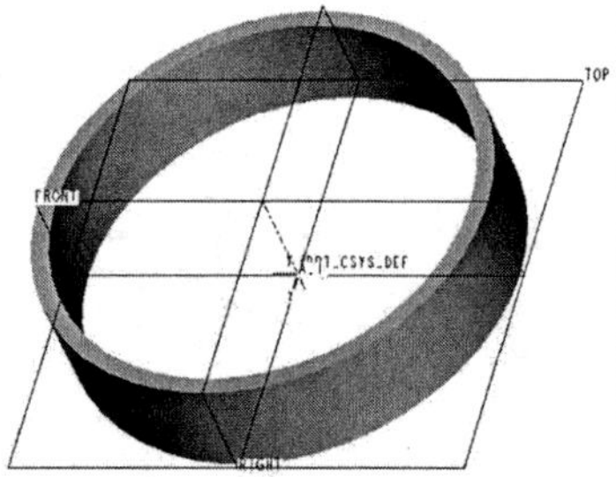

STEP II: Create the displacement graph

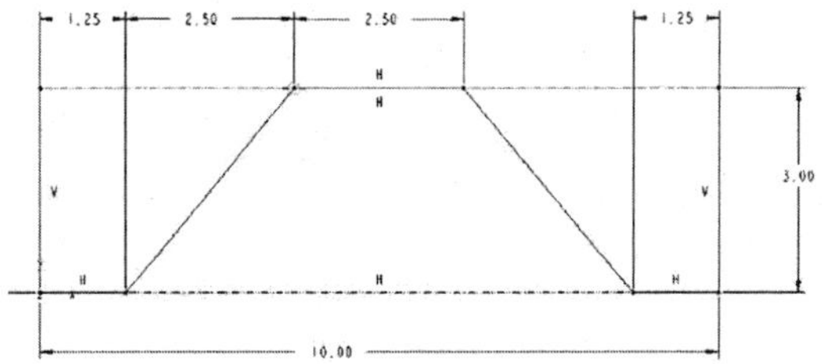

STEP III: Create two datum circles on the outer surface

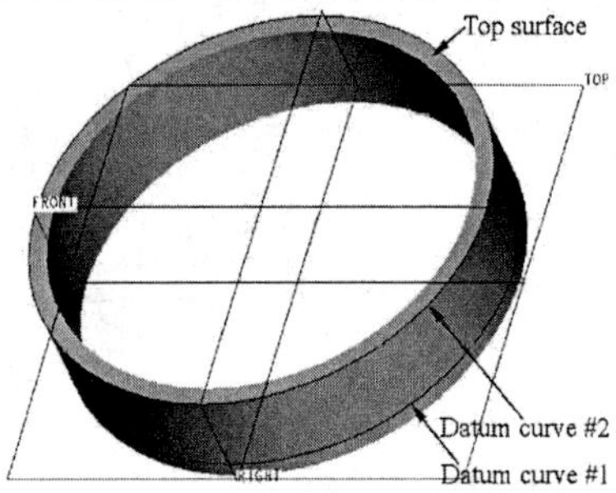

SEQUENCE OF STEPS

STEP IV: Create a track

1. Start "Variable Section Sweep - Cut" feature.
2. Select the origin- and x-trajectories.
3. Draw the track section.

STEP V: Create a rib

1. Start "Variable Section Sweep - Protrusion" feature.
2. Select the origin- and x-trajectories.
3. Draw the rib section.

Goal	Step	Commands
	IN NOTEPAD OR EXCEL	
Create cam profile data points	1. Open Notepad (or VI editor) or Excel.	
	2. Enter data points.	**Enter data points** Refer Fig. 18.1.
	3. Save file.	**FILE → SAVE AS →** (File name) **"profile.pts"** (If the name is enclosed in quotes, then Windows will not attach any extension to the file name.) → (Encoding) **ANSI → Save → FILE → EXIT** Refer Fig. 18.2.
	IN ProE	
Open a new file for the face cam part	4. Set up the working directory.	**FILE → SET WORKING DIRECTORY →** ***Select the working directory*** **→ OK**
	5. Open a new file.	**FILE → NEW →** ***Part*** **→** ***Solid*** **→ groovedcam → OK**
Create the base cylinder	6. Start "Extrude" feature.	
	7. Define the sketching plane.	**Placement → Define →** ***Select the FRONT datum plane*** **→ Sketch**

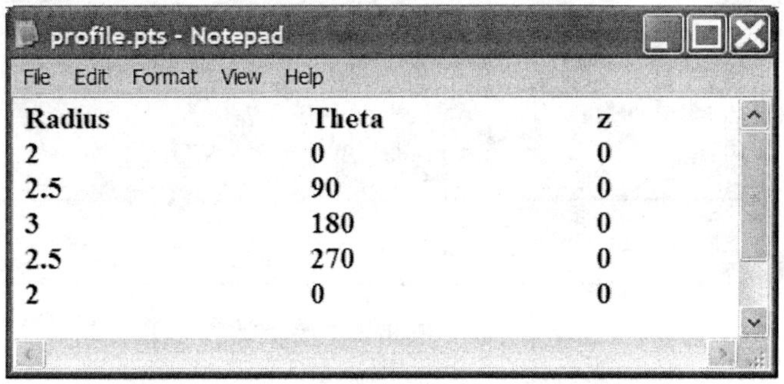

Fig. 18.1.

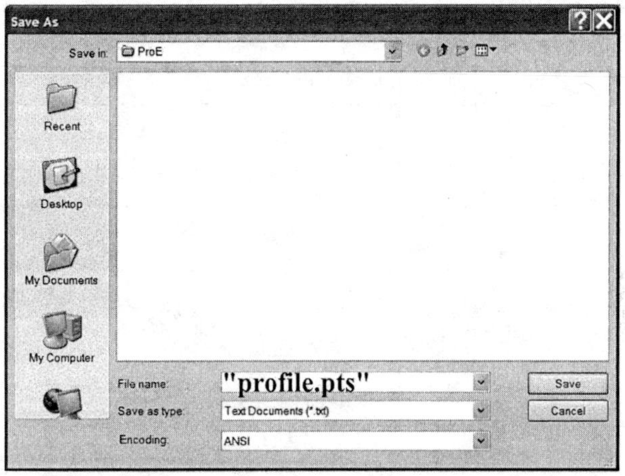

Fig. 18.2.

Goal	Step	Commands
Create the base cylinder (continued)	8. Draw a circle.	→ ***Select the center of the circle as the intersection of the TOP and RIGHT datum planes → Select a point to define the outer edge of the circle*** Refer Fig. 18.3.
	9. Modify the diameter.	→ ***Double click the diameter dimension →*** **<u>8</u>→ *<u>ENTER</u>***
	10. Exit sketcher.	
	11. Define the depth.	(Depth) **<u>1</u>** → ***<u>ENTER</u>***
	12. Accept the feature creation.	→ **VIEW → ORIENTATION → STANDARD ORIETATION** Refer Fig. 18.4.
Create the groove for the cam follower	13. Start "Extrude - Cut" feature.	→
	14. Select the sketching plane.	**Placement → Define →** ***Select the front surface of the cam (that is away from the front datum plane) →*** **Sketch** Refer Fig. 18.5.
	15. Define a coordinate system.	→ → ***Select the intersection of RIGHT and TOP datum planes***
	16. Create a spline.	→ ***Pick points 1, 2, 3, 4 and 1*** Refer Fig. 18.6.

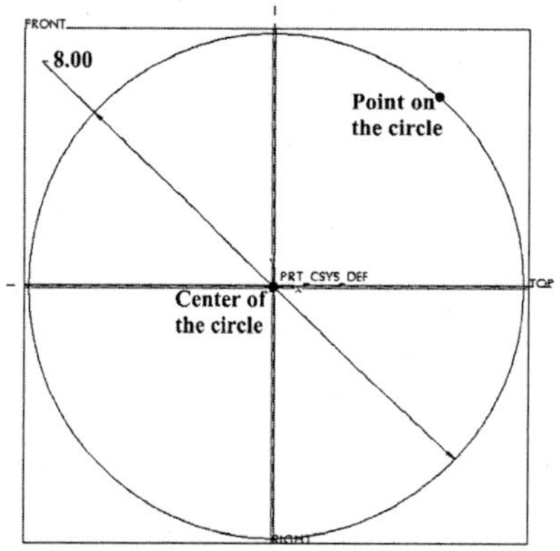

Fig. 18.3.

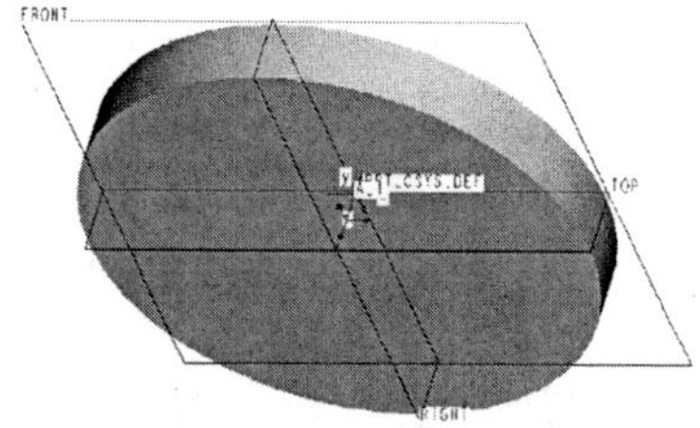

Fig. 18.4.

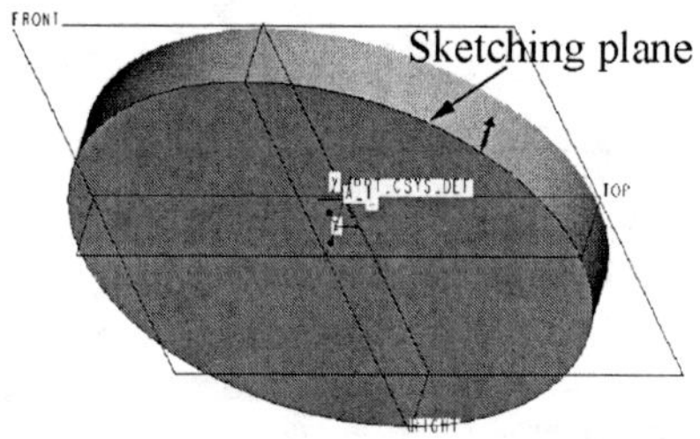

Fig. 18.5.

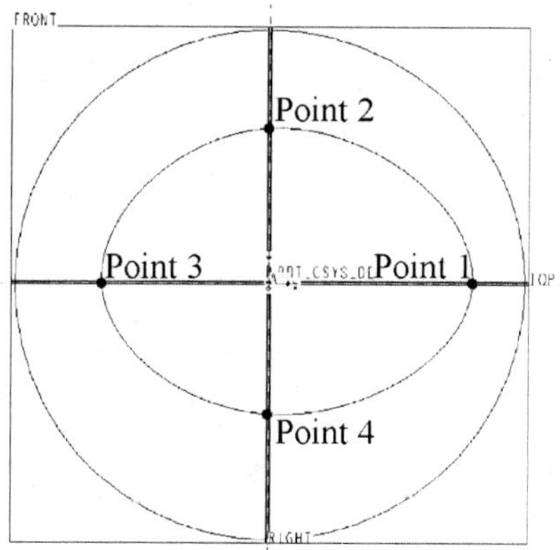

Fig. 18.6.

Goal	Step	Commands
Create the groove for the cam follower (continued)	17. Modify the endpoint dimension.	→ ***Double click on the distance between the coordinate system and point 1*** → **2** → ***ENTER*** Refer Fig. 18.7.
	18. Select and assign the coordinate system.	→ ***Select the spline*** → → **File (in the dash)**→ ***Click on*** ***(in the dash)*** → ***Select the coordinate system*** → ***Select polar coordinate system*** Refer Fig. 18.8.
	19. Read data points.	→ **If ProE prompts: Cannot modify spline with dimensions to internal points. Delete dimensions? Click YES** → ***Select PROFILE.PTS*** → **OPEN** → **(in the dash)**
	20. Exit sketcher.	
	21. Define the cut.	(Depth) **0.5** → → (Thickness **0.5** (next to thicken icon) Refer Fig. 18.9.
	22. Accept the feature creation.	→ **VIEW** → **ORIENTATION** → **STANDARD ORIETATION** Refer Fig. 18.10.

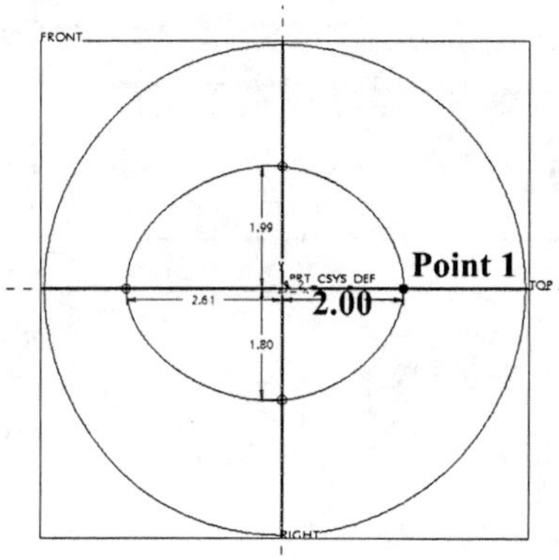

Fig. 18.7.

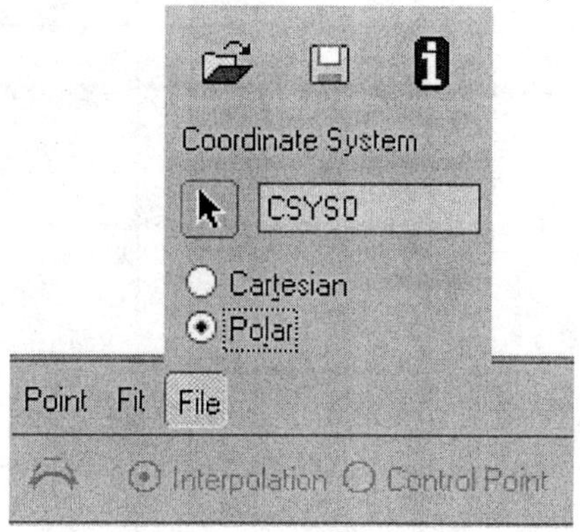

Fig. 18.8.

Fig. 18.9.

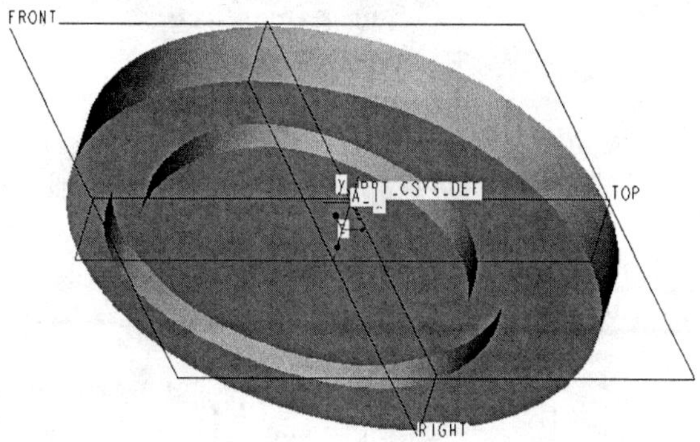

Fig. 18.10.

Goal	Step	Commands
Create UDF feature	23. Open plate cam file.	**FILE → OPEN →** ***Select "platecam.prt"*** **→ OPEN**
	24. Create a User Defined Feature (UDF).	**TOOLS → UDF LIBRARY → Create → holepattern →**
	25. Define UDF options.	**Stand Alone → Done** **(Include original part) Yes → Yes**
	26. Select the features.	**Add → Select → Pick →** ***Select the axial hole and patterned holes (the last two features in the model tree)*** **→ Done → Done/Return**
	27. Define the prompts.	**Single → Done/Return →** **the placement plane → →** **Secondary reference 1 → →** **Single → Done/Return →** **Secondary reference 2 → →** Read the prompt and displayed reference. If it needs to be changed, click Enter prompt, or else click Next. After ensuring correct prompts, select: **Done/Return**

In the stand-alone option, ProE copies the required information at the time of the UDF creation. On the other hand, the subordinate option copies the information from the original part at the run time. The second option is very useful in making sure that the holes of mating parts line up.

In the "single" option, a single prompt appears for the reference used by several features. The "multiple" option prompts references for each feature in the UDF.

Goal	Step	Commands
Create UDF feature (continued)	28. Define the variable parameters.	***Select Var Dims in "UDF: Holepattern, Standalone" window* → Define →** Refer Fig. 18.11. **Add → Select Dim → Zoom in →** ***Select the patterned hole depths (1.0 and 0.375 respectively.) →*** The depths should be highlighted. Refer Fig. 18.12. **Done/Return → Done/Return →** (Enter prompts) **<u>cam thickness</u>** (if 1.0 is highlighted) → → **<u>the depth of countersunk hole</u>** (if 0.375 is highlighted) → → If you are not sure whether the prompts correspond to their respective dimensions, click on Dim Prompts and follow instructions. **OK**
	29. Close the window	**FILE → ERASE → CURRENT → YES**

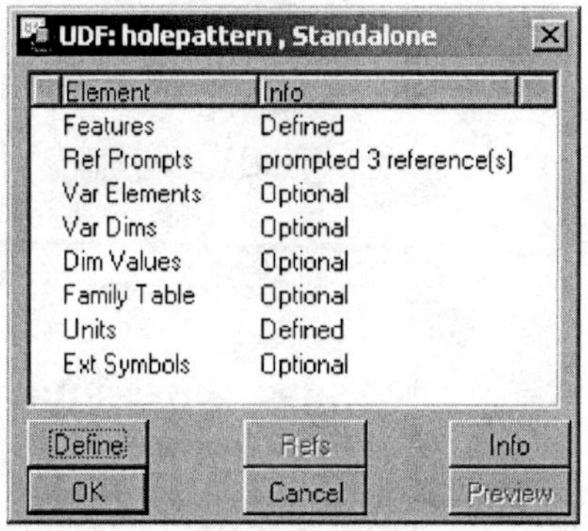

Fig. 18.11.

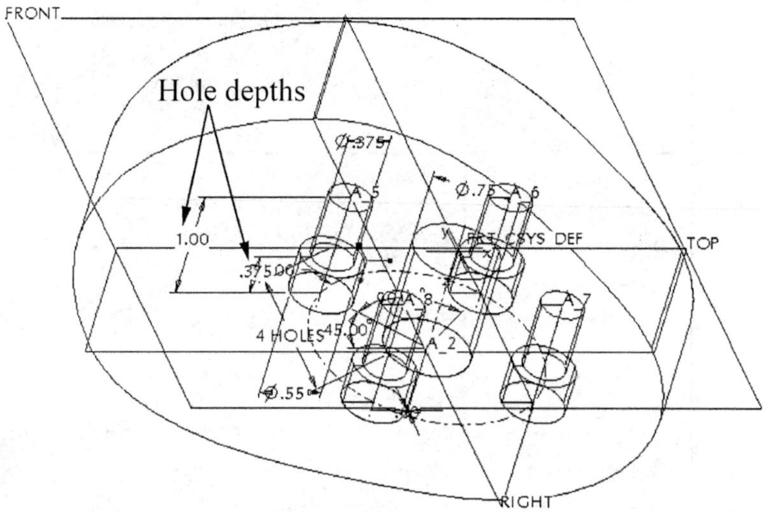

Fig. 18.12.

Goal	Step	Commands
Activate grooved cam window	30. Activate “groovedcam” window.	**WINDOW → GROOVEDCAM.PRT**
Insert the UDF	31. Start “holepattern” UDF.	**INSERT → USER DEFINED FEATURE → *Select holepattern* → Open → *Select view source model* → OK** Refer Fig. 18.13. ProE opens the reference part in another window. This helps in picking the corresponding datum planes.
	32. Select references.	***Select each placement reference in the window & select the corresponding reference in the model (front surface, RIGHT and TOP datum planes) →*** Refer Figs. 18.14 and 18.15.
	33. Define the UDF options.	***Select variables tab*** → (Enter the cam thickness) **1** → (Enter the countersunk hole depth) **0.25** → ✔ → ***Select the front surface*** → **Done** Refer Figs. 18.16 and 18.17.
Save the file and exit ProE	34. Save the file and exit ProE.	**FILE → SAVE → GROOVEDCAM.PRT → OK → FILE → EXIT → Yes**

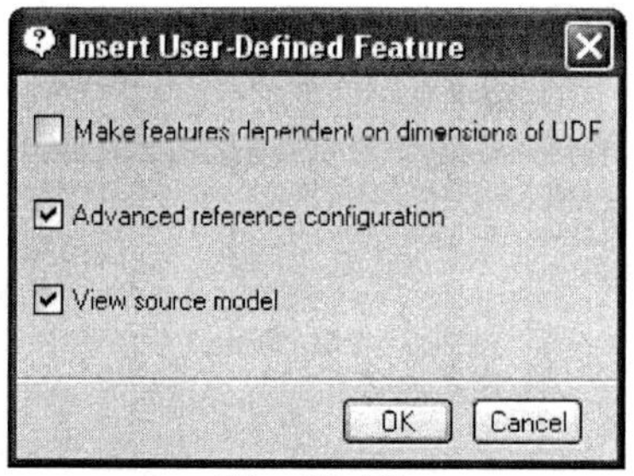

Fig. 18.13.

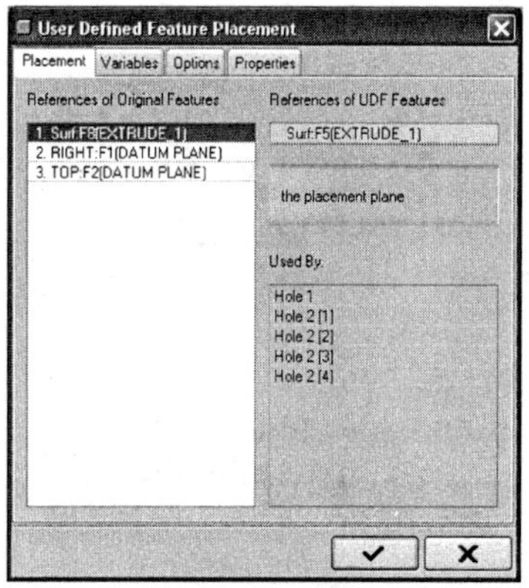

Fig. 18.14.

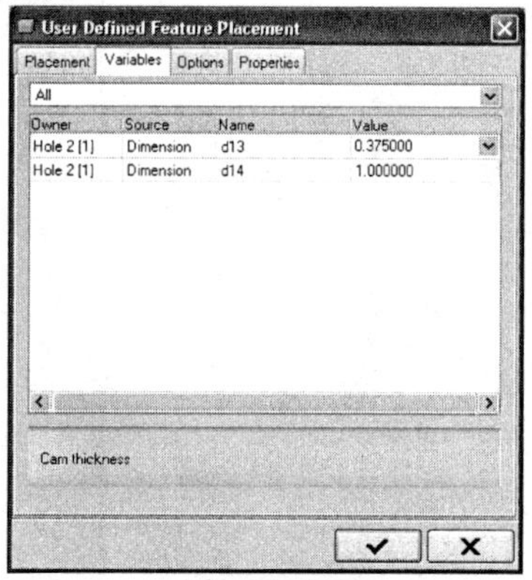

Fig. 18.16.

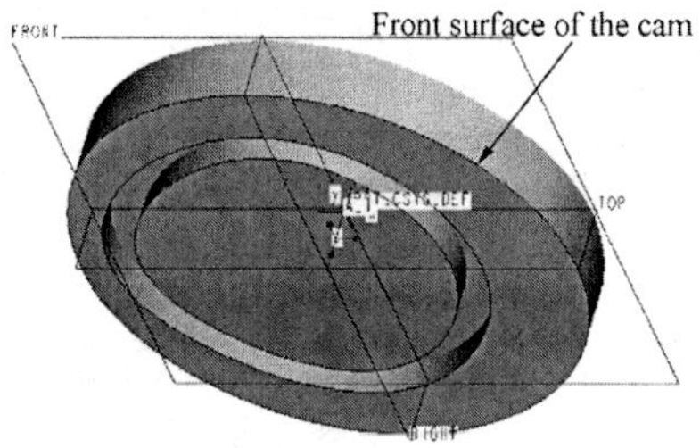

Fig. 18.15.

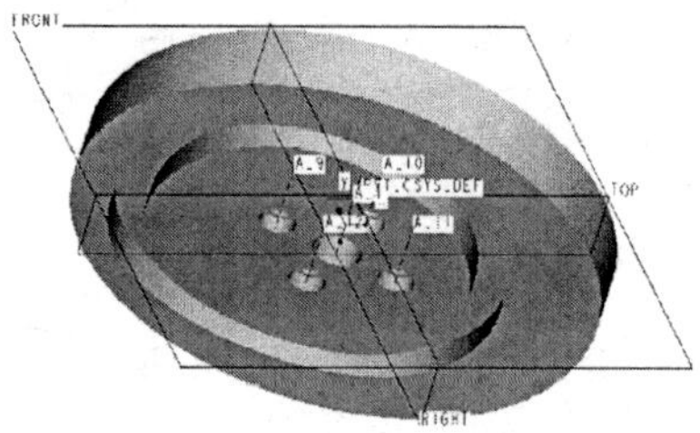
Fig. 18.17.

EXERCISE

Problem 1

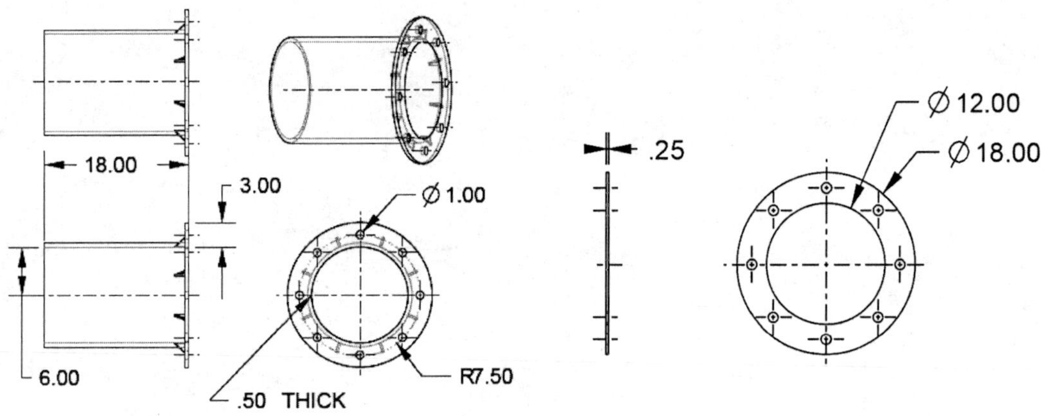

(Rib details not shown)

Hints:

1. Create the pipe part with the flange by using "Revolve – Thicken" option.
2. Create a radial hole and pattern the hole.
3. Creating ribs: Start the rib feature (INSERT → RIB). Then, create a datum on the fly though the axis of the cylinder and at 22.5 from the TOP datum plane ( ). Resume the feature creation. Sketch a line as shown in the figure below (References → Define in the dash).

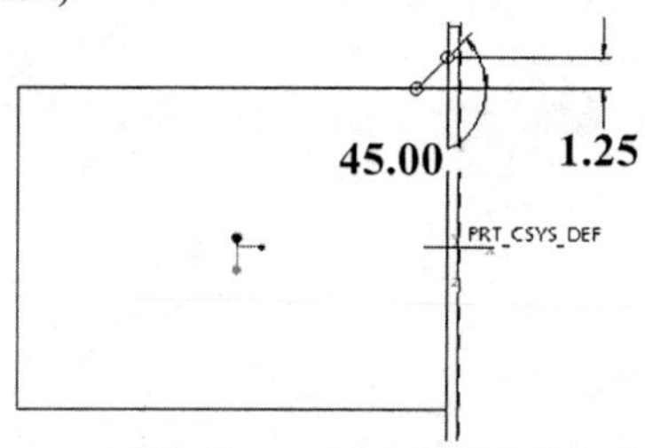

If necessary flip the material add direction by clicking on the in the references. Also change the thickness option to both sides. Define the thickness as 0.25.

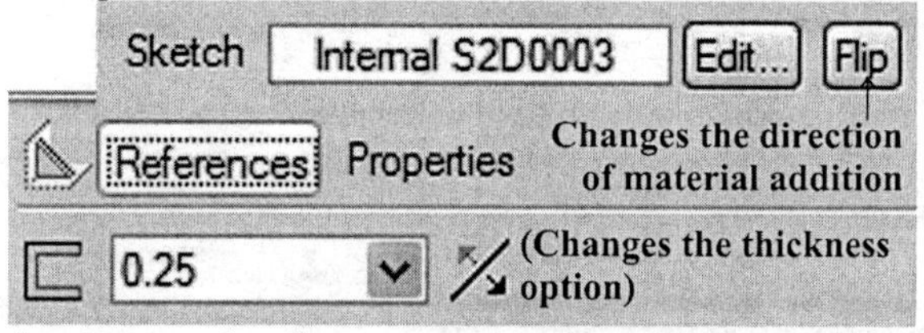

4. Pattern the rib.
5. Create the sealing ring. Use UDF feature to copy the hole pattern from the pipe to the ring.
6. Assemble the ring and then, the two pipes. Use repeat feature in the assembly.

NOTES:

LESSON 19
BOLT HEADS

Learning Objectives

- Understand ***Family Tables*** and their application in design.
- Use ***Sketches*** in the part creation.
- Practice ***Relations***.
- Practice ***Extrude*** feature.

Family Tables

Family tables provide a systematic means of organizing and storing a large database of information about similar components. The user must create a generic instance that captures the common geometric characteristics of a set of similar components. Then, the user can pick a specific instance by selecting its characteristic dimensions.
In a family table, columns define items that may change and rows define the values for these items which are used to generate each instance.

Background Information

A good application for family tables is the selection of bolts. While the head may be different, the shank and the thread specification are common characteristics of any bolt. The dimensions of these features may vary. Family tables allow the user to create a single database of bolts. The user can then pick a specific instance by selecting the type of bolt head and specifying the relevant dimensions.

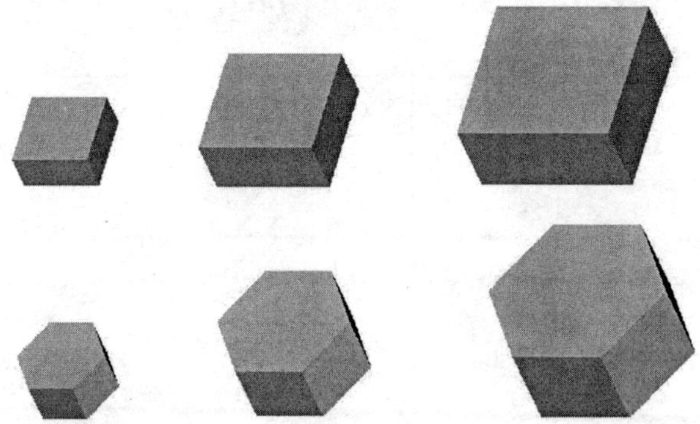

SEQUENCE OF STEPS

STEP I: Create a hexagonal section

1. Create a construction circle.

2. Create the hexagon.

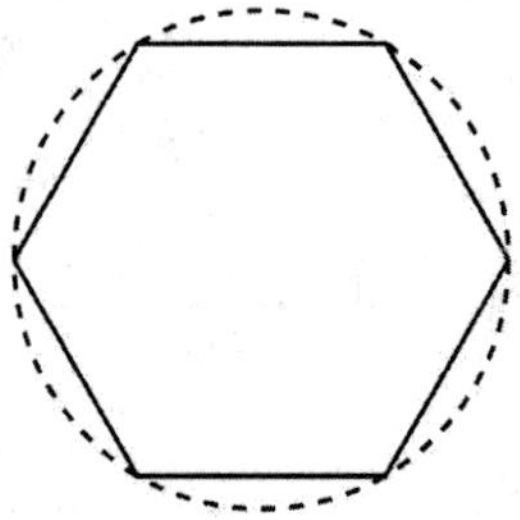

STEP II: Create a square section

1. Create a square section.

2. Add relations to center the square.

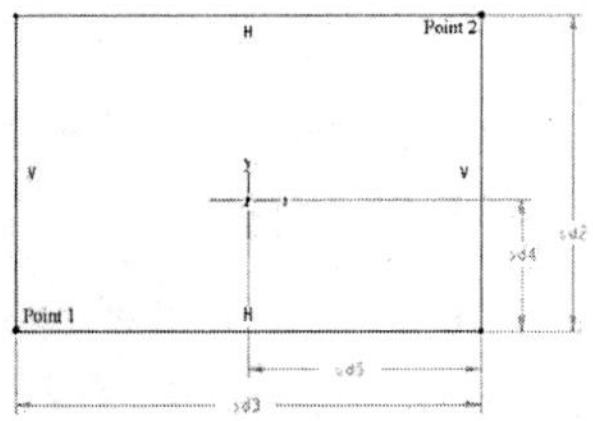

STEP III: Create the hexagonal head

1. Import the hexagonal section.

2. Define the direction and the depth of extrusion.

3. Name the hexagonal head feature and its dimensions.

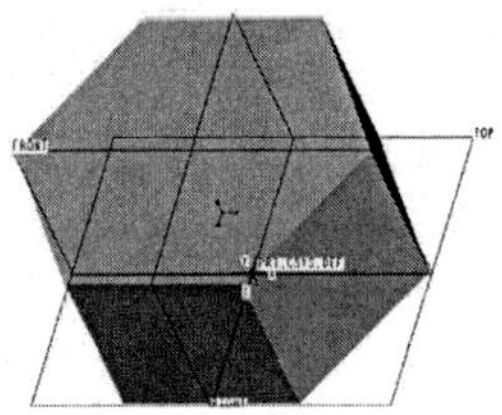

STEP IV: Create the square head

1. Import the square section.
2. Define the direction and the depth of extrusion.
3. Name the square head feature and its dimensi

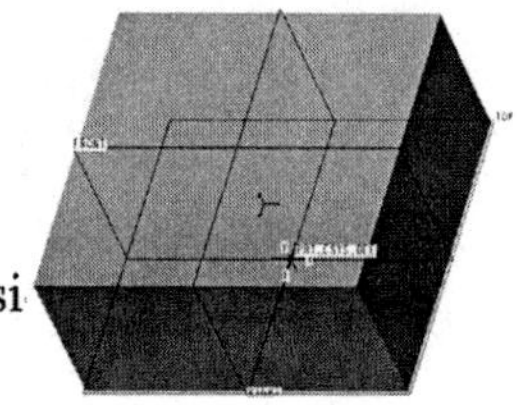

STEP V: Create the family table

1. Add features and dimensions to the family table.
2. Add new instances to the family table.
3. Patternize the family table to create several instances.

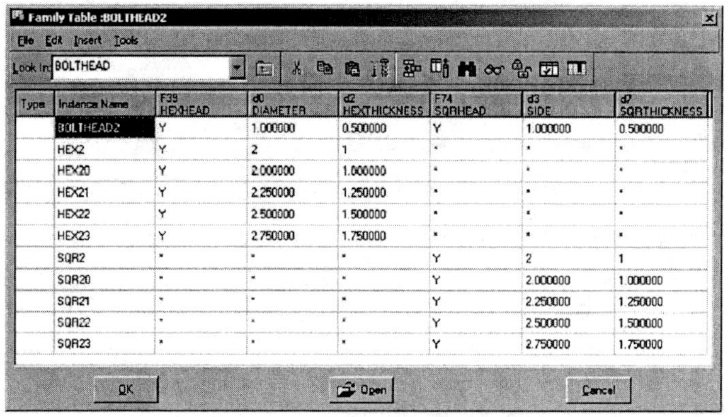

Type	Instance Name	F39 HEXHEAD	d0 DIAMETER	d2 HEXTHICKNESS	F74 SQRHEAD	d3 SIDE	d7 SQRTHICKNESS
	BOLTHEAD2	Y	1.000000	0.500000	Y	1.000000	0.500000
	HEX2	Y	2	1	*	*	*
	HEX20	Y	2.000000	1.000000	*	*	*
	HEX21	Y	2.250000	1.250000	*	*	*
	HEX22	Y	2.500000	1.500000	*	*	*
	HEX23	Y	2.750000	1.750000	*	*	*
	SQR2	*	*	*	Y	2	1
	SQR20	*	*	*	Y	2.000000	1.000000
	SQR21	*	*	*	Y	2.250000	1.250000
	SQR22	*	*	*	Y	2.500000	1.500000
	SQR23	*	*	*	Y	2.750000	1.750000

Goal	Step	Commands
Open a new file	1. Set up the working directory.	**FILE → SET WORKING DIRECTORY →** ***Select the working directory*** **→ OK**
	2. Open a new file.	**FILE → NEW →** ***Part*** **→** ***Solid*** **→ bolthead → OK**
Create the hex head	3. Start "Extrude" feature.	
	4. Set up the sketching plane.	**PLACEMENT → DEFINE →** ***Select the TOP datum plane*** **→ Sketch**
	5. Insert the hexagonal section.	***→ Select the hexagon section → Double click on section → Click in the graphics window to place the section***
	6. Center the section.	***Drag the section by holding it at the center and drop it on the PRT_CSYS_DEF (The center of the section must lie on the PRT_CSYS_DEF)*** Refer to Fig. 19.1.
	7. Define the scale.	(scale) **1** → (rotate) **0** → → **VIEW → ORIENTATION → REFIT → CLOSE** Refer to Fig. 19.2.
	8. Exit sketcher.	
	9. Define the depth.	(Depth) **0.5**
	10. Accept the feature creation.	**→ VIEW → ORIENTATION → STANDARD ORIETATION** Refer to Fig. 19.3.
	11. Rename the feature.	***Double click on the extrude feature name in the model tree →*** **HexHead →** ***ENTER*** Refer to Fig. 19.4.

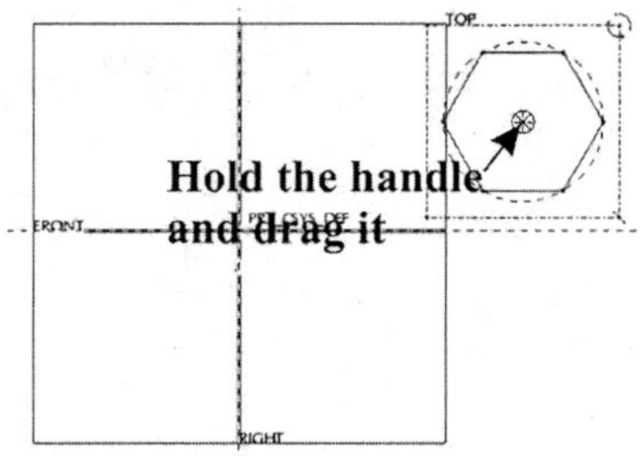

Fig. 19.1.

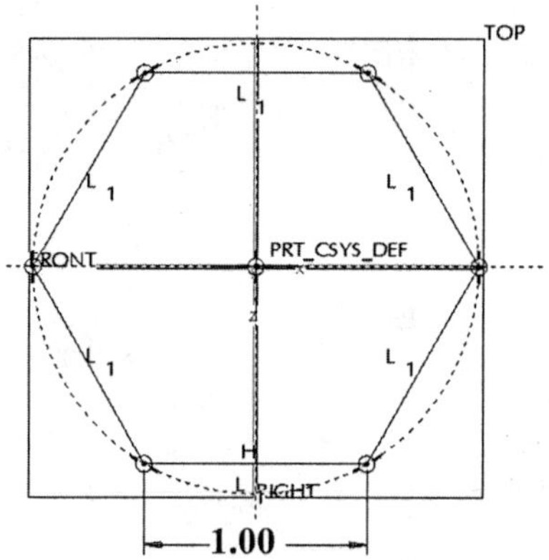

Fig. 19.2.

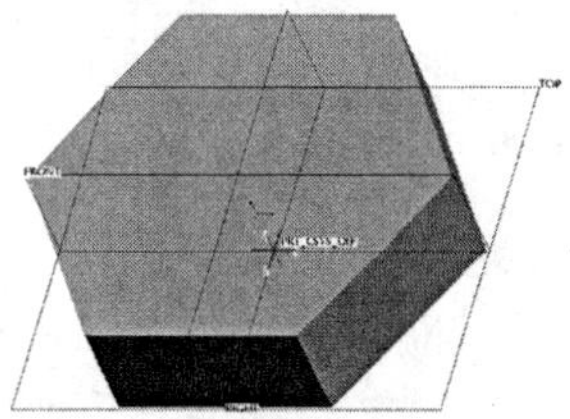
Fig. 19.3.

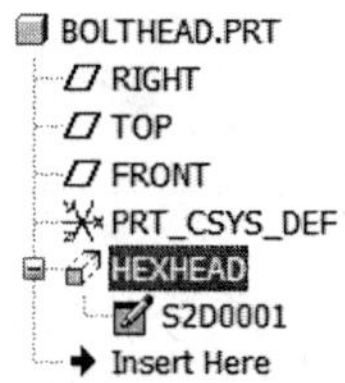

Fig. 19.4.

Goal	Step	Commands
Create the hex head (Continued)	12. Rename the dimensions.	***Select HexHead from the model tree* → *Right Mouse* → Edit → *Select the side (1.00) dimension* → EDIT → PROPERTIES →** ProE opens the "Dimension Properties" window. ***Select the Dimension Text tab* →** (Name) **<u>HexSide</u> → OK →** Refer to Fig. 19.5. **Select the thickness (0.5) dimension → *Right Mouse (Hold)* → *Properties* → *Select the Dimension Text tab* →** (Name) **<u>HexThickness</u> → OK**
Suppress the hex head	13. Suppress the hex head feature.	***Select the HexHead feature from the model tree* → *Right Mouse (Hold)* → Suppress → OK**
Create a square head	14. Start "Extrude" feature	
	15. Set up sketching plane.	**PLACEMENT → DEFINE → *Select the TOP datum plane* → Sketch**
	16. Insert the square section.	 ***→ Select the square section → Double click on section → Click in the graphics window***
	17. Center the section.	**Drag the section by holding it at the center and drop it on the PRT_CSYS_DEF (The center of the section must lie on the PRT_CSYS_DEF)** Refer to Fig. 19.6.
	18. Define the scale.	(scale) **<u>1</u> →** (rotate) **<u>0</u> →**  **→ VIEW → ORIENTATION → REFIT → CLOSE**

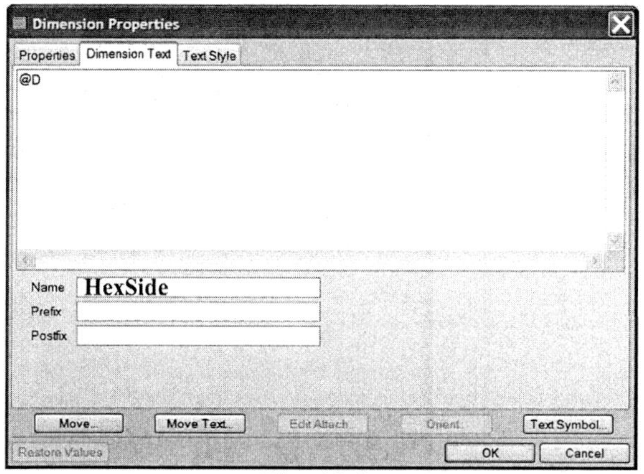

Fig. 19.5.

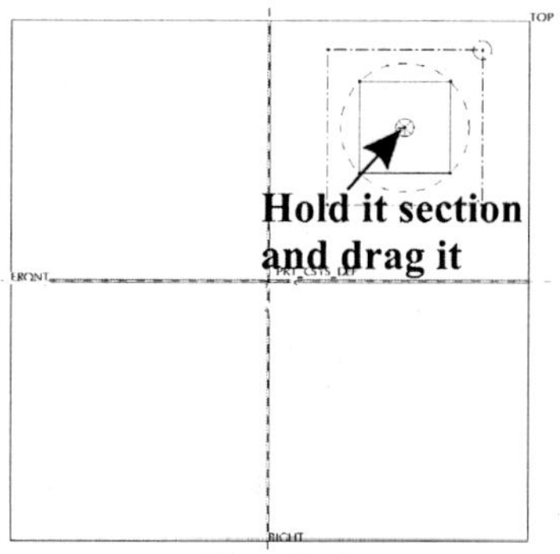

Fig. 19.6.

Goal	Step	Commands
	19. Change the placement dimensions.	→ ***Select each placement dimension* (0.50) →** ***Right Mouse* → Strong → TOOLS → RELATIONS →** **<u>Add relations shown in Fig. 19.7</u> → OK** Note that the name of parameters can be different your model.
	20. Exit sketcher.	
	21. Define the depth.	(Depth) **<u>0.5</u>**
	22. Accept the feature creation.	**→ VIEW → ORIENTATION → STANDARD ORIETATION** Refer to Fig. 19.8.
Create a square head (Continued)	23. Rename the feature.	***Double click on the protrusion feature from the model tree* → <u>SqrHead</u> → <u>ENTER</u>** Refer to Fig. 19.9.
	24. Rename the side dimension.	***Select SqrHead from the model tree* → *Right Mouse (Hold)* → Edit →** ***→ Select the side dimension (1.00) → Right Mouse (Hold) → Properties →*** ***Select the Dimension Text tab* →** (Name) **<u>SqrSide</u> → OK →** Refer to Fig. 19.10. ***Select the thickness (0.5) dimension → Right Mouse (Hold) → Properties → Select the Dimension Text tab* →** (Name) **<u>SqrThickness</u> → OK**

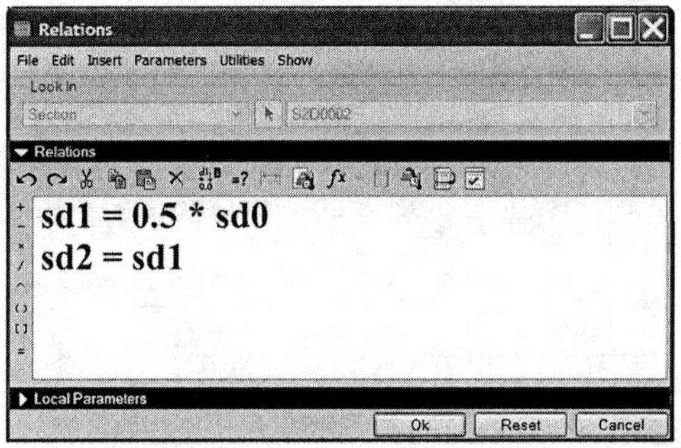

Fig. 19.7.

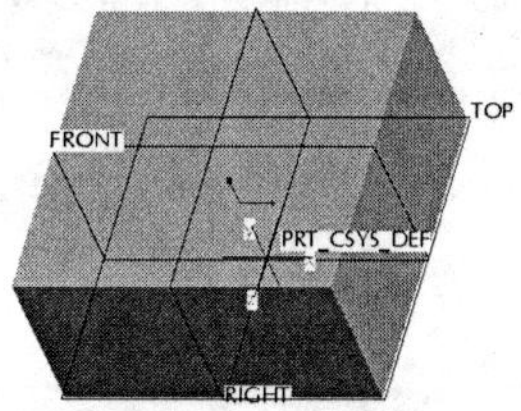

Fig. 19.8.

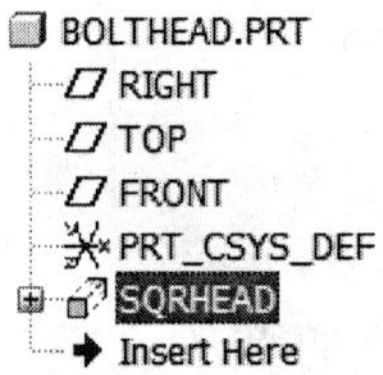

Fig. 19.9.

Fig. 19.10.

Goal	Step	Commands
Resume all features	25. Resume the hex head feature.	**EDIT → RESUME → RESUME ALL** HexHead feature should reappear in the model tree. SqrHead feature is not visible as it is insider the HexHead feature.
Create the family table	26. Start the Family Table command.	**TOOLS → FAMILY TABLE** ProE opens the Family Table window. Refer to Fig. 19.11.
	27. Add features and dimensions to the family table.	→ ProE opens the "Family Items" window. ***Select feature in the add item subwindow → Select → Select HexHead feature from the Model Tree →*** ***Select dimension in the add item subwindow → Select HexHead feature → Select the side and thickness dimensions →*** ***Select feature in the add item subwindow → Select → Select SqrHead feature from the Model Tree →*** ***Select dimension in the add item subwindow → Select SqrHead feature → Select the side dimension → Select the thickness dimension → OK*** Refer to Figs 19.12 and 19.13.

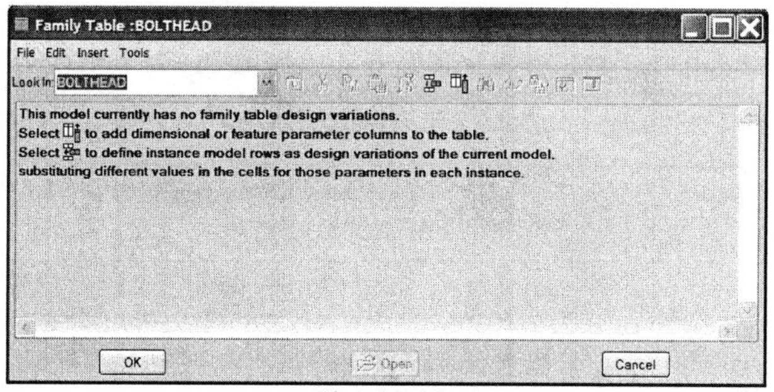

Fig. 19.11.

In a family table, columns define items that may change and rows define the values for these items which are used to generate each instance.

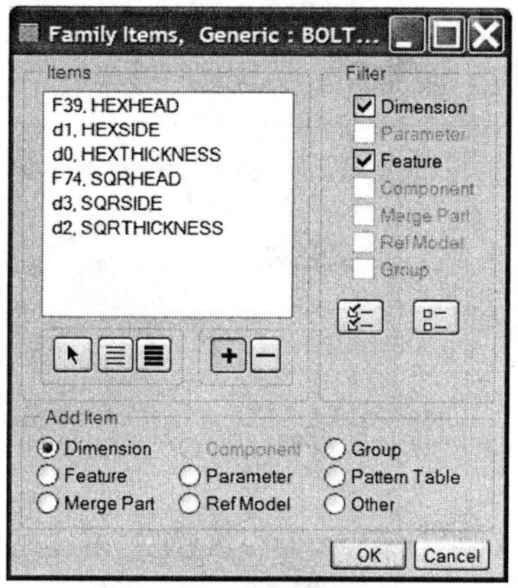

Fig. 19.12.

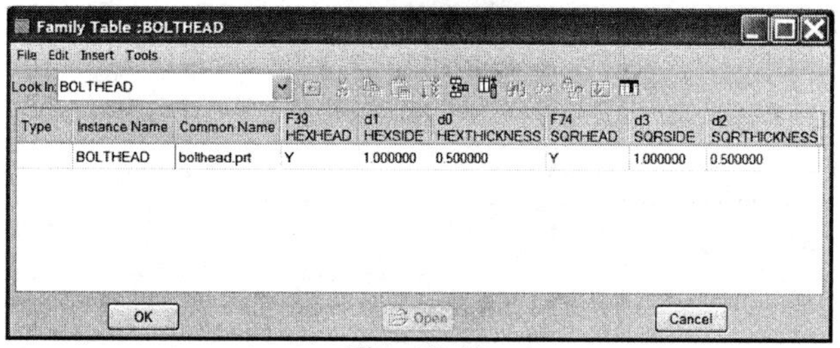

Fig. 19.13

Goal	Step	Commands
Create the family table (Continued)	28. Add new instances to the table.	→ (Instance Name) **Hex2** → (HexHead) **Y** → (HexSide) **2** → (HexThickness) **1**→ (SqrHead) **N** → (Instance Name) **Sqr2** → (SqrHead) **Y** → (Side) **2** → (SqrThickness) **1** → (HexHead) **N** Refer to Fig. 19.14.
	29. Create more instances (patternize the table).	***Select Hex2*** → → (Quantity) **4** → ***Select HexThickness*** → >> → (Increment) **0.25** → ***ENTER*** → ***Select the HexSide*** → >> → (Increment) **0.25** → ***ENTER*** → **OK** → Refer to Fig. 19.15. ***Select SQR2*** → → (Quantity) **4** → ***Select SqrThickness*** → >> → (Increment) **0.25** → ***ENTER*** → ***Select the SqrSide*** → >> → (Increment) **0.25** → ***ENTER*** → **OK** → Refer to Fig. 19.16. **OK** Refer to Fig. 19.17.

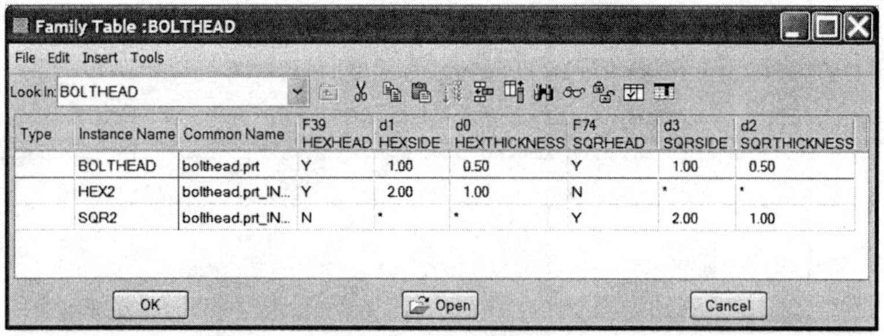

Fig. 19.14.

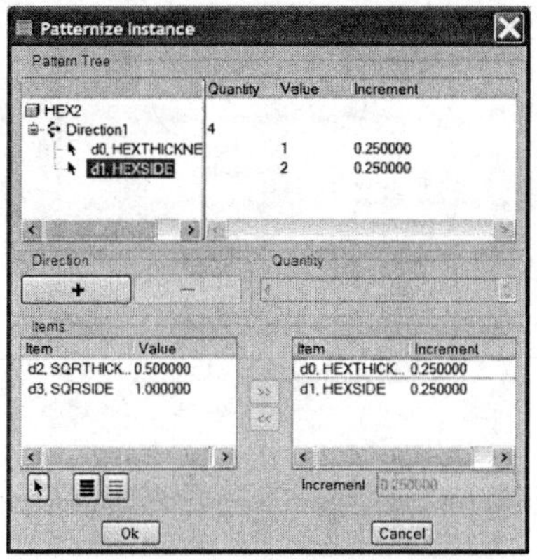

Fig. 19.15.

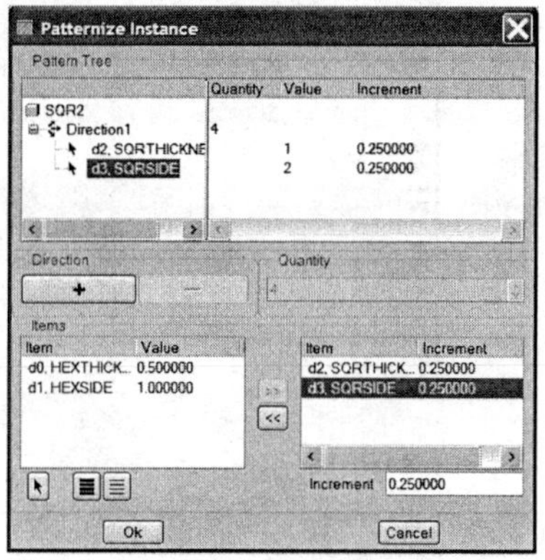

Fig. 19.16.

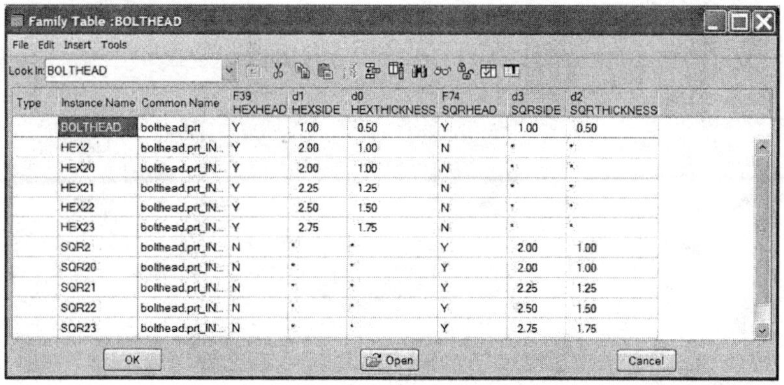

Fig. 19.17.

Goal	Step	Commands
Save the file and exit the window	30. Save the file and erase the window.	**FILE → SAVE → BOLTHEAD.PRT → OK → FILE → ERASE → CURRENT → YES**
Open the bolt file	31. Open the bolt file.	**FILE → OPEN → *Select BOLTHEAD.PRT* → *Select any one instance* → OPEN** Note that it is possible to select an instance by choosing the values for different parameter specification by clicking on the Parameter Tab. Refer to Figs. 19.18 and 19.19.
Exit ProE	32. Exit ProE.	**FILE → EXIT → YES**

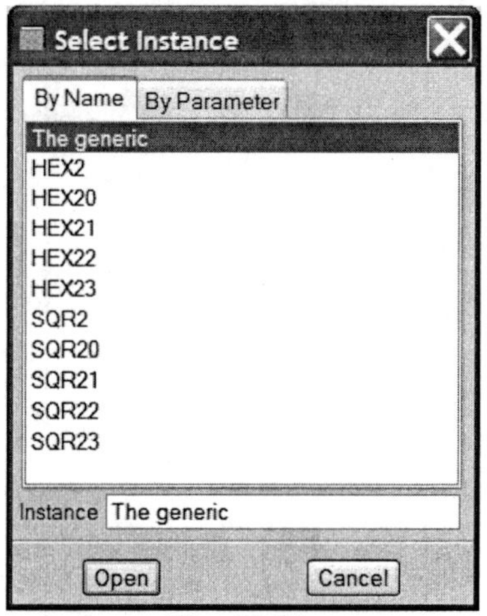

Fig. 19.18.

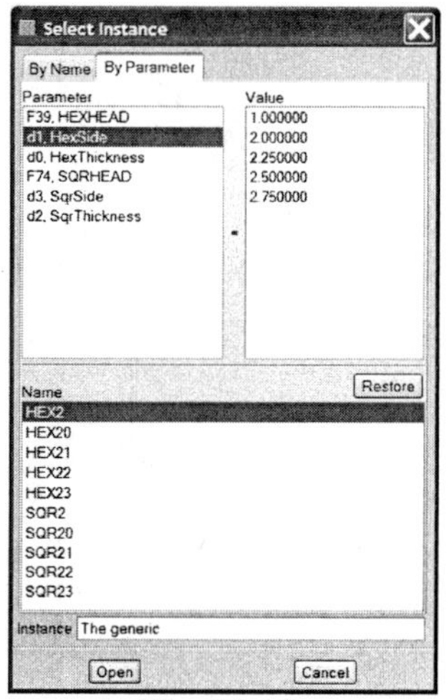

Fig. 19.19.

Exercise

Problem 1

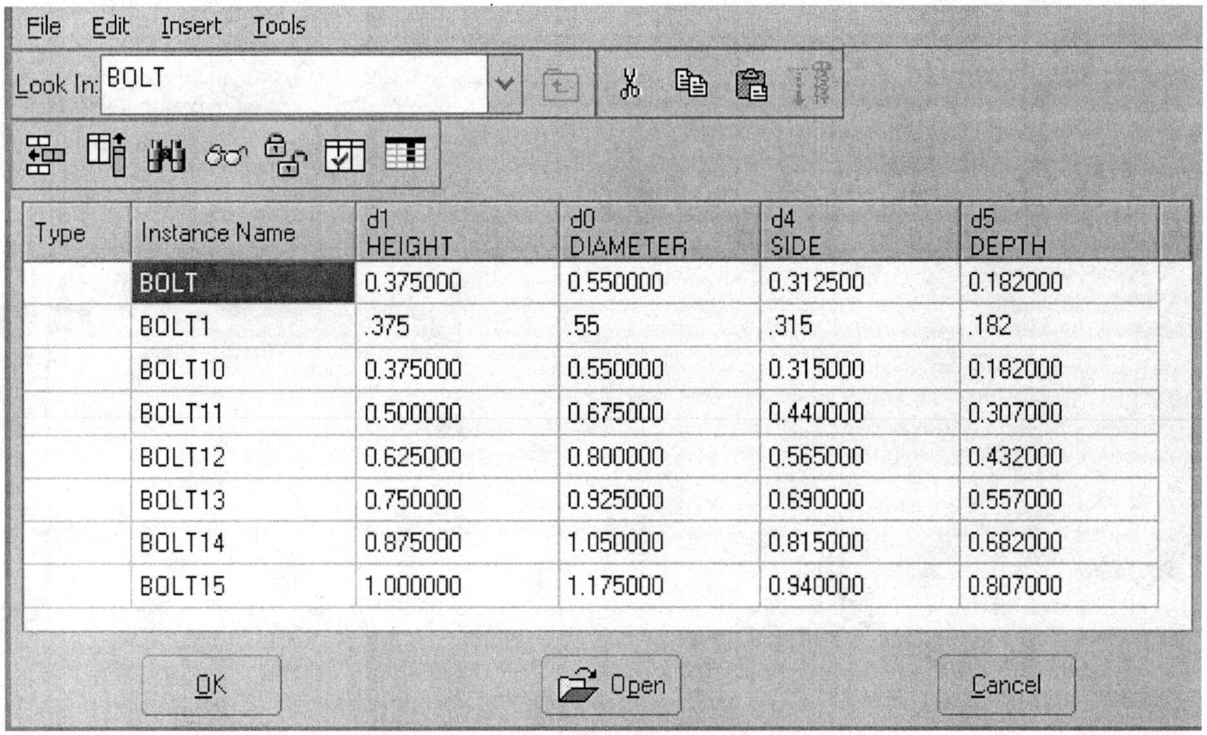

Type	Instance Name	d1 HEIGHT	d0 DIAMETER	d4 SIDE	d5 DEPTH
	BOLT	0.375000	0.550000	0.312500	0.182000
	BOLT1	.375	.55	.315	.182
	BOLT10	0.375000	0.550000	0.315000	0.182000
	BOLT11	0.500000	0.675000	0.440000	0.307000
	BOLT12	0.625000	0.800000	0.565000	0.432000
	BOLT13	0.750000	0.925000	0.690000	0.557000
	BOLT14	0.875000	1.050000	0.815000	0.682000
	BOLT15	1.000000	1.175000	0.940000	0.807000

Hints:

1. Use the part created in Chapter 8 and suppress the shank and cosmetic threads features.
2. Change the name of the dimensions.
3. Create the family table (note the increments are 0.125 on all dimensions)

Problem 2

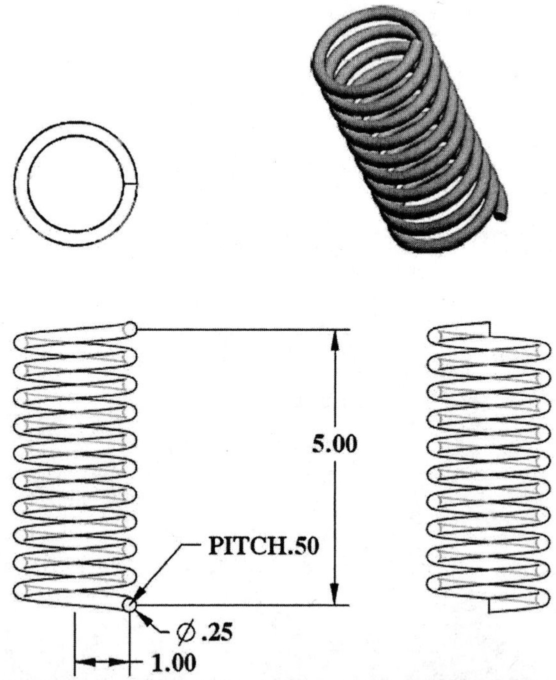

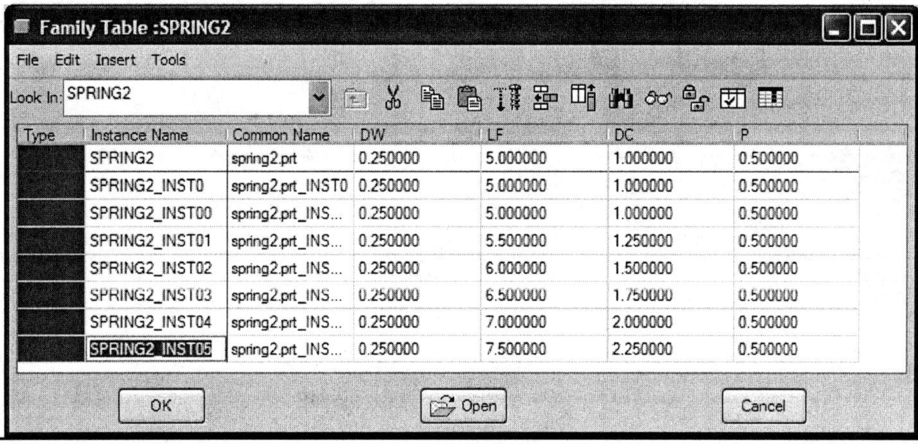

Type	Instance Name	Common Name	DW	LF	DC	P
	SPRING2	spring2.prt	0.250000	5.000000	1.000000	0.500000
	SPRING2_INST0	spring2.prt_INST0	0.250000	5.000000	1.000000	0.500000
	SPRING2_INST00	spring2.prt_INS...	0.250000	5.000000	1.000000	0.500000
	SPRING2_INST01	spring2.prt_INS...	0.250000	5.500000	1.250000	0.500000
	SPRING2_INST02	spring2.prt_INS...	0.250000	6.000000	1.500000	0.500000
	SPRING2_INST03	spring2.prt_INS...	0.250000	6.500000	1.750000	0.500000
	SPRING2_INST04	spring2.prt_INS...	0.250000	7.000000	2.000000	0.500000
	SPRING2_INST05	spring2.prt_INS...	0.250000	7.500000	2.250000	0.500000

Hints:

1. Naming parameters may be tricky. You may want to create the parameters first and the use them while creating the spring. The parameters are dw (wire diameter), dc(coil diameter), lf (free length) and p (pitch). Create a spring.
2. Create the family table using "Add item – Parameter."

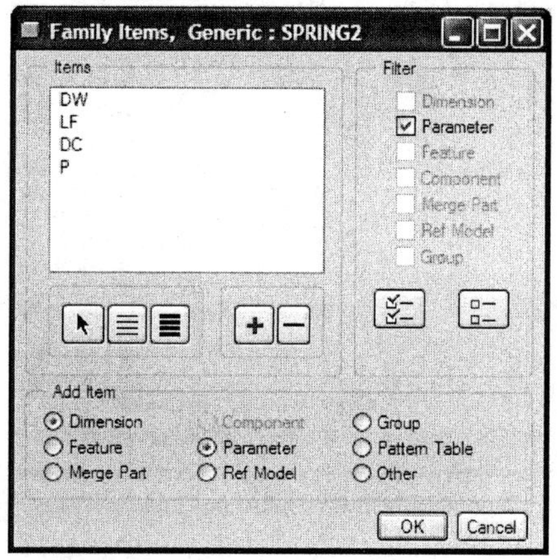

Problem 3 – Lego blocks - Pattern table - Family Table

1. Create a cube. The sketch is shown below. Delete the coincident constraints to get the 0.00 dimensions from the FRONT and RIGHT datums	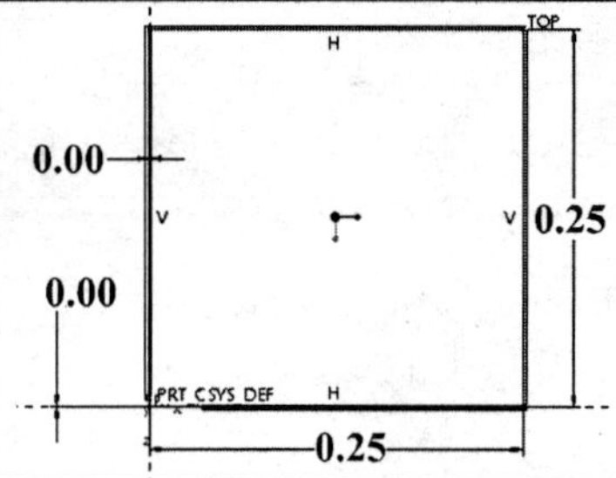
2. Create the cylinder part. Reference it from the edges of the cube (NOT THE DATUM PLANES). Extrusion depth 0.0625.	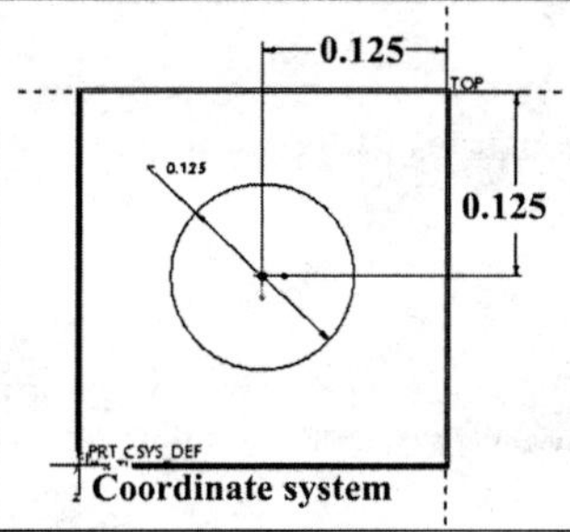
3. Group the two features.	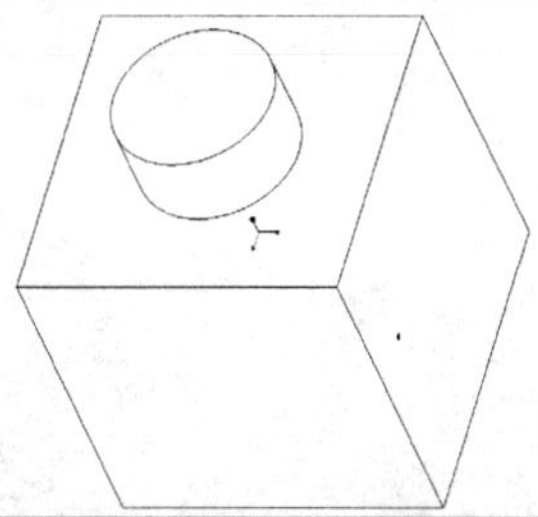
4. Pattern the group. In the menu, select table from the pattern type drop down menu.	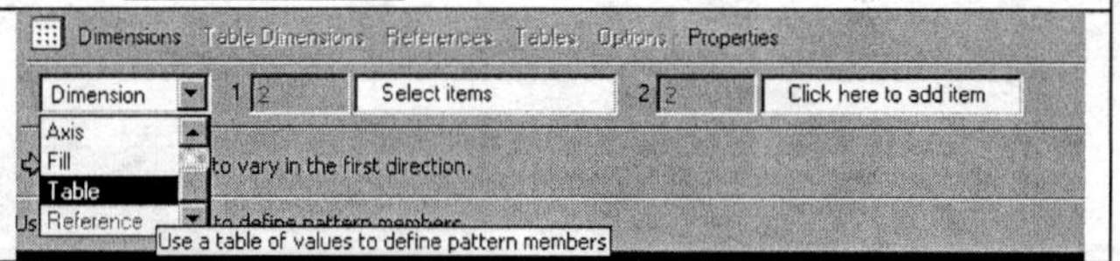
5. Holding ***CTRL*** select the two 0.00 placement dimensions (refer the sketch in hint 1).	
6. Select "Tables" button to access the tables menu. Right-click in the menu to select "Add":	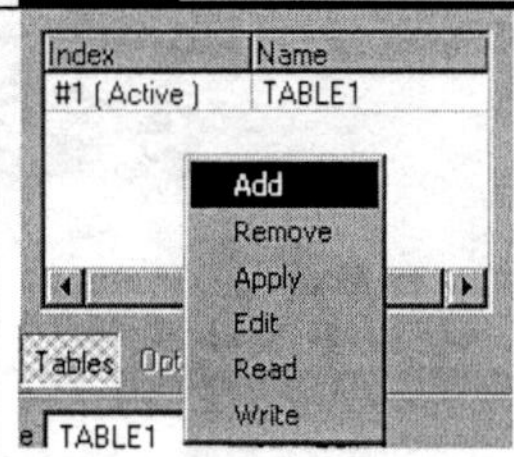

7. Add four tables. Rename them as “one_by_two”, “one_by_three”, “two_by_two”, and “two_by_three”. Then, edit each table to contain an appropriate number of instances and dimensions.

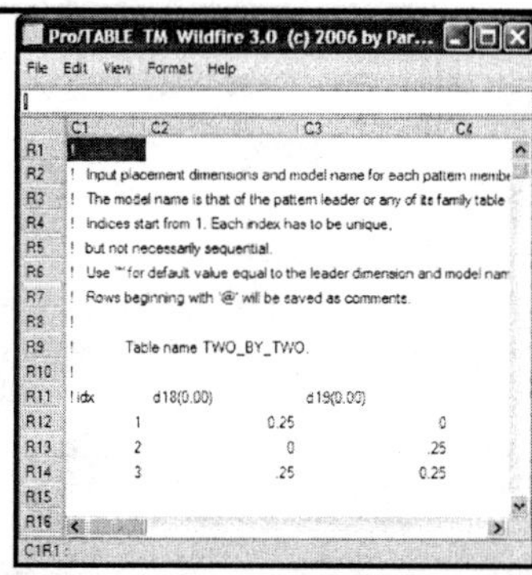

Table for two_by_two

8. Create the shell feature with shell thickness 0.01.

9. Start family table. A new column to the table. Under the “Add Item” heading select “Pattern Table.” Select the group patterned feature from the model tree and click “OK”.

10. In the family table screen, add four rows to give four versions of the part. Renames for the instances and enter the names of the tables.

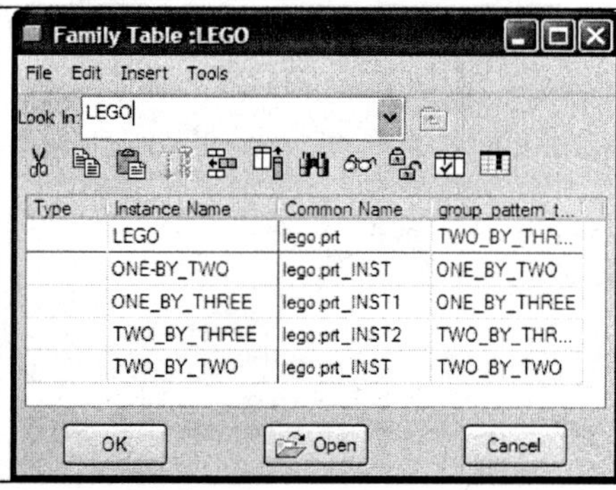

11. Save and close the part. When, open the part and you choose exactly any lego

OPEN-ENDED DESIGN

Create a family table to select an appropriate dumbbell (5 lb, 10 lb, 20 lb).

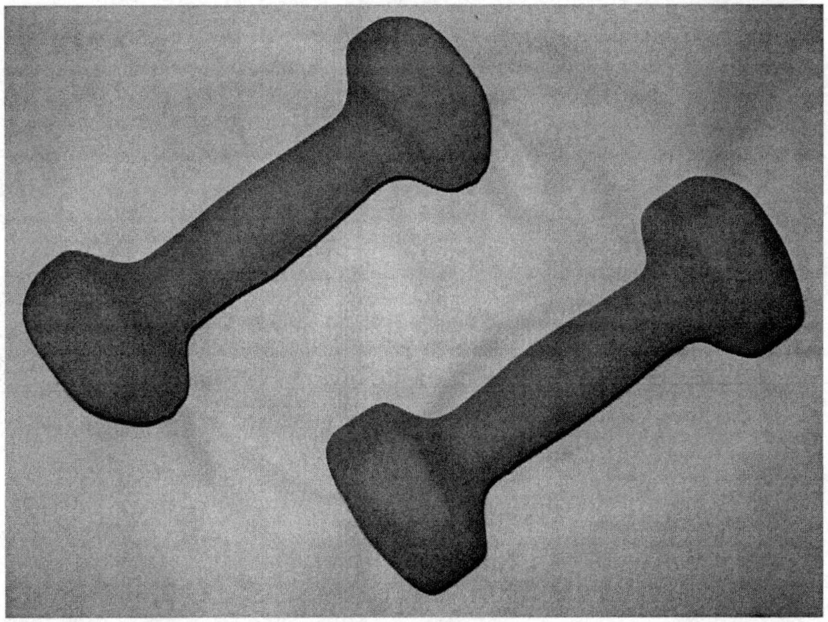

NOTES:

LESSON 20
ELECTRICAL FUSE ASSEMBLY

Learning Objectives

- Learn to setup a ***Layout file***.
- Practice creating parts in the assembly mode.
- Learn the use of ***Tables***.
- ***Import*** and ***Export*** to IGES files.

Layout

A layout is useful to capture and represent the design intent. It provides a single interface consisting of sketches, drawings, and parametric tables to control the geometry of various assemblies and parts. While it looks like a drawing, instead of providing details of the part, it serves the opposite useful purpose of providing an overall big picture of the design and the design intent. The magnitude of various parameters defined in the layout determines the geometry of individual components and assemblies. Tables in a layout provide a useful way to organize the information about various parameters and their magnitude, and control or modify the values. Once, the layout is declared in the part/assembly, regenerate command automatically updates the part/assembly and makes it consistent with the layout file. As creating two-dimensional drawings or sketches is tedious, an easy alternative is to export drawing files as an IGES (or dxf or dwg) file and then, import it into the layout. The layout file has an extension ".lay".

Background Information:

Sand-filled electrical fuses are used to protect electric mains and feeders, circuit breakers, heating and lighting circuits, motors, transformers, semiconductors and more, against current surges. The components of a sand-filled fuse are: Fuse element, End-caps, Fiberglass casing and sand. Sand fills the space in the casing around the fuse element and helps in dissipating the energy during the short-circuit conditions. The cavity volume, a key design parameter, determines the amount of sand that can be filled. Several fuses are made with very similar geometry and a different number of weak spots. This lesson shows how to use layouts to control the model.

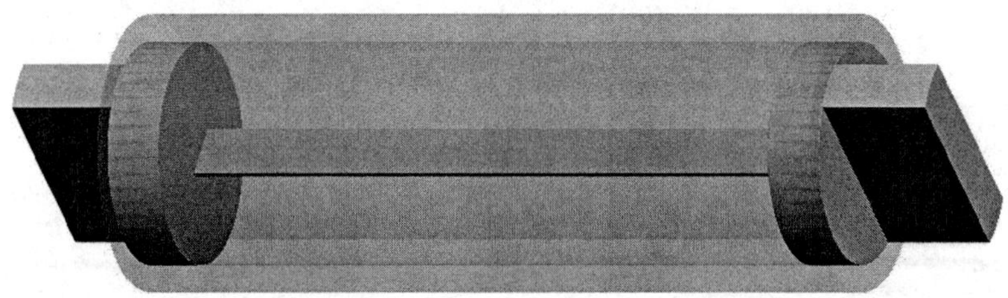

SEQUENCE OF STEPS

Step I - Create the end bell part

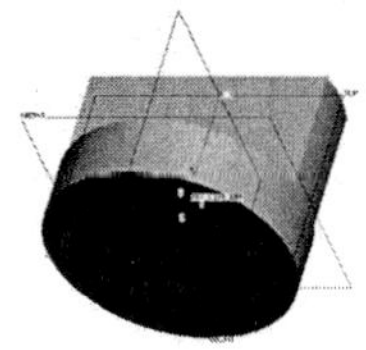

Step II - Create a drawing for the end bell part

1. Create the drawing
2. Export the drawing to an IGES file

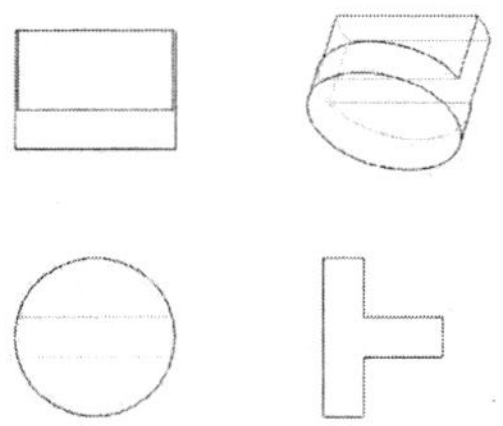

Step II - Create a layout

1. Import the end bell drawing
2. Sketch and dimension the fuse cavity
3. Add parameters
4. Create the data table

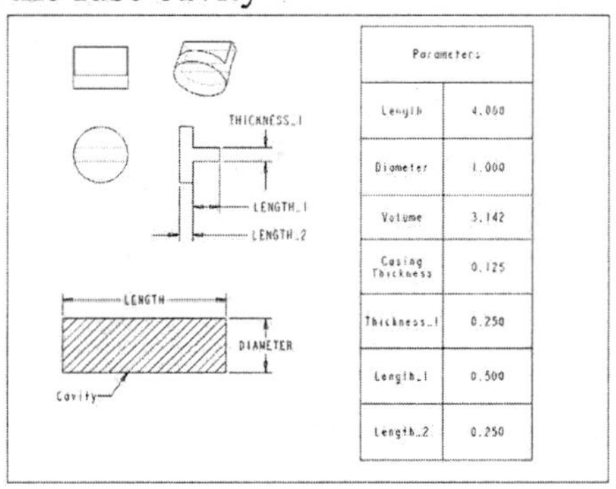

Step IV - Create the fuse assembly

1. Create the casing part in the assembly
2. Assign the layout to the casing part

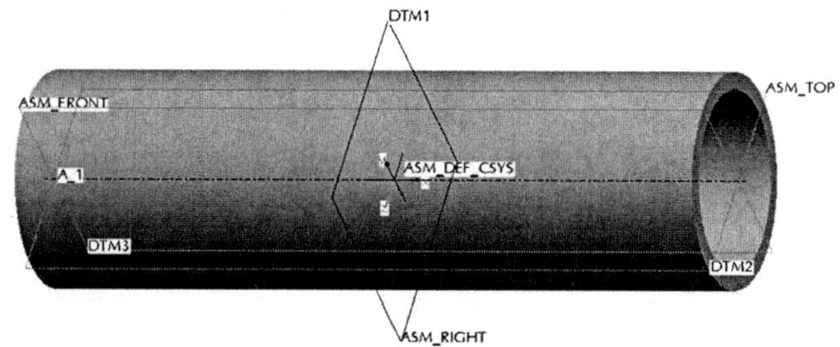

3. Declare the layout for the end bell part
4. Assemble the end bell

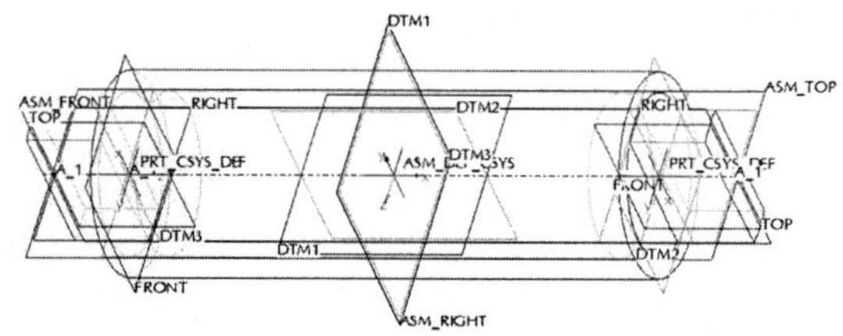

5. Create the fuse element
6. Setup the display

Goal	Step	Commands
Open a new file for the end bell part	1. Set up the working directory.	**FILE → SET WORKING DIRECTORY → *Select the working directory* → OK**
	2. Open new file for the end bell part.	**FILE → NEW → *Part* → *Solid* → endbell → OK**
Create the end bell part	3. Start "Extrude" feature.	
	4. Select the sketching plane.	**Placement → DEFINE → *Select the FRONT datum plane* → Sketch**
	5. Sketch a circle.	→ *Select the center of the circle at the intersection of TOP and RIGHT datum planes* → *Select a point to define the circle*
	6. Modify the dimensions.	→ ***Double click the diameter dimension* → 1 → *ENTER*** Refer to Fig. 20.1.
	7. Exit sketcher.	
	8. Define the extrusion depth.	(Depth) **0.25 → ENTER**
	9. Accept the feature creation.	**→ VIEW → ORIENTATION → STANDARD ORIENTATION** Refer to Fig. 20.2.
	10. Start "Extrude" feature.	
	11. Select the sketching plane.	**Placement → DEFINE → *Use Previous***
	12. Add new references.	**SKETCH → REFERENCES → *Select the circle* → CLOSE** Refer to Fig. 20.3.

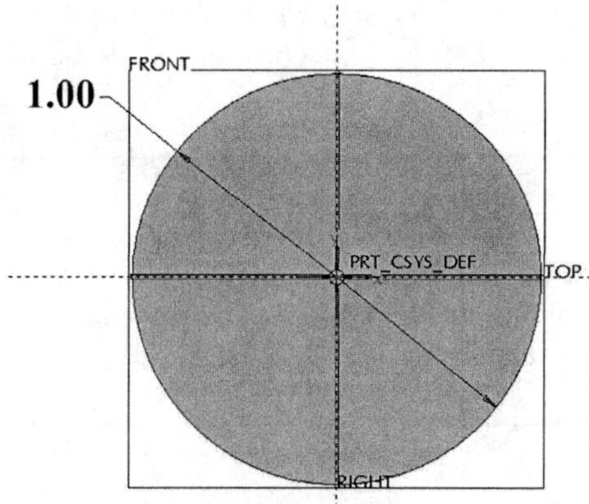

Fig. 20.1.

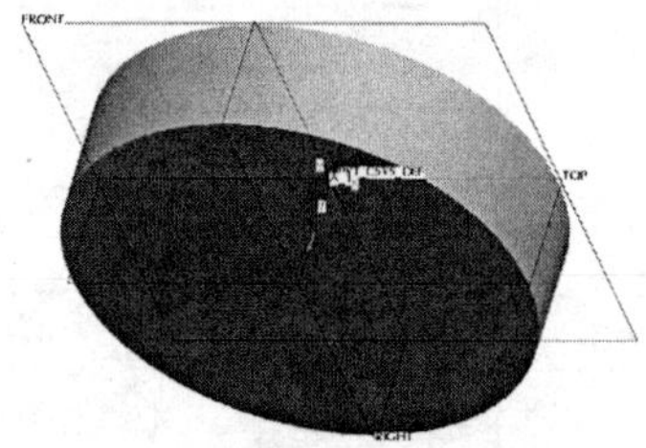
Fig. 20.2.

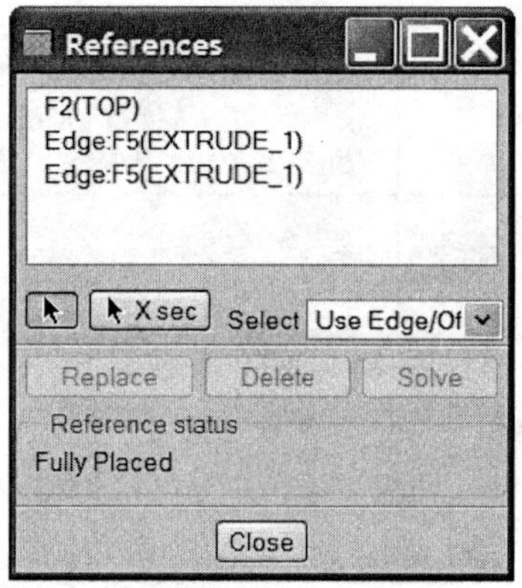

Fig. 20.3.

Goal	Step	Commands
Create the end bell part (continued)	13. Create two lines.	→ ***Pick points 1 and 2 → Middle Mouse → Pick points 3 and 4 → Middle Mouse*** Refer to Fig. 20.4.
	14. Dimension the lines from the TOP datum plane.	→ ***Select line 1 and the TOP datum → Middle Mouse → Select line 2 and the TOP datum → Middle Mouse*** Refer to Fig. 20.4.
	15. Add a relation.	**TOOLS → RELATIONS → <u>sd3 = sd2</u> → OK** Refer to Fig. 20.4.
	16. Use edge command to sketch a circle.	→ **Loop** → ***Select the circle***
	17. Divide the circle at Points 1, 2, 3 and 4.	→ → ***Select points 1, 2, 3 and 4***
	18. Delete arc segments 1 and 2.	→ ***Select arcs 1 and 2 → <u>DELETE</u>*** Refer to Fig. 20.5.
	19. Modify the dimensions.	→ ***Double click the distance dimension → <u>0.125</u> → <u>ENTER</u>***
	20. Exit sketcher.	
	21. Define the extrusion depth.	→ **DEFAULT ORIENTATION →** (Depth) **<u>0.5</u> →**
	22. Accept the feature creation.	Refer to Fig. 20.6.
Save the end bell part	23. Save the part.	**FILE → SAVE → ENDBELL.PRT → OK**

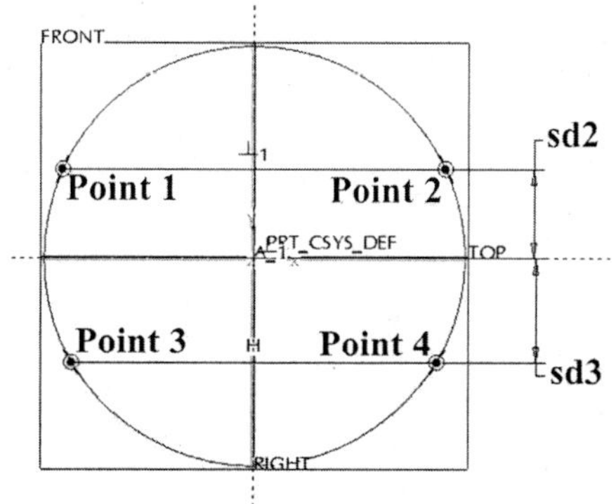

Fig. 20.4.

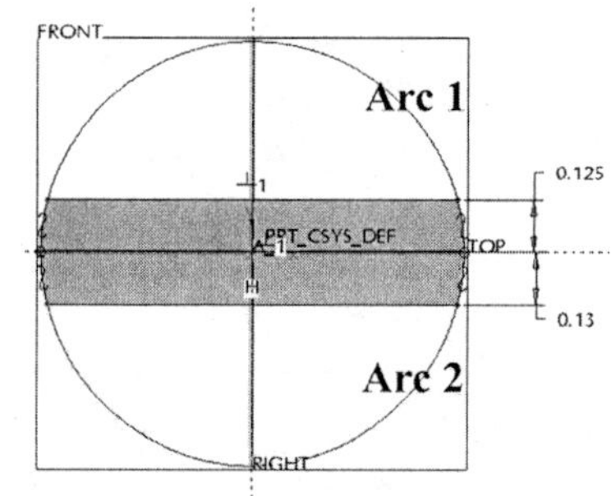

Fig. 20.5.

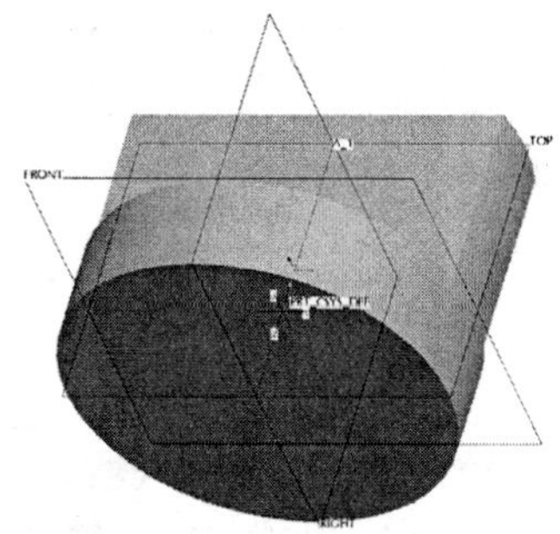

Fig. 20.6.

Goal	Step	Commands
Open a drawing file for the end bell part	24. Open a drawing file for the end bell part.	**FILE → NEW → *Drawing* → ENDBELL → OK →** (Default Model) **ENDBELL.PRT → Use default template → OK → Use template → a_drawing → OK** Refer to Figs. 20.7 and 20.8.
Create the end bell drawing	25. Turn off datum planes.	(Turn off datum planes and coordinate system) →
	26. Add a trimetric view for visualization.	→ ***Select the position for the general view* → APPLY → *View display* → *(Display style) Hidden* → OK** Refer to Figs. 20.9 and 20.10.
	27. Arrange the views.	→ ***Select and move the view (so that the views close to one another)*** Refer to Fig. 20.10.
Save and export the drawing	28. Save and export the drawing.	**FILE → SAVE → ENDBELL.DRW → OK → FILE → SAVE A COPY → (Type) Iges → ENDBELL → OK → OK**

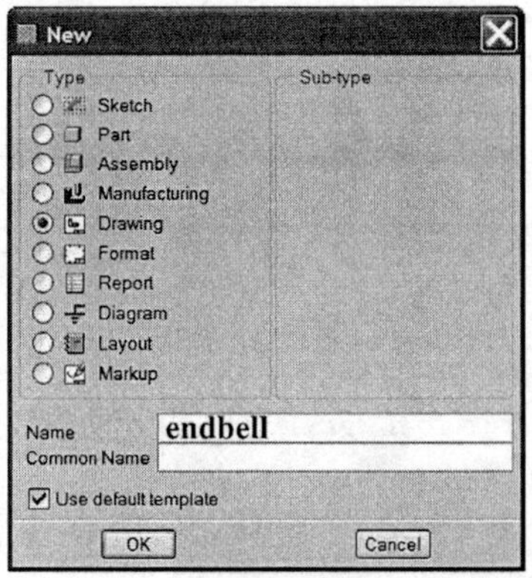

Fig. 20.7.

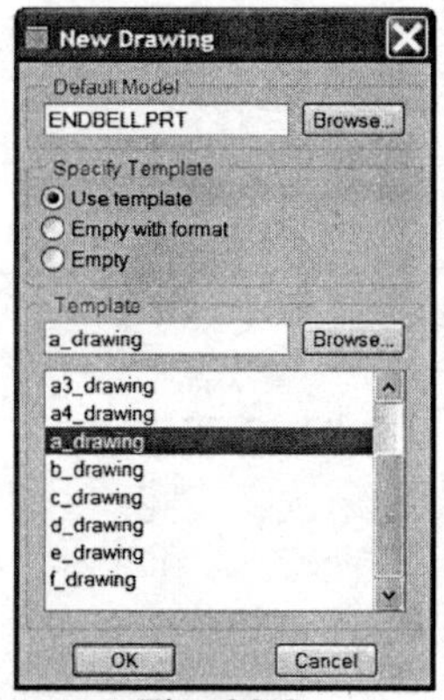

Fig. 20.8.

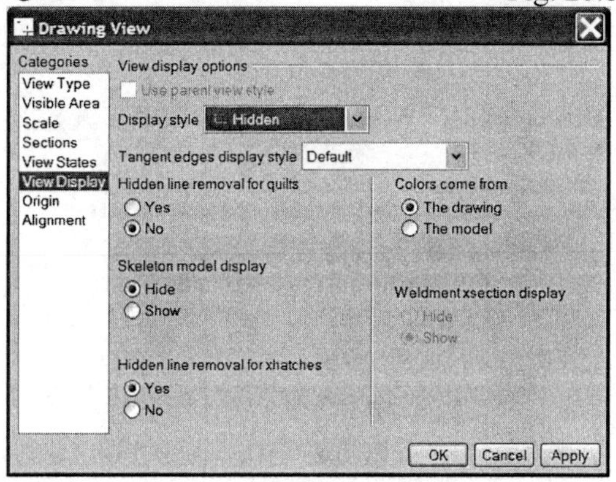

Fig. 20.9.

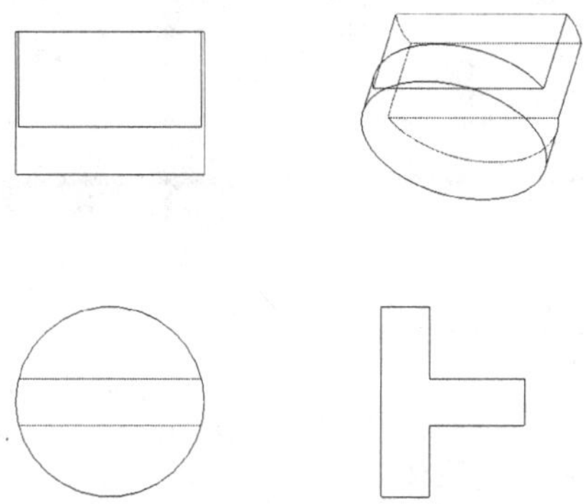
Fig. 20.10.

Goal	Step	Commands
Open a new file for the fuse layout	29. Open a new file for the fuse layout.	**FILE → NEW →** ***Layout*** **→ <u>fuse</u> → OK** Refer to Fig. 20.11. ***Select Landscape → Select A size →*** **OK** Refer to Fig. 20.12.
Import the end bell drawing	30. Append the end bell drawing to the model.	**INSERT → SHARED DATA → FROM FILE →** ***Select endbell.iges*** **→ Open → →** ***Select Import User Colors*** **→ OK →** Refer to Fig. 20.13.
	31. Move the drawing in the window.	↖ ***→ Pick two points to define the diagonal of the selection box → Drag the drawing to the corner point*** Refer to Fig. 20.14.
Sketch and dimension the fuse cavity	32. Create line 1.	**SKETCH → SKETCHER PREFERENCE → CHAIN SKETCHING → CLOSE → SKETCH → LINE → LINE → SKETCH → SPECIFY → ABSOLUTE COORDINATES →** (x) **<u>1</u>** → (y) **<u>2</u>** → ✓ **→ SKETCH → SPECIFY → ABSOLUTE COORDINATES →** (x) **<u>1</u>** → (y) **<u>3</u>** → ✓
	33. Create line 2.	(x) **<u>4</u>** → (y) **<u>3</u>** → ✓
	34. Create line 3.	(x) **<u>4</u>** → (y) **<u>2</u>** → ✓
	35. Create line 4.	(x) **<u>1</u>** → (y) **<u>2</u>** → ✓ → ✕ Refer to Fig. 20.14.
	36. **Optional Step:** If you make any mistakes, then delete excess lines.	↖ ***→ Select the lines to be deleted →*** ***<u>DELETE</u>*** (to start new line creation)

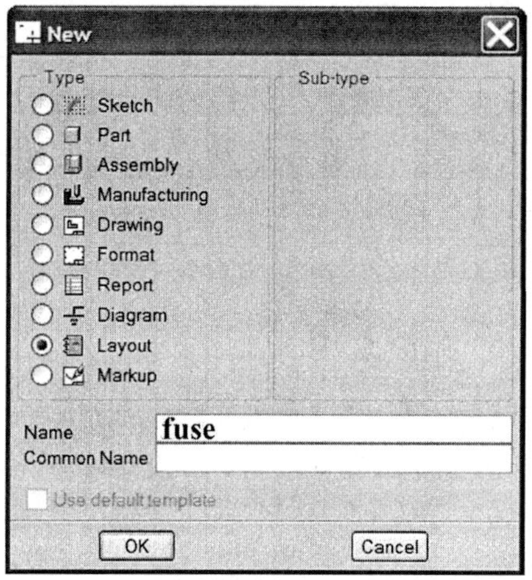

Fig. 20.11.

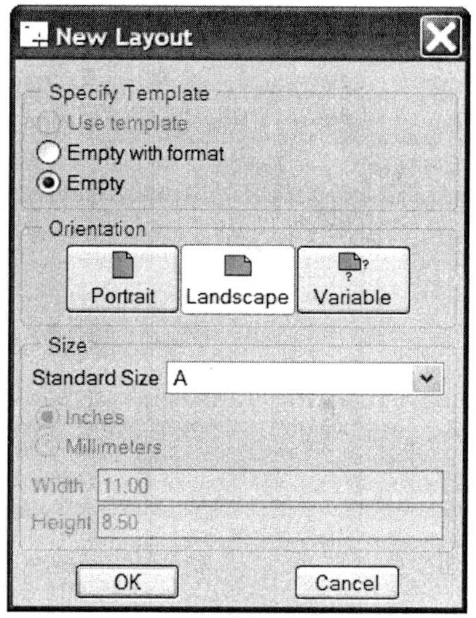

Fig. 20.12.

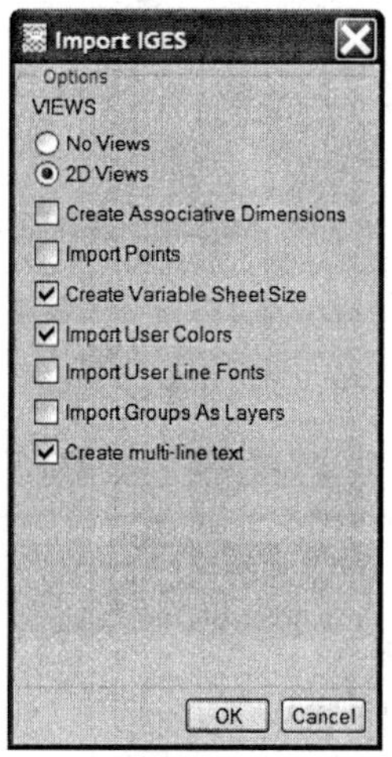

Fig.20.13.

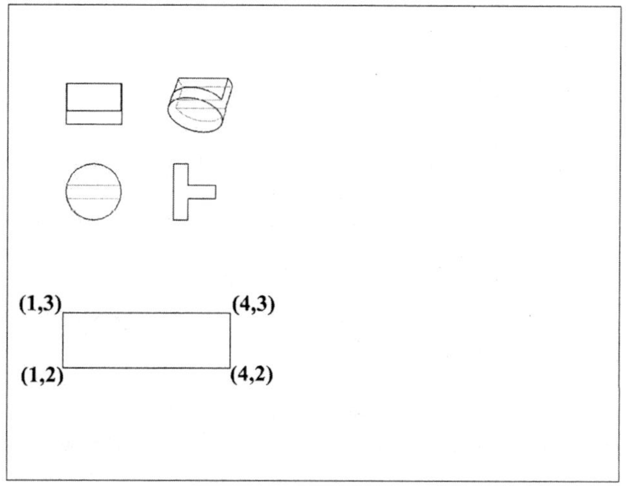

Fig. 20.14.

Goal	Step	Commands
Sketch and dimension the fuse cavity (continued)	37. Hatch the cavity.	→ ***Select the four lines*** → **EDIT** → **HATCH/FILL** → **Cavity** → → **Spacing** → **Overall** → **Half** → **Half** → **Half** → **Done** Refer to Fig. 20.15.
Sketch and dimension the fuse cavity (continued)	38. Dimension the cavity.	**INSERT** → **DIMENSION** → **NEW REFERENCES** → **On Entity** → ***Select line 1*** → ***Middle Mouse*** → **Diameter** → → **2** → → ***Select line 2*** → ***Middle Mouse*** → **Length** → → **4** → → **Return** Refer to Fig. 20.16.
	39. Name the cavity region.	**INSERT** → **NOTE** → **With Leader** → **Enter** → **Horizontal** → **Standard** → **Default** → **Make Note** → **On Entity** → **Arrow Head** → ***Select the bottom edge of the cavity (line 3)*** → **Done** → **Pick Pnt** → ***Select the starting point for the text note*** → **Cavity** → → → **Done/Return** Refer to Fig. 20.16.
	40. Add new parameters.	**TOOLS** → **PARAMETERS** → → **Volume** → → **Thickness_C** → **0.125** → **OK** Refer Fig. 20.17. Thickness_C refers to the casing thickness.
	41. Add a new relation.	**TOOLS** → **RELATIONS** → **Volume = pi * diameter^2 * length/4** → **OK**

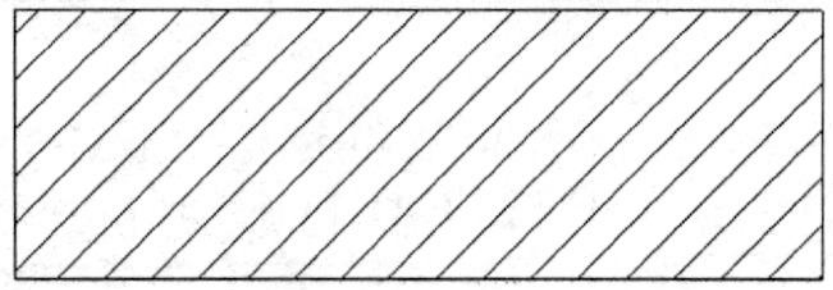

Fig. 20.15.

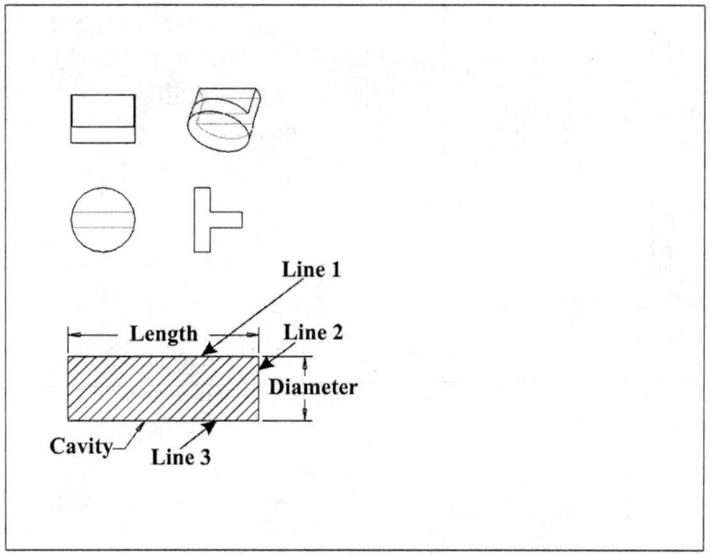

Fig. 20.16.

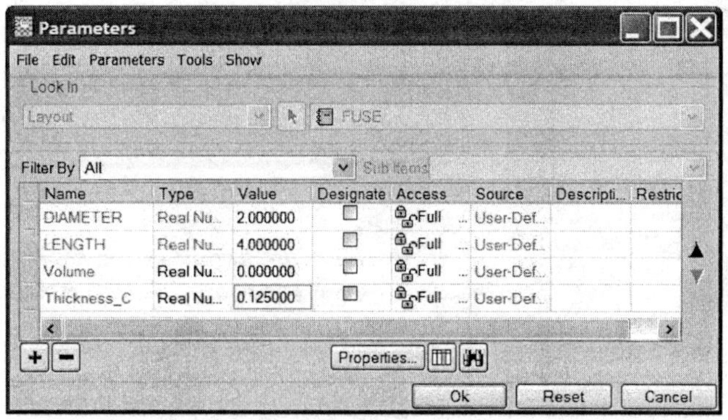

Fig. 20.17.

Goal	Step	Commands
Add dimensions to the end bell	42. Add dimensions to the end bell part.	**INSERT → DIMENSION → NEW REFERENCES → On Entity →** ***Select thickness_1 line → Middle Mouse →*** **<u>Thickness_1</u> →**  **→ <u>0.25</u> →**  **→ On Entity →** ***Select length_1 line → Middle Mouse →*** **<u>Length_1</u> →**  **→ <u>0.5</u> →**  **→ On Entity →** ***Select thickness_2 line → Middle Mouse →*** **<u>Length_2</u> →**  **→ 0.25 →**  **→ Return** Refer to Fig. 20.18.
	43. Arrange the dimensions.	 ***→ Select each dimension and move it to an appropriate location*** Refer to Fig. 20.18.
Add a data table	44. Create a table with eight rows and two columns.	**TABLE → INSERT → TABLE → Descending → Rightward → By Num Chars → Pick Pnts →** ***Select the upper left corner of the table → Mark off the width of the first column as 12 characters → Mark off the width of the second column as 12 characters → Middle Mouse → Mark off the height of the each row by clicking on 4 (Create 8 rows) → Middle Mouse*** Refer to Fig. 20.19.

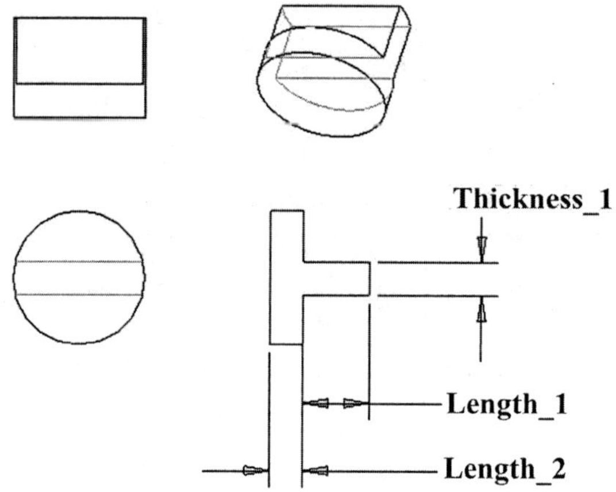

Fig. 20.18.

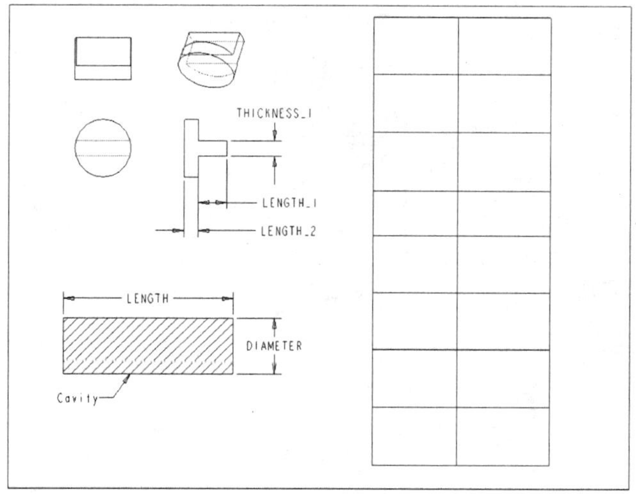

Fig. 20.19.

Goal	Step	Commands
Add a data table (continued)	45. Merge the two cells in the first row.	**TABLE → MERGE CELLS → Rows & Cols → *Select the first two cells*** Refer to Fig. 20.20.
	46. Enter the parameter names.	***→ Double click in each cell in the first column → Enter the corresponding parameter names (Split long names into two lines) → Click on Text Style tab → Select Center and Middle for alignment*** **→ OK** Refer to Figs. 20.20 and 20.21.
	47. Define the parameter values.	***Double click in each cell in the second column, enter the parameter names with the prefix "&" (example: &length for length) (&Thickness_C denotes the casing thickness) → Click on Text Style tab → Select Center and Middle for alignment*** **→ OK** Refer to Figs. 20.19 and 20.21.
Save the layout	48. Save the layout.	**FILE → SAVE → FUSE.LAY → OK**
Open a new file for the fuse assembly	49. Open a new file for the fuse assembly.	**FILE → NEW → Assembly → Design → Fuse → OK**
Declare the layout	50. Examine the existing relations.	**TOOLS → RELATIONS →** The relations window shows no relations **→ OK**
	51. Declare the layout.	**FILE → DECLARE → Declare Lay → Fuse**
	52. Examine the existing relations.	**TOOLS → PARAMETERS → OK** Note that the parameters include the list from the fuse layout.

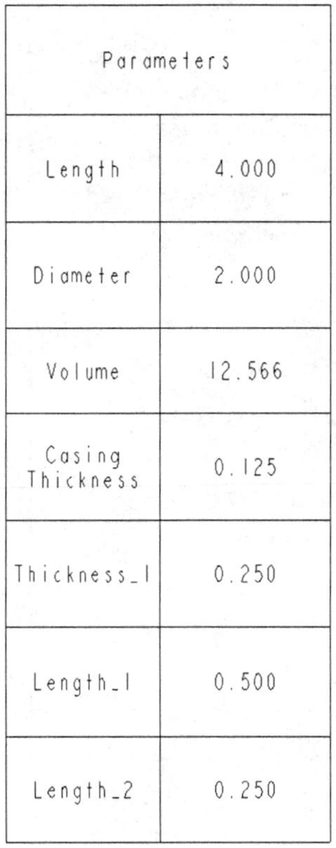

Fig. 20.20.

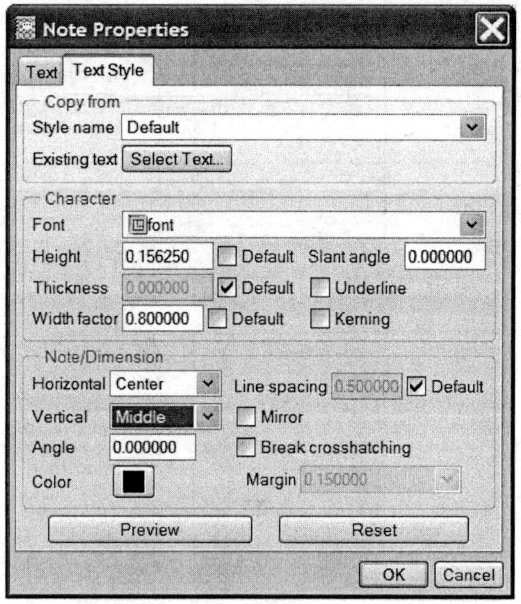

Fig. 20.21.

Goal	Step	Commands
	53. Start creating the casing.	**INSERT → COMPONENT → CREATE → Part → Solid → <u>casing</u> → OK →** ***Locate Default Datums → Three Planes*** **→ OK** Refer to Fig. 20.22.
	54. Create the datum planes.	***Select the ASM_RIGHT datum plane → Select the ASM_TOP datum plane → Select the ASM_FRONT datum plane → Select the casing part in the model tree to display its datum planes*** Refer to Fig. 20.23.
	55. Specify the extrusion options.	→ → **(Thickness) <u>0.1</u> →** ***<u>ENTER</u>*** **→ Placement → DEFINE →** ***Select DTM1*** **→ SKETCH**
Create the casing part in the assembly	56. Create a circle.	→ *Select the center of the circle → Select a point to define the circle*
	57. Modify the dimensions.	→ ***Double click the diameter dimension → <u>1</u> → <u>ENTER</u>*** Refer to Fig. 20.24.
	58. Exit sketcher.	
	59. Select the direction of material creation.	(Next to the thickness icon) (Click this icon until the cylinder is as large as possible – in other words, material will be added to the outer side)
	60. Define the depth.	→ (Depth) <u>**4**</u> →
	61. Accept the feature creation.	→ **VIEW → ORIENTATION → STANDARD ORIENTATION** Refer to Fig. 20.25.

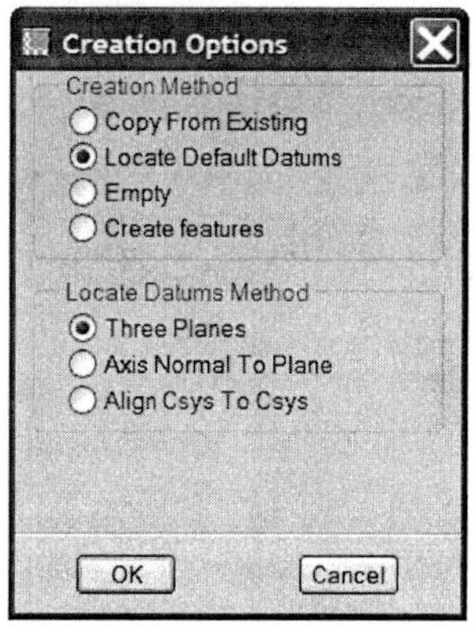

Fig. 20.22.

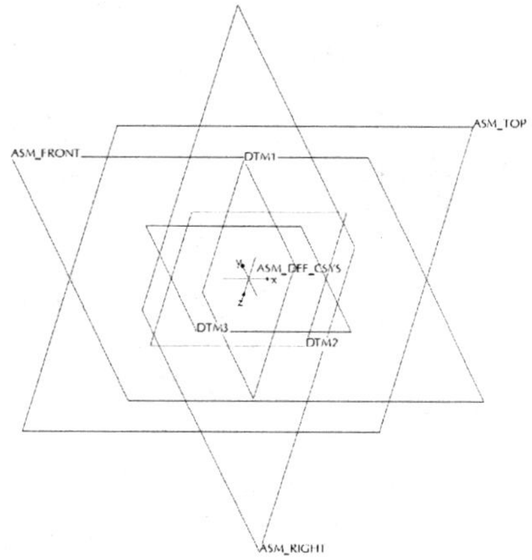

Fig. 20.23

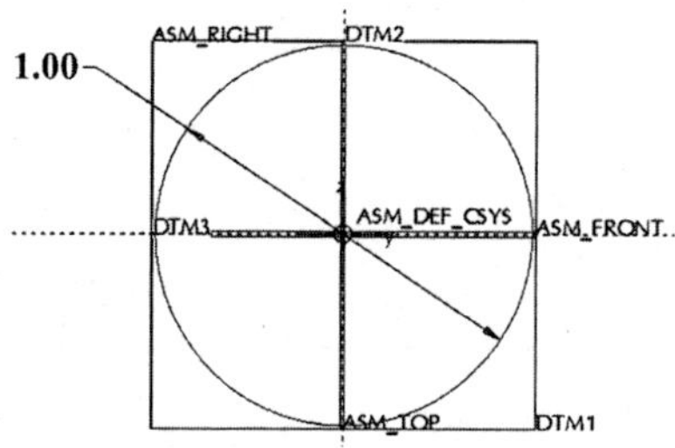

Fig. 20.24.

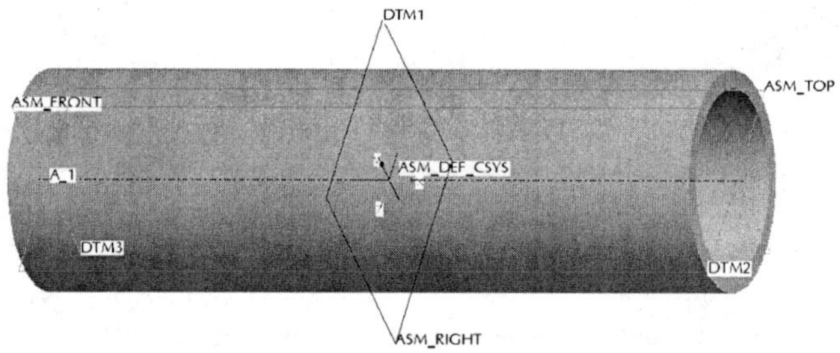

Fig. 20.25.

Goal	Step	Commands
Assign the layout for the casing part	62. Open the part in a new window.	***Right mouse on the casing part*** (in the model tree hold the right mouse) → ***Open*** ProE opens the part in a new window.
	63. Declare the layout.	**FILE → DECLARE → Declare Lay → Fuse**
	64. Add relations.	**TOOLS → RELATIONS →** ***Select the protrusion*** **→** Refer to Figs. 20.26 and 20.27. **Input the relations shown in Fig. 20.27.** → OK
	65. Regenerate the casing.	**EDIT → REGENERATE** (Note the changes.) **WINDOW → FUSE.LAY →** ***Double click on the diameter value in the table*** **→ 1 →** ***ENTER*** **→ EDIT → REGENERATE →** **WINDOW → CASING.PRT → EDIT → REGENERATE**
Assign the layout for the end bell part	66. Activate the end bell part window.	WINDOW → ENDBELL.PRT
	67. Declare the layout.	FILE → DECLARE → Declare Lay → Fuse
	68. Add relations.	TOOLS → RELATIONS → *Select the two protrusions* → **Refer Fig. 20.29.** Input the relations shown in Fig. 20.29. Note that d1, d2, d3 and d8 may be different for your model → UTILITIES → REORDER RELATIONS → OK → OK

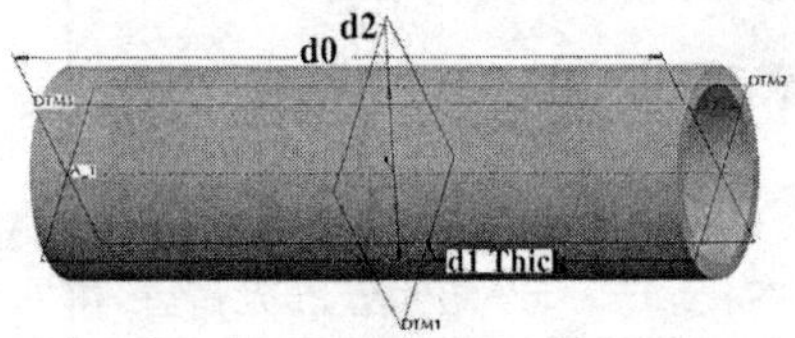

Fig. 20.26.

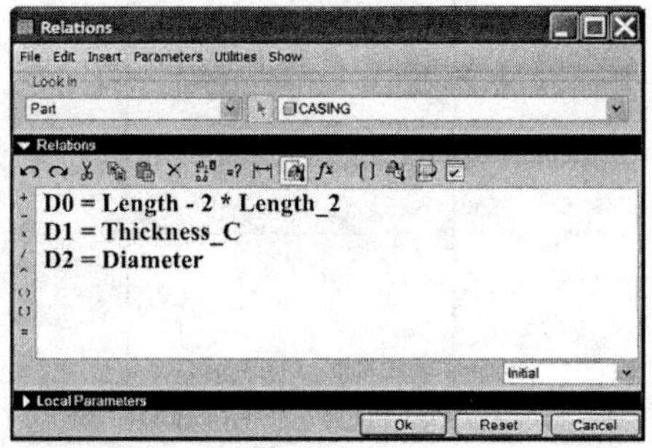

Fig. 20.27.

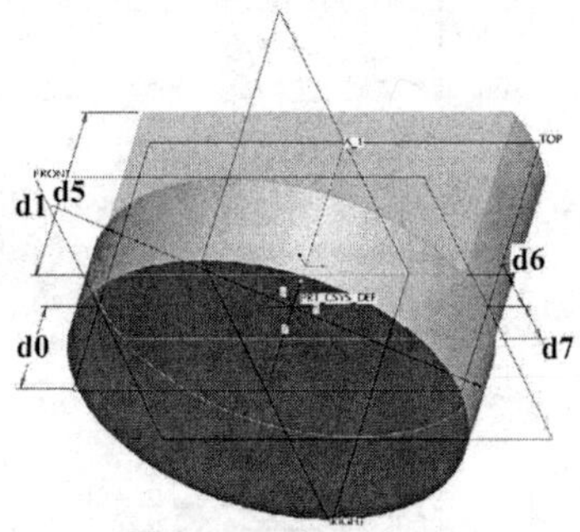

Fig. 20.28.

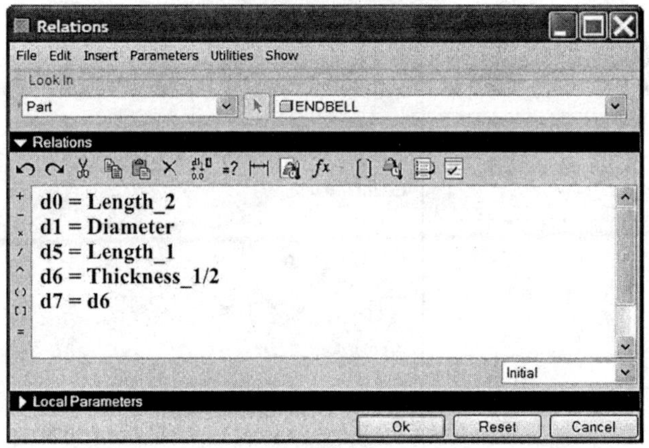

Fig. 20.29.

Goal	Step	Commands
Assign the layout for the end bell part (continued)	69. Regenerate the end bell.	**EDIT → REGENERATE**
	70. Switch the active window back to assembly.	**WINDOW → FUSE.ASM**
Assemble the end bells	71. Start assembling the end bell.	→ ***In Session → Select endbell.prt →*** **Open**
	72. Establish the constraints.	**Placement →** (Constraint Type) ***Align → →*** (Offset) ***Coincident → Select the axis of the end bell → Select the axis of the casing →*** Refer Figs. 20.30 and 20.31. **New Constraint →** (Constraint Type) **Align →** (Offset) ***Coincident → Select the outer surface of the end bell*** *(Refer Fig. 20.31)* ***→Select the outer surface of the casing*** *(Refer to Fig. 20.31)* **→ Accept → 0 → *ENTER* → OK** Refer to Fig. 20.32.
	73. Place the second end bell.	***Select the end bell part from the model tree*** **→ EDIT → REPEAT** ***Select the "Align Surface Surface" constraint*** Refer to Fig. 20.33. **ADD → Select →** ***Select the other end surface of the casing*** *(highlighted in Fig. 20.34)* **→ Confirm →** Refer to Fig. 20.35.

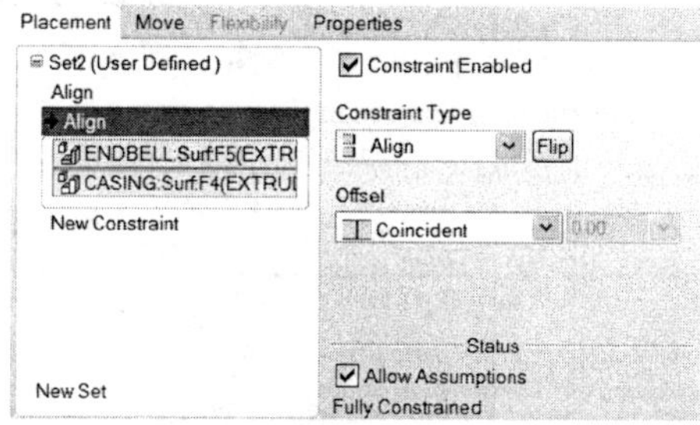

Fig. 20.30.

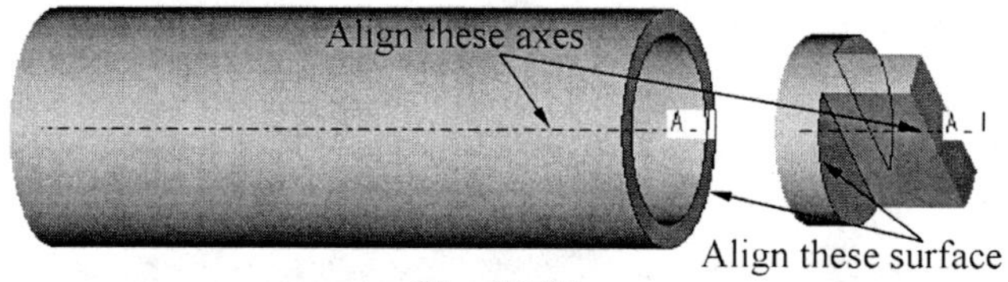

Fig. 20.31.

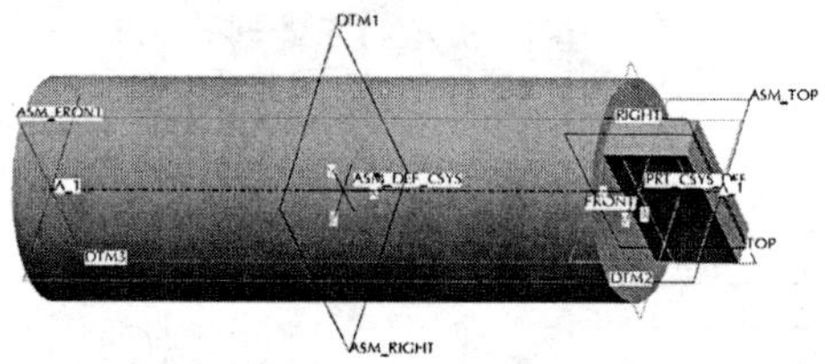

Fig. 20.32.

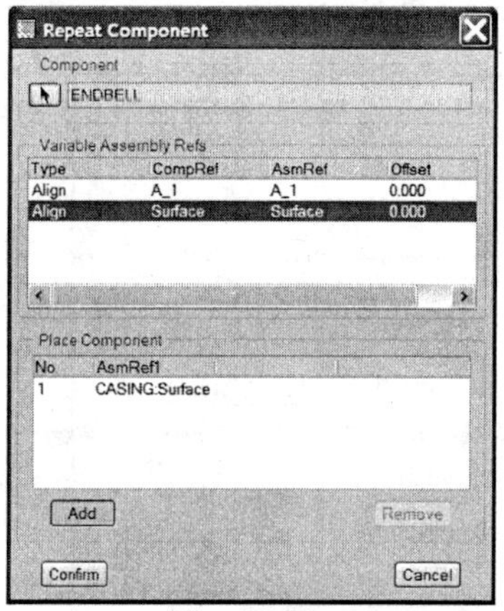

Fig. 20.33.

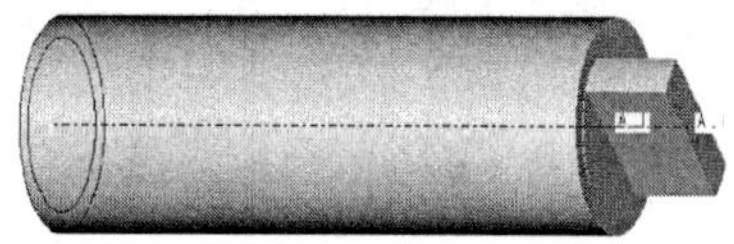

Fig. 20.34.

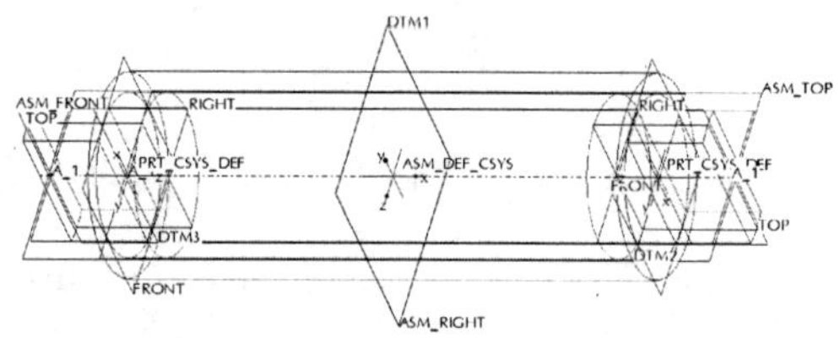

Fig. 20.35.

Goal	Step	Commands
Create the fuse element	74. Start creating the fuse element.	**INSERT → COMPONENT → CREATE → *Part* → *Solid* → element → OK →** ***Locate Default Datums → Three Planes*** **→ OK**
	75. Define the datum planes.	***Select the ASM_TOP datum plane → Select the ASM_FRONT datum plane → Select the ASM_RIGHT datum plane → Select the fuse element part in the model tree to display its datum planes*** Refer to Fig. 20.36.
	76. Start "Protrusion – Extrude" feature.	**→ Placement → DEFINE →** ***Select DTM1 OF THE ELEMENT PART →*** (Orientation) **TOP → Sketch**
	77. Add new references.	**SKETCH → REFERENCES →** ***Select the right end of the left end bell and the left end of the right end bell*** Refer to Fig. 20.37.
	78. Sketch the section.	**→** ***Pick points 1 and 2*** Refer to Fig. 20.38.
	79. Modify the dimensions.	**→** ***Double click the width dimension → 0.25 → ENTER → Double click the half-width dimension → 0.125 → ENTER***
	80. Exit sketcher.	✓
	81. Define the depth.	→ (Depth) **0.02**
	82. Accept the feature creation.	**→ VIEW → ORIENTATION → STANDARD ORIENTATION** Refer Fig. 20.39.

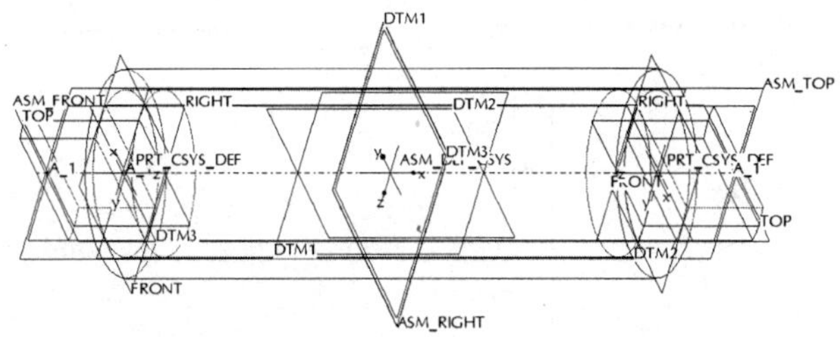

Fig. 20.36.

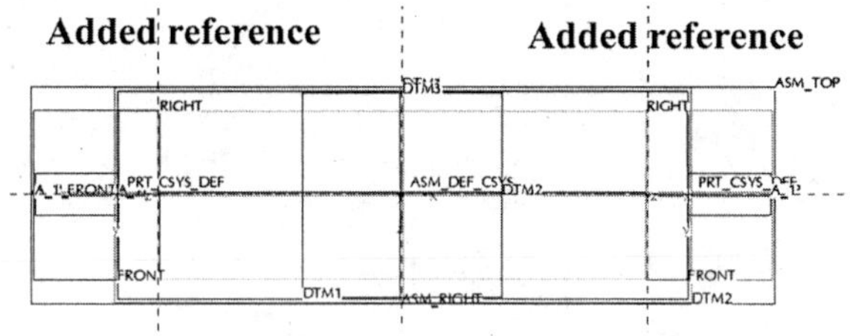

Fig. 20.37.

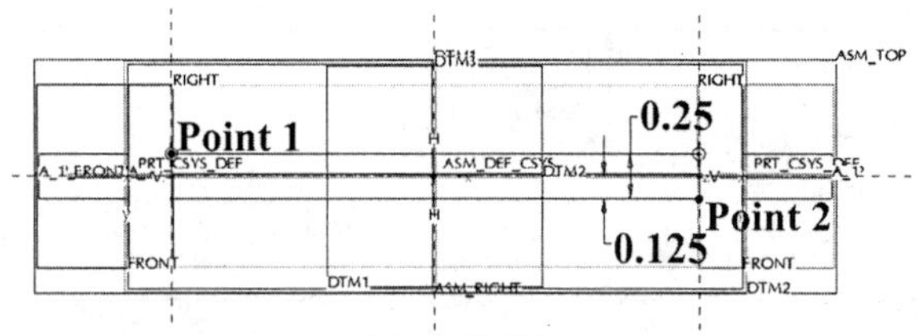

Fig. 20.38.

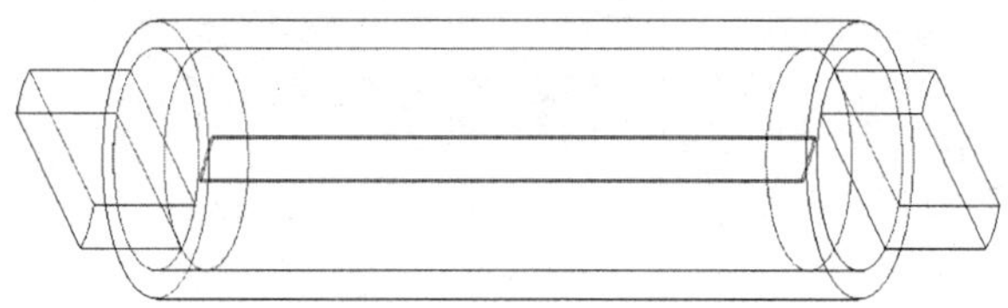
Fig. 20.39.

Goal	Step	Commands
Setup color	83. Define the model color.	**VIEW → COLOR AND APPEARANCES →** [+ icon] **→** ***Click on the white area →*** Refer to Fig. 20.40. ***Click on Color wheel → Select a suitable color in the color editor window →*** **CLOSE** ***→ Add three more colors → Select a color →*** **Components →** ***Select the components →*** **OK → APPLY → Set the colors for all the components except the casing →** ***Select a suitable color for the casing → Click on the Advanced tab → Slide the transparency tab →*** **Components →** ***Select the casing →*** **OK → APPLY → Close →** [icon] Refer to Figs. 20.41 and 20.42.
Save the files and exit ProE	84. Save the element part.	***Select the element part in the model tree → Right Mouse → Open →*** **FILE → SAVE → ELEMENT.PRT → OK**
	84. Save the file and exit Pro|ENGINEER.	**WINDOWS → FUSE.ASM → FILE → SAVE → FUSE.ASM → OK → FILE → EXIT → YES**

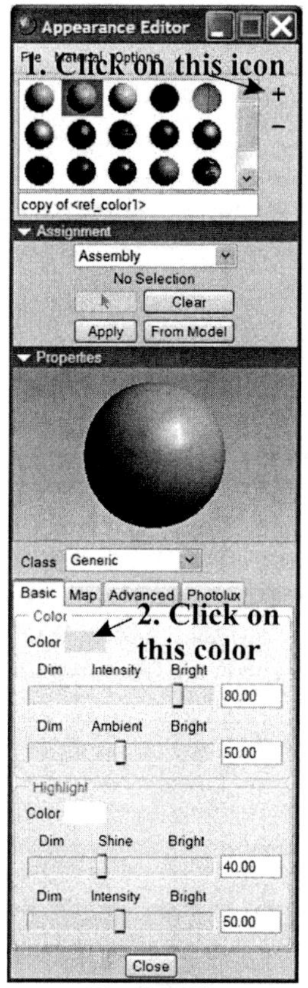

Fig. 20.40.

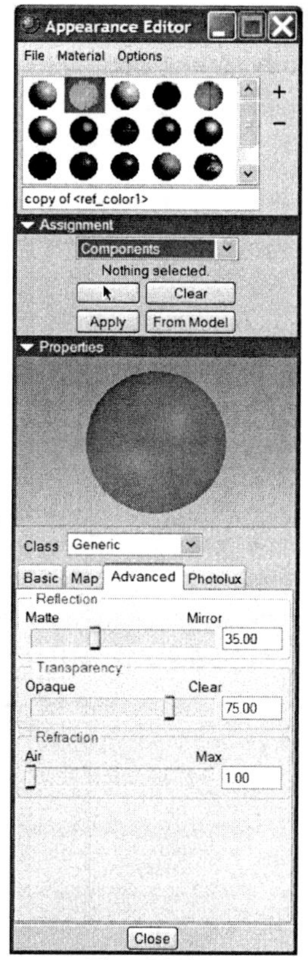

Fig. 20.41.

Fig. 20.42.

OPEN-ENDED DESIGN

Create a Swiss Army knife. There are many varieties with varying degrees of complexity.

OPEN-ENDED DESIGN

Setup a layout to create two sizes of legos (big blocks for small children and small blocks for big kids).

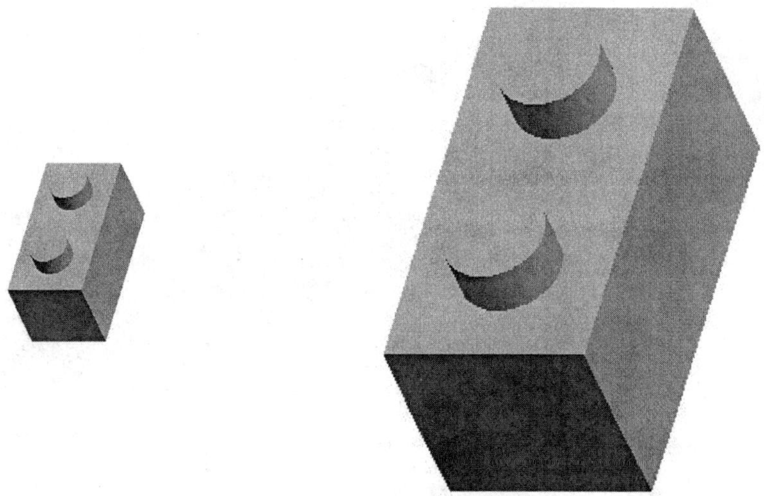

OPEN-ENDED DESIGN

Create a complex assembly with several parts and control it with layout.

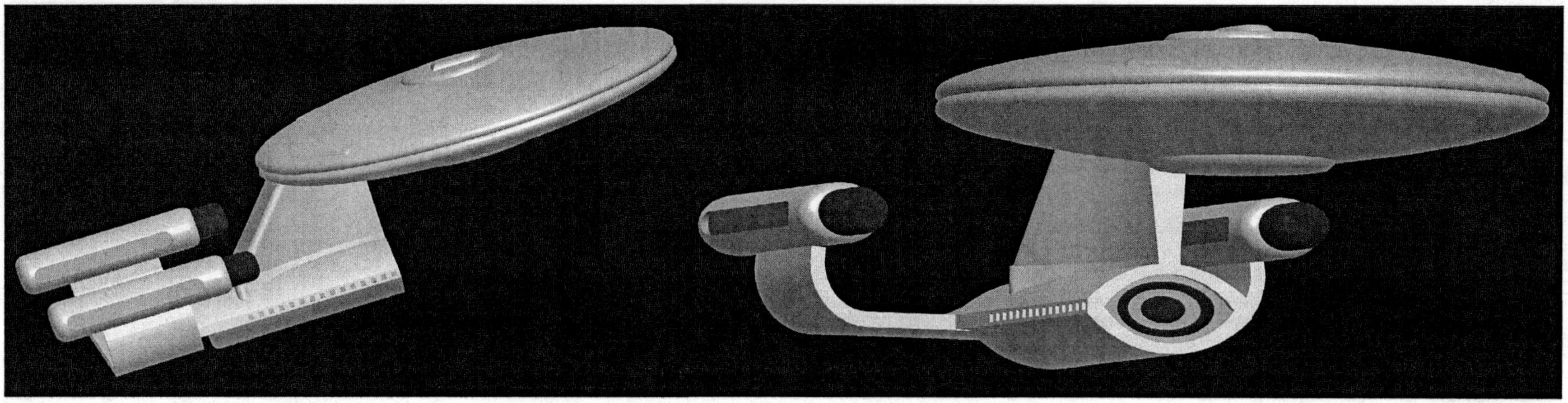